A MANUAL OF
ENGLISH PROSE LITERATURE

BIOGRAPHICAL AND CRITICAL

DESIGNED MAINLY TO SHOW
CHARACTERISTICS OF STYLE

WILLIAM MINTO

ATLANTIC PUBLISHERS AND DISTRIBUTORS

Published by
ATLANTIC PUBLISHERS AND DISTRIBUTORS
B-2, Vishal Enclave, New Delhi-110 027
Phones 5413460, 5429987

Sales Office
4346/4C, Ansari Road, Darya Ganj,
New Delhi-110 002
Phones 3273880, 3285873
Fax 91-11-3285873

ISBN 81-7156-547-6

Typeset at
APD Computer Graphics, Delhi-110 006
Printed in India at
Fine Offset Press, Delhi-110 002

PREFACE

THE main design of this book is to assist in directing students of English composition to the merits and the defects of our principal writers of prose. It is not, however, merely a collection of received critical opinions. It may be of some value to the inquirer after general information, as well as to readers more advanced than those kept specially in view.

The characteristics of the work are briefly these. It deals with prose alone, assigning books of fiction to the department of poetry; it endeavours to criticise upon a methodical plan, fully explained in an Introduction; it selects certain leading authors for full criticism and exemplification; and it gives unusual prominence to three select authors of recent date.

Little need be said to justify taking up Prose by itself. In criticising Poetry we are met by very different considerations from those that occur in the other kinds of composition. What is more, many people not particularly interested in Poetry are anxious for practical purposes to have a good knowledge of Prose style; and when Prose and Poetry are discussed in the same volume, Prose is generally sacrificed to Poetry.

In excluding Romance or Fiction from a Manual of

Prose Literature, I follow a division suggested by the late Professor George Moir, in his treatises on Poetry, Romance, and Rhetoric. Romance has a closer affinity with Poetry than with Prose: it is cousin to Prose but sister to Poetry; it has the Prose features, but the Poetical spirit.

The advantages of criticising upon a methodical plan in terms previously defined, will be at once apparent. Criticising methodically is like ploughing in straight lines: we get over the field not only sooner, but to much better purpose; besides, it is easier to see both what we accomplish and what we miss. As regards the defining of critical terms, it was a favourite position with De Quincey that "before absolute and philosophic criticism can exist, we must have a good psychology." The present work makes little pretension to be philosophic, much less to be absolute; but it is an attempt to apply in criticism some of the light thrown upon the analysis of style by the newest psychology. I am aware that methodical critical dissection is considered by many a cold disenchanting process. But however cold and disenchanting, it is indispensable to the student: it is part of the apprenticeship that every workman must submit to. Before learning to put a complicated mechanism together, we must take it to pieces, and study the parts one by one. If the student goes to work at random, picking up a hint here and a hint there, he is completely at the mercy of every pedantry that comes to him under the sanction of a popular name. The only true preservative against literary crotchets and affectations, is a comprehensive view of the principal arts and qualities, the principal means and ends, of style.

It may be said that criticism on a uniform plan tends to destroy individuality; that a book constructed on such a plan can be nothing but a featureless inventory. This can happen only if the plan is narrow, and if specific modes of the various qualities of style are not distinguished with sufficient delicacy. Uniformity of plan, so far from destroying individuality, is really the best way to bring individual characteristics into clear prominence: if all are subjected to the same examination, the range of the questions being sufficiently wide, individualities are thrown into relief with much greater distinctness than they possibly could be by any other process. Comparison is the soul of criticism. In the following work, the account of each author contains a preliminary sketch of his character; the analysis that follows may be viewed as a means of tracing the outcome of that character in his style, and of making his peculiarities felt more vividly by bringing him into extended comparison with others.

The student should be warned emphatically against such blind guides as declaim against the cramping influence of rules for composition, and urge us to work out our own individuality without regard to the precepts of the schools. Sound principles of composition do not repress genius, but rather do genius a service by preventing it from dissipating itself in unprofitable eccentricities. There is every room for variety within the conditions adopted in the following work: indeed their chief recommendation is that they recognise diversity of style according to diversity of subject and purpose. Students often put the question, What should we do to acquire a good style? A principal aim in this Manual is to make students familiar with the fact that there are varieties of good style. Instead of aiming blindly at the acquisition of "a good style," the writer or the speaker should first study his audience, and consider how he wishes to affect them; and then inquire how far the rhetorical precepts that he has learnt will help him to accomplish his purpose, and how far rhetorical teachers can direct him to the causes of success in those that have best accomplished the same ends in the same circumstances.

Regarding the prominence given to the modern authors, I have only to repeat that the work is intended mainly for students, and to say that the most rewarding study for them, in the first instance at least, lies in the more recent (which are also the higher) developments of prose style. With the same eye to the primary destination of the work, I have said comparatively little about prose writers anterior to the age of Elizabeth.

The biographies of the various writers are brief; but every pains has been taken to make them accurate. The biographies of the three selected modern men will be found to be more complete than any hitherto published.

PREFACE TO SECOND EDITION

THE alterations that I have made in revising this book for a second edition have been mainly in one direction. I have here and there omitted or modified passages that might have seemed to countenance the idea that goodness or badness in style might be pronounced upon, without reference to the effect aimed at by the writer. This I have done to prevent the slightest suspicion that the criticisms in this book consist in the dogmatic application of any absolute standard of style. In spite of the tolerably plain disclaimer in my first Preface, this absoluteness of view has been not only suspected, but alleged. It is true I have not been able, after diligent search, to find the quotations by which the allegation was supported; nevertheless, I wish to place the purpose of the book in this respect beyond the possibility of honest misapprehension.

Since the first edition was issued, Mr Trevelyan's biography of Lord Macaulay has appeared, and Mr H. A. Page has published two volumes on the Life and Writings of De Quincey. My sketches of Macaulay and De Quincey can, in consequence, no longer pretend to be "more complete than any hitherto published."

CONTENTS.

INTRODUCTION.

PART I.

DE QUINCEY—MACAULAY—CARLYLE.

CHAP. I.—THOMAS DE QUINCEY.

PART II.

PROSE WRITERS IN HISTORICAL ORDER.

CHAP I.—PROSE WRITERS BEFORE 1580.

CHAP. II.—FROM 1580 TO 1610.

CHAP. III.—FROM 1610 TO 1640.

CHAP. IV.—FROM 1640 TO 1670.

CHAP. V.—FROM 1670 TO 1700.

CHAP. VI.—FROM 1700 TO 1730.

CHAP. VII.—FROM 1730 TO 1760.

CHAP. VIII.—FROM 1760 TO 1790.

CHAP. IX.—FROM 1790 TO 1820.

CHAP. X.—SELECT WRITERS OF THE EARLY PART OF THIS CENTURY.

A MANUAL

OF

ENGLISH PROSE LITERATURE.

INTRODUCTION.

In the case of the authors chosen for full examination, and to some extent also in the case of the others, the various peculiarities of Style are taken up in a fixed order; and it may help the reader's memory to state this order at the beginning.

The preliminary account of each author's Character is intended mainly as an introduction to the characteristics of his style; and while it gratifies a natural curiosity in repeating what is known of his appearance or personality, does not profess to be a complete account of the man in all his relations, public and domestic.

The analysis of the style proceeds upon the following order: Vocabulary, Sentence and Paragraph, and Figures of Speech, which may be called the ELEMENTS OF STYLE; Simplicity, Clearness, Strength, Pathos, Melody, Harmony, and Taste, the QUALITIES OF STYLE; Description, Narration, Exposition, Persuasion, the KINDS OF COMPOSITION. Upon each of these subdivisions we shall make some remarks, endeavouring to justify the arrangement wherever it seems to be open to objection or misapprehension.

ELEMENTS OF STYLE.

VOCABULARY.

Command of language is the author's first requisite. A good memory for words is no less indispensable to the author than a good memory for forms is to the painter. Words are the material that the author works in, and it is necessary above everything that he should have a large store at his command.

Probably no man has ever been master of the whole wealth of the English vocabulary. The extent of each man's mastery can be ascertained with exactness only by an actual numerical calculation, such as has been made for the poetry of Shakspeare and Milton. This has not yet been attempted for any of our great prose writers; and until some enthusiast arises with sufficient industry for such a labour, we must be content with a vague estimate, formed upon our general impression of freshness and variety of diction.

The simple fact of holding a place among the leaders of literature is a proof of extraordinary mastery of language. But can we, without actual numeration, distinguish degrees of mastery? Most probably we can. We could have told from a general impression, without actually counting, that Shakspeare uses a greater variety of words than Milton. We can perceive, without referring to the enlargement of dictionaries, that our language has increased in scope and flexibility since the middle of last century. In like manner we can fix relatively any author's command of words. We may say with confidence that Defoe is more copious and varied than Addison, and Burke than Johnson; and, although our judgment of modern writers is more liable to error, we may venture to say that De Quincey, Macaulay, and Carlyle show a greater command of expression than any prose writers of their generation.

It is interesting, also, to observe on what special subjects an author's expression is most copious and original. Perhaps no one has an equal abundance of words for all purposes. From the inevitable limitation of human faculties, no man, however "myriad-minded," can give his attention to everything. Inevitably every man falls into special tracks of observation, reflection, and imagination; and each man accumulates words, and expresses himself with fluency and variety, concerning the subjects that are oftenest in his thoughts. Were we to apply the test of arithmetic, we should find that two men using very much the same number of words upon the whole, have the depths and shallows of their verbal wealth at very different places.

To mark out fully where a vocabulary is weak and where it is strong, we should have to anticipate the qualities of style and the kinds of composition. A man that can write freely and eloquently in one strain or in one species of composition, may be dry and barren in another strain or another species of composition. Most writers have some one vein that they peculiarly and obviously excel in. Thus Addison is rich in the language of melodious and and elegant simplicity, Paley in the language of homely simplicity,

De Quincey in the language of elaborate stateliness, Macaulay in the language of brilliant energy.

Here it may be well to point out—and the caution is of such importance that it may have to be repeated—that the divisions in the following analysis are not, in the language of the logicians, mutually exclusive. Following Professor Bain's Rhetoric we consider style under three different aspects—approach it from three different sides; but we do not treat of different things. In each of the divisions, the same things are examined, only from different points of view. Each of these divisions, were our examination to be ideally thorough, should exhibit every possible excellence and defect of style. We might take up all the notable points in an author's style under what we have called the "Elements of Style"—the choice of words, plain and figurative, and the arrangement of these in sentences and paragraphs. We might, again, take up everything remarkable under the "Qualities of Style"—simplicity, clearness, and so forth: a style is good or bad according as it produces, or fails to produce, certain effects. Finally, we might comprehend the whole art of style under the "Kinds of Composition:" every excellence of style is either good description, good narration, good exposition, good persuasion, or good poetry. The divisions are far from being mutually exclusive. Were we to say in one department all that might be said, we should leave nothing for the others. The sole justification of having three, and not one, is practical convenience. There must of necessity be occasional repetitions, but each department has certain arts of style that are best regarded from its own particular point of view.

THE SENTENCE.

The construction of sentences is an important part of style. Sometimes, indeed, it is expressed by the word *style*, as if it constituted the whole art. With a nearer approach to accuracy, it is sometimes called the *mechanical* part of style. This designation may be allowed, if sentence-building is loosely taken to include the construction of paragraphs and the general method of a discourse. It is probably true that the construction of sentences and of paragraphs may be subjected to more precise rules than any other processes of the art of composition. And this being so, they may, if a term is wanted to express this distinction, conveniently be called mechanical.

Special Artifices of Construction.—One may doubt whether it would be practicable to make anything like a comprehensive collection of all the forms of sentence possible in English. At any rate, it has not yet been done. Writers on composition have hitherto attempted nothing more than to distinguish a few well-marked modes of construction.

I. The Periodic Structure.—"A period," says Campbell, "is a complex sentence, wherein the meaning remains suspended till the whole is finished. . . . The criterion of a period is this: If you stop anywhere before the end, the preceding words will not form a sentence, and therefore cannot convey any determined sense." This is the common definition of a period, and it is probably difficult to go farther without committing one's self to general statements that will not apply to every period. At the risk of being slightly inaccurate, it might be well to go a little deeper into the substance of the periodic structure. What exactly do we imply by saying that the meaning is suspended till the close? We imply that the reader's interest is kept in suspense till the close. And how is this done? Generally, it may be said, by bringing on predicates before what they are predicated of, and, which is virtually a similar process, qualifications before what they qualify; letting us know descriptive adjuncts, results, conditions, alternatives, oratorical contrasts, of subjects, states, or actions, before we formally know the particular subjects, states, or actions, contemplated by the writer. Thus, in the following sentence—

> "On whatever side we contemplate Homer, what principally strikes us is his invention;"

the subject—in this case the key-word—is reserved to the last, and the adverbial adjuncts of the predicate are stated before the predicate itself. A statement is made in a form showing that it has a bearing upon something to follow, and our curiosity is awakened to know what something is. "On whatever side we contemplate Homer." The next statement, "what principally strikes us," contracts our curiosity into a more definite field, and thereby sharpens our interest. Still it points us forward. There is a progress from the indefinite to the definite, and, in the case of this particular period, a growing interest, which is not relieved till we reach the very last word. In a loose structure of sentence, which may be called the natural or usual structure in English, the predicate follows the subject, and qualifying adjuncts follow what they qualify: we know the subject before we know the attribute predicated of it or annexed to it. In a period, on the other hand, the writer, stating the predicate or qualifying adjuncts of a word before the word itself, may be said to circumvent that word, to make (as the Greek *periodos* signifies) a "circuit" about it, to bring its predicate or its adjuncts, as the case may be, from behind it and place them before it.

Campbell speaks of the period as a "complex" sentence. If the above view of the period is accepted as substantially correct, "complexity," in the grammatical sense, must be regarded as an accident of the period, and not part of its essence. The statements of other writers on composition warrant us in applying the term period to sentences that are not complex. Professor Bain simply says that, "In a periodic sentence, the meaning is suspended until the close," and makes no mention of a periodic sentence being necessarily complex. And Whately gives, as an example of periodic structure, the following "simple" sentence: "One of the most celebrated of men for wisdom and for prosperity was Solomon."

It would be well if the application of the term periodic were a little extended. When qualifying adjuncts are brought in before their exact bearing is known, and in such a way as to stimulate curiosity, a peculiar effect is produced; and we should be justified by the derivation of the word "periodic" in applying it to all marked cases of such anticipation. Practically, indeed, the word is applied in the wider sense. If Campbell's definition were rigorously adhered to, the term periodic could be applied only to sentences that keep the reader in suspense up to the very last word. But, as a matter of fact, the term is applied much more widely. We speak of writers as having a periodic style, although their works contain few complete periods, according to Campbell's "criterion of a period." Since, therefore, the narrow definition of the term is practically disregarded, it would be well to come to a formal understanding of its latitude. The term "period" might still be retained for a periodic sentence, rigorously complete or nearly so. But it would probably better suit the prevailing application of the term "periodic" to accept it as a name for such anticipations as I have roughly indicated—to call every style "periodic" where such anticipations habitually occur. Of this periodic style, the most eminent of modern masters is De Quincey.

In the *loose sentence*—in a sentence so constructed as to be noticeably "loose"—qualifying and explanatory adjuncts are tacked on after the words they refer to. This might be copiously exemplified from the writings of Carlyle, and, in a less degree, from Addison.

The effect of the periodic structure is to keep the mind in a state of uniform or increasing tension until the *dénouement.* This is the effect stated in its ultimate and most general form. The effect that a reader is conscious of receiving varies greatly with the nature of the subject-matter. When the subject is easy and familiar, the reader, finding the sentence or clause come to an end as soon as his expectations are satisfied, receives an agreeable impression of neatness and finish. When the subject-matter is unfamiliar, or when the suspense is unduly prolonged, the periodic structure is intolerably tedious, or intolerably exasperating, according to the temper of the reader. In impasssioned writing the period has a moderating effect, the tension of the mind till the key-word is reached preventing a dissipation of excitement.

Dr Blair says that the periodic style is "the most pompous, musical, and oratorical manner of composing," and that it "gives an air of gravity and dignity to composition." The Doctor probably had in his eye such periodic writers as Hooker, Sir Thomas Browne, and Johnson. Undoubtedly long periodic sentences give great scope for pomp, music, gravity, dignity, and such effects, but these are not necessary attributes of the period. A period, as we have defined it, need not be long; and a lively interest may be sustained as well as a grave interest.

Advantages and disadvantages of the periodic structure.—To some extent we have anticipated these in considering the effect of the period.

In light subjects, neatness or finish is generally regarded as an advantage. Yet even in this a caution is needed; rounded neatness, if it recurs too frequently, may become tiresome. The caution can probably be given in no more definite form than Hamlet's. Be not too *periodic* neither, but let your own discretion be your tutor.

In unfamiliar subjects, care must be taken that the considerations kept in suspense be not too numerous or too abstruse. De Quincey has vividly described "the effect of weariness and repulsion which may arise from this single vice of unwieldy comprehensiveness in the structure of sentences." "Those who are not accustomed to watch the effects of composition upon the feelings, or have had little experience in voluminous reading pursued for weeks, would scarcely imagine how much of downright physical exhaustion is produced by what is technically called the *periodic* style of writing. It is not the length, the ἀπεραντολογία, the paralytic flux of words. It is not even the cumbrous involution of parts within parts, separately considered, that bears so heavily upon the attention. It is the suspense, the holding on of the mind until what is called the ἀπόδοσις, or coming round of the sentence, commences. This it is which wears out the faculty of attention. A sentence, for example, begins with a series of *ifs;* perhaps a dozen lines are occupied with expanding the conditions under which something is affirmed or denied. Here you cannot dismiss and have done with the ideas as you go along; for as yet all is hypothetic—all is suspended in air. The conditions are not fully to be understood until you are acquainted with the dependency: you must give a separate attention to each clause of this complex hypothesis, and yet, having done *that* by a painful effort, you have done nothing at all; for you must exercise a reacting attention through the corresponding latter section, in order to follow out its relations to all parts of the hypothesis which sustains it." These remarks point to the abuse rather than to the use of the periodic style, and were directed against a prevailing style in newspaper "leaders." It is obviously necessary, for the avoiding of perplexity, not to bring in too many or too abstruse considerations before their bearing is made known. A writer with the least regard for his readers, should see that by so doing he exacts too severe an effort of attention. It may safely be laid down that the longer a period is, the simpler should be both the language and the matter of the suspended clauses.

Mr Herbert Spencer in his 'Essay on the Philosophy of Style,' and Professor Bain in his Rhetoric, advocate what we have defined as periodic structure, on the ground that it enables us to apprehend the meaning of a complex statement with less risk of confusion. The advantage of placing qualifying words before the object that they qualify is briefly stated in Bain's Rhetoric, under the "order of words."

The legitimate use of the periodic structure in impassioned prose is best seen in the so-called "prose fantasies" of De Quincey.

II. Sentences studiously Long and studiously Short.—No small element in the mechanical art of sentence-building is the adjustment of the length of the sentence. One of the greatest faults in our early writers is that their sentences are too long. They did not know when to stop. They seem to have been afraid to let a sentence out of their hands till they had tacked on all the more important qualifications of the main statement. They thus frequently ran on to a most cumbrous length; and when they did proceed to a new sentence, frequently took no pains to connect it with the preceding main statement, but started off in pursuit of some subordinate idea suggested by one of the qualifying statements. So defective, indeed, were they in sentence-structure, that it is dangerous for a beginner in composition to spend much time in their company. And one great part of this deficiency was, that they did not know when to end a sentence, or, in other words, that they had not the art of beginning a new sentence at the proper point.

It would be absurd to prescribe a definite limit for the length of sentences, or even to say in what proportion long and short should be intermixed. Here, too, discretion is the tutor. Only it must be borne in mind that a long series either of very short sentences or of very long sentences is tiresome.

The distinction between the "periodic style" (*style périodique*) and the "abrupt style" (*style coupé*) depends to a great extent upon the length of the sentences. The Periodic style (as we see from its description by De Quincey) implies something more than the use of the periodic structure; it implies *long* periods, elaborately constructed, holding "a flock of clauses" in suspense, and moving with a stately rhythm. So in the Abrupt style, the short sentence is an important feature, although, as appears in the style of Macaulay, it is not the only feature.[1]

The use of a startling series of short sentences may almost be said to be a feature of English oratory. We find it in the journals of the Elizabethan Parliaments; and, later, in the writings of Bolingbroke, in the published speeches of Chatham, and in the speeches and writings of Burke.

The long sentence, formed of several members gradually increasing in length so as to make a climax in sound, would universally be designated oratorical. It was much affected by Cicero.

III. The Balanced Sentence.—"When the different clauses of a compound sentence are made similar in form, they are said to be balanced.

The artifice of constructing successive clauses upon the same plan is said to have been introduced into our language from the Italian. Wherever it came from, it begins to appear noticeably about the middle of the sixteenth century. In Elizabeth's reign, it became very fashionable. It was one feature of Lyly's "Euphuism." It held its ground through the reign of James, appearing even in booksellers' advertisements and in the titles of maps. One of John Speed's maps is entitled, 'A new and accurate map of the world, drawn according to the *truest descriptions*, *latest discoveries*, *and best observations*, that have been made by English or strangers.'

The advantages of the balanced structure are pointed out briefly, but fully, in Bain's Rhetoric. It is a pleasure in itself; when not carried to excess, it is a help to the memory; and, when the balanced clauses stand in antithesis, it lends emphasis to the opposition. We find also in practice that it serves as a guide to the proper arrangement of the important words. Under a natural sense of effect the important word is often reserved for the last place, the best position for emphasis. Further, in impassioned prose, as in Raleigh's invocation to Death, and De Quincey's imitations—the invocations to Opium and to Solitude, balance has something of the effect of metre.

In the case of balance, much more than in the case of the periodic structure, it is necessary to beware of going to excess. There is almost no limit to the means of disguising the periodic structure. The reader may be entertained with such variety in the parts of a period, that he enjoys its bracing effects without knowing the cause. But the balanced structure cannot be so disguised: it is like metre—to disguise it is to destroy it. Clauses

[1] While speaking of these general distinctions of style, we may note a third, the Pointed style, consisting in "the profuse employment of the Balanced Sentence, in conjunction with Antithesis, Epigram, and Climax." How far these distinctions are from being distinctive, in the sense of indicating incompatible modes of composition, may be judged from the fact that Dr Johnson often employs all the three "styles" in one paragraph.

are constructed on the same plan, or they are not; corresponding words occupy corresponding places in their respective clauses, or they do not. And while the balanced structure is prominent, and thus apt to fatigue the ear, it is very catching; it has a great power of enslaving whoever employs it heedlessly. Several of our writers, such as Johnson, "Junius," and Macaulay, allowed their ear to be captivated, and not only employed balanced forms to excess, but often added tautologous and otherwise questionable clauses from an irresistible craving for the familiar measure.

IV. The Condensed Sentence.—"This is a sentence abbreviated by a forced and unusual construction."

Anything so violently artificial as this can be used but seldom without giving offence. It was a favourite artifice with Gibbon. In the present day, when used at all, it is used chiefly for comic purposes. Readers of Dickens and his imitators are familiar with such terms as "drew tears from his eyes and a handkerchief from his pocket." Occasionally we find it in works of more serious pretensions, as in Mr Forster's Life of Goldsmith; but nobody now uses it for serious purposes so often as Gibbon did.

GENERAL CONSIDERATIONS.—**I. The Emphatic Places of a Sentence.**—"As in an army on the march, the fighting columns are placed front and rear, and the baggage in the centre, so the emphatic parts of a sentence should be found either in the beginning or in the end, subordinate and matter-of-course expressions in the middle."

There is nothing more urgently required for the improvement of our sentences than a constant study to observe this principle. The special artifices that we have mentioned are good only for certain modes of composition and for particular purposes, and become offensive when too often repeated; but it is difficult to conceive when there would be an impropriety in placing important words where the reader naturally expects to find them. The reader's attention falls easily and naturally upon what stands at the beginning and what stands at the end, unless obviously introductory in the one case, or obviously rounding off in the other. The beginning and the end are the natural places for the important words. This arrangement is conducive both to clearness and to elegance: it prevents confusion, and is an aid to justness of emphasis. As important words need not occupy absolutely the first place nor absolutely the last, but at the beginning may be preceded by qualifying clauses, and at the end may be followed by unemphatic appendages that are not of a nature to distract attention, we are not required to make unnatural inversions or to take unidiomatic liberties of any kind. If a writer finds a construction stiff and unnatural, he may be sure that he has not succeeded in throwing the emphasis where it should be thrown; if he has not buried the important words in the depths of the sentence, he has probably done worse: he has probably drawn off the reader's attention from the words altogether, and fixed it where it should seldom or never be fixed — upon the form.

The following out of this principle is not so easy as it appears. One is safe to assert that it will never be carried out thoroughly till it is made an important part of school drill. Without some such long and early training, a scrupulous purist in this respect might hang as long over his sentences as Mr Tennyson is said to hang over his lines, and commit blunders after all. In bringing sentences into harmony with this principle of arrangement alone, there is a field for endless variety of school exercises in composition.

II. Unity of Sentence. — Upon this point it is especially dangerous to lay down any abstract rule. Irving's statements, that "a sentence or period ought to express one entire thought or mental proposition," and that "it is improper to connect in language things which are separated in reality," are much too dogmatic and cramping. Separate particulars must often be brought together in the same sentence.

The only universal caution that can be given is, to beware of distracting from the effect of the main statement by particulars not immediately relevant. "Every part should be subservient to one principal affirmation."

The advice not to overcrowd a sentence may have to yield to a law of the paragraph concerning the due subordination in form of whatever is subordinate in meaning. "A statement merely explanatory or qualifying, put into a sentence apart, acquires a dangerous prominence."

Most of the faults specified by Blair as breaches of "unity" occur in connection with other arts of sentence-structure. "Excess of parenthetical clauses" is an abuse of the periodic structure, objectionable only in so far as it imposes too severe a strain upon the retentive powers of the reader. It is a fault often committed by De Quincey, whose own powers of holding several things in the mind at once without confusion sometimes betrayed him into forgetting that all are not equally gifted. The fault of not "bringing the sentence to a full and perfect close"—so flagrant in our early writers—is not likely to be committed by any one aware of the value of the end of a sentence as the place for important words.

The specialties of the sentence in Narrative and in Description are examined at length in Bain's Rhetoric (THE SENTENCE, sec. 25). He says that "the only rule that can be observed in distinguishing the sentences is to choose the larger breaks in the sense."

THE PARAGRAPH.

Professor Bain was the first, so far as I am aware, to consider how far rules can be laid down for the perspicuous construction of paragraphs. Other writers on composition, such as Campbell, Lord Kames, Blair, and Whately, stop short with the sentence.

De Quincey, a close student of the art of composition, felt the importance of looking beyond the arrangement of the parts of a sentence, and philosophised in a desultory way concerning the bearing that one sentence should have upon another. "It is useless," he says, in one of his uncollected papers, "to judge of an artist until you have some principles in the art. The two capital secrets in the art of prose composition are these: 1st, The philosophy of transition and connection; 2dly, The way in which sentences are made to modify each other; for the most powerful effects in written eloquence arise out of this reverberation, as it were, from each other, in a rapid succession of sentences; and because some limitation is necessary to the length and complexity of sentences, in order to make this interdependency felt: hence it is that the Germans have no eloquence." These "two capital secrets" correspond very much with Professor Bain's two first rules of the paragraph.

I have examined at considerable length the paragraph arrangement of Macaulay. Very few writers in our language seem to have paid much attention to the construction of paragraphs. Macaulay is perhaps the most exemplary. Bacon and Temple, from their legal and diplomatic education, are much more methodical than the generality. Johnson is also entitled to praise. But none of them can be recommended as a model.

FIGURES OF SPEECH.

In most treatises on composition, the consideration of figurative language occupies a large space. Of the small portion of Aristotle's Rhetoric devoted to composition purely, it constitutes about one half. So in the works of Campbell, Kames, and Blair, particularly in Kames's 'Elements of Criticism,' the origin, nature, limits, minute divisions, the uses and the abuses of figures of speech, are examined and exemplified at great length. And yet these later writers profess to be much more concise than "the ancient critics and grammarians," and to have discarded many vexatiously subtle subdivisions.

The chief thing wanted in the ancient divisions and subdivisions was some broad principle of classification. This is supplied by referring figures to their origin in the operations of the intellect. A proper basis for a classification is found in the ultimate analysis of these operations. When the classes thus instituted—Figures of

Similarity, Figures of Contiguity, and Figures of Contrast—have gathered up all the figures that belong to them respectively, very few remain unclassified. Some of those that do remain are distinguished from the others on a different principle. Such figures as interrogation, exclamation, and apostrophe, are departures from the ordinary structure of sentences, and thus are distinguished from such figures as are departures from the ordinary application of words. According to the distinction of the old grammarians, they are "figures," as distinguished from "tropes." So much for the classification of figures. It is not quite complete—it leaves hyperbole, climax, innuendo, and irony unclassified; but it is a great improvement upon the old chaos.

The truth is, that the subjects included in books of composition under the head of Figures of Speech do not admit of a logical classification. Under that head rhetoricians have gradually accumulated all artifices of style that do not belong to the choice of plain words and the structure of sentences. Such an accumulation could hardly be other than heterogeneous.[1]

One of the ancient terms it might be well to revive and redefine in accordance with its derivation and original application—namely, the word "trope." At present, when used at all, it is used loosely as a kind of general synonym for a figure of speech. By Quintilian it was defined as an opposition to the term figure—designating, as we have just seen, extraordinary applications of individual words in contrast to irregular constructions of sentence. Such a distinction is of no practical value—it would be useful to have a special term for irregular constructions of sentence; but it would be impossible to restrict the word figure to such an application. Apart from that, the word trope is not treated with much delicacy when set up as an expression for all "figures of speech" (in the wide sense), *except* irregular constructions of sentence. I would propose to rescue the word from an application so promiscuous, and to settle it in its original application as a name for a much narrower class of artifices.

Interpreted by its derivation, *trope* signifies a word "turned," diverted from its ordinary application, and pressed, as it were, into special service. Now only a limited number of figures of speech consist in this extraordinary use of *single words*; it would be convenient to have a common designation for them. What could be more proper than to use for that designation the existing word *trope?*

To vindicate the restriction of a term to a special class of figures,

[1] Had paragraph structure been sooner recognised, the so-called figure of speech, "climax," would probably have been referred to the paragraph as a special artifice in paragraph construction. Climax is no more a figure of speech than the periodic, the balanced, or the condensed structure of sentence.

even when that restriction is warranted by the derivation of the term, we must show that occasions arise for speaking of that class of figures collectively. In this case such a vindication is easy. There are writers, such as De Quincey, who use comparatively few formal similitudes, and yet use metaphors, personification, synecdoches, or metonymy, in almost every sentence. On the other hand there are writers, such as Macaulay, whose diction in its general texture is plain, but who employ a great many formal similitudes. Both classes of writers are figurative, but the one class is rich in *tropes*, the other in *similes*.

The want of such a word as trope, thus defined, has led to an abuse of the word metaphor by popular writers. Metaphor has been taken to supply the want. In strict language, metaphor means a similitude implied in the use of a single word, without the formal sign of comparison; but it is often loosely used as a common designation for synecdoches and metonymies as well. The temptation to such an abuse is withdrawn by reviving the original meaning of the word trope.

The chief points that we shall notice under Figures of Speech, besides the profusion of any one figure or class of figures, are the sources of similitudes and compliance with the conditions of effective comparison. The sources of an author's similitudes are often peculiarly interesting, as affording a means of measuring the circumference of his knowledge. We cannot, to be sure, by such means, take a very accurate measure, but we can tell what books a man has dipped into, may discover what writers he has plagiarised from, and may be able to guess how his interests are divided between books and the living world. What casts doubt upon our conclusions is the fact, that so many writers are similitude-hunters, are very often on the watch for good similitudes; and the consequent presumption that they utilise a large proportion of their knowledge. Thomas Fuller is one of the most versatile, as he is one of the most delightful, masters of allusion. He would seem to have turned almost every item of his knowledge to account, and thus has a greater appearance of learning than many men of really profounder erudition and wider knowledge of the world.

The conditions of effective comparison exhaust all that can be said in the way of advice concerning the use of figures. When a similitude is addressed to the understanding—is intended merely to make one's meaning more perspicuous—care must be taken that the point of the comparison be clear, that there be no distracting circumstances, and that the comparison be more intelligible to those addressed than the thing compared. When a similitude is intended to elevate or to debase an object by displaying its high or its low relations, care must be taken that the comparison be, in the estimation of those addressed, really higher or (as the case may be) lower than the object; farther, that it be not extravagantly and offensively out of level, and that it be fresh. These are the main conditions of effective comparison for purposes of exposition, and for persuasive eulogy or ridicule. In comparisons designed only for embellishment, the conditions are novelty and harmony, or, as it might also be called, propriety. As regards the number of figures employed, every writer must be guided by his own discretion. The critic of style can only remark, that if writers were always careful to make their comparisons effective for a purpose of some kind, the number would be considerably reduced.

In treating of an author's figures, as in treating of his vocabulary, we might anticipate most of the qualities of his style. Figures may be simple, or stirring, or grand, or touching, or witty, or humorous. A full account of a man's figurative language would display nearly all his characteristics.

As a sort of postscript to the Elements of Style, we may easily define the mutual relation of two terms often used in contradistinction—MANNER and MATTER. As distinguished from matter, manner includes everything that we have designated by the general title Elements of Style—not only the choice of words and the structure of the parts of a discourse, but everything superinduced upon the subject of discourse by way either of comparison or of contrast.

QUALITIES OF STYLE.

The division of qualities into purity, perspicuity, ornament, propriety, is open to the objection of being too vague. This appears in amendments of the scheme proposed by different critics. Some would strike off "propriety" as being common to all the other qualities. Others, confining propriety to the choice of individual words, would retain it and strike off "purity," as being a part of propriety thus restricted. Others still would dispense with "ornament," as a separate division, and discuss ornaments under perspicuity and propriety. And Blair maintains that "all the qualities of a good style may be ranged under two heads, perspicuity and ornament."

Such vague fumbling is inevitable so long as qualities of style are viewed in the abstract, and without reference to their ends. Campbell was the first to suggest a substantial principle of classification by considering style as it affects the mind of the reader. His analysis is not perfect, but he was upon the right track. "It appears," he says, "that besides purity, which is a quality entirely grammatical, the five simple and original qualities of style, *considered as an object to the understanding, the imagination, the pas-*

sions, and the ear, are perspicuity, vivacity, elegance, animation, and music." That so many writers on composition should have fallen back from this comparatively thorough analysis to bad versions of the old analysis, is not much to their credit.

One of the causes of imperfection in Campbell's analysis was his desire to separate rigidly between the effects of style or manner, and the effects of the subject-matter. This cannot be done: the manner must always be viewed in relation to the matter. In order to get at qualities of style, we must first make an analysis of the effects of a composition as a whole—matter and manner together; not till then are we in a position to consider how far the effect is due to the manner and how far to the matter. For example, if a composition is readily intelligible, we consider how far this is due to the familiarity of the subject-matter, and how far to the author's treatment, to his choice and arrangement of words, and to his illustrations. Nothing could be more absurd than Blair's confident assertion that the difficulty of a subject can never be pleaded as an excuse for want of perspicuity; that if an author's ideas are clear, he should always be able to make them perspicuous to others. Perspicuous, as Blair understands the word, means *easily* seen through; and it may be doubted whether any powers of style could make the generalisations of a science easily and immediately apparent to a mind not familiar with the particulars. Style can do much, but it has a limit. It can never make a subject naturally abstruse as easily understood as a subject naturally simple, a treatise on Logic as perspicuous as a statement of familiar facts. So with compositions that address the feelings; the master of style cannot but work at a disadvantage when his subject is not naturally impressive.

The chief aim of the following brief remarks on Qualities of Style is to define prevailing critical terms as closely as may be with reference to the ultimate analysis here adopted.

INTELLECTUAL QUALITIES OF STYLE—SIMPLICITY AND CLEARNESS.

Aristotle recognises but one intellectual quality, clearness. The first requisite of composition is that it be clear. So Quintilian: "The first virtue of eloquence is perspicuity." In Campbell's scheme, also, "the first and most essential of the qualities of style is perspicuity."

Blair, while he reduced all qualities to perspicuity and ornament, was led, in his consideration of perspicuity, to another intellectual quality—namely, precision. He described precision as "the highest part of the quality denoted by perspicuity," and then made the following contrast between precision and perspicuity "in a qualified sense." "It appears," he said, "that an author may, *in a qualified sense*, be perspicuous, while yet he is far from being precise. He uses proper words and proper arrangements; he gives you the idea as clear as he conceives it himself,—and so far he is perspicuous: but the ideas are not very clear in his own mind; they are loose and general, and therefore cannot be expressed with precision. All subjects do not equally require precision. It is sufficient, on many occasions, that we have a general view of the meaning. The subject, perhaps, is of the known and familiar kind; and we are in no hazard of mistaking the sense of the author, though every word which he uses be not precise and exact. Few authors, for instance, in the English language, are more clear and perspicuous, on the whole, than Archbishop Tillotson and Sir William Temple; yet neither of them are remarkable for precision."

The fact is, that if the words are taken in their ordinary senses, precision is not a mode of perspicuity, but a quality in some measure antagonistic to perspicuity. Blair might have drawn a line between perspicuity and precision, and made them two separate intellectual qualities. The division would not have been the best, but it would have been a real division, and better than none at all.

Aristotle's single virtue of "clearness" or "perspicuity" needs to be analysed before we can characterise authors with discrimination. We need two broad divisions, simplicity and clearness, and a subdivision of clearness into general clearness and minute clearness. This more exact division I shall briefly explain: it is not arbitrary dictatorial sequestration of terms to unfamiliar applications, but a breaking up of such sequestrations, and a reconciliation of the language of criticism with the language of familiar speech.

When designations of merit are loose and indeterminate, they may sometimes be cleared up by a reference to designations of demerit. It is so in this case. What are the *faults* of style as a means of communicating knowledge? We at once say abstruseness and confusion. Returning, then, to the positive side, we ask ourselves what are the corresponding merits—what are the opposites of abstruseness and confusion—and we have no difficulty in seeing that the main intellectual "virtues" of style are simplicity and clearness.

Simplicity and abstruseness are relative terms. Whatever is hard to understand is not simple, is abstruse, recondite; and what is hard for one man may be easy for another. The phraseology of natural science or of medicine is hard to the unlearned reader, but easy as a primer to the naturalist or the physician. Abstract terms are generally unpopular, and generally disliked as dry, bookish, scholastic; yet they are said to come to Scotchmen more naturally than the concrete language of common things. Want of simplicity is not an absolute fault; it is a fault only in relation to the persons addressed. A writer addressing himself purposely to a learned audience only wastes his strength by beating about the bush for language universally familiar.

Clearness, as opposed to confusion, is not so much relative to the capacity of the persons addressed. Ambiguous language—words so arranged as to convey an impression different from what the writer intends, may mislead learned and unlearned alike. Confused expression is not justifiable under any circumstances, unless, indeed, it is the writer's deliberate purpose to mislead. The educated reader will guess the meaning sooner than the uneducated; but neither educated nor uneducated should be burdened with the effort of guessing.

Clearness, as we have said, may conveniently be subdivided into general clearness and minute clearness—minute clearness being expressed by such words as distinctness, exactness, precision. There is a marked line of separation between these subdivisions. Accuracy in the general outlines is a different thing from accuracy in the details. In truth, the two are somewhat antagonistic. To dwell with minute precision on the details tends rather to confuse our impressions as to the general outlines. After our attention has been turned to minute distinctions, we find it difficult to grasp the mutual relations of the parts so distinguished when we endeavour to conceive them as a whole. Again, minute distinctness is opposed to simplicity. The general outlines of things can be conveyed in familiar language; but when we desire to be exact, we must have recourse to terms that are technical and unfamiliar. To say that the earth is "round" is a sufficiently clear description of the form of the earth in a general way—and the word is familiar to everybody; but when we are more exact, and describe the earth as "a sphere flattened at the poles," we remove ourselves from the easy comprehension of many of our countrymen.

We are now in a better position to discuss the critical and popular use of the word perspicuity. It is evident, from Campbell's account of the faults against perspicuity, that he understands by the term a certain amount of clearness combined with simplicity. He includes in his list of offences not only confusion of thought, ambiguity—using the same word in different senses—and uncertain reference in pronouns and relatives, which are offences against clearness, but also technical terms and long sentences, which are offences against simplicity. This is also the popular use of the term. Such writers as Addison and Macaulay are said to be perspicuous, because they are at once simple or easily understood, and free from obvious confusion. Their ideas are expressed in popular language, and sufficiently discriminated for popular apprehension.

Popularly, therefore, as well as in some rhetorical treatises, perspicuity stands for a clear, unambiguous, unconfused structure of simple language. But why should the term be confined to a clear structure of *simple* language? We can easily see how it came to be so confined. A general reader does not receive clear impressions from a work couched in abstruse language, however perspicuous may be the arrangement. The effort of realising the words is too much, and he lets them slip through his mind vaguely. For him an abstruse style cannot be perspicuous—simplicity is indispensable to perspicuity. But while we see how the word came to be so confined, we cannot see why it should be kept so confined. Johnson's arrangement is clearer and more free from ambiguity than Addison's or Tillotson's. Why should he not be called a perspicuous writer?

But some of our readers will say that Johnson *is* called a perspicuous writer. This is true, but he is not so by Campbell's definition, for he uses technical terms and long sentences; nor is he so by the verdict of those that are loosely called general readers. He is called perspicuous because his words are apt to his meaning, and because the general structure of his discourses is clear. His language is not simple; he is not perspicuous if simplicity be considered a part of perspicuity.

Here, therefore, seems to arise a clash between the general reader and the reader more familiar with abstract and learned phraseology. But the disagreement is more apparent than real. The general reader applies the term perspicuous to a clear choice and construction of simple language, of language familiar to him; the more learned reader applies the term to a clear choice and structure of language, abstruse perhaps to the generality, but still familiar to *him*. In point of fact, the two classes of readers use the word perspicuous with the same meaning. Both have in view, not the familiarity of the language or the structure, but the clearness of it, its freedom from ambiguity and confusion. The intellectual qualities of such writers as Tillotson, Locke, Addison, Macaulay, are not fully distinguished by the single word perspicuous—the style of such writers is perspicuous *and simple*. Johnson and De Quincey are also perspicuous in their choice of words, and in their general structure; but their diction, as a whole, is abstruse.

We said a little ago that clearness might be subdivided into general clearness and minute clearness. At that time we mentioned no single word for general clearness. In our consideration of the word perspicuity, we have seen that, when hunted down to its real signification, it proves to be the very word required. Perspicuity, or lucidity, will thus stand for general clearness, unambiguous, unconfused structure—what may loosely be called general accuracy of outline. For minute accuracy, careful discrimination of terms—demanding from the reader an effort to make sure that his ideas are not vague, but rigidly defined—we have the terms precision, exactness, and distinctness.

A distinct, exact writer may be perspicuous; but, as we have said, he runs a risk of not being so. When a writer is scrupulously anxious that his readers understand every detail exactly as he conceives it, there is a danger that he put too severe a strain upon them, and confuse their comprehension of the general aspect of his theme. De Quincey is an example of a writer at once exact and perspicuous; and the secret is, that he is aware of his danger, and frequently presses upon his reader a general view of what he is doing.

Precision and simplicity are in a measure antagonistic. When Socrates began to cross-examine the people of Athens, he found that they could not define the meaning of words that they were using every day. They used language in a loose way for purposes of social intercourse, and did not trouble themselves to be rigidly exact. The case is not much altered among us. A very exact writer cannot but be abstruse to the generality.

EMOTIONAL QUALITIES OF STYLE—STRENGTH, PATHOS, THE LUDICROUS.

The emotional qualities of style are not so difficult to distinguish as the intellectual qualities. Had Campbell not been needlessly anxious to isolate the style from the subject-matter, he would never have thought of huddling together all the emotional qualities under the name of vivacity.[1] There are three broadly distinguished emotional qualities — strength, pathos, and the ludicrous; and each of these is a general name for distinct varieties.

Under the general name of Strength are embraced such varieties as animation, vivacity, liveliness, rapidity, brilliancy; nerve, vigour, force, energy, fervour; dignity, stateliness, splendour, grandeur, magnificence, loftiness, sublimity

Between the extremes in the list—animation and sublimity—there is a wide difference; yet sublimity is more appropriately classed with animation than with any mode of pathos. So with rapidity and dignity. The contrast between strength and pathos is as the contrast between motion and rest. The effect of a calm, sustained motion is nearer to the effect of absolute repose than it is to the effect of a restless, rapid, abrupt motion; yet the calm, sustained motion is considered as a state of motion, and not as a state of rest. In like manner, an overpowering sense of sublimity approaches nearer to a sense of depression and melancholy than it does to animation or vivacity; yet it is essentially a mode of strength, and not a mode of pathos.

[1] Longinus's celebrated treatise περὶ ὕψους, mistranslated "On the Sublime" through the Latin *De Sublimitate,* falls into the same excess of abstraction. *Hypsos,* according to De Quincey, means everything tending to elevate composition above commonplace.

In the above list I have attempted some kind of subordinate division, throwing together the terms that seem more nearly synonymous. It would not be possible to define them exactly without incurring the charge of making one's own feelings the standard for all men. The terms are used with considerable latitude, partly because few people take the trouble to weigh their words, but partly also because different men have different ideals of animation, different ideals of energy, different ideals of sublimity. All can understand, upon due reflection, the common bond between these qualities—their common difference from the qualities comprehended under pathos; but no amount of explanation can give two men of different character the same ideas of animation, energy, dignity, or sublimity. The utmost that explanation can do is to disabuse their minds of the idea that the one is wrong and the other right, and to persuade them that they are simply at variance. At the same time, the application of the terms is not absolutely chaotic. Take the universal suffrage, and you find a considerable body of substantial agreement between the loose borders.

One great cause of the licentious abuse of these terms is the desire of admirers to credit their favourites with every excellence of style. Could we subtract all the abuses committed under this impulse, we should find the popular applications of terms very much at one. All agree in describing Macaulay as animated, rapid, and brilliant. There is not so much unanimity in accrediting him with dignity—at least with dignity of the highest degree; and he is seldom credited with sublimity. Readers would probably be no less unanimous in calling Jeremy Taylor fervid, Dryden energetic, Temple dignified, Defoe nervous, Johnson vigorous, Burke splendid, and De Quincey's "prose fantasies" sublime.

Perhaps none of the above words are so shifting in their application as the word sublimity. In an account of De Quincey's character I have tried to distinguish two opposite modes of sublimity. No critical term is more in need of definition. De Quincey denies it of Homer, and ascribes it in the highest degree to Milton, seeming to understand by it the exhibiting of vast power to adoring contemplation.

Pathos is contrasted with the sentiment of power, and is said to be "allied to inaction, repose, and the passive side of our nature." According to this definition, whatever excites or agitates is not pathetic.

This distinction, like every attempt at analysis of mental states, is open to endless dispute. It will be almost unanimously allowed as regards tender feelings awakened by the representation of "objects of special affection, displays of active goodness, humane sentiments, and gentle pleasures." But it may stagger many as applied to the representations of pain and misery. Are these not agitating? and are they not justly called pathetic?

To answer all conceivable difficulties in the way of understanding the above definition of pathos would be hopeless within our present limits. It may remove some difficulties to remind the reader that we have here to do not with tender feeling as awakened by actual objects, but with tender feeling as awakened by verbal representations. Pathos, as here discussed, is the quality of a style that awakens tender feelings—not another name for tender feeling as it arises in actual life. I do not mean that the feelings arising from these two sources differ otherwise than in degree; I mean only that the reality is usually more agitating than the verbal representation. The report of a railway accident may be read with a certain luxurious horror by a delicate person, whom the actual sight would throw into fits.

But still the question returns, Are not verbal representations of pain and misery often agitating? The answer to this question is, that not every representation of pain and misery is pathetic.

To speak technically, there are two different uses of painful scenes in composition—the description of misery is adapted to two distinct ends. These may be defined, with sufficient accuracy, as the persuasive end and the poetic end. When a writer or a speaker wishes, by a painful description or a painful story, to persuade to a course of action, he dwells upon the particulars that agitate and excite. A pleader wishing to excite pity for his client, so as to procure acquittal, dwells upon the harrowing side of the case—the destitution of the man's family, and suchlike. He does not cater for the pleasure of the jurors, but does his best to make them uncomfortable. So the preacher of a charity sermon, if he wishes to draw contributions from his audience, must not throw a sentimental halo over the miseries of the poor, but must drag into prominence hunger, dirt, and nakedness, in their most repulsive aspects, horrifying his hearers with pictures that haunt them until they have done their utmost to relieve the sufferers. Very different is the end of the poet. His object is to throw his reader into a pleasing melancholy. He withholds from his picture of distress all disgusting and exciting circumstances, reconciles us to the pain by dwelling upon its alleviations, represents misery as the inevitable lot of man, exhibits the authors of misery as visited with condign punishment, expresses impassioned sympathy with the unfortunate victims. By some artifice or other—I have mentioned only a few for illustration—he contrives to make us acquiesce in the existence of the misery represented. He has failed in his end if he leaves us dissatisfied and uncomfortable, because the misery was not relieved or cannot be relieved now. If we are not reconciled to the existence of the misery, disposed simply to mourn over it and be content, the composition is not pathetic, but painful. For this luxurious treatment of painful things the poet is often heavily censured by the preacher. Sterne's 'Sentimental Journey' was reprobated by Robert Hall; and in our own day we are familiar with Carlyle's denunciation of "whining, puling, sickly sentimentality."

To this distinction between the painful end of persuasion and the pathetic end of poetry, we may add a little by way of anticipating the more obvious objections.

It will be said that a preacher's object is to persuade people to action, and yet that sermons are often called pathetic. This fact need not disturb our definition. For, 1°, While it is *one* of a preacher's objects to persuade to action, it is not his only object: the pulpit has also a function of consolation—and consolation, the reconciling of people to their miseries, is by our definition essentially pathetic. 2°, Supposing a sermon admirably adapted to set beneficence in motion—supposing it to present a picture of most harrowing distress—the hearers cannot take measures for relief at once; and meantime, if not so excited as to be thoroughly uncomfortable, they may indulge in pathetic dreams of the relief that they intend to give. 3°, The effect of a composition depends very much upon the recipient—a tale of woe that makes one man uncomfortable for days, may supply another with a luxurious feast of mournful sentiment. It is chiefly this last consideration that makes the application of the term pathos shifting—that causes the difficulty of drawing any "objective" line between pathos and horror. Few persons skilled in analysing their feelings would object to the above definition of pathos, but there would be considerable difference of opinion as to what is agitating or horrible and what is truly pathetic.

Again, it may be said that a tragic poem is agitating, and yet that it is pathetic. To which we answer that in a tragedy, while isolated scenes are tempestuously agitating, the effect may yet be pathetic on the whole. Tragedy "purifies the mind by pity and terror;" the atmosphere is shaken with tempests, only to subside at the end into a purer and more perfect calm. Painful incidents, thrilling transports of grief, keep alive our interest in the plot: we do not see the pathetic side of these painful representations till we look back upon them from the repose of the conclusion.

I need not dwell on the terms for varieties of the Ludicrous. The only nicety is the distinction between wit and humour. Much has been written on this distinction. One can see, from the examples quoted, that critics are very much at one, though they generally fail in definition, owing to the vagueness of their psychological language. Professor Bain's theory is that *humour* is simply the laughable degradation of an object without malice, in a genial, kindly, good-natured way; and that *wit* is "an ingenious and unexpected play upon words." The two qualities are not opposed, not incompatible. A good deal of the confusion about them has arisen from viewing them as two contrasted and inconsistent qualities. Wit may be humorous, or it may be derisive, malicious. I have somewhere seen it laid down that humour "involves an element of the subjective." When we call a writer humorous, we have regard to the *spirit* of his ludicrous degradation; we imply that he is good-natured—that he bears no malice. When we call a writer witty, we have regard simply to the cleverness of his expression; he may be sarcastic, like Swift—or humorous, like Steele. The proper antithesis to humour is satire: wit is common to both.

Such is the true definition of humour, but in the actual application there may be as much inconstancy as in the application of the term pathos, and from the same reason. What appears kindly and good-natured to one man, may not appear so to another. Addison is generally classed among the humorists; yet only the other day his kindliness was described as an affectation put on to sharpen the sting of his ridicule. Johnson spoke of his "malevolent wit and humorous sarcasm;" and the present writer believes that it would be difficult to find, among all Addison's papers, half-a-dozen in which the wit may not fairly be characterised as malicious. He is a humorist to us, but he could hardly have appeared a humorist to his victims.

There is another cause of difference among critics as respects particular compositions. A reader may refuse to acknowledge a degradation, however comical. He may view an object too seriously to allow that it should be trifled with. A recent critic professes himself blind to the humour of De Quincey, and sees in his playful liberties with distinguished names nothing but frivolous impertinence. In all such cases, as De Quincey himself says, "not to sympathise is not to understand."

ELEGANCIES OF STYLE—MELODY, HARMONY, TASTE.

"In the harmony of periods," says Blair, "two things may be considered. First, agreeable sound, or modulation in general without any particular expression. Next, the sound so ordered as to become expressive of the sense."

Instead of expressing qualities so different by a single term, it is better to provide a term for each. In accordance with the acceptation of melody and harmony in the vocabulary of music, we may describe "agreeable sound or modulation in general" as

Melody, and "the sound so ordered as to become expressive of the sense" as *Harmony*. If a single designation is wanted for the two qualities together, we may, agreeably to Campbell's list of qualities, call them the *music* of composition.

Under Melody there are two things that we may consider. First, whether an author conforms to the general laws of melody,—the avoiding of harsh effects; the alternation of long and short, emphatic and unemphatic syllables; the alternation of consonants among themselves, and vowels among themselves; the avoiding of unpleasant alliterations; the cadence at the close. Second, what is his prevailing rhythm, *tune* or *strain*, and how far this is varied.

To examine how far an author observes the general rules of melody would be a good school exercise. It is not easy to give an idea of an author's favourite strain. The only means open to us is to produce characteristic specimens. We have as yet no scheme of nomenclature or notation for describing it technically.

Some writers, perhaps the majority, can impart no characteristic swing to their language—either having no natural preference for a particular rhythm, or giving their whole attention to the expression of the meaning, or being overruled by habitual combinations. Only such as have, first, a decided ear for effects of cadence, and, secondly, a copious choice of words, can attain to a melody that shall be either characteristic or effective.

As regards Harmony. There is such a thing as harmony, or adaptation of sound to sense, even in prose. At the same time, change of strain or movement to suit change of theme is not so marked in prose as in poetry, and for a very obvious reason. The writer of verse can suit himself to variations of feeling by choice of metre, but the writer of prose has no such fixed steps to help him to vary his pace. Besides, the prose writer's habits of construction are accommodated to his prevailing rhythm; the phrases that most readily occur to him are in pace with this rhythm,—so that, along with a greater difficulty than the verse writer in changing his pace, owing to the want of a standard metre, he has a farther difficulty that besets none but verse writers accustomed only to one metre.

Accordingly, we find that prose writers having a characteristic rhythm, can vary it but slightly to harmonise with the subject-matter.

The word *taste* is used in two different senses; and when we meet with the word, and are disposed to challenge its application, we do well to make sure in which signification our author employs it. In its widest sense it is equivalent to artistic sensibility—as Blair defines it, "the power of receiving pleasure from the beauties of nature and of art." In its narrower sense it may be expressed as artistic judgment, being identical with what Blair and others define as "delicacy" and "correctness" of taste. By writers of the present day the word seems to be generally used in the narrower sense; and in this sense it is used in the following work.

As regards what artistic judgment is there may be wide differences of opinion. Many men, many tastes; one man's liking may be another man's loathing. Still, when all has been said that can be said concerning differences of taste, it cannot be denied that there is a considerable body of agreement. To take the elements of style separately. There is a tolerably unanimous public opinion against interlarding English composition with foreign words or idioms, Latin, French, or German; against needless coining of new words; and against setting up of unidiomatic combinations. No writer could make an excessive use of any artifice of construction —balanced sentences, short sentences, condensed sentences, abrupt and startling transitions—without incurring general censure. So as regards figures of speech: a style too ornate, too hyperbolical, too declamatory, is condemned as such by the critics with very considerable unanimity. Marked abuses of the elements of style are very generally recognised as abuses. To be sure, if a writer is otherwise fresh and vigorous, all read him; and even fastidious critics wink at his eccentricities as an agreeable break in the general monotony of composition; but few venture to hold up his eccentricities for general imitation.

Concerning the emotional qualities of style we find much less agreement. There are always a few of wider literary knowledge and superior discernment who groan inwardly, some of them outwardly, at the judgment of the multitude in the matter of sublimity, pathos, and humour. And these apart, writers and their admirers separate naturally into different schools. Taste "varies with the emotional constitution, the intellectual tendencies, and the education of each individual. A person of strong tender feelings is not easily offended by the iteration of pathetic images; the sense of the ludicrous and of humour is in many cases entirely wanting; and the strength of humane and moral sentiment may be such as to recoil from inflicting ludicrous degradation. A mind bent on the pursuit of truth views with distaste the exaggerations of the poetic art. Each person is by education attached more to one school or class of writers than to another."

KINDS OF COMPOSITION.

Five "kinds of composition" are set down in Bain's Rhetoric—description, narration, exposition, persuasion, poetry.[1] Each of

[1] The design of the present work excludes Poetry both with and without the accompaniment of metre.

these kinds has a special method, a special body of rules. The student who has mastered everything that has been given under the "Elements" and the "Qualities" of style, has still something to learn.

We have already remarked that the three divisions adopted in this work are distinguished not as separate component parts, but only as different aspects or different ways of approach. We have said that under either the "Elements of Style," the "Qualities of Style," or the "Kinds of Composition," a complete survey might be taken of all the arts of style. When we come to consider the kinds of composition, we see that this remark needs a farther limitation. The kinds of composition may be subdivided, and under each of the subdivisions might be included a complete survey of the arts of style. Every precept of style laid down under the "Elements" and the "Qualities" might be repeated under Description, Narration, and Exposition. Whoever wishes to describe well, narrate well, and expound well, would be all the better for knowing every good advice that can be given in the departments prior in the order of our sketch. Persuasion, again, embraces everything prior to it. There is no precept of style that may not be useful to the orator or the persuasive writer. "Rhetoric" is another name for the whole art of composition.

DESCRIPTION, NARRATION, EXPOSITION.

These three kinds of composition may be roughly distinguished as follows: Description embraces all the means of representing in words particular "objects of consciousness," whether external things or states of mind; narration, all the means of representing particular sequences of events; exposition, all the means of representing general propositions. These may be taken as rough definitions of them in their elemental purity; in actual composition they are almost always mixed.

For the simplest forms of description, narration, and exposition, special rules would be of no practical use—would be affected and superfluous. It is only in the more complicated and difficult forms that precepts become of service, and then they may be said to be indispensable.

The main difficulty in description arises "when we have to describe a varied scene—the array of a battle, a town, a prospect, the exterior or interior of a building, a piece of machinery, the geography of a country, the structure of a plant or an animal." It is to this difficulty that the special rules of description apply. Burke and Macaulay are often said to possess great descriptive power. But, as we shall see, this can mean only that they present with vividness the individual particulars or striking aspects of a scene. Neither of them possesses great descriptive method. Carlyle may be said to have raised the standard of descriptive method; Alison also, and later Mr Kinglake, are very studied in their descriptions.

The principles of description, as stated in Bain's Rhetoric, are perhaps the best defined and the least liable to exception of all precepts relating to composition. No person can describe a complicated scene well without consciously or unconsciously satisfying these conditions; and a person with a moderate command of language, by adhering to these conditions, will surpass—at least as regards the first essential of drawing a clear picture—the undisciplined efforts of very high genius.

No such exactness of plan is attainable for the narration of complicated events. Still, it is possible to point out to the historian his chief liabilities to confusion, and put him so far upon his guard.

We defined the fundamental idea of narration as being the representation of particular sequences of events. But History in its actual development is a much more complex affair. De Quincey recognises three modes of history: Narrative (a record of public transactions); Scenical (a study of picturesque effects); and Philosophical (a reasoned explanation of events). These are real distinctions, and we are not sure that they might not be multiplied. Not that extant histories may be divided into these three classes—such a work as Macaulay's 'History of England' attempts to combine the three modes—but these distinctions point to three different functions of History. The historian may simply record public transactions without attempting to explain them or draw lessons from them, and without any effort to describe splendid spectacles or interesting incidents. He may give his principal care to making the record of events instructive, may have a studious eye to the lessons of political and social wisdom, or he may give his principal care to making the record of events scenically or dramatically interesting. Now, without saying that these three functions should be kept distinct—that a history should be either plainly narrative, or philosophical, or scenical, and should not aspire to be all three at once—there is an advantage in considering a history under these three aspects separately. We observe first by what arts the historian makes his narrative simple and perspicuous—whether he follows the order of events, where and with what justification he departs from that order, what provision he makes for keeping distinct in our minds the several concurring streams of events in complicated transactions, what skill he shows in the construction of summaries, and other minor points. His skill in explaining events by general principles, and in deducting general lessons, forms a separate consideration. And still another consideration is his scenical and dramatic skill; his word-painting, plot-arrangement, and other points of artistic treatment.

Apart from the objects of critical remark thus grouped together may be placed, as a thing for special consideration, the particular form of historical chapter or book that undertakes to delineate the whole social state of a people at some one epoch. The most celebrated example of this is the third chapter of Macaulay's History.

For the statement of simple generalities, presenting no difficulty to the apprehension of the reader, little direction can be given. The rules of exposition apply only to the more abstruse generalities. The four leading arts of statement and illustration are iteration, obverse iteration, exemplification, and comparison. The popular expositor must also study the arts of imparting interest to dry subjects, and must learn to appreciate the difficulties of the tyro, and to take every advantage of the previous knowledge of his readers.

The arts of PERSUASION, rhetoric proper, open up a still wider field. We have said that all the arts of style are of service to the orator. There are times, perhaps, when the speaker may choose to set the precepts of clear expression on one side. Instead of trying to express himself clearly, he may seek to mislead and cheat his audience with studied ambiguity; but he will do this all the better if he is able, upon occasion, to express himself clearly and attractively.

The principal things to attend to in criticising oratory are the orator's knowledge and power of adapting himself to the persons addressed, his verbal ingenuity as shown in happy turns of expression, his argumentative power, and his skill in playing upon special emotions.

In the examination of the leading authors, we follow the order of this introductory sketch. We do not take up, in the case of every author, every point here mentioned; we remark only upon the prominent features in each individual case; but we take up the various points in the order of our preliminary analysis.

PART I.

DE QUINCEY. MACAULAY.
CARLYLE.

CHAPTER I.

THOMAS DE QUINCEY,

1785—1859.

Among the most eminent prose writers of this century is Thomas de Quincey, best known as *The English Opium-Eater*.

The family of De Quincey, as we learn from this its most famous modern representative, was originally Norwegian, played a distinguished part in the Norman Conquest, and flourished through nine or ten generations as one of the houses of nobility, until its head, the Earl of Winchester, was attainted for treason. For more than a century before the birth of the "Opium-Eater," none of his name had borne a title of high rank. His father was an opulent merchant in Manchester, who died young, leaving his widow a fortune of £1600 a-year.

We know the particulars of the earlier part of De Quincey's life from his 'Confessions of an Opium-Eater,' and his 'Autobiographic Sketches.' The fifth son of a family of eight, he was born on the 15th of August 1785, at Greenhay, then an isolated house about a mile from Manchester. He has recorded his earliest recollections; and he was so precocious, that these date from the middle of his second year. His autobiography contains few incidents that depart strikingly from the ordinary course of the world. In his own record, things that are insignificant as objects of general interest assume the proportions that all human beings must assign to the events of their own life.

His first great affliction was the death of a favourite sister when he was about six years old. Were we to measure him by the standard of ordinary children, we should refuse to believe what he tells us of the profound gloom thrown over him by this bereavement—"the night that for him gathered upon that event ran after his steps far into life." "Well it was for me at this period," he says, "if well it were for me to live at all, that from any continued contemplation of my misery I was forced to wean myself, and suddenly to assume the harness of life."

From these "sickly reveries" he was suddenly withdrawn, and "introduced to the world of strife." A "horrid pugilistic brother," five or six years older than himself, whose "genius for mischief amounted to inspiration," returned home from a public school. The character of this brother is drawn in the Sketches with exquisite humour and fondness. He was a boy of amazing spirits and volubility. He maintained a constant war with the boys of a neighbouring factory, and compelled little Thomas to bear a part. He kept the nursery in a whirl of excitement and wonder with war bulletins, ghost stories, tragic theatricals, and burlesque lectures "on all subjects known to man, from the Thirty-nine Articles of our English Church down to pyrotechnics, legerdemain, magic—both black and white—thaumaturgy, and necromancy."

After two years of this excitement, William left Greenhay, and Thomas, then in his eighth year, relapsed into his quiet life, and steadily pursued his studies under one of his guardians, finding in that guardian's family other objects for his precocious sympathy and meditation. When he was eleven years old his mother removed to Bath, and placed him at the grammar-school there. He had made such progress under his guardian's tutorship that at Bath his Latin verses were paraded by the head-master as an incitement to the older boys. This distinction led to his removal from the school. His austere mother was so shocked at the compliments he was receiving, that, after two years, she sent him to a private school in Wiltshire, "of which," he says, "the chief recommendation lay in the religious character of the master." At Winkfield he remained but a year. Then came a pleasant interlude in his school life. He spent the summer travelling in Ireland with Lord Westport, a young friend of his own age, and on his return stayed for three months at Laxton, the seat of Lord Carbery, where he studied Greek and talked theology with the beautiful Lady Carbery. But his pleasures were again interrupted by the higher powers. His guardians decided that he should go for three years to Manchester grammar-school before proceeding to Oxford. Some boys would have hailed the change with pleasure, but young De Quincey, though then but fifteen and a few months more, was premature in the expansion of his mind, and had begun to think boyish society intolerable. He went to Manchester in 1800, but he could not bring himself to be content with his situation. In the course of two years his health gave way, and, no longer able to endure the restraint, he took his departure one day without warning. His wanderings did not last long. He walked straight to Chester; and, while hanging about his mother's house trying to get an interview with his sister, was caught by an easy stratagem. He was not, however, sent back to school, but remained at his mother's house till his guardians should decide what was to be done with him.

Soon followed the great adventure of his life, the most interesting part of his Confessions. Obtaining some money from his mother for a pedestrian tour in Wales, he tired of the mountain solitudes, and shaped his course to London, in hopes of being able to borrow two hundred pounds on his expectations. Here he went through hard experiences. His errand brought him under the vexatious extortions and delays of a money-lender. He was reduced to the brink of starvation. On one occasion, indeed, he might have perished but for the kindness of a companion in misfortune, the poor outcast Anne, whom in happier days he vainly sought to trace. Fortunately he was discovered and taken home again. He remained at home about a year; but being taunted by his uncle with wasting his time, he undertook to go to Oxford upon £100 of an annual allowance, and proceeded thither in the October of 1803.

The 'Autobiographic Sketches,' as republished, terminate with his sudden resolution to go to Oxford. In their original form, as contributions to 'Tait's Magazine,' three more papers undertake to describe his life at Oxford, but these consist mostly of rambling digressions on the idea of an English University, on the Greek orators, on Paley, and suchlike, and contain very little personal narrative. This much we may glean, that he lived a hermit kind of life, and did not conform in the least to the studies of the place. He "sequestered himself" so completely that (to quote his own expression), "for the first two years of my residence in Oxford, I compute that I did not utter one hundred words." He had but one conversation with his tutor. "It consisted of three sentences, two of which fell to his share, one to mine." In all senses he was justified in exclaiming, "Oxford, ancient mother! hoary with ancestral honours, time-honoured, and, haply it may be, time-shattered power, I owe thee nothing! Of thy vast riches I took not a shilling, though living among multitudes who owed to thee their daily bread." In the matter of study, he was a law to himself. He told his tutor in that notable conversation that he was reading Paley; but in point of fact he had been "reading and studying very closely the 'Parmenides.'" As a schoolboy he had attained to an unusual mastery over the Greek language, "moving through all the obstacles and resistances of a Greek book with the same celerity and ease as through those of the French and Latin"—and he read Greek daily; "but any slight vanity which he might connect with a power so rarely attained, and which, under ordinary circumstances, so readily transmutes itself into a disproportionate admiration of the author, in him was *absolutely swallowed up in the tremendous hold taken of his entire sensibilities at this time by our own literature.*"

In his 'Recollections of Coleridge' he says, "From 1803 to 1808 I was a student at Oxford." This probably means that for those five years he remained formally on the books of Worcester College. How much of this time he spent in actual residence is not recorded, and in all likelihood cannot be ascertained. When we consider his self-determined habits of study, we see that it matters comparatively little to know where he lived. There is a tradition that he once submitted to the written part of the Final Examination, but abruptly left Oxford without offering himself for the oral part.

In the intervals of his residence at Oxford, he began to make occasional visits to London, and to get introductions to literary society. He had always been especially anxious to see Coleridge and Wordsworth. When he ran away from school, he would have gone to the Lake district, had he not scrupled to present himself in the character of a fugitive schoolboy. About Christmas 1804-5 he had gone to London with an introduction to Charles Lamb, his final object being to procure through Lamb an introduction to Coleridge. His wishes were not gratified till later than this. He first saw Coleridge at Bristol in the autumn of 1807, and Wordsworth later in the same year, at the poet's cottage in the Vale of Grasmere.

In the winter of 1808-9 he took up his residence at the Lakes. Wordsworth had quitted his cottage in Grasmere for the larger house of Allan Bank, and De Quincey succeeded this illustrious tenant. He retained this cottage for seven-and-twenty years, and up to 1829 it was his principal place of residence. "From this era," he says, "through a period of about twenty years in succession, I may describe my domicile as being amongst the lakes and mountains of Westmoreland. It is true, I often made excursions to London, Bath, and its neighbourhood, or northwards to Edinburgh; and perhaps, on an average, passed one-fourth part of each year at a distance from this district; but here only it was that henceforwards I had a house and small establishment." A good many interesting particulars about the society of the Lakes, and his way of passing his time, are given in some papers that have not been republished ('Tait's Magazine,' 1840).

From the time of his settling at the Lakes, a habit grew upon him which powerfully influenced his life. Some four years after he took up his residence at Grasmere, he became a confirmed and daily opium-eater. The rise and progress of this habit, the pleasures and the pains of the "pernicious drug," and the miseries of his struggle to leave it off, are related in his Opium Confessions. He had first tasted opium in 1804, as a cure for toothache. From that date up to 1812 he took opium as an occasional indulgence, "fixing beforehand how often, within a given time, and when, he would commit a debauch of opium." It was not till 1813 that opium became with him an article of daily diet; in that year he multiplied the laudanum drams to allay "an appalling irritation of the stomach." The large doses once begun, he could not break off. He went on from one degree of indulgence to another, till in 1816 he was taking as much as 8000 drops of laudanum per day. Probably in view of his approaching marriage, he succeeded in reducing his allowance to 1000 drops. He married towards the close of 1816. Up to the middle of 1817 he "judges himself to have been a happy man;" and he draws a beautiful picture of the interior of his cottage in a stormy winter night, with "warm hearth-rugs, tea, a fair tea-maker, shutters closed, curtains flowing in ample draperies on the floor, whilst the wind and rain are raging audibly without." Again he seems to have lapsed into over-indulgence—to have succumbed to the "Circean spells" of opium. The next four years he spent in a kind of intellectual torpor, utterly incapable of sustained exertion. "But for misery and suffering," he says, "I might indeed be said to have existed in a dormant state. I seldom could prevail on myself to write a letter. An answer of a few words to any that I received was the utmost that I could accomplish; and often *that* not until the letter had lain weeks, or even months, on my writing-table." At length in 1821, with the increasing expenses of his household, his affairs became embarrassed, and he was called upon by the strongest inducements to shake off this dead weight upon his energies. He succeeded. Unable wholly to renounce the use of opium, he yet reduced the amount so far as to be capable of literary exertion.[1]

His first production was the 'Confessions of an English Opium-Eater.' This appeared in the 'London Magazine' in the autumn of 1821, and was reprinted in a separate form in the following year.

From 1821 to 1825, though he still spent the greater part of his time at Grasmere, he was often in London, his lodgings being in York Street, Covent Garden. During that time he was a frequent contributor to the 'London Magazine.' He speaks of his "daily task of writing and producing something for the journals;" calls

[1] The Opium Confessions, as they stand in the final edition, convey the impression, though not in specific words, that he had wholly renounced the use of opium, and he is usually accused of having pretended to a self-command that he never absolutely acquired. Had the appendix to the first edition of the Confessions been reprinted, he might have been spared this accusation. He there explains why, in the narrative as originally written in the 'London Magazine,' he wished to convey the impression that he had wholly renounced the use of opium; and says that in suffering his readers to think of him as a reformed opium-eater, he left no impression but what he shared himself.

himself "one of the *corps littérataire;*" and says that the following writers were in 1821-2-3 "amon t his *collaborateurs*" in the 'London Magazine'—Charles Lamb, Hazlitt, Allan Cunningham, Hood, Hamilton, Reynolds, Carey. In his 'Noctes Ambrosianæ,' Christopher North says that the magazine failed because De Quincey's papers were glaringly superior to the other contributions—a whimsical gibe at the other contributors. A performance of his in the autumn of 1824 may be mentioned as showing how thoroughly he had identified himself with the literary brotherhood. It was, as he says, "the most complete literary hoax that ever can have been perpetrated." A German bookseller had published a novel in German under the title of 'Walladmoor,' professing that it was a translation from Sir Walter Scott. De Quincey reviewed the pseudo-translation hurriedly, and spoke of it in rather high terms, chance having directed him to the only tolerable passages in the work. Thereupon a London firm conceived the idea of translating it, and employed De Quincey as translator. When he came to go through the work in detail, he found it, as he says, "such 'almighty' nonsense (to speak *transatlantice*)" that translating it was out of the question; and accordingly he rewrote the greater part of it. All the same, his composition was given to the English world as a translation from the German. His dedication of the performance to the German forger is a very fine piece of humour. His industry in London does not seem to have been sufficiently rewarded to relieve him from his embarrassments. In a letter to Professor Wilson, dated from London, 1825, he expresses himself as being in dread of apprehension for debt.

After 1825 his literary activity was directed almost entirely to Edinburgh. He was probabl drawn there by his friendship with Wilson. In 1826 he began, in 'Blackwood's Magazine,' a series of papers under the title of "Gallery of German Prose Classics;" but opium-eaters, as he said, "though good fellows upon the whole, never finish anything"—and the Gallery never received more than two celebrities, Lessing and Kant, the series ending with the third instalment. From 1825 to 1849 he wrote a great deal for 'Blackwood,' contributing altogether about fifty papers that have been reprinted, three or four sometimes upon one subject. Among the most famous of these 'Blackwood' papers were—"Murder considered as one of the Fine Arts" (1827), "Toilette of a Hebrew Lady" (1828), "Dr Parr and his Contemporaries, or Whiggism in its Relations to Literature" (1831), "The Cæsars" (1832-3-4), "The Essenes" (1840), "On Style" (1840-1), "Homer and the Homeridæ" (1841), "Coleridge and Opium-Eating" (1845), "Suspiria de Profundis" (1845), "The Mail-Coach," and "The Vision of Sudden Death" (1849).

In 1834 he formed another very fertile literary connection,

becoming a contributor to 'Tait's Magazine.' This connection is better known than his earlier and longer-continued connection with Blackwood, because his papers were not anonymous, but bore either his own name or the well-known *alias*, "The English Opium-Eater." He contributed very regularly up to 1841, and again in 1845 and 1846. He sent in altogether nearly fifty separate papers, of which about two-thirds have been reprinted. The most famous were his "Sketches of Life and Manners, from the Autobiography of an English Opium-Eater," contributed at intervals up to 1841. For some unexplained reason, not more than one-half of these have been reprinted. About thirty of his contributions to 'Tait' were personal reminiscences. These are represented in his collected works by two volumes—'Autobiographic Sketches' (vol. xiv.) and 'Recollections of the Lakes' (vol. ii.) Apart from these, his best-known papers in 'Tait' were "A Tory's Account of Toryism, Whiggism, and Radicalism" (1835-36).

Little seems to be known about his place of residence from 1830 to 1843. Up to 1829 he lived chiefly at Grasmere. He spent the year 1830 with Professor Wilson in Edinburgh. In 1835 he gave up his cottage at Grasmere. In 1843 he settled with his family at Lasswade, a small village near Edinburgh. It is probably to this interval that we must refer Mr John Hill Burton's somewhat overdone sketch of his habits and personal appearance in the 'Book-Hunter,' where De Quincey appears as "Thomas Papaverius," a "mighty book-hunter."

During 1842-3-4 he sent nothing to 'Tait,' and very little to 'Blackwood;' and in 1844 appeared the only work of his that first saw the light as an independent book—'The Logic of Political Economy.' It is not a complete exposition of political economy, but, as the title imports, of certain first principles—the doctrines of value, market-value, wages, rent, and profits.

As in the case of Macaulay, Carlyle, and others, his scattered contributions to periodical literature were first republished in America. The collection was begun by the firm of Ticknor, Reed, & Fields, Boston, in 1852, without the author's knowledge; but the publishers generously made him a sharer in the profits of the publication, and he ultimately gave his assistance to the work of collecting the scattered papers. The first English edition, "in fourteen volumes crown 8vo, was published by Messrs Hogg of Edinburgh, during the eight years 1853-60; and all the papers it contained, with the exception of a few in the last volume, enjoyed the author's revision and correction."

His last productions were some papers on China, contributed to 'Titan' (a continuation of 'Hogg's Instructor') in 1856-57. They are not included in his collected works, but are republished separately.

He died at Edinburgh, December 8, 1859, in his seventy-fifth year.

We have several descriptions of De Quincey's personal appearance. He was a slender little man, with small, clearly chiselled features, a large head, and a remarkably high, square forehead. "In addition," says Professor Masson, "to the general impression of his diminutiveness and fragility, one was struck with the peculiar beauty of his head and forehead, rising disproportionately high over his small, wrinkly visage, and gentle, deep-set eyes." There was a peculiarly high and regular arch in the wrinkles of his brow, which was also slightly contracted. The lines of his countenance fell naturally into an expression of mild suffering, of endurance sweetened by benevolence, or, according to the fancy of the interpreter, of gentle, melancholy sweetness. All that met him seem to have been struck with the measured, silvery, yet somewhat hollow and unearthly, tones of his voice, the more impressive that the flow of his talk was unhesitating and unbroken.

"Although a man considerably under height and slender of form, he was capable of undergoing great fatigue, and took constant exercise." His having been the travelling companion of Christopher North about the English lakes is a sufficient certificate. The weak point in his bodily system, as he frequently tells us, was his stomach. This weakness he often pleads as the justification of his opium-eating. Opium was "the sole remedy potent enough to control his distress and irritability." He sometimes humorously exaggerates his infirmity. "A more worthless body than his own, the author is free to confess, cannot be. It is his pride to believe that it is the very ideal of a base, crazy, despicable human system, that hardly ever could have been meant to be seaworthy for two days under the ordinary storms and wear and tear of life; and, indeed, if that were the creditable way of disposing of human bodies, he must own that he should almost be ashamed to bequeath his wretched structure to any respectable dog."

As often happens,[1] the impoverishment of certain bodily organs was accompanied, if not caused, by an enormous and disproportionate activity of intellect. It may be doubted whether we have ever seen in this quarter of the globe a man so completely absorbed in mental operations, and so far removed from our ordinary way of looking at the world. He resembled the contemplative sages of India more than the intellectual men of rough, practical England.

[1] "In general," says our author, "a man has reason to think himself well off in the great lottery of this life if he draws the prize of a healthy stomach without a mind, or the prize of a fine intellect with a crazy stomach; but that any man should draw both is truly astonishing, and, I suppose, happens only once in a century."

Of no man can it be absolutely true that he does nothing but observe, read, meditate, imagine, and communicate the results; but this may be affirmed of De Quincey with a nearer approach to truth than it can be affirmed of any other great name in our literature.

In reading his works, one of the first things that strike us is the extreme multifariousness of his knowledge. When we compare him even with writers of a high order, we cannot help being astonished at the force of a memory that could hold so much in readiness for immediate use. He was noted for conversational powers; and, as he himself explains, one of his peculiar advantages for conversation was "a prodigious memory" and "an inexhaustible fertility of topics."

In his writings this retentive capacity often makes us pause and wonder. For some of his most curious freaks of scholarship, indeed, his "Toilette of a Hebrew Lady" and his "Casuistry of Roman Meals," he took most of the materials at second-hand from the German. Still, if we were to assemble all his digressions, quotations, notes, and allusions, we should be sufficiently convinced of the immense and eccentric range of his reading, and at the same time of his tenacious hold of what he had read. Indeed, if we were to make such a collection, we should be no less astonished at the extent of another field of his memory. We should find that he was a close observer of human character, and that he noted and remembered characteristic peculiarities and expressions of feeling with Boswellian minuteness. In the course of his wanderings he met persons of all ranks and conditions, and he seldom mentions a name without giving some characteristic particulars of the person.

Then, as regards the other great intellectual force—the power of recovering analogous circumstances or detecting hidden resemblances—De Quincey had a very remarkable, perhaps a still more remarkable, endowment. Speaking of his conversational powers, he says that in addition to the advantage of a prodigious memory, he had "the far greater advantage of a logical instinct for feeling in a moment the secret analogies or parallelisms that connected things else apparently remote." And again, writing of his powers of memory, he says, "I mention this in no spirit of boasting. Far from it; for, on the contrary, amongst my mortifications have been compliments to my memory, when, in fact, any compliment that I had merited was due to the higher faculty of an electric aptitude for seizing analogies, and, by means of those aerial pontoons, passing over like lightning from one topic to another."[1] This power appears in his writings in several shapes. The quotations and allusions that show his wide knowledge of books and men are very obvious signs of the activity of his analogical faculty. His numerous illustrations, and the metaphorical cast of his language are no

[1] Blackwood's Magazine, April 1845.

less striking. Less obtrusive evidences of the faculty, but still more valuable as being evidences of its strength, are his power of breaking through routine views, and the ingenious plausibility of his arguments. He very rarely assumes a traditional view without some note of exception, and this evidently not from a rough love of paradox—as is sometimes alleged by careless readers—but from his strong and delicate sensibility to the exact relations of things. Nothing can be more exquisite than his subtlety in distinguishing wherein things agree and wherein they differ—in what respects a traditional view is warrantable, and in what respects it is erroneous. Equally charming to the lover of intellectual subtlety are his deliberate arrays of argument in support of a favourite thesis, as seen in such performances as his paper on the Essenes, or his attempt to whitewash the character of Judas Iscariot. His skill in urging every circumstance favourable to his opinion, and in explaining away everything that bears against it, gives to the English reader an idea of elaborate ingenuity not to be obtained from any other of our recognised "leaders of literature."

Were De Quincey's writings the outcome of nothing more generally attractive than profound erudition, intellectual subtlety, and powers of copious expression, they would not have taken such a hold of public interest. But he was not an arid philosopher, a modern Duns Scotus or Thomas Aquinas. He tells us that he read "German metaphysicians, Latin schoolmen, thaumaturgic Platonists, and religious Mystics," but he tells us also that at one time "a tremendous hold was taken of his entire sensibilities by our own literature." Though he "well knew that his proper vocation was the exercise of the analytic understanding," he spent perhaps the greater part of his time in the exercise of the imagination, taking profound delight in "the sublimer and more passionate poets," in "the grand lamentations of Samson Agonistes, or the great harmonies of the Satanic speeches in 'Paradise Regained.'"

He described himself as a Eudæmonist or Hedonist—averse to everything that did not bring him immediate enjoyment; and this half-humorous description may be allowed, if we take care not to forget that his enjoyments were of a peculiar nature. His pleasures were not boisterous—not dependent upon a flow of animal spirits. He was an intellectual Hedonist, or pleasure-seeker. During a considerable part of his time he was rapt in his favourite studies, in works of the analytic understanding, of history, and of imagination. But even in daily life, in intercourse with the world, his imagination seems to have been preternaturally active. He was a close observer of character, as we can see both from his works and from the testimony of those that knew him. But, as we also know from both sources, his imagination was constantly active in shaping his surroundings into objects of refined pleasure, ranging through many varieties of grave and gay. He applied this transfiguring process to the incidents of his own life—not inventing romantic or comical incidents, but dwelling upon certain features of what really took place, and investing them with lofty, tender, or humorous imagery. So with his friends and casual acquaintances. He was sufficiently observant of what they really did and said, was remarkably acute in divining what passed in their minds, and felt the disagreeable as well as the agreeable points of their character; but he had the power of abstracting from the disagreeable circumstances. He fixed his imagination upon the agreeable side of an acquaintance, and transmuted the mixed handiwork of nature into a pure object of æsthetic pleasure.[1]

His pleasures, we have said, were not boisterous. He had not the constitution for hearty enjoyment of life. In his Sketches he describes himself as being, in his boyhood, "the shiest of children," "constitutionally touched with pensiveness," "naturally dedicated to despondency." From his repose of manners he was a privileged visitor to the bedroom of his dying father. He was passionately fond of peace, had "a perfect craze for being despised"—considering contempt as the only security for unmolested repose—and always tried to hide his precocious accomplishments from the curiosity of strangers. All his life through he retained this shyness. He had splendid conversational powers, and never was silent from timidity, at least when under the influence of his favourite opium; and yet he rather avoided than courted society. He humorously tells us how he was horrified at a party in London when he saw a large company of guests filing in one after the other, and divined from their looks that they had come to "lionise" the Opium-Eater. Mr Hill Burton represents the difficulty of getting him out to literary parties in Edinburgh in spite of his most solemn promises; and we have from Professor Masson a pleasant instance of his shyness to recognise a new acquaintance in the street, and of his nervousness when he found himself the subject of observation.

Such a man often contracts strong special attachments. In some of the impassioned records of the Confessions and the 'Autobiographic Sketches,' we have evidence of the strength of De Quincey's affections. In writing of living friends, he usually practises a delicate reserve, and veils his tenderness under the mask of humour. Yet even to this there are some exceptions, such as the touching address to his absent wife in the Opium Confessions. In writing of departed friends, he pours out his feelings without reserve. His sister Elizabeth, the outcast Anne,

[1] It is not meant that he was so unlike other men as to be doing this constantly; only that he seized upon and transfigured actual objects into ideals much more than the generality of intellectual men.

the infant daughter of Wordsworth, and his unfortunate friend Charles L——,[1] may be mentioned as objects that at different periods of his life engrossed his affections, and whose loss he deplores with impassioned sorrow.

He has sometimes been accused of letting his imagination dwell too favourably upon himself—of being especially vain. Now we call a man vain when he pretends to something that he does not possess, or when he makes an ostentatious display of his possessions. It has not been alleged that De Quincey was vain in the first and worst sense; he has never been accused of exaggerating for the purpose of extorting admiration. But it is alleged that he was vain in the second sense; that he makes a complacently ostentatious display of his ancestral line, of his aristocratic connections, of his romantic adventures, of his philosophical knowledge, of his wonderful dreams. Such a charge could hardly be made but by a hasty or an undiscriminating reader. In the 'Autobiographic Sketches' we are never complacently invited to admire. We never think of the writer as a self-glorified hero, unless we are all the more jealous of being thrown into the shade. We are taken into his confidence, but he challenges our sympathy, not our admiration. He often speaks of himself humorously, but never with ostentatious complacency. He treats himself with no greater favour than any of the other subjects of his narrative. The truth seems to be, that he who observed and speculated upon every human creature that came under his notice, observed and speculated most of all upon himself as the human creature that he was best acquainted with. He was too discerning a genius to be unconscious of his own excellence, and too little of a humbug to pretend that he was.

As he has been accused of vanity, so he has sometimes been accused of arrogance, upon a still graver misconception of his shy, retiring nature, and his humorous self-irony. His dogmatic judgments of Plato, Cicero, Dr Johnson, and other eminent men, and his strong expressions of national and political prejudice, are sometimes quoted as signs of a tendency to domineer. It may safely be asserted that whoever takes up this view has not penetrated far into the peculiar personality of De Quincey. Whatever might be the strength of his expressions, and these were often exaggerated for comic effect, there have been few men of equal power more unaffectedly open to reasonable conviction. When he had made up his mind, he took a pleasure, usually a humorous pleasure, in putting his opinion as strongly as possible; but that was no index as regarded his susceptibility to new light. This we may reasonably infer from his character as revealed in his works; and if we need further evidence, we have it in the words

[1] The two last are mentioned in papers that have not been reprinted.

of his personal acquaintance Mr Burton, who speaks of his "gentle and kindly spirit," and his boyish ardour at making a new discovery. Equally mistaken is the charge of jealousy, which comes from some admirers of Wordsworth and Coleridge. He always, and with obvious sincerity, professed an admiration for the extraordinary qualities of these men, but he knew exactly where their strength lay; he knew that both were men of special strength combined with special infirmity, and in his "Recollections" of them, while doing all justice to their merits, he did not scruple to expose their faults. On this ground he is charged with jealousy. But before we admit a charge so inconsistent with what we know of his character otherwise, it must be shown that his criticisms are unfair, or that they contain anything that can be construed into an evidence of malice. Had De Quincey been a jealous, irritable man, instead of being "gentle and kindly" as he was, the universally attested arrogance and contemptuous manner of Wordsworth would have driven him to take part with the 'Edinburgh Review,' and in that case the great poet's reputation might have been considerably delayed.

I have dwelt at disproportionate length upon two qualities that are *not* marked in De Quincey's character, simply for the reason that unappreciative critics have described them as the ruling emotions of his personal reminiscences. To discuss them at such length without a guarding statement would create misconception. We may say, in loose terms, that two kinds of emotion almost engrossed his imagination, and that these, in the peculiar form they assumed in De Quincey, were diametrically antagonistic and inevitably destructive to emotions so petty as vanity or jealous egotism. These two ruling emotions may be vaguely described as humour and sublimity.

Though naturally unfitted for rough merriment, for Teufelsdroeckh laughter, De Quincey had a keen sense of the ridiculous. None of his papers are without humorous strokes, and some of them are extravagantly humorous from beginning to end. Christopher North began to take opium, but desisted upon finding, as he said, that it destroyed his moral sensibilities, and put him into such a condition of mind that he was ready to laugh at anything, no matter how venerable. It is sometimes said that opium had a similar effect upon De Quincey. But, as he would have delighted to point out, a distinction must be drawn as regards laughter at things venerable: the laugh may be malicious, designed to bring a venerable object into contempt, or it may be humorous, revolving simply upon its own extravagance—degradation of the object being manifestly serious and ill-natured in the one case, and manifestly whimsical and good-natured in the other. There is not a trace of malice in De Quincey's laughter. It is, as he described it himself, merely "humorous extravagance." He is a humorist, not a satirist. Sometimes he treats venerable persons or institutions with playful banter. Sometimes, by a kind of inverse process, he takes a pleasure in speaking of mean occupations with expressions of mock dignity. One unique vein of his humour consists in speaking with affection or admiration, or with a dry business tone, concerning objects usually regarded with horror and indignation. Whatever he does, as we shall see when we come to exemplify his humour, he does all with good-nature. He seldom applies his banter to living persons, and then in such a way that none but very touchy subjects could take offence. Indeed, so playful and stingless is his humour, that many profess themselves unable to see anything to laugh at in his peculiar extravagances. In humour, of course, everything depends upon the reader's attitude of mind. De Quincey's own answer to his censors is complete: "*Not to sympathise is not to understand;* and the playfulness which is not relished, becomes flat and insipid, or absolutely without meaning."

His genius for the sublime is unquestioned. He was singularly open to impressions of grandeur. As in his humour, so in his susceptibility to sublime effects, it is difficult for an energetic people like us to lower ourselves into this peculiar state of mind. I say to *lower* ourselves, for the effort implies a diminution of our active energies and the intensifying of our passive susceptibilities. One of the best ways of understanding De Quincey in his sublime moods is to contrast him with Carlyle in his so-called hero-worship. The attitude of mind in worship, as usually understood, is a passive attitude—an attitude of reverential prostration, of adoring contemplation. If this be so, the term worship is incorrectly applied to Carlyle's attitude, and applies with much greater propriety to De Quincey's. Carlyle's state of mind seems to be a state of exalted *activity.* A man of force and vigour, he seems to *sympathise with the efforts* of his heroes—to feel himself, in thinking of them, exalted to the same pitch of victorious energy. Now this is not a state of prostration, of adoration, but the highest possible state of ideal activity—the moment of success in imaginary Titanic effort. On the contrary, De Quincey's attitude is essentially an attitude of adoration, of awe-struck *passivity.* He lies still, as it were,—remains quiescent; passively allows magnificent conceptions to enter his mind and dwell there. Carlyle's hero-worship is more the intoxication of power than the worship of power, the sublime of egotism more than the sublime of adoration. The vision of great manifestations of power seems to act upon the one as a stimulant, upon the other as a narcotic, conspiring with the subduing influence of "all-potent opium."

The power that walks in darkness, that leaves for the imagination a wide margin of "potentiality," is more impressive than power with a definite limit. Accordingly De Quincey tells us that "his nature almost demanded mystery."

The pleasing astonishment inspired by visions of grandeur is nearly allied to awe, and awe passes readily into panic dread. This De Quincey experienced in his opium-dreams. "Clouds of gloomy grandeur overhung his dreams at all stages of opium, and, in the last, grew into the darkest of miseries." His dreams were tumultuous — "with dreadful faces thronged and fiery arms." Sometimes gorgeous spectacles, "such as never yet were beheld by waking eye," suddenly gave place to "hurrying trepidations." Sometimes he was filled with apprehensions of frightful disaster, while kept motionless by "the weight of twenty Atlantics."

As regards the sensuous framework of De Quincey's emotions, it is interesting to notice his peculiar sensibility to the luxuries and grandeurs of the ear. He was not insensible to the "pomps and glories" of the eye, but the ear was his most highly endowed sense. This is his own analysis. He recognised, he said, his sensibility to music as rising above the common standard by various tests—"by the indispensableness of it to his daily comfort, the readiness with which he made any sacrifices to obtain a 'grand debauch' of that nature, &c. &c." He might have mentioned as a good confirmation that he broke through the traditional explanation of Æschylus's "multitudinous laughter of the boundless ocean," as referring to the visual appearance of the waves, and asked whether it might not refer to the sounds of the ocean. For him the image would have had a greater charm if referred to the ear. One of his favourite pleasures of "imagination" (if we may use the word in a sense not exactly warranted by its derivation) was to construct ideal music out of the sounds of nature. "Often and often," he says, "seating myself on a stone by the side of the mountain-river Brathay, I have stayed for hours listening to the same sound to which so often C—— L—— and I used to hearken together with profound emotion and awe—the sound of pealing anthems, as if streaming from the open portals of some illimitable cathedral; and many times I have heard it of a quiet night, when no stranger could have been persuaded to believe it other than the sound of choral chanting—distant, solemn, saintly."

When we view De Quincey on the active side, we find a great deficiency, corresponding to his intense occupation with the exercise of the analytic understanding and the imagination, both in the study and in the actual world. He was signally wanting in the pushing activity of the English race. Very characteristic is what he tells us of his boyhood, that when he was ordered to do a thing, instead of forthwith rushing off to do it, or stubbornly refusing obedience, like an active English child, he first made sure that he exactly understood the mandate, bothering his superior to express himself with scrupulous precision of language.

He took little interest in the practical "questions" of the day. He is said to have written, about 1821, a criticism of Lord Brougham under the title of "Close Comments on a Straggling Speech;" but this, one may guess, was more humorous than practical. On one occasion he professed to "descend from his long habits of philosophical speculation to a casual intercourse with fugitive and personal politics"—namely, in 1835, when he wrote his "Account of Toryism, Whiggism, and Radicalism" for 'Tait's Magazine.' Here, however, quite as much as elsewhere, he is still the abstract philosopher, not the man of practice: he expressly refuses to discuss the policy of the rival parties on any particular question, and confines himself to an original exposition of their abstract creeds, their mutual relations to the British Constitution. So little practical interest did he take in the current business of the nation, that at one time he acknowledges that he had not read a newspaper for three years. One must almost suppose that he informed himself of the proceedings of existing parties with no livelier interest than he took in the proceedings of parties in ancient Greece or Rome.

His habits seem to have been very irregular. He did not want steadiness of application to special studies; he did not roam restlessly from field to field, but set himself down to a subject, and mastered it, not content till he had read everything that he could find upon the particular subject. But he hated the labour of producing, at times with an absolute loathing. He wrote nothing till forced by pecuniary embarrassment. In the course of some remarks on Coleridge, he says that it is characteristic of an opium-eater to finish nothing that he begins; and his own works to some extent bear out this humorous principle.

Mr Hill Burton gives an interesting picture of his indifference to the ordinary ways of human business. "Only immediate craving necessities could ever extract from him an acknowledgment of the common vulgar agencies by which men subsist in civilised society." "Those who knew him a little might call him a loose man in money matters; those who knew him closer, laughed at the idea of coupling any notion of pecuniary or other like responsibility with his nature."

As regards his Opinions. He professed himself a Tory in politics, and spoke with sternness, and even ferocity, concerning Whigs, Radicals, Republicans, Revolutionists, and "the faction of Jacobinism through its entire gamut." He objected to the Reform

Bill of 1832 that it had "ruffianised" Parliament—"introduced a Kentucky element" into an assembly conducted with more than Roman dignity. Theoretically, he held that both Whigs and Tories were necessary to the British Constitution, as guiding the two opposed forces of the nation, the one the democratic, the other the aristocratic; that, properly understood, they were as two hemispheres, the one incomplete without the other. In their views of current questions, one party must be right and the other wrong, at least so far; but as regarded their reasons for existing, it was absurd to ask which was right and which was wrong—both *must* exist. He belonged himself by birth to the aristocratic party, and probably in his philosophic way he considered it his duty to criticise Radicals from the aristocratic point of view, using strong language without any corresponding strength of feeling.

As a literary critic, his catholicity of spirit and breadth of view were unique among the men of his time. Rarely indeed, if ever, has a mind so calm, unprejudiced, and comprehensive, been applied to the work of criticism. In his own day he was usually numbered among the "Lakers," or partisans of Wordsworth, Coleridge, and Southey. He was so only in the sense of treating these remarkable men with justice. He, better than Jeffrey himself, knew the shortcomings of Wordsworth, condemned his theory of poetic diction, and made fun of absurdities in "The Excursion;" but he felt the shortcomings with calm discrimination, and was not misled by them into undervaluing the striking originality of Wordsworth's genius. He was one of the most devout of the admirers of Shakspeare, and, as we have seen, entered with passionate rapture into the majestic harmonies of Milton; but he had no part in the common bond of the Lakers—their wholesale contempt for Pope. He says, in one of his "uncollected" papers:—

"In the literature of every nation, we are naturally disposed to place in the highest rank those who have produced some great and colossal work—a 'Paradise Lost,' a 'Hamlet,' a 'Novum Organum'—which presupposes an effort of intellect, a comprehensive grasp, and a sustaining power, for its original conception, corresponding in grandeur to that effort, different in kind, which must preside in its execution. But, after this highest class, in which the power to conceive and the power to execute are upon the same scale of grandeur, there comes a second, in which brilliant powers of execution, applied to conceptions of a very inferior range, are allowed to establish a classical rank. Every literature possesses, besides its great national gallery, a cabinet of minor pieces, not less perfect in their polish, possibly more so. In reality, the characteristic of this class is elaborate perfection—the point of inferiority is not in the finishing, but in the compass and power of the original creation, which (however exquisite in its class) moves within a smaller sphere. To this class belong, for example, 'The Rape of the Lock,' that finished jewel of English literature; 'The Dunciad' (a still more exquisite gem); 'The Vicar of Wakefield' (in its earlier part): in German, &c."

He has been charged with an open depreciation of Keats and Shelley. But this we cannot reconcile with his papers on these poets. Without even giving him the benefit of his plea, that the papers were "slight impromptus, peremptorily excluding a comprehensive view of the subject," and disregarding his statement when they were reprinted that "in the case of Keats there is something which (after a lapse of several years) I could wish unsaid, or said more gently," we may take them as they stand. He charges Keats with "trampling upon his mother-tongue as with the hoofs of a buffalo," and says of "Endymion" that it exhibits "the very midsummer madness of affectation, of false vapoury sentiment, and of fantastic effeminacy." But this judgment of the earlier poem did not prevent him from calling the "Hyperion" "imperishable," and ascribing to it "the majesty, the austere beauty, and the simplicity of a Grecian temple enriched with Grecian sculpture." As for any depreciation of Shelley, *that* I have been unable to find. He makes fun, in a kindly spirit, of Shelley's youthful confidence in waging war against the ruling powers, but at the same time he praises the youth's sincerity, pronounces him "the least false of human creatures," and speaks of "the profound respect due to his exalted powers." The truth is, that the charges made against De Quincey's criticisms are due to his unusual comprehensiveness of view and his sensibility to diversities of gifts. He was, to borrow his own words, "a large estimator of things as they are—of natural gifts, and their infinite distribution through an infinite scale of degrees, and the compensating accomplishments which take place in so vast a variety of forms." Hence came numerous misapprehensions. Too many critics, in his day no less than now, credited their idols with every excellence of composition, every excellence of head and heart, every propriety of conduct in their several relations as superiors, inferiors, and equals. When De Quincey, who was never blind to a man's genuine claims to superiority, drew these claims into stronger relief by recording attendant defects, outcries arose on every hand that he was stealthily undermining established reputations. People refused to understand that a writer "hopelessly inferior in one talent" could yet be "vastly superior in another."

A word on his estimates of foreign writers. His exposure of weak points in such universally established names as Homer, Plato, Cicero, and Goethe, is set down to no higher motive than a love of paradox, a passion for inspiring wonder. Of this every reader must judge for himself. Only when we criticise the criticisms of De Quincey, we must bear in mind the unparalleled extent of his reading. This unique preparation for valuing literary powers entitles him to be criticised with reverence and modesty.

In his "Brief Appraisal of the Greek Literature in its foremost pretensions" (which has not been reprinted), he is an unqualified assertor of the superiority of modern to ancient literature. "It is," he said, "a pitiable spectacle to any man of sense and feeling, who happens to be really familiar with the golden treasures of his own ancestral literature, and a spectacle which moves alternately scorn and sorrow, to see young people squandering their time and painful study upon writers not fit to unloose the shoes' latchets of many amongst their own compatriots; making painful and remote voyages after the drossy refuse, when the pure gold lies neglected at their feet." "We engage to produce many scores of passages from Chaucer, not exceeding 50 to 80 lines, which contain more of picturesque simplicity, more tenderness, more fidelity to nature, more felicity of sentiment, more animation of narrative, and more truth of character, than can be matched in all the Iliad or the Odyssey." Again,—"To our Jeremy Taylor, to our Sir Thomas Browne, there is no approach made in the Greek eloquence. The inaugural chapter of the 'Holy Dying,' to say nothing of many another golden passage; or the famous passage in the 'Urn Buriall,' beginning, 'Now, since these bones have rested under the drums and tramplings of three conquests,'—have no parallel in literature." Finally, "For the intellectual qualities of eloquence, in fineness of understanding, in depth and in large compass of thought, Burke far surpasses any orator, ancient or modern."

In another paper, also excluded from his collected works, he exposes the "dire affectation" of many enthusiastic admirers of Greek and Latin writers:—

"Raised almost to divine honours, never mentioned but with affected rapture, the classics of Greece and Rome are seldom read—most of them never; are they indeed the closet-companions of any man? Surely it is time that these follies were at an end; that our practice were made to square a little better with our professions; and that our pleasures were sincerely drawn from those sources in which we pretend that they lie."

ELEMENTS OF STYLE.

Vocabulary.

De Quincey ranges with great freedom over the accumulated wealth of the language, his capacious memory giving him a prodigious command of words. His range is perhaps wider than either Macaulay's or Carlyle's, as he is more versatile in the "pitch" of his style, and does not disdain to use the "slang" of all classes, from Cockney to Oxonian.

In his diction, taken as a whole, there is a great preponderance of words derived from the Latin. Lord Brougham's opinion that "the Saxon part of our English idiom is to be favoured at the expense of that part which has so happily coalesced from the Latin or Greek," he puts aside as "resembling that restraint which some metrical writers have imposed upon themselves—of writing a long copy of verses from which some particular letter, or from each line of which some different letter, should be carefully excluded." From various causes, he himself makes an excessive use of Latinised phraseology. First, his ear was deeply enamoured of a dignified rhythm; none but long words of Latin origin were equal to the lofty march of his periods. Secondly, by the use of Latinised and *quasi* technical terms, he gained greater precision than by the use of homely words of looser signification. And thirdly, it was part of his peculiar humour to write concerning common objects in unfamiliar language.

The strong point in his diction is his acquaintance with the language of the thoughts and feelings, with the subjective side of the English vocabulary. A writer naturally accumulates words in the line of his strongest interest; and De Quincey had a paramount interest in the characters, thoughts, and affections of man—human nature may be said to have been his constant study.

A systematic student in none of the sciences, except perhaps metaphysics and political economy, he nevertheless had gleaned technical terms from every science. He was indeed ever on the watch for a good word; sciences, arts, and even trades, all alike he laid under greater or less occasional contributions.

Sentences.

Although De Quincey complained of the "weariness and repulsion" of the periodic style, he carried it to excess in his own composition. His sentences are stately, elaborate, crowded with qualifying clauses and parenthetical allusions, to a degree unparalleled among modern writers.

In reviewing Whately's Rhetoric, he naturally objected to the dogma that "elaborate stateliness is always to be regarded as a worse fault than the slovenliness and languor which accompany a very loose style." He maintained, and justly, that "stateliness the most elaborate, in an *absolute* sense, is no fault at all, though it may be so in relation to a given subject, or to any subject under given circumstances." Whether in his own practice he always conforms to circumstances, is a question that must be left to individual taste. There is a certain stateliness in his sentences under almost all circumstances—a stateliness arising from his habitual use of periodic suspensions. To take two examples from his Sketches:—

"Never in any equal number of months had my understanding so much expanded as during this visit to Laxton."

When we throw this out of the elaborately periodic form, we, as it were, relax the tension of the mind, and destroy the stately effect. Thus—

"My understanding expanded more during this visit to Laxton than during any three months of my life."

Again—

"Equally, in fact, as regarded my physics and my metaphysics; in short, upon all lines of advance that interested my ambition, I was going rapidly ahead."

The statement has a very different effect when the periodic arrangement is reversed.

Criticism of single sentences cannot easily be made convincing, and the critic is apt to forget the paramount principle that regard must be had to the context, to the nature of the subject, to the effect intended by the writer. When a single sentence is put upon its trial, there are many casuistical considerations that may legitimately be pleaded by the counsel for the defence. Still, if we try De Quincey by his own rule against "unwieldy comprehensivness," we must convict him of many violations. In almost every page we find periods that cannot be easily comprehended except by a mind of more than ordinary grasp; and in many cases where, viewed with reference to the average capacity, he cannot be said to overcrowd, he is yet upon the verge of overcrowding. The following sentence may be quoted as one that stands upon the verge. It calls for a considerable effort of attention, and a long succession of such sentences would be exasperating. He is speaking of his youthful habit of scrupulously making sure of the meaning of an order:—

"So far from seeking to 'pettifogulise'—*i.e.*, to find evasions for any purpose in a trickster's minute tortuosities of construction—exactly in the opposite direction, from mere excess of sincerity, most unwillingly I found, in almost everybody's words, an unintentional opening left for double interpretations."

In this case the familiarity and the close connection of the ideas makes the effort of comprehension considerably less. When the subject-matter is so easy, the interspersion of such periods here and there cannot be called a fault. It is, on the contrary, to most ears an agreeable relief to the monotony of ordinary forms of sentence. But for the general reader, for the average capacity of easy understanding, such sentence-forms are multiplied to an intolerable degree in De Quincey's writing. And he does not always escape the besetting fault of long and crowded sentences—intricacy.

As regards the length and elaboration of De Quincey's sentences, it is interesting to compare the first edition of the Opium Confessions with the final revision. Many alterations consist in filling out the sentences; and, in a good many cases, two sentences are amalgamated into one. Take the following example, the first few sentences of the section entitled, "The Pleasures of Opium." In the original edition this stands—

"It is so long since I first took opium, that if it had been a trifling incident in my life, I might have forgotten its date; but cardinal events are not to be forgotten, and from circumstances connected with it, I remember that it must be referred to the autumn of 1804. During that season I was in London, having come thither for the first time since my entrance at college. And my introduction to opium arose in the following way. From an early age I had been accustomed to wash my head in water at least once a-day," &c.

In the revised edition we read—

"It is very long since I first took opium; *so* long, that if it had been a trifling incident in my life, I might have forgotten its date; but cardinal events are not to be forgotten, and from circumstances connected with it, I remember that this inauguration into the use of opium must be referred to the spring or to the autumn of 1804, during which seasons I was in London, having come thither for the first time since my entrance at Oxford. And this event arose in the following way: From an early age I had been accustomed," &c.

The four sentences of the original are amalgamated into two, without any condensation of the original bulk. On the contrary, additions are made, one for the sake of emphasis, another for the sake of a more formal connection.

Unity of Sentence.—A casuist would find no difficulty in arguing that De Quincey's sentences are not *over*-crowded. None of the qualifications or parenthetic allusions could be said to be altogether irrelevant; and the difficulty of grasping the meaning being set on one side, it might be pleaded that, as regards the main purpose of the sentence, and its place among the other sentences of the composition, they are all of them indispensable.

De Quincey, however, often offends beyond the possibility of justification, overloading his sentences in a gossiping kind of way with particulars that have no relevance whatsoever to the main statement. Of this habit I quote two examples, italicising the irrelevant clauses, and placing one of them in small capitals as being an offence of double magnitude, a second irrelevance foisted in upon the back of the first. The first sentence relates to the exposure of infants in ancient Greece; the second explains itself.

"And because the ancients had a scruple (no scruple of mercy or of relenting conscience, but of selfish superstition) as to taking life by violence from any creature not condemned under some law, the mode of death must be by exposure on the open hills, where either the night air, or the fangs of a wolf, oftentimes of the great dogs—*still preserved in most parts of Greece (and traced back to the days of Homer as the public nuisances of travellers)*—usually put an end to the unoffending creature's life."

"It is asserted, as a general affection of human nature, that it is impossible to read a book with satisfaction until one has ascertained whether the author of it be tall or short, corpulent or thin; and, as to complexion, whether he be a 'black' man (which, in the 'Spectator's' time, was the absurd expression for a swarthy man), or a fair man, or a sallow man, or perhaps a green man, *which Southey affirmed to be the proper description of many stout artificers in Birmingham too much given to work in metallic fumes;* ON WHICH ACCOUNT THE NAME OF SOUTHEY IS AN ABOMINATION TO THIS DAY IN CERTAIN FURNACES OF WARWICKSHIRE."

The excrescences on the last sentence might be justified on the ground that they are humorous, although in severe exposition the humour would probably be ill-timed; but the parenthetic information in the first is pedantic, and insufferably out of harmony with the rest of the sentence.

Paragraphs.

We have seen in our Introduction that De Quincey studied "the philosophy of transition and connection." He is scrupulously elaborate, almost too elaborate, in explaining the point of his statements.

No quotation can be made from De Quincey that does not exemplify this. Still the analysis of a short passage may help to put the student upon the proper track for seeing how large a part of his composition is taken up with phrases of connection:—

"*So it will always be.* Those who (*like Madame Dacier*) possess no accomplishment but Greek, will of necessity set a superhuman value upon *that literature in all its parts, to which their own narrow skill becomes an available key.*"

The expressions in italics are all connective. A rapid writer, such as Macaulay, would have omitted "like Madame Dacier," and in place of the connective periphrasis at the end, would have said briefly and pointedly "Greek literature," leaving the reader to pass on without the labour of formally comprehending the connection. To continue:—

"Besides that, over and above this coarse and conscious motive for overrating that which reacts with an equal and answerable overrating upon their own little philological attainments, there is another agency at work, and quite unconsciously to the subjects of that agency, in disturbing the sanity of any estimate they may make of a foreign literature."

This sentence is wholly connective, joining together the two inducements to overrate the value of a foreign literature—the second being stated as follows:—

"It is the habit (well known to psychologists) of transferring to anything created by our own skill, or which reflects our own skill, as if it lay causatively and objectively in the reflecting thing itself, that pleasurable power which in very truth belongs subjectively to the mind of him who surveys it, from conscious success in the exercise of his own energies. Hence it is that we see daily without surprise young ladies hanging enamoured over the pages of an Italian author, and calling attention to trivial commonplaces, such as, clothed in plain mother English, would have been more repulsive to them than the distinctions of a theologian or the counsels of a great-grandmother. They mistake for a pleasure yielded by the author what is in fact the pleasure attending their own success in mastering what was lately an insuperable difficulty."

This explicitness of connection is the chief merit of De Quincey's paragraphs. He cannot be said to observe any other principle. He is carried into violations of all the other rules by his inveterate habit of digression. Often upon a mere casual suggestion he branches off into a digression of several pages, sometimes even digressing from the subject of his first digression. The enormity of these offences is a good deal palliated by his being conscious that he is digressing, and his taking care to let us know when he strikes off from the main subject and when he returns. Some of his papers are professedly "discursive," especially the 'Autobiographic Sketches.'

The following is an example of his way of apologising for a digression. It illustrates, at the same time, his capital excellence of explicit connection. In a paper professedly on Demosthenes, he comes across Lord Brougham's Rectorial Address at Glasgow, and at once, leaving Demosthenes, proceeds to discuss several things mentioned in the address. At the close of this excursus he says:—

"I have used my privilege of discursiveness to step aside from Demosthenes to another subject, not otherwise connected with the Attic orator than, first, by the common reference of both subjects to rhetoric; but, secondly, by the accident of having been jointly discussed by Lord Brougham in a paper which (though now forgotten) obtained at the moment most undue celebrity."

The apology, however, becomes the occasion of another offence. Before returning to Demosthenes, he throws in a few sentences of comment on the fact that in England the utterances of eminent public men on subjects beyond their province and their acquirements are received with a deference not accorded to men "speaking under the known privilege of professional knowledge."

Should these digressions, obviously breaches of strict method, be imitated or avoided? The experienced writer will please himself, and consult the effect that he intends to produce. But if he digresses after the model of De Quincey, he may rest assured that he will be accused of affectation, and will offend all that read for direct information concerning the subject in hand.

Figures of Speech.

De Quincey may be described as a very "tropical" writer (see INTRODUCTION, p. 13). He uses comparatively few formal similitudes, but his pages are thickly strewn with "tropes," with metaphors, personifications, synecdoches, and metonymies.

His most characteristic and peculiar figure is personification. He makes a constant practice of applying predicates to names of inanimate things, and even to abstract nouns, as if they were names of living agents.

This mannerism pervades all De Quincey's writings, and is so characteristic that we at once think of him when we find it appearing strongly in another writer. A few examples give but a faint impression compared with what we receive when we read his volumes and meet with an example in every other sentence. It is peculiarly striking in the case of abstract nouns—above all, when one abstraction is represented as acting upon another; thus—

"Here I had terminated this chapter as at a natural pause, which, while shutting out for ever my eldest brother from the reader's sight and from my own, necessarily at the same moment worked a permanent revolution in the character of my daily life. Two such changes, and both so abrupt, indicated imperiously the close of one era and the opening of another. The advantages, indeed, which my brother had over me in years, in physical activities of every kind, in decision of purpose, and in energy of will—all which advantages, besides, borrowed a ratification from an obscure sense, on my part, of duty as incident to what seemed an appointment of Providence—inevitably *had* controlled, and for years to come *would have* controlled, the free spontaneous movements of a dreamer like myself."

This treatment of abstractions as living agents may be studied also in the following passage, concerning the civilising influence of Athens through her theatre:—

"But if it were a vain and arrogant assumption to illuminate, as regarded those primal truths which, like the stars, are hung aloft, and shine for all alike, neither vain nor arrogant was it to fly her falcons at game almost as high. If not life, yet light; if not absolute birth, yet moral regeneration and fructifying warmth—these were quickening forces which abundantly she was able to engraft upon truths else slumbering and inert. Not affecting to teach the new, she could yet vivify the old. Those moral echoes, so solemn and pathetic, that lingered in the ear from her stately tragedies, all spoke with the authority of voices from the grave. The great phantoms that crossed her stage, all pointed with shadowy fingers to shattered dynasties and the ruins of once regal houses, Pelopidæ or Labdacidæ, as monuments of sufferings in expiation of violated morals, or sometimes—which even more thrillingly spoke to human sensibilities—of guilt too awful to be expiated. And in the midst of these appalling records, what is their ultimate solution? From what key-note does Athenian Tragedy trace the expansion of its own dark impassioned music? Ὕβρις (*hybris*)—the spirit of outrage coupled with the spirit of insult and arrogant self-assertion—in that temper lurks the original impulse towards wrong; and to that temper the

Greek drama adapts its monitory legends. The doctrine of the Hebrew Scriptures as to vicarious retribution is at times discovered secretly moving through the scenic poetry of Athens. His own crime is seen hunting a man through five generations, and finding him finally in the persons of his innocent descendants."

The tropical applying of abstractions to words expressing movement—see in the above passage "lurking," "moving," "hunting," &c.—is a prominent De Quinceyism. Ideas "lurk under" terms; distinctions "move obscurely" in the minds of men; revolutions "travel leisurely through their stages;" "the guardianship of civilisation suddenly unfolds itself like a banner" over particular nations; a danger "approaches and wheels away—threatens, but finally forbears to strike," &c. &c.

The Sources of his Similitudes.—De Quincey's similitudes are drawn from an immense sphere of reading and observation. Without pretending to be exhaustive, we may mention separately some of his principal fields.

(1.) The characteristics of lower animals. He very often enlivens an adjective of quality by appending a comparison to some animal possessing the quality in an extreme form. We are constantly meeting such phrases as "restless as a hyena;" "rare as a phœnix;" "by original constitution strong as one of Meux's dray-horses;" "Burke, a hunting leopard, coupled with Schlosser, a German poodle." In owning himself baffled to find any illustration of Richter's activity of understanding, he shows how deliberately he ransacked his knowledge in pursuit of similitudes:—

"What then is it that I claim? Briefly, an activity of understanding so restless and indefatigable that all attempts to illustrate, or express it adequately, by images borrowed from the natural world, from the motions of beasts, birds, insects, &c., from the leaps of tigers or leopards, from the gambolling and tumbling of kittens, the antics of monkeys, or the running of antelopes and ostriches, &c., are baffled, confounded, and made ridiculous by the enormous and overmastering superiority of impression left by the thing illustrated."

(2.) Works of travel. A great reader of books of travel, he found in the customs and natural phenomena of foreign countries extreme examples, and thus was able to give to his similes a peculiar finish, and at times an independent value, such as attaches to some of the similes of Milton. Where for an image of hopeful change a less accomplished artist would simply make comparison to the opening of spring, De Quincey is able to cite the opening of spring in *Sweden*, and dwells upon a gorgeous picture of the sudden vernal outburst in that country. An unfinished book that another would compare simply to an unfinished building, he compares to "a *Spanish* bridge or aqueduct begun upon too great a scale for the resources of the architect;" opening up remote collateral reflections to the reader that has time to pause and consider.

Again, illustrating how soon we forget the features of dead or distant friends, he says—

"The faces of infants, though they are divine as flowers on a savanna of Texas, or as the carolling of birds in a forest, are, like flowers in a savanna of Texas, or the carolling of birds in a forest, soon overtaken by the pursuing darkness that swallows up all things human."

Again—

"Yes, reader, countless are the mysterious handwritings of grief or joy which have inscribed themselves successively upon the palimpsest of your brain; and like the annual leaves of aboriginal forests, or the undissolving snows on the Himalaya, or light falling upon light, the endless strata have covered up each other in forgetfulness."

Once more—

". . . 'the anarchy of dreams' presides in German philosophy; and the restless elements of opinion, throughout every region of debate, mould themselves eternally, like the billowy sands of the desert, as beheld by Bruce, into towering columns, soar upwards to a giddy altitude, then stalk about for a minute, all aglow with fiery colour, and finally unmould and 'dislimn,' with a collapse as sudden as the motions of that eddying breeze under which their vapoury architecture had arisen."

This last image was a favourite with him. He first used it in the article on Dr Parr:—

"The brief associations of public carriages or inns are as evanescent as the sandy columns of the Great Desert, which the caprices of the wind build up and scatter, shape and unshape, within the brief revolution of a minute."

He used it again in the preface to his 'Political Economy:'—

". . . or, like the fantastic architecture which the winds are everlastingly pursuing in the Arabian desert, would exhibit phantom arrays of fleeting columns and fluctuating edifices, which, under the very breath that had created them, would be for ever collapsing into dust."

(3.) He very often compares individuals to celebrated personages in literature, by a kind of synecdoche. One specimen must suffice:—

"Here at this time was living Mr Clarkson,—that son of thunder, that Titan, who was, in fact, the one great Atlas that bore up the Slave Trade Abolition cause—now resting from his mighty labours and nerve-shattering perils."

(4.) The feats of magic furnish him with several expressions of astonishment. "Thaumaturgic" is a favourite word; he speaks of the "rhabdomantic" power of Christianity in evoking dormant feelings; and he compares the transformation worked by a lady upon her husband to the achievements of "some mighty caliph or lamp-bearing Aladdin."

(5.) From music he draws some very favourite metaphors. Thus: He knows "human despondencies through all their infinite *gamut.*" Christopher North at Oxford "enjoyed an unlimited favour with an infinite *gamut* of friends and associates, running through every *key*, the *diapason* closing full in groom, cobbler, and stable-boy." Ceylon is "a *panorganon for modulating through the whole diatonic scale* of climates."

(6.) He takes many metaphors from the technical language of law and trade. The question as to the comparative value of ancient and modern learning is "the great pending suit between antiquity and ourselves." "Such as these were the habits and the *reversionary* consolations of Pompey." "The other historic person on whom I shall probably be charged with *assault and battery* is Josephus." "The Jew did not receive the bribe first and then perpetrate the treason, but trusted to Roman *good faith at three months after date.*" Writing of Pope's composing satire at the instigation of Warburton, he says:—

"To enter a house of hatred as a junior partner, and to take the stock of malice at a valuation (we copy from advertisements), *that* is an ignoble act."

These metaphors are very often humorous. Thus—

"A Canadian winter for my money; or a Russian one, where every man is but a co-proprietor with the north wind, in the fee-simple of his own ears."

(7.) Sometimes he takes a fancy to draw upon mathematics, medicine, or physical science. Thus—

"As to Symmons, he was a *Whig;* and his covert purpose was to secure Milton for his own party, before that party was fully secreted by the new tendencies beginning to move amongst the partisanships of the age. Until Dr Sacheverel came, in Queen Anne's reign, the crystallisations of Whig and Tory were rudimental and incomplete. Symmons, therefore, was under a bias, and a morbid kind of deflection."

How far he observes the **conditions of effective comparison.**— De Quincey is a model of exact comparison. To point out with deliberate—some would say with tedious—scrupulosity the resembling circumstances in the things compared, peculiarly suits his subtilising turn of mind. He never seems to be in a hurry, and does not aspire to hit off a similitude in a few pregnant words; his characteristic is punctilious accuracy, regardless of expense in the matter of words.

Out of numerous available examples may be quoted his comparison of the distribution of men in Ceylon to the distribution of material in a peach:—

"But strange indeed, where everything seems strange, is the arrangement of the Ceylonese territory and people. Take a peach: what you call the flesh of the peach, the substance which you eat, is massed orbicularly round a central stone—often as large as a pretty large strawberry. Now, in Ceylon the central district, answering to this peach-stone, constitutes a fierce little Lilliputian kingdom, quite independent, through many centuries, of the lazy belt, the peach-flesh, which swathes and enfolds it, and perfectly distinct by the character and origin of its population. The peach-stone is called Kandy, and the people Kandyans."

Seeing that he possessed an extraordinary power of "elevating" by means of similitudes, it is natural to ask whether he is ever guilty of undue exaggeration. When this question is put concerning De Quincey, attention turns at once to his Opium Confessions and his 'Autobiographic Sketches.' In these works he describes his own feelings in metaphors taken from the language of the great operations of Nature, and draws elaborate comparisons between momentous epochs in his own life, and such imposing phenomena as the uncontrollable migrations of the buffalo herds. Are these similitudes extravagantly hyperbolical? Do they offend the reader as rising extravagantly above the dignity of the subject? Much depends upon our point of view. If we view the autobiographer unsympathetically, from the stand-point of our own personality—if we regard him simply as a unit among the millions of mankind, a speck upon "the great globe itself,"—we shall undoubtedly be shocked at his venturing to compare revolutions within his own insignificant being to revolutions affecting vast regions of the earth. But if we view him as he means that we should view him, sympathetically, from the stand-point of *his* personality, we shall not be shocked at the audacity of his similitudes—we shall not consider them extravagant, or out of keeping with the feelings proper to the occasion. Epochs and incidents in our own life are more important to us, bulk more largely in our eyes, than epochs and incidents in the history of a nation. The violent death of a near and dear relative or friend touches us more profoundly than an earthquake at Lisbon, a massacre at Cawnpore, or a revolution in Paris. De Quincey says nothing that has not been felt more or less dimly by all human beings when he says, that on his entering Oxford the profound public interest concerning the movements of Napoleon "*a little* divided with me the *else monopolising awe attached to the solemn act of launching myself upon the world.*"

Concerning the novelty or originality of his similitudes. He has never been accused of plagiarising. When he borrows a figure of speech, he gives a formal acknowledgment; at least he does so in some cases, and I have never seen any clandestine appropriations charged against him. "As I have never allowed myself," he says, "to covet any man's ox, nor his ass, nor anything that is his, still less would it become a philosopher to covet other people's images or metaphors." And if he had, we might say, as he said of Coleridge's plagiarisms, that such robbery would have been an honour to the person robbed. We may be sure, from the unique finish of his similitudes, that the stolen property would have improved in value under his hands.

QUALITIES OF STYLE.

Simplicity.

De Quincey cannot be ranked among simple writers. His style has certain elements of simplicity, but, at the same time, it has, in a considerable degree, every element of abstruseness specified in a manual of composition.

(1.) He makes an excessive use of Latinised, scholarly, and technical terms. Thus—

"I myself, who have never been a great wine-drinker, used to find that half-a-dozen glasses of wine *advantageously affected* the *faculties*, brightened and *intensified the consciousness*, and gave to the mind a feeling of being '*ponderibus librata suis.*'"

Concerning his 'Logic of Political Economy,' Mr M'Culloch says —"It would have been more popular and successful had it been less scholastic. It is right to be logical, but not to be perpetually obtruding logical forms and technicalities on the reader's attention."

(2.) In his choice of subjects he prefers the recondite—offering, in this respect, a great contrast to Macaulay.

In his Essays "addressed to the understanding as an insulated faculty," he runs after the most abstruse problems. Take the examples quoted in his preface to the first volume of his 'Collected Works.' In the "Essenes," he defends a new speculation on a puzzling subject with considerations familiar only to archæologic theologians. In his "Cæsars," his purpose is not so much a condensed narrative as an elucidation of doubtful points. His "Essay on Cicero" deals with problems of the same nature. And so with many others of his articles. The volume on 'Leaders in Literature,' wherever it keeps faithful to its title, is taken up mainly with the "traditional errors affecting them." Even his 'Autobiographic Sketches' turn aside upon various incidents to the pursuit of subtle speculations, such as disquisitions on the possible issues of an action, recondite analysis and conjecture of motives, consideration of delicate points of taste, nice investigation of the sources of the influence of a poem or a picture. His 'Logic of Political Economy' deals with the most puzzling and abstruse principles of the science.

(3.) So far from shirking—as is the manner of simple writers —every call to modify a bare assertion, he revels in nice distinctions and scrupulous qualifications. This is a part of his exactness.

(4.) We have already noticed his excessive use of abstract terms and forms of expression. What we exemplified as his favourite figure is not good for rapid perusal. When a transaction is represented as taking place, not between living agents, but between abstract qualities of those agents, a mode of statement so unfamiliar is not to be comprehended without a considerable effort of thought.

(5.) His general structure is not simple. Long periods, each embodying a flock of clauses, are abstruse reading. Even his explicitness of connection has not its full natural effect of making the effort of comprehension easy. He connects his statements with such exactness that the explicitness becomes a burden.

Certain things may be said in extenuation of this neglect of the ordinary means of simplicity.

I. With all his abstruseness he does observe certain points of a simple style.

(1.) He often repeats in simpler language what he has said with characteristic abstractness of phrase. Thus, in the case of his cardinal distinction between the literature of knowledge and the literature of power—

"In that great social organ which, collectively, we call literature, there may be distinguished two separate offices that may blend, and often *do* so, but capable, severally, of a severe insulation, and naturally fitted for reciprocal repulsion. There is, first, the literature of *knowledge;* and secondly, the literature of *power*. The function of the first is to *teach;* the function of the second is to *move*. The first is a rudder; the second, an oar or a sail."

(2.) In dealing with dates and statistics, he has a commendable habit of devising helps to the reader's memory by means of familiar comparisons. Thus—

"This was in 1644, the year of Marston Moor, and the penultimate year of the Parliamentary war."

Again—

"Glasgow has as many thousands of inhabitants as there are days in the year. (I so state the population in order to assist the reader's memory.)"

In like manner he helps us to remember the territorial extent and the population of Ceylon by a comparison with Ireland and Scotland.

(3.) A characteristic figure with him is a figure taken from simple movements:—

"This growth of intellect, *outrunning* the capacities of the physical structure;" "by night he succeeded in *reaching the farther end* of his duties;" "he *walked* conscientiously *through* the services of the day." "Extraordinary erudition, even though *travelling* into obscure and sterile fields, has its own peculiar interest. And about Dr Parr, moreover, there *circled* another and far different interest."

It must, however, be admitted that such forms of expression, though intrinsically simple, are abstruse to the majority from not being familiar.

II. His technical terms can often justify their existence on the plea that they give greater precision. Thus—

"There was a prodigious ferment in the first half of the seventeenth century. In the *earlier bisection of the second half* there was a general settling or *deposition* from this ferment."

So in giving the dimensions of the famous Ceylon pillar—

"The pillar measures six feet by six—*i.e.*, thirty-six square feet—*on the flat quadrangular tablet of its upper horizontal surface.*"

Once more, writing of the impossibility of translating certain words by any single word, he says—

"To take an image from the language of eclipses, the correspondence between the *disk* of the original word and its translated representative is, in thousands of instances, not *annular;* the centres do not coincide; the words overlap."

In all these cases there is no denying that the expression is superlatively precise, although perhaps all the precision required under the circumstances might have been given in more familiar language.

Such are some of the circumstances that compensate his abstruseness. Imitators should see that they make equal compensation. The assertion may be hazarded that writers aiming at wide popularity are not safe to use so much abstruse language as De Quincey, whatever may be their powers of compensating.

Clearness.

Perspicuity.—To readers that find no difficulty in the abstruseness of his diction, De Quincey is tolerably perspicuous. His virtues in this respect are summed up in the capital excellence of his paragraphs, explicitness of connection. If we find his diction easy, he is so scrupulous in keeping before us the general arrangement of his composition, as well as the bearing of particular statements, and even, as we have seen, of his numerous digressions, that we are seldom in danger of confusion.

Exactness, however, rather than perspicuity, is his peculiar merit. On this he openly prides himself. In an article on Ceylon, having said that a young officer, marching with a small body of men through the island, *took* Kandy in his route, he appends a footnote to the word "took":—

"This phrase is equivocal; it bears two senses—the traveller's sense and the soldier's. But *we* rarely make such errors in the use of words; the error is original in the government documents themselves."

He certainly had reason to glory. None of our writers in general literature have shown themselves so scrupulously precise. His works are still the crowning delicacy for lovers of formal, punctilious exactness.[1]

Of this exactness we have already given several illustrations. We have illustrated the exactness of his comparisons, and the fact that he often purchases exactness at the price of simplicity. Reference may also be made to the account of his opinions and the passage there quoted.

His minuteness in modifying vague general expressions is particularly worthy of notice, and, when not pushed to a pedantic extreme, worthy of imitation. He seldom says that a thing is remarkable without adding in what respects. A man's life is "notable in two points;" has "two separate claims upon our notice:"—

"A man of original genius, shown to us as revolving through the leisurely stages of a biographical memoir, lays open, *to readers prepared for such revelations, two separate theatres of interest;* one in his personal career, the other in his works and his intellectual development."

In like manner, "that sanctity which settles on the memory of a great man, ought, *upon a double motive*, to be vigilantly sustained by his countrymen." When he predicates a superlative, he is exemplarily scrupulous to let us know what particulars it applies to. Aristotle's Rhetoric is "the best, *as regards* the primary purpose of the teacher; *though otherwise*, for elegance," &c. Jeremy Taylor and Sir T. Browne are "undoubtedly the richest, the most dazzling, and, *with reference to their matter*, the most captivating of all rhetoricians." When he puts the question, "Was Cæsar, upon the whole, the greatest of men?" he does not at once pronounce roundly "Yes" or "No." He first explains in what sense he means great:—

"Was Cæsar, upon the whole, the greatest of men? We restrict the question, of course, to the classes of men great in *action;* great by the extent of their influence over their social contemporaries; great by throwing open avenues to extended powers that previously had been closed; great by making obstacles once vast to become trivial; or prizes that once were trivial to be glorified by expansion."

As an example of this "pettifogulising" on the larger scale, we may quote his footnote on the maxim "*De mortuis nil nisi bonum:*"—

[1] With a legitimate feeling of his own innocence, he often censures the lax practice of other writers. He is angry with Dr Johnson for not further explaining what he meant by calling Pope "the most correct of poets." "Correctness," he exclaims, "in what? Think of the admirable qualifications for settling the scale of such critical distinctions which that man must have had who turned out upon this vast world the single oracular word 'correctness' to shift for itself, and explain its own meaning to all generations!"

"This famous canon of charity (*Concerning the dead, let us have nothing but what is kind and favourable*) has furnished an inevitable occasion for much doubtful casuistry. The dead, as those pre-eminently unable to defend themselves, enjoy a natural privilege of indulgence amongst the generous and considerate; but not to the extent which this sweeping maxim would proclaim,—since, on this principle, in cases innumerable, tenderness to the dead would become the ground of cruel injustice to the living: nay, the maxim would continually counterwork itself; for too inexorable a forbearance with regard to one dead person would oftentimes effectually close the door to the vindication of another. In fact, neither history nor biography is able to move a step without infractions of this rule; a rule emanating from the blind kindliness of grandmothers, who, whilst groping in the dark after one individual darling, forget the collateral or oblique results to others without end. These evils being perceived, equitable casuists began to revise the maxim, and in its new form it stood thus—'*De mortuis nil nisi verum*' ('*Concerning the dead, let us have nothing but what is true*'). Why, certainly, that is an undeniable right of the dead; and nobody in his senses would plead for a small *percentage* of falsehood. Yet, again, in that shape the maxim carries with it a disagreeable air of limiting the right to truth. Unless it is meant to reserve a small allowance of fiction for the separate use of the living, why insist upon truth as peculiarly consecrated to the dead? If all people, living and dead alike, have a right to the benefits of truth, why specify one class, as if in silent contradistinction to some other class, less eminently privileged in that respect? To me it seems evident that the human mind has been long groping darkly after some separate right of the dead in this respect, but which hitherto it has not been able to bring into reconciliation with the known rights of the living. Some distinct privilege there should be, if only it could be sharply defined and limited, through which a special prerogative might be recognised as among the sanctities of the grave."

Strength.

De Quincey's style, as the reader has doubtless remarked in preceding extracts, is not animated—meaning by animation the presentation of ideas in rapid succession—it stands, in fact, to use a phrase of his own, in "polar antithesis" to the animated style. His prevailing characteristic is elaborate stateliness. He finds the happiest exercise of his powers in sustained flights through the region of the sublime.

I. Let us first exemplify his elevation of style as applied to the ordinary subjects of lofty composition, such as men of extraordinary powers, secret machinations, great natural phenomena, scenes of horror and confusion.

He had not, like Carlyle, a formal gallery of historical heroes. He seldom lends his powers of style to glorifying the great men of history. His tendency was rather to discover and develop lurking objects of admiration or astonishment—the daring of Zebek Dorchi against the "mighty behemoth of Muscovy," the energetic hardihood of the slave that attempted to assassinate the Emperor Commodus, the erection of a statue to the slave Æsop, and suchlike.

The following is his account of "Walking Stewart," whom almost anybody else would have passed by as a hare-brained enthusiast:—

"His mind was a mirror of the sentient universe—the whole mighty vision that had fleeted before his eyes in this world—the armies of Hyder Ali and his son Tippoo, with oriental and barbaric pageantry; the civic grandeur of England; the great deserts of Asia and America; the vast capitals of Europe—London, with its eternal agitations, the ceaseless ebb and flow of its 'mighty heart;' Paris, shaken by the fierce torments of revolutionary convulsions; the silence of Lapland; and the solitary forests of Canada; with the swarming life of the torrid zone; together with innumerable recollections of individual joy and sorrow that he had participated in by sympathy,—lay like a map beneath him, as if eternally co-present to his view; so that, in the contemplation of the prodigious whole, he had no leisure to separate the parts or occupy his mind with details."

The machinations of secret societies had a great charm for him. Here is a passage concerning the Hetæria of Greece:—

"It cannot be denied that a secret society, with the grand and almost awful purposes of the Hetæria, spite of some taint which it had received in its early stages from the spirit of German mummery, is fitted to fill the imagination, and to command homage from the coldest. Whispers circulating from mouth to mouth of some vast conspiracy mining subterraneously beneath the very feet of their accursed oppressors—whispers of a great deliverer at hand whose mysterious *Labarum*, or mighty banner of the Cross, was already dimly descried through northern mists, and whose eagles were already scenting the carnage and 'savour of death' from innumerable hosts of Moslems—whispers of a revolution which was again to call, as with the trumpet of resurrection, from the grave, the land of Timoleon and Epaminondas; such were the preludings, low and deep, to the tempestuous overture of revolt and patriotic battle which now ran through every nook of Greece, and caused every ear to tingle."

The following is an example of his description of sublime natural phenomena. It occurs as a similitude:—

"Has the reader witnessed, or has he heard described, the sudden burst —the explosion, one might say—by which a Swedish winter passes into spring, and spring simultaneously into summer? The icy sceptre of winter does not there thaw and melt away by just gradations: it is broken, it is shattered, in a day, in an hour, and with a violence brought home to *every* sense. No second type of resurrection, so mighty or so affecting, is manifested by nature in southern climates. Such is the headlong tumult, such the 'torrent rapture' by which life is let loose amongst the air, the earth, and the waters under the earth. Exactly what this vernal resurrection is in manifestations of power and life, by comparison with climates that have no winter; such, and marked with features as distinct, was," &c.

As an example of his power of depicting horrors, take his account of the sack of Enniscorthy—

"Next came a scene which swallowed up all distinct or separate features in its frantic confluence of horrors. All the loyalists of Enniscorthy, all the gentry for miles around who had congregated in that town as a centre of security, were summoned at that moment, not to an orderly retreat, but to instant flight. At one end of the street were seen the rebel pikes, and bayonets, and fierce faces, already gleaming through the smoke; at the other end volumes of fire, surging and billowing from the thatched roofs, and blazing rafters beginning to block up the avenues of escape. Then began the agony and uttermost conflict of what is worst and what is best in human nature. Then was to be seen the very delirium of fear, and the very delirium of vindictive malice—private and ignoble hatred, of ancient origin, shrouding itself in the mask of patriotic wrath; the tiger-glare of just vengeance, fresh from intolerable wrongs and the never-to-be-forgotten ignominy of stripes and personal degradation; panic, self-palsied by its own excess; flight, eager or stealthy, according to the temper and the means; volleying pursuit; the very frenzy of agitation, under every mode of excitement; and here and there the desperation of maternal love victorious and supreme above all lower passions. I recapitulate and gather under general abstractions many an individual anecdote reported by those who were on that day present in Enniscorthy; for at Ferns, not far off, and deeply interested in all those transactions, I had private friends, intimate participators in the trials of that fierce hurricane, and joint sufferers with those who suffered most."

It is this "recapitulation and gathering under general abstractions" that raises the passage above those hideous accumulations of horrible particulars faithfully reported by newspaper correspondents from seats of war. His "Revolt of the Tartars" is a good example of sustained grandeur of narrative and description; there also he abstains from individual horrors, and raises the imagination to dwell with awe upon the passions raging through the strife.

II. Let us now constitute a special section for his peculiar flights of sublimity, not because they are essentially different from the preceding, but because they really have, what they claim to have, a slight element of peculiarity; because, in short, they are experimental.

It is sometimes said that De Quincey claims to be the originator of impassioned prose. He makes no such claim. He knew as well as anybody that impassioned prose had been written long before his day, by Jeremy Taylor, Sir Thomas Browne, Milton, Burke, and others.[1] What he did claim was to be the author of a "*mode* of impassioned prose ranging under no precedents that he was aware of in any literature." He speaks of the utter sterility of universal literature, not in impassioned prose, but in "*one department* of impassioned prose." That department may be described with sufficient precision as "impassioned autobiography."

Why call this a special department, and speak of it as a hazardous experiment? The specialty consists in describing incidents of purely personal interest in language suited to their magnitude as they appear in the eyes of the writer; and the danger is, as we have had occasion to notice incidentally (p. 59), that readers be unsympathetic, and refuse to interest themselves in the writer's

[1] Two, at least, of his impassioned apostrophes are modelled upon Sir Walter Raleigh's famous apostrophe to Death.

personal feelings. The specialty is undoubtedly considerable, and so is the danger. That De Quincey succeeded was shown by the popularity of his autobiographical works.

The mere splendour of such a style as De Quincey's would, to readers prepared to enjoy it, overcome a great amount of distastefulness in the subject. But apart from the mechanical execution, he showed himself sensible of the chief danger in the treatment of such themes. That danger is, the intrusion of personal vanity. "Any expression of personal vanity, intruding upon impassioned records, is fatal to their effect, as being incompatible with that absorption of spirit and that self-oblivion in which only deep passion originates, or can find a genial home." If the autobiographer steps aside from the record of his feelings to compare them with the feelings of other people, and to make out that he has been honoured, afflicted, or agitated above other people, every reader's self-conceit takes the alarm, and forthwith scans the writer with cynical antipathy. De Quincey is on his guard against making such a blunder. He does not, as Mr Tennyson sometimes does, exhibit his sufferings in comparison with the sufferings of other men, and claim for the incidents of his life an affinity with the most tragical events incident to frail humanity. He represses every suggestion that he regards the events of his life as other than commonplace in the eye of an impartial observer. He is intent upon expounding them simply as they affected him; conscious all the time that to other men the events of their life are of equal magnitude, and that he must not egotistically challenge comparison; knowing, as an artist, that any expression of personal vanity, any appearance of pluming himself upon his experience, is fatal to the effect of the composition.

We need not fill up our limited space with quotations from a book so well know as the Opium Confessions, and now published at sixpence. One only will be given, and that as having already been alluded to. The reader will notice that our author is wholly engrossed with his suffering and his sudden resolution, and endeavours only to make his case vividly intelligible; there is no trace of boastful comparison with the experience of other people:—

"But now, at last, came over me, from the mere excess of bodily suffering and mental disappointments, a frantic and rapturous reagency. In the United States the case is well known, and many times has been described by travellers, of that furious instinct which, under a secret call for saline variations of diet, drives all the tribes of buffaloes for thousands of miles to the common centre of the 'Salt-licks.' Under such a compulsion does the locust, under such a compulsion does the leeming, traverse its mysterious path. They are deaf to danger, deaf to the cry of battle, deaf to the trumpets of death. Let the sea cross their path, let armies with artillery bar the road, even these terrific powers can arrest only by destroying; and the most frightful abysses, up to the very last menace of engulfment, up to the very instant of absorption, have no power to alter or retard the line of their inexorable advance.

"Such an instinct it was, such a rapturous command—even so potent, and, alas! even so blind—that, under the whirl of tumultuous indignation and of new-born hope, suddenly transfigured my whole being. In the twinkling of an eye, I came to an adamantine resolution—not as if issuing from any act or any choice of my own, but as if positively received from some dark oracular legislation external to myself."

Pathos.

From the prevailing majesty of his diction, De Quincey's pathos is rarely of a homely order. In some of his papers, as in the "Military Nun," there are touching little strokes of half-humorous tenderness. But his most characteristic pathos is impassioned regret for departed nobleness; in which case he blends with his expressions of sorrow a splendid glorification of the object, so that the mind is at once saddened and filled with ideas of sublimity.

The impassioned apostrophes of the Opium Confessions are tolerably well known. We may therefore choose an example from a composition less generally known—his paper on "Joan of Arc:"—

"What is to be thought of *her?* What is to be thought of the poor shepherd girl from the hills and forests of Lorraine, that—like the Hebrew shepherd boy from the hills and forests of Judea—rose suddenly out of the quiet, out of the safety, out of the religious inspiration, rooted in deep pastoral solitudes, to a station in the van of armies, and to the more perilous station at the right hand of kings? . . . Pure, innocent, noble-hearted girl! whom, from earliest youth, ever I believed in as full of truth and self-sacrifice, this was amongst the strongest pledges for *thy* truth, that never once—no, not for a moment of weakness—didst thou revel in the vision of coronets and honour from man. Coronets for thee! Oh no! Honours, if they come when all is over, are for those that share thy blood. Daughter of Domremy, when the gratitude of thy king shall awaken, thou wilt be sleeping the sleep of the dead. Call her, king of France, but she will not hear thee! Cite her by thy apparitors to come and receive a robe of honour, but she will be found *en contumace.* When the thunders of universal France, as even yet may happen, shall proclaim the grandeur of the poor shepherd girl that gave up all for her country, thy ear, young shepherd girl, will have been deaf for five centuries. To suffer and to die, that was thy portion in this life; that was thy destiny; and not for a moment was it hidden from thyself. Life, thou saidst, is short; and the sleep which is in the grave is long. Let me use that life, so transitory, for the glory of those heavenly dreams destined to comfort the sleep which is so long. This pure creature —pure from every suspicion of even a visionary self-interest, even as she was pure in senses more obvious—never once did this holy child, as regarded herself, relax from her belief in the darkness that was travelling to meet her. She might not prefigure the very manner of her death; she saw not in vision, perhaps, the aerial altitude of the fiery scaffold, the spectators without end on every road pouring into Rouen as to a coronation, the surging smoke, the volleying flames, the hostile faces all around, the pitying eye that lurked but here and there, until nature and imperishable truth broke loose from artificial restraints,—these might not be apparent through the mists of the hurrying future. But the voice that called her to death, *that* she heard for ever."

As an example of a pathetic apostrophe, in a less touching but still impressive key, take his reminiscence of Edward Irving, from one of his unreprinted papers :—

"He was the only man of our times who realised one's idea of Paul preaching at Athens, or defending himself before King Agrippa. Terrific meteor! unhappy son of fervid genius, which mastered thyself even more than the rapt audiences which at one time hung upon thy lips! were the cup of life once again presented to thy lips, wouldst thou drink again? or wouldst thou not rather turn away from it with shuddering abomination? Sleep, Boanerges, and let the memory of man settle only upon thy colossal powers, without a thought of those intellectual aberrations which were more powerful for thy own ruin than for the misleading of others!"

Humour.

Our author's "Murder considered as one of the Fine Arts," belongs to a vein of irony peculiarly his own—the humour of bringing the ideas of Fine Art and ordinary business into ludicrous collision with solemn or horrible transactions. An extract or two from the beginning of this paper will give an idea of its character. It is preceded by an "Advertisement of a man morbidly virtuous," which begins thus—

"Most of us who read books, have probably heard of a society for the promotion of vice, of the Hell-Fire Club, founded in the last century by Sir Francis Dashwood, &c. At Brighton, I think it was, that a society was formed for the suppression of virtue. That society was itself suppressed; but I am sorry to say that another exists in London, of a character still more atrocious. In tendency, it may be denominated a society for the encouragement of murder; but, according to their own delicate *εὐφημισμὸς*, it is styled, The Society of Connoisseurs in Murder. They profess to be curious in homicide; amateurs and dilettanti in the various modes of carnage; and, in short, murder-fanciers. Every fresh atrocity of that class which the police annals of Europe bring up, they meet and criticise as they would a picture, statue, or other work of art. But I need not trouble myself with any attempt to describe the spirit of their proceedings, as the reader will collect *that* much better from one of the monthly lectures read before the society last year. This has fallen into my hands accidentally, in spite of all the vigilance exercised to keep their transactions from the public eye."

The "morbidly virtuous" advertiser concludes by saying that he has not yet heard of the society offering prizes for a well-executed murder, but that "undoubtedly their proceedings tend to that." The atrocious lecture thus exposed to the eye of the public begins as follows :—

"GENTLEMEN,—I have had the honour to be appointed by your committee to the trying task of reading the Williams' Lecture on Murder considered as one of the Fine Arts,—a task which might be easy enough three or four centuries ago, when the art was little understood, and few great models had been exhibited; but in this age, when masterpieces of excellence have been executed by professional men, it must be evident, that in the style of criticism applied to them, the public will look for something of a corresponding improvement. Practice and theory must advance *pari passu*. People begin to see that something more goes to the composition of a fine murder than two blockheads to kill and be killed—a knife—a purse—and a dark lane. Design, gentlemen, grouping, light and shade, poetry, sentiment, are now deemed indispensable to attempts of this nature. Mr Williams has exalted the ideal of murder to all of us; and to me, therefore, in particular, has deepened the arduousness of my task. Like Æschylus or Milton in poetry, like Michael Angelo in painting, he has carried his art to a point of colossal sublimity; and, as Mr Wordsworth observes, has in a manner 'created the taste by which he is to be enjoyed.' To sketch the history of the art and to examine his principles critically, now remains as a duty for the connoisseur, and for judges of quite another stamp from his Majesty's Judges of Assize."

The humour is kept up through fifty-seven pages.[1]

The "Williams' Lecture" is the crowning achievement of his humour. His works contain many occasional touches in the same vein. He is frequently jocular on the subject of death. Thus—

"In like manner, I do by no means deny that some truths have been delivered to the world in regard to opium: thus, it has been repeatedly affirmed by the learned that opium is a tawny brown in colour—and this, take notice, I grant; secondly, that it is rather dear, which also I grant—for in my time East India opium has been three guineas a-pound, and Turkey eight; and, thirdly, that if you eat a good deal of it, most probably you must do what is disagreeable to any man of regular habits—viz., die."

Again, alluding to Savage Landor's contumacy at school:—

"'*Roberte the Deville:*' see the old metrical romance of that name: it belongs to the fourteenth century, and was printed some thirty years ago, with wood engravings of the illuminations. Roberte, however, took the liberty of murdering *his* schoolmaster. But could he well do less? Being a reigning Duke's son, and after the rebellious schoolmaster had said—

'Sir, ye bee too bolde:
And therewith took a rodde hym for to chaste.'

Upon which the meek Robin, without using any bad language as the schoolmaster had done, simply took out a long dagger '*hym* for to chaste,' which he did effectually. The schoolmaster gave no bad language after that."

It must not be supposed that De Quincey's humour consists solely in this playing with dread ideas. His works, as we noticed in sketching his character, overflow with good-natured humour of every description. It is often of that strongly individual kind which only intimate sympathisers can tolerate; strangers call it impertinent, flippant, affected. Take, for example, one of his playful apostrophes to historical names:—

"Sam Parr! I love you. I said so once before. But *perstringing*, which was a favoured word of your own, was a no less favoured act. You also in

[1] The paper occurs in vol. iv. of the Collected Edition. This volume, containing also the "Revolt of the Tartars," the "Templar's Dialogues," and the "Vision of Sudden Death," affords good examples of all the qualities of his style.

your lifetime perstringed many people, some of whom perstringed you, Sam, smartly in return."

"I (said Augustus Cæsar) found Rome built of brick; but I left it built of marble. Well, my man, we reply, for a wondrously little chap, you did what in Westmoreland they call a good *darroch* (day's work); and if *navvies* had been wanted in those days, you should have had our vote to a certainty. But Caius Julius, even under such a limitation of the comparison, did a thing as much transcending this," &c.

We must also give a specimen of his humorous "slangy" outrages on the dignity of criticism. The following occurs in his "Brief Appraisal of Greek Literature," which has not been reprinted:—

"But all this extent of obligation amongst later poets of Greece to Homer serves less to argue his opulence than their penury. And if, quitting the one great blazing jewel, the Urim and Thummim of the Iliad" [Achilles], "you descend to individual passages of poetic effect; and if amongst these a fancy should seize you of asking for a specimen of the *sublime* in particular, what is it that you are offered by the critics? Nothing that we remember beyond one single passage, in which the God Neptune is described in a steeplechase, and 'making play' at a terrific pace. And certainly enough is exhibited of the old boy's hoofs, and their spanking qualities, to warrant our backing him against a railroad for a rump and dozen; but, after all, there is nothing to grow frisky about, as Longinus does, who gets up the steam of a blue-stocking enthusiasm, and boils us a regular gallop of ranting, in which, like the conceited snipe upon the Liverpool railroad, he thinks himself to run a match with Sampson; and whilst affecting to admire Homer, is manifestly squinting at the reader to see how far he admires his own flourish of admiration; and, in the very agony of his frosty raptures, is quite at leisure to look out for a little private traffic of rapture on his own account. But it won't do; this old critical posture-master (whom, if Aurelius hanged, surely he knew what he was about) may as well put up his rapture pipes, and (as Lear says) 'not squiny' at us; for let us ask Master Longinus, in what earthly respect do these great strides of Neptune exceed Jack with his seven-league boots? Let him answer that, if he can. We hold that Jack has the advantage."

Melody and Harmony.

The melody of De Quincey's prose is pre-eminently rich and stately. He takes rank with Milton as one of our greatest masters of stately cadence, as well as of sublime composition. If one may trust one's ear for a general impression, Milton's melody is sweeter and more varied; but for magnificent effects, at least in prose, the palm must probably be assigned to De Quincey. In some of De Quincey's grandest passages the language can be compared only to the swell and crash of an orchestra.

It need hardly be added that the harmony between his rhythm and his subject-matter is most striking in the sublime flights.

Taste.

De Quincey has been accused of crossing the bounds of good

taste in certain respects. His digressions and footnotes have been objected to. His punctilious precision in the use of terms has been called pedantic. He has been censured for carrying to excess what we have described as his favourite figure. But especially he has been visited with severe condemnation for his offences in the pursuit of comic effect—more particularly in the use of slang. A recent critic has gone the length of describing his "slangy" apostrophes as "exquisite foolery."

KINDS OF COMPOSITION.

Description.

Though so many of De Quincey's papers are descriptive, and are properly designated sketches, he has really left us very little detailed description of external nature. The reason is to be found in his character. His interest was almost wholly engrossed by man. The description that he excelled in was description of the human form, feelings, and manners.

Where he does attempt the description of still life, notwithstanding his natural clearness and order, he is much inferior to Carlyle. He has one or two good points. He gives right and left in his pictures, and brings in such touches of precision as—"standing on a different radius of my circular prospect, but at nearly the same distance:"—which is very significant, if not too scholastic. But if we take even such a studied piece as his description of the valley of Easedale, at the beginning of his "Recollections of the Lakes," vol. ii., we miss the vividness of a master of the descriptive art. We receive no idea of such a fundamental fact as the size of the valley: we are, indeed, presented rather with the feelings and reflections of a poetically-minded spectator, than with the material aspects of the scene.

Generally speaking, he describes nature only in its direct or figurative relations to man. A scene is interesting as "the very same spectacle, unaltered in a single feature, which once at the same hour was beheld by the legionary Roman from his embattled camp, or by the roving Briton in his 'wolf-skin vest.'" A hamlet of seven cottages clustering together round a lonely highland tarn, is interesting as suggesting seclusion from the endless tumults and angry passions of human society; the declining light of the afternoon, from its association with the perils and dangers of the night. Thus it happens that often, instead of describing he really expounds — expounds the thoughts that arise from the general features of a scene by force of association or of similitude. We see this in his description of the English Lake scenery:—

"But more even than Anne Radcliffe had the landscape-painters, so many and so various, contributed to the glorification of the English Lake district; drawing out and impressing upon the heart the sanctity of repose in its shy recesses—its Alpine grandeur in such passes as those of Wastdalehead, Langdalehead, Borrowdale, Kirkstone, Hawsdale, &c., together with the monastic peace which seems to brood over its peculiar form of pastoral life, so much nobler (as Wordsworth notices) in its stern simplicity and continual conflict with danger hidden in the vast draperies of mist overshadowing the hills, and amongst the armies of snow and hail arrayed by fierce northern winters, than the effeminate shepherd's life in the classical Arcadia, or in the flowery pastures of Sicily."

An indifferent observer of nature, De Quincey was minute and precise in his observation of human beings. Every face that he met he seems to have watched with the vigilant attention of a Boswell. He has described the persons of many of his contemporaries. His most careful portraits are, perhaps, his Lake companions—Wordsworth, Coleridge, Southey, and Wilson. To these must be added his delineation of the notorious murderer Williams. The reader that desires to see how watchful an eye he had for the smallest particularities of shape, look, and bearing, will do well to read his prefatory note on Coleridge, vol. xi.

It is in the description of the feelings that he particularly excels. Not only is he deeply learned in the proper vocabulary of the feelings; he had acquired by close study, and employs with exquisite skill, a profound knowledge of the outward manifestations of feeling in tone, feature, gesture, and conduct. In reading motives from what he would have called the dumb hieroglyphics of observed or recorded behaviour, and in tracing the succession of feelings that must have passed under given circumstances, he is one of our greatest masters. In this point more perhaps than in any other, he challenges the closest attention of the student.

A good specimen of his power is the passage in the Marr murder where he pictures Mary's feelings on her returning to the door and finding it locked:—

"Mary rang, and at the same time very gently knocked. She had no fear of disturbing her master or mistress; *them* she made sure of finding still up. Her anxiety was for the baby, who, being disturbed, might again rob her mistress of a night's rest; and she well knew that with three people all anxiously awaiting her return, and by this time, perhaps, seriously uneasy at her delay, the least audible whisper from herself would in a moment bring one of them to the door. Yet how is this? To her astonishment—but with the astonishment came creeping over her an icy horror—no stir nor murmur was heard ascending from the kitchen. At this moment came back upon her, with shuddering anguish, the indistinct image of the stranger in the loose dark coat whom she had seen stealing along under the shadowy lamplight, and too certainly watching her master's motions. Keenly she now reproached herself that under whatever stress of hurry she had not acquainted Mr Marr with the suspicious appearances. Poor girl! she did not then know that, if this communication could have availed to put Marr upon his guard, it had reached him from another quarter; so that her own omission, which had in reality arisen under her hurry to execute her master's commission, could not be charged with any bad consequences. But all such reflections this way or that were swallowed up at this point in overmastering panic. That her double summons *could* have been unnoticed—this solitary fact in one moment made a revelation of horror. One person might have fallen asleep, but two—but three—*that* was a mere impossibility. And even supposing all three together with the baby locked in sleep, still how unacountable was this utter—utter silence! Most naturally at this moment something like hysterical horror overshadowed the poor girl; and now, at last, she rang the bell with the violence that belongs to sickening terror. This done, she paused. Self-command enough she still retained, though fast and fast it was slipping away from her, to bethink herself that, if any overwhelming accident *had* compelled both Marr and his apprentice-boy to leave the house in order to summon surgical aid from opposite quarters—a thing barely supposable—still, even in that case, Mrs Marr and her infant would be left, and some murmuring reply, under any extremity, would be elicited from the poor mother. To pause, therefore, to impose stern silence upon herself, so as to leave room for the possible answer to this final appeal, became a duty of spasmodic effort. Listen, therefore, poor trembling heart; listen, and for twenty seconds be as still as death. Still as death she was; and during that dreadful stillness, when she hushed her breath that she might listen, occurred an incident of killing fear, that to her dying day would never cease to renew its echoes in her ear."

Narrative.

De Quincey never attempted any continuous history. Taking his own division of history into Narrative, Scenical, and Philosophical, we see that he had special qualifications for the two last modes. But he wanted industry to take up a national history and pursue it continuously through all its stages. What he might have done we can guess only from speculations recorded incidentally in such papers as his account of the Cæsars, or of Cicero, or Charlemagne, and from the spectacular sketch of the Revolt of the Tartars.

He wrote several short biographies. In these he has at least the negative merit of not chronicling unimportant facts. They can hardly be called narratives; there is in them as little as possible of anything that could be called narrative art. They are, properly speaking, discussions of perplexities that have gathered about the story of the individual life, and descriptions of the various features of the character.

In his most imaginative tales, such as the "Spanish Military Nun," the facts are altogether secondary to the poetical embellishments—are but the bare cloth on which he works his many-coloured tapestry of pathos, humour, and soaring rhapsodies.

Exposition.

De Quincey possessed some of the best qualities of an expositor, coupled with considerable defects.

The great obstacle to his success in exposition was the want of simplicity. He was, as we have seen, too persistently scholastic for the ordinary reader, making an almost ostentatious use of logical forms and scientific technicalities.

As his studious clearness is marred by an unnecessary use of unfamiliar words and forms of expression, so others of his merits in exposition must be stated with some abatement.

He was aware of the value of iterating a statement. "A man," he says, "who should content himself with a single condensed enunciation of a perplexed doctrine, would be a madman and a *felo de se*, as respected his reliance upon that doctrine." Yet he considered iteration a departure "from the severities of abstract discussion." "In the senate, and for the same reason in a newspaper, it is a virtue to reiterate your meaning: tautology becomes a merit; variation of the words, with a substantial identity of the sense and dilution of the truth, is oftentimes a necessity." But in a book, he held, repetition is rather a blemish, seeing that the reader may "return to the past page if anything in the present depends upon it." In this he was probably unpractical: doubtless the reader is saved much weariness by judicious repetition, although of course less is needed in a book than in a speech.

He knew also the value of stating the counter-proposition. In upholding the Ricardian law that the value of a thing is determined by the *quantity* of the labour that produces it, he broadly declares that the mere statement of the doctrine brings the student not one step nearer the truth, unless he is told what it is designed to contradict—namely, that the value of the thing is not determined by the *value* of the producing labour.

When he is thoroughly in earnest, and resolved to make an abstruse point clear to the meanest capacity, he knows how to proceed by means of simple examples and illustrations. This is well shown in his Dialogues on Political Economy. The misfortune is, that he is not always alive to the abstruseness of the question he happens to be dealing with, and consequently wears to many readers an air of repulsive incomprehensibility.

His power of clothing a dry subject with interest appears advantageously in his "Templar's Dialogues on Political Economy." In respect of varied interest, this fragment is equal to the dialogues of Plato.

In consequence chiefly of his abstruseness, he cannot be recommended as a model to the popular expositor. Yet his command of language, his precision, and his power of imparting interest, make him a profitable study if the student knows what to imitate and what to avoid.

CHAPTER II.

THOMAS BABINGTON MACAULAY,

1800—1859.

THIS most popular of modern prose writers was born on the 25th of October 1800, at Rothley Temple in Leicestershire, the residence of his uncle-in-law and name-father, Thomas Babington.

His father, Zachary Macaulay, was a man of some note, and was judged worthy of a monument in Westminster Abbey. The son of a Scotch minister in Dumbartonshire, he made a moderate fortune in Jamaica and Sierra Leone, and on his return to England in 1799, became a principal supporter of the Society for the Abolition of Slavery. A dry taciturn man, writing a plain terse style, he bore little outward resembance to his distinguished son; but he had the same untiring powers of work, and the same extraordinary strength of memory. He edited the newspaper of the Abolitionists, and was the great master of the statistics employed for the agitation of the public mind. The historian's mother, a pupil of the sisters of Hannah More, was also a person of talent; to her he seems to have owed his buoyant constitution.

Never, to use his own favourite mode of expression, was a child brought into this world under circumstances more favourable to the development of literary talent. His parents belonged to a small sect of earnest and accomplished persons, closely knit together by a common object, and zealously devoted to their adopted mission. With the earliest dawn of intelligence he heard imperial policy discussed at his father's table, and the affairs of the nation arranged, not by ideal politicians, but by men actively engaged in public business—such men as Henry Thornton, Thomas Babington, and Wilberforce. He saw his father preparing their printed organ, and at an early age was taught by that encyclopedic statistician the argumentative value of facts. There being the closest intercourse between the families of the Clapham sect, a boy of promising abilities met with much attention, and many willing instructors of his youthful curiosity. Besides, young "Tom," bright and loquacious, was an especial favourite with Hannah More, "the high priestess of the brotherhood," and had his fancy quickened and his ambition fired by her anecdotes of the literary men of last century.

He was not sent to any of the great public schools. He received his earliest instruction at a small school in Clapham. "At the age of twelve he was placed under the care of the Rev. Mr Preston, first at Shelford, afterwards near Buntingford, in the neighbourhood of Cambridge." With Mr Preston he seems to have remained until ready to enter the University.

In his nineteenth year he began residence at Trinity College, Cambridge. In after-life he used to mention with regret that at College he spent very little time on the prevailing study of mathematics; but classics he prosecuted with such success, that in 1821 he gained the high distinction of the Craven scholarship. A large part of his time was given to pursuits not so strictly academical; he was a distinguished orator at the Union, and twice carried away the Chancellor's medal for English verse—in 1819 for a poem on Pompeii, and in 1821 for a poem on Evening. He took his degree of B.A. in 1822, and in October 1824 was elected Fellow of his College.

Very soon after taking his degree, and while waiting in College for his fellowship, he set himself strenuously to fulfil his ambition in literature. His first efforts were contributed to 'Knight's Quarterly Magazine,' between June 1823 and November 1824. From these early productions we can see that he did not work at random, but to some extent pursued definite objects. Thus, in his "Fragments of a Roman Tale," and his "Scenes from Athenian Revels," we can discern a purpose—a purpose that he often recommends as the highest aim of the historian,—namely, to realise the *private* life of the bygone generations. Again, from his studies of Dante, Petrarch, Cowley, Milton, and the Athenian orators, we may infer that he worked upon the orthodox plan for literary aspirants, of making himself familiar with the leading masters of style in different languages. Then we have an indication of a mechanical plan of working. His contributions appear in pairs—a grave composition coupled with something lighter. If this was not the arrangement of the publisher, we may suppose that he sought the relief of variety, and that from the first he worked upon a deliberate resolve to excel in all kinds of composition.

In 1824 he made his first appearance as a public speaker. At an Abolitionist meeting in Freemasons' Hall, he seconded one of the resolutions, and his speech is said to have created some talk among outsiders.

The performance that first brought him conspicuously into notice was his article on Milton, contributed to the 'Edinburgh Review' in August 1825. He was called to the bar in 1826; but though he took chambers in the Temple and joined the Northern Circuit, he probably gave little time to legal business, and he made no name as a barrister. It was his literary power that found him patronage. In 1827 he received from Lord Lyndhurst a commissionership of bankrupts. And in 1830, through the influence of Lord Lansdowne, he was returned for the borough of Calne, and entered the House of Commons.

In the Reform debates of 1831 and 1832 he was one of the most effective speakers. He went strongly and unreservedly with the Whigs. In 1832, as an acknowledgment of his zeal for Reform, he was returned by the newly enfranchised borough of Leeds. In the same year he was appointed Secretary to the Board of Control. In the first session of the Reformed Parliament he spoke against the repeal of the union with Ireland, in favour of a bill for removing the civil disabilities of the Jews, and in favour of a bill for depriving the East India Company of their exclusive trade with China and other commercial privileges. In 1834 he was made president of a new law commission for India, and a member of the Supreme Council of Calcutta. In discharge of the duties of these lucrative offices he spent two years and a half in India, returning in 1838.

On his return from India he professed himself anxious to withdraw from politics, and devote his whole time to literature. He had not ceased, even when in India, to contribute to the 'Edinburgh Review'; but he wished now to settle down to his great project, the 'History of England from the Accession of James II.' This could not be. His party could not yet dispense with him. He was requested to stand for Edinburgh, and was elected in 1839, after very little opposition.

Re-entering Parliament, he was appointed Secretary at War, and retained the office till the fall of the Melbourne Ministry in 1841. In the general election of 1841 he was re-elected for Edinburgh without opposition. On the return of the Whigs to power in 1846, he obtained the office of Paymaster-General, and a seat in the Cabinet of Lord John Russell. Neither in office nor in opposition was he a silent member. His voice was heard on all questions of importance. On all party questions he stood by his party. He defended the war with China in 1840, assisted in beating down the Chartists, assailed Lord Ellenborough's administration of India, supported Lord John Russell's motion for an inquiry into the state of Ireland, and argued against loading slave-grown sugar with heavy duties. On questions less strictly matters of party, he showed his natural liberality of spirit—supported the increased Maynooth Grant and the abolition of Theological Tests in the Scottish Universities, and resented in very strong language the attempt to deprive certain Dissenters of their chapels on the ground that they did not hold the opinions of the original possessors. In 1841 he carried a change in the laws of copyright. In 1846 he supported an unsuccessful bill for limiting the labour of young persons in factories to ten hours a-day.

In 1842 he published his 'Lays of Ancient Rome.' Both before and after this he wrote occasional verses. Though not quite so popular as his prose, his poetry was very widely read. Yet most people would gladly forego his Lays for another volume of the History.

In 1844 he wrote the last of his brilliant essays to the 'Edinburgh Review.' Ambitious of distinction as an orator and a statesman, he had never renounced his literary ambition. It was chiefly on his writings that he depended for durable fame. Even during his official residence in India he found time to write for the Review. These periodical contributions were now stopped, not because he henceforth threw himself into politics with undivided ardour, but because he was setting in earnest to his projected History.

In 1846 he was at the height of his political success. In 1847 came a change. He had kept his seat for Edinburgh since 1839. He had been re-elected in 1841 without opposition. But of late his conduct had been far from satisfactory to the mass of the electors. He had given deep offence to churchmen of all sects by the breadth of his views. He had spoken in most contemptuous terms of the persecution of Sir David Brewster by the Established clergy; he had roused the hatred of the Evangelicals by advocating the Maynooth Grant, and still more by his derisive mention of the "bray" of Exeter Hall, and the "prescriptive right" of its frequenters "to talk nonsense." In the general election of 1847, therefore, he stood third on the poll. This may be considered the end of his political life. He refused to offer himself for another seat, and retired to his study and his books. In 1852 the electors of Edinburgh returned him at their own expense, unasked, and without putting him to the troubles of a canvass; but he took little part in the business of the House. His only memorable speech was on the exclusion of the Master of the Rolls from the House of Commons, on which occasion he is said to have turned the scale by a hundred votes.

In 1849 appeared the first two volumes of his History. Very few books have been bought with such avidity. There was a demand for the work such as had not been known since the days of Byron and Scott.

The second two volumes were not published till 1855. Expectation had been on tiptoe, and the rush was almost greater than for the first instalment.

While carrying on his History, he turned aside to write for the 'Encyclopedia Britannica' some biographies that he had more or less crudely sketched in his 'Essays'—the Lives of "Atterbury" (1853), "Bunyan" (1854), "Goldsmith" (1856), "Johnson" (1856), and "Pitt" (1859). These works are highly finished, and are considered by many to be the most favourable specimens of his style.

Meantime honours were coming in to crown his labours. In 1849 he was elected Lord Rector of the University of Glasgow, and was made a Fellow of the Royal Society. The year 1857 was especially fruitful of such rewards to successful toil. In that year he was elected a Foreign Member of the French Academy, and of the Prussian Order of Merit, High Steward of Cambridge; and in the autumn he was raised to the peerage as Baron Macaulay of Rothley—the first literary man to receive such a distinction.

He did not long enjoy his honours. His multifarious labours began to tell upon him. He was threatened with one of the maladies that too surely follow upon a life of excitement and overstrained energy—derangement of the action of the heart. Latterly he was prohibited from public speaking: at his installation as High Steward of Cambridge he simply bowed his acknowledgments, and made no speech. He had drafted and partly written a fifth volume of his History, but did not live to publish it. The last composition published during his life was his biography of Pitt. He died at his residence, Holly Lodge, Kensington, on the 28th of December 1859.

We cannot say of Macaulay himself what he said of Johnson —that we are as familiar with his personal appearance as with the faces that have surrounded us from childhood. The explanation probably is, that there was nothing in his appearance to draw particular attention. He seems to have been a fair-complexioned, good-looking man, about the middle height, full-bodied, and with a tolerably firm carriage. He is described as "robust-looking." Crabb Robinson says that his features were regular, but that they had not the delicacy one expects to see in men of genius and fine sensibility. His voice was strong and commanding, but its effect was marred by a quick and excited articulation.

He had a vigorous constitution. He was one of the favoured few that draw, as De Quincey says, the double prize of a fine intellect and a healthy stomach. Had he been more economical of his strength, he might have lived much longer in full exercise of his faculties.

It is often said that a man's powers cannot be fairly valued till several generations after his death; that his contemporaries and their immediate posterity can seldom judge with impartiality. Many persons repeat this dictum in something like the above form without ever asking themselves, What kind of powers do we mean? If power is taken to mean intellectual power as displayed in books, the dictum is probably true. We can probably judge better of the amount of intellect in a book than could have been done by the writer's contemporaries. But while posterity may give a juster award as respects the intellectual power shown in a book, it is much more likely to be unfair in its judgment of a man's general energy of intellect. Intellect may be thrown into other things than books, and if a man dazzles the judgment of his contemporaries, and obtains unmerited praise of his literary productions, the reason in all likelihood is that literature is not his only field of intellectual display.

Macaulay's brilliant command of expression, and confident and plausible deliverances on every subject of human interest, furnish a sufficient explanation of the extraordinary popularity of his works. Bnt undoubtedly the popular admiration of the man's abilities was heightened by the current traditions of his oratory, his powers of conversation, and his astonishing feats of memory. Everything combined to convey the impression of amazing versatility. Now, when his books are calmly judged, and his work estimated by special authorities in the various fields that he traversed with such confidence, there is a danger that we undervalue his powers, and estimate his whole intellectual force by the part of it that was spent upon his books. If he wished his fame to rest upon the quality, and not upon the quantity, of his literary productions, he should have chosen a more limited field, and not voraciously aspired to be pre-eminent in three such departments as poetry, history, and criticism. And if he wished his fame to rest upon his literary productions alone, whether in their quantity or in their quality, he should not have dissipated his energies so profusely in directions that are of little avail for permanent literary renown. He aspired to eminence not only as a man of letters, but as an orator and as a legislator. Besides all this, attested by substantial documents, he spent, if we may credit circulating traditions, an ordinary man's allowance of energy in the excitement of conversation, and in the indulgence of an incontinent appetite for reading. In conversation he did not give and take like De Quincey: once started on a theme, he ran on as in a set prelection, without break or pause. As regards his reading, the report is that besides what he read for his literary works, he went through thousands of novels, kept abreast of the ballad literature of the streets, and attempted such freaks as reading the bulky volumes of Chrysostom. With all necessary allowance for exaggeration, it is evident that his literary performances are far from representing the whole of his dissipated intellectual force.

Numerous testimonies are on record concerning his extraordinary powers of memory. The hyperbolical expression that he forgot nothing, while it goes very far beyond the truth, indicates significantly what an impression he made on his contemporaries. It is the kind of exaggeration that makes heroes out of pre-eminent men. In his history he often quotes the substance of a document instead of giving the exact words; and the reason was, that he often quoted from memory. Several of his essays, involving extensive ranges of matter of fact, were written, by his own statement, at a distance from books. Concerning his conversation, we have several authentic anecdotes. We learn from the historian Prescott that he did not go prepared on a particular subject, and watch his opportunity to bring it forward, but fluently quoted a profusion of facts and dates on subjects introduced by others. Washington Irving relates that, in historical combats with Hallam, Macaulay quoted chapter and section as if he had had the books before him. Another acquaintance tells us that, being on one occasion convicted of a misquotation from 'Paradise Lost,' he soon after offered himself for examination, undertaking to quote any passage suggested to him in the whole poem. Moore's Diary contains several expressions of wonder at the power of his memory. At one time in particular, says the poet, "he astonished us by repeating old Irish slang ballads as glibly as I used to do when a boy."

With such a plenitude of sheer retentiveness, he combined a large share of the analogical faculty. He ranged freely through the immense store of particulars that he had accumulated, drawing parallels, analogies, and figurative comparisons with vivacious facility. Assert a proposition in art, politics, social science, indeed in any department of human knowledge, and without a moment's hesitation he would place before you similar propositions from various authors, and hosts of confirmatory or contradictory particulars. He would then, perhaps, state a view held by himself, and support his position by a fertile array of instances, analogies, and similitudes.

These brilliant powers were not without their natural weaknesses. He was so hurried a thinker, he was so enamoured of mere movement, that he could not rest to analyse minutely, or to make certain that his instances and comparisons were exactly to the point. True, he had strong sense, and with his wide command of facts was not likely to go far astray on practical questions. But compare him with a calm, meditative, original writer like De Quincey, and you become vividly aware of his peculiar deficiency, as well as his peculiar strength; you find a more rapid succession of ideas and greater wealth of illustration, but you miss the subtle casuistry, the exact and finished similitudes, and the breaking up of routine views. No original opinion requiring patient consideration or delicate analysis is associated with the name of Macaulay. It better suited his stirring and excitable nature to apply his dazzling powers of expression and illustration to the opinions of others. He was quick to expose false generalisations by producing contradictory instances, and he often generalised for himself with the utmost boldness; but none of his original generalisations possess any importance. The life of a misunderstood man like Goldsmith is a good test of a writer's power of breaking through false traditions. Macaulay's Life of Goldsmith repeats many vulgar errors, and contains nothing new except the opinion that Goldsmith was not an ill-used man, but might have lived comfortably had he been provident—an opinion resulting from strong unsentimental sense, coupled with a special eye for plain matters of fact. In his similitudes and otherwise, he often errs against exact congruity. Describing Dante's countenance, he places a "sullen and contemptuous curve" upon the lip, a "haggard and woful stare" in the eye—sullenness and contempt upon one feature, and hopeless compassion upon another. Expounding the peculiarities of Milton's similes, and enlarging especially upon "the extreme remoteness of the associations by which he acts upon the reader" —an expression, by the way, somewhat vague—he illustrates his meaning by saying that the poet "strikes the key-note, and expects his hearers to make out the melody"—a feat that "every schoolboy" knows to be absurdly impossible, there being hundreds of different melodies starting from the same key-note.

As regards the emotional side of the man. In his writings he appears buoyant and hopeful, an optimist, looking on the bright side of things, enthusiastic in his desire of progress, exultingly sure of its fulfilment in these latter days, confident in his opinions, warm and open in his expressions of like and dislike; a man "radiant," as Carlyle says, "with pepticity," without a trace of misgiving, despondency, or sourness. His sympathies go all with the vigorous and hopeful side of human nature; he ignores the miseries and difficulties of this life. He would have us believe that human comfort is rapidly on the increase; that we are rapidly nearing his millennium, where "employment is always plentiful, wages always high, food always cheap, and a large family is considered not as an encumbrance but as a blessing." "From the oppressions of illiterate masters, and the sufferings of a degraded peasantry," his mind always turns with delight to such conceptions as "the vast magnificent cities, the ports, the arsenals, the villas, the museums, the libraries, the marts filled with every article of comfort or luxury, the factories swarming with artisans, the Apennines covered with rich cultivation up to their very summits, the Po wafting the harvests of Lombardy to the granaries of Venice, and carrying back the silks of Bengal and the furs of Siberia to the palaces of Milan."

We spoke of De Quincey as a man of ever-active imagination, often engaged in transmuting the scenes and characters of his daily life into food for his æsthetic sensibilities. There does not seem to have been much of this day-dreaming turn in Macaulay. His energies were engrossed with actualities, and in his overpowering love of movement he hurried eagerly from one thing to another, without staying to overlay them with superstructures of the imagination. In his study he did not lie dreaming on a rug before the fire with a book in his hand, subjecting every new idea to a mental chemistry of analysis and synthesis, and using it as a starting-point for speculations of his own, but sat in his chair or walked through the room reading, writing, and revising with his whole strength. The chief work of his imagination—using the word in a loose popular sense—was to picture the scenes and personages of ancient times and distant countries as they really were—the work of what may be called the historical imagination. Of æsthetic imagination—imagination properly so called, imagination as a creative or modifying faculty engaged in building up objects of Fine Art—he had little share. It was, one may say, pushed aside by other mental activities, and what work it did was done in a hurry. His warmest admirers cannot claim for him a high degree of æsthetic culture. He was too much occupied with facts to have time for it. His 'Lays of Ancient Rome' are interesting rather historically than æsthetically. They afford us vivid glimpses of Roman life and Italian scenery. The incidents, the sayings, and the doings are of the garish order that captivates the inexperienced taste.

Concerning his Opinions. In practical politics, as we have seen, Macaulay adhered to the Whigs; and generally, in questions not identified with party, showed himself a friend to religious liberty, and to measures calculated to improve the condition of the poorer classes. While he supported the Reform Bill, he was averse to sweeping constitutional changes. The Radical party was his especial aversion.

Theoretical politics he professed to regard with abhorrence. He scoffed at "metaphysical" and "abstract" theories of government, and treated with scorn the idea that the lawgiver can derive any light from general principles of human nature. Doubtless he was prejudiced against political theorists, because the chief theorists in his day were Radicals. He himself theorised abundantly upon general principles of human nature—as, for example, in his account of the Italian States in the essay on Machiavelli; and he theorised under the disadvantage of not knowing that he did theorise.

In his historical verdicts, he is accused of allowing his judgment to be warped by party feeling. Perhaps too much has been made of this. His attachment to certain ideas was probably stronger than his attachment to party. He loved liberty, justice, toleration, and the fair fame of England, with the warmth of an ardent nature: whoever did violence to these ideas, he hated as if a personal enemy. He hated Laud as a bigot, and Charles as a tyrant. He admired Cromwell as the destroyer of a tyranny. He had not the heart to denounce Cromwell's usurpation, partly because the usurper used his power with moderation, and did not show a narrow partiality for his own sect, but, above all, because during the Protectorate the name of England was dreaded and respected on the Continent. He was a most ardent patriot; to be patriotic was an unfailing passport to his favour: and such as had betrayed their country were subjected to a jealous valuation, and let off with scant acknowledgment of their virtues, and a thorough exposure of their crimes.

He has left comparatively little literary criticism, and that little is not at all valuable. His deliverance against Pope's "correctness," in his Essay on Byron, is sometimes quoted. That his pungent analogies drive very wide of the mark, the student will see by reading the late Mr Conington's Essay on Pope, Oxford Essays, 1858.

Though in no sense a man of science, he pronounces with his usual confidence on questions of philosophy. He eulogises modern science because it does not "disdain the humble office of ministering to the comforts of mankind." But he sees little good in the Inductive Method. It has, he says, "been practised ever since the beginning of the world by every human being." He overlooks the all-important fact that it has been practised only in simple cases, and in those imperfectly, and that its sole pretension is to make available for complicated problems principles that have been acted upon and established in cases of greater simplicity. The following is a sharp criticism from the pen of Sir George Cornewall Lewis, a determined enemy of superficial knowledge:—

"I have read Macaulay's article on Lord Bacon in the 'Edinburgh Review.' It is written in his usual sparkling, lively, antithetical style, and the historical part of it is interesting and amusing. His remarks on the ancient philosophy are for the most part shallow and ignorant in the extreme; his objections to the utility of logic are the stale commonplaces which all the enemies of accurate knowledge, and the eulogists of common-sense, practical men, &c., have always been setting forth."

ELEMENTS OF STYLE.

Vocabulary.

There is little to remark upon in Macaulay's vocabulary except its copiousness. He has no eccentricities of diction like De Quincey or Carlyle; he employs neither slang nor scholastic technicalities, and he never coins a new word. He cannot be said to use an excess of Latin words, and he is not a purist in the matter of Saxon.

His command of expression was proportioned to the extraordinary compass of his memory. The copiousness appears not so much in the Shakspearian form of accumulating synonyms one upon another, as in a profuse way of repeating a thought in several different sentences. This is especially noticeable in the opening passages of some of his Essays. In his review of Southey, for example, he starts an opinion that the laureate's forte was sentiment rather than reason, and luxuriates as if he never would have done with his voluptuous repetitions of the titillating doctrine.

Sentences.

Macaulay's is a style that may truly be called "artificial," from his excessive use of striking artifices of style—balanced sentences, abrupt transitions, and pointed figures of speech.

The peculiarities of the mechanism of his style are expressed in such general terms as "abrupt," "pointed," "oratorical." We shall not attempt to gather together separately all the elements that justify these epithets; but, following the order indicated in the Introduction, the various particulars that go to the making of the "abruptness" and the "point" will be noticed as we proceed.

His sentences have the compact finish produced by the frequent occurrence of the periodic arrangement. He is not uniformly periodic; he often prefers a loose structure, and he very rarely has recourse to the forced inversions that we find occasionally in De Quincey. Yet there is a sufficient interspersion of periodic arrangements to produce an impression of firmness. Taken as a whole, his style is one of the last that we should call loose.

We here speak of the periodic arrangement or structure as defined in our Introduction (p. 5). If we take the word periodic in its restricted sense, we cannot describe Macaulay as a composer in the periodic style. The "periodic style," in its narrower sense, implies long and heavy-laden sentences, and Macaulay's tendency is towards the short and light.

Occasionally he uses the long oratorical climactic period, consisting of a number of clauses in the same construction gradually increasing in length so as to form a climax. Thus—

"The energy of Innocent the Third, the zeal of the young orders of Francis and Dominic, and the ferocity of the Crusaders, whom the priesthood let loose on an unwarlike population, crushed the Albigensian Churches."

Again, in a sketch of the Reformation—

"The study of the ancient writers, the rapid development of the powers of the modern languages, the unprecedented activity which was displayed in every department of literature, the political state of Europe, the vices of the Roman Court, the exactions of the Roman Chancery, the jealousy with which the wealth and privileges of the clergy were naturally regarded by laymen, the jealousy with which Italian ascendancy was naturally regarded by men born on our side of the Alps—all these things gave to the teachers of the new theology an advantage which they perfectly understood how to use."

In the last example there are two climaxes in sound.

A large proportion of his sentences contain words and clauses in formal balance; but the effect of this would not be so striking were it not that his composition contains so much antithesis in other modes. The general predominance of antithesis we shall consider in its place under Figures of Speech; here we have to do properly with balanced forms, whether embodying antithesis or not.

He makes considerable use of conventional balanced phrases for amplifying the roll of the sentence. Thus—"After full inquiry, and impartial reflection;" "men who have been tried by equally strong temptations, and about whose lives we possess equally full information;" "no hidden causes to develop, no remote consequences to predict;" "very pleasing images of paternal tenderness and filial duty;" and so forth.

The following is an example of balance without antithesis. It is valuable as an artificial mode of giving separate emphasis to two things involved in the same argument—a preventive against confusion:—

"Now it does not appear to us to be the first object that people should always believe in the established religion, or be attached to the established government. A religion may be false. A government may be oppressive. And whatever support governments give to false religions, or religion to oppressive governments, we consider as a clear evil."

While this mode of statement has undeniably its advantages, it is obviously too startling an artifice to be often employed. The two short sentences, interjected without connectives, are examples of one element of our author's abruptness.

The following passages show balance combined with antithesis:—

"Thus the successors of the old Cavaliers had turned demagogues; the successors of the old Roundheads had turned courtiers. Yet was it long before their mutual animosity began to abate; for it is the nature of parties to retain their original enmities far more firmly than their original principles. During many years, a generation of Whigs, whom Sidney would have spurned as slaves, continued to wage deadly war with a generation of Tories whom Jeffreys would have hanged for Republicans."

"With such feelings, both parties looked into the chronicles of the middle ages. Both readily found what they sought; and both obstinately refused to see anything but what they sought. The champions of the Stuarts could easily point out instances of oppression exercised on the subject. The defenders of the Roundheads could as easily produce instances of determined and successful resistance offered to the Crown. The Tories quoted from ancient writings expressions almost as servile as were heard from the pulpit of Mainwaring. The Whigs discovered expressions as bold and severe as any that resounded from the judgment-seat of Bradshaw. One set of writers adduced numerous instances in which kings had extorted money without the authority of Parliament. Another set cited cases in which the Parliament had assumed to itself the power of inflicting punishment on kings. Those who saw only one half of the evidence would have concluded that the Plantagenets were as absolute as the Sultans of Turkey; those who saw only the other half would have concluded that the Plantagenets had as little real power as the Doges of Venice; and both conclusions would have been equally remote from the truth."

It is a pretty general opinion among critics that Macaulay overdid this artifice of style. Even his apologist in the 'Edinburgh Review' admitted that his sentences were sometimes "too curiously balanced." As he himself said of Tacitus—"He tells a fine story finely, but he cannot tell a plain story plainly. He stimulates till stimulants lose their power." The worst of it is that exact balance cannot long be kept up, as in the above passage, without a sacrifice of strict truth; both sides are extremely exaggerated to make the antithesis more telling.

Paragraphs.

1. The striking characteristic of *abruptness* in Macaulay's style is caused chiefly by his peculiar ways of transition and connection. He does not conduct us from one statement to another with the deliberate formality of De Quincey. We are seldom left in doubt as to the bearing of his statements; but we are often kept in suspense, and generally we must make out connections for ourselves without the help of explicit phrases.

Let us, for example, study his way of introducing the general proposition italicised in the middle of the following passage:—

"The state of society in the Neapolitan dominions, and in some parts of the Ecclesiastical State, more nearly resembled that which existed in the great monarchies of Europe. But the governments of Lombardy and Tuscany, through all their revolutions, preserved a different character. *A people when assembled in a town is far more formidable to its rulers than when dispersed over a wide extent of country.* The most arbitrary of the Cæsars found it necessary to feed and divert the inhabitants of their unwieldy capital at the expense of the provinces. The citizens of Madrid have more than once besieged their sovereign in his own palace, and extorted from him the most humiliating concessions. The Sultans have often been compelled to propitiate the furious rabble of Constantinople with the head of an unpopular vizier. *From the same cause there was a certain tinge of democracy in the monarchies and aristocracies of Northern Italy.*"

The general proposition is introduced abruptly. We are expecting a statement about the governments of Lombardy and Tuscany, when, with a sudden jerk, the circle of our vision is widened, and we are presented with a general comparison between the government natural to cities and the government natural to country districts. If we are familiar with the subject, and if our attention is fully awake, we at once have a dim perception of the writer's drift, and read on till it is distinctly enunciated. But undoubtedly the sudden transition has an abrupt effect. It has not the equable smoothness of De Quincey's transitions. The artifice is not unlike the common practice of beginning an essay with a statement that has no obvious connection with the title. We feel a momentary astonishment, and we are put upon our mettle to anticipate the application. To be sure, these unapplied generalities have not quite so much of an abrupt effect when they come upon us at the beginning. At the beginning our attention is supposed to be free. Nothing has gone before to preoccupy us except the title. At any point in the body of the essay our attention is supposed to be engrossed with the particular subject of exposition; and we start when the expected flow of the discourse is suddenly checked, and we are jerked upon a new line.

So much for the abrupt introduction of generalities. Any page of Macaulay will furnish the reader with other examples. The first sentence of the above passage illustrates another mode of abrupt transition. The subject of the paragraph is the government of the States of Lombardy and Tuscany; but the paragraph opens with a statement concerning the government of the Neapolitan dominions. Instead of laying down directly the state of society in Lombardy and Tuscany, he begins with an independent assertion about the state of society in the Neapolitan dominions. He has been describing Lombardy and Tuscany; and the reader is expected to understand, without any explicit connective, that the assertion about the Neapolitan States is meant as a contrast. The effect is very much the same as is produced by the sudden introduction of a generality. We presently see the drift of the statement, yet we experience a momentary astonishment. This mode of construction is much in favour with Macaulay. We are constantly being jerked away from the immediate subject, and jerked back with a "but." Thus, in a disquisition on the dramatists of the Restoration, he suddenly opens a new paragraph with the statement—

"In the old drama there had been much that was reprehensible."

This is not, as we might suppose, the opening of a digression on the old drama. He is merely taking a step out of the subject that he may return with greater force. The next sentence is—

"But whoever compares even the least decorous plays of Fletcher with those contained in the volume before us, will see how much the profligacy which follows a period of overstrained austerity goes beyond the profligacy which precedes such a period."

In the same Essay a paragraph on the morality of Greek writings proceeds as follows:—

"The immoral English writers of the seventeenth century are indeed much less excusable than those of Greece and Rome. *But* the worst English writings of the seventeenth century are decent, compared with much that has been bequeathed to us by Greece and Rome. Plato, we have little doubt, was a much better man than Sir George Etherege. *But* Plato has written things at which Sir George Etherege would have shuddered."

The effect of these sudden interruptions of continuity is still more abrupt when the contrasting statement is introduced, as it were, in fragments. Thus, towards the close of a flowing declamation on the beneficial influence of the Roman Catholic Church in the dark ages, he staggers us by abruptly declaring—

"The sixteenth century was comparatively a time of light."

Of this fragmentary statement we can make nothing. We stumble on, bewildered, to the next:—

"Yet even in the sixteenth century a considerable number of those who quitted the old religion followed the first confident and plausible guide who offered himself, and were soon led into errors far more serious than they had renounced."

Now we can guess at his drift, and pass lightly over a sentence of examples—

"Thus Matthias and Kniperdoling, apostles of lust, robbery, and murder, were able for a time to rule great cities"—

reaching the explicit statement of the idea in the following sentence:—

"In a darker age such false prophets might have founded empires; and Christianity might have been distorted into a cruel and licentious superstition, more noxious not only than Popery, but even than Islamism."

Apart from the abruptness of these sudden and discontinuous changes of subject, the introduction of generalities, contrasting statements, qualifications, and suchlike, before we know formally their bearing upon the subject in hand, has something of the effect of the periodic structure upon a larger scale: we are, as in an expanded period, kept in suspense until the application is fully developed.

2. The rule of *Parallel Construction* is that "when several consecutive sentences iterate or illustrate the same idea, they should, as far as possible, be formed alike." Macaulay observes this rule better perhaps than any of our popular writers. With his natural sense of perspicuous effect, he felt the advantage of keeping the principal subject prominent throughout all the sentences of a paragraph.

He is far, indeed, from being perfect. Thus, in the passage recently quoted concerning the Italian States, the illustrations of the general principle invert the position of the principal subject. The general proposition is made concerning the people, and two of the illustrations are stated as if the subject of discourse had been the despots and their hardships. Let us amend, for instance, the first illustration :—

"The most arbitrary of the Cæsars found it necessary to feed and divert the inhabitants of their unwieldy capital at the expense of the provinces."

Here the phrase "at the expense of the provinces" is improperly prominent: who paid the bill is a matter of no importance; the point is that the inhabitants of Rome extorted the treat. Let us put it as follows :—

"The inhabitants of the unwieldy capital of the Cæsars exacted expensive bounties of food and diversion from the most arbitrary of their masters."

Our amendment may be less elegant, but, in that particular connection, it is more perspicuous.

Though open to improvement, Macaulay undoubtedly owes not a little of his perspicuity to the observance of this rule. Whole paragraphs might be quoted containing little or nothing to alter; particularly when he exerts himself to give a sustained account of an institution or an individual—the Roman Catholic Church or Hyder Ali. When he does not give the leading place to the principal subject, he awards it to some subject introduced in his peculiar way for purposes of contrast, and for the time occupying the foreground in the exposition.

The uses of parallel structure may be studied to advantage in Macaulay. Usually but slight alterations are required, and no harm need be done to the variety of his expression. The following is another good case where some slight changes make an obvious improvement. The passage occurs in an exposition of the theme that "No men occupy so splendid a place in history as those who have founded monarchies on the ruins of republican institutions" :—

"In nations broken to the curb, in nations long accustomed to be transferred from one tyrant to another, a man without eminent qualities may easily gain supreme power. The defection of a troop of guards, a conspiracy of eunuchs, a popular tumult, might place an indolent senator or a brutal soldier on the throne of the Roman world. Similar revolutions have often occurred in the despotic States of Asia. But a community which has heard the voice of truth and experienced the pleasures of liberty, in which the merits of statesmen and of systems are freely canvassed, in which obedience is paid not to persons but to laws, in which magistrates are regarded not as the lords but as the servants of the public, in which the excitement of party is a necessary of life, in which political warfare is reduced to a system of tactics; such a community is not easily reduced to servitude."

The subject being the grandeur of men that have made themselves absolute over free institutions, it would obviously conduce to perspicuity to make that subject prominent throughout, as it is in the first sentence. The conclusion of the last sentence drops the usurper altogether, and lets the pervading idea slip out of clear comprehension into vagueness. Let us try the effect, as regards clearness, of some such alterations as the following:—

"In the Roman world an indolent senator or a brutal soldier might be placed on the imperial throne by the defection, &c.; and similar revolutions have often occurred in the despotic States of Asia. But in a community, &c.; in a community thus free and enlightened, only men of rare genius for command can hope to obtain the mastery."

3. The opening sentence in his paragraphs is not always a clue to the main subject. Of this we have had an example.

One of his great arts of surprise is to occupy the first sentences of the paragraph with circumstances leading us to expect the opposite of what is really the main statement. Very often all the sentences up to the last are a preparation for the shock of astonishment administered at the close. We are told what ought to have happened, what was expected to happen, or what happened in some other age or country under similar circumstances, before we reach the gist of the paragraph, which is to tell us what really happened in some particular case. The following paragraph is constructed on this plan:—

"No part of the system of the old Church had been more detested by the Reformers than the honour paid to celibacy. They held that the doctrine of Rome on this subject had been prophetically condemned by the apostle Paul as a doctrine of devils; and they dwelt much on the crimes and scandals which seemed to prove the justice of this awful denunciation. Luther had evinced his own opinion in the clearest manner, by espousing a nun. Some of the most illustrious bishops and priests who had died by fire during the reign of Mary had left wives and children. Now, however, it began to be rumoured that the old monastic spirit had reappeared in the Church of England; that there was in high quarters a prejudice against married priests; that even laymen, who called themselves Protestants, had made resolutions of celibacy which almost amounted to vows; nay, that a minister of the established religion had set up a nunnery, in which the psalms were chanted at midnight by a company of virgins dedicated to God."

In such paragraphs, to indicate the drift at the beginning would alter the character of the composition. But in many cases the delay of the main proposition is purposeless, and serves only to confuse. Thus, in a paragraph detailing the circumstances that made it impossible to transfer to the King of England the ecclesiastical supremacy of the Pope, he begins—

"The immediate effect of the Reformation in England was by no means favourable to political liberty. The authority which had been exercised by the Popes was transferred almost entire to the King. Two formidable powers which had often served to check each other were united in a single despot. If the system on which the founders of the Church of England acted could have been permanent, the Reformation would have been in a political sense the greatest curse that ever fell on our country. But that system carried within it the seeds of its own death." (And so on through a long paragraph.)

We do not catch the drift of the paragraph until we reach the fourth sentence, and we do not know that it is the key to the subject till we have read the whole. An ordinary reader, asked to summarise such a paragraph after a single perusal, would give but a poor account of it. He would naturally recall the first sentences, and comparing these with the tenor of the latter part of the paragraph, would almost to a certainty founder in the attempt to reconcile them. It would have been far better to begin with the fourth sentence. This, though not a direct statement of the substance of the paragraph, states it by implication. The three first sentences should be thrown into their natural position of subordination. We should then have some such opening as follows:—

"If the system on which the founders of the Church of England acted could have been permanent, the Reformation would have been in a political sense the greatest curse that ever fell on our country. At first, indeed, it seemed by no means favourable to political liberty. The authority exercised by the Popes was transferred almost entire to the King. Two formidable powers that had often served to check each other were united in a single despot. But this union could not last; the appearance of danger soon vanished."

His paragraphs often begin with one or more short sentences, recapitulating the previous paragraph. It is a good deal a matter of taste; but probably most authorities would prefer that these short sentences were prefixed to the real substance of the paragraph in the form of clauses. Thus, take his account of the reaction of public feeling after the warm reception of William and Mary:—

"The ill-humour of the clergy and of the army could not but be noticed by the most heedless; for the clergy and the army were distinguished by obvious peculiarities of garb. 'Black coats and red coats,' said a vehement Whig in the House of Commons, 'are the curses of the nation.' But the discontent was not confined to the black coats and the red coats."

Now the discontent among the other classes being the subject of the paragraph, many would prefer to have all the above condensed into one sentence, in some such way as follows:—

"Although the ill-humour of the clergy and the army could not fail to be most remarked, distinguished as they were from other classes by their peculiar garb ('black coats and red coats,' said a vehement Whig in the House of Commons, 'are the curses of the nation'), yet the clergy and the army were not the only discontented classes."

4. *Dislocation.* — In delineating a character, or in giving an account of a town, he would not seem to have bestowed much attention on the order of the circumstances in his statement.

To take an example from the celebrated third chapter of his History:—

"Norwich was the capital of a large and fruitful province. It was the residence of a bishop and of a chapter. It was the chief seat of the chief manufacture of the realm. Some men distinguished by learning and science had recently dwelt there; and no place in the kingdom, except the capital and the universities, had more attractions for the curious. The library, the museum, the aviary, and the botanical garden of Sir Thomas Browne, was thought by the Fellows of the Royal Society well worthy of a long pilgrimage. Norwich had also a court in miniature."

(Here follows a picturesque account of the mansion of the Dukes of Norwich; their state—the golden goblets, silver tongs and shovels, paintings, gems; a picturesque description of the festive reception of Charles II. in 1671; a similar description of the return of the Duke of Norwich. After this the paragraph closes abruptly with the statement—)

"In the year 1693, the population of Norwich was found, by actual enumeration, to be between twenty-eight and twenty-nine thousand souls."

Now here the statement that Norwich was the chief seat of the chief manufacture of the realm deserved to be made more prominent. Further, there is some confusion in thrusting it in between the bishop and the literary celebrities; it has more natural affinity with the largeness and fruitfulness of the province, and, if it is useful to preserve continuity of ideas, should have been placed next to the first sentence. The number of the population comes in very abruptly: seeing that he makes the population his first care in this chapter, and maintains it to be the most important fact, one is surprised that he did not observe on the small scale what he considered advisable on the great scale.

The paragraphs of this same third chapter are a very good study upon this point of arrangement, and afford scope for a great deal of casuistry. If we take the chapter as a whole, the order and proportion of the statements are open to many objections. It may, indeed, be doubted whether there is in the chapter any principle either of order or of proportion. One statement seems to suggest another; at the end the reader feels that he has passed through a brilliant muddle; whether he has obtained the complete Pisgah-view promised him at the beginning, he cannot say; he is only sure that he has been highly entertained.

5. *Unity.*—His natural clearness taught him the propriety of confining each paragraph to a single subject. He is, however, open to considerable improvement, as students will have no difficulty in seeing when they take him rigidly to task.

As regards irrelevant digressions, he is singularly correct. He is one of our most consecutive writers—perhaps among writers of popular literature the most consecutive. This makes him a most profitable study for the distribution of matter into paragraphs: the general run of his composition being consecutive, slight alterations bring him into conformity with the most rigid rules.

6. Some of the peculiarities already commented on involve a breach of the sixth rule of the paragraph—namely, that *subordinate statements should be kept in their proper place.*

His trick of taking an explanatory statement out of the sentence, and stating it by itself as an independent fact, is a blemish of this kind. The abrupt defect is due to its unexpected and undue prominence.

His short sentences often err against the same canon. A number of examples that should be comprised in one sentence receive a sentence each. A statement is repeated in two parts, and each part is honoured with a separate sentence.

These transgressions are seldom of a kind to cause confusion, and many people who like to be startled by such rattling fireworks will think the breach of the rule more admirable than the observance. The student must judge for himself, and be fully persuaded in his own mind. If he take a paragraph of Macaulay's, he will find that by slight changes, sometimes by a change of punctuation, he can moderate the abrupt statements into their fitting harmony with the main theme; let him return to the passage after a time, compare his own version with the original, and judge as impartially as he can which of the two has the most pleasing effect.

A wider consideration might be raised under this head. Does not Macaulay, in the exuberance of his powers of language and illustration, sometimes dwell longer than necessary on a simple topic? Doubtless he does illuminate with superfluous profusion subjects that stand in no great need of illumination. The fluent abundance of examples and comparisons, while it puts his meaning beyond doubt, is often greater than the subject demands. Instance is piled upon instance and comparison upon comparison, where a bare statement would be enough to make the meaning clear to the smallest capacity. For example, in his Essay on Addison, he takes occasion to controvert Dr Johnson's account of Boileau's views concerning modern Latin. Boileau, he says, had not an "injudicious contempt for modern Latin;" he only "thought it probable that in the best modern Latin a writer of the Augustan age would detect ludicrous improprieties;" and he was quite right in thinking so. This, one would think, is tolerably clear without farther expansion. But Macaulay goes on to cite no less than three parallel cases of the difficulty of mastering a foreign idiom.

"What modern scholar can honestly declare that he sees the smallest impurity in the style of Livy? Yet is it not certain that in the style of Livy, Pollio, whose taste had been formed on the banks of the Tiber, detected the inelegant idiom of the Po? Has any modern scholar understood Latin better than Frederic the Great understood French? Yet is it not notorious that Frederic the Great, after reading, speaking, writing French, and nothing but French, during more than half a century, after unlearning his mother tongue in order to learn French, after living familiarly during many years with French associates, could not, to the last, compose in French, without imminent risk of committing some mistake which would have moved a smile in the literary circles of Paris?"

In like manner, the works of Scott and Robertson contain Scotticisms "at which a London apprentice would laugh."

This excess of particularity is an error on the right side for popular success. The multiplication of instances may be overdone; but if the language is fresh and varied, general readers will take a good deal before they complain of a surfeit. The language, however, *must* be fresh and varied; of this condition a writer should make sure before trying to imitate Macaulay.

If the student wishes to conform his style to the general judgment of critics, he must not imitate Macaulay too absolutely; he must endeavour to be more varied in the forms of his sentences, to aim less frequently at contrasts, to study more carefully the placing of important words, and, above all, to make a more moderate use of abrupt transitions.

Figures of Speech.

"*Splendour of Imagery.*"—The eulogists of Macaulay's style rarely fail to include among its beauties great "splendour of imagery." Now, if under "imagery" may be included comparisons and contrasts of every description, as well as every kind of picturesque circumstances, he is no doubt fully entitled to the phrase. But if imagery means no more than pictorial similitudes, then, compared with such writers as Carlyle and Burke, he cannot be called a master of splendid imagery.

In his earlier essays, he shows an obvious straining after ingenious conceits. His Essay on Milton is, as he said himself in later years, "overloaded with gaudy and ungraceful ornament." In essays written before he was thirty, there are probably twice as many similes as in all his subsequent writings. His "Milton" contains as many as any six of his later essays. The History is studiously plain, so far at least as regards figurative ornament.

Undoubtedly, his similitudes are often brilliantly ingenious, and expressed with his usual richness and felicity of language. But they are too artificial and gaudy finery to be worthy of serious imitation.

Real Comparisons.—Out of the resources of his prodigious memory, Macaulay was able to elucidate a point much more vividly than by figurative comparisons. Whatever he undertakes to depict, whether persons, places, or things, he is able to compare them at all points with other objects of the same kind; he is able to make what are technically called "real comparisons;" and thus conveys a livelier impression of their salient attributes than if he compared them with objects having less in common. It is needless to multiply examples of what may be found in almost every page. We take as specimens four from the first few pages of his History:—

"Hengist and Horsa, Vortigern and Rowena, Arthur and Mordred, are mythical persons, whose very existence may be questioned, and whose adventures must be classed with those of Hercules and Romulus."

"What the Olympian chariot-course and the Pythian oracle were to all the Greek cities, from Trebizond to Marseilles, Rome and her bishop were to all Christians of the Latin communion, from Calabria to the Hebrides."

"The same atrocities which had attended the victory of the Saxon over the Celt were now, after the lapse of ages, suffered by the Saxon at the hand of the Dane."

"The Court of Rouen seems to have been to the Court of Edward the Confessor what the Court of Versailles long afterwards was to the Court of Charles the Second."

Perhaps the most forcible of his comparisons are those intended to reverse a common prejudice, or drive home an unfamiliar view. Thus, in the beginning of his History, he falls foul of English historians for expatiating with exultation on the power and splendour of our French kings:—

"This," he says, "is as absurd as it would be in a Haytian negro of our time to dwell with national pride on the greatness of Lewis the Fourteenth, and to speak of Blenheim and Ramilies with patriotic regret and shame. . . . One of the ablest among them, indeed, attempted to win the hearts of his English subjects by espousing an English princess. But by many of his barons this marriage was regarded as a marriage between a white planter and a quadroon girl would now be regarded in Virginia."

So, to illustrate how completely the popular element had been subverted in the monarchies of the Continent, he says—

"The privileges of the States-General, of the States of Brittany, of the States of Burgundy, are now matters of as little practical importance as the constitution of the Jewish Sanhedrim or of the Amphictyonic Council."

Very often the comparisons are made in an abbreviated form,

like the figure of *synecdoche*, in which an individual stands as the type of a species. Thus—

"Scotsmen, whose dwellings and whose food were as wretched as those of the Icelanders of our time, wrote Latin verse with more than the delicacy of Vida, and made discoveries in science which would have added to the renown of Galileo. Ireland could boast of no Buchanan or Napier."

In like manner, but, to speak technically, with more of the genuine *Antonomasia*, he says that had Bacon given to Literature the time that he gave to Law and Politics, "he would have been not only the *Moses* but the *Joshua* of philosophy." William could have gained the cordial support of the Whigs only "by becoming the most factious man in his kingdom, a *Shaftesbury* on the throne."

Further, the greater number of his comparisons are not allegations of similarity. The characteristic Macaulayan comparison is more a contrast than a parallel—is, indeed, the form of secondary contrast specified as the contrast between the individual members of a comprehensive class. Thus, take poets: he seems to have poets and their productions ranged on a scale of merit; and when a particular poet or production comes up, he places them above or below some other, or between some two. Machiavelli's "Mandragola is superior to the best of Goldoni, and inferior only to the best of Molière." Byron's letters from Italy "are less affected than those of Pope and Walpole; they have more matter in them than those of Cowper." Addison's Epistle to Lord Halifax "contains passages as good as the second-rate passages of Pope, and would have added to the reputation of Parnell or Prior." Again, "We need not hesitate to admit that Addison has left us some compositions which do not rise above mediocrity, some heroic poems hardly equal to Parnell's, some criticism as superficial as Dr Blair's, and a tragedy not very much better than Dr Johnson's." What he does with poets, he does in a greater or less degree with statesmen, generals, and all sorts and conditions of men that cross his narratives.

Figures of Contrast.—We have already noticed incidentally our author's lavish use of antithesis. The contrasts are really more numerous than might be thought at first glance; the bare framework is so overlaid and disguised by the extraordinary fulness of expression that many of them escape notice. When we look narrowly, we see that there is a constant play of antithesis. Not only is word set off against word, clause against clause, and sentence against sentence. There are contrasts on a more extensive scale; one group of sentences answers to another, and paragraphs are balanced against paragraphs. His pages are illuminated not only by little sparks of antithesis, but by broad flashes.

Enough has been given in illustration of the minuter play of antithesis. Pupils in composition may be exercised in referring examples to the various modes of antithesis, extreme and secondary. Here it may not be superfluous to dwell at some length upon a few of our author's more prominent ways of manufacturing this stage-lightning in its ampler forms.

He deals very largely in what is technically known as obverse statement; and gives it a peculiar abrupt point by denying the negative before affirming the positive. In explaining his abrupt transitions we called attention to something of this nature: we remarked on one example (p. 88), that before affirming that a certain form of government prevailed in one tract of country, he affirmed that it did *not* prevail in *another*. As another example, take the following passage from a disquisition on the style of Johnson:—

"Mannerism is pardonable, and is sometimes even agreeable, when the manner, though vicious, is natural. Few readers, for example, would be willing to part with the mannerism of Milton or of Burke. But a mannerism which does not sit easy on the mannerist, which has been adopted on principle, and which can be sustained only by constant effort, is always offensive. And such is the mannerism of Johnson."

There is a good deal of antithetic pungency in thus taking the obverse first. We expect, from the general tone of his remarks, that he means to condemn the mannerism of Johnson, and we start with surprise when he abruptly declares that "mannerism is pardonable." "What!" flashes across our mind, "Johnson's mannerism?" We eagerly read on, and are pleasingly reassured when we see the qualification—"when the manner, though vicious, is natural." Nor is this the only startle we receive in the course of the short paragraph; there is another shock in reserve to keep our attention awake. We have been called away from some minute particulars about Johnson to this general principle, and the illustration of it from remote quarters. At the end of the paragraph we are brought abruptly back to Johnson—"And such is the mannerism of Johnson." Many writers would have executed neither of these brilliant turns. Many would have *begun* by saying that the mannerism of Johnson is unpardonable, and would then have proceeded to state why it is so, and then, perhaps, by way of counter-illustration, would have explained when mannerism *is* pardonable. Macaulay's order of statement would thus have been inverted, and the contrast, brought in by an equable transition, would have produced a much less flashing effect.

A favourite and characteristic way of getting up an antithesis is, before narrating an event, to recount all the circumstances that concurred to make it different from what it ultimately proved to be. Thus, before narrating Frederick the Great's breach of faith with Maria Theresa, he describes the Pragmatic Sanction, and dilates upon the considerations weighing with the various European Governments to make them observe what they had stipulated. In like manner, he contrasts the general expectation before an event with the event itself. A good example of this is his account of the disbanding of Cromwell's veterans :—

"The troops were now to be disbanded. Fifty thousand men, accustomed to the profession of arms, were at once thrown on the world; and experience seemed to warrant the belief that this change would produce much misery and crime, that the discharged veterans would be seen begging in every street, or would be driven by hunger to pillage. But no such result followed. In a few months there remained not a trace indicating that the most formidable army in the world had just been absorbed into the mass of the community. The Royalists themselves confessed that in every department of honest industry, the discarded warriors prospered beyond other men; that none was charged with any theft or robbery; that none was heard to ask an alms; and that, if a baker, a mason, or a waggoner attracted notice by his diligence and sobriety, he was in all probability one of Oliver's old soldiers."

Another favourite device is in the course of his narrative to speculate what might have happened had the circumstances been different. He does this at every turning-point in English history. The struggle between Crown and Parliament might have come on early in the reign of Elizabeth, had not intestine quarrels been suspended in the face of a common danger. Had the administration of James been able and splendid, the Parliament might have been suppressed, and the Crown become absolute. In like manner, upon the execution of Charles I., the fall of Richard Cromwell, the Restoration, and the Revolution, he pauses to imagine what might have been the course of events had they been directed by men of different character. The same vein of reflection is continually cropping up in all his narratives.

Everywhere in his writings we can trace the dominating love of antithesis. His "celebrated third chapter" sustains the excitement of paradox through more than a hundred pages. In his History the conflict of opposing parties affords him constant opportunities. What the one party thought of a particular measure is set off against what the other party thought; "the temper of the Whigs" is contrasted with the "temper of the Tories." We are kept in the seat of judgment till we have heard the historian plead first on the one side, and then, still more convincingly, on the other.

In the delineation of characters he finds greater scope for his favourite effect. In these pictures, the scintillations of antithesis are almost incessant.

Antithesis is such an undeniable advantage in the statement of a fact, as a means of awakening us to its full import, that it is hard to say in any particular case that Macaulay was at fault in using an antithetic form of statement. That he was not too pointed for the mass of readers was shown by their eagerness in running after his productions. That he was too abrupt and startling for refined judges of composition is no less apparent by the unanimity of their condemnation. We have seen what the 'Edinburgh Review' said about the "too curious balance" of his sentences: the same presumably partial authority allows that he employed "unnecessary antithesis to express very simple propositions."

The great objection to the frequent use of antithesis, as already observed, is the danger of its betraying a writer into exaggerations, into deepening the shadow and raising the light. It is not denied that Macaulay has a tendency to make slight sacrifices of truth to antithesis. The chapter on the state of society in 1685 has been convicted of many exaggerated statements by less dazzling antiquarians. In his numerous comparisons between different men, he unquestionably tampers with the realities for the sake of enhancing the effect. He exaggerates the melancholy of Dante's character on the one hand, and the cheerfulness of Milton's on the other; he puts too strongly the purely illustrative character of Dante's similes in contradistinction to the purely poetic or ornamental character of Milton's. So he probably overstates the shallowness and flippancy of Montesquieu, to heighten by contrast the solidity and stateliness of Machiavelli.

He seems to have been aware of his turn for exaggeration, and provides an excuse for it. A slightly over-coloured statement rouses lethargy, and does not leave upon the mind a false impression. The hurried reader remembers but faintly. The impression carried away from an exaggerated statement is probably nearer the truth than if the statement had been literally exact.

Such doctrine is, to say the least of it, dangerous. There is, however, one case where antithetic exaggeration may be useful. A skilful writing-master, when dealing with pupils that have a tendency to write a cramped hand, trains them to a more flowing penmanship by giving them liberty to make extravagant flourishes, and by encouraging them to exaggerate the final limbs of their *m*s and *n*s. On the same principle, a teacher of composition, dealing with tame pupils, may train them to a bolder movement by allowing them to exaggerate freely for purposes of antithesis.

Epigram.—Macaulay delights in epigrams. There is a dash of epigram in his unexpected transitions. His antithesis often takes an epigrammatic point. The arts of surprise being so predominant in his style, we may quote a few specimens of this the most piquant of those arts:—

"Cranmer could vindicate himself from the charge of being a heretic only by arguments which made him out to be a murderer."

"They valued a prayer or a ceremony, not on account of the comfort which it conveyed to themselves, but on account of the vexation which it gave to the Roundheads; and were so far from being disposed to purchase union by concession, that they objected to concession, chiefly because it tended to produce union."

"One thing, and one thing only, could make Charles dangerous—a violent death. . . . His subjects began to love his memory as heartily as they had hated his person; and posterity has estimated his character from his death rather than from his life."

"The great ruling principle of his [Robert Walpole's] public conduct was indeed a love of peace, but not in the sense in which Archdeacon Coxe uses the phrase. The peace which Walpole sought was not the peace of the country, but the peace of his own administration."

"There can be no greater error than to imagine that the device of meeting the exigencies of the State by loans was imported into our Island by William the Third. From a period of immemorial antiquity it had been the practice of every English Government to contract debts. What the Revolution introduced was the practice of honestly paying them."

"The town of Bedford probably contained more than one politician who, after contriving to raise an estate by seeking the Lord during the reign of the saints, contrived to keep what he had got by persecuting the saints during the reign of the strumpets; and more than one priest who, during repeated changes in the discipline and doctrines of the Church, had remained constant to nothing but the benefice."

"The Puritan hated bear-baiting, not because it gave pain to the bear, but because it gave pleasure to the spectators. Indeed he generally contrived to enjoy the double pleasure of tormenting both spectators and bear."

The art of the following is essentially epigrammatic. The piquancy arises from the unexpected deliverance of such incongruities in the same sentence:—

"They therefore gave the command to Lord Galway, an experienced veteran, a man who was in war what Molière's doctors were in medicine, who thought it much more honourable to fail according to rule, than to succeed by innovation, and who would have been very much ashamed of himself if he had taken Monjuich by means so strange as those which Peterborough employed. This great commander conducted the campaign of 1707 in the most scientific manner. On the plain of Almanza he encountered the army of the Bourbons. *He drew up his troops according to the methods prescribed by the best writers, and in a few hours lost eighteen thousand men, a hundred and twenty standards, all his baggage, and all his artillery.*"

Climax.—A rhetorician of so decided a turn as Macaulay could not fail to use the rhetorician's greatest art. In every paragraph that rises above the ordinary level of feeling, we are conscious of being led on to a crowning demonstration.

His arts of contrast already exemplified have the effect of making a climax. See particularly the quotations at pp. 92, 100. He seems to pause in the course of his narrative or his argument, and go back for a race that will carry him sweepingly over the next obstacle. As another example of this climactic use of contrast, take the following about Burke. He is comparing Bacon and Burke as two men whose later writings are more ornamented than their earlier:—

"In his youth he wrote on the emotions produced by mountains and cascades, by the masterpieces of painting and sculpture, by the faces and necks of beautiful women, in the style of a parliamentary report. In his old age he discussed treaties and tariffs in the most fervid and brilliant language of romance. It is strange that the 'Essay on the Sublime and Beautiful,' and the 'Letter to a Noble Lord' should be the productions of one man. But it is far more strange that the essay should have been a production of his youth and the letter of his old age."

In stating, as his manner is, the various motives that impel different parties at particular conjunctures, he is careful to reserve the most telling for the end, and artfully prepares the way for the final resolution.

One of his most studied attempts at climax is the famous passage about Charles in the Essay on Milton.

The only other Figure of Speech that is a marked ingredient in Macaulay's style is *Hyperbole.* An exaggerated turn of expression is one of the main elements of his animated manner: it will be fully discussed under the quality of *Strength.*

QUALITIES OF STYLE.

Simplicity.

Macaulay's composition is as far from being abstruse as printed matter can well be. One can trace in his writing a constant effort to make himself intelligible to the meanest capacity. He loves to dazzle and to argue, but above everything he is anxious to be understood. His ideal evidently is to turn a subject over on every side, to place it in all lights, and to address himself to every variety of prejudice and preoccupation in his audience.

Yet his simplicity is very different from the simplicity of such writers as Goldsmith and Paley. His is far from being a homely style. He does not studiously affect Saxon terms. Without being so scholastic and technical as De Quincey, he is not scrupulous about using words of Latin origin, and admits many terms that Dean Alford would have excluded from "the Queen's English." Besides, although he were an Anglo-Saxon Pharisee in his choice of words, his turns of expression are not simple in the sense of being familiar and easy. His balanced sentences, abrupt transitions, pointed antitheses, and climactic arrangement, elevate him out of the ranks of homely authors, and constitute him, as we have said, pre-eminently artificial.

What is it, then, that makes him so easily understood? For one thing, he seldom meddles with abstruse problems. He does not, like De Quincey, delight to match his ingenuity against difficulties; he does not choose a subject because it has baffled everybody else: his pleasure is to do brilliantly what everybody can do in a manner. De Quincey wrote upon Pope and Shakspeare because perplexities had settled upon their lives. Macaulay takes up only biographies whose principal incidents are known and read by all men — the lives of Atterbury, Bunyan, Goldsmith, Johnson, Pitt. He does not covet openings for nice speculation. When a recondite question crosses his path, he provides an answer so simple and easy that the cautious reader doubts whether it is complete. He makes Shakspeare the result of the Reformation; Wordsworth the result of the French Revolution; Byron "the interpreter between Wordsworth and the multitude." In discussing the life of Bacon, he finds it necessary to give his opinion of the inductive method. The opinion is very plausible; but scientific authorities pronounce it "ignorant and shallow in the extreme." In his life of Machiavelli, he undertakes to account for the peculiar state of Italian society in the fourteenth century. The explanation is most simple: the Italians were given to commerce and literature; they employed mercenaries to fight their battles; the mercenaries were treacherous, — hence they ceased to depend upon war for effecting their desires: they came to despise courage and honour intrigue; to think it contemptible to do by force what could be done by fraud. With all its simplicity, the application is far from satisfactory; it begins at too late a point. It does not explain why the Italians turned to commerce and literature, and paid the natives of ruder countries to do their fighting. If we knew *that*, we should probably find that the treachery of the mercenaries encouraged, and did not originate, cowardice and intrigue: a people originally indisposed to fight their own battles were not likely at any time to excel in the active virtues. Further, the employment of mercenaries was only one of many causes tending to encourage the practice and admiration of dishonest dexterity.

In like manner in his History, with all his unexampled knowledge of facts, and of every variety of opinion avowed by opposite parties, he still shows a disposition to put up with pat and easy explanations of events. For example, he explains the hostility of the clergy to the Revolution by the fact that it controverted flatly all their favourite doctrines about non-resistance and passive obedience. This is a most acceptable theory; it refers us to a well-known weakness of human nature: yet who that has read

Macaulay's own picture of the multitude of conflicting interests then prevalent will believe that this was the sole cause of the clerical disaffection ?

Another example of his love of simple explanations is seen in the prominence he everywhere gives to the doctrine of reaction. The discontent under Cromwell and under William is compared to the discontent under Moses; and all such cases are spoken of as reactions of feeling. So the "appalling outbreak of licentiousness" after the Restoration is explained as the natural result of the Puritan austerity. In all these instances the alleged law is a familiar fact of our nature; and we are willing to accept it as a full explanation, though it is far from being so.

He is, then, readily understood, because he deals with familiar subjects, and explains difficulties by a reference to familiar things. But this is only a small element of his intelligibility. The main element is his close and constant adherence to the concrete.

The terse abstract statement so familiar to the reader of Johnson, occurs but rarely in Macaulay, and only as a variety of expression. He discusses everything in the concrete. When he states an abstract proposition, unless it is all the more familiar, he follows it up with a plethora of particular cases. We have seen (p. 95) that his prodigious knowledge of particulars betrays him into a superfluity of illustration.

In describing the conduct of individuals, he is not content with general terms: he does not simply style them brave, or just, or sagacious; he compares them with some well-known embodiment of these qualities, or relates significant circumstances. Thus, in a passage already referred to, he says that "had the administration of James been able and splendid, it would probably have been fatal to our country." Many writers would have been content with this plain statement, but Macaulay goes on to say:—

> "Had he been, like Henry the Fourth, like Maurice of Nassau, or like Gustavus Adolphus, a valiant, active, and politic ruler, had he put himself at the head of the Protestants of Europe, had he gained great victories over Tilly and Spinola, had he adorned Westminster with the spoils of Bavarian monasteries and Flemish cathedrals, had he hung Austrian and Castilian banners in Saint Paul's, and had he found himself, after great achievements, at the head of fifty thousand troops, brave, well disciplined, and devotedly attached to his person, the English Parliament would soon have been nothing more than a name."

In conveying an idea of the doctrines of the Church of England, instead of plunging into details and bald generalities, he hits them off boldly by stating the position of the Church of England relatively to other Churches, and enlivens the comparison with the names of representative men:—

"To this day the constitution, the doctrines, and the services of the Church, retain the visible marks of the compromise from which she sprang. She occupies a middle position between the Churches of Rome and Geneva. Her doctrinal confessions and discourses, composed by Protestants, set forth principles of theology in which Calvin or Knox would have found scarcely a word to disapprove. Her prayers and thanksgivings, derived from the ancient liturgies, are very generally such that Bishop Fisher or Cardinal Pole might have heartily joined in them. A controversialist who puts an Arminian sense on her articles and homilies, will be pronounced by candid men to be as unreasonable as a controversialist who denies that the doctrine of baptismal regeneration can be discovered in her liturgy."

In stating quantity or dimension, he adds to the dry unrememberable ciphers a comparison with some similar case in the lump. His "third chapter" is much indebted to this art of relieving the tedious quotation of figures. Thus—

"Cornwall and Wales at present yield annually near fifteen thousand tons of copper, worth near a million and a half sterling—that is to say, worth about twice as much as the annual produce of all English mines of all descriptions in the seventeenth century."

In like manner he substitutes familiar ways of reckoning time in place of the precise notation by dates. Thus, in describing the amalgamation of races after the Conquest, he says:—

"The great-grandsons of those who had fought under William, and the great-grandsons of those who had fought under Harold, began to draw near to each other in friendship; and the first pledge of their reconciliation was the Great Charter, won by their united exertions and framed for their common benefit."

His way of dealing with cumbrous qualifications, explanations, and examples, is not an unmixed gain in the direction of simplicity. His method is, as we have seen, to make all such statements in separate sentences, instead of joining them to the main statement in the same sentence. So far this is a gain: the mind is engaged with one thing at a time; it is asked to take in the several statements one at a time, instead of getting them all at once along with an indication of their relationships. But this very severality of statement leads to confusion: the mind having grasped the separate facts, receives no clue to their mutual bearings, and is placed in danger of bewilderment.

There is a way out of the difficulty—namely, to make the qualifications and explanations as few as possible. This is hardly legitimate; yet we have seen that Macaulay is suspected of adopting it.

Clearness.

In the Introduction (p. 17) we mentioned Macaulay as one of the writers whose style justifies a subdivision of Clearness into Perspicuity and Precision. He is perspicuous, but not precise.

To say that "not an ambiguous sentence is to be found throughout his works," is attributing a perfection hardly possible for mortal writer. Doubtless very few of his sentences are ambiguous, even at first glance; and in several that do mislead on first inspection, the meaning is not hard to find. His general method is decidedly perspicuous, although, as we have seen in discussing his paragraphs, it also comes sort of perfection, and is open to amendment. His numerous examples and comparisons conduce greatly to perspicuity. And, finally, his extraordinary number of contrasts is a help in the same direction.

While Macaulay is one of the most perspicuous of English writers, he has no claim to the merit of being minutely exact. We have seen that, after stating a general principle, he makes his meaning perspicuous—clear in its leading outlines—by a free quotation of examples. But he quotes his examples roundly and confidently; he very seldom pauses to take note of casuistical objections, of special circumstances making a particular case doubtful as an example of his general assertion: Frederick the Great is a typical German, and commits blunders in French that would have moved a smile in the literary circles of Paris; Sir Walter Scott is a typical Scotsman, and he perpetrates Scotticisms that a London apprentice would laugh at; Ben Jonson was a great man, Hoole a very small man—yet Ben Jonson's verse was rugged, and Hoole, *as coming after Pope*, poured out decasyllabic verses in thousands, "all as well turned, as smooth, and as like each other as the blocks which have passed through Mr Brunel's mill in the dockyard at Portsmouth." In like manner his comparisons are perspicuous, are good as broad indications of his general meaning; but they have the same defect—a defect for certain purposes at least—of not being nicely pointed to the relevant circumstances, of not entering into exact details. We get but a vague notion of the doctrines of the Church of England from the statement that "she occupies a middle position between the Churches of Rome and Geneva;" and little distinct information about Addison's Epistle from the statement that "it contains passages as good as the second-rate passages of Pope, and would have added to the reputation of Parnell or Prior." It is not by such rough assertions that accurate knowledge is imparted; they convey rather the conceit of knowledge than the reality; they are simple but vague.

When we insist upon Macaulay's want of minute exactness, of all pretension to be called an accurate writer, it is but fair to notice that minute exactness, scrupulous accuracy, did not accord with the popular design of his works. He wrote for hurried readers, and more to amuse or interest than to instruct. He considered that "laborious research and minute investigation" belonged to authors by profession. We can excuse a want of exactness in a writer so anxious to make his language perspicuous. For his perspicuity he certainly deserves all praise; and it is always right to point out that from this very quality his inexactness is easily discovered, and that he passes for shallow in many quarters where a more shallow and at the same time more obscure writer would pass for profound. Particularly is he admirable for his profuseness of exemplification: he often supplies us with the means of correcting his own indistinct generalities. Even his comparisons to individuals and specific institutions, though vague, are seldom misleading: if they convey little substantial knowledge, they at least convey no error. For such comparisons it may always be pleaded that they awaken curiosity, and set the inquirer on the right track; if we desire fuller information, they direct us where to look for it. In a hasty review of the doctrines of the Church of England, it is perhaps best to incite the reader to compare them with the doctrines of other Churches; and where limits preclude a full discussion, to furnish no more detail than an index map.

Strength.

In the quality of strength, Macaulay offers a great and obvious contrast to De Quincey—the contrast between brilliant animation and stately pomp. His movement is more rapid and less dignified. He does not slowly evolve his periods, "as under some genial instinct of incubation:" he never remits his efforts to dazzle; and in his most swelling cadences, he always seems to be perorating against an imaginary antagonist.

Most of the elements of his peculiar animation have already been noticed in other connections. We have already commented upon the varied expression, the abrupt transitions, the constant play of antithesis, the perspicuous method, and the lively array of concrete particulars. We have also noticed implicitly the exhilarating pace both of the language and of the thoughts, the rapidity of the rhythm—as determined by shortness of phrase, clause, and sentence—and the quick succession of the ideas.

As regards his animated "objectivity," or concreteness, there is one thing that might be brought out more fully—namely, his art of enlivening condensed narrative by pictorial, or at least concrete, circumlocutions. We quote as an example part of his account of Strafford:—

"He had been one of the most distinguished members of the Opposition, and felt towards those whom he had deserted *that peculiar malignity which has, in all ages, been characteristic of apostates.* He perfectly understood the feelings, the resources, and the policy of the party to which he had lately belonged, and had formed a vast and deeply meditated scheme *which very nearly confounded even the able tactics of the statesmen by whom the House of Commons had been directed.* . . . His object was to do for England *all, and more than all, that Richelieu was doing in France;* to make Charles *a monarch as absolute as any on the Continent,*" &c.

These frequent allusions to actual men and things would alone make the style vivacious; the rapid succession of particulars is in itself exhilarating.

He had a great command over the proper vocabulary of strength. He is very vehement in his epithets. Whole pages might be quoted that contain hardly a single adjective under the degree of enormous. One of his favourite themes is the corruption and profligacy of the Restoration times. Whenever he has occasion to speak of this, he seems to fall into a passion, and uses the strongest language that propriety will allow. And this subject is only one out of many that provoke his vehemence to an equal degree. On every subject, indeed, he expresses himself with confidence, and in language habitually bordering on the extreme.

He has been much taken to task for the violence of his invective. Certainly, when he conceived a dislike to an individual or to an institution, he expressed his feelings without reserve. And he disliked a great many characters. He disliked all the English statesmen of the Revolution period for their treachery and want of patriotism. Sir William Temple he pronounces to be "the most respectable" of them. Yet even Temple, he declares, "was not a man to his taste;" he "had not sufficient warmth and elevation of sentiment to deserve the name of a virtuous man." Judge Jeffreys he regards with the most absolute loathing, and holds up to contempt and hatred with an indignation as cordial as if one of his own family had been among the bloody monster's many victims. Concerning this part of the History, Mr Croker said in the 'Quarterly Review' that the historian had almost realised Alexander Chalmers's 'Biographia Flagitiosa; or, the Lives of Eminent Scoundrels.' "He hates," said Mr Croker further, "nearly everybody but Cromwell, William, Whig exiles, and Dissenting parsons." The last sneer goes perhaps too far; the insinuation is hardly correct: Macaulay was much more impartial in his hatred than this would imply. He hated some of the French Republicans as heartily as he hated any of our English ancestors, whether Whig or Tory. He has written nothing stronger than his condemnation of Barrère. Barrère "approached nearer than any person mentioned in history or fiction, whether man or devil, to the idea of consummate and universal depravity." This is very strong, but becomes stronger still as the historian proceeds. Here he makes Barrère an approximation to unqualified depravity: a little further, and he drops the slight reservation. "All the other chiefs of parties had some good qualities, *and Barrère had none.*" "Barrère had not a single virtue, *nor even the semblance of one.*"

Sometimes, in his contemptuous and derisive moods, he uses a studied meanness of expression that reminds us of the coarse familiarity of Swift. Thus, speaking of Boswell, he says—"If he had not been a great fool, he would never have been a great writer." So of Chatham, he says—"He was not invited to become a placeman, and he therefore stuck firmly to his old trade of patriot." This homely order of expression he often employs with great effect in the way of derisive refutation. Thus, in ridiculing Southey's sentimental views on questions of political economy, he says—"We might ask how it can be said that there is no limit to the production of paper money, when a man is hanged if he issues any in the name of another, and is forced to cash what he issues in his own?"

It is difficult to draw the line between such strength of language and the figure of speech known as hyperbole. The italicised expressions in the following passages are unmistakably hyperbolical. Such expressions are very common in Macaulay, and, read along with the context, do not strike us as rising far above the general level of his language:—

"The house of Bourbon was at the summit of human greatness. England had been outwitted, and found herself in a situation at once degrading and perilous. The people of France, not presaging the calamities by which they were destined to expiate the perfidy of their sovereign, *went mad with pride and delight. Every man looked as if a great estate had just been left him.*"

"His own reflections, his own energy, were to supply the place of *all Downing Street and Somerset House.* . . . The preservation of an empire from a formidable combination of foreign enemies, the construction of a government in all its parts, were accomplished by him, while every ship brought out *bales of censure* from his employers, and while the records of every consultation were *filled* with acrimonious minutes by colleagues."

One of his modes of exaggeration is almost a mannerism. Whatever he happens to be engaged with is in some respect or other the most wonderful thing that ever existed. The following are his two most common forms for expressing such a conviction:—(1.) "No election ever took place under circumstances so favourable to the Court." (2.) "Of all the many unpopular steps taken by the Government, the most unpopular was the publishing of this declaration."

He is sometimes betrayed into making the same extreme statement about two different persons. Thus he says of Clarendon—"No man ever laboured so hard to make himself despicable and ludicrous;" and it is notorious that he makes a like remark about Boswell.

So much for the animation of Macaulay's manner. As regards his choice of subjects, it may be said in general that he is careful to take up only such as have an independent interest to the mass of English readers. Consequently his charms of style operate at every advantage; they have no dead weight to overcome; they are required only to support the natural interest of the matter. A History of England, if written with moderate spirit, would always have an attraction for every Englishman; written with Macaulay's glowing patriotism and brilliant style, it proved more attractive than the most captivating novel. Similarly with his Essays. His article on Milton placed him at once in the first rank of popular favourites; an extraordinary success resulting, not so much from the display of his literary knowledge, as from the happy application of his glittering rhetoric to a theme much canvassed at the time. All his essays are upon men of first-rate interest: any particulars about Machiavelli, Byron, Johnson, Bacon, Pitt, or Frederick the Great, are eagerly read, if there is any appearance of novelty in the manner of relating them.

Great men and great events—these are the favourite themes of Macaulay. When such matter is handled in such a manner, no wonder that the writer is the most popular author of his day.

Animation is our author's distinguishing quality; but often from the grandeur of his subject, and of the objects that he brings into comparison with it from all countries and from all times, his style takes a loftier tone.

There is something more than animating in his easy manner of ranging through space and time. To be transported with such freedom from continent to continent, from dynasty to dynasty, and from age to age; to pass judgment on the rival pretensions of the foremost men and the most august empires that have appeared in the world,—this, unless we have a very frivolous conception of what we are doing, should elevate us to the highest heights of sublimity. Macaulay's abrupt manner is sometimes antagonistic to the finest effects that might be accomplished by these ambitious surveys. But very often his eloquence is lofty and imposing.

Thus, in advocating with wonted enthusiasm the apotheosis of Lord Clive:—

"From Clive's second visit to India dates the political ascendancy of the English in that country. His dexterity and resolution realised, in the course of a few months, more than all the gorgeous visions which had floated before the imagination of Dupleix. Such an extent of cultivated territory, such an amount of revenue, such a multitude of subjects, was never added to the dominion of Rome by the most successful proconsul. Nor were such wealthy spoils ever borne under arches of triumph, down the Sacred Way, and through the crowded Forum, to the threshold of Tarpeian Jove. The fame of those who subdued Antiochus and Tigranes grows dim when compared with the splendour of the exploits which the young English adventurer achieved at the head of an army not equal in numbers to one half of a Roman legion."

Perhaps his noblest flight of sublimity is his eulogy of the

Roman Catholic Government. This is in every way an admirable specimen of his style. There is just one break in the sustained grandeur of the passage. He should not have introduced the numerical comparison between the different creeds—a tag of statistics is very chilling and repulsive amidst the glowing flow of admiration. Macaulay's abundance of hard information often betrays him into violations of Art.

Pathos.

In Macaulay's style, as in his nature, there was more vigour than tenderness or delicacy. The abruptness and rapidity of transition, and the unseasonable intrusion of hard matters of fact, which we have just referred to as being fatal to sustained sublimity, were no less fatal to sustained pathos. The following account of the death of Hampden illustrates the beauties and the faults of his pathetic narration :—

"Hampden, with his head drooping, and his hands leaning on his horse's neck, moved feebly out of the battle. The mansion which had been inhabited by his father-in-law, and from which in his youth he had carried home his bride Elizabeth, was in sight. There still remains an affecting tradition that he looked for a moment towards that beloved house, and made an effort to go thither to die. But the enemy lay in that direction. He turned his horse towards Thame, where he arrived almost fainting with agony. The surgeons dressed his wounds. But there was no hope. The pain which he suffered was most excruciating. But he endured it with admirable firmness and resignation. His first care was for his country. He wrote from his bed several letters to London concerning public affairs, and sent a last pressing message to the headquarters, recommending that the dispersed forces should be concentrated. When his public duties were performed, he calmly prepared himself to die. He was attended by a clergyman of the Church of England, with whom he had lived in habits of intimacy, and by the chaplain of the Buckinghamshire Green-coats, Dr Spurton, whom Baxter describes as a famous and excellent divine."

The galloping short sentences in the middle of the passage are sadly out of harmony with the occasion, and nothing could be more uncongenial than the ostentatious scrap of antiquarian knowledge foisted in at the end.

His reflections on St Peter's Ad Vincula, where Monmouth was buried, are solemn and touching. He warns us that—

"Death is there associated, not, as in Westminster Abbey and St Paul's, with genius and virtue, with public veneration, and with imperishable renown ; not, as in our humblest churches and churchyards, with everything that is most endearing in social and domestic charities,—but with whatever is darkest in human nature and in human destiny, with the savage triumph of implacable enemies, with the inconstancy, the ingratitude, the cowardice of friends, with all the miseries of fallen greatness and of blighted fame"—

and he then proceeds to record a long line of illustrious and unfortunate dead. The art of such a passage is of the simplest order. To us it is affecting as a vivid representation of the lapse of time, and of the disasters that wait upon greatness: but to the narrator it is little more than an exercise of historical memory.

The Ludicrous.

Macaulay's wit and humour are the wit and humour usually ascribed to "The True-Born Englishman." He has no command either of biting insinuation or of delicate raillery. His laugh is hearty and confident; unsparing contempt, open derision, broad and boisterous humour. Of each of the three qualities thus loosely expressed, we shall produce examples: his portrait of Archbishop Laud, for whom he "entertained a more unmitigated contempt than for any character in our history;" a short extract from his review of Mitford's 'History of Greece;' and the beginning of his review of Nares's 'Life of Lord Burleigh:'—

"Bad as the Archbishop was, however, he was not a traitor within the statute. Nor was he by any means so formidable as to be a proper subject for a retrospective ordinance of the Legislature. His mind had not expansion enough to comprehend a great scheme, good or bad. His oppressive acts were not, like those of the Earl of Strafford, parts of an extensive system. They were the luxuries in which a mean and irritable disposition indulges itself from day to day, the excesses natural to a little mind in a great place. The severest punishment which the two Houses could have inflicted on him would have been to set him at liberty, and send him to Oxford. There he might have stayed, tortured by his own diabolical temper—hungering for Puritans to pillory and mangle; plaguing the Cavaliers, for want of somebody else to plague, with his peevishness and absurdity; performing grimaces and antics in the Cathedral; continuing that incomparable Diary, which we never see without forgetting the vices of his heart in the imbecility of his intellect, minuting down his dreams, counting the drops of blood which fell from his nose, watching the direction of the salt, and listening for the note of the screech-owls. Contemptuous mercy was the only vengeance which it became the Parliament to take on such a ridiculous old bigot."

"The principal characteristic of this historian, the origin of his excellences and his defects, is a love of singularity. He has no notion of going with a multitude to do either good or evil. An exploded opinion, or an unpopular person, has an irresistible charm for him. The same perverseness may be traced in his diction. His style would never have been elegant, but it might at least have been manly and perspicuous; and nothing but the most elaborate care could possibly have made it so bad as it is."

"The work of Dr Nares has filled us with astonishment similar to that which Captain Lemuel Gulliver felt when first he landed in Brobdingnag, and saw corn as high as the oaks in the New Forest, thimbles as large as buckets, and wrens of the bulk of turkeys. The whole book, and every component part of it, is on a gigantic scale. The title is as long as an ordinary preface; the prefatory matter would furnish out an ordinary book; and the book contains as much reading as an ordinary library. We cannot sum up the merits of the stupendous mass of paper which lies before us better than by saying that it consists of about two thousand closely printed quarto pages, that it occupies fifteen hundred inches cubic measure, and that it weighs sixty pounds avoirdupois. Such a book might, before the deluge, have been considered as light reading by Hilpa and Shalum. But, unhappily, the life of man is now threescore years and ten; and we cannot but think it somewhat unfair in Dr Nares to demand from us so large a portion of so short an existence.

"Compared with the labour of reading through these volumes, all other labour, the labour of thieves on the treadmill, of children in factories, of negroes in sugar-plantations, is an agreeable recreation," &c.

His masterpieces of broad ridicule are found in his literary reviews. He makes unmerciful game of Southey's Political Economy, Robert Montgomery's Poems, and Croker's edition of Boswell.

Melody, Harmony, Taste.

Macaulay's rhythm is fluent, rarely obstructed by harsh combinations, but it is not rich and musical like De Quincey's. Though often abrupt and always rapid, at times, as we have seen, it swells into more flowing cadences; yet, at best, the melody of his sentences is the melody of a fluent and rapid speaker, not the musical roll of a writer whose ear takes engrossing delight in the luxuries of sound.

Beyond amplifying the roll of his sentences when he rose to more stately declamations, he does not appear to have studied much the adaptation of sound to sense. His rhythm is well suited to the general vigour of his purposes; it is not much in harmony with quiet and delicate touches.

Like De Quincey and Carlyle, he has certain salient mannerisms. The general voice of persons of cultivated taste is against his abruptness, his hyperbolical turn of expression, and his needless employment of antithesis. In these particulars he has transgressed the general rule of not carrying pungent and striking artifices to excess. Objection may also be taken to the unmitigated force of his derision and his humour. "There is too much horse-play in his raillery."

KINDS OF COMPOSITION.

Description.

In one of his earlier essays, Macaulay lays down the opinion that mere descriptions of scenery are tiresome, and that still life needs associations with human feeling to make it interesting. This explains why his writings contain so few descriptions of natural scenery.

When engaged on his History he made it a point of conscience to visit and describe from personal observation the scenes of the most memorable events. He visited the battle-field of Sedgmoor, and describes the general appearance of the country at the present day as seen from the church-tower of Bridgewater. But the description is rather an analysis of the landscape into its general elements, mingled with various historical reminiscences, than a composition of those elements into a definite picture. In like manner he wrote on the spot a description of the Irish towns round which the Englishry rallied at the Revolution—Kenmare, Enniskillen, and Londonderry. In describing Kenmare, he simply notes the general features of the district—"the mountains, the glens, the capes stretching far into the Atlantic, the crags on which the eagles build, the rivulets brawling down rocky passes, the lakes overhung by groves, in which the wild deer find covert;" elements, certainly, of gorgeous scenery, but left to the reader to form into a coherent landscape. His description of Londonderry is perhaps his most vivid effort. Yet even this is vague compared with the luminous word-painting of Carlyle.

In his Essays he neglects many opportunities that a master of descriptive art would have eagerly seized. Had Carlyle written an essay on Lord Clive, he would have luxuriated in realising to English readers the novel aspects of Indian scenery; he would have put forth all his powers of imagery to convey a distinct impression of the shape and dimensions of the table-lands and the great valleys, and would have placed vividly before us the exact "lie" of the hill-fortresses and the magnificent cities of the plains, the appearance of the surrounding country, and, as far as language can express such things, even the variations of sky and atmosphere.

But is not Macaulay always spoken of as a great pictorial artist? True, he is so; but in a very different sense from such artists as Carlyle. The dictum quoted above is the key to his choice of subjects. What he delights to group and to delineate is not inanimate things, but the condition, actions, and productions of man. When he describes a town he is concerned less with its shape and its position relatively to the surrounding landscape, than with its political or commercial importance, the number and character of its population, or the splendour of its buildings. The description of Benares is a fair specimen of his manner:—

"His first design was on Benares, a city which in wealth, population, dignity, and sanctity, was among the foremost of Asia. It was commonly believed that half a million of human beings was crowded into that labyrinth of lofty alleys, rich with shrines, and minarets, and balconies, and carved oriels to which the sacred apes clung by hundreds. The traveller could scarce make his way through the press of holy mendicants, and not less holy bulls. The broad and stately flights of steps which descended from these swarming haunts to the bathing-places along the Ganges, were worn every day by the footsteps of an innumerable multitude of worshippers. The schools and temples drew crowds of pious Hindoos from every province where the Brahminical faith was known. . . . Commerce had as many pilgrims as religion. All along the shores of the venerable stream lay great fleets of vessels laden with rich merchandise. From the looms of Benares went forth the most delicate silks that adorned the balls of St James's and of the Petit Trianon; and in the bazaars the muslins of Bengal and the sabres of Oude were mingled with the jewels of Golconda and the shawls of Cashmere."

There is thus no lack of pictorial matter in Macaulay. The peculiarity is, that so much of it has a direct connection with human beings, and that though of a strongly objective turn of mind, he had no natural bent for the description of still life. It was vigorous, stirring movement—"the rush and the roar of practical life"—that chiefly engaged his interest. He is nowhere more in his element than in describing a gorgeous pageant, or the demonstrations of an excited mob. He enters with great zest into the reception of Charles I. at Norwich, the "Progress" of James II., the procession of William and Mary along the Strand, the ceremony of the coronation, and suchlike. He describes the accompanying festivities with gusto; the illuminations, the bells ringing, the "conduits spouting wine," the "gutters running with ale." There is probably no prose passage that has been oftener committed to memory than his account of the trial of Hastings. One of his most vivid pictures is his detail of the prolonged excitement of London during the persecution and trial of the seven Bishops, and the burst of joy upon their acquittal:—

"Sir Roger Langley answered 'Not guilty!' As the words passed his lips, Halifax sprang up and waved his hat. At that signal, benches and galleries raised a shout. In a moment ten thousand persons, who crowded the great hall, replied with a still louder shout, which made the old oaken roof crack; and in another moment the innumerable throng without set up a third huzza, which was heard at Temple Bar. The boats which covered the Thames gave an answering cheer. A peal of gunpowder was heard on the water, and another, and another; and so, in a few moments the glad tidings were flying past the Savoy and the Friars to London Bridge, and to the forest of masts below. As the news spread, streets and squares, market-places and coffee-houses, broke forth into acclamations. Yet were the acclamations less strange than the weeping. For the feelings of men had been wound up to such a point, that at length the stern English nature, so little used to outward signs of emotion, gave way, and thousands sobbed aloud for very joy. Meanwhile, from the outskirts of the multitude, horsemen were spurring off to bear along all the great roads intelligence of the victory of our Church and nation."

As regards the method of such descriptions. They follow very much the same rules as the description of scenery. The describer should begin with a comprehensive view of his subject. In this respect Macaulay is, as a rule, exemplary. In his description of Benares, for instance, the first sentence is a summary introduction to what follows. Further, the describer should observe a method in the details; he should place together all that are connected, and should give them either in the direct or in the inverse order of importance: he should, at least, consider what is the most luminous methd in the particular case. This Macaulay is not sufficiently careful to do: we saw (p. 94) that his order of statement is sometimes confused. The description of the London rejoicings is of the nature of a description from the traveller's point of view.

After all, the objective character of our author's style consists more in the pictorial touches brought in by a side wind than in the direct description of objects. We have already seen, that instead of making a plain statement of fact, he states some suggestive circumstance. Instead of saying that nobles and even princes were proud of a University degree, he says that they "were proud to receive from a University *the privilege of wearing the doctoral scarlet.*" Instead of saying that the Dutch would never incur the risk of an invasion, he says that "they would never incur the risk of *seeing an invading army encamped between Utrecht and Amsterdam.*" Such concrete circumstances are very instrumental in keeping up the pictorial air of his pages—imparting all the more splendour that, as a rule, they are loud and glaring, rather than quiet and significant.

In the important process of describing the feelings, he displays his usual objectivity. He tells what people said, what they did, how they looked, what visions passed through their imaginations, and leaves the particularities of their state of feeling to be inferred from these material indications. Carlyle represents Johnson "with his great greedy heart and unspeakable chaos of thoughts; stalking mournful on this earth, eagerly devouring what spiritual thing he could come at." Macaulay represents him with more of concrete circumstances: "ransacking his father's shelves," "devouring hundreds of pages," "treating the academical authorities with gross disrespect," standing "under the gate of Pembroke, haranguing a circle of lads, over whom, in spite of his tattered gown and dirty linen, his wit and audacity gave him an undisputed ascendancy."

Narrative.

Whatever be the ultimate judgment of able critics regarding the merits of Macaulay's 'History of England,' viewed as a philosophical history or as a solid narrative of public events, there can be no doubt that it was and is an eminently popular work. It gained the popular favour not by slow degrees, but at a leap; five editions, numbering in all about 18,000 copies, were sold in six months. In the following remarks, we cannot profess to anaylse all the ingredients of his extraordinary charm for English readers, but only to observe how far he fulfils certain conditions of perspicuous, instructive, and interesting narrative.

The affairs of England during the reigns of James and William were considerably involved, and without skilful arrangement a history of that period could hardly fail to be confused. Macaulay's exhibition of the movements of different parties, the different aspects of things in the three parts of the kingdom, the complicated relations between James and William, and the intrigues of different individuals, is managed with great perspicuity.

He is exemplary in keeping prominent the main action and the main actor. After the death of Charles, our interest centres in James. We are eager to know how the change of monarch was received in London and through the country, and how James stood in his relations with France and Rome, with Scotland, and with the English clergy and the Dissenters. Macaulay follows the lead of this natural interest, and does not leave James until he is fairly settled on the throne. James once established, our interest in him is for the time satisfied, and we desire to know the proceedings of his baffled opponents. Accordingly, the historian transports us to the asylum of the Whig refugees on the Continent, describes them, and keeps their machinations in Holland, and their successive invasions of Britain, prominent on the stage until the final collapse of their designs and the execution of their leaders. That chapter of the History ends with an account of the cruelties perpetrated on the aiders and abettors of the western insurrection under Monmouth. Then the scene changes to Ireland, the next interesting theatre of events. And so on: there were various critical junctures in the history of the Government, and the events leading to each are traced separately.

The arrangement is so easy and natural, that one almost wonders to see it alleged as a merit. But when we compare it with Hume's arrangement of the events of the same period, we see that even a historian of eminence may pursue a less luminous method. Hume relates, first, all that in his time was known of James's relations with France; then the various particulars of his administration in England, down to the insurrection of Monmouth; then the state of affairs in Scotland, including Argyle's invasion and the conduct of the Parliament. He goes upon the plan of taking up events in local departments, violating both the order of time and the order of dependence. Macaulay makes the government of James the connecting rod or trunk, taking up, one after another, the difficulties that successively besiege it, and, when necessary, stepping back to trace the particular difficulty on hand to its original, without regard to locality. By grappling thus boldly with the complicacy of events, he renders his narrative more continuous, and avoids the error of making a wide separation between events that were closely connected or interdependent. He does not, like Hume, give the descent of Monmouth in one section, and the descent of Argyle upon Scotland, an event prior in point of time, in another and subsequent section. James, after his accession, put off the meeting of the English Parliament till the more obsequious Parliament of Scotland should set a good example. Macaulay tells us at once James's motive for delaying the meeting of the English Parliament, and details what happened in Scotland during the fortnight of delay. In Hume's History, we do not hear of the proceedings instituted by the Scottish Parliament till after the execution of Argyle, by which time we are interested in another chain of events, and do not catch the influence of the proceedings in Scotland upon the proceedings in England.

In the explanation of events, Macaulay is simple, perspicuous, and plausible, but does not strike us as being precisely correct. When he can produce a broad and obvious motive, he does not refine upon the proportionate influence of minor motives. Upon this tendency we remarked in treating of the intellectual qualities of his style. If it does not add to his scientific value, it adds at least to his popularity.

As compared with the historians of last century—Hume, Gibbon, Robertson—Macaulay is superior in the use of summaries, prospective and retrospective, to help our comprehension of details. As compared with Carlyle, he is inferior in this respect. Before entering into the detail of an incident, he usually favours us with a general sketch of its nature, and its bearing on what has been or what is about to be related; but he is not so exemplary in prefiguring the course of events on the larger scale. You can usually tell from the beginning of a paragraph the general substance of what is to follow; you cannot always tell from the beginning of a chapter what may be the nature of its contents.

The interest excited by the 'History of England' on its first appearance was doubtless due partly to its controversial tone, and its able support of a popular side. With his hatred of abstract principles of government, it was not to be supposed that he would shape his narrative with a view to drawing from the facts any general political lessons, such as a caution against the evils of arbitrary government. What he wished to enforce was not an abstract lesson, but a strongly cherished opinion amounting briefly to this, that the government of the Stuarts was a curse to the country, and that the Revolution was a blessing.

The History has been wittily called "The Whig Evangel," and we have seen it described as "An Epic Poem, of which King William is the Hero." To the one title it may be objected that our author shows the Whig statesmen of the Revolution to have been quite as discreditable as the Tory statesmen; and to the other, that the work is more rhetorical and polemic than poetical.

If we must have a caricature secondary title for the book, it would perhaps be more accurately described as "A Plea for the Glorious Memory," or "A short and easy Method with the Stuarts."

One of Macaulay's pet theories, advocated with his usual enthusiasm, was his view as to the proper method of writing history. He was eager for the admission of greater scenical interest. He loses no opportunity of striking at "the dignity of history," which would confine the historian to "a detail of public occurrences—the operations of sieges—the changes of administrations—the treaties—the conspiracies—the rebellions." He would "intersperse the details which are the charm of historical romances." "The perfect historian is he in whose work the character and spirit of an age is exhibited in miniature." "We should not have to look for the wars and votes of the Puritans in Clarendon, and for their phraseology in 'Old Mortality;' for one half of King James in Hume, and for the other half in the 'Fortunes of Nigel.'"

Following out this theory, he gives to his work a strong tincture of personal interest. Even in the introductory summary, when briefly sketching the Commonwealth and the Restoration, he does not forget his ideal; he brings up the "great characteristics of the age, the loyal enthusiasm of the brave English gentry, the fierce licentiousness of the swearing, dicing, drunken reprobates, whose excesses disgraced the royal cause—the austerity of the Presbyterian Sabbaths in the city, the extravagance of the Independent preachers in the camp, the precise garb, the severe countenance, the petty scruples, the affected accent, the absurd names and phrases which marked the Puritans,"—and so on. When he enters on the reign of James II. he turns aside much more from public transactions to the details of private life. He resuscitates all the Court gossip of the period. He draws the character of every courtier of any note—rakes up their foibles, repeats their choicest strokes of wit. He read thousands of forgotten tracts, sermons, and satires in order to revive for us the personalities of the age. He devotes fifteen pages to the last illness and death of Charles II., and forty to the persecution and trial of the Seven Bishops.

It may well be asked whether with all this infusion of personal interest he comes near his ideal of presenting a miniature of the age. If any one had objected to him that he shows us the life of the courtiers and the clergy rather than the life of the people, he would probably have pointed to the passage in his History where he despatches all that he has to say about the people in six pages, with the remark that so little is known concerning "those who held the ploughs, who tended the oxen, who toiled at the looms of Norwich, and squared the Portland stone for St Paul's."

The interest of personality is not the only interest in his narrative. He has a natural tendency to give it a dramatic turn. When he introduces his personages, and explains what part they are playing, he drops a hint that by-and-by they may be found playing a very different part. We have already seen how inveterate is his habit of deferring an event till he has told us what ought to have happened or what might have happened. This bears a strong resemblance to dramatic plotting, and excites very much the same interest; it is one of the best recognised means of raising expectation and keeping it in suspense. In like manner he expatiates on all the preliminaries of an action till he has awakened in us something like the excitement of those that are watching and waiting for the event.

Another great charm in Macaulay's narrative is his hopeful tone, his hearty sympathy with progress, and confident belief in the fact. He has no faith in the dogma that former times were better than the present; he maintains with great variety of eloquence that mankind is steadily and rapidly moving forward. Sanguine minds are never weary of quoting the triumphal opening of his History, and in particular his unhesitating declaration that "the history of our country during the last hundred and sixty years is eminently the history of physical, of moral, and of intellectual improvement."

For English readers this charm is increased by the historian's patriotism. The world is advancing, and England is walking in the van.

The "celebrated Third Chapter."—This chapter professes to give a picture of the social condition of "the England which Charles II. governed." It is interesting as an elaborate attempt to delineate a cross section of history.

Many of the details have been challenged. He has been accused of colouring facts to suit his prejudice in favour of modern cultivation, and to gratify his favourite passion for antithesis. His accounts of the country squire and the country clergyman, of Buxton, of the suburbs of London, and of one or two other things, are said to be greatly exaggerated. He is charged with taking the lampoons of the time as documents of literal fidelity.

Without pronouncing upon the merits of these charges, which the historian's defenders declare to be trivial, we may enter two objections to the chapter.

(1.) The information is far from complete; it gives a very imperfect view of the state of society during the period chosen. A preference is given to flash and startling facts—to the material that is good for pictures and for dazzling paradoxes. Hardly anything is told us concerning the machinery of commerce, the machinery of government, or the system of ranks; he says nothing about that important social fact how far it was possible to pass from one station in life to another. The chapter remains a great achievement for a historian who was not also a special antiquarian, and who did not make even history his exclusive work; but it is far from being a complete sketch of the period.

(2.) There is, as already noticed, no principle of order—no endeavour to help the reader's memory. When we study the chapter, we can trace in the succession of subjects a certain train of association; but there is slight connection apparent upon the surface, and one's impression at the end of the whole is not a little confused. The population leads him to speak of the taxation as the only reliable means of getting at the population; the taxation suggests the public expenditure; the public expenditure the public resources, agriculture and mining; agriculture leads to rent; rent to the country squire; the squire to the clergyman,—and so on. On such a method, or rather no-method, there could be nothing but intricacy and confusion.

Exposition.

We have already seen how far Macaulay possesses the gifts of an able expositor. With his mastery of language, he can repeat his statements in great variety of forms. In his love of antithesis he often has recourse to the obverse form of repetition. He has an incomparable command of examples and illustrations. Thus, of all the four great arts of exposition he is a master.

Yet he cannot rank as an expositor with such a writer as Paley. This is partly on account of a deduction that must be made from his powers of accurate exposition. He is too fond of extreme and "sensational" examples, and of easy concrete illustrations not restricted to the relevant point. But the great detraction is, that he did not exhibit his powers, like Paley, on subjects of considerable inherent difficulty.

Macaulay's bent was naturally towards subjects of popular interest. Whatever he cared to master he could expound with the utmost clearness; but he had little inclination for hard abstract principles. His 'Notes on the Indian Penal Code' are hardly an exception. He has to support the provisions of the Code by general considerations, and his statement of these considerations is very clear and very interesting. But the subject is not naturally dry and repulsive. There is no greater temptation to make the Notes abstruse than there is to make a critical essay abstruse. He makes them interesting and animated by exactly the same arts of style as give such interest and animation to his essays. He mixes up the statement of the general principles with particular cases: sometimes, without stating the principle at all, he merely suggests it by saying that the particular provision he is defending rests on the same principle as some familiar rule of English law. He finds ample scope for antithesis in contrasting other Penal Codes with the various provisions of the Code recommended for India. Not even paradoxes are wanting; he surprises us at times by finding unsuspected reasons for departing from some familiar practice—such as the practice of allowing in certain cases an option between fine and imprisonment.

Persuasion.

Macaulay was a very popular orator. Soon after he entered Parliament, he spoke in the same debate with the late Lord Derby; and Sir James Mackintosh describes their speeches as "two of the finest speeches ever spoken in Parliament." And many men still living confess that their prejudices against the Reform Bill of 1832 were first overcome by his eloquent and perspicuous arguments.

His speeches are not the only evidence of his debating power. He is essentially a controversialist: it is hardly an exaggeration to say that he never makes a statement without attempting to prove it. His history is a protracted argument in favour of the Revolution. The "Third Chapter" is a broadside against the superiority of former days. When he has no real opponent to refute, no actual prejudice to overturn, he imagines all sorts of objections for the purpose of proving them to be groundless. His 'Notes on the Indian Penal Code' are defences against supposed objections. His Essay on Warren Hastings is a plea under the disguise of a judicial summing up. Not that he argues solely from the love of argument; always in earnest, he is eager to bring others round to his own views—ever bent upon convincing and converting.

This determination to persuade is at the root of his efforts to make himself understood by everybody, already noticed as the main cause of his simplicity of style. He is not content to utter an opinion in a form intelligible from his own point of view: having constantly before him the desire to convince all classes of minds, he asks how the opinion will be regarded by people of opposite sentiments, and shapes his statement accordingly.

Knowledge of those addressed.—Macaulay's audience may be said to have been the whole English-speaking world. That he knew many favourite maxims and ways of looking at things, is sufficiently proved by his wide popularity.

He humoured in an especial manner two feelings that are said to be peculiarly English—love of the practical as opposed to the theoretical, and love of material progress. He "distrusts all general theories of government;" he was intensely inimical to

James Mill's Essay on Government. He loves gradual changes; he professes a horror of revolutions and a contempt for Radicals. And while a stanch friend to intellectual and moral progress, he is far from seeing any danger to either in the multiplication of physical comforts: he exults in the English "public credit fruitful of marvels;" and one of the ideals that he "wishes from his soul" to see realised is, "employment always plentiful, wages always high, food always cheap, and a large family considered not as an encumbrance, but as a blessing."

Another thing that could not fail to endear him is his outspoken pride of country. By the mixture of races in our island was formed, he says, "a people inferior to none existing in the world." Englishmen "were then, as they are still, a brave, proud, and high-spirited race, unaccustomed to defeat, to shame, or to servitude."

Means of Persuasion.—(1.) Always perfectly master of the facts of his subject, he displays the highest rhetorical ingenuity in giving happy turns to opposing arguments. This was one great secret of his success in the Reforming Parliaments of 1831 and 1832. Hardly an argument could be advanced but he turned it against the speaker—maintaining with all his paradoxical point that it was precisely the consideration that led him to advocate Reform. The Reformers were taunted with a leaning to universal suffrage. "Every argument," returns Macaulay, "which would induce me to oppose universal suffrage, induces me to support the plan which is now before us. I am opposed to universal suffrage because I think that it would produce a destructive revolution. I support this plan because I am sure that it is our best security against a revolution." Again, in answer to the hackneyed appeal to the wisdom of our ancestors, he says, "We talk of the wisdom of our ancestors; and in one respect, at least, they were wiser than we. They legislated for their own times. They looked at the England which was before them. They did not think it necessary to give twice as many members to York as they gave to London, because York had been the capital of Britain in the time of Constantius Chlorus;" and so on. Again, "It is precisely because our institutions are so good that we are not perfectly contented with them; for they have educated us into a capacity for enjoying still better institutions." Once more—the promoters of the Anatomy Bill were accused of trying to make a law to benefit the rich at the expense of the poor. "Sir," said Macaulay, "the fact is the direct reverse. This is a bill which tends especially to benefit the poor;" and he proceeded to prove his assertion by examples.

Another of the devices of his fertile ingenuity and perfect acquaintance with his subject is to accuse his Conservative opponents of holding dangerous principles. He carries the war into the enemy's country. "If," cries the Member for the University of Oxford—"if we pass this law, England will soon be a Republic. The Reformed House of Commons will, before it has sate ten years, depose the King and expel the Lords from their House."

"Sir," returns Macaulay, "if my honourable friend could prove this, he would have succeeded in bringing an argument for democracy infinitely stronger than any that is to be found in the works of Paine. My honourable friend's proposition is in fact this: that our monarchical and aristocratical institutions have no hold on the public mind of England; that these institutions are regarded with aversion by a decided majority of the middle class. . . . Now, sir, if I were convinced that the great body of the middle class in England look with aversion on monarchy and aristocracy, I should be forced, much against my will, to come to this conclusion, that monarchical and aristocratical institutions are unsuited to my country."

So when they opposed the disfranchisement of the Rotten Boroughs on the ground that it was spoliation of property, Macaulay warned them of the danger of such a principle:—

"You bind up two very different things in the hope that they may stand together. Take heed that they do not fall together. You tell the people that it is as unjust to disfranchise a great lord's nomination borough as to confiscate his estate. Take heed that you do not succeed in convincing weak and ignorant minds that there is no more injustice in confiscating his estate than in disfranchising his borough."

(2.) His powers of drawing a strong and vivid picture are of great service in helping him to make out his case. In arguing on the Reform Bill, he was at great pains to make a powerful statement of the inequalities of the existing system of representation, and sketched with his best vigour the following strong example:—

"If, sir, I wished to make such a foreigner clearly understand what I consider as the great defects of our system, I would conduct him through that immense city which lies to the north of Great Russell Street and Oxford Street—a city superior in size and in population to the capitals of many mighty kingdoms; and probably superior in opulence, intelligence, and general respectability to any city in the world. I would conduct him through that interminable succession of streets and squares, all consisting of well-built and well-furnished houses. I would make him observe the brilliancy of the shops, and the crowd of well-appointed equipages. I would show him that magnificent circle of palaces which surrounds the Regent's Park. I would tell him that the rental of this district was far greater than that of the whole kingdom of Scotland at the time of the Union. And then I would tell him that this was an unrepresented district."

To take another well-known instance. In answer to the common objection that the Reform Bill would not be final, he argued that finality was not to be expected—that a changed state of society might again call for a change in the representation. His manner of putting the possibilities of change was characteristic:—

"Another generation may find in the new representative system defects such as we find in the old representative system. Civilisation will proceed. Wealth will increase. Industry and trade will find out new seats. The same causes which have turned so many villages into great towns, which have turned so many thousands of square miles of fir and heath into cornfields and orchards, will continue to operate. *Who can say that a hundred years hence there may not be, on the shore of some desolate and silent bay in the Hebrides, another Liverpool with its docks and warehouses and endless forests of masts? Who can say that the huge chimneys of another Manchester may not rise in the wilds of Connemara?* For our children we do not pretend to legislate."

(3.) His great powers of debate appear chiefly in refutation. He is critical rather than constructive. He takes delight in exposing false analogies and false generalities, and in showing that anticipations are not warranted by previous experience.

When he can put a doctrine upon the horns of a dilemma, he tosses it with great spirit. A good instance is his assault on primogeniture; which also illustrates his habit of referring all generalities to the fundamental particulars, and his favourite manner of retorting that the facts prove exactly the opposite of what is asserted:—

"It is evident that this theory, though intended to strengthen the foundations of Government, altogether unsettles them. Did the divine and immutable law of primogeniture admit females or exclude them? *On either supposition, half the sovereigns of Europe must be usurpers*, reigning in defiance of the commands of heaven, and might be justly dispossessed by the rightful heirs. These absurd doctrines received no countenance from the Old Testament; for in the Old Testament we read that the chosen people were blamed and punished for desiring a king, and that they were afterwards commanded to withdraw their allegiance from him. Their whole history, far from favouring the notion that primogeniture is of divine institution, *would rather seem to indicate that younger brothers are under the special protection of heaven.* Isaac was not the eldest son of Abraham, nor Jacob of Isaac, nor Judah of Jacob, nor David of Jesse, nor Solomon of David. Indeed, the order of seniority among children is seldom strictly regarded in countries where polygamy is practised."

Examples, actual cases, which he lays down in such numbers, often have the effect of a proof, being the actual foundation of the general proposition. His illustration in the debate on the Anatomy Bill of the assertion that the poor suffer more by bad surgery than the rich, has something of this effect:—

"Who suffers by the bad state of the Russian school of surgery? The Emperor Nicholas? By no means. The whole evil falls on the peasantry. If the education of a surgeon should become very expensive, if the fees of surgeons should consequently rise, if the supply of regular surgeons should diminish, the sufferers would be, not the rich, but the poor in our country villages, who would again be left to mountebanks, and barbers, and old women, and charms, and quack medicines."

Perhaps the best example of his irresistible use of facts to enforce his views is to be seen in his speeches on the proposals to extend Copyright. He runs over the principal men in English literature, and examines how the law would have operated with them. Would it have induced Dr Johnson to labour more assiduously had he known that a bookseller, whose grandfather had purchased the copyright of his works from his residuary legatee Black Frank, would be in 1841 drawing large profits from the monopoly? Would it have induced him to give one more allegory, one more life of a poet, one more imitation of Juvenal?

Very often his concrete comparisons are of the nature of arguments by analogy. His speech on the war with China, defending the Government from the charge of having brought on the war by mismanagement, abounds in comparisons of this sort. One of the charges was that the instructions sent to the superintendent were vague and meagre, to which Macaulay replied that it would be pernicious meddling to attempt to direct in detail the action of a functionary fifteen thousand miles off:—

"How indeed is it possible that they should send him directions as to the details of his administration? Consider in what a state the affairs of this country would be if they were to be conducted according to directions framed by the ablest statesman residing in Bengal. A despatch goes hence asking for instructions while London is illuminating for the peace of Amiens. The instructions arrive when the French army is encamped at Boulogne, and when the whole island is up in arms to repel invasion. A despatch is written asking for instructions when Buonaparte is at Elba. The instructions come when he is at the Tuilleries. A despatch is written asking for instructions when he is at the Tuilleries. The instructions come when he is at St Helena. It would be just as impossible to govern India in London as to govern England at Calcutta."

Here we have substantially an argument by analogy. Another of the charges brought against Government was, that they made no exertion to suppress the opium trade. This Macaulay met with the assertion that it was impossible, supporting his assertion with the following plausible parallel:—

"In England we have a preventive service which costs us half a million a-year. We employ more than fifty cruisers to guard our coasts. We have six thousand effective men whose business is to intercept smugglers. And yet . . . the quantity of brandy which comes in without paying duty is known to be not less than six hundred thousand gallons a-year. Some people think that the quantity of tobacco which is imported clandestinely is as great as the quantity which goes through the custom-house. . . . And all this, observe, has been done in spite of the most effective preventive service that, I believe, ever existed in the world. . . . If we know anything about the Chinese Government, we know this, that its coast-guard is neither trusty nor efficient; and we know that a coast-guard as trusty and as efficient as our own would not be able to cut off communication between the merchant longing for silver and the smoker longing for his pipe."

Any attempt at prevention, he says further, would turn the smugglers into pirates—

"Have not similar causes repeatedly produced similar effects? Do we not know that the jealous vigilance with which Spain excluded the ships of other nations from her transatlantic possessions turned men who would otherwise have been honest merchant adventurers into buccaneers? The same causes which raised up one race of buccaneers in the Gulf of Mexico would soon have raised up another in the China sea."

The same sense of the effect of dealing with propositions in the concrete appears in another form. He is anxious to reduce vague and general charges to a statement of facts, with a view to show the insufficiency of the real grounds. Thus he reduces Sir James Graham's charge of Government maladministration in China to the following:—

"The charge against them therefore is this, that they did not give such copious and particular directions as were sufficient, in every possible emergency, for the guidance of a functionary who was fifteen thousand miles off."

His habit of immediately looking to the facts when a generality was asserted, often enabled him to point out that certain circumstances had not been taken into account. Thus, in the Reform debate, a member argued that it was unjust to disfranchise Aldborough, because the borough was as populous now as in the days of Edward III., when it was constituted an elective borough. True, replied Macaulay, but it ought to be much more populous now than then, if it would keep its position. Other towns have been growing enormously, while Aldborough has been standing still.

(4.) Though habitually gladiatorial, and always eager to convince by argument, he shows considerable tact in recommending his own view to the feelings of the persons addressed.

Throughout his History he seeks favour for his own favourites by representing them as the champions of English glory. His account of Cromwell may be studied for artful touches of this sort. One of his most splendid paragraphs is his account of the supremacy of England during the Protectorate. In equally enthusiastic terms he celebrates the superiority of Cromwell's pikemen:—

"The banished Cavaliers felt an emotion of national pride when they saw a brigade of their countrymen, outnumbered by foes and abandoned by allies, drive before it in headlong rout the finest infantry of Spain, and force a passage into a counterscarp which had just been pronounced impregnable by the ablest of the marshals of France."

In the Reform debates his principal card was the fear of provoking the people to a revolution. Again and again he reiterated that there were grounds for such a fear. When Lord John Russell hinted at the danger of disappointing the expectations of the nation, he was accused of threatening the House. Macaulay defended the obnoxious expression as quite "parliamentary and decorous," and repeated his own belief in the reality of the danger:—

"I, sir, do entertain great apprehension for the fate of my country. I do in my conscience believe that unless the plan proposed, or some similar plan, be speedily adopted, great and terrible calamities will befall us. Entertaining this opinion, I think myself bound to state it, not as a threat, but as a reason."

In more than one of the debates he held up the French Revolution as a warning:—

"The French nobles delayed too long any concession to the popular demands. Because they resisted reform in 1783, they had to resist revolution in 1789. They would not endure Turgot, and they had to endure Robespierre."

In one speech he drew a vivid picture of the destruction of the nobility, and asked—

"Why were they scattered over the face of the earth, their titles abolished, their escutcheons defaced, their parks wasted, their palaces dismantled, their heritages given to strangers? Because they had no sympathy with the people, no discernment of the signs of their time; because, in the pride and narrowness of their hearts, they called those whose warnings might have saved them theorists and speculators; because they refused all concession until the time had arrived when no concession would avail."

CHAPTER III.

THOMAS CARLYLE,

Born Dec. 4, 1795.

Thomas Carlyle, "The Censor of the Age," as he has been called, is an author by profession. In his famous petition on the Copyright Bill, written in 1839, he described himself as "a writer of books."

His early life was not particularly checkered; and since he adopted the profession of literature, the principal epochs of his career have been the dates of his various books.

His education was the education of hundreds of young Scotchmen in the same generation. His father, who is spoken of as a shrewd and intelligent man, had a farm near the village of Ecclefechan, in Dumfriesshire. Thomas, the eldest son, was sent with other little boys to the parish school; and in 1810, after some training in the higher branches of learning at the burgh school of Annan, proceeded to the University of Edinburgh.

When he entered the University, he had not quite completed his fifteenth year. Some of his professors were men of note: Dunbar, Professor of Greek; Leslie, Professor of Mathematics; Playfair, Professor of Natural Philosophy; Thomas Brown, Professor of Logic and Moral Philosophy. Young Carlyle was a hard student. He applied himself diligently to classics. To Brown's lectures he probably gave little attention, having a strong distaste for the analytic mode of dealing with mind, but the lectures in science he mastered thoroughly: natural liking for the subject, or the professor's enthusiasm, or accident, led him to make mathematics his principal study. He prosecuted the high mathematics for a long time with the greatest ardour. It was in his devotion to this subject that he first injured his naturally robust health.

He became a mathematical teacher, and at one time was a candidate for the Professorship of Astronomy in Glasgow. Traces of these studies appear not only in his figurative allusions, but in an amount of scientific method far beyond what is generally found in writers of high imagination.

In the end of May 1814 he quitted Edinburgh, having gone through the usual curriculum in arts; and, by competitive trial at Dumfries, got the teachership of mathematics in the burgh school of Annan, where, as we have mentioned, he had himself been a scholar. After two years' service in that post, he was, through the recommendation of his Edinburgh professors, offered the teachership of mathematics and classics in the burgh school of Kirkcaldy, and held that appointment also for about two years. In Kirkcaldy he made the intimate acquaintance of Edward Irving, who, like himself, had been a schoolboy at Annan, and who for some years was master of a "venture school" in Kirkcaldy, known as "The Academy."

The time spent by Carlyle in schoolmastering, and its probable influence on his habits of thought and feeling, have been a little exaggerated. He was barely three-and-twenty when he gave it up. In the end of 1818 he left Kirkcaldy, and went across to Edinburgh, with no definite prospects, but with a vague leaning towards literature. He spent some three years in Edinburgh mainly in what he would call "stony-ground husbandries." His only known literary work during those years was the composition of certain articles for Brewster's 'Edinburgh Encyclopedia." It is probably to this period especially that we must refer the rumours of his unprecedented reading in the University library; he devoured extraordinary numbers of books on history, poetry (in a moderate degree), romance, and general information as to all countries, and all things of popular interest. In 1821 he became tutor to Charles Buller, an appointment that probably relieved him from a good deal of distasteful drudgery.

In 1823 he sent to the 'London Magazine' the first instalment of his 'Life of Schiller.' In 1824 his publications were numerous; he finished his 'Life of Schiller,' and produced a translation of 'Legendre's Geometry,' with an original Essay on Proportion, as well as his first notable work, the translation of 'Wilhelm Meister.' During the next two years he laboured at translations from the German, "honest journey-work, not of his own suggesting or desiring." In 1825 his Schiller appeared in a separate form. In 1826 he married Miss Jane Welsh, only daughter of Dr Welsh, a lineal descendant from John Knox, and lived with his wife in Edinburgh till he had completed and published four volumes of translations from German romance. He then (in 1828) retired to the farm of Craigenputtoch, in Dumfriesshire, a small property belonging to his wife, situated about a day's journey east of his native Ecclefechan.

When he married he resigned his tutorship, and henceforth devoted his whole time to letters. At Craigenputtoch he lived about six years. His manner of life he described in an often-quoted letter to Goethe, with whom he had been brought into correspondence by his translation of 'Wilhelm Meister.' He had retired to his own "bit of earth" to "secure the independence through which he could be enabled to remain true to himself." "Six miles from any one likely to visit him," "in the loveliest nook of Scotland," he yet kept himself informed of what was passing in the literary world; he had, "piled upon the table of his little library, a whole cartload of French, German, American, and English journals and periodicals." He was "uncertain about his future literary activity."

At Craigenputtoch he wrote for various periodicals—'The Edinburgh Review,' 'The Foreign Quarterly,' 'Fraser's Magazine'—the essays reprinted in the three first volumes of his 'Miscellanies.' Two of these are estimates of British writers; the Essay on Burns (1828), mentioned in his letter to Goethe as the only thing of importance he had written during his first year at Craigenputtoch; and his Essay on Boswell's 'Life of Johnson.' The others are estimates of German and French authors—Richter, Werner, Goethe, Heine, Novalis, Schiller, Voltaire, Diderot. His own line of literary activity being yet undeveloped, he occupied himself in measuring the literary activity of others. But during this period of criticism he had been revolving and finishing an original work in a peculiar vein, the 'Sartor Resartus,' which, after being rejected by several publishers, at length saw the light as a series of articles in 'Fraser's Magazine,' 1833-34. The singularity and force of the Sartor drew upon the author more attention than he had hitherto received.

In 1834 he removed to the London suburb now associated with his name. The "Seer of Chelsea" is now as familiar a synonym as "the glorious Dreamer of Highgate." His fame was then in a rapid ascendant. The Sartor was much admired in America; it and his fugitive essays were reprinted at Boston in 1836. In 1837 he gave to "a very crowded, yet a select, audience" in London a course of six public lectures on German literature; in 1838 a course of twelve "On the History of Literature, or the Successive Periods of European Culture;" in 1839 a course on "the Revolutions of Modern Europe;" in 1840 a course on "Heroes, Hero-Worship, and the Heroic in History."[1] These lectures made a sensation in fashionable literary circles; the rugged English, the Scotch accent, the emphatic sing-song cadence, combined with the

[1] The last course only has been published.

loftiness and originality of the matter, drew crowds to hear the new prophet. "It was," said Leigh Hunt, "as if some Puritan had come to life again, liberalised by German philosophy and his own intense reflections and experiences."

Meanwhile his master-works began to appear. In 1837 he produced 'The French Revolution,' the first work that bore his name. In 1838 'Sartor Resartus,' "hitherto a mere aggregate of Magazine articles," emerged from its "bibliopolic difficulties," and became a book. The same year witnessed the first edition of his 'Miscellanies.' In 1839 he published, under the title of 'Chartism,' his first attack on the corruption of modern society, and the futility of all extant projects of reform. In 1843 he followed up 'Chartism' with 'Past and Present.' In 1845 he published his 'Cromwell's Letters and Speeches,' which met with a more rapid sale than any of his previous works. In 1850 he returned, in his 'Latter-Day Pamphlets,' to the condition of society, pouring forth unmeasured contempt on "The Nigger Question," "The Present Time," "Model Prisons," "Downing Street," "The New Downing Street," "Stump Orators," "Parliaments," "Hudson's Statue," "Jesuitism." Next year appeared his 'Biography of John Sterling.' Thereafter he was occupied exclusively with his great historical work, 'The History of Frederick II., commonly called The Great.' The two first volumes were published in 1858, other two in 1862, and in 1865 the work was completed.

In the session of 1865-66 he was elected Lord Rector by the students of Edinburgh University; and on April 2, 1866, delivered to a crowded and enthusiastic audience his famous Installation Address. He was not suffered long to enjoy the most affecting public manifestations that have ever honoured his name. His wife died before his return to London: in the very hour of his public triumph came the stroke of calamity; and the old man mourned that "the light of his life was quite gone out."

Of late years he has published no large work. Now and then he makes his voice heard on questions of passing interest. In 1867 he wrote for 'Macmillan's Magazine' a very gloomy anticipation of the consequences of the Reform Bill, with the suggestive title, "Shooting Niagara, and After?" In 1869 he sent to the newspapers a letter on his favourite "Emigration." His last utterance was in 1870, on the war between France and Germany, rejoicing over the French defeat, and quoting history to show that it had been well deserved.

In his Rectorial Address at Edinburgh, being then a patriarch of seventy, he addressed a kindly warning to his youthful hearers against the physical dangers of too severe study. His own strong frame and great constitutional robustness were early impaired by injudicious closeness of application. During the whole of his later life he suffered from dyspepsia. It says much for the native energy of his system that, in spite of this depressing—if not debilitating—disorder, he accomplished such an amount of solid work, retaining his powers to old age, and writing with unabated vigour at the extreme age of seventy. He had sufficient strength of will to sustain what De Quincey always recognised as the best remedy for *his* "appalling stomachic derangement"—namely, regular habits of active exercise.

We spoke of Macaulay as a man whose intellectual energies were to some extent dissipated upon various fields of exertion. Carlyle's energies have been to a much greater degree concentrated upon his books. For nearly half a century he gave the best part of his working time to literature, pursuing his appointed tasks with the utmost regularity and method. Probably more intellectual force has been spent upon the production of Carlyle's books than upon the productions of any two other writers in general literature.

His powers of memory were not of the same universally and immediately dazzling order as Macaulay's. Every person that met Macaulay went away in astonishment at "the stores which his memory had at instantaneous command." In private society Carlyle impresses his hearers by talk very much resembling the general texture of his writings. The first notice that we have of him is in De Quincey's 'Autobiographical Sketches,' where "a young man introduced by Irving" is said to have delivered a eulogy on Mahomet, and to have had a joke passed upon him by Charles Lamb in consequence. He had not Macaulay's wide-ranging readiness of recollection, could not quote with the same instantaneous fluency, and could not trust his memory so confidently without a written note. Again—to compare him in this particular with De Quincey—he does not strike us as possessing great multifarious knowledge. He makes comparatively few allusions beyond the circle of subjects that he has specially studied. His scrupulous love of accuracy may have hampered the flowing display of his knowledge; but within the circles of his special studies, his memory is pre-eminently wonderful. To hold in mind the varied materials of his vivid historical pictures was a strain of retentive force immeasurably greater than was ever required of either De Quincey or Macaulay for the production of their works. His memory is singularly catholic as regards the kind of thing remembered; he remembers names, dates, scenical groupings, and the characteristic gestures and expressions of whole societies of men, to all appearance with equal fidelity.

Carlyle is sometimes loosely spoken of as a great "thinker," but his power does not lie in the regions of the dry understanding, in analysis, argument, or practical judgment. In his youth he was distinguished as a mathematician; but when he turned to the study of men, he took fire: on anything connected with man, he felt too profoundly to reason well. His whole nature rose in rebellion against cold-blooded analysis and matter-of-fact argument. In his works he is never tired of sneering at "Philosophism," the "Dismal Science" of Political Economy, "Attorney Logic," and suchlike. He had a natural antipathy to such ways of approaching men and the affairs of men. He was naturally incapable of De Quincey's pursuit of character or meaning into minute shades, and of Macaulay's elaborate refutations by copious instance and analogy. Take, for example, his Hero-worship. Instead of analysing, as De Quincey might have done, the elements of greatness in his heroes, or of producing, as Macaulay might have done, argumentative arrays of actual undeniable achievements as the proof of their title to admiration, he exercises his ingenuity in representing their greatness under endless varieties of striking images; the hero is "a flowing light-fountain of native original insight, of manhood and heroic nobleness;" "at all moments the Flame image glares in upon him;" "a messenger he, sent from the Infinite Unknown with tidings to us."

Though deficient as an analyst and as a debater, he shows in other forms abundance of the elementary intellectual force principally concerned in analysis and debate. Had his feelings been less dominant, he might have developed into a profound professor of what he calls the Dismal Science, and might even, with unprecedented persuasive skill, have converted the world to the practice of Malthusianism. But feeling and natural impulses chained his great intellect to their service; and instead of scientific analysis and solid argument, the result is a splendour and originality of imagery and dramatic grouping that entitle him to rank with Shakspeare, or with whoever may be placed next to our received ideal of the incomparable.

A man of feeling and impulse, his feelings and impulses were very different from what we find in natures constitutionally fitted for enjoyment, in the born lovers of existence, his own "eupeptic" men. In his works we encounter something very different from Macaulay's uniform glow of buoyant hopefulness, hearty belief in human progress, and confident plausible judgment of men and events. We find gloomy views of man and his destiny, a stern gospel of work, judgments passed in strong defiance of conventional standards, and towering egotism under the mask of humour.

In another aspect he strikes us as offering a considerable contrast to De Quincey. The Opium-Eater, though not by any means a eupeptic man, was an avowed Eudæmonist, "hated an inhuman moralist like unboiled opium," and was a lover of repose and of the softer motions. In Carlyle, on the contrary, the central and commanding emotion is Power; he is all for excitement and energy. We have already seen the difference in their ways of viewing great men; that De Quincey admires them in a passive attitude, while Carlyle is raised by the thought of their achievements to the loftiest heights of ideal energy. We have no means of knowing how Carlyle would have enjoyed the actual control of human beings as a commander or a civic ruler—like Cromwell, Frederick, Mirabeau, or Dr Francia; but he shows a most thorough enjoyment of commanding authority in the imagination. His thirst for the ideal enjoyment seems insatiable, and drives him to exaggerate the influence of his chosen heroes, and to suppress and understate the influence of their coadjutors. "Universal History, the history of what man has accomplished in this world, is at bottom the history of the Great Men who have worked there." "All things that we see standing accomplished in the world are properly the outer material result, the practical realisation and embodiment of thoughts that dwelt in the Great Men sent into the world: the soul of the whole world's history, it may justly be considered, were the history of these."

A good way of representing the difference between two such writers is to look through their works, and piece together their conceptions of the universe in their highest moods of sublimity. De Quincey sees midsummer moving over the heavens like an army with banners; hears cathedral music in the confused noise of mountain-streams; loves to contemplate calmly in the mirror of such minds as 'Walking Stewart's' the whole mighty vision of the sentient universe, oriental pageantry, revolutionary convulsions, civic splendour; and occasionally lifts his mind to travel in the same calm way through the illimitable grandeurs of astronomical spaces. Contrast this repose of attitude with the violent excitement of Carlyle's favourite conceptions: the world pictured as a dark simmering pit of Tophet, wild puddle of muddy infatuations, of irreconcilable incoherences, bottomless universal hypocrisies, an ungenuine phantasmagory of a world, full of screechings and gibberings, of foul ravening monsters, of meteor-lights and Bacchic dances, the wild universe storming in upon man infinite vague-menacing.

Carlyle's love of powerful excitement finds a magnificent outlet in his humour and derision. Psychologists tell us that the basis of laughter is a sudden accession of pleasure in the shape of the special elation of power and superiority. Carlyle avowedly approves of laughter—sets up hearty laughter as a criterion of genuine human worth; and, as we shall see when we come to his qualities of style, he is self-indulgent, if not intemperate, in the exercise of his own sense of the ludicrous. His mirth is robust

—as he says himself, in describing the Norsemen, "a great broad Brobdingnag grin of true humour."

His pathos is of the kind that goes naturally with such excessive indulgence in the excitement of power. Wherever there is a height there is a corresponding hollow; the lover of intoxicating excitement too surely pays the penalty in intervals of exhaustion, of unutterable depression and despondency. With all his fire, his gospel of work, and his denunciation of unproductive sentimentality, Carlyle has his inevitable fits of the melting mood. We shall see that at times he is overpowered with sadness at the thought of human miseries and perplexities, and that he bemoans with more than Byronic despondency the irresistible movement of time.

We have already spoken of the amount of intellectual effort spent upon the production of our author's books. The grand duty of work that he preaches with such earnestness he seems to have been no less earnest in performing. In reading his books we cannot but be struck with the many evidences of faithful labour. Take, for example, any page of his 'French Revolution,' and consider what pains he must have expended upon the mere composition, the choice of the language, the structure of the sentences, and the studied figures of speech; upon the various arts of original, clear, and forcible expression: then, putting this aside as involving no small effort, as something not to be done in a hurry, consider the labour that it must have cost him to form from scattered documents and by patient exercise of the historical imagination, his own vivid conceptions of the scenes that he delineates so vividly.

He does not seem to have done his work with the fitful irregularity of Christopher North, but rather to have acted on the Virgilian plan of so much manuscript each day. Such work as his could hardly have been accomplished without the steadiest concentration of endeavour. It is known that in composing the 'French Revolution' he set himself daily to produce so much, and in all probability he composed his other works on the same rigid method. In this respect he is a much safer model to the general run of students than the versatile and discursive Macaulay.

Opinions.—Carlyle's doctrines are the first suggestions of an earnest man, adhered to with unreasoning tenacity. As a rule, with no exception that is worth naming, they take account mainly of one side of a case. He was too impatient of difficulties, and had too little respect for the wisdom and experience of others, to submit to be corrected; opposition rather confirmed him in his own opinion. Most of his practical suggestions had already been tried and found wanting, or had been made before and judged impracticable upon grounds that he did not or would not understand. His modes of dealing with pauperism and crime were in full operation under the despotisms of Henry VII. and Henry VIII. His theory of a hero-king, which means in practice an accidentally good and able man in a series of indifferent or bad despots, has been more frequently tried than any other political system: Asia at this moment contains no government that is not despotic. His views in other departments of knowledge also, are chiefly determined by the strength of unreasoning impulses.

This will appear when we state his opinions in some detail. We throw them for convenience into a few familiar divisions.

Psychology.—He disclaims the ordinary mental analysis. He speaks with great contempt of "motive-grinding." He sat through Thomas Brown's lectures with perpetual inward protest, declaring that he did not want the mind to be taken to pieces in that way.

We need not therefore look in his writings for any large views of the mind, or any enunciations of doctrines of a comprehensive kind. In his partiality for everything German, he adopts with unquestioning faith some Kantian and other transcendentalisms of German origin. His own original views of the mind are fragmentary and somewhat fanciful.

We may apply the title "Psychological" to some of his doctrines about the indissoluble union of certain qualities. For one example, take his theory of Laughter as the criterion of goodness. "Readers," he says, "who have any tincture of Psychology, know . . . that no man who has once heartily and wholly laughed can be altogether irreclaimably bad." Again, "Laughter, also, if it come from the heart, is a heavenly thing." As another example, take his doctrine that Intellect is the true measure of worth. "Human Intellect, if you consider it well, is the exact summary of Human Worth." "A man of intellect, of real and not sham intellect, is by the nature of him likewise inevitably a man of nobleness." "The able man is definable as the born enemy of Falsity and Anarchy and the born soldier of Truth and Order."

Such doctrines are, it is hardly necessary to say, far from clear. Very bad men often laugh heartily enough, in the ordinary sense of the words; and very able men, in the ordinary sense of the word "able," are often very great scoundrels. Carlyle's unreserved admirers probably bring themselves to accept such dogmas by laying stress on the saving clauses,—"if it comes from the heart;" "if you consider it well;" and suchlike. But none of these clauses will save the doctrines if they are taken in the ordinary meaning of their words; and one may well doubt whether great writers are to be allowed the privilege of throwing the ancient boundaries of words into confusion.

Other examples of his habit of attaching laudatory predicates to what he has a liking for, without much regard to the fitness of the application, are such as the following: "All deep things are song. It seems somehow the very central essence of us, Song; as if all the rest were but wrappings and hulls;" "You may see how a man would fight by the way in which he sings;" "'The imagination that shudders at the hell of Dante,' is not that the sàme faculty, weaker in degree, as Dante's own?" "Your genuine poet is the real Encyclopedist," &c. &c. All these involve indifferent psychology, and they are but samples of more of the same kind.

Ethics.—Doctrines in Ethics we shall keep as far as possible distinct from doctrines in Theology; although many of our author's doctrines are two-sided.

(1.) According to Carlyle, the chief end of life is the performance of Duty. He is full of contempt for the pursuit of happiness, and pours out his most indignant eloquence against the theory of life that would make happiness the end. "In all situations out of the Pit of Tophet, wherein a living man has stood or can stand, there is actually a prize of quite *infinite* value placed within his reach—namely, a *Duty* for him to do: this highest Gospel . . . forms the basis and worth of all other Gospels whatsoever."

His stern creed allows no collateral support to the discharge of duty. If men labour in hope of reward, they are still unconverted, still in darkness. They must recognise that they deserve nothing. To Methodism, "with its eye for ever turned on its own navel," and torturing itself with the questions—'Am I right, am I wrong? Shall I be saved, shall I be damned?'—he gives the lofty advice—"If thou be a man, reconcile thyself" to the fact "that thou *art* wrong; thou art like to be damned;" "then first is the devouring Universe subdued under thee," and there breaks upon thee "dawn as of an everlasting morning." On the same principle of acknowledging utter worthlessness, and recognising that nothing too bad can befall us, we are advised—"Fancy that thou deservest to be hanged (as is most likely), thou wilt feel it happiness to be only shot; fancy that thou deservest to be hanged in a hair-halter, it will be a luxury to die in hemp." In short, our only consolation in life is to be the sense of doing our duty; as regards everything else, we must expect nothing, lest we should be disappointed.

(2.) But Duty is an abstraction, an empty Ideal: does Carlyle recommend any duties in particular? Yes.

The first great duty is the duty of Work—Action, Activity. This eminent feature in his preaching has been called "The Gospel of Labour." According to this gospel, all the "peopled, clothed, articulate-speaking, high-towered, wide-acred World" has been "made a world for us" by work; the individual that does not lend a hand fails in his duty as a denizen of the

Universe. Man's greatest enemy is Disorder; his most imperative and crying duty is to subdue disorder, convert chaos into order and method; the able-bodied or able-minded man that stands idle deserves unspeakable contempt,—he is a dastard, a fool, a *simulacrum;* he does not fulfil his destiny as a man. Wherefore, "Do thy little stroke of work; this is Nature's voice, and the sum of all the commandments, to each man."

To the question, What is to be done? he answers peremptorily, "'Do the duty which lies nearest thee,' which thou knowest to be a duty." "Produce! Produce! Were it but the pitifullest infinitesimal fraction of a Product, produce it in God's name. . . . Whatsoever thy hand findeth to do, do it with thy might." He never recommends or brings prominently forward care in the choice of a vocation; he is so eager and impetuous to have something done, that he has no thought of cautioning against the hasty adoption of unsuitable work. He evidently considers there is much more danger in idleness. We must "live and not lie sleeping while it is called to-day." "Something must be done, and soon." Doubt is removed only by activity.

He upholds the dignity of work at all points. "All true work is religion." "'*Laborare est orare*'—work is worship." The "Captains of Industry" are the true aristocracy. The great army of workers, "Ploughers, Spinners, Builders; Prophets, Poets, Kings; Brindleys and Goethes, Odins and Arkwrights;"—this grand host is "noble, every soldier in it; sacred, and alone noble." "Two men he honours, and no third"—"the toilworn Craftsman who conquers the Earth," and "him who is seen toiling for the spiritually indispensable."

He sets off his own Gospel of Work against other pretended Gospels. He despatches the Stoics in the person of Epictetus by telling them that "*the end of man is an Action and not a Thought*, though it were the noblest." He taunts those that make happiness the end of life with the declaration, that "the night once come, our unhappiness, our happiness — it is all abolished; vanished, clean gone; a thing that has been." "But our work—behold, that is not abolished, that has not vanished: our work, behold, it remains, or the want of it remains;—for endless Times and Eternities, remains." He is also vigorous against what he calls sentimentalism, which he dubs "twin-sister to Cant." "The barrenest of all mortals is the sentimentalist;" "in the shape of work he can do nothing."

Another great duty is the duty of Obedience. Not only is obeying the best discipline for governing, and as such extolled in Abbot Samson, and recommended to the Duke of Logwood, but "Obedience is our universal duty and destiny; wherein whoso will not bend must break." Too early and too thoroughly we cannot be trained to know that "Would in this world of ours is as mere zero to Should." Again to the same effect—"Obedience is the primary duty of man. No man but is bound indefeasibly with all force of obligation to obey."

There is nothing peculiar upon the face of these precepts, except their strength; they might almost stand in the Institutions of the Jesuits. Here and there throughout his works we meet with qualifications. He denounces the obedience of the Jesuits—"Obedience to what is wrong and false?—good heavens! there is no name for such a depth of human cowardice and calamity." It is the heroic, the divine, the true, that he would have us obey. When the powers set over us are no longer anything divine, resistance becomes a deeper law of order than obedience.

If we ask how we are to know the heroic, the divine, we are left to understand that it will make itself manifest. The true King "carries in him an authority from God, or man will never give it him." "He who is to be my Ruler, whose will is to be higher than my will, was chosen for me in heaven."

Another duty is the duty of Veracity, of Sincerity as opposed to Cant, the duty of being Real and not a Sham. On these virtues and their opposites, on those that observe them and those that violate them, he expends much eloquence. The 'French Revolution' is almost a continued sermon on the evils of insincerity, hollowness, quackery, and on the good of the corresponding virtues. And in none of his works can we read far without encountering some declamation on Truth, Sincerity, Reality, Falsehood, Cant, Puffery, Sham.

On one point his preaching of Truth may mislead. He does not seem to think that Truth requires a man to make a frank and open declaration of his beliefs. For his own part, at least, he is very reticent as to his real opinions, on matters of religion for instance; and he praises Goethe's example of wrapping up opinions in mysterious oracles. The fact would seem to be, that all his requirements of Veracity, Sincerity, Reality, are satisfied by one thing, the conscientious performance of one's appointed work. This, if we look beneath the gorgeous verbal opulence of the preacher, would seem to be the whole duty of man. If he engages to cut thistles, let him cut them with all his might. If he engages to review authors, let him read their works conscientiously. If he engages to write history, let him diligently search out its facts.

His characteristic love of reality appears in his preference of Fact to Fiction, and his condemnation of Fine Art as Dilettantism.

Religion.—His religious views are worded obscurely. To extract definite opinions from his vague declamations on the subject, would inevitably be to misrepresent him. He intimates plainly enough that he has departed from the received orthodoxy of this country; of this he makes no secret. He himself gave up studying for the Scottish Church; and he records his opinion "in flat reproval" of John Sterling's resolution to take orders in the English Church. "No man of Sterling's veracity, had he clearly consulted his own heart, or had his own heart been capable of clearly responding, and not been dazzled and bewildered by transient fantasies and theosophic moonshine, could have undertaken this function." Elsewhere he pities Sterling in this "confused epoch of ours," with "the old spiritual highways and recognised paths to the Eternal, now all torn up and flung in heaps, submerged in unutterable boiling mud-oceans of Hypocrisy and Unbelievability, of brutal living Atheism, and damnable dead putrescent Cant." But while he is thus severe alike on Infidelity and on Orthodoxy, he never says with an approach to intelligibility what is his own belief. John Sterling gives the following account of the Religion or No-Religion of the Sartor:—

"What we find everywhere, with an abundant use of the name of God, is the conception of a formless Infinite whether in time or space; of a high inscrutable Necessity, which it is the chief wisdom and virtue to submit to, which is the mysterious impersonal base of all Existence—shows itself in the laws of every separate being's nature, and for man in the shape of duty."

We may perhaps rank among his religious opinions his acceptance of Fichte's idea that the "*true* literary man" is "the world's Priest," "continually unfolding the Godlike to men," "sent hither especially that he may discern for himself, and make manifest to us, this same Divine Idea." By way of defining the "true" man of letters, he says that "whoever lives not wholly in this Divine Idea is . . . no Literary Man."

Politics.—His political views connect themselves partly with his ideas about Work, Reality, Sincerity, and suchlike; and partly with his Hero-King. All the miseries in this life are due to Idleness, Imposture, Unveracity. This he explicitly declares. "Quack-ridden; in that one word lies all misery whatsoever. Speciosity in all departments usurps the place of reality, thrusts reality away. . . . The quack is a Falsehood incarnate." He does indeed say elsewhere that "it is the feeling of *injustice* that is insupportable to all men; "but then he explains that injustice "is another name for disorder, for unveracity, unreality." This being so, what does he propose as remedies for imposture, unreality, &c.? We come upon two specific remedies hidden away under masses of declamation—emigration and education: emigration—to provide work for industrious men that can get no employment; education—for no stated reason. He simply recommends that "the mystery of alphabetic letter should be imparted to all human souls in this realm." These are his only constructive views in politics, and they can hardly be said to be his. For the rest, through his 'Chartism,' 'Past and Present,' 'Latter-Day Pamphlets,' and incidentally through his other works, he deplores the present state of things, denounces existing Kings, Aristocracies, Churches, and specially declaims against modern political movements. We did wrong to emancipate the negroes; they find the necessaries of life cheap, work little, and let the sugar crops rot. We are too lenient with our criminals (see p. 155). He would take more work out of them. He considers the transaction of Government business to be in a wretched state—hampered by "blind obstructions, fatal indolences, pedantries, stupidities;" the Colonial Office "a world-wide jungle of red-tape, inhabited by doleful creatures." He would have none but men of ability in important posts. He disapproves strongly of Parliaments elected by the people; sneers at voting and "ballot-boxes;" asks whether a crew that settled every movement by voting would be likely to take a ship round Cape Horn. His ideal of government is to have a king (which he is constantly deriving from *Can* through König, and constantly translating "Ableman") at the head of affairs, and capable, obedient officials under him through all degrees of importance. How to realise the ideal he does not show; and, as we have said, he takes no account of the endeavours of human communities towards this ideal, or of the uncontrollable forces that make it an impossibility.

Criticism.—Of literary criticism in the ordinary sense of the word—in the sense of noting faults and merits of style, of showing what to avoid and what to imitate—Carlyle's writings contain next to nothing. He published, as we have seen, under the title of 'Critical and Miscellaneous Essays,' remarks on various great men of letters—German, French, and English. But in these essays he does not occupy himself with style, or with the statement and illustration of critical canons. He deals rather with life, character, and opinions; declaims on his favourite topics—Mystery, Reverence, Industry, Veracity; rails at reviewers, logicians, historical philosophers, sceptical philosophers, atheists, and other favourite objects of aversion. He ranks authors, not according to their literary power, but according to as they possess his cardinal virtues. Goethe and Johnson he extols above measure as being men of power, and, at the same time, industrious, veracious, and reverential towards the mystery of the world. In consideration of this he passes over in Goethe some minor iniquities that elsewhere he condemns in the abstract, and passes over in Johnson what some writers are pleased to call his intolerant prejudices and narrow canons of criticism. Voltaire and Diderot he finds industrious and veracious, but terribly wanting in reverence. Accordingly, he refuses to call them great men—finds in Voltaire *adroitness* rather than greatness, and styles him a master of *persiflage.*

One or two of his precepts may be called literary, though they scarcely belong to minute criticism. He warns writers to beware of affectation; to study reality in their style. One of the chief merits of Burns is his "indisputable air of reality." He further recommends them to write slowly; points out the evils of Sir Walter Scott's extempore speed, and affirms that no great thing was ever done without difficulty. Once more, he stands up for a style that does not show its meaning at once, that becomes intelligible slowly and after much laborious study. On this ground he praises Goethe and Novalis, saying that no good book or good thing of any sort shows itself at first. Still another literary notion, already alluded to, is his idea that, in the present day, men should write prose and not poetry, and history rather than fiction.

ELEMENTS OF STYLE.

Vocabulary.

His command of words must be pronounced to be of the highest order. Among the few that stand next to Shakspeare he occupies a very high place.

As his peculiar feelings are strongly marked, so are the special regions of his verbal copiousness. As a matter of course, he was specially awake to, and specially retained, expressions suiting his peculiar vein of strength, rugged sublimity, and every form of ridicule and contempt down to the lowest tolerable depths of coarseness. It would be interesting to collect the various forms that he uses to express his sense of the confusion, the chaotic disorder, of these latter days. An estimate of his abundance on that or any other of his favourite topics would give the reader the most vivid idea of his lingual resources.

Having a strong natural bent for the study of character, he is a consummate master of the requisite phraseology. In the language needful for describing character, he probably comes nearer Shakspeare than any other of our great writers. To be convinced of this, we have only to look at his opulence in bringing out the leading features of such a man as John Sterling. Between the subjective and the objective side, the language of feeling and the language of gesture and action, he is pretty evenly divided—a master of both vocabularies.

In the use of Latinised terms, as against Saxon, he follows the Shakspearian type of an indifferent mixture. He does not particularly affect either extreme. Often on themes where other writers would use solemn words of Latin origin, he prefers what Leigh Hunt calls a "noble simplicity," and which others would call "profane familiarity;" but he employs liberally the Latinised vocabulary when it suits his purpose. His acquaintance with technical names is considerable. He makes frequent metaphorical and literal application of the language of mathematics and natural philosophy—his favourite studies when a young man. He knew also the vocabulary of several industries, as well as of the social mechanism and institutions.

Two circumstances in particular make his command of acknowledged English appear less than it really is. First, revelling in his immense force of Comparison or Assimilation, he shows a prodigious luxuriance of the figures of similarity—nicknaming personages, applying old terms to new situations, and suchlike. He often substitutes metaphorical for real names when the real are quite sufficient, and perhaps more suitable for the occasion. Now this habit, not to speak of its lowering the value and freshness of his genius by over-doing and over-affecting originality of phrase, often makes it appear as if he did not know the literal and customary names of things, and were driven to make shift with these allusive names. Another circumstance produces the same impression. He is most liberal in his coinage of new words, and even new forms of syntax. For this he was taken to task by his friend John Sterling,[1] part of whose criticism we quote :—

"A good deal of the language is positively barbarous. 'Environment,' 'vestural,' 'stertorous,' 'visualised,' 'complected,' "and others I think to be found in the first thirty pages, are "words, so far as I know, without any authority; some of them "contrary to analogy; and none repaying by their value the disadvantage of novelty. To these must be added new and erroneous locutions: 'whole other tissues' for *all the other*, and similar "uses of the word *whole*; 'orients' for *pearls*; 'lucid' and "'lucent' employed as if they were different in meaning; 'hulls' "perpetually for *coverings*, it being a word hardly used, and then "only for the husk of a nut; 'to insure a man of misapprehension;' "'talented,' a mere newspaper and hustings word, invented, I believe, by O'Connell. I must also mention the constant recurrence of some words in a quaint and queer connection, which "gives a grotesque and somewhat repulsive mannerism to many "sentences. Of these the commonest offender is 'quite;' which "appears in almost every page, and gives at first a droll kind of "emphasis; but soon becomes wearisome. 'Nay,' 'manifold,'

[1] Carlyle's Life of Sterling, 276.

"'cunning enough significance,' 'faculty' (meaning a man's rational "or moral *power*), 'special,' 'not without,' haunt the reader as if "in some uneasy dream, which does not rise to the dignity of "nightmare."

In this passage, which Carlyle himself has given to the world, some of his most striking peculiarities of diction are noticed. To give an adequate view of his verbal eccentricities, would be no small labour. He extends the admitted licences of the language in every direction, using one part of speech for another, verbs for nouns, nouns for verbs, adverbs and adjectives for nouns. His coinages often take the form of new derivatives—"benthamee," "amusee." He abuses the licence of giving plurals to abstract nouns: thus "credibilities," "moralities," "theological philosophies," "transcendentalisms and theologies."

This excess of metaphors, new words, and grammatical licences is in favour of the reader's enjoyment, but not so much in favour of the student's instruction. It belongs to the inimitable, unreproducible part of the style; the student cannot take the same liberties without bearing the charge of copying an individual manner, instead of deriving from the common fund of the language. So far it may stimulate to do likewise in one's own independent sphere; but close imitation is little better than parody, and imitation of any kind runs some danger of ridicule.

Sentences.

In his essays, particularly in the earlier essays and in his 'Life of Schiller,' Carlyle shows none of the irregularity of structure that appears in his matured style. He has an admirable command of ordinary English, and constructs his sentences to suit the motion of a massive and rugged, yet musical rhythm.

Even in his essays, though himself writing with great care, he speaks slightingly of painstaking in the structure of sentences. What he really objects to is making sentences after an artificial model, of a particular length, or with a particular cadence, or with a particular number of members; but he speaks as if he condemned all labour in the arrangement of words, and lays himself open to be quoted by any that would shirk the trouble of making themselves as intelligible as possible to their readers.

The sentences of his later manner we can describe in his own words. Among his editorial remarks on the style of Teufelsdroeckh is the following:—

"Of his sentences perhaps not more than nine-tenths stand straight on their legs; the remainder are in quite angular attitudes, buttressed up by props (of parentheses and dashes), and ever with this or the other tag-rag hanging from them; a few even sprawl out helplessly on all sides, quite broken-backed and dismembered."

From this figurative description one would suppose his sentences to be extremely involved and complicated. As a matter of fact, they are extremely simple in construction — consisting, for the most part, of two or three co-ordinate statements, or of a short direct statement, eked out by explanatory clauses either in apposition or in the "nominative absolute" construction. These apposition and absolute clauses are the "tag-rags," and it is in the connection of them with the main statement that we find the "dashes and parentheses." This character of his sentences is so obvious that few examples will suffice:—

"Whatsoever sensibly exists, whatsoever represents Spirit to Spirit, is properly a Clothing, a suit of Raiment, put on for a season and to be laid off. Thus in this one pregnant subject of CLOTHES, rightly understood, is included all that men have thought, dreamed, done, and been: the whole External Universe and what it holds is but Clothing; and the essence of all Science lies in the PHILOSOPHY OF CLOTHES."

In this explanation of the Philosophy of Clothes, the sentences are free from intricacy. The second sentence exemplifies a very common form with Carlyle in his less irregular moods, although he sneers at some sentence-makers because they are very curious to have their sentence consist of three members; yet he seems to have been himself a lover of this peculiar cadence.

He very often uses the sentence of two members, one explanatory of the other—avoiding the error of joining them by a conjunction. Thus in his description of John Sterling's mother:—

"The mother was a woman of many household virtues; to a warm affection for her children, she joined a degree of taste and intelligence which is of much rarer occurrence."

As examples of his practice of *apposition*, take the following:—

"Biography is by nature the most universally profitable, universally pleasant of all things: especially Biography of distinguished individuals."

Speaking of John Sterling, he says:—

"To the like effect shone something, a kind of childlike, half-embarrassed shimmer of expression, on his fine vivid countenance; curiously mingling with its ardours and audacities."

The Crown-Prince's imprisonment by his father is thus described:—

"Poor Friedrich meanwhile has had a grim time of it these two months back; left alone, in coarse brown prison-dress, within his four bare walls at Cüstrin; in uninterrupted, unfathomable colloquy with the Destinies and the Necessities there."

In the following long sentence abundant use is made both of participle and of nominative absolute:—

"Eminent swill of drinking, with the loud coarse talk supposable, on the part of Mentzel and consorts, did go on, in this manner, all afternoon; in the evening drunk Mentzel came out for air; went strutting and staggering about; emerging finally on the platform of some rampart, face of him huge and red as that of the foggiest rising Moon;—and stood, looking over into the Lorraine Country; belching out a storm of oaths as to his taking it, as to his doing this and that; and was even flourishing his sword by way of accompaniment; when, lo, whistling slightly through the summer air, a rifle-ball from some sentry on the French side (writers say, it was a French drummer, grown impatient, and snatching a sentry's piece) took the brain of him or the belly of him; and he rushed down at once, a totally collapsed monster, and mere heap of dead ruin, never to trouble mankind more."

We have seen that Macaulay's style may in an especial degree be called artificial, inasmuch as he makes prodigal use of special artifices of composition. Carlyle is artificial in a different sense; at least he uses artifices of a different kind. His structure of sentence is extremely loose—is an extravagant antithesis to the periodic. His studied ruggedness and careless cumulative method are incompatible with measured balance of clause or sentence. We may say, with a rough approximation to truth, that Macaulay's artificiality lies in departing from ordinary colloquial structure, Carlyle's in departing from the ordinary structure of written composition.

In his 'Life of Schiller,' and in his earlier essays, Carlyle builds up his composition with elaborate care in the ordinary literary forms. The following periodic sentences are constructed with Johnsonian formality, and with more than Johnsonian elaboration:—

"Could ambition always choose its own path, and were will in human undertakings always synonymous with faculty, all truly ambitious men would be men of letters. Certainly, if we examine that love of power, which enters so largely into most practical calculations—nay, which our Utilitarian friends have recognised as the sole end and origin, both motive and reward, of all earthly enterprises, animating alike the philanthropist, the conqueror, the money-changer, and the missionary—we shall find that all other arenas of ambition, compared with this rich and boundless one of Literature, meaning thereby whatever respects the promulgation of Thought, are poor, limited, and ineffectual. For dull, unreflective, merely instinctive as the ordinary man may seem, he has nevertheless, as a quite indispensable appendage, a head that in some degree considers and computes; a lamp or rushlight of understanding has been given him, which, through whatever dim, besmoked, and strangely diffractive media it may shine, is the ultimate guiding light of his whole path: and here as well as there, now as at all times in man's history, Opinion rules the world."

In this earlier style he sometimes also composes elaborate balanced parallels after the model of Pope's comparison between Homer and Virgil. We quote a short comparison between Alfieri and Schiller, where the imitation of Pope is very apparent:—

"Alfieri and Schiller were again unconscious competitors in the history of Mary Stuart. But the works before us give a truer specimen of their comparative merits. Schiller seems to have the greater genius; Alfieri the more commanding character. Alfieri's greatness rests on the stern concentration of fiery passion, under the dominion of an adamantine will: this was his own make of mind; and he represents it with strokes in themselves devoid of charm, but in their union terrible as a prophetic scroll. Schiller's moral force is commensurate with his intellectual gifts, and nothing more. The mind of the one is like the ocean, beautiful in its strength, smiling in the radiance of summer, and washing luxuriant and romantic shores: that of the other is like some black unfathomable lake placed far amid the melancholy mountains; bleak, solitary, desolate; but girdled with grim sky-piercing cliffs, overshadowed with storms, and illuminated only by the red glare of the lightning. Schiller is magnificent in his expansion, Alfieri is overpowering in his condensed energy; the first inspires us with greater admiration, the last with greater awe."

Paragraphs.

In his more rhapsodical works, such as 'Chartism' and the 'Latter-Day Pamphlets,' he is an indifferent observer of paragraph method. The reader is bewildered by the introduction of reflections without any hint of their bearing on the theme in hand. Some pages remind us of his vivid descriptions of chaotic inundations that hide or sweep away all guiding-posts. Very seldom can we gather from the beginning of a paragraph what is to be its purport. No attempt is made to keep a main subject prominent. Whenever anything occurs to suggest one of his favourite themes of declamation, he embraces the opportunity, and lets his main business drop.

This applies to his "prophetical" utterances, where his great natural clearness both in matter and in manner seems to be abandoned. In his history the case is very different. There his arrangement is almost the perfection of clearness. He is at pains to make everything easy to the reader. When the bearing of a statement is not apparent, he is careful to make it explicit. In each paragraph the main subject is for the most part kept prominent—his defiance of ordinary syntax giving him great facilities for a distinct foreground and background. He begins his paragraphs with some indication of their contents. Further, he is consecutive, and keeps rigidly to the point.

Figures of Speech.

Teufelsdroeckh is made to say, concerning style, that plain words are the skeleton, and metaphors [1] "the muscles and tissues and living integuments;" further, that his own style is "not without an apoplectic tendency."

This might be quoted against Carlyle's own dictum, that "genius is unconscious of its excellence." His profusion of figurative language is perhaps the most striking monument of his originality and power.

[1] Metaphor is here probably used for "trope," as that word is defined in the Introduction.

Figures of Similarity.—His similitudes, forcibly hunted out from every region of his knowledge of nature and of books, are not merely fanciful embellishments—most of them go to the making of his vivid powers of description. The character, or personal appearance, or action of an individual; the character of a nation, a state of society, a political situation; the relative position of two belligerents,—everything, in short, that needs describing, he brings vividly before us in its leading features by some significant simile or metaphor.

This wealth of illustration is very noticeable in the description of character. For every personage of marked character he exerts himself to find a vivid similitude. "Acrid, corrosive, as the spirit of sloes and copperas, is Marat, Friend of the People." Lafayette is "a thin constitutional Pedant; clear, thin, inflexible, as water turned to thin ice, whom no Queen's heart can love." The Countess of Darlington, George I.'s fat mistress, is "a cataract of tallow, with eyebrows like a cart-wheel, and dim coaly disks for eyes." She is contrasted with the Duchess of Kendal, the lean mistress, "poor old anatomy or lean human nailrod."

Every kind of situation, individual or social, is set forth in the same way. The 'French Revolution' is a blazing heap of similitudes; they meet us at every page in twos and threes. They are often very homely. The following, taken at random, are tolerably fair specimens:—

"Your Revolution, like jelly sufficiently boiled, needs only to be poured into shapes of Constitution, and 'consolidated' therein."

"Military France is everywhere full of sour inflammatory humour, which exhales itself fuliginously, this way or that; a whole continent of smoking flax, which, blown on here or there by any angry wind, might so easily start into a blaze, into a continent of fire."

"Such Patriotism as snarls dangerously and shows teeth, Patrollotism shall suppress; or, far better, Royalty shall soothe down the anger of it by gentle pattings, and, most effectual of all, by fuller diet."

The History of Friedrich is illuminated no less effectively. He speaks incidently of the French Revolution as—

"That whirlwind of the universe—lights obliterated—and the torn wrecks of Earth and Hell hurled aloft into the Empyrean—black whirlwind which made even apes serious, and drove most of them mad."

The above is a characteristic figure. The following, along with a characteristic similitude, introduces one of his favourite personifications:—

"As the History of Friedrich, in this Cüstrin epoch, and indeed in all epochs and parts, is still little other than a whirlpool of simmering confusions, dust mainly, and sibylline paper-shreds, in the pages of poor Dryasdust, perhaps we cannot do better than snatch a shred or two (of the partly legible kind, or capable of being made legible) out of that hideous caldron;

pin them down at their proper dates; and try if the reader can, by such means, catch a glimpse of the thing with his own eyes."

His account of old Friedrich's violence to young Friedrich upon the attempted "desertion," is a fair sample of his figurative manner at its acme:—

"Friedrich Wilhelm's conduct, looked at from without, appears that of a hideous royal ogre, or blind anthropophagous Polyphemus fallen mad. Looked at from within, where the Polyphemus has his reasons, and a kind of inner rushlight to enlighten his path, and is not bent on man-eating, but on discipline in spite of difficulties,—it is a wild enough piece of humanity, not so much ludicrous as tragical. Never was a royal bear so led about before by a pair of conjuring pipers in the market, or brought to such a pass in his dancing for them."

Two other things must be noticed before we have a complete idea of his employment of similitudes. One is a habit, already partially alluded to, of keeping up descriptive metaphors, and using them instead of the literal names, or along with the literal names as a kind of permanent Homeric epithet. Thus, he never mentions the Countess of Darlington without designating her as the "cataract of tallow;" or the Duchess of Kendal without something equivalent to "Maypole or lean human nailrod." The other noticeable thing is his frequent repetition, with or without variations, of certain favourite figures. Perhaps the most characteristic is his stock of metaphors and similes drawn from the great features of the material world to illustrate the moral; his "pole-star veiled by thick clouds," his earthquakes, mad foam-oceans, Noah's deluge, mud-deluges, cesspools of the Universe, Pythons, Megatheriums, Chimæras, Dead-Sea Apes, and suchlike.

He has also certain favourite *personifications*, which are made to do a great deal of service. Such are the Destinies, the Necessities, the dumb Veracities, the Eternal Voices, Fact, Nature, all which are so many synonyms for the homely phrase, "circumstances beyond our control." We have seen that when Friedrich was shut up alone at Cüstrin, he was left in "colloquy with the Destinies and the Necessities there." In another passage he is said to be "shut out from the babble of fools, and conversing only with the dumb Veracities, with the huge inarticulate moanings of Destiny, Necessity, and Eternity." When he submits to his father, he is said to be "loyal to Fact," which means that he yields to what he cannot overcome. In like manner, Democracy, "the grand, alarming, imminent, indisputable Reality," is "the inevitable Product of the Destinies:" whoever refuses to recognise that the world has come to this, is "disloyal to Fact." "All thinking men, and good citizens of their country," "have an ear for the small still voices and eternal intimations;" in other words, discern the best course that circumstances will admit of. "The eternal regulations of the Universe," "the monition of the gods in regard to our affairs," "which, if a man know, it is well with him," are other figurative expressions to the same effect.

One of Carlyle's favourite inferior personages is Dryasdust, whom we have already introduced. He represents any and every historian that takes an interest in what our author finds it convenient to pronounce "dry." He is abused sometimes for knowing Rymer's 'Fœdera' and India Bills, sometimes for knowing Court gossip. He is one of Carlyle's standing butts.

Figures of Contiguity.—If we apply this designation to every case of indicating a thing, not by its literal name, but by use of expressive parts and expressive collaterals, Carlyle luxuriates in such figures as much as in figures of similarity.

To take an instance: his metonymies for Death are as numerous as Homer's. "The all-hiding earth has received him." "Low now is Jourdan the Headsman's own head." "So dies a gigantic Heathen and Titan; stumbling blindly, undismayed, down to his rest. . . . His suffering and his working are now ended." "These also roll their fated journey." Danton "passes to his unknown home." "Our grim good-night to thee is that" (address to the German scoundrel upon his execution).

As with similitudes, so with choice circumstances, he has a way of repeating them, keeping them under the reader's notice, as often as he mentions the subject. Thus, in his pamphlet on "The Nigger Question," he is perpetually renewing the image of the "beautiful blacks sitting up to their beautiful muzzles in pumpkins." In the pamphlet on "The Present Time," he repeatedly presents the reforming Pope as "the good Pope with the New Testament in his hand." In like manner he takes hold of a title or expression that provokes his mirth, and turns it to ridicule by frequent repetition; thus he talks of Parliament as the "Collective wisdom."

Figures of Contrast are not a marked feature in his style. He has a sense of the effect of explicit contrast, and sometimes employs it as a means of strength; but his studied effects are not in the direction of sharp antithetical point.

He makes considerable use of the telling oratorical contrast, the juxtaposition of strikingly incongruous circumstances. In his Essay on Voltaire he contrasts the blazing glory of Tamerlane with the humble industry of Johannes Faust, the inventor of movable types; pointing out that the humble man's influence was in the end much the more powerful of the two. So he contrasts the loud triumphant proclamation of the Champs de Mars Federation with the signing of the Scottish Solemn League and Covenant in a dingy close of the Edinburgh High Street, and with "the frugal supper of thirteen mean-dressed men in a mean Jewish dwelling." The 'French Revolution' is peculiarly rich in such contrasts. He makes a fine thing of Robespierre's resigning a judgeship in his younger days because he could not bear to sentence a human creature to death. The sad end of Marie Antoinette is contrasted with her prosperous days; the tragic heroism of Charlotte Corday is made more touching by a fine description of her personal beauty. And in the "sports of fickle fortune" with many of the leading revolutionists, he finds the utmost scope for Rembrandt lights and shadows.

Epigram is not much in his way. He occasionally indulges in word-play, but it is hardly epigrammatic; it has more of an affinity with punning. His oft-repeated derivation of king—"*Kön-ning*, Can-ning, or Man that is Able"—is a mixture of philology and pun. Some of his puns are less doubtful. Thus, "Certain Heathen Physical-Force Ultra-Chartists, 'Danes' as they were then called, coming into his territory with their 'five points,' or rather with their five-and-twenty thousand *points* and edges too—of pikes, namely, and battle-axes," &c. So he says that the Lancashire and Yorkshire factories are a monument to Richard Arkwright, "a true *pyr*amid or *flame*-mountain."

Minor Figures and Figures Proper. Hyperbole.—Our author's hyperboles consist partly in the use of exaggerating similitudes, partly in unrestrained torrents of extreme epithets. His exaggerations as to the confusion and dishonesty of these "latter-days," the general tumble-down and degradation of the whole system of modern society, are the most familiar specimens. "Days of endless calamity, disruption, dislocation, confusion worse confounded." "Bankruptcy everywhere; foul ignominy, and the abomination of desolation, in all high places." "Social affairs in a state of the frightfulest embroilment, and as it were of inextricable final bankruptcy, unutterable welter of tumbling ruins." "Never till now, I think, did the sun look down on such a jumble of human nonsenses." He is conscious of this hyperbolic turn, as, indeed, he shows himself conscious of most of his peculiarities. He speaks of Teufelsdroeckh's having "unconscionable habits of exaggeration in speech."

When strong epithets, metaphors, similes, and contrasts, put in plain forms of speech, come short of the intensity of his feelings, he avails himself to an unprecedented degree of the bolder licences of style. Much of his peculiar manner is made up of the special figures of Interrogation, Exclamation, and Apostrophe.

Interrogation is a large element in his mannerism. It is not merely an occasional means of special emphasis; it is a habitual mode of transition, used by Carlyle almost universally for the vivid introduction of new agents and new events. Thus—

"But on the whole, Paris, we may see, will have little to devise; will only have to borrow and apply. And then, as to the day, what day of all the calendar is fit, if the Bastille Anniversary be not?"

After the Queen's execution, he asks, "Whom next, O Tinville?"

In like manner, recounting some of the proceedings in the Parliamentary war, he says—

"Basing is black ashes, then: and Langford is ours, the Garrison 'to march forth to-morrow at twelve of the clock, being the 18th instant.' And now the question is, Shall we attack Dennington or not?"

With these vivid epic interrogations, there is usually, as in the above examples, a mixture of something like the figure called *Vision*. He supposes himself present at the deliberation of a scheme, the preparation of a great event, and suggests ideas as an interested spectator. Thus, after representing how Louis deliberated whether he should try to conciliate the people, or canvass for foreign assistance, he asks—"Nay, are the two hopes inconsistent?" Again, he apostrophises the National Assembly expecting a visit from the King, with—

"Think therefore, Messieurs, what it may mean; especially how ye will get the Hall decorated a little. . . . Some fraction of velvet carpet, cannot that be spread in front of the chair, where the Secretaries usually sit?"

One or two instances give but a faint impression of what is so prominent in his style.

Exclamation occurs in every mood. Sometimes in wonder and elation; sometimes in derision and contempt; sometimes in pity, sometimes in fun, sometimes in real admiration and affection. An example or two may be quoted. Thus—"How thou fermentest and elaboratest, in thy great fermenting-vat and laboratory of an Atmosphere, of a World, O Nature!" Many such exclamations of wonder occur in his Sartor. His exclamations of derision are addressed, not to individuals, but to imaginary personages, as when he addresses Dryasdust,—"Surely at least you might have made an index for these books;" or to collective masses, as when he exclaims of duellists—"Deuce on it, the little spitfires!" Towards individuals he seldom if ever expresses either reverential wonder on the one hand, or contempt on the other. The scenes of the French Revolution often call forth exclamations of pity and horror. "Miserable De Launay!" "Hapless Deshuttes and Varigny!"—such expressions are frequent. At times, also, we come across such exclamations as—"Horrible, in lands that had known equal justice!" As an instance of a humorous touch, take his exclamation on one of the Kaisers—"Poor soul, he had six-and-twenty children by one wife; and felt that there was need of appanages!" His expressions of admiration for his heroes are numerous. On Mirabeau he exclaims—"Rare union: this man can live self-sufficing—yet lives also in the lives of other men; can make men love him, work with him; a born king of men!" Of Sterling he says—"A beautiful childlike soul!" Oliver and Friedrich he frequently salutes with expressions of sympathising admiration. Sometimes, as he has a habit of doing with all his strong effects—in a kind of deprecating way—he puts the exclamations into the mouths of other people—"'Admirable feat of strategy! What a general, this Prince Carl!' exclaimed mankind." "'Magnanimous!' exclaim Noailles and the paralysed French gentleman: 'Most maganimous behaviour on his Prussian Majesty's part!' own they."

Apostrophe.—The apostrophising habit is perhaps the greatest notability of his mannerism. His make of mind impels him to adopt this art of style, apart from his consciousness of the power it gives him as a literary artist. It provides one outlet among others for his deep-seated dramatic tendency. Farther, it suits his active turn of mind and favourite mode of the enjoyment of power; it gives scope for his daring familiarity with personages, whether for admiration or for humour, and meets with no check from any regard for offended conventionalities. Not so frequently does he address in tones of pity; still, in the moving scenes of the French Revolution, and elsewhere, some of his apostrophes are very touching.

His style in its final development affords innumerable examples. The 'French Revolution' is particularly full of dramatic apostrophes, as indeed of the irregular figures generally. The author sees everything with his own eyes, and addresses the actors in warning, exhortation, reproof, or whatever their actions call for. Usher Maillard is shown crossing the Bastille ditch on a plank, and warned—"Deftly, thou shifty Usher: one man already fell; and lies smashed, far down there, against the masonry!" When De Launay is massacred, the revolutionists are reproved with—"Brothers, your wrath is cruel!" "Up and be doing!" "Courage!" "Quick, then!" Such ejaculations are frequent; to every movement, in fact, he contributes the cries of an excited bystander.

As an example of his more declamatory apostrophes, take the following, which is indeed an imaginary speech:—

"Away, you! begone swiftly, ye regiments of the line! in the name of God and of His poor struggling servants, sore put to it to live in these bad days, I mean to rid myself of you with some degree of brevity. To feed you in palaces, to hire captains, and schoolmasters, and the choicest spiritual and material artificers to expend their industries on you,—No, by the Eternal! . . . Mark it, my diabolic friends, I mean to lay leather on the backs of you," &c.

The following is an example of his pathetic apostrophes. In the destruction of the Bastille a prisoner's letter was discovered with a passionate inquiry after his wife, to which Carlyle replies:—

"Poor prisoner, who namest thyself *Quéret-Démery*, and hast no other history,—she is *dead*, that dear wife of thine, and thou art dead! 'Tis fifty years since thy breaking heart put this question; to be heard now first, and long heard, in the hearts of men."

His characteristic manner of drawing the attention of the hearer with an imperative, is a mode of apostrophe—

"Now, therefore, judge if our patriot artists are busy; taking deep counsel how to make the scene worthy of a look from the universe."

It will have been noted that many of the above-quoted apostrophes are of the nature of the figure called *Vision*. Carlyle's histories are, indeed, prolonged visions; throughout he treats the past as present, and makes us, as it were, actual spectators of the events related.

His *irony* is a department in itself. It often turns up in such passing touches as—"Our Nell Gwyn defender-of-the-faith;" "Christ's crown soldered on Charles Stuart's;" "most Christian kingship, and most Talleyrand bishopship;" Shakspeare, "whom Sir Thomas Lucy, *many thanks to him*, was for sending to the treadmill." In his treatment of modern society, irony is often kept up through long passages; thus "The Nigger Question" is full of irony. It is to be noted that his irony can always be known as such. He has none of the De Foe irony that runs a danger of being mistaken for earnest. The following is a short specimen, on the New Poor-Law, from 'Chartism':—

"To read the reports of the Poor-Law Commissioners, if one had faith enough, would be a pleasure to the friend of humanity. One sole recipe seems to have been needful for the woes of England—'refusal of outdoor relief.' England lay in sick discontent, writhing powerless on its fever-bed, dark, nigh desperate, in wastefulness, want, improvidence, and eating care, till, like Hyperion down[1] the eastern steeps, the Poor-Law Commissioners arose, and said, Let there be workhouses, and bread of affliction and water of affliction there! It was a simple invention; as all truly great inventions are. And see, in any quarter, instantly as the walls of the workhouse arise, misery and necessity fly away, out of sight, out of being, as is fondly hoped, dissolve into the inane; industry, frugality, fertility, rise of wages, peace on earth and goodwill towards men do,—in the Poor-Law Commissioners' reports,—infallibly, rapidly or not so rapidly, to the joy of all parties, supervene."

QUALITIES OF STYLE.

Simplicity.

(1.) Our author, as we remarked in speaking of his vocabulary, uses a fair admixture of homely words. When hard to under-

[1] "Down" is a small blunder; it should be *up*.

stand, he is so not from the use of technical and scholastic terms, but from the use of words of his own coining. A reader of Carlyle, not knowing Latin, has often to consult a dictionary, and consults it in vain. It is a jest about him that he aspires to the honour conferred upon Jean Paul Richter, of having a dictionary written for himself.

As regards his similitudes, we have already seen that many of them are homely and graphic, while the few stock figures connected with his fanciful conception of the universe, the action of the Destinies, Eternal Voices, and suchlike, rather perplex than render comprehension easy. It should, however, be noticed, that to those once initiated into the circle of these figures they present a really simple, because very undiscriminating, way of expressing complicated circumstances. "Loyalty to facts" becomes a very glib figure to those that have once mastered its meaning.

His sentence-structure is favourable to simplicity, being free from involution and intricacy. The want of concatenation and consecutiveness mars, as has been said, the intelligibility of his rhapsodical 'Pamphlets' and his 'French Revolution.' These drawbacks do not occur so much in the Friedrich.

(2.) His subjects are far from abstruse, being narratives and familiar questions of practice. The difficulty of the 'Sartor Resartus' is due, not so much to the nature of the subject, as to the intentional mystification, and the substitution of allusions and figures for plain statements. If it were stript of its gorgeous imagery and "boiled down," the residuum would probably be more intelligible than interesting.

(3.) Occasionally, for the sake of effects of comprehensive strength, he uses abstract expressions; but his diction is upon the whole concrete to a degree rarely found among writers of prose. Even when he uses abstractions, he violates grammar (p. 146) to give them plurals, and thereby treat them as class names; he vivifies some of them further (p. 151) by treating them as personalities. His love of the concrete often appears in his repeating a number of suggestive particulars or circumstances instead of one general designation. Thus, in his 'Chartism,' when discussing the discontent of the working classes, he refers to it again and again by mentioning significant symptoms—"Glasgow Thuggery, Chartist torch-meetings, Birmingham riots, Swing conflagrations;" or again, "Chartism with its pikes, Swing with his tinder-box." When he has to state his conviction that much misery is caused by poor Irish labourers finding no work in Ireland, and coming to England in search of it, he does so in very picturesque terms:—

"But the thing we had to state here was our inference from that mournful fact of the third Sanspotatoe, coupled with this other well-known fact, that the Irish speak a partially intelligible dialect of English, and their fare across by steam is fourpence sterling! Crowds of miserable Irish darken all our towns. The wild Milesian features, looking false ingenuity, restlessness, unreason, misery, and mockery, salute you on all highways and byways. The English coachman, as he whirls past, lashes the Milesian with his whip, curses him with his tongue: the Milesian is holding out his hat to beg."

When he desires a more comprehensive effect, he personifies this influx of Irish destitution under the name of the Irish giant Despair, and thus describes him:—

"I notice him in Piccadilly, blue-visaged, thatched in rags, a blue child on each arm; hunger-driven, wide-mouthed, seeking whom he may devour."

With regard to this picturesque statement, the remark may be made that, while each particular is immediately and easily understood, it may be doubted whether the meaning that the writer professedly wishes to convey is so easily apprehended as it would be in the driest general statement. Upon the whole, this excess of concreteness is perhaps not in favour of our understanding the general drift, but the reverse. Most readers complain that Carlyle is bewildering in his prophetical utterances. The excess of figures and the absence of plain generalities is perhaps partly the cause. Let any reader of ordinary analytic power try, after reading 'Chartism,' to recall the train of argument, and he will find his confused recollection of individually vivid figures rather against than in favour of the effort.

Clearness.

Perspicuity.—In his expressly didactic or prophetic works, he shows, as we have seen, little concern to impart his views without confusion. Nor are his essays so perspicuous as the essays of Macaulay. The History of Friedrich is, however (see p. 170), a clearer narrative than the 'History of England;' it lifts us more above the confusion of details by means of comprehensive summaries and divisions with descriptive titles, and it brings leading events into stronger relief by assigning to subordinate events a subordinate place in the narrative.

Precision.—He is not an exact writer. Hating close analysis, his aim always is to give the broad general features rather than the minute details. He has little of the hair-splitting, dividing and distinguishing mania of De Quincey; no desire to sift his opinions on a topic, and say distinctly what they are and what they are not. Some idea of the difference between them in this respect is obtained by comparing Carlyle's various lucubrations on Jean Paul Richter with De Quincey's article on the same subject. But we see the utter antagonism of manner as regards precision at its height when we reflect how De Quincey would have treated such a subject as the discontent of the working classes. If Carlyle had been at pains to reduce his political views to distinct heads as De Quincey would have done, one would have been better able to judge of their universally alleged poverty.

Strength.

We have already touched on a good many of the peculiarities of Carlyle's singular force of style. The language that Sterling calls "positively barbarous"—the rugged derivatives and quaint solecisms—is very stimulating when it is intelligible. Among his figures of speech we meet with many elements of strength—powerful and original similitudes, bold metaphors, vivid handling of abstractions, choice of telling circumstances, sensational contrasts, habitual exaggeration of language, and daring liberties with ordinary forms of speech. Here we have for the production of telling literary effects a catalogue of instrumentalities that will hardly be paralleled from any writer after Shakspeare. And this is not all. The comprehensive summaries, already mentioned as his principal instruments of perspicuity, embracing as they do a great range of particulars, more than any other of his arts, lift up and dilate the mind with a feeling of extended power.

The crowning feat of strength is the combination of circumstances in effective groups—the imagination of impressive situations. Carlyle's power in this respect is nearly, if not quite, equal to Shakspeare's—equal, that is, in degree, though not perhaps in kind. It was first revealed in his 'Sartor Resartus'; and none of his later works surpass this first great production in the imagination of rugged grandeur. Take, for example, his picture of "Teufelsdroeckh at the North Pole":—

"More legitimate and decisively authentic is Teufelsdroeckh's appearance and emergence (we know not well whence) in the solitude of the North Cape, on that June Midnight. He has a 'light-blue Spanish cloak' hanging round him, as his 'most commodious, principal, indeed sole upper-garment;' and stands there on the World-promontory, looking over the infinite Brine, like a little blue Belfry (as we figure), now motionless indeed, yet ready, if stirred, to ring quaintest changes.

"'Silence as of death,' writes he; 'for Midnight, even in the Arctic latitudes, has its character: nothing but the granite cliffs ruddy-tinged, the peaceable gurgle of that slow-heaving Polar Ocean, over which in the utmost North the great Sun hangs low and lazy, as if he too were slumbering. Yet is his cloud-couch wrought of crimson and cloth-of-gold; yet does his light stream over the mirror of waters, like a tremulous fire-pillar, shooting downwards to the abyss, and hide itself under my feet. In such moments, Solitude also is invaluable; for who would speak, or be looked on, when behind him lies all Europe and Africa, fast asleep, except the watchmen; and before him the silent Immensity, and Palace of the Eternal, whereof our Sun is but a porch-lamp?'"

Another fair specimen of his combining power is seen in Teufelsdroeckh's "own ideas with respect to duels." This also shows a spice of cynicism:—

"Few things, in this so surprising world, strike me with more surprise. Two little visual Spectra of men, hovering with insecure cohesion in the midst of the UNFATHOMABLE, and to dissolve therein, at any rate, very soon,—make pause at the distance of twelve paces asunder; whirl round; and, simultaneously by the cunningest mechanism, explode one another into Dissolution; and off-hand become Air, and Non-extant! Deuce on it (*verdammt*), the little spitfires!—Nay, I think with old Hugo von Trimberg: 'God must needs laugh outright, could such a thing be, to see His wondrous Manikins here below!'"

In one of his later Miscellanies, iv. 315, there is a "Fragment on Duelling" (of date 1850), where the actual fights are described with startling spirit, and the surroundings drawn with almost incomparable power. This also is a good specimen of his style.

Let us take a brief glance at the principal themes or occasions that excite his powers of gorgeous expression. (1.) He puts forth all his powers to extol his favourite recipes for clearing the world of confusion. One or two fragments of such eloquence have been already given. Above all, he is ever on the watch for an opportunity of enforcing his gospel of Work, the panacea which alone brings order out of confusion, cosmos out of chaos. Such passages as the following may be described as "bracing." The general effect of such a gospel is to exalt the sense of active vigour, to disturb, if not dispel, the indolent mood compatible with adoring reverence or tender sentiment:—

"Any law, however well meant as a law, which has become a bounty on unthrift, idleness, bastardy, and beer-drinking, must be put an end to. In all ways it needs, especially in these times, to be proclaimed aloud that for the idle man there is no place in this England of ours. He that will not work, and save according to his means, let him go elsewhither; let him know that for him the Law has made no soft provision, but a hard and stern one; that, by the Law of Nature, which the law of England would vainly contend against in the long-run, *he* is doomed either to quit these habits, or miserably be extruded from this earth, which is made on principles different from these. . . . A day is ever struggling forward, a day will arrive in some approximate degree, when he who has no work to do, by whatever name he may be named, will not find it good to show himself in our quarter of the solar system."

His eulogy of the heroes, the men that he pronounces to have done genuine work in the world, has the same bracing tone. Prostrate adoration, as we have seen, does not suit his temperament; he "fraternises" with the heroes, holds up them and their works as patterns to all men of the heroic mould. True, he commands the multitude to worship, and declaims against them if they refuse; but he is rarely found in the adoring attitude himself.

(2.) Perhaps his richest vein is his unmeasured invective against everything that defeats the hero's efforts to redress the universal confusion, and his overcharged pictures of that confusion. He does not assail individuals for single acts—*that* would have a narrow and rancorous effect. When an offender crosses his path, he denounces him not personally, but as one of "the Devil's Regiment," as adding his little contribution to the "bellowing chaos," "the wide weltering confusion." Most of his stormy warfare of words is directed against the evils of this life gathered up under abstractions familiar to the most incidental reader of his books—Shams, Unveracities, Speciosities, Phantasms, and suchlike. We must be content for examples with fragments already quoted. (See pp. 140, 153).

(3.) He describes with fearful power the grand operations of Nature in her terrible aspects. He is not insensible to beneficent grandeurs, but his temperament inclines him more to the gloomy side—to the "tropical tornado" more than to the "rainbow and orient colours." At times he represents that a God, an Order, a Justice, presides over the "wild incoherent waste;" that to a man understanding the Sphinx riddle (another variety for the "eternal regulations of the Universe"), Nature is "of womanly celestial loveliness and tenderness;" that "Nature, Universe, Destiny, Existence, however we name this grand unnameable fact in the midst of which we live and struggle, is as a heavenly bride and conquest to the wise and brave." But on this aspect of Nature he dwells less than on the opposite. More often "the wild Universe storms in on Man infinite, vague-menacing." It is on this aspect of the Universe that he has accumulated his "Titanic" grandeurs of expression.

As an example of his luxurious revelling in "sulphur, smoke, and flame," may be quoted the following from his 'Chartism':—

"It is in Glasgow among that class of operatives that 'Number 60,' in his dark room, pays down the price of blood. Be it with reason or with unreason, too surely they do in verity find the time all out of joint; this world for them no home, but a dingy prison-house, of reckless unthrift, rebellion, rancour, indignation against themselves and against all men. Is it a green flowery world, with azure everlasting sky stretched over it, the work and government of a God; or a murky, simmering Tophet, of copperas-fumes, cotton-fuz, gin-riot, wrath and toil, created by a Demon, governed by a Demon? The sum of their wretchedness, merited and unmerited, welters, huge, dark, and baleful, like a Dantean Hell, visible there in the statistics of Gin; Gin, justly named the most authentic incarnation of the Infernal Principle in our times, too indisputably an incarnation; Gin, the black throat into which wretchedness of every sort, consummating itself by calling on Delirium to help it, whirls down; abdication of the power to think or resolve, as too painful now, on the part of men whose lot of all others would require thought and resolution: liquid Madness sold at tenpence the quartern, all the products of which are and must be, like its origin, mad, miserable, ruinous, and that only! If from this black, unluminous, unheeded *inferno*, and prison-house of souls in pain, there do flash up from time to time some dismal widespread glare of Chartism or the like, notable to all, claiming remedy from all," &c.

Pathos.

Carlyle's writings are not without gleams of pathos, all the more touching from the surrounding ruggedness. A man of strong special affections, he dwells with most moving tenderness on the life and character of his friends Edward Irving and John Sterling. To his heroes—Mirabeau, Cromwell, Friedrich, Burns—he seems to have been bound by something of the same personal attachment; and he records their death as with the deep sorrow of a surviving friend.

He often waxes wroth with "puking and sprawling Sentimentalism;" and the thought of human misery seems usually to rouse his indignation against idleness as the cause of misery, and to excite him to a more vehement enforcement of his panacea, the gospel of Work. Yet sometimes the thought of human misery does unnerve him, and throw him into the melting mood. Thus, when he stands with Teufelsdroeckh in the porch of the "Sanctuary of Sorrow," he cries:—

"Poor, wandering, wayward man! Art thou not tried, and beaten with stripes, even as I am? Ever, whether thou bear the royal mantle or the beggar's gabardine, art thou not so weary, so heavy-laden? and thy Bed of Rest is but a Grave. O my Brother, my Brother! why cannot I shelter thee in my bosom, and wipe away all tears from thy eyes?"

His most characteristic pathos is his subdued sorrow at the irresistible progress of time. The tired labourer mourns wearily that he can do so little, that time is so short. This weary feeling often crosses his page. "Agamemnon, the many Agamemnons, Pericleses, and their Greece; all is gone now to some ruined fragments—dumb, mournful wrecks and blocks." Jocelin of Brakelond is "one other of those vanished existences whose work is not yet vanished; almost a pathetic phenomenon, were not the whole world full of such!" So (to give one more example) he moralises as follows on the glimpse of Cromwell's cousin in one of the Letters:—

"Mrs St John came down to breakfast every morning in that summer visit of the year 1638, and Sir William said grave grace, and they spake polite devout things to one another; and they are vanished, they and their things and speeches,—all silent, like the echoes of the old nightingales that sang that season, like the blossoms of the old roses. O Death! O Time!"

The Ludicrous.

His sense of the ludicrous runs riot; it may be said to be present everywhere in his writings. When not absolutely predominant, it makes itself felt as a condiment, adding a grotesque flavour even to his serious declamations. A few modes of the quality may be specified:—

(1.) His cyncism.—While he often dilates on the grandeurs of human destiny, he not unfrequently sneers at mankind with dry contempt. It is not the fierce cynicism of Timon; he is too magnanimous for that. He surveys mankind from an Olympian height, and is tickled by their doings. See the "little spitfires" and "manikins" in the passage on duels, p. 160. Compare also this godlike cynicism with the despondency of Hamlet. To Hamlet the world is "a sterile promontory," "a pestilent congregation of vapours;" to Teufelsdroeckh in certain moments the world seems "a paltry dog's cage."

(2.) His derision is, however, usually more boisterous, less notably *dry*. He is not personal and rancorous; he does not rail against individuals. His favourite butts are certain abstractions, institutions, and opinions; a whole pandemonium of Shams,—sham Authorities, sham secretaries of the Pedant species, &c.—"vile age of Pinchbeck," "wild Anarchy and Phallus-Worship;" the Church, Parliament, Downing Street, galvanised Catholicism, Kings, Aristocracy; Reform movements, Exeter Hall Philanthropic movements, Puseyism, Logic, Political Economy, Benthamee Radicalism, Leading Articles. In truth, he seems to dislike all existing institutions and all existing opinions, with the exception of one set. He has thus absolutely unlimited scope for his riotous derisive humour; his field is the world. And it cannot be denied that he turns his position to the best account.

One of his most characteristic proceedings is to heap contemptuous nicknames upon the object of his dislike. His command of language here stands him in good stead. See his "Nigger Question," "The Dismal Science," "Pig-Philosophy," "Horsehair and Bombazeen Procedure." Any page of his declamations on modern society will give abundance of examples. Another favourite device is to set up representative men with ridiculous names, as M'Croudy, the Right Honourable Zero, the Hon. Hickory Buckskin, the Duke of Trumps, and many others, not to mention the unquenchable Dryasdust.

It is to be observed that whether his ridicule be quiet or boisterous, the absence of personal spleen makes it essentially humorous, not vindictive, bitter, rancorous. The man places himself at such a height above other mortals, and is so sublimely confident in his views, that difference of opinion rather amuses than provokes him, and leaves him free to turn his opponent into ridicule "without any ill feeling."

(3.) In his *apostrophes* we have seen what humorous liberties he takes with individuals. In all these ludicrous degradations there is a redeeming touch of kindness. The kindness is always there, whatever be the form of it — whether grim, grotesque, whimsical, or playfully affectionate. Even towards scoundrels of easy morality, like *Wilhelmus Sacrista* in 'Past and Present,' he shows some relenting when they come before him in their personality as individuals. Poor William, given to "libations and *tacenda*," is deposed by Abbot Samson, and, in spite of all his idleness, gets from our author the following kindly parting:—

"Whether the poor Wilhelmus did not still, by secret channels, occasionally get some slight wetting of vinous or alcoholic liquor,—now grown, in a manner, indispensable to the poor man? — Jocelin hints not; one knows not how to hope, what to hope! But if he did, it was in silence and darkness; with an ever-present feeling that teetotalism was his only true course."

His nicknames for individuals are moderated to the same kindly tone of humour. Karl August is very objectionable in the abstract; yet Carlyle gives him no harder nickname than "August the Physically Strong;" and in his older days, "August the Dilapidated-Strong."

(4.) In his 'Sartor Resartus,' and elsewhere, he shows himself capable of the humour of driving fun at himself. The chapter on Editorial Difficulties is a sample. The humour is much more self-asserting than De Quincey's; it amounts in substance to this, that he fathers his most extravagant eccentricities upon a feigned name, and criticises them from an ordinary point of view — a device for stating, without the appearance of extravagance, opinions that the general public might think bombastic were they delivered in the author's own person.

(5.) In a writer of such brilliant execution as Carlyle, the quality of the humour is much enhanced by the pleasure arising from the freshness of the language. When the ludicrous overthrow of dignitaries would otherwise be apt to raise serious feelings, the enjoyment of the language is conciliating, and disposes the reader to laugh rather than be angry.

Melody—Harmony—Taste.

As respects the melodious combination of words, Carlyle, though not below average, is by no means a model. He despises all study to avoid harsh successions; he considers such art to be mere trifling in the present age. In his own attempts to "sing"—that is, to write verses before he fully discovered that his strength lay in prose—the rhythm is conspicuously bad.

Still his prose has a peculiar strain—a characteristic movement. From such passages as have been given, the reader with an ear for cadence will have no difficulty in making it out. It corresponds to the emphatic sing-song intonation of his voice; a stately sort of rhythm, after a fashion of stateliness that differs from De Quincey's in the rugged unmelodious flow, and the frequent recurrence of emphasis.

As regards *Harmony* between the rhythm and the sense, with Carlyle, as with other impassioned writers, the agreement is most perfect when he is writing at full swing in his favourite mood.

He has an ostensible and paraded contempt for the idea of art, or of composition intended to please. Himself nothing if not artistical, he insists on being supposed to wear no garb but the mantle of the prophet. Though thus formally disavowing art, he really does, consciously or unconsciously, sacrifice even truth to be artistical. Not to review him as an artist, is to do him an injustice.—As an artist, he errs chiefly in carrying his favourite effects to excess.

In the pursuit of strength, he sometimes intrudes expressions that approach the confines of rant. Thus, in the following extract he ruins a passage of real pathos with one of his extravagantly sensational mannerisms :—

"For twenty generations here was the earthly arena where powerful living men worked out their life-wrestle,—looked at by Earth, Heaven, and Hell. Bells tolled to prayers; and men, of many humours, various thoughts, chanted vespers, matins;—and round the little islet of their life rolled for ever (as round ours still rolls, though we are blind and deaf) the illimitable Ocean, tinting all things with *its* eternal hues and reflexes; making strange prophetic music! How silent now! all departed, clean gone. The World-Dramaturgist has written, *Exeunt*. The devouring Time-Demons have made away with it all: and in its stead, there is either nothing; or what is worse, offensive universal dust-clouds, and grey eclipse of Earth and Heaven, from 'dry rubbish shot here.'"

From this passage, which opens with such beauty, common taste would probably banish the World-Dramaturgist and the Time-Demons; and the concluding expression would generally be regarded as the unseasonable mirth of excitement gone beyond control. One class of his offences, then, may be set down to the temporary dulling of the artistic sense by over-excitement.

Farther, his humour betrays him into violations of taste. This is done deliberately, in cold blood, not from over-excitement. A humorous turn is given to a declamation on a grave subject—such a subject as overwhelms the ordinary mind with seriousness. The conclusion of the passage on duelling is an example. If an explanation of this is sought, probably none will be found except the pleasure, natural to strong nerves, of treating with levity what weaker brethren cannot help treating with gravity. Partly to the same motive may be referred his humorous treatment of the more serious outbreaks of the elder Friedrich. On this have been passed some of the severest comments that our author has received in the course of his career as a writer. His humour causes him to offend on another side. Some of his fun is quite as broad as the taste of the period will allow. In such figures as "owl-droppings," and "the ostrich turning its broad end to heaven," he goes beyond the standing limits of this century. In 'Sartor Resartus,' the name "Teufelsdroeckh" and the "Nobleman's Epitaph" would hardlly be tolerated if rendered in the vernacular.

Under errors in Taste might also be reckoned his barbarisms and solecisms of language. Farther, almost universally he is charged with abusing his vast figurative resources, with carrying his figurative manner to excess. He would seem to have been conscious of his liability to this charge before it was made: in a passage already quoted from the Sartor, he speaks of labouring under figurative plethora. At the same time, it is undoubtedly to the freshness and variety of his figures that he owes a great part of his reputation.

KINDS OF COMPOSITION.

Description.

In Carlyle's powers of description lies one of his most indisputable claims to high literary rank. He seems to have studied the art most elaborately. We can gather from his various books that all his life long he had watched human beings and natural scenery with an eye to the rendering of their peculiarities into language. Especially in his later writings he describes with incomparable felicity.

In the delineation of external nature, "his peculiarities are to bring forward in strong relief the comprehensive aspects, to impress these by iteration and by picturesque comparisons, to use the language of the associated feelings, and in the shape of harmonious groupings to introduce some of the elements of poetry." The following, from the last volume of 'Friedrich,' exemplifies his statement, repetition, and illustration of the general features of a scene:—

"Torgau itself stands near Elbe; on the shoulder, eastern or Elbeward shoulder, of a big mass of Knoll, or broad Height, called of Siptitz, the main eminence of the Gau. Shoulder, I called it,[1] of this Height of Siptitz; but more properly it[1] is on a continuation, or lower ulterior height dipping into Elbe itself, that Torgau stands. Siptitz Height, nearly a mile from Elbe, dips down into a straggle of ponds; after which, on a second or final rise, comes Torgau dipping into Elbe. Not a shoulder strictly, but rather a *cheek*, with *neck* intervening;—neck *goitry* for that matter, or quaggy with ponds! The old Town stands high enough, but is enlaced on the western and southern side by a set of lakes and quagmires, some of which are still extensive and undrained. The course of the waters hereabouts, and of Elbe itself, has had its intricacies; close to north-west, Torgau is bordered, in a straggling way, by what they call *Old Elbe;* which is not now a fluent entity,

[1] The two *its* with different references are awkward. In place of "I called it," he should have used some such expression as "I said," without the *it*.

but a stagnant congeries of dirty waters and morasses. The Hill of Siptitz abuts in that aqueous or quaggy manner; its fore-feet being, as it were, at or in Elbe River, and its sides, to the south and to the north for some distance each way, considerably enveloped in ponds and boggy difficulties."

The following, from his article on Dr Francia, illustrates his dexterity in making a description vivid by imagining the feelings of a spectator:—

"Few things in late war, according to General Miller, have been more noteworthy than this march. The long straggling line of soldiers, six thousand and odd, with their quadrupeds and baggage, winding through the heart of the Andes, breaking for a brief moment the old abysmal solitudes! For you fare along, on some narrow roadway, through stony labyrinths; huge rock-mountains hanging over your head on this hand, and under your feet on that; the roar of mountain-cataracts, horror of bottomless chasms;—the very winds and echoes howling on you in an almost preternatural manner. Towering rock-barriers rise sky-high before you, and behind you, and around you; intricate the outgate! The roadway is narrow; footing none of the best. Sharp turns there are, where it will behove you to mind your paces; one false step, and you will need no second; in the gloomy jaws of the abyss you vanish, and the spectral winds howl requiem. Somewhat better are the suspension-bridges, made of bamboo and leather, though they swing like see-saws: men are stationed with lassos, to gin you dexterously, and fish you up from the torrent, if you trip there."

This passage is also a good example of a description where the particulars support each other: along with towering rocks and a narrow roadway we naturally expect huge abysses and roaring waters. The mention of the hollow winds shows his sensibility to harmonious poetical effects.

"A description is more easily and fully realised when made individual—that is, presented under all the conditions of a particular moment of time." Our author fully understands this: it is one of his cardinal arts. His works abound in picturesque allusions to seasons and times, to temporary attitudes of things and persons. Thus, in his 'Life of Sterling':—

"One day in the spring of 1836, I can still recollect, Sterling had proposed to me, by way of wide ramble, useful for various ends, that I should walk with him to Eltham and back, to see this Edgeworth, whom I also knew a little. We went accordingly together; *walking rapidly*, as was Sterling's wont, *and, no doubt, talking extensively.* It probably was in the end of February; *I can remember leafless hedges, grey driving clouds, procession of boarding-school girls in some quiet part of the route.*"

Again—

"At length some select friends were occasionally admitted; signs of improvement began to appear; and, *in the bright twilight, Kensington Gardens were green, and sky and earth were hopeful*, as one went to make inquiry. The *summer brilliancy was abroad over the world* before we fairly saw Sterling again *sub dio.*"

In his account of Walter Raleigh's execution one sentence is

"*A cold hoar-frosty morning.*" Such touches as the following are pretty frequent:—

"The Scots delivered their fire with such constancy and swiftness, it was as if the whole air had become an element of fire—*in the ancient summer gloaming there.*"

In describing the tumults after the capture of the Bastile, he suddenly breaks in—

"*O evening sun of July, how, at this hour, thy beams fall slant* on reapers amid peaceful woody fields; on old women spinning in cottages; on ships far out in the silent main; on Balls at the Orangerie of Versailles, where high-rouged Dames of the Palace are even now dancing with double-jacketed Hussar-officers,—and also on this roaring Hell-porch of a Hôtel-de-Ville!"

One of his most effective groupings is the bivouac of the army that we have just seen described in their passage over the Andes—

"What an entity, one of those night-leaguers of San Martin; all steadily snoring there in the heart of the Andes *under the eternal stars!* Wayworn sentries with difficulty keep themselves awake; tired mules chew barley rations, or doze on three legs; the feeble watch-fire will hardly kindle a cigar; *Canopus and the Southern Cross glitter down;* and all snore steadily, *begirt by granite deserts, looked on by the Constellations in that manner.*"

His narratives are eminently pictorial. At every step in the succession of events we are stopped to look at some posture of the actors or their surroundings. This is one of the most striking features in the 'French Revolution;' it may be called a historic word-tapestry, a series of significant word-pictures; it rather describes events in order than relates the order of events. A short example can give but a faint idea of the character of such a work; the following specimen is taken at random. It describes the storming of the palace of Versailles by a mob:—

"Woe now to all body-guards, mercy is none for them! Miomandre de Sainte-Marie pleads with soft words, on the grand staircase, 'descending four steps' to the roaring tornado. His comrades snatch him up, by the skirts and belts; literally from the jaws of Destruction; and slam-to their door. This also will stand few instants; the panels shivering in, like potsherds. Barricading serves not: fly fast, ye body-guards! rabid Insurrection, like the Hellhound Chase, uproaring at your heels!

"The terror-struck body-guards fly, bolting and barricading; it follows. Whitherward? Through hall on hall: woe, now! towards the Queen's suite of rooms, in the furthest room of which the Queen is now asleep. Five sentinels rush through that long suite; they are in the ante-room knocking loud: 'Save the Queen!' Trembling women fall at their feet with tears: are answered: 'Yes, we will die; save ye the Queen!'

"Tremble not, women, but haste: for, lo, another voice shouts far through the outermost door, 'Save the Queen!' and the door is shut. It is brave Miomandre's voice that shouts this second warning. He has stormed across imminent death to do it; fronts imminent death, having done it. Brave Tardivet du Repaire, bent on the same desperate service, was borne down with pikes; his comrades hardly snatched him in again alive. Miomandre and Tardivet: let the names of these two Body-guards, as the names of brave men should, live long.

"Trembling Maids of Honour, one of whom from afar caught glimpse of Miomandre, as well as heard him, hastily wrap up the Queen; not in robes of state. She flies for her life, across the Œil-de-Bœuf; against the main-door of which, too, Insurrection batters. She is in the King's apartment, in the King's arms; she clasps her children amid a faithful few. The imperial-hearted bursts into mother's tears: 'O my friends, save me and my children! O mes amis, sauvez moi et mes enfans!' The battering of Insurrectionary axes clangs audible across the Œil-de-Bœuf. What an hour!"

We might institute a comparison between Macaulay and Carlyle as regards the description of human beings. Take equal portions of their historical works and you find a greater abundance of concrete circumstances in Carlyle than in Macaulay. As a pictorial artist Carlyle is of the two the more studied and elaborate. Hardly an individual crosses Carlyle's page that is not made to appear in some characteristic attitude, or under some significant image: a much greater proportion of Macaulay's personages are mere names and functionaries. But let us take any individual that plays a prominent part in the narrative, and we shall probably find that Macaulay, in his diffuse way, records the greater number of facts concerning him. We have seen that it is so in the case of Johnson (p. 117). Macaulay's narrative contains fewer concrete circumstances upon the whole, but more concerning any prominent individual.

This difference between our two authors connects itself with a deeper difference. Carlyle is more subjective than Macaulay: he systematically attempts to picture the inner man. Partly as a consequence of this, he gives fewer circumstances: the diffuse Macaulay, taking no trouble to group circumstances about a few leading qualities of mind, gives freely out of the abundance of his memory; but Carlyle gives only circumstances that he sees to be characteristic, that he is able to read into consistency with his ideas of the man's nature. Macaulay gives numerous outward particulars, sayings, and doings gathered with confident hand from all manner of anecdotes and reminiscences, and leaves readers very much to their own inferences as to the thoughts and feelings that passed underneath these appearances. He is pre-eminently objective, and his record of circumstances is given in an easy excursive way. Carlyle, on the other hand, laboriously masters the characters of the leading personages in the events that he relates, and struggles to conceive and to represent how they felt and how they expressed their feelings in the various situations touched upon in his narrative: he is too intensely concentrated upon the immediately relevant situations to go gossiping away into previous incidents in the lives of the personages concerned.

Take as a faint illustration one particular case. Macaulay's account of the English Revolution is much less pictorial upon the whole than Carlyle's 'French Revolution.' But Macaulay gives us a great many more particulars concerning the principal statesmen at the Court of Charles II. than Carlyle gives us concerning the principal statesmen at the Court of Louis XV. Carlyle takes up a particular moment, the illness of Louis XV., and dramatically represents how this fact was regarded by various personages and classes throughout Paris according to their several characters: the abundant pictorial matter is given chiefly in illustration of characteristic thoughts and feelings.

Narrative.

As already incidentally remarked (p. 158), Carlyle's narrative method is seen to most advantage in his 'Friedrich.' In the 'French Revolution' there are many defects afterwards overcome. The introduction of new personages is there less carefully attended to. There also he errs greatly in the excess of his moralisings and preachings, which perpetually interrupt the narrative.

In the 'Friedrich,' through his intense desire to be lucid, to put himself in the reader's place, and appreciate difficulties, the minor arts of narrative are carefully observed. His ordinary narrative paragraph, although never absolutely perfect, is seldom perplexed by the confusion of the persons acting. He always notices the appearance or disappearance of important agents, and, knowing the difficulties of description, does not unguardedly shift the scenes. His long introduction to the history of Friedrich's reign, extending through two volumes, is exemplary in these respects: whatever may be said of the wild phantasmagoric or pantomimic character of the narrative, it certainly has the merit of making us distinctly aware when new figures appear, and when they depart, and of not only bringing but keeping under our attention the place and the circumstances. He also understands well the necessity of supporting the main story in its place of prominence, of indicating collateral and dependent events in their proper character, and of making all his transitions broad and apparent. His imaginary authorities, Dryasdust and Sauerteig, and "the well-known hand" that contributes subordinate narratives, have this to be said as a justification of their existence, that they do help to keep separate what the author considers of inferior from what he considers of superior importance. Dryasdust gives numerous particulars of small consequence about the private life of the prince, and does such dry business as "A peep into the Nosti-Grumkow Correspondence caught up in St Mary Axe:" Sauerteig gives wild views about the proper persons to write history, and does the unpalatable work of defending old Friedrich's character in the loftiest

Carlylian manner; the "well-known hand" gives us in small print Prince Karl's operations on the Rhine, the account of Skipper Jenkins, the life of Voltaire, and suchlike particulars subsidiary to the main narrative.

One great help to the lucidity of his narrative is the titular summaries, or labels, as he calls them. They lighten the heavy body of the narrative, giving the reader a natural break or stop, an opportunity for looking back and forward. Every book has its descriptive heading—"Double-Marriage Project, and Crown Prince, going adrift under the Storm-winds, 1727-1730:" "Fearful Shipwreck of the Double-Marriage Project, February—November 1730:" "Crown-Prince Retrieved; Life at Cüstrin, November 1730—February 1732." By these more comprehensive headings, we are enabled to run over the general succession of events without confusion. Then, the books are subdivided into chapters, each with a descriptive "label;" and within the chapters there are divisions of still smaller compass. Thus, the leading subject of one chapter is "Death of George I.:" as a minor subject we have—"His Prussian Majesty falls into one of his Hypochondriacal Fits." The leading title of another chapter is "Visit to Dresden;" the minor "labels" are—"The Physically strong pays his Counter Visit;" and—"Of Princess Wilhelmina's Four Kings and other Ineffectual Suitors." With this care in dividing and subdividing, the table of Contents becomes a vertebrate skeleton of the work, instead of being merely an analysis without any discrimination of degrees of importance.

Upon the whole it may safely be affirmed that by one means or another, ordinary and extraordinary, he makes his narratives the most lucid productions of their kind. It may be a question whether he has not made sacrifices to distinctness, and whether he might not have been equally lucid without being offensively eccentric.

In the *Explanation of Events*, he proceeds with his natural perspicacity, though he grumbles a good deal at being obliged to explain. Thus, he enters at considerable length into the sources and the progress of the quarrel between old Friedrich and George II., enumerating separately five causes. His manner of explanation is thoroughly his own. Dry analysis being distasteful to him, he proceeds dramatically, disclosing the moving springs of events in supposed soliloquies, and personal communications oral and verbal between the leading agents, himself being usually present, and putting in his word after the fashion of a Greek chorus. How different his manner is from the ordinary way of writing history, need hardly be pointed out.

Two short passages from his account of the above-mentioned

quarrel "between the Britannic and Prussian Majesties" are all we have room for:—

"'My Brother the *Comödiant*' (George II.) 'quietly put his Father's Will in his pocket, I have heard; and paid no regard to it (except what he was compelled to pay, by Chesterfield and others). Will he do the like with his poor Mother's Will?' Patience, your Majesty: he is not a covetous man, but a self-willed and a proud,—always conscious to himself that he is the soul of honour, this poor brother King."

"Very soon after George's accession there began clouds to rise; the perfectly accomplished little George assuming a severe and high air towards his rustic Brother-in-law. 'We cannot stand these Prussian enlistments and encroachments; rectify these in a high and severe manner!' says George to his Hanover officials. George is not warm on his throne till there comes in, accordingly, from the Hanover officials, a complaint to that effect, and even a List of Hanoverian subjects, who are, owing to various injustices, now serving in the Prussian ranks. 'Your Prussian Majesty is requested to return us these men!'

"This List is dated 22d January 1728; George only a few months old in his new authority as yet. The Prussian Majesty grumbles painfully responsive: 'Will, with eagerness, do whatever is just; most surely! But is his Britannic Majesty aware? Hanover officials are quite misinformed as to the circumstances;' and does not return any of the men. Merely a pacific grumble, and nothing done in regard to the complaints. Then there is the meadow of Clanrei which we spoke of: 'That belongs to Brandenburg you say? Nevertheless, the contiguous parts of Hanover have rights upon it.' Some 'eight cartloads of hay,' worth, say, almost 5*l.* or 10*l.* sterling: who is to mow that grass I wonder?

"Friedrich Wilhelm feels that all this is a pettifogging, vexatious course of procedure; and that his little cousin, the Comödiant, is not treating him very like a gentleman. 'Is he, your Majesty!' suggests the Smoking Parliament."

His deep-seated dramatic tendency leads him to such forms, when he does condescend to "motive-grinding." Explanation on the larger scale he scouts; he has no patience with "philosophical" histories. He does not want to have great events traced to their chief causes; he prefers that they should remain in mystery. He lays his ban on all attempts to give reasons for the 'French Revolution.'

"To gauge and measure this immeasurable Thing, and what is called *account for it*, and reduce it to a dead logic-formula, attempt not! . . . As an actually existing Son of Time, look with unspeakable manifold interest, oftenest in silence," &c.

Yet in the dramatic form, he does, as a matter of fact, give the commonplace explanation, that the masses found the yoke of their superiors intolerable.

Carlyle has his doubts about the propriety of making History a schoolmistress. "Before Philosophy can teach by Experience," he says, "the Philosophy has to be in readiness, the Experience must be gathered and intelligibly recorded." Yet, like most other historians, he makes use of history to illustrate his peculiar doctrines, ethical, religious, and political. Not that he is, like Macaulay, continually building up arguments in support of his views. He does not argue, he declaims. He sets up certain men, Oliver Cromwell and the two Friedrichs, as shining examples of Duty, Veracity, and Justice, and upon every colourable opportunity extols them for their exercise of these, his favourite virtues. He is drawn to the Great Rebellion, because it affords "the last glimpse of the Godlike vanishing from this England; conviction and veracity giving place to hollow cant and formulism." He loves and praises old Friedrich in spite of his ungovernable temper, because "he went about suppressing platitudes, ripping off futilities, turning deceptions inside out;" because "the realm of Disorder, which is Unveracity, Unreality, what we call Chaos, has no fiercer enemy." He writes the history of young Friedrich, although "to the last a questionable hero," because he was an able ruler, and "had nothing whatever of the Hypocrite or Phantasm." In every case he takes for granted the excellence of his favourite virtues; more than that, he tacitly assumes and maintains that they atone for every other immorality. His excuses of old Friedrich's severities on the score of justice, have called out loud expressions of indignation from the reviewers of his History.

Farther, he has not escaped the imputation of colouring characters and garbling facts under the bias of his narrow standard of morality. In the opinion of a distinguished French critic, he has misconceived and distorted the history of the French Revolution from a habitual effort to vilify whoever has a different theory of life from himself.

For such as are not repelled by his many eccentricities and arrogant judgments, Carlyle's histories possess an intense charm. Without recurring to the elements of power in his style, we here glance briefly at his use of the opportunities peculiar to narrative.

The interest of his narrative is very largely personal. Scenery and military movements he describes with the most graphic power; but he is constantly at the right hand of individuals rejoicing in their strength as the prime movers of great transactions. He records public transactions, but he keeps his heroes in the foreground or stays with them in the background as the centres of power. In our small quotations to show his mode of explaining events, this appears incidentally; but no illustration could bring out fully what is so pervading a character of all his histories. He gives the prominence to individuals on principle: assigning to "great men," "heroes," a prodigious influence on the affairs of the world, he carries this so far as to think their sayings and doings alone worthy of permanent record. Tittle-tattle about inferior personages, Acts of Parliament, and suchlike, he makes over to Dryasdust; and certainly his intensely personal method has the advantage in point of sensational interest. His exaltation of heroes, if not the most accurate way of representing human transactions, is doubtless the most artistic: every drama requires a central figure.

With his strong sense of dramatic effect Carlyle's plot would be almost as absorbing as a sensational novel, were we not generally aware beforehand from other sources what is to be the upshot. Judge by reading, for example, his account of the Crown-Prince's attempted flight from the cruelties of old Friedrich. Note also, generally, his art of introducing a name with some such phrase as "Mark this man well; we shall perhaps hear of him again."

The interest in the progress of mankind, so notable in Macaulay, is greatly wanting in Carlyle. There could hardly be a greater contrast than between the glowing optimist and the despairing prophet; between the hopeful opening of the 'History of England' and the doleful opening of the 'Letters and Speeches of Oliver Cromwell.' In Carlyle's histories, the absorbing interest of succession, of gradual development, is not wanting; but it is the interest of plot, of suspended expectation, not the cheering interest of increase in human wellbeing. To the patriotic Prussian, indeed, his 'History of Friedrich' would be exhilarating, as showing the gradual advance of the House of Brandenburg: and even the philanthropist might rejoice to see the people prospering under the rule of Friedrich. But little encouragement to jubilation of any kind is given by the sardonic historian. His eye is rather on the Phantasms that remain, than on the Phantasms that have been trodden under foot.

Exposition.

From Carlyle the student will learn no delicate arts of exposition. In considering the intellectual qualities of his style, simplicity and clearness, we saw what he does to make himself readily and distinctly intelligible. With his immense command of words he is able to repeat his doctrines in great variety of forms. He is most profuse in similitudes. The two great drawbacks to his powers of exposition are, (1) that he deliberately prefers imperfect hints and figurative sayings to complete and plain expression; and (2) that his examples are not typical cases, but selected for stage effect.

His character-drawing is one of his chief distinctions. It is elaborately studied, and in many points the execution is admirable. His sketch of the outward man seldom fails to be felicitous; not groping about confusedly in minor details of feature or of figure, but dashing off the general likeness with bold comprehensive strokes.—See his description of George's two mistresses (p. 151), and Mentzel (p. 147). His description of Leibnitz is also good as regards the externals, though perhaps it would bear filling out in other respects: "Sage Leibnitz, a rather weak, but hugely ingenious old gentleman, with bright eyes and long nose, with vast black peruke and bandy legs." These are but slender specimens of his art, probably far from being the best that could be produced; but the reader will have no difficulty in finding others; he describes every person that crosses his pages.

As a rule, he is satisfied with a few suggestive strokes; but occasionally he fills in the picture. When he does so, he gives the general view first, and then tells of particular after particular, deliberately, and with some similitude or collateral circumstance to fix each particular distinctly in the mind. His description of Friedrich in the two first pages of his history, is one of his most finished delineations.

He carries the same art of clear broad touches into his description of character. He is not perverted by likes or dislikes from trying to give the broad outlines truly; as a rule, he looks at a character only with the eye of an artist: and as a rule, his vigorous portraiture of the general temperament is true to nature. An example or two will show how he always aims at comprehensive general views. We take them at random:—

"This Jocelin, as we can discern well, was an ingenious and ingenuous, a cheery-hearted, innocent, yet withal shrewd noticing quick-witted man; and from under his monk's cowl has looked out on that narrow section of the world in a really human manner; not in any *simial*, canine, ovine, or otherwise inhuman manner," &c.

"The eupeptic, right-thinking nature of the man; his sanguineous temper, with its vivacity and sociality, an ever-busy ingenuity, rather small perhaps, but prompt, hopeful, useful, always with a good dash, too, of Scotch shrewdness, Scotch *canniness;* and then a loquacity, free, fervid, yet judicious, *canny,*—in a word, natural vehemence, wholesomely covered over and tempered (as Sancho has it) in 'three inches of old Christian *fat!*'—all these fitted Baillie to be a leader in General Assemblies," &c.

In these short dashing portraitures, perhaps the only thing worth objecting to is a certain want of order. It is when we come to the minute detail of character that we become conscious of a weakness in the scientific foundations. Carlyle's failure should warn all of the danger of despising psychological analysis, and at the same time producing an analysis made out by common-sense with the assistance of capricious fancy. De Quincey had too clear an insight to fall into such a blunder; he had no hope even of criticism, unless it was to be based on accurate psychology. Contempt for psychology usually implies bad psychology; contempt for analysis, bad analysis. Emphatically is it so with Carlyle. Avowing a contempt for analysis, he rushes with analytic assertions into regions where the ablest analyst treads with caution, and commits blunders that the poorest analyst would be ashamed of. We had occasion to note (p. 138) his view about the association of intellect with moral worth, and of a sense of the ridiculous with moral worth. Take this other statement of his favourite doctrine:—

"The thinking and the moral nature, distinguished by the necessities of speech, have no such distinction in themselves; but rightly examined, exhibit in every case the strictest sympathy and correspondence; are, indeed, but different phases of the same indissoluble unity—a living mind."

Now, here the division into thinking nature and moral nature is an analysis, just as the division into intellect and worth and a faculty of laughter is an analysis. These are distinguished, he says, by the necessities of speech; but does he suppose that the psychologist makes any other than a verbal distinction? The difference is this: the scientific analyst distinguishes with care, common speech distinguishes without care. To prefer the common-speech analysis to the scientific, is to prefer unskilled labour to skilled labour; amateur analysis is not likely to be much more valuable than amateur shoemaking.

Persuasion.

Carlyle's way of making converts is, as we have seen, the way of the declaiming prophet, not of the supple plausible debater, or of the solid logician. He appeals almost exclusively to the feelings, not to the reason; and issues his lamentations and denunciations, his Jeremiads and Isaiads, without the slightest attempt to conciliate opponents.

His oratory is employed partly on political, partly on moral subjects. His political influence has been insignificant, smaller perhaps than has been exercised by any political adviser of moderate ability; his moral influence has been considerable.

What chiefly cripples his influence, is the arrogant tone of his assertions, his total disregard for the feelings and cherished opinions of those addressed. A prophet after this strain can win over at first only the few accidentally predisposed to agree with him. With these few all his grandeur and copiousness is overwhelming; they become at once his intense admirers and adherents.

For bringing over such as are not prepared to jump to his conclusions, he exerts little influence, except the intrinsic attractions of his style. A reader is disposed to view with favour opinions clothed in a vesture so brilliant: in admiring the fresh original diction, the gorgeous figures, the soaring declamations, the vivid powers of description and narration, one is in danger of being made captive to the doctrines. With those that do not admire the style, whose teeth are set on edge by the outrages on propriety of expression, the prophet's force tells the other way. To many, also, his vituperative eloquence, in spite of its undercurrent of geniality, is offensive. With readers so disposed he is far from gaining ground; every fresh effusion widens the breach.

One of the most amiable features in his preaching is the consoling of the humble worker under difficulties. He has many ingenious turns of thought and expression for coining good out of evil, and beguiling the miserable out of their distresses. He comforts the feeble by assuring them with his utmost grandeur of language that in the end right becomes might; that justice, however long delayed, will at length visit the oppressor. He contends with Plato that the victim of wrong suffers less than the wrong-doer; and talks of "only *suffering* inhumanity not *being it* or *doing it.*" If a man has genius, "he is admitted into the *West-End of the Universe.*" "Man's unhappiness comes of his greatness." Had we "half a universe," "there would still be a dark spot in our sunshine." He sets the performance of Duty high above every other consideration. He often declaims against conventional standards of respectability; and cheers the poverty-stricken with such "wine and oil" as the following:—

"And now what is thy property? That parchment title-deed, that purse thou buttonest in thy breeches-pocket? Is that thy valuable property? Unhappy brother, most poor insolvent brother, I without parchment at all, with purse oftenest in the flaccid state, imponderous, which will not fling against the wind, have quite other property than that! I have the miraculous breath of Life in me, breathed into my nostrils by Almighty God."

PART II.

ENGLISH PROSE WRITERS IN HISTORICAL ORDER.

CHAPTER I.

PROSE WRITERS BEFORE 1580.

FOURTEENTH CENTURY.

Sir John Mandeville, 1300-1371.—The earliest book of prose able to take for itself a place in our literature, was a book of Travels by Sir John Mandeville.

In the various manuscript collections of Early English compositions are to be found prose fragments written before Mandeville's work. Some of these have been printed by the Early English Text Society—namely, Homilies of the Twelfth and Thirteenth Centuries; the Ayenbyte of Inwyt, illustrating the Kentish dialect in 1340; also, from a MS. of the fifteenth century, some fragments by the ascetic Yorkshire preacher, Richard Rolle de Hampole, who died in 1349. But these fragments are inconsiderable; and seeing that they had not vitality enough to keep themselves alive, they must not be allowed to take away from Mandeville the honour of being the Father of English Prose. Mr Henry Morley calls him "our first prose writer in formed English," and says "that with him and Wiclif begins, at the close of the period of the Formation of the Language, the true modern history of English Prose."

Mandeville professes to write what he had seen and heard in the course of thirty-four years of travel in the East. Nearly all that is known of his life may be given in his own words:—

"I, John Maundevylle, knyght, alle be it I be not worthi, that was born in Englond, in the Town of Seynt Albones, passed the See in the Zeer of our Lord Jesu Crist MCCCXXII., in the day of Seynt Michelle; and hidre to have ben longe tyme over the See, and have seyn and gon thorghe manye dyverse Londes, and many Provynces and Kingdomes, and Iles, and have passed thorghe Tartarye, Percye, Ermonye the litylle and the grete; thorghe Lybye, Caldee, and a gret partie of Ethiope; thorghe Amazoyne, Inde the lasse and the more, a gret partie; and thorghe out many othere Iles, that ben abouten Inde; where dwellen many dyverse Folkes, and of dyverse Maneres and Lawes, and of dyverse Schappes of Men."

Besides this, we know that before leaving England he studied physic, a branch of knowledge that the traveller would find serviceable wherever he went. He is said to have returned to England in 1356, and to have then written his book in Latin, in French, and in English:—

"And zee schulle undirstonde, that I have put this Boke out of Latyn into Frensche, and translated it azen out of Frensche into Englyssche, that every Man of my Nacioun may undirstonde it."

His book completed, he seems to have been again seized with his passion for travel. He is said to have died at Liège in 1371.

There being no printing-press in England till the last quarter of the fifteenth century, Mandeville's book of Travels was not printed till more than a century after his death; but immediately upon its composition, it began to circulate widely in manuscript. It was translated into Italian by Pietro de Cornero, and printed at Milan in 1480. It was first printed in England in 1499, when an edition was issued by Wynkyn de Worde.

Geoffrey Chaucer, 1328-1400.—Of the 'Canterbury Tales' two are in prose—the "Parson's Tale" and the "Tale of Melibœus." The "Parson's Tale" is a long and somewhat tedious discourse on the Seven Deadly Sins; the "Tale of Melibœus" (and his wife Prudence) is an allegory, closely translated from a French treatise. Neither of them has the spirit of Chaucer's verse, and they would hardly have been preserved had they appeared in less illustrious company.

Besides these tales, he wrote in prose a translation of the 'De Consolatione Philosophiæ of Boethius,' date unknown; a 'Treatise on the Astrolabe,' addressed to his son Lewis, conjectured date 1391; and 'The Testament of Love.'

John de Wycliffe, Wicliffe, or **Wiclif,** the Reformer, **1324-1384,** is usually mentioned among writers of English prose in the fourteenth century. But if we trust recent researches—and they have every appearance of being trustworthy—he can keep this place only by courtesy and repetition. He wrote mostly in Latin; and the few English pieces usually ascribed to him are no longer his by undivided consent. His latest biographer, Mr Shirley, maintains that "half the English religious tracts of the fourteenth and fifteenth centuries have been assigned to him in the absence of all external, and in defiance of all internal evidence;" and, in particular, affirms that writings against the mendicant orders, universally ascribed to Wicliffe, are ascribed to him against contemporary authority. As regards the translation of the Bible associated with Wicliffe's name, in *that* he would seem to have received assistance; and we have no certain means of distinguishing Wicliffe's own work from the work of his assistants.

In the narrative of Wicliffe's life, Mr Shirley is at variance with some traditional views. One of his chief points is that Wicliffe has been confounded with another man of the same name, and that it was this other Wicliffe whose appointment to the Wardenship of Canterbury Hall in 1365 was disputed, and finally set aside by the Pope. According to Mr Shirley, the following are the chief facts in Wicliffe's life: He was a Yorkshireman, born in 1324 at Spreswell or Ipswell, near Wyclif. He studied at Oxford; but no particulars of his life are known till 1361, when he appears as Master of Balliol. In this year he was presented to the rectory of Fylingham in Lincolnshire, and shortly after went there to reside. In 1363, having taken a doctor's degree, he used the privilege of lecturing in divinity at Oxford. At this date he broached no doctrinal heresy, but assailed abuses in Church government, especially recommending himself to the Court by his attacks on the temporal power of the Pope, and by defending Parliament's refusal to recognise the Pope's claim for arrears of tribute. In 1368, to be nearer Oxford, he obtained the living of Ludgershall in Buckinghamshire. In 1374 he was one of a legation sent by Edward III. to arrange some difficulties with the Pope. On his return he was presented to the living of Lutterworth in Leicestershire, which was his home for the remainder of his life. So long as he attacked only the pretensions of Church dignitaries, he was supported by the Court against their attempts at revenge. But when in 1381 he began to attack the doctrines of the Church, and proclaimed his heresy on transubstantiation, the Court dared no longer support him. He was banished from Oxford; and nothing but his death in 1384 could have saved him from further persecutions.

That it should be difficult to identify Wicliffe's writings is not to be wondered at, when we remember that in those days tracts and books circulated only in manuscript. Wicliffe towering so high above other theologians of the time, his name could not fail to become a nucleus for all writings of a reforming tenor. His translation of the Bible, completed in 1383, and used as the basis for subsequent versions, was not printed for centuries. His New Testament first appeared in 1731, and the Old Testament was never printed till so late as 1850.

The whole of the New Testament is said to be by Wicliffe's own hand. It can be conveniently seen and compared with other early versions in Bagster's 'English Hexapla.'

The only other name usually mentioned among the prose writers of the fourteenth century is **John de Trevisa,** who in 1387 translated Higden's 'Polychronicon.' The translation was printed in 1482 by Caxton, who took upon him "to change the rude and old English"— an evidence of the rapid growth of the language. Trevisa is said to have made other translations from the Latin. Of a translation of the Scriptures said to have been executed by him nothing is now known.

FIFTEENTH CENTURY.

Prose writers in this century are not numerous, and their works contain little to tempt anybody but the antiquary. Indeed, up to the last quarter of this century there was little inducement to cultivate the vernacular. A work, as we have said, circulated only in manuscript; and the learned, chiefly clergymen, addressed their brethren in Latin. Doubtless hundreds of Latin manuscripts have perished; we cannot suppose that the itch for writing was altogether extinct. The following are the most famous of those that wrote in the mother tongue.

Reynold Pecock, 1390-1460.—The Bishop of St Asaph is no unworthy successor to Wicliffe, and stands alone in his century as an advocate of tolerance and ecclesiastical freedom. He followed Wicliffe in denying the infallibility of the Pope, and in upholding the Scriptures as the sole rule of faith. He also questioned the doctrine of transubstantiation. In one respect he was far before his time, and probably before Wicliffe. He opposed the persecution of the Lollards; and urged that the Church should reason them out of their heresy, not burn them. When taken to task for these heterodoxies, he recanted; and thus escaping martyrdom, was imprisoned for the rest of his life in Thorney Abbey. His chief extant work is called the 'Repressor of overmuch blaming of the Clergy,' 1449.

Sir John Fortescue, 1395-1483.—Legal and political writer, author of a Latin work, 'De Laudibus Legum Angliæ' (concerning the excellence of the laws of England), and an English work, 'The Difference between an Absolute and a Limited Monarchy, as it more particularly regards the English Constitution.' These are perhaps the first works that avow in their title the strong English pride of country. The one extols the English upon the ground of their civil law, and the other sets forth the superiority of the English people to the French.

In his 'De Laudibus,' Fortescue calls himself *Cancellarius Angliæ*, Chancellor of England; but this title seems to have been no better than the titles conferred by James VIII. at St Germains. He was Chief-Justice of the King's Bench in the reign of Henry VI., fled with that prince after the battle of Towton, was probably made Chancellor when in exile, returned with Margaret and Prince

Edward, was taken prisoner at Tewkesbury in 1471, made his submission to Edward IV., and spent the close of his life in retirement at Ebrington in Gloucestershire.

His 'Monarchy' was first printed in 1714 by his descendant, Baron Fortescue, the friend of Pope. The 'De Laudibus' is more famous; it was translated into English in 1516, and subsequently annotated by Selden, the antiquary.

John Capgrave, 1393—, born at Lynne, educated probably at Cambridge, made Provincial of the Order of Austin Friars in England, was one of the most learned men of his time, a voluminous author in Latin, and wrote a biography and a chronicle in English. The 'Chronicle of England' is reprinted in the Master of the Rolls series of Chronicles. It begins with the Creation, and is distinguished by its conciseness.

William Caxton, the Printer, **1420-1492.**—Caxton was a London mercer, driving a business so considerable that he had to make frequent journeys into the Low Countries, and other Continental seats of manufacture and merchandise. Having literary tastes, he also took an interest in printing, which had been introduced into Holland a little before the middle of the century. In 1464 he was one of two commissioners for negotiating a commercial treaty between England and Charles of Burgundy; and soon after, on the marriage of Charles with Lady Margaret of York, he received a post in her household. In his leisure he turned to his favourite pursuits, translated Le Fevre's 'History of Troy,' and had both original and translation printed for him, or perhaps partly by himself, at some press in the Netherlands or in Germany. He is supposed to have set up as a printer in London in 1474, his first production being a translation from the French by himself, entitled, 'The Game and Playe of the Chesse.' He was fairly established in 1477. From that date till his death, in 1492, he translated and printed indefatigably.

Caxton's printing-press gave an immense impulse to writing in the English tongue. In the first ten years after its establishment, probably more English was written for publication than had been written in the two preceding centuries. His press gave to the world no less than sixty-four books, nearly all in English.

His publications were mostly translations from French and Latin, many of them made by himself. They include religious books of a popular cast—'Pilgrimage of the Soul,' 'The Golden Legend' (Lives of the Saints), 'The Life of St Catherine of Sens:' books of romance—'Godfrey of Boloyn,' 'The Book of the Order of Chivalry,' 'The History of the Noble, Right Valiant, and Right Worthy Knight Paris, and of the Fair Vienne:' and some of the works of Chaucer, Gower, and Lydgate.

Robert Fabyan, or **Fabian,** who died in 1512, is usually counted among the authors of this century. His 'Concordaynce of Stories,' generally known as Fabyan's Chronicle, is the first attempt to write history in English prose. An alderman and a sheriff of London, he seems to have pursued literature to the damage of his business; for in 1502 he withdrew from office on the ground of poverty. In all likelihood he had composed his Chronicle after his retirement from the cares of official life.

The Concordance, compiled from older sources, as the name indicates, narrates the history of Britain from the landing of Brutus the Trojan down to 1485. It is most minute in the detail of facts and fictions, making no attempt to distinguish between great events and small. One of its most authentic records is a full and particular account of the successive Lord Mayors of London. —The book was not published till 1516, four years after the author's death.

One or two other names of this century have been preserved. **Juliana Berners** (of uncertain date, supposed 1390-1460) deserves mention as the first of her sex to publish a book in English. She was prioress of Sopewell Nunnery, near St Albans, was—very unlike a nun—fond of hawking and hunting, and wrote a treatise on these sports. **Sir Thomas Malory** (fl. 1470) is known as the translator and compiler of the 'History of King Arthur,' printed by Caxton in 1485. To this century belong also translations of various romances from the French, occupied chiefly with the acts of the Round Table Knights and the Seer Merlin; also the **Paston Letters,** supposed date 1422.

The following are Mr Marsh's general remarks on the prose literature of the fifteenth century: "The English prose litera-" ture of the fifteenth century consists, in large proportion, of " translations, and these always partake more or less of the colour " of the sources from which they were borrowed. There is, in " fact, so little native English of that period extant in a printed " form, that it is not easy to determine how far the prevalence of " Gallicisms in the translations printed by Caxton is to be ascribed " to the influence of French originals upon the style of the trans-" lator, and how far it was a characteristic feature of the language " of the time."

FIRST HALF OF SIXTEENTH CENTURY.

With the sixteenth century our prose literature begins a new era, though the writers are still far from being of any use as models of style. In spite of the encouragement given to English writing by the establishment of printing, some of the most distinguished authors of the time wrote chiefly in Latin, being ambitious of a wider audience than the English-reading public. The high-minded Bishop FISHER, who in 1535, at the age of seventy-five, was put to death for denying the king's ecclesiastical supremacy, wrote copiously in Latin in defence of the Catholic tenets, and left only a few sermons in English. Bishop BALE, a generation later (1495-1563), a champion on the Protestant side, is known chiefly by his 'Lives of Eminent English Writers, from Japhet down to 1559,' a work written in Latin. He wrote in English some bitter controversial tracts, and an account of the examination and death of the Protestant martyr Sir John Oldcastle. Sir Thomas More wrote his 'Utopia' in Latin. Still, this century begins with a greatly increased activity in the production of original English works.

John Bourchier, Lord Berners, 1474-1532, is known chiefly as the translator of 'Froissart's Chronicles.' He was Chancellor of the Exchequer and Governor of Calais, and undertook the translation, which was published in 1523, at the request of the king. It was reprinted in 1812 in the series of English Chronicles. Berners made one or two other translations from French and Spanish. As an educated man and a courtier, he wrote without pedantry the best English of the time. "This translation," says Mr Marsh, "is doubtless the best English prose style which had yet appeared. . . . The dialogistic style of the English of Lord Berners is as racy and nearly as idiomatic as had yet appeared."

Sir Thomas More, 1480-1535, first layman Chancellor of England, author of 'Utopia,' is perhaps the first of our writers whose prose displays any genius; and his 'Life of Edward V.' is pronounced by Mr Hallam to be "the first example of good English language, pure and perspicuous, well chosen, without vulgarisms or pedantry."

More's life is well known; he ranks with Sir Philip Sidney as one of the most popular characters in our history. His father was Sir John More, a judge of the Court of King's Bench. Admitted as a page to the household of Cardinal Morton at the age of fifteen, he was sent thence to Oxford, where he made the acquaintance of Erasmus. Under his pleasant exterior there was a vein of gravity and asceticism; and after leaving Oxford he had thoughts of becoming a monk. This desire passed away; he settled down to the practice of the law, soon rose to distinction, was made under-sheriff of London, and obtained a seat in Parliament in 1504. He offended Henry VII. by opposing a subsidy; and, retiring from public life, probably busied himself with his 'Life of Edward V.,' till the accession of Henry VIII. let him resume his profession. With Henry he became a great favourite, and in 1529, on the fall of Wolsey, was made Chancellor. A stanch adherent to the Church of Rome, he is said to have practised in his chancellorship severities against the Reformers very inconsistent with the theory of the 'Utopia.' When Henry broke with Rome, the Chancellor would not follow him, and suffered death rather than take an oath affirming the validity of the King's marriage with Anne Boleyn. He was beheaded in 1535, acting up to his Utopian precept that a man should meet death with cheerfulness.

The 'Utopia,' written, as we have said, in Latin, was first printed in 1516 at Louvain. His principal English work is the 'Life and Reign of Edward V. and of his Brother, and of Richard III.,' our first prose composition worthy of the title of history. He was also a voluminous writer of controversy, publishing more than 1000 pages folio against Tyndale; and a letter to his wife that has chanced to be preserved is often quoted.

The 'Utopia,' though written in Latin, is always reckoned as an English work, and is the chief support of More's place in English literature. The dramatic setting of the work is done with great ingenuity and humorous circumstantiality. More professes to be only a transcriber; he simply writes down what he remembers of a conversation with a restless traveller, Raphael Hythloday. Ralph had met in his travels with the commonwealth of Utopia (Nowhere), and More draws him out to give an account of it. Ralph is thus an earlier Teufelsdroeckh, as Utopia is an earlier Weissnichtwo. Under the dramatic guise, disclaiming all responsibility for the opinions, More utters freely political advice that might have been unpalatable but for its witty accompaniments of time, place, and circumstance.

The work is full of graphic personal descriptions, and of humour that has a freshness almost unique after such a lapse of time. As a small sample of his picturesque description, take the first appearance of Hythloday. On leaving church at Antwerp one day, sauntering out—

> "I chanced to espy this foresaid Peter (Giles) talking with a certain stranger, a man well stricken in age, with a black sunburnt face, a long beard, and a cloak cast homely about his shoulders, whom by his favour and apparel forthwith I judged to be a mariner."

A fair specimen of his humour is his pretended difficulties in finding out exactly where Utopia lay. He let off Raphael without minute questioning, so occupied was he with the peculiarities of the place; then he wrote to his friend Giles, who found the traveller, and asked the particulars of latitude and longitude; but unfortunately at the critical moment a servant came and whispered Raphael, and when the story was taken up again after this interruption, some person in the room had a fit of coughing, so that Giles lost "certain of the words." Throughout Robinson's translation of the 'Utopia,' the translator is so full of admiration that he cannot refrain from marginal remarks, such as, "O wittie head," "a prettie fiction and a wittie," "mark this well."

Of late years the 'Utopia' has been sometimes quoted as containing lessons for the present day. As a matter of fact, More gives us no lesson that we do not get from living preachers in forms more directly adapted to our time—the main pleasure in reading him apart from his humour and picturesqueness is the surprise of finding in the 'Utopia' doctrines that have been preached in these latter days and considered novel. Curiously enough, the chief author of our time anticipated by the "merry, jocund, and pleasant" More, is the grimly humorous, vehement, and defiant "Seer of Chelsea," Mr Carlyle. The difference of manner makes the coincidence of matter all the more striking. We find realised in the 'Utopia' Mr Carlyle's main political doctrines: his hatred of idleness and love of steady industry, his model aristocracy, his "Captains of Industry," his treatment of malefactors, and his grand specific for an overcrowded country—emigration. The Utopians are a sober, industrious, thrifty people; jewellery and fine clothes they put away with childhood; they have no idle rich, they leave hunting to the butchers; the chief duty of their magistrates the Syphogrants is, "to see and take heed that no man sit idle;" they enslave their malefactors, give them a peculiar dress, cut off the tips of their ears, hire them out to work, and punish desertion with death; when their children become too numerous, they found a colony.

All this is a curious anticipation of the 'Latter-Day Pamphlets;' and in More we meet with many other things that we are accustomed to think peculiarly modern. He makes some pleasant play on the pedantic worship of antiquity, and the over-honoured "wisdom of our ancestors." He brings against the capital punishment of theft the same argument that Macaulay, in the Indian Penal Code, urged against the capital punishment of rape. Some years ago we heard much about the depopulation of the Highlands of Scotland to make deer-parks: More has a similar complaint to make; in his day the high price of English wool tempted landlords to eject husbandmen, and turn arable land into sheep-pastures.

The 'Utopia' was first translated by Ralph Robinson in 1551. It was again translated by Bishop Burnet in 1684. Both translations have often been reprinted, and others have been made. Robinson's translation is included in the series of 'English Reprints,' 1869.

If we compare Robinson's translation with the original or with Burnet's translation, we are struck with a peculiarity characteristic of our literature up to and including the age of Elizabeth. Robinson seldom translates an epithet with a single word; he repeats two or even three words that are nearly synonymous. It would seem as if he distrusted the expressiveness of the new language, and sought to convey the Latin meaning by showing it in as many aspects as our language permitted. "Plain, simple, and homely," "merry, jocund, and pleasant," "disposition or conveyance" of the matter, might be explained in this way. But the greater number of the tautologies are the incontinence arising from want of art; couples are often used where the meaning of one would be amply apparent: thus—"I grant and confess," "I reckon and account," "tell and declare," "win and get," and so forth.

Sir Thomas Elyot, 1487-1546, a man of admired integrity and of a genial didactic turn, who was employed by Henry VIII. on two of his most important embassies, was a miscellaneous writer of considerable range. His most famous work is 'The Governor,' which deals chiefly with the subject of education. Besides this he wrote a medical and dietetic work, 'The Castle of Health,' composed 'Bibliotheca Eliotæ' (probably a work on the choice of books), and pretended to translate from the Greek a work called 'The Image of Governance.'

With More and Elyot may be mentioned their friend, though considerably their junior, **John Leland** (1506-1552), scholar and antiquary, author of 'The Itinerary.'

Edward Hall, 1500-1547, is often coupled with Fabyan as one of the two beginners of English prose history. The title of his work is 'The Union of the two Noble and Illustrious Families of Lancaster and Yorke.' There is no particular reason for coupling him with Fabyan. More comes between them as a historian with his Edward V. Hall was a man of better education than Fabyan; studied at Cambridge, went to the bar, and rose to be one of the judges of the sheriff's court. His style is not equal to More's, and better than Fabyan's.

Sir Roger Ascham says that in "Hall's Chronicle much good matter is quite marred with indenture English and . . . strange and inkhorn terms."

The work was reprinted among the English Chronicles in 1809.

George Cavendish, 1495 (?)-1562 (?), gentleman-usher to Cardinal Wolsey, and after Wolsey's death to Henry VIII., wrote a biography of the Cardinal, which is reprinted in Wordsworth's 'Ecclesiastical Biography' as a standard authority. Apart from its own worth, it is interesting as having furnished Shakspeare with particulars for his 'Henry VIII.'

An edition, published by Mr Singer in 1825, was accompanied with a proof that the author was *George* Cavendish, and not *William*, as commonly reported.

John Bellenden, Ballenden, or **Ballentyne,** Archdean of Moray, is the first Scotch writer of prose. He translated Boece's 'History of Scotland' (1536) and the first five books of Livy. His diction is very little different from the ordinary English diction of that time.

Translators of the Bible.—Between 1537 and 1539 appeared in rapid succession four translations of the Bible, Tyndale's, Coverdale's, Matthew's, and Cranmer's.

William Tyndale, 1484-1536.—*Translation of New Testament, published at Antwerp*, 1526.—Little is known of Tyndale's family. He was a native of Gloucestershire, his birthplace probably North Nibley. He was educated at Oxford, and continued there probably as a tutor till 1519. Thereafter, being tutor in the family of Sir John Walsh, of Little Sodbury, in his native county, his anti-Popish views became known, exposed him to threats of censure, and finally made England too hot for him, and drove him to Hamburg, 1523-24. Here he laboured at his translation of the Scriptures, holding, with the Reformers of Germany and Switzerland, that the Bible should be in every hand, not in the exclusive keeping of the Church. In 1524-25 he printed two editions of the New Testament by snatches at different places, subject to vexatious interruptions. In 1526 an edition was deliberately printed at Antwerp, and every endeavour used to smuggle it into England. Turning next to the Old Testament, he translated the five books of Moses, which he published in 1530. He revised his New Testament in 1534. Hitherto he had escaped the agents sent to hunt him out and apprehend him. At last, in 1535, an emissary of the English Popish faction tracked him to Antwerp, obtained a warrant from the Emperor, and lodged him in prison. In 1536 he was led to the stake at Antwerp, strangled, and burnt. At that very time, the change having come in Henry's relations with the Pope, the King's printer in London was printing the first English edition of his New Testament.

"Tyndale's translation of the New Testament is the most important philological monument of the first half of the sixteenth century, perhaps, I should say, of the whole period between Chaucer and Shakspeare, both as a historical relic and as having more than anything else contributed to shape and fix the sacred dialect, and establish the form which the Bible must permanently assume in an English dress. The best features of the translation of 1611 are derived from the version of Tyndale, and thus that remarkable work has exerted, directly and indirectly, a more powerful influence on the English language than any other single production between the ages of Richard II. and Queen Elizabeth." —(Marsh's 'Lectures on the English Language.')

Miles Coverdale, 1488-1569, published a translation of the whole Bible in 1537. His life was more prosperous than Tyndale's. Hardly any mention is made of him before the date of his translation: he would seem to have worked in silence, until the times became favourable to open activity in the cause of the Reformed faith. He was made Bishop of Exeter in 1551. During the reign of Mary he prudently retired to the Continent, returning on the accession of Elizabeth to his former dignity. He is said to have been a native of Yorkshire. His version of the New Testament differs but slightly from Tyndale's. He also wrote several tracts, now much in request among book-hunters.

Matthew's Bible, so called from the name on the title-page, was issued under the superintendence of **John Rogers,** the proto-martyr of the reign of Mary. It is not a new translation, but a revised edition of Tyndale's Pentateuch and New Testament, with an amended version of Coverdale's translation for the rest of the Bible. Rogers was a native of Warwickshire, was educated at Cambridge, and became the disciple and friend of Tyndale at Antwerp, where he was chaplain to the English merchants. He married a German wife, and left ten children.

Cranmer's Bible (1540) took its name from the celebrated Archbishop **Cranmer, 1489-1556.** It is substantially a new edition of Matthew's, revised by collation with the original Hebrew and Greek.

Hugh Latimer, 1491-1555, one of the foremost champions of the Reformation, burnt by Queen Mary at Oxford, along with Cranmer and Ridley. He was born at Thurcaston in Leicestershire, the son of a well-to-do yeoman. In 1505 he was sent to Cambridge, where in due course he became a resident Fellow. Always vehement and enthusiastic, he distinguished himself, like another Paul, by his strong attachment to the prevailing faith and his denunciations of the new light. About 1521 he was converted by a priest whom he calls "Little Bilney," and immediately made himself obnoxious to "divers Papists in the University" by the new direction of his zealous and powerful eloquence. He was brought before Wolsey, but the Cardinal found nothing amiss in his preaching, and sent him away in triumph. When Henry wished to invalidate his marriage with Catherine, Latimer sat upon the question as one of a University Commission, and decided in the King's favour. Soon thereafter, in 1530, he was invited to Court, made a royal chaplain, and in 1535, on the elevation of Cranmer to the see of Canterbury, Bishop of Worcester. Never inclined to look at the world on its favourable side, he signalised his preferment by denouncing, with characteristic vehemence, the abuses of the time, declaring that "bishops, abbots, priors, parsons, canons resident, priests and all, were strong thieves—yea, dukes, lords, and all;" and that "bishops, abbots, with such other," should "keep hospitality to feed the needy people, not jolly fellows with golden chains and velvet gowns." In 1539 he got into trouble for refusing to sign the six Romanistic articles, resigned his bishopric, sought to retire into private life, but was seized, put in the Tower, and "commanded to silence." His voice is not heard again till the reign of Edward VI., when he blazes out as the most stirring of the Reforming preachers, and a man of importance at Court. When Edward died, everything was changed, and Latimer, with other conspicuous Protestants, suffered the last extreme of persecution.

Latimer's sermons are still read with interest. They present an extraordinary contrast to modern sermons. In those days the ministers of the Word did not confine themselves to exegesis and morality in the abstract; they addressed hearers by name, and singling out particular classes, told them with some minuteness how to regulate their lives. Latimer took the utmost advantage of this licence of the pulpit,—told my Lord Chancellor of certain cases that he should attend to personally; warned the King against having too many horses, too many wives, or too much silver and gold; and admonished bishops and judges of their duty in the plainest terms. This was not all: in the *matter* he probably did not go beyond the time; in the manner, he was led by his excess of energy into eccentricities of diction and illustration rendered tolerable only by the power and freshness of his genius. His contemporaries looked upon him much as the present generation looks on Thomas Carlyle. Many could not endure his open defiance of conventionality, and could not speak of him with patience. These he outraged still more by replying to them from the pulpit. He says—

"When I was in trouble, it was objected and said unto me that I was singular, that no man thought as I thought, that I loved a singularity in all that I did, and that I took a way contrary to the King and the whole Parliament, and that I was travailed with them that had better wits than I; that I was contrary to them all."

He then goes on to compare his case with Christ's, and draws a humorous ironical parallel between himself and Isaiah, with a quaint drollery, almost buffoonery, not likely to conciliate those already offended by his eccentric power.

He is often praised for his "vigorous Saxon." It is undoubtedly vigorous, and his illustrations have the stamp of genius. But to his cultivated hearers, the homely turns must have sounded like Yorkshire or broad Scotch in a modern discourse. It is not to be supposed that the Court of Edward VI. heard the following without a smile:—

"In the VII. of Jhon the Priests sent out certain of the Jews to bring Christ unto them violently. When they came into the temple and heard Him preach, they were so moved with His preaching that they returned home again and said to them that sent them, *Nunquam sic locutus est homo ut hic homo.* There was never man spake like this man. Then answered the Pharisees, *Num et vos seducti estis?* *What, ye brain-sick fools, ye hoddy pecks, ye doddy polls, ye huddes, do ye believe Him?* *Are you seduced also?*"

Or the following:—

"Germany was visited XX. years with God's Word, but they did not earnestly embrace it, and in life follow it, but made a mingle-mangle and a hotch-potch of it.

"I cannot tell what, partly Popery, partly true religion, mingled together. They say in my country when they call their hogs to the swine trough: '*Come to thy mingle-mangle; come pyr, come pyr,*'—even so they made mingle-mangle of it."

Latimer's "Sermon on the Plougher," and his "Seven Sermons before Edward VI.," are in the series of English Reprints. Several editions of his sermons were issued in the sixteenth century.

John Foxe, 1517-1587, author of the 'Book of Martyrs,' a native of Lincolnshire. Having studied at Oxford and gained a fellowship, he became openly Protestant, and was expelled in 1545. After various distresses, he had been but a short time comfortably settled as tutor to the Earl of Surrey when Mary ascended the throne, and he had to flee to the Continent and support himself by correcting proofs. After Mary's death he returned and received a prebendary. His 'Book of Martyrs' is an interesting record, reprinted by various religious societies: the facts are not much to be relied on, being based upon popular report, evidently little sifted.

Sir John Cheke, 1514-1557, Professor of Greek at Cambridge, is best known by the impulse he gave to the study of Greek. His life was troubled; he had difficulties with Gardiner about certain innovations in the pronunciation of Greek, and on the accession of Mary had to flee the country for his religion. After some years' precarious wandering, he was caught at Antwerp and brought back; was offered the alternative of recantation or death; recanted, and soon after died of shame and grief.

His only English work is written against the insurrection of Ket the Tanner. Its title is, 'The Hurt of Sedition, how grievous it is to a Commonwealth.'

THIRD QUARTER OF SIXTEENTH CENTURY.

Roger Ascham, 1515-1568, is one of the best-known men of his century. He was more fortunate in his life than More, Latimer, or Cheke. He enjoyed a pension under Henry and Edward, had his pension not only continued but increased by Mary, was made her Latin secretary; after her death became a favourite with Elizabeth, continued to enjoy pension and secretaryship, taught Latin and Greek to the learned Queen, and lived to write that, "*in our fore-*

fathers' time, Papistry as a standing pool covered and overflowed all England." The secret of his success was, that he held no strong opinions in religion, or, at any rate, kept them to himself. When at Cambridge he nearly lost his fellowship by indiscreetly speaking against the Pope. Escaping shipwreck that time, he was careful never to offend again by an obtrusive profession of his faith. A Yorkshireman, son of Lord Scroop's steward, he had little of the Yorkshire vigour; a man of delicate constitution, of gentle and polished manners; noted for his fine penmanship and elegant scholarly acquirements, and having not a little of the dexterity of the courtier.

The 'Toxophilus' (1545) is a dialogue on archery, sustained by Philologus and Toxophilus—Lover of the Book, and Lover of the Bow. It gives the history of the bow, compares archery with other recreations, recommends it as an exercise for the student, tells the best kind of wood for the bow, discusses the art of shooting, &c.; above all, it declares what England owes to the bow, and urges every Englishman to practise the national weapon. Upon the merits of this side of the treatise he received his pension from Henry. The 'Schoolmaster' (published in 1570, after his death) discusses the readiest means of acquiring a knowledge of Latin, and criticises the style of Varro, Sallust, Cicero, and Cæsar. In both 'Toxophilus' and the 'Schoolmaster' he takes great liberty of digression, but does little to redeem his promise of great things under modest titles. He announced a 'Book of the Cockpit,' in defence of his frequenting that place of amusement, but the work was never published. His chief service to English prose is the example he sets, as a scholar and a courtier, of writing in the vernacular. This service is acknowledged by Dr Nathan Drake. Thomas Fuller says of him—"He was an honest man, and a good shooter. Archery was his pastime in youth, which, in his old age, he exchanged for cock-fighting. His 'Toxophilus' is a good book for *young* men; his 'Schoolmaster' for *old;* his 'Epistles' for *all* men."

A collected edition of his English works was published in 1761. Another reprint in 1815 is modernised, not only in the spelling but in the language.

Thomas Wilson, d. 1581, writer on *Rhetoric*, *Logic*, &c.—His 'System of Rhetoric and Logic,' pub. 1553, is the first systematic treatise on the English language. He was a man of position, said to have been Dean of Durham, and to have held offices of state under Elizabeth. He made a stand for the purity of the "King's English."[1] He ridiculed fops and scholars for talking Chaucer, and for larding their speech with French-English, with Italianated terms, with inkhorn terms, with "far-fetched colours of gay antiq-

[1] He is, so far as we are aware, the first writer to use this expression.

uity." "The unlearned or foolish fantastical . . . will so Latin their tongues that the simple . . . think surely they speak by some revelation."

Among the many eloquent preachers and able men of business connected with the Church of England in the beginning of the reign of Elizabeth, the two most celebrated writers were **Thomas Becon** (1511-1567) and **John Jewel** (1522-1571). Both had to flee to the Continent during the reign of Mary, and both were rewarded upon the accession of Elizabeth. Becon inclined to be Puritan and Presbyterian, and received no higher preferment than a stall in Canterbury Cathedral. He wrote voluminously, chiefly books of devotion and poetry. One of his devotional works, 'The Sick Man's Salve,' became a popular household book, and is frequently alluded to by Ben Jonson and contemporary dramatists. Jewel was made Bishop of Salisbury. He was one of the ablest of Elizabeth's bishops. When comparatively a young man, he was chosen by the University of Oxford to deliver a congratulatory address to Queen Mary upon her accession. His famous 'Apology for the Church of England,' written in elegant Latin, was much admired throughout Europe, and at once adopted by the Church as a conclusive defence of her faith.

Sir Thomas North, a collateral ancestor of the Guildfords, issued in 1579 an English version of 'Plutarch's Lives,' rendered from the French translation by Amyot. The work was very popular, until superseded by Dryden's translation. It is closely followed by Shakspeare in 'Coriolanus,' 'Julius Cæsar,' and 'Antony and Cleopatra.'

Holinshed's 'Chronicle,' published about 1580, is known to many readers only from being similarly utilised by Shakspeare, who made Holinshed's translation of Boece the basis of 'Macbeth.' In the composition of his 'Chronicles,' which profess to be a complete history of Great Britain and Ireland, Holinshed, himself a man of uncertain biography, had several assistants, whose lives are equally obscure. The prefatory account of England in the sixteenth century, the most valuable part of the work, was written by **William Harrison**; the history and description of Ireland by **Richard Stanihurst. John Hooker,** the Chamberlain of Exeter, and uncle of "the judicious Hooker," is also said to have given some assistance.

CHAPTER II.

FROM 1580 TO 1610.

SIR PHILIP SIDNEY,

1554—1586.

In the prose works of Sir Philip Sidney we discern an advance on the style of all preceding writers. The advance is not perhaps great :—we are not to suppose that prose style departed from the usual law of gradual progress :—still, whatever the difference may be in the ultimate analysis, undeniably his prose is nearer the present style of English than any prose of anterior date. His style has a flow and elevation not to be found in any prose work before his time. On that ground, although he is "a warbler of *poetic* prose," his literary fame resting chiefly on a romance, it is desirable to analyse his style simply as a prose style at some length.

As the "Hero of Zutphen," Sidney is one of the most popular characters in English history; and in his own day, at a very early age, was celebrated all over Europe for his discretion, courage, and accomplishments. It is said that he was mooted as a candidate for the throne of Poland, and that Elizabeth put her veto on the rising negotiation, because she could not part with "the jewel of her time." He was born at Penshurst in Kent; son of Sir Henry Sidney—a knight who became a favourite with Elizabeth, and was famed as an administrator of Ireland; and nephew to the Earl of Leicester. He was educated at Shrewsbury, and at Christ Church, Oxford. In 1572, at the age of seventeen, he set out with three years' leave of absence to travel on the Continent; was in Paris during the massacre of St Bartholomew, and went thence to Frankfort, Vienna, and the chief cities of Italy. During these travels, unlike most travellers of his rank, he associated with scholars and statesmen, making an earnest study of European politics. Introduced at Court in 1575, his mixed courtesy and gravity at once made him a favourite. In 1577, at the age of twenty-two, being sent as ambassador in great state to congratulate the new Emperor of Germany, and discover as far as possible his tendencies, he met William the Silent of Orange, who pronounced him one of the ripest statesmen in Europe. During the eight following years he had no public employment, and lived chiefly at Court. In 1578 he wrote his masque 'The Lady of the May,' performed at Elizabeth's reception by his uncle the Earl of Leicester. Probably about the same time he began his sonnets to 'Stella,' the daughter of the Earl of Essex, afterwards married to Lord Rich. In the same year he had Spenser living with him at Penshurst. In 1580 he wrote the 'Arcadia,' dedicated to his celebrated sister, the Countess of Pembroke. In the following year he is supposed to have written the 'Apologie for Poetrie.' After this he became too much engaged in politics to have time for literature. As a statesman, he devoted himself to the policy of humbling the power of Spain. He had boldly written to Elizabeth in 1580, dissuading her from the marriage with Anjou, and now he was eager that the Queen should take active part with the Continental Protestants. This not being done, he impatiently planned with Drake a secret expedition to strike at the Spanish colonies in America, but was interdicted just at starting. At last Elizabeth resolved to stir, and in the fall of 1585 sent him to the Netherlands as Governor of Flushing along with an army under Leicester. Commencing operations in spring, Sidney showed great enterprise and skill, but was mortally wounded in a rencounter at Zutphen, and died Oct. 17, 1586. The touching incident that has endeared his memory, and made him known to every schoolboy, occurred as he rode wounded from the battle.

Though he was well known as a writer, and widely esteemed as a patron of literary men during his life, none of his works were published till after his death. The 'Arcadia' was first printed in 1590, the 'Apologie for Poetrie' in 1595.

In personal appearance Sidney was tall and handsome, with clear complexion, and hair of a dark amber colour. By Spenser's testimony he excelled in athletic sports—"in wrestling nimble, and in running swift; in shooting steady, and in swimming strong; well made to strike, to throw, to leap, to lift." He was of such prowess in the tournament, that on the occasion of a great festival he was selected as one of four champions to keep the lists in honour of England against all comers.

It is not often that we find in union with such physical prowess any remarkable powers of mind. In Elizabeth's Court there were many able men both physically and mentally, but none of those that were a match for Sidney in the tournament could have written the 'Arcadia' or the 'Apology for Poetry.' Even in his healthy active boyhood Sidney was remarkably studious; "his talk," says his schoolfellow Fulke Greville, "ever of knowledge, and his very play tending to enrich the mind." When he grew to manhood, his sagacity in practical affairs soon won him golden opinions from more than one veteran statesman. If we look to his writings, we find abundant proofs of intellectual vigour. His diction is copious and felicitous, unmistakably significant of mental quickness and force. In his 'Arcadia' we are constantly struck with the extreme volatility and subtlety of his fancy. In the Apology, along with a similar sprightliness, we meet with passages suggestive of more solid power. In defending poetry against the Puritans, it shows considerable rhetorical perspicacity to claim the Psalms of David as "divine poems." And there is no small discernment in his maintaining that a poem might be written in prose; that "verse is but an ornament and no cause to poetry." Taken all in all, his works bear evidence of versatile, fresh, and vigorous intellect, and support what is recorded of his adroit courtesy and sagacious observation of affairs.

As regards his emotional character, were we to judge solely from his writings, we should take him to have been a man of ebullient spirits, tempered by extraordinary sweetness and warmth of disposition. This is the impression left by the soft exuberant humour of the Apology, and its strong expressions of delight in the works of the poet. He seems to have been a pleasant companion, although not of the rollicking, pleasure-loving temper that perpetually craves for society. Gay with the gay among his boon companions, he could also be serious with the serious. He loved to exchange thoughts in private colloquy with such men as Languet and Spenser. At times he courted solitude, and would even seem to have undergone fits of melancholy and despondency, as when, before leaving England for the last time, he expressed a presentiment that he should never return. To the creations of art he turned with ever fresh delight. He was not an optimist; he did not find enduring satisfaction, abundant means of enjoyment, in the actual world; he took refuge from facts in the regions of imagination—"Nature's world," he said, "is brazen, the poet's only golden." The ruling emotion in his creative efforts, as we shall see when we come to analyse the qualities of his style, is tenderness—not the wild passionate tenderness of the Celtic nature, but a soft and courtly phase of the emotion. His imagination did not dwell sadly upon the sorrowful side of life, but joyfully spent itself in playful humour, in graceful fancies, in pictures of beautiful women and beautiful scenery, and in deeds of romantic devotion. The 'Arcadia' gives little evidence of delight in the mere excitement of power. It contains great variety of incidents and characters; but everything is transfigured by the all-pervading sweetness and warmth—everything is seen through this atmosphere. His heroes—young men of irresistible prowess—are beautiful as gods. In recounting their most valiant achievements, he never suffers us to forget that they are in love; either they are fighting to rescue their fair ladies, or the ladies are listening with admiration to the story of their brave adventures. If he enters with spirit into the description of a storm, a battle, a tournament, a duel, a popular tumult, or the speeches at a trial, not only does he mingle pretty fancies with his description or narrative, but he seldom keeps long out of view the tender interests at stake.

Men so lavishly endowed otherwise as Sidney, with such capacities and self-contained means of enjoyment, are often indifferent to the aims of ambition, and even rash and imprudently generous. A less bountiful natural outfit is more serviceable for rising and remaining high in the world. He did not push for favour and office at Court: a slight rebuff drove him to the country; and he might have spent his life in retirement had not his foreign friend Languet impressed him with the gravity of the political situation in Europe, and urged him to take a part. Once resolved upon a course of action, he moved with fearlessness and vigour. Few men would have ventured on his bold remonstrance to Elizabeth against the French marriage. Naturally sweet-tempered, he was haughty and imperious when provoked, and ready to put out his hand to execute his will: witness his giving the lie to the Earl of Oxford, his challenge to the unknown asperser of his uncle Leicester, and his threatening to "thrust his dagger into" poor secretary Molyneux, whom he suspected of tampering with his letters. He owed his death to an impulse of romantic generosity. The Lord-Marshal happening to enter the field of Zutphen without greaves, Sidney cast off his also, to put his life in the same peril, and so exposed himself to the fatal shot.

The opinions of the Apology call for some notice. It is a light humorous production, with here and there flashes of lofty beauty; but beneath all this, there is a foundation of serious doctrine. The author is full of humour and eloquence in behalf of the delights of poetry, but he shows also a serious interest in the cause, a genuine zeal to convince and convert. Very much contrary to the modern theory that makes the "interpretation of nature" the poet's chief end, is the saying above quoted, that "nature's world is brazen, the poet's only golden." "Nature never set forth the earth in so rich tapestry as divers poets have done, neither with pleasant rivers, fruitful trees, sweet-smelling flowers, nor whatsoever else may make the too much loved earth more lovely." He eloquently defends the usefulness of poetry: it furnishes speaking pictures of virtue more perfect than even history can show; to make vice attractive is the abuse and not the use of poetry. To those that accuse poets of lying, he ingeniously answers that they affirm nothing as true, and therefore cannot lie.

His criticisms of existing English poetry show a fine taste. He objects to outrageous infraction of the unities (see p. 209); to violent mixture of serious and comic — "your mongrel tragi-comedy;"—and to making ridicule of human weakness, of "an extreme show of doltishness," or of "strangers because they speak not English as we do." He objects also to Lyly's surfeit of similitudes, accusing him of "rifling up all Herbarists, all stories of Beasts, Fowls, and Fishes," which, he says, is "an absurd surfeit to the ears," "rather overswaying the memory than any whit informing the judgment."

ELEMENTS OF STYLE.

Vocabulary. — "It is marvellous," says Mr William Stigant, author of an essay on Sidney in the 'Cambridge Essays' for 1858, "with what a delicate tact he had divined the capacity of the English language for prose composition, and how few obsolete words he has made use of, writing in advance of the great Elizabethan epoch. He reads indeed more modern than any author of that century." Sidney escapes free from Thomas Wilson's censure; his terms are neither French, nor Italianate, nor inkhorn words of Latin origin. The idiom, too, is purely English: he differs but seldom from modern idiom, and then from using English idioms that have become obsolete, not from any affectation of foreign syntax.

As a master of the living English of his time, he must rank among the highest. Even to modern readers his diction is rich and varied; the fitting word is chosen with an apparent ease that implies a great power over the language.

Sentences. — Nathan Drake's criticisms of Sidney's style as "nerveless and incompact," can apply only to the sentences. The component clauses are framed with great versatility, sometimes with a rich long-drawn melody, sometimes with pointed neatness, sometimes with proverbial conciseness. In putting the clauses together, he is certainly careless. He does not, like Jeremy Taylor, pour them out breathlessly without any syntax whatever, but he rambles on without much regard to unity, or to the symmetrical distribution of his matter. In our various quotations, the reader will see his ordinary sentences; the following is a specimen of his worst form :—

"The country Arcadia among all the provinces of Greece, hath ever been had in singular reputation; partly for the sweetness of the air, and other natural benefits, but principally for the well-tempered minds of the people, who (finding that the shining title of glory, so much affected by other nations, doth indeed help little to the happiness of life) are the only people, which, as by their justice and providence give neither cause nor hope to their neighbours to annoy; so are they not stirred with false praise to trouble others' quiet, thinking it a small reward for the wasting of their own lives in ravening, that their posterity should long after say, they had done so."

Paragraphs.—Our author's paragraph arrangement is very irregular, though not worse than the average of his time. Sometimes, when he ought to begin a new paragraph, he does not even begin a new sentence. The following passage is an example of his want of strict method:—

"Poesy, therefore, is an art of imitation, for so Aristotle termeth it in his word *Mimesis,* that is to say, a representing, counterfeiting, or figuring forth: to speak metaphorically, a speaking picture: with this end, to teach and delight; of this have been three several kinds. The chief, both in antiquity and excellency, were they that did imitate the inconceivable excellencies of God. Such were, David in his Psalms; Solomon in his Song of Songs, in his Ecclesiastes, and Proverbs; Moses and Deborah in their hymns, and the writer of Job; which, beside other, the learned Emanuel Tremilius and Franciscus Junius do entitle the poetical part of the Scripture. Against these none will speak that hath the Holy Ghost in due holy reverence.

"In this kind, though in a wrong divinity, were Orpheus, Amphion, Homer in his hymns, and many other, both Greeks and Romans; and this Poesy must be used, by whosoever will follow S. James his counsel, in singing Psalms when they are merry; and I know is used with the fruit of comfort by some, when in sorrowful pangs of their death-bringing sins, they find the consolation of the never-leaving goodness.

"The second kind is of them that deal with matters philosophical; either moral, as, &c.: . . . which who mislike, the fault is in their judgments quite out of taste, and not in the sweet food of sweetly uttered knowledge. But because this second sort is wrapped within the fold of the proposed subject, and takes not the course of his own invention, whether they be properly Poets or no, let Grammarians dispute: and go to the third, indeed right Poets, of whom," &c.

Minor niceties, of course, we need not look for. It is, however, interesting to meet the following example of a set comparison, where the order of the balance is better kept than in some of the celebrated later efforts after the same plan. He is describing "the two daughters of King Basilius, so beyond measure excellent in all the gifts allotted to reasonable creatures, that we may think they were born to show that nature is no step-mother to that sex, how much soever some men (sharp-witted only in evil-speaking) have sought to disgrace them:"—

"The elder is named *Pamela;* by many men not deemed inferior to her sister: for my part, when I marked them both, methought there was (if at least such perfections may receive the name of more) more sweetness in

Philoclea, but more majesty in *Pamela*. Methought love played in *Philoclea's* eyes, and threatened in *Pamela's:* methought *Philoclea's* beauty only persuaded, but so persuaded as all hearts must yield. *Pamela's* beauty used violence, and such violence as no heart could resist. And it seems that such proportion is between their minds; *Philoclea* so bashful, as if her excellencies had stolen into her before she was aware; so humble that she will put all pride out of countenance; in sum, such proceeding as will stir hope, but teach hope good manners. *Pamela* of high thoughts, who avoids not pride with not knowing her excellencies, but by making that one of her excellencies to be void of pride; her mother's wisdom, greatness, nobility, but (if I guess aright) knit with a more constant temper."

Figures.—Sidney is wholly free from what he condemns in Lyly—excess of similes and parallels. He makes comparatively few formal similitudes. Some of those that he does make are singularly apt. The saying that Chevy Chase "moved him like the sound of a trumpet," is as familiar as any of Shakspeare's. Another similitude borrowed or stolen from him is scarcely less famous. A combat between two of his heroes he describes as being like a battle between a Spanish galleon and an English man-of-war. The figure is well known as applied by Fuller to Ben Jonson and Shakspeare.

While comparatively free from gaudy and fantastic embellishments, one of the worst vices of the Elizabethan style, he is not a plain writer. His peculiar affectation consists in an excessive use of fanciful personifications and fanciful antitheses; fancies usually sweet and graceful, and palling only from overmuch repetition. We touched on this in the brief account of his character; we shall find abundant examples in the quotations that follow. When the subject-matter is beautiful and pleasing, these graceful fancies are an additional charm; when the subject is grave or lofty, they are inharmonious and out of place.

Perhaps the most pleasing use of his personifications is in the description of nature. He often expresses the time of the day euphemistically. For example: "About the time that the candles began to inherit the sun's office;" "seeing the day begin to disclose her comfortable beauties;" "as soon as the morning had took a full possession of the element;" and suchlike. In describing landscape, he follows no descriptive method; merely overlaying the various particulars of a scene with his "flowers of poetry," "sugared" epithets, and pleasing figurative conceits. Thus he describes how Musidorus and Clitophon came to "a pleasant valley, on either side of which high hills *lifted up their beetle brows, as if they would overlook the pleasantness of the under prospect.*" And how "they laid them down hard by the murmuring music of certain waters, which spouted out of the side of the hills, and in the bottom of the valley made of many springs a pretty brook, *like a commonwealth of many families.*"

The following longer passage is really an example of his favourite figures, rather than an illustration of any descriptive art:—

"It was indeed a place of delight; for through the midst of it there ran a sweet brook, which did both hold the eye open with her azure streams, and yet seek to close the eye with the purling noise it made upon the pebble stones it ran over: the field itself being set in some places with roses, and in all the rest constantly preserving a flourishing green: the roses added such a ruddy show unto it, as though the field were bashful at his own beauty: about it, as if it had been to enclose a theatre, grew such sort of trees, as either excellency of fruit, stateliness of growth, continual greenness, or poetical fancies, have made at any time famous. In most part of which there had been framed by art such pleasant arbours, that, one answering another, they became a gallery aloft from tree to tree almost round about, which below gave a perfect shadow; a pleasant refuge then from the choleric look of Phœbus."

QUALITIES OF STYLE.

Simplicity and Clearness.—Sidney's style, as we have said, is free alike from the "inkhorn" technical words of the learned pedant, and from the French and "Italianate" words of the travelled man of fashion. His meaning is also less cumbered and interrupted with superfluous quotations than was common at the time.

The order of topics in the Apology shows little sense of the value of good arrangement. There is a kind of rough method on the large scale. He first sets out the true nature and value of poetry, then answers objections, and concludes with a criticism of existing poetry. But within these divisions he jumps from one thing to another without restraint.

Precision in the use of words was little attended to till much later in the history of our language.

Strength.—The 'Arcadia' being a chivalrous romance, is an excellent field for a powerful style. In the imagination of thrilling adventures, reckless braving of danger, exploits of superhuman heroism, our author shows a keen enjoyment of vigorous action. Musidorus and Pyrocles perform the most wonderful achievements—leading armies, quelling tumults, fighting single combats, passing from chains and imprisonment to victorious command,—achievements well fitted to exercise the highest powers of vigorous narrative and description.

We have seen (p. 199) how this stirring and imposing activity is qualified and softened down. Partly there is a large admixture of gentler elements in the plot, the exploits being for the most part either done at the instigation of love, or recited to gratify the curiosity of fair hearers. But what we are concerned with here is not so much the subject-matter as the manner of presentation. As already noted incidentally, Sidney's style is deliberately the reverse of exciting or elevating. Whether he is reciting grim deeds of battle, or describing the most terrific phenomena of nature, he tempers the account with soft and humorous fancies. He wrote the 'Arcadia' more to amuse himself and his sister than to set forth thrilling and heroic incidents in their appropriate language. The following are two examples of his treatment of exciting themes. The manner as a whole would not be tolerated in the present age, and even as a relic of antiquity will hardly be enjoyed if read as a serious effort. We must keep in mind that the youthful knight wrote for the entertainment of his sister and her lady friends; and that, with all his softness and courtesy, he took pleasure in occasionally shocking his gentle readers with somewhat grim humour:—

"But by this time there had been a furious meeting of either side: where after the terrible salutation of warlike noise, the shaking of hands was with sharp weapons; some lances, according to the metal they met and skill of the guider, did stain themselves in blood; some flew up in pieces, as if they would threaten heaven because they failed on earth. But their office was quickly inherited, either by (the prince of weapons) the sword, or by some heavy mace, or biting axe; which hunting still the weakest chace, sought ever to light there where smallest resistance might worse prevent mischief. The clashing of armour, and crushing of staves, the justling of bodies, the resounding of blows, was the first part of that ill-agreeing musick, which was beautified with the grisliness of wounds, the rising of dust, the hideous falls and the groans of the dying. The very horses angry in their master's anger, with love and obedience, brought forth the effects of hate and resistance, and with minds of servitude did as if they affected glory. Some lay dead under their dead masters, whom unknightly wounds had unjustly punished for a faithful duty. Some lay upon their lords by like accident, and in death had the honour to be borne by them, whom in life they had borne. Some having lost their commanding burthens, ran scattered about the field, abashed with the madness of mankind. The earth itself (wont to be a burial of men) was now, as it were, buried with men: so was the face thereof hidden with dead bodies, to whom death had come masked in divers manners. In one place lay disinherited heads dispossessed of their natural seignories; in another, whole bodies to see to, but that their hearts wont to be bound all over so close, were now, with deadly violence, opened: in others, fouler deaths had uglily displayed their trailing guts. There lay arms, whose fingers yet moved, as if they would feel for him that made them feel; and legs which, contrary to common reason, by being discharged of their burthen, were grown heavier. But no sword payed so large a tribute of souls to the eternal kingdom as that of *Amphialus;* who, like a tiger from whom a company of wolves did seek to ravish a new-gotten prey, so he (remembering they came to take away *Philoclea*) did labour to make valour, strength, choler, and hatred to answer the proportion of his love, which was infinite."

"But by that the next morning began a little to make a gilded show of a good meaning, there arose even with the sun, a vail of dark clouds before his face, which shortly, like ink poured into water, had blacked over all the face of heaven; preparing as it were a mournful stage for a tragedy to be played on. For forthwith the winds began to speak louder, and as in a tumultuous kingdom, to think themselves fittest instruments of commandment; and blowing whole storms of hail and rain upon them, they were sooner in danger than they could almost bethink themselves of change. For then the traitorous sea began to swell in pride against the afflicted navy, under which, while the heaven favoured them, it had lain so calmly, making mountains of itself, over which the tossed and tottering ship should climb, to be straight carried down again to a pit of hellish darkness; with such cruel blows against the sides of the ship that, which way soever it went, was still in his malice that there was left neither power to stay, nor way to escape. . . . But in the ship wherein the princes were, now left as much alone as proud lords be when fortune fails them, though they employed all industry to save themselves, yet what they did was rather for duty to nature than hope to escape so ugly a darkness as if it would prevent the night's coming, usurped the day's right: which accompanied sometimes with thunders, always with horrible noises of the chasing winds, made the masters and pilots so astonished that they knew not how to direct; and if they knew they could scarcely, when they directed, hear their own whistle. For the sea strove with the winds which should be louder, and the shrouds of the ship, with a ghastful noise to them that were in it, witnessed, that their ruin was the wager of the other's contention, and the heaven roaring out thunder the more amazed them as having those powers for enemies. There was to be seen the divers manner of minds in distress; some sat upon the top of the poop weeping and wailing, till the sea swallowed them; some one more able to abide death than the fear of death, cut his own throat to prevent drowning; some prayed; and there wanted not of them which cursed, as if the heavens could not be more angry than they were."

Pathos.—In the 'Arcadia' there are very few passages to gratify the taste for the pathos of tender regret. Pitiable incidents occur very often, but they serve to keep alive the stir of the plot, and do not invite us to shut the book and indulge in melancholy tenderness. The misery of the sufferers is too intense to be pathetic. They suffer from the pangs of despised love, from the agony of bereavement, from the rage of remorse; they are not resigned to their fate.

The following are two exceptions to the above general statement —two pitiful incidents that have no influence on the plot, and are good subjects for pathetic treatment. One is the death of young Agenor, related with genuine pathos. Had the death of the gay youth been wilful, it would have moved us with horror; being an accident, it touches us with sorrow as for an unavoidable and irremediable misfortune:—

"His name was *Agenor*, of all that army the most beautiful; who having ridden in sportful conversation among the foremost, all armed, saving that his beaver was up, to have his breath at more freedom, seeing *Amphialus* come a pretty way before his company, neither staying the commandment of his captain, nor reckoning whether his face were armed or no, set spurs to his horse, and with youthful bravery casting his staff about his head, put it then in his rest, as careful of comely carrying it as if the mark had been but a ring and the lookers-on ladies. But *Amphialus's* lance was already come to the last of his descending line, and began to make the full point of death against the head of this young gentleman; when *Amphialus*, perceiving his youth and beauty, compassion so rebated the edge of choler that he spared that fair nakedness, and let his staff fall to Agenor's vampalt: so as both with brave breaking should hurtlessly have performed that match, but that the pitiless lance of *Amphialus* (angry with being broken) with an unlucky counterbuff, full of unsparing splinters, lighted upon that face, far fitter for the combats of Venus; giving not only a sudden but a foul death, leaving scarcely any tokens of his former beauty; but his hands abandoning the reins and his thighs the saddle, he fell sideward from the horse."

The other is the death of Parthenia—a lady who, when her husband was slain, put on armour, challenged his victor, and perished in the fight. Sidney overlays this painful subject with his favourite figures. It is difficult to feel in what mood such an incident could appear a suitable ground for such embroidery:—

"But the head-piece was no sooner off, but that there fell about the shoulders of the overcome knight the treasure of fair golden hair, which with the face (soon known by the badge of excellency) witnessed that it was *Parthenia*, the unfortunately virtuous wife of *Argalus;* her beauty then, even in despight of the passed sorrow, or coming death, assuring all beholders that it was nothing short of perfection. For her exceeding fair eyes, having with continual weeping gotten a little redness about them, her round sweetly-swelling lips a little trembling, as though they kissed their neighbour death; in her cheeks the whiteness striving by little and little to get upon the rosiness of them; her neck, a neck indeed of alabaster, displaying the wound, which with most dainty blood laboured to drown his own beauties; so as here was a river of purest red, there an island of perfectest white, each giving lustre to the other, with the sweet countenance, God knows, full of an unaffected languishing: though these things to a grossly conceiving sense might seem disgraces, yet indeed were they but apparelling beauty in a new fashion, which all looked upon through the spectacles of pity, did even increase the lines of her natural fairness; so as *Amphialus* was astonished with grief, compassion, and shame, detesting his fortune that made him unfortunate in victory."

Sidney's true pathos lies chiefly in pictures of beauty and devotedness. With such subjects his fancies are more in keeping. We have seen (p. 203) with what sweetness he can describe natural scenery. In his descriptions of female beauty, he is sometimes a little more sensuous than the taste of our period thinks becoming. But there is much of his description that none need hesitate to read. The following hyperbolical passage contains what is probably the original of one of Shakspeare's sweetest fancies:—

"Her breath is more sweet than a gentle south-west wind, which comes creeping over flowery fields and shadowed waters in the extreme heat of summer; and yet is nothing compared to the honey-flowing speech that breath doth carry; no more all that our eyes can see of her (though when they have seen her, what else they shall ever see is but dry stubble after clover-grass) is to be matched with the flock of unspeakable virtues, laid up delightfully in that best-builded fold."

His personifications appear to advantage in such passages as this:—

"And as the ladies played there in the water, sometimes striking it with their hands, the water (making lines on his face) seemed to smile at such beating, and, with twenty bubbles, not to be content to have the picture of their face in large upon him, but he would in each of those bubbles set forth the miniature of them."

The 'Arcadia' is brimful of chivalrous devotion. Every personage is one of a pair of lovers—Pyrocles and Philoclea, Musidorus and Pamela, Helen and Amphialus, Amphialus and Pamela, Argalus and Parthenia, Phalantus and Artesia, &c. The friendship of Pyrocles and Musidorus is like the friendship of Pylades and Orestes. When the one is supposed to be drowned, the other is restrained only by force from casting himself into the sea. When the one is seized and threatened with death, the other insists upon taking his place. It would indeed be difficult to make any alteration in the plot that should bring out more numerous or more striking acts of devotedness.

Humour.—Sidney's humour is hearty, joyous—bordering sometimes upon farce, but usually refined by the wit of the expression. In the 'Arcadia' he has one or two humorous characters, notably Dametas and Mopsa;[1] and describes some exquisitely ludicrous scenes, such as the fight between the two cowards Dametas and Clinias, and Mopsa in the wishing-tree. The following passage, occurring in the description of a riot, is very farcical, without much wit to give it refinement:—

"Yet among the rebels there was a dapper fellow, a tailor by occupation, who fetching his courage only from their going back, began to bow his knees, and very fencer-like to draw near to Zelmane. But as he came within her distance, turning his sword very nicely about his crown, Basilius struck off his nose. He (being suitor to a seamstress's daughter, and therefore not a little grieved for such a disgrace) he stooped down, because he had heard that if it were fresh put to, it would cleave on again. But as his hand was on the ground to bring his nose to his head, Zelmane with a blow sent his head to his nose."

There is a boyish freshness and simplicity about the humour of the Apology. In the beginning, by way of anticipating the criticism that he is a prejudiced enthusiast in favour of poetry, he tells a humorous story to bring out that "self-love is better than any gilding to make that seem gorgeous wherein ourselves are parties." He tells us how he and a friend took lessons of a riding-master in Vienna, and that this gentleman, "according to the fertileness of the Italian wit, did not only afford us the demonstration of his practice, but sought to enrich our minds with the contemplations therein, which he thought most precious." He then recounts some of Pugliano's bravuras about the value of horsemanship—"skill of government was but a pedanteria in comparison"—and repeats some of his eloquent praises of the horse:—

[1] Mopsa is borrowed by Shakspeare.

"The only serviceable courtier without flattery, the beast of most beauty, faithfulness, courage, and such more, that if I had not been a piece of a logician before I came to him, *I think he would have persuaded me to have wished myself a horse.*"

His argument for the unities is enlivened by a similar spirit of boisterous mockery :—

"For where the stage should always represent but one place, and the uttermost time presupposed in it should be, both by Aristotle's precept and common reason, but one day: there is both many days and many places, inartificially imagined. But if it be so in Gorboduc, how much more in all the rest? Where you shall have Asia of the one side, and Afric of the other, and so many other under-kingdoms that the Player, when he cometh in, must ever begin with telling where he is: or else the tale will not be conceived. Now ye shall have three ladies walk to gather flowers, and then we must believe the stage to be a Garden. By-and-by we hear news of shipwreck in the same place, and then we are to blame if we accept it not for a Rock.

"Upon the back of that, comes out a hideous monster with fire and smoke, and then the miserable beholders are bound to take it for a Cave. While in the mean time, two armies fly in, represented with four swords and bucklers, and then what hard heart will not receive it for a pitched field? Now, of time they are much more liberal, for ordinary it is that two princes fall in love. After many traverses she is got with child, delivered of a fair boy, he is lost, groweth a man, falls in love, and is ready to get another child, and all this in two hours space: which how absurd it is in sense," &c.

This must have been very amusing ridicule [1] of the stage as it existed in Sidney's time, though from the change of circumstances it has not the same effect for us. The mock-heroic close of the Apology has not yet lost its force, though even it is perhaps too exuberant for modern taste :—

"Thus doing, your name shall flourish in the Printer's shops; thus doing, you shall be of kin to many a poetical preface; thus doing, you shall be most fair, most rich, most wise, most all,—you shall dwell upon superlatives. . . . But if (fie of such a But) you be borne so near the dull-making *Cataphract* of *Nilus* that you cannot hear the Planet-like Music of Poetry, if you have so earth-creeping a mind, that it cannot lift itself up to look to the sky of Poetry; or rather, by a certain rustical disdain will become such a Mome, as to be a Momus of Poetry: then, though I will not wish unto you the Ass's ears of Midas, nor to be driven by a Poet's verses (as Bubonax was) to hang himself, nor to be rhymed to death, as is said to be done in Ireland; yet thus much curse I must send you, in the behalf of all Poets, that while you live, you live in love, and never get favour, for lacking skill of a Sonnet; and when you die, your memory die from the earth for want of an Epitaph."

Melody. Harmony.—We have already remarked (*Sentences*, p. 201) that Sidney is versatile in the movement of his language. Every reader must notice how readily he adapts his rhythm to pointed wit or flowing declamation. Few of our writers surpass him in soaring and bringing out a full melodious cadence. The last-quoted sentence is as measured and stately in its movement as

[1] It may have suggested the incomparable fun of the play before Theseus in Midsummer Night's Dream.'

could well be found. In some of the tender passages, the music of the language is such as can hardly be imitated under present laws of taste as regards epithets. The following is an instance—"the nightingales one with the other striving which could *in most dainty variety recount their wrong-caused sorrow.*"

It is needless to review Sidney's style at length under the kinds of composition. We have seen that he has no descriptive method—that the only merit of his description lies in the graces of his style. As a *Narrator*, he relates events with clearness; but the different lines of events are so numerous and interwoven that it is difficult to avoid getting confused among them. To those that do not enjoy the beauties of his language, the numerous speeches and meditations must appear a tedious impediment to the action. As regards *Exposition*, all has been said under the intellectual qualities. In the way of *Persuasion*, his Apology would tell partly by its clear and ingenious arguments, partly by its winning playfulness of manner and impetuous exuberance of spirits.

RICHARD HOOKER, 1553-1600.

The following estimate of Hooker by the author of the 'Introduction to the Literature of Europe' is often quoted: "So stately "and graceful is the march of his periods, so various the fall of his "musical cadences upon the ear, so rich in images, so condensed in "sentences, so grave and noble his diction, so little is there of vul-"garity in his racy idiom, of pedantry in his learned phrase, that "I know not whether any later writer has more admirably dis-"played the capacities of our language, or produced passages more "worthy of comparison with the splendid monuments of antiquity." Though this eloquent panegyric is an extreme exaggeration, and could never have been written by any person keeping his eye on the facts, the 'Ecclesiastical Polity' does undoubtedly, as is often said, "mark an era in English prose." In some respects superior, in some inferior to Sidney's, Hooker's style is the first specimen of good prose applied to the weightier purposes of literature.

According to Izaak Walton, in one of his well-known "Lives," Hooker was born at Heavitree, in or near Exeter. His parents were poor, but of respectable family; his uncle John was Chamberlain of Exeter. His father designed to apprentice him to a trade; but his schoolmaster, seeing the boy's abilities, was solicitous that he should get learning, and spoke to the chamberlain uncle. The uncle spoke to Jewel, Bishop of Salisbury, who examined the young prodigy, found him all that the good schoolmaster represented, gave him a pension, and in 1567 got him admitted as a Clerk (sizar, servitor, or bursar) to Corpus Christi, Oxford. In 1571 his patron died, and Hooker was greatly dejected, and even in fears, about his future subsistence. From this he was relieved by the President of the College, who promised to be his friend; and some nine months after, through the recommendation of his late patron, he got as a pupil Edwin, son of Bishop Sandys, whose influence was afterwards of great service to him. For some ten years after this, he remained at Oxford, being admitted Fellow of his College in 1577, appointed to read Hebrew lectures in 1579, and in the same year temporarily expelled along with Reynolds for some reason now unknown. During this time he was an industrious reader, "enriching," says Walton, "his quiet and capacious soul with the precious learning of the philosophers, casuists, and schoolmen; and with them the foundation and reason of all laws, both sacred and civil; and indeed with such other learning as lay most remote from the track of common studies." In 1581, going to preach in London, he was led to make an unhappy marriage; and about the same time settled with his wife in the living of Drayton Beauchamp, in Buckinghamshire. In 1584-85, at the recommendation of Sandys, whose son had seen and pitied the unhappiness of his old tutor's married life, Hooker was taken in hand by Archbishop Whitgift, and through his influence appointed Master of the Temple, in the Episcopal interest, and against a Presbyterian champion of the name of Travers. Here began Hooker's labours in defence of Episcopacy. Travers, a bold preacher, with a popular manner, was Afternoon Lecturer in the Temple, and maintained in the pulpit Presbyterian views of Church government. Hooker preaching in the forenoon, "the pulpit," as Fuller said, "spake pure Canterbury in the morning, and Geneva in the afternoon." Travers, silenced by Whitgift on the ground of insufficient ordination, continued the war in print; Hooker replied—but, unfit for the worry of controversy, begged from his patron some quiet post in the country, and in 1591 removed to the living of Boscombe, near Salisbury. Here in peace and privacy he meditated his 'Ecclesiastical Polity,' and published the first four Books in 1594. Translated in 1595 to the better living of Bishopsborne, near Canterbury, he sent a fifth Book to the press in 1597. He died in 1600, leaving three more Books of the Polity. The genuineness of these later books is doubted by Walton. On his and other evidence it is contended that the Sixth Book was mutilated by the Presbyterian friends of Hooker's wife, and interpolated with other matter taken from Hooker's papers; also that the Seventh and the Eighth received a bias from Presbyterian hands. The evidence of fraud, though not improbable, is scarcely conclusive. The good faith of Hooker's Episcopal friends is shown by their publishing what they believed to be mutilated copies. The Sixth and Eighth Books were first published in 1651, the Seventh in 1662.

From Walton we have a circumstantial description of Hooker as "a man in poor clothes, his loins usually girt in a coarse gown or canonical coat; of a mean stature, and stooping, and yet more lowly in the thought of his soul; his body worn out, not with age, but study and holy mortifications; his face full of heat-pimples, begot by his inactivity and sedentary life." This account of his poor *physique* is borne out by other authorities. Dr Spenser says that his body was spent with study, and Fuller that his voice was low and his stature little. To complete his bodily infirmities, "though not purblind, he was short or weak sighted."

Impartial critics will not join the devoted admirers of Hooker in placing him among the greatest intellects of the nation. All his life through he was a most industrious student, and his acquisitions as a scholar were undeniably profound. But his original force, whether as a thinker or as an expositor, was not great. As a champion of Episcopacy, he added little or nothing to the arguments of Jewel and Whitgift. Even his high flights of eloquence are not always original; in many cases the ideas and the images are borrowed, the diction only being his own. In the application of his scholarship he is often very ingenious. His great fault, and it is fatal to the high pretensions set up for him, is a want of coherence. He seems incapable of the effort of closely concatenating his thoughts. As he writes, a quotation occurs to him having some dim application to his present subject; he puts down the quotation, but leaves its bearing vague and indistinct. Something like this is admitted, as it must be admitted, by his warmest eulogists. The explanation probably lies in his constitutional languor. What his intellect might have done in a more vigorous constitution of body, can be only a matter of speculation.—One thing may be noted by way of parenthesis. If in controversy his constitutional feebleness interfered with the clear and telling application of his scholarship, in another respect it gave him a great advantage over his opponents. It left him free from the impulses of vehement attachment; no impetuosity of conviction hurried him into unreason; he could always approach his subject with judicial calmness, and take a circumspect survey of his ground. This dispassionate habit strikes us in every sentence; it is Hooker's chief distinction amidst the fiery partisanship of the time. Whether his judgment was sound or unsound, he was eminently free from vehement prejudice, "or mist of passionate affection."

Perhaps the chief cause of the over-estimation of Hooker's intellectual force is the extraordinary musical richness of his language. Most of us are more influenced by mere pomp of sound than we might be willing to allow; and the melody of Hooker's periods is of the richest order. Like De Quincey, he was extremely susceptible to the "luxuries of the ear." This we can see from his own account of how music affected him: "We are at the hearing of some more inclined unto sorrow and heaviness, of some more mollified and softened in mind; one kind apter to stay and settle us, another to move and stir our affections; there is that draweth to a marvellous grave and sober mediocrity; there is also that carrieth, as it were, into ecstasies, filling the mind with a heavenly joy, and for the time in a manner severing it from the body."

Though the Polity is professedly an argumentative work, and does contain some very solid dispassionate argument, his mind was perhaps more poetical than scientific. Special emotions do not assert themselves in marked individual luxuriance. The poverty of his nature in vital power was not favourable to the growth of emotion. We meet in the Polity neither rancorous invective nor passionate sentimental philanthropy, neither hero-worship nor exuberant self-confident vivacity. The work is as utterly deficient in these more obtrusive forms of emotion as could well be conceived. The basis of the peculiar poetic vein of the work is his intense fear of every mode of confusion, strife, agitation; his passionate longing for quiet and tranquillity. He dilates with an approach to rapture on "the glorious inhabitants of those sacred palaces, where nothing but light and blessed immortality, no shadow of matter for tears, discontentments, griefs, and uncomfortable passions to work upon, but all joy, tranquillity, and peace, even for ever and ever doth dwell." In the spirit of this craving for peace, and weary impatience of conflict and excitement, he dwells upon the prevalence of order throughout nature, upon the blessings of regularity and authority wherever they exist; and passionately deprecates every appearance of insubordination. He is earnest with all dissenters from the established faith, worship, or government, to give up "private discretion," "private fancies," which can lead only to anarchy, disturbance, tumult. He would have them mature their views, submit these to constituted authority, and abide by the decision. Meantime let them obey in silence.

What we know of his demeanour and active habits confirms the view of his character that one naturally forms from reading his works. "God and nature," says Izaak Walton, "blest him with so blessed a bashfulness, that as in his younger days his pupils might easily look him out of countenance; so neither then, nor in his age, did he ever look any man in the face; and was of so mild and humble a nature, that his poor parish clerk and he did never talk but with both their hats on, or both off, at the same time." All circumstances show Hooker to have been an unusually shy, sensitive, feeble little man, with very little activity, and very low constitutional power. He entered the controversies of his time unwittingly; and, after a short experience, begged for "peace and privacy." When forced to vindicate what he had said in his sermons, he did so, not with the heat of a strongly persuaded man of energy, but with the meekness and charity of a retiring nature. How much he leant upon others appears in the narrative of his college life—so different from the sturdy self-reliance of Johnson. Still more does this come out in Walton's well-known account of his visit to the "Shunamite's House" in London, when he went up from Oxford to preach. Reaching London on the back of a horse that would not or could not run, wet, weary, weather-beaten, numb with wind and rain, he bitterly refused to be persuaded that he could preach within two days; but the Shunamite, Mrs Churchman, by cosy nursing, "enabled him to perform the office of the day," and having given him such a taste of the comfort of womanly ministration, persuaded him that he needed a wife, drew from the unresisting man in his gratitude a commission to procure one, and provided him with her own daughter.—There is hardly to be found in history a more extreme instance of a man wanting in self-will, and submitting himself passively to the disposal of others.[1]

Opinions.—One of the many eulogistic sayings concerning Hooker is that, "should the English Constitution in Church and State be unhappily ruined, . . . the book" ('Ecclesiastical Polity') "probably contains materials sufficient for repairing and rebuilding the shattered fabric." A less glowing admirer represents him as "the one adequate exponent of the religious ideas and policy of the age and reign of Elizabeth." Even this needs an explanation. Hooker was not, as this would imply, an impartial chronicler of all existing views of Church doctrine, ritual, and government. He was the champion of a religious party—of the adherents to Episcopacy. He expounded their views, and with such acceptance, that for more than 250 years he has been honoured as a main bulwark of the Church of England. Certainly he has a good claim to his title—"the judicious Hooker!" The profound scholarship of the work, its "earnest longing desire to see things brought to a peaceable end," its entire freedom from partisan heat, and consequent appearance of impartiality, go a long way to account for his extraordinary popularity as a doctrinal writer.

Another cause may have helped in some small degree. We have

[1] The story is doubted by Mr Keble, who also, by way of exalting Hooker's virtue, maintains that his meekness and patience under his wife was not constitutional, but a painfully acquired self-command. Had old Izaak Walton's ideal of virtue been the same as Mr Keble's, we should probably never have heard of Hooker's passive obedience in domestic life; but if we doubt this fact, we must doubt many others that confirm it. In Walton's Biography—and it is our only external authority—Hooker appears as an inactive man of feeble constitution, yielding willingly to the guidance of others. That he should show signs of an irritable temper in his writings is hardly to the purpose, if it could be established. Self-assertion upon paper and self-assertion in an actual presence are two very different things.

already mentioned his occasional vagueness, his hazy application of general principles and parallel citations. This dimness of expression has had curious results. Men of diametrically opposite opinions have sought to strengthen their cause with his authority. James II. was wont to say that Hooker's Polity converted him to Romanism. Bishop Hoadley, a Church polemic of Queen Anne's reign, cited Hooker in confirmation of his views, that the form of Church government is a matter of Christian expediency. In extreme opposition to this, the High Church party re-edited Hooker as a main instrument in keeping the Anglican Church "near to primitive truth and apostolical order," as upholding the divine right of Episcopacy, and the doctrine of apostolical succession. Had Hooker expressed himself with greater distinctness, his reputation might have been less universal.

ELEMENTS OF STYLE.

Vocabulary.—Hooker's diction is not so modern as Sidney's. A glossary to Hooker would be at least ten times as large as a glossary to an equal amount of writing by Sidney. In great measure, of course, this is due to the difference of subject. By Swift he is coupled with Parsons the Jesuit as writing a purer style than other theologians of his time. He did not coin words like Jeremy Taylor, nor employ them in meanings warranted by derivation but not by usage—very common errors among his more pedantic contemporaries. His usages are not peculiar and eccentric. Some of his words—such as "civil" for *civilised*, "regiment" for *regimen* or *government*, "put in ure" for put in *use* or *practice*—are now obsolete, but they were good current English in his day. His command of words is good, but he has not the rich variety of Sidney, much less of Bacon.

Sentences.—Hooker affords our first example of an elaborate, high-sounding "periodic style." His sentences, in their general character, are long and involved—an extreme contrast to the light and pointed style of John Lyly, though of their kind they are quite as finished. With all their excellences, they are not good models for English periods. In writing our first elaborate theological treatise, his fine ear was irresistibly caught by the rhythm of Latin models; and while he learned from them a more even proportion of sentence, he learned also to build an elaborate rhythm at the expense of native idiom.[1] The following example of his "elaborate collocation" is quoted by Dr Drake:—

[1] We have seen Hallam's conception of our author's sentences. Dr Drake's is more moderate, and nearer the facts: "Though the words for the most part are well chosen and pure, the arrangement of them into sentences is intricate and harsh, and formed almost exclusively on the idiom and construction of the Latin. Much strength and vigour are derived from this adoption; but perspicuity, sweetness, and ease are too generally sacrificed."

"Though for no other cause, yet for this, that posterity may know we have not loosely, through silence, permitted things to pass away as in a dream, there shall be for men's information, extant this much concerning the present state of the Church of God established amongst us, and their careful endeavours which would have upheld the same."

Here the last clause is very awkwardly placed. In the following sentence the first clause is still more awkward, and towards the end the influence of Latin models is still more apparent :—

"And beyond seas, of them which fled in the days of Queen Mary, some contenting themselves abroad with the use of their own service-book *at home authorised before their departure out of the realm,* others liking better *the Common Prayer-book of the Church of Geneva translated, those smaller contentions before begun were by this means somewhat increased.*"

In the parts italicised the violation of English idiom and order is peculiarly marked. As at least one-half of the Polity is written in this style, Hallam must have been thinking of very select passages when he spoke of Hooker's "racy idiom."

Sometimes, in his more animated moments, he surprises us with a run of shorter sentences. These occur but rarely, and are not long sustained. The following is an example :—

"But wise men are men, and the truth is truth. That which Calvin did for establishment of his discipline, seemeth more commendable than that which he taught for the countenancing of it established. Nature worketh in us all a love to our own counsels. The contradiction of others is a fan to inflame that love. Our love set on fire to maintain that which once we have done, sharpeneth the wit to dispute, to argue, and by all means to reason for it. Wherefore a marvel it were if a man of so great capacity," &c.

Here he returns to his usual length of sentence. Occasionally we meet with balanced passages. In such cases, from aiming at point, he is more idiomatic and also less intricate. The following comes much nearer the modern standard than our previous extracts :—

"These men in whose mouths at the first sounded nothing but mortification of the flesh, were come at the length to think they might lawfully have their six or seven wives apiece ; they which at the first thought judgment and justice itself to be merciless cruelty, accounted at the length their own hands sanctified with being imbrued in Christian blood ; they who at the first were wont to beat down all dominion, and to urge against poor constables 'kings of nations ;' had at the length both consuls and kings of their own erection amongst themselves : finally, they which could not brook at the first that any man should seek, no not by law, the recovery of goods injuriously taken or withheld from him, were grown at the last to think they could not offer unto God more acceptable sacrifice, than by turning their adversaries clean out of house and home, and by enriching themselves with all kind of spoil and pillage ; which thing being laid to their charge, they had in a readiness their answer, that now the time was come, when according to the Saviour's promise 'the meek ones must inherit the earth ;' and that their title hereunto was the same which the righteous Israelites had unto the goods of the wicked Egyptians."

His inversions sometimes have the effect of putting the emphatic words in the emphatic places; for example, in the following harsh construction:—

"That which by wisdom he saw to be requisite for that people, was by as great wisdom compassed."

Now quite as good emphasis might be had without such a sacrifice of euphony and idiom. But apart from this, the theory that all his inversions have this object is not tenable. His construction is ruled chiefly by fascination for the rhythm that goes with the Latin idiom. Thus, in a sentence quoted at p. 213, he weakens the emphasis by reserving the verb "doth dwell" to the end, after the fashion of the Latin, and that, too, when English idiom permitted the inversion. "Wherein doth dwell nothing but light and blessed immortality," &c., would have been perfectly good English idiom, and would have given better emphasis. But Hooker's ear was tuned to a foreign rhythm. A close examination of almost any passage would show great room for improvement in the way of emphasis. In no era of English style has much regard been paid to the placing of words except for rhythm.

In the distribution of his matter into sentences, Hooker is more correct than Sidney is in the Apology. He observes much better the requirements of unity; his aiming at the period prevented rambling. In this respect he will bear comparison with any writer of the seventeenth century; it helps greatly to give him a modern air.

Paragraphs.—Attention to clearness and simplicity in the structure of paragraphs was a thing unknown in the age of Elizabeth, and Hooker was in this respect neither better nor worse than the good writers of his time. Sometimes when he is dealing confusedly with an obscure subject, the connection between one sentence and another becomes very difficult to trace. Every sentence stands on its own bottom. It would be hard to find a more hopelessly perplexed paragraph than the following. After close scrutiny, we find that each sentence contains a different idea from its predecessor:—

"Wherefore to return to our former intent of discovering the natural way, whereby rules have been found out concerning that goodness wherewith the Will of man ought to be moved in human actions; as every thing naturally and necessarily doth desire the utmost good and greatest perfection whereof Nature hath made it capable, even so man. Our felicity therefore being the object and accomplishment of our desire, we cannot choose but wish and covet it. All particular things which are subject unto action, the Will doth so far incline unto, as Reason judgeth them the better for us, and consequently the more available to our bliss. If Reason err, we fall into evil, and are so far forth deprived of the general perfection we seek. Seeing therefore that for the framing of men's actions the knowledge of good from evil is necessary, it only resteth that we search how this may be had.

Neither must we suppose that there needeth one rule to know the good and another the evil by. For he that knoweth what is straight doth even thereby discern what is crooked, because the absence of straightness in bodies capable thereof is crookedness. Goodness in actions is like unto straightness; wherefore that which is done well we term *right*. For as the straight way is most acceptable to him that travelleth, because by it he cometh soonest to his journey's end; so in action, that which doth lie the evenest between us and the end we desire must needs be the fittest for our use. Besides which fitness for use, there is also in rectitude, beauty; as contrariwise in obliquity, deformity. And that which is good in the actions of men, doth not only delight as profitable, but as amiable also. In which consideration the Grecians most divinely have given to the active perfection of men a name expressing both beauty and goodness, because goodness in ordinary speech is for the most part applied only to that which is beneficial. But we in the name of goodness do here imply both."

Figures of Speech.—So far from being, as Hallam says, "rich in figures," Hooker is for his age singularly devoid of ornament. As among the great Elizabethan writers his languid vitality is a marked contrast to the general plenitude of life, so his unadorned gravity of style is a contrast to the general figurative exuberance. Similitudes might be quoted from him—some very apposite, and some very pleasing; but the vein is neither abundant nor original. His habitual personification of nature is the manner of the time. If we regard law in its strict scientific meaning as an express command sanctioned by threat of punishment, Hooker's extension of the term to the order of nature, the angelic manner of life, and suchlike, is metaphorical; but the metaphor neither began nor ended with Hooker.

QUALITIES OF STYLE.

Simplicity.—In this as in other respects Hooker is very unequal. Taken all in all, and compared with the best English standards, his style is not readily intelligible to a modern reader: apart from obsolete words, which might soon be mastered, the unfamiliar Latin idiom, and the elaborate accumulation of clauses, make it stiff and perplexing. This is the general character of his style; occasional passages are more flowing and idiomatic, and may be read almost as fluently as good modern prose.

As compared with the average of his contemporaries, he appears to advantage. He is nearly, if not quite, free from some of their prevailing vices; he has few, if any, pedantic barbarisms; and his pages are not encumbered with superfluous quotation and illustration.

Clearness.—Speaking of Sidney, we remarked that in English literature, as in every other, exact expression is a thing of later growth. In such subjects as occupied our earliest writers, narratives, practical treatises—on hawking, chess, shooting—sermons on moral duties, and the like, precision is not so much a requisite; there is little risk of confusion. It needs obscure and complicated subjects to test powers of expression. Not till we come to controversial books on Church doctrine do we feel the want of clearness, and impatiently consider how many tedious folio pages might have been anticipated by a little rigorous definition of terms at the beginning, and a strict adherence to the definitions throughout. The war of creeds and forms having been waged for the most part in the universal Church Latin, Hooker's 'Ecclesiastical Polity' is the first English work that makes us painfully aware of the confused thinking and confused expression of the time.

On an easy subject Hooker is clear and orderly. In expounding a given body of opinions, he is comprehensive and lucid: witness his account of the doctrines of the Anabaptists. Under a severe strain of thought, he breaks down; he is incapable of reducing confusion into order. His Puritan opponents, Cartwright and Travers, were prejudiced in favour of narrow principles that his calmer mind readily felt to be narrow. But when he tried to rest his practical doctrines on broader principles, he only made confusion worse confounded. His opponents made their meaning unmistakable; Hooker's real meaning remains somewhat of a problem to this day. They held that Scripture is the only rule of human conduct, and that Scripture lays down the Presbyterian form of Church government. Hooker's purpose seemingly was to maintain that Scripture is *not* the *only* rule of human conduct; but this he does so vaguely that not many years ago this purpose was triumphantly produced as "the key to the philosophy" of his book. Had we not happened to know from history what were the doctrines he sought to refute, the exact drift of the First Book would have remained a puzzle to all generations. In various places he declares his design, but in very perplexing language:—

> "Lest therefore any man should marvel whereunto all these things tend, the drift and purpose of all is this, even to show in what manner, as every good and perfect gift, so this very gift of good and perfect laws is derived from the Father of lights; to teach men a reason why just and reasonable laws are of so great force, of so great use in the world; and to inform their minds with some method of reducing the laws whereof there is present controversy unto their first original causes, that so it may be in every particular ordinance, thereby the better discerned, whether the same be reasonable, just, and righteous, or no."

In another place he declares his purpose to be to show that "Scripture is not the only law whereby God has opened His will touching all things that may be done." Some study enables us to reconcile in some sort the two declarations of purpose; but in the book itself he loses all sight of this purpose, and frames it as—what he elsewhere declares it to be—an introduction to solve "a number of doubts and questions about the nature, kinds, and qualities of laws in general."

This confusion of expression is a thing apart from any confusion of thought; on that we do not enter here. A farther evidence of Hooker's imperfect expression is seen in the opposite theories that are fathered upon him. That so many should take shelter under his authority is a proof of their respect, but not of his clearness.

The emotional qualities of Hooker's style may be dismissed briefly. He is for the most part intent upon quiet argument, quoting authorities and expounding principles. It is in the First Book chiefly that we find occasional passages having a poetical glow.

Strength.—Viewed as a definition and exposition of the various modes of law, this First Book drew from the scrupulously clear and exact John Austin the strong epithet of "fustian;" but whatever be its value in a scientific point of view, undoubtedly several parts are written in a highly poetical strain of subdued grandeur, in admirable harmony with the sonorous dignity of the rhythm. The exciting causes of these warmer passages are the author's admiration of beneficent cosmic power, and his dread of what might happen were this power withdrawn. He shrinks with his whole heart from every form of jarring irregularity, from everything that disturbs and agitates; he worships whatever keeps these horrors in subjection, and admires warmly whatever follows a quiet and peaceable course. His conception of the operations of nature would be very impressive and poetical were it not so familiar by repetition:—

"Although we are not of opinion, therefore, as some are, that nature in working hath before her certain exemplary draughts or patterns, which subsisting in the bosom of the Highest, and being thence discovered, she fixeth her eye upon them, as travellers by sea upon the pole-star of the world, and that according thereunto she guideth her hand to work by imitation: although we rather embrace the oracle of Hippocrates, that 'each thing, both in small and in great, fulfilleth the task which destiny hath set down;' . . . nevertheless, forasmuch as the works of nature are no less exact than if she did both behold and study how to express some absolute shape or mirror always present before her; yea, such her dexterity and skill appeareth, that no intellectual creature in the world were able by capacity to do that which nature doth without capacity and knowledge. It cannot be but nature hath some director of infinite knowledge to guide her in all her ways."

In the above, the glow of his admiration for order is chilled by his being compelled to own that nature is an unconscious instrument. He finds more congenial scope in admiring the perfect obedience of the "huge, mighty, and royal armies" of angels.

His apprehension of a collapse of the order of nature contains some good expressions; but the conclusion, as a piece of art, is very lame and ineffectual—indeed, an anti-climax:—

"Now if nature should intermit her course, and leave altogether, though it were but for a while, the observation of her own laws; if those principal and mother elements of the world, whereof all things in this lower world are made, should lose the qualities which now they have; if the frame of that heavenly arch erected over our heads should loosen and dissolve itself; if celestial spheres should forget their wonted motions, and by irregular volubility turn themselves any way as it might happen; if the prince of the lights of heaven, which now as a giant doth run his unwearied course, should, as it were, through a languishing faintness, begin to stand and to rest himself; if the moon should wander from her beaten way, the times and seasons of the year blend themselves by disordered and confused mixture, the winds breathe out their last gasp, the clouds yield no rain, the earth be defeated of heavenly influence, the fruits of the earth pine away as children at the withered breasts of their mother no longer able to yield them relief;—what would become of man himself, whom these things now do all serve? See we not plainly that obedience of creatures unto the law of nature is the stay of the whole world?"[1]

Pathos.—In nearly every exhibition of feeling in Hooker's works there is a tinge of pathos. His craving for rest, quiet, and order is perpetually appearing. When, in his office at the Temple, he conceived the design of writing a final defence of Episcopacy, and had read many books, he made the following pathetic appeal to Whitgift:—

"But, my lord, I shall never be able to finish what I have begun, unless I be removed into some quiet country parsonage, where I may see God's blessings spring out of my mother earth, and eat mine own bread in peace and privacy."

Throughout his Polity we trace the working of the same spirit. There is a large mixture of pathos in the examples that we have quoted of his loftier flights. The rhapsody on law, which was so distasteful scientifically to John Austin, we regard with a kindlier feeling when we keep in mind the character of the man. We see a feeble, dependent soul clinging with ecstasy to an idea that gives him comfort and strength:—

"Of law, there can be no less acknowledged than that her seat is the bosom of God, her voice the harmony of the world. All things in heaven and earth do her homage; the very least as feeling her care, and the greatest as not exempted from her power. Both angels and men, and creatures of what condition soever, though each in different sort and manner, yet all with uniform consent, admiring her as the mother of their peace and joy."

[1] This passage is an instance of Hooker's want of originality and native power. The imagined confusion of the world is translated particular for particular from Arnobius,—an unacknowledged plagiarism pointed out by Keble. Besides the noble rhythm, no part of the vigorous conception is Hooker's except the concluding particular. Arnobius supposes the earth to be too dry for seeds to germinate; Hooker too dry to "yield relief to her fruits."

Another favourite subject in a similar vein is the desirability of peace and unity between Puritan and Prelatist:—

"Far more comfort it were for us (so small is the joy we take in these strifes) . . . to be joined with you in bonds of indissoluble love and amity, to live as if our persons being many our souls were but one, rather than in such dismembered sort to spend our few and wretched days in a tedious prosecuting of wearisome contentions."

The Ludicrous.—Such a genuine lover of peace as Hooker was not likely to exasperate by keen sarcasm. And, on the other hand, a man of his feeble constitution was not likely to have a genial flow of humour, or a broad, hearty sense of the ludicrous. Such humour as he has is very faint, and takes a sarcastic, ironical turn. In answering the Puritans he states their doctrines gravely, very seldom allowing any trace of ridicule to cross his statement, and even then making the ridicule apparent, not by epithets, but by bringing ludicrous incongruities to the surface in his exposition. His manner was very different from the boisterous wit of Tom Nash, a champion on the same side. We have seen one example of his irony (p. 216). Here is another:—

"Where they found men in diet, attire, furniture of house, or any other way, observers of civility and decent order, such they reproved as being carnally-minded. Every word otherwise than severely and sadly uttered seemed to pierce like a sword through them. If any man were pleasant, their manner was presently with deep sighs to repeat those words of our Saviour Christ, 'Woe be to you which now laugh, for ye shall lament.' So great was their delight to be always in trouble, that such as did quietly lead their lives, they judged of all other men to be in most dangerous case."

To quote one or two passages like this without any of the context would give an exaggerated idea of the power of Hooker's irony. Read with the grave body of context, they strike us as but a very slight departure from the general gravity. In the above, which is a favourable example, the point is not brought out with equal force in all the sentences.

Melody.—The general movement of Hooker's language is stiff cumbrous, but richly musical. Here and there, as we have seen, his stiffness relaxes, and he warms into flowing strains of solemn melody. The majority of our quotations are favourable examples of his rhythm. The opening sentence of the Polity (p. 216)—"Though for no other cause, yet for this," &c.—is a fine example of a *crescendo* effect. The first sentence of his paragraph on the angels—"But now that we may lift up our eyes (as it were) from the footstool to the throne of God," &c.—has something of the movement of the sentence in Sir Thomas Browne's 'Hydriotaphia' that drew such exclamations of delight from De Quincey.

The great cause of clumsiness in his general rhythm is an excessive use of heavy relative constructions:—

"That which hitherto we have set down is (I hope) sufficient to show their brutishness which imagine that religion and virtue are only as men will account of them."

"Of what account the Master of Sentences was in the Church of Rome, the same and more amongst the preachers of Reformed Churches Calvin had purchased; so that the perfectest divines were judged they which were skilfullest in Calvin's writings. . . . Till at length the discipline, which was at the first so weak, that without the staff of their approbation, who were not subject unto it themselves, it had not brought others under subjection, began now to challenge universal obedience, and to enter into open conflict with those very churches, which in desperate extremity had been relievers of it."

Even these passages are not without a certain musical charm, especially if we disregard the meaning and attend only to the succession of the syllables.

KINDS OF COMPOSITION.

Exposition.—Hooker's powers of exposition are tested by the book on Law, his most abstruse subject. Viewed simply as a piece of exposition, this book contains little to profit the student. In this particular respect, it is bad even by the standard of the time. Its main faults have been specified under the *Paragraph* and the quality of *Clearness.* The paragraph on the discovery of rules of action, quoted to illustrate his worst, is a piece of very confused writing. On a subject requiring closeness of thought, he has not the qualities that made up for bad method in some of his contemporaries; he has neither felicity nor variety of expression, nor fulness of example and illustration. These remarks apply chiefly to the First Book: his imperfect expression is most apparent there. In his arguments on ritual and doctrine he is more on beaten ground, and proceeds with less confusion.

Persuasion.—The 'Ecclesiastical Polity' is said to have had great influence. It is a good example to show how much in persuasion depends upon the manner. Hooker added little or nothing to what Whitgift had urged against the Presbyterian champion, Cartwright; and in clearness, terseness of expression, and logical force, is far inferior to his patron. His main contribution is his elaborate and (in a logical point of view) clumsy attempt to prove what Whitgift had simply asserted or taken for granted, that not everything required for the conduct of human affairs is to be found in Scripture. His arguments in the first two Books had little weight with the Puritans. Once they saw his drift, they admitted the general propositions, but questioned his implied conclusions. Law was a good thing, and should be obeyed, but not bad law; not everything was found in Scripture—but the Presbyterian government, and their views about liturgies, vestments, and sacraments, *were* found in Scripture. While Hooker's arguments were neither new nor convincing, his moderation, singular in that age, gained him a hearing, and his earnest advocacy of the blessings of union and order was like oil on the troubled waters. Whitgift's strenuous hostility and unsparing rigour of argument set his opponents on edge, and steeled them against conviction; Hooker's mild and occasionally hazy statement of the same arguments won the doubtful at once, and by degrees made friends out of decided enemies.

JOHN LYLY or LILLIE, 1554-1606.

This ingenious writer deserves a place of minor prominence in a history of prose—partly from the intrinsic merits of his style, and partly from the voluminous controversy that has been raised upon it. He is generally known as "The Euphuist," and his style is called Euphuism. We shall analyse this Euphuism, and try to make out what it is, where its elements came from, and what influence it had upon its age as a model of composition.

Few particulars of Lyly's life are on record. We know only that he was born in Kent, that he was a student at Magdalen, Oxford, that he was patronised by Lord Burghley, and that from 1577 to 1593 he was a hanger-on at Court and wrote plays. His plays had no small reputation, coming immediately before Shakspeare. Ben Jonson gives him honourable mention; and, in a bookseller's puff of the next generation, he is described as "the only rare poet of that time, the witty, comical, facetiously quick and unparalleled John Lilly, Master of Arts." His chief work in prose, apart from prose dramas and some assistance to Tom Nash in the Marprelate controversy, is a moral romance known as 'Euphues' (whence his name Euphuist). It is in two parts, 'Euphues, the Anatomy of Wit' (1579), and 'Euphues and his England' (1580). Euphues, a gay young Athenian of good family, travels in the first part to Naples, in the second part to England; the plot is subservient to the development of the young man's moral nature, and gives occasion for discourses on religion, education, friendship, and other virtues, with a great many love-passages. The book suited the taste of the time, and was popular: according to Blount the bookseller, "all our Ladies were then his Scholars; and that Beauty in Court which could not parley Euphuism was as little regarded as she which now" (1632) "speaks not French." With all his popularity the ingenious, gentle, humorous little man received no solid patronage. There are extant two petitions of his to the Queen complaining of his deferred hopes of favour. He had hung on for thirteen years in hopes of getting the Mastership of the Revels; and in his second petition (1593), despairing of this, he begs—

"Some land, some good fines, or forfeitures that should fall by the just fall of these most false traitors, that seeing nothing will come by the Revels, I may prey upon the Rebels. Thirteen years your Highness' servant, but yet nothing. Twenty friends that though they say they will be sure I find them sure to be slow. A thousand hopes but all nothing; a hundred promises but yet nothing. Thus casting up the inventory of my friends, hopes, promises, and times, the *summa totalis* amounteth to just nothing. My last will is shorter than mine invention: but three legacies, patience to my creditors, melancholy without measure to my friends, and beggary without shame to my family."

What were his fortunes after this, whether Elizabeth heard his petition, is not known. Probably the frugal Queen gave him some relief. His admiring bookseller says, though without express reference to the petition, that he was "heard, graced, and rewarded." He died at the comparatively early age of fifty-two.

The interest in Lyly was revived in this century by Sir Walter Scott's attempt to reproduce a Euphuist in the person of Sir Piercie Shafton. In the heat of attacking and defending Lyly and his style, of arguing as to whether he invented Euphuism or only fell in with a ruling taste, whether he vitiated our language or caught a taint, the disputants have not always kept in view what peculiarly belongs to Lyly's mannerism and what does not. His style has good points and bad points, peculiar affectations and affectations common to the age. A discussion on Euphuism becomes hopelessly tangled and complicated unless the leading elements of his manner are kept distinct. Here it may be well, without pretending to give an exhaustive analysis, to distinguish some particulars that should not be confused. Three or four may be specified.

(1.) *Neatness and finish of sentence.*—Lyly's sentences are remarkably free from intricacy and inversion, much shorter, more pithy and direct than was usual. We must come down at least a century before we find a structure so lucid. To be sure, his matter was not heavy, and did not tempt him to use either weighty sentences or learned terms: still, credit to whom credit is due; his sentences, as sentences, though not in perfect modern form, are the most smooth and finished of that time. His chief fault is the want of variety, "an eternal affectation of sententiousness," says an old critic, "keeps to such a formal measure of his periods as soon grows tiresome, and so by confining himself to shape his sense so frequently into one artificial cadence, however ingenious or harmonious, abridges that variety which the style should be admired for."

(2.) *Fanciful antithesis and word-play.*—The passage above quoted from his petition to Elizabeth is an extreme example. In the 'Euphues' there are few passages so fantastically antithetical; the antithesis of the 'Euphues' is more a kind of balance in the clauses, with or without opposition in the matter. Thus, when young Euphues is counselled by aged Philantus, he replies :—

"Father and friend (your age showeth the one, your honesty the other), I am neither so suspicious to mistrust your goodwill, nor so sottish to mislike your good counsel. As I am therefore to thank you for the first, so it stands upon me to think better on the latter. I mean not to cavil with you as one loving sophistry : neither to control you, as one having superiority; the one would bring my talk into the suspicion of fraud, the other convince me of folly."

When Euphues rejects the good advice, Lyly moralises thus :—

"Here ye may behold, Gentlemen, how lewdly wit standeth in his own light, how he deemeth no penny good silver but his own, preferring the blossom before the fruit, the bud before the flower, the green blade before the ripe ear of corn, his own wit before all men's wisdoms. Neither is that reason, seeing for the most part it is proper to all those of sharp capacity to esteem of themselves as most proper : if one be hard in conceiving, they pronounce him a dolt; if given to study, they proclaim him a dunce: if merry, a jester : if sad, a saint : if full of words, a sot : if without speech, a cipher. If one argue with them boldly, then he is impudent : if coldly, an innocent : if there be reasoning of divinity, they cry, *Quæ supra nos, nihil ad nos ;* if of humanity, *sententias loquitur carnifex.*"

Lyly did not invent this measured balance : like Johnson, he only took up, trimmed, and carried to excess a structure that others used in a rougher form and less frequently. The whim for antithesis and playing upon words is said to have been imported from Italy[1] by scholars and travelled men of fashion. It appears in our literature long before Lyly. It would seem to have been encouraged by Elizabeth. We see how Lyly strained his wit to gain her favour ; and in 1567, a quarter of a century before, we find Roger Ascham exerting himself as follows. The letter is addressed to Elizabeth, though she is in the third person, and has the same object as Lyly's petition :—

"I wrote once a little book of shooting : King HENRY, her most noble father, did so well like and allow it, as he gave me a living for it ; when he lost his life I lost my living ; but noble King Edward again did first revive it by his goodness, then did increase it by his liberality ; thirdly, did confirm it by his authority under the great seal of England, which patent all this time was both a great pleasure and profit to me, saving that one unpleasant word in that patent, called 'during pleasure,' turned me after to great displeasure ; for when King EDWARD went, his pleasure went with him, and my whole living went away with them both."

Here we have the same striving at verbal conceits—differing from Lyly's only in being less ingenious and polished. Lyly, it is clear, cannot be charged either with inventing this affectation or with introducing it to Court.

(3.) *Excess of similitudes, parallels, and instances.*—This is the

[1] Morley's English Writers, Introduction.

most striking part of Lyly's mannerism. It is for this that he is censured by Sidney, and accused of "rifling up all Herbarists, all stories of beasts, fowls, and fishes." To the same effect he is attacked by Michael Drayton: while Sidney is praised because he—

"Did first reduce
Our tongue from Lillie's writing then in use;
Talking of stones, stars, plants, of fishes, flies,
Playing with words, and idle similies."

Not only does Lyly ransack natural history for comparisons, he even goes the length of inventing natural history; at least, whether he is the inventor or not, many of his comparisons refer to fabulous properties. The following are examples. Take first "Euphues to the Gentlemen Scholars of Athens."

"The merchant that travelleth for gain, the husbandman that toileth for increase, the lawyer that pleadeth for gold, the craftsman that seeketh to live by his labour—all these, after they have fatted themselves with sufficient, either take their ease, or less pain than they were accustomed. *Hippomanes* ceased to run when he had gotten the goal. *Hercules* to labour when he had obtained the victory. *Mercury* to pipe when he had cast *Argus* in a slumber. The ant, though she toil in summer, yet in winter she leaveth to travail. The bee, though she delight to suck the fair flower, yet is she at last cloyed with honey. The spider that weaveth the finest thread ceaseth at the last when she hath finished her web. But in the action and study of the mind (Gentlemen) it is far otherwise, for he that tasteth the sweet of learning endureth all the sour of labour. He that seeketh the depth of knowledge, is as it were in a *Labyrinth,* in the which the farther he goeth, the farther he is from the end: or like the bird in the lime-bush, which, the more she striveth to get out, the faster she sticketh in. And certainly it may be said of learning as it was feigned of *Nectar*, the drink of the Gods, the which the more it was drunk, the more it would overflow the brim of the cup; neither is it far unlike the stone that groweth in the river of Caria, the which the more it is cut the more it increaseth. And it fareth with him that followeth it as with him that hath the dropsy," &c.

Euphues having been rather sharply reproached with inconsistency by his friend Philantus, makes the following reply:—

"The admonition of a true friend should be like the practice of a wise physician, who wrappeth his sharp pills in fine sugar; or the cunning Chirurgeon, who lancing a wound with an iron, immediately applieth to it soft lint; or as mothers deal with their children for worms, who put their bitter seeds into sweet raisins, if this order had been observed in thy discourse, that interlacing sour taunts with sugared counsel, bearing as well a gentle rein as using a hard snaffle, thou mightest have done more with the whisk of a wand, than now thou canst with the prick of the spur, and avoid that which now thou mayest not, extreme unkindness. But thou art like that kind judge which Propertius noteth, who condemning his friend, caused him for the more ease to be hanged with a silken twist. And thou like a friend cuttest my throat with a razor, not with a hatchet, for my more honour. But why should I set down the office of a friend, when thou, like our *Athenians*," &c.

The following is what we may suppose to have been imitated by the gallants of the Court :—

"For as the hop, the pole being never so high, groweth to the end, or as the dry beech kindled at the root never leaveth until it come to the top : or as one drop of poison disperseth itself into every vein, so affection having caught hold of my heart, and the sparkles of love kindled my liver, will suddenly, though secretly, flame up into my head, and spread itself into every sinew."

"What cruelty more unfit for so comely a lady than to spur him that galloped, or to let him blood in the heart, whose vein she should have staunched in the liver? But it fared with me as with the herb basil, the which the more it is crushed, the sooner it springeth ; or the rue, which the oftener it is cut the better it groweth ; or the poppy, which the more it is trodden with the feet, the more it flourisheth."

It serves no good purpose to apply the term Euphuism to anything but the tricks of style characteristic of Lyly, the author of 'Euphues.' We only make confusion when we apply the name to quaint punning and antithesis, or to superabundance of illustration and exemplification. These faults, such as they were, Lyly shared with his time. His peculiarity lay not so much in hosts of parallels and instances, as in the sententious pointed way of expressing them. That is the Euphuistic *form:* the Euphuistic substance is the copious illustration of everything pertaining to man from animals, plants, and minerals, real or fabulous. The form and substance taken together constitute Euphuism proper, the real invention of Lyly, and, it would appear, for some short time the fashionable affectation at Court.

If by Euphuism we understand, as seems most reasonable, the peculiar manner of the author of 'Euphues,' we cannot accept Mr Marsh's statement that "the quality of style called Euphuism has more or less prevailed in all later periods of English literature.' It is quite true that ingenious playing upon words has been a favourite practice "in all later periods of English literature." But Lyly's style had very little influence on literature, either for evil or for good. All sorts of antithetical pranks with words prevailed before he wrote, especially in the language of gallantry, ridiculed in 'Love's Labour Lost.' To this affectation he probably added nothing but greater polish of form. His similitudes from nature, whether simple, far-fetched, or spurious, were so overdone that the evil wrought its own cure. There were probably Euphuists in private circles and among inferior writers; but in higher, and even in middling literature, the affectation was too excessive to last, too characteristic to be imitated. Further, even the good points were not imitated. Mannerists like Johnson, Macaulay, or Carlyle, have an influence for good on many that do not adopt their most startling peculiarities. But Lyly's example carried no weight ; his lucid neatness of sentence, and orderly way of producing instances, perished with his worthless affectations. English style immediately after him was not less prolix and intricate, nor less overburdened with clumsy quotations, than it was before him.

It is hardly necessary to say that the style of Scott's "Piercie Shafton" is far from being a reproduction of Euphuism as it is in Lyly. Perhaps the nearest prototype of Shafton is Sidney's caricature of a pedantic schoolmaster "Rhombus" in 'The Lady of the May.'[1]

OTHER WRITERS.

CHURCH CONTROVERSIALISTS—1580-1600.

Some of the writers now to be mentioned wrote before the year 1580; all of them wrote after it. The struggle between the two Church parties passed through a crisis in the latter part of Elizabeth's reign. Hooker, as we have seen, was the chief literary champion of Episcopacy: in their capacity as writers, the others may be clustered round him.

John Whitgift, Archbishop of Canterbury, **1530-1604,** did probably more than any one man to establish the Church of England. He was born in Lincolnshire, and studied at Cambridge. During the first half of Elizabeth's reign he rose to distinction, filling important offices in the University. He was made Archbishop of Canterbury in 1583, and distinguished himself by his rigorous policy against the Presbyterians. His 'Defence of his Answer to Cartwright's Admonition,' first published in 1574, is reprinted by the Parker Society. A strenuous, sagacious man, he writes a vigorous, straightforward, and clear style, seasoned with open personal invective and ridicule. His sentences, without being made after any peculiar form, are short and simple: he keeps too close a grasp on the argument, and is too eagerly bent upon refuting, to have time for the elaboration of periods.

Thomas Cartwright (1535-1603), "the incarnation of Presbyterianism," and for some time a thorn in the side of Whitgift, was born in Hertfordshire. He encountered Whitgift at Cambridge, and was worsted, being deprived of the Lady Margaret Professorship and of his fellowship in Trinity, and thus driven from the University in 1572. After spending some years as English Chaplain at Antwerp, he returned, got into trouble with the Church, and was imprisoned. In his later years he seems to have been conciliated by Whitgift, and to have made a less violent opposition. His works are—'An Admonition to Parliament,' 1572; 'An Admonition to the People of England,' 1589; 'A Brief Apology,' 1596; also 'A Directory of Church Government,' and 'A Body of Divinity,' published after his death. Cartwright was a very pop-

[1] Lyly's 'Euphues' is issued in Mr Arber's series of English Reprints, with a useful Introduction, containing several notices of Euphuism at different dates.

ular preacher. He writes with great fervour, but his style is much more involved and antiquated than Whitgift's, and he has much less argumentative force.

Martin Marprelate wrote some virulent, coarsely humorous personal tracts on the Puritan side about the time of the Spanish Armada (1588). Martin's real name is a greater mystery than Junius; the latest conjecture is that he was a Jesuit. At one time he was identified with John Penry, who seems to have been a mild, much-suffering Puritan Welshman, quite incapable of anything so boisterous. The titles of the tracts are such as "The Epitome," "The Supplication," "Hay any Work for a Cooper?" Martin was answered in an equally personal strain by "witty TOM NASH," who chose such titles as "An Almond for a Parrot" (equivalent to "A sop for Cerberus") and "Pap with a Hatchet"[1] (an expression for doing a kind thing in an unkind way).

Robert Parsons or **Persons (1546-1610)**, the daring and skilful pioneer of the Jesuits in England, is praised by Swift for the purity and vigour of his English style. A native of Somersetshire, he was educated at Oxford, and became a celebrated tutor. Being expelled from his College in 1574 (according to Fuller, for embezzlement of College money), he joined the Jesuits, and was the moving spirit of the Popish plots against Elizabeth before the Spanish Armada. In his later years he presided over the English College at Rome.

CHRONICLES, HISTORY, ANTIQUITIES.

The series of *Chroniclers* is continued in this period by **John Stow (1525-1605)** and **John Speed (1552-1629)**, both tailors by trade. Stow, a genial industrious creature, after publishing a 'Summary of English Chronicles' in 1565, became ambitious to write a great chronicle of England that should surpass every other in number and accuracy of facts, quitted his tailor's board, and walked through England searching for documents that had been dispersed by the suppression of the monasteries. His great work was never published, but in 1598 he brought out a 'Survey of London,' which was the basis of subsequent accounts of the metropolis, and in 1600 'Flores Historiarum,' The Flowers of the Histories (of England). In his last years he received from King James a recommendation to the charity of the public, and stood in churches to receive alms—so ill was his humble industry rewarded. With all his diligence he is said to have been able to add little to the stock of chronicled facts.—Speed seems to have lived more comfortably, and, working with equal industry, to have been more

[1] Sometimes ascribed to Lyly, the Euphuist.

discriminating in his choice of authorities.[1] He published a 'History of Great Britain' in 1614. Previously, in 1606, he had published a Collection of Maps, including maps of the English shires, each map curiously bordered with drawings of inhabitants, towns, notable buildings, &c. The balanced structure of his titles is characteristic of the time. His Map of the World is "drawn according to the truest descriptions, latest discoveries, and best observations that have been made by English or strangers;" the outlines of the Great Southern Continent "rather show there is a land, than descry either land, people, or commodities."

Three writers, who pretend to a weightier style than Stow or Speed, may be called HISTORIANS. **Sir John Hayward (1560-1627)**, LL.D. of Cambridge, was patronised by Essex, imprisoned by Elizabeth, knighted by James, and made one of the two historiographers of the abortive Chelsea College. He wrote a 'Life and Reign of Henry IV.' (1599); 'Lives of the three Norman Kings of England' (1613); and a 'Complete History of Edward IV.,' with 'Certain Years of Queen Elizabeth's Reign,' published in 1630 after his death. Hayward was the subject of one of Bacon's apothegms. Elizabeth, much incensed at his history, asked "Whether there were no treason contained in it?" "No, madam," answered Bacon, "for treason, I cannot deliver opinion that there is any, but very much felony." "How and wherein?" "*Because he has stolen many of his sentences and conceits out of Cornelius Tacitus.*" Jeremy Taylor in return did Hayward the honour to steal some ideas from his 'Sanctuary of a Troubled Soul.' **Richard Knolles (1549-1610)**, Fellow of Lincoln, Oxford, and Master of the Free School at Sandwich, wrote a 'History of the Turks,' and other works relating to the Ottoman Empire. Johnson, who read Knolles for his 'Irene,' in a paper on History ('Rambler,' 122), says: "None of our writers" (of history) "can, in my opinion, justly contest the superiority of Knolles, who, in his 'History of the Turks,' has displayed all the excellencies that narration can admit. His style, though somewhat obscured by time, and sometimes vitiated by false wit, is pure, nervous, elevated, and clear. A wonderful multiplicity of events is so artfully arranged, and so distinctly explained, that each facilitates the knowledge of the next. Whenever a new personage is introduced, the reader is prepared by his character for his actions; when a nation is first attacked, or city besieged, he is made acquainted with its history or situation; so that a great part of the world is brought into view." The estimate is excessive, even as made in Johnson's time.

[1] Speed's superior accuracy and rejection of fables is no doubt partly due to his having had the advice of *Sir Robert Cotton* (1570-1631), a man of property and good position, who made it his hobby to collect every sort of document relating to the history of England.

The distinctness of arrangement, and the geographical sketches, were due more to the character of the subject than to any superiority of method: these "excellencies" were easy in narrating the steps of a conquest through a foreign country. Knolles's sentences are long and rambling—prolonged by successive relative clauses starting each from the one that goes before. **Samuel Daniel (1562-1619)**, the poet, wrote a 'History of England from the Conquest to the Accession of Henry VII.' It is praised by Hallam for its purity of diction, being written in the current English of the Court, and free from scholarly stiffness and pedantry. The structure of the sentences is easy to the extent of negligence.

Two or three ANTIQUARIES are usually mentioned among the prose writers of this period; perhaps because, though they wrote chiefly in Latin themselves, they furnished materials for the English prose of other writers. **William Camden (1551-1623)**, Headmaster of Westminster School, wrote the 'Britannia,' and founded a Chair of History in Oxford. **Sir Henry Spelman (1562-1604)**, Sheriff of Norfolk, a legal and ecclesiastical antiquary, is famed as a restorer of Saxon literature, having founded a Saxon Professorship at Cambridge. **Sir Robert Cotton** has been already mentioned as a collector of historical documents; he is not said to have written anything.

CHRONICLERS OF MARITIME DISCOVERY.—The enterprising naval worthies in the reigns of Elizabeth and James, if they had no poet, were not without their chroniclers. Many of their voyages to "descry new lands" in America, or in the Southern Continent, have been put on record. The chief of this department of history is **Richard Hakluyt (1553-1616)**, Lecturer on Cosmography at Oxford, and an active correspondent with the foreign geographers, Ortelius and Mercator. In 1598, 1599, and 1600, he published 'The Principal Navigations, Voyages, Traffiques, and Discoveries of the English Nation, made by Sea or over Land, to the Remote and Farthest Distant Quarters of the Earth, within the compass of these 1500 years.' Very interesting reading for persons with the proper taste for their subject-matter, Hakluyt's narratives have no charms of style. The same may be said of **Samuel Purchas (1577-1628)**, 'Hackluytus Posthumus,' B.D. of Cambridge, who continued Hackluyt, and wrote 'Purchas his Pilgrimage,' containing an account of all the religions of the world.

Some of the hardy mariners told their own story—as John Davis (of Davis Straits, an early searcher for the North-West Passage), and Sir Richard Hawkins, who went in quest of land to the south. Sir Walter Raleigh, the "discoverer of Guiana," will be mentioned presently.

MISCELLANEOUS.

The versatile **Sir Walter Raleigh (1552-1618)** wrote some of the most flowing and modern-looking prose of this period; and had his subject-matter been less antiquated, we should have gone over his peculiarities at some length. He is, perhaps, the most dazzling figure of his time: his high position at the Court of Elizabeth, gained not by birth, but by personal charms and merits; his conduct against the Armada and at Cadiz; his American enterprises; his two new imports, tobacco and the potato; his unjust imprisonment by King James,—made him to the people of London the most wonderful of living men; and he still holds the highest rank among our traditional heroes. His principal writings are—'The Discovery of the large, rich, and beautiful Empire of Guiana,' published in 1596, and his 'History of the World,' composed during his imprisonment. The 'Discovery' is a matter-of-fact record of his own voyage, his dealings with the natives, and his impressions of the scenery. It was much ridiculed at the time by his jealous enemies, but there is nothing incredible in what he professes to have seen, though he was too sanguine in his beliefs as to the splendour of the parts of the empire that he had not seen. As regards the style, he "neither studied phrase, form, nor fashion;" yet at times he shows his natural power of graphic description. The following is perhaps his best; he describes the "overfalls of the river of Caroli, which roared so far off:"—

"When we ran to the tops of the first hills of the plains adjoining to the river, we beheld that wonderful breach of waters, which ran down *Caroli*; and might from that mountain see the river how it ran in three parts, above twenty miles off, and there appeared some ten or twelve overfalls in sight, every one as high over the other as a church tower, which fell with that fury, that the rebound of waters made it seem as if it had been covered all over with a great shower of rain; and in some places we took it at the first for a smoke that had risen over some great town."

The 'History of the World' is a work of erudition rather than a narrative—going off into general dissertations on the origin of government, the nature, use, and abuse of magic, &c.; comparing the personages of Scripture with the personages of heathen mythology; discussing at great length such vexed questions as the site of Paradise, the place where the ark rested, the local dispersion of the sons of Noah, &c.; and in the classical history criticising accounts of battles and campaigns with the sagacity of a practical man. The only parts of the book that any modern reader would care to peruse are some parts of the Greek, Macedonian, and Roman history—where his estimates of events in war and in policy are entitled to respect;—the preface to the work; and the conclusion. Only the preface and the conclusion have much literary value;

they are among the finest remains of Elizabethan prose. Critics often incautiously speak as if the whole work were written in the same strain. A grave melancholy runs through them, the natural mood of an ambitious spirit and a strong confident wit chastened but not broken by slander and imprisonment, writing in "the evening of a tempestuous life." Especially remarkable are the passages on Death. In the preface he says:—

"But let every man value his own wisdom, as he pleaseth. Let the rich man think all fools, that cannot equal his abundance; the Revenger esteem all negligent that have not trodden down their opposites; the Politician, all gross that cannot merchandise their faith: Yet when we once come in sight of the Port of death, to which all winds drive us, and when by letting fall that fatal Anchor, which can never be weighed again, the navigation of this life takes end: Then it is, I say, that our own cogitations (those sad and severe cogitations, formerly beaten from us by our health and felicity) return again, and pay us to the uttermost for all the pleasing passages of our life past."

In the same strain he concludes his history:—

"It is therefore death alone that can suddenly make man to know himself. He tells the proud and insolent that they are but Abjects, and humbles them at the instant; makes them cry, complain, and repent; yea, even to hate their forepassed happiness. He takes the account of the rich, and proves him a beggar; a naked beggar, which hath interest in nothing, but in the gravel that fills his mouth. He holds a Glass before the eyes of the most beautiful, and makes them see therein their deformity and rottenness; and they acknowledge it.

"O eloquent, just, and mighty Death! whom none could advise, thou hast persuaded; what none hath dared, thou hast done; and whom all the world hath flattered, thou only hast cast out of the world and despised; thou hast drawn together all the far-stretched greatness, all the pride, cruelty, and ambition of man, and covered it all over with these two narrow words, *Hic jacet.*"

Raleigh's other works are a treatise on Ship-building, 'Maxims of State,' the 'Cabinet Council,' the 'Sceptic,' and 'Advice to his Son.' In worldly wisdom, this last is equal to Bacon's Essays, though the subjects of advice are more commonplace.

William Cecil, Lord Burleigh (1522-1598), like Raleigh, wrote advice for his son under the title 'Precepts or Directions for the Well-ordering and Carriage of a Man's Life,' a digest of commonplace advice on the choice of a wife, the management of a household, the danger of suretiship, and suchlike.

Thomas Dekker, the dramatist, an antagonist of Ben Jonson's, wrote 'Seven Deadly Sins of London' (1606), 'The Gull's Hornbook' (1609), and other ephemeral productions—burlesque satires of the extreme fashionable world, of the bucks and girls of the period.

King James I. had a literary turn: he wrote 'A Counterblast to Tobacco,' and a work on 'Demonology.' Neither of these pedantic compositions would have survived had they been written by a less distinguished personage.

The unfortunate **Sir Thomas Overbury (1581-1613)**,—who, after figuring brilliantly at the Court of James as the favourite of the King's favourite, Robert Carr, was mysteriously cut off by slow poison, in consequence of his opposing Carr's marriage with the Countess of Essex,—wrote 'Characters of Witty Descriptions of the Properties of Sundry Persons.' Fanciful word-play, we have seen, existed at Court before Lyly's 'Euphuism:' the sermons of the King's admired preachers are one evidence that it continued when the temporary fashion of Euphuism was gone; Overbury's characters are another and a stronger. Take as a sample his description of a *tinker*:—

"He seems to be very devout, for his life is a continual pilgrimage; and sometimes in humility goes barefoot, therein making necessity a virtue. His house is as ancient as Tubal-Cain's, and so is a renegade by antiquity; yet he proves himself a gallant, for he carries all his wealth upon his back; or a philosopher, for he bears all his substance about him. . . . So marches he all over England with his bag and baggage; his conversation is irreprovable, for he is ever mending. He observes truly the statutes, and therefore had rather steal than beg, in which he is irremovably constant, in spite of whips or imprisonment. . . . Some would take him to be a coward, but, believe it, he is a lad of mettle. . . . He is very provident, for he will fight with but one at once, and then also he had rather submit than be counted obstinate."

CHAPTER III.

FROM 1610 TO 1640.

FRANCIS BACON,

1561—1626.

WERE we to place authors strictly according to age, we should include Bacon in the same generation with Sidney and Hooker. But we have an eye rather to the dates of the composition of their works; and most of Bacon's works were written after 1610.

As the "founder of Inductive Philosophy," his great reputation is literary rather than scientific; he advanced Science as an advocate, not as a labourer in the field. He recalled men from speculation, and urged them to study facts. He was an eager and acute observer, whenever he found time; but only a fraction of his time was devoted to Science. His service lay not so much in what he did himself, as in the grand impulse he gave to others.

The merits of his style, as of every other style in that age, are variously estimated. Addison praises his grace, Hume calls him stiff and rigid, and many persons would be unable to see that either of these criticisms has any peculiar application. But all admit that he is one of the greatest writers of prose during the reigns of Elizabeth and James.

His father, Sir Nicholas Bacon, was Elizabeth's Lord Keeper; his mother, Anne Cooke, a woman of Lady Jane Grey accomplishments, translated Bishop Jewel's 'Apology' in 1564. Born at his father's house in London, Francis was sent at the age of twelve to Trinity College, Cambridge, and remained there for two years and a half under the care of Whitgift, then Master of Trinity. Of these early days little is known, except that he was an exceedingly grave and precocious child, and was called by Elizabeth her "young Lord Keeper;" it is said, also, that before he left Cambridge he had begun to dislike Aristotle as being barren of practical fruit. Previous to his father's death in 1579, he had spent more than two years in Paris with the English ambassador there. His ideal at this time seems to have been to make statecraft his profession, and reserve a considerable part of his time for study. But his father's death leaving him without adequate provision, and his uncle Burleigh refusing to find him a sinecure, he was compelled to take up the profession of law. He was admitted as an utter barrister in 1582; and thenceforth his time was distributed between the practice of law, public business, and his great literary projects. Under Elizabeth his promotion was not rapid: the Queen thought him "showy and not deep" in law; he had enemies at Court in his uncle and cousin; and his generous patron, Essex, did him more harm than good by indiscreet urgency. He got nothing but the reversion of the Clerkship of the Star-Chamber, which did not fall in for twenty years; he applied in vain for the Attorney-Generalship, the Solicitor-Generalship, and the Mastership of the Rolls. Under James, he became Solicitor-General in 1607, Attorney-General in 1613, Lord Chancellor in 1617. In 1620 appeared the 'Novum Organum.' In 1621 he underwent the well-known censure of Parliament, being fined and deprived of the Great Seal. The remainder of his life was passed in studious retirement, during which he composed the greater part of his literary works. In the spring of 1626 he caught a chill when experimenting with snow, and died on Easter-day, April 9.

His chief English works are the 'Essays,' the 'Advancement of Learning,' the 'History of Henry VII.,' the 'New Atlantis,' and 'Sylva Sylvarum.' Of the Essays there were three different issues: ten essays in 1597, under the title 'Essays, Religious Meditations, Places of persuasion and dissuasion;' thirty-eight in 1612, entitled 'The Essays of Sir Francis Bacon, Knight, the King's Solicitor-General;' fifty-eight in 1625, entitled 'The Essays or Counsels, Civil and Moral, of,' &c. The 'Advancement of Learning' (which he translated into Latin, and enlarged during his retirement, calling it 'De Augmentis Scientiarum') was published in 1605. The 'History of Henry VII.' was his first work after he was banished from Court. The 'New Atlantis' was written about the same time; it is a romance somewhat after the manner of More's 'Utopia,' the design being to describe a college fully equipped for the study of Nature on the inductive method. 'Sylva Sylvarum' or the 'Natural History,'—a collection of facts touching the qualities of bodies, made partly from observation, partly from books—was the last work of his life.

Bacon seems to have been in person a little, broad, square-shouldered, brown man, thin and nervous-looking. He had a large head and small features.

It would be presumptuous to attempt anything like an exact valuation of Bacon's intellectual power. We state only what lies upon the surface when we say that the character and products of his intellect are very often as much over-estimated upon one side as they are under-estimated upon another. He is frequently praised as if he had originated and established the inductive method, as if he had laid down the canons appealed to in modern science as the ultimate conditions of sound induction. This is going too far. Bacon was an orator, not a worker; a Tyrtæus, not a Miltiades. He rendered a great service by urging recourse to observation and experiment rather than to speculation; but neither by precept nor by example did he show *how* to observe and experiment well, or so as to arrive at substantial conclusions. Not by precept; for if modern inductive method were no better than Bacon's inductive method, Macaulay's caricature of the process would not be so very unlike the reality. Nor by example; for the majority of his own generalisations are loose to a degree. To call Bacon the founder of scientific method is to mistake the character of his mind, and to do him an injustice by resting his fame upon a false foundation. Unwearied activity, inexhaustible constructiveness—that, and not scientific patience or accuracy, was his characteristic. He had what Peter Heylin calls "a chymical brain;" every group of facts that entered his mind he restlessly threw into new combinations. We over-estimate the man upon one side when we give him credit for scientific rigour; his contemporary Gilbert, who wrote upon the magnet, probably had more scientific caution and accuracy than he. And we under-estimate him upon another side when we speak as if the Inductive Philosophy had been the only outcome of his ever-active brain. His projects of reform in Law were almost as vast as his projects of reform in Philosophy. In Politics he drew up opinions on every question of importance during the forty years of his public life, and was often employed by the Queen and Lord Burleigh to write papers of State. All this was done in addition to his practical work as a lawyer. And yet his multiplex labours do not seem to have used up his mental vigour; his schemes always outran human powers of performance. His ambition was not to make one great finished effort and then rest; his intellectual appetite seemed almost insatiable.[1]

[1] It is a curious problem to make out why an intellect so acute and active revolted from the subtleties of the schoolmen, and did not rather turn to them as its most congenial element. Part of the explanation is doubtless to be found in the high development of his senses, in the strong arrest of his mind upon the outer world. A meditative man will walk for miles through the country, and be unable to describe minutely any one object that he has seen. Bacon's eye

In a man with such prodigious activity of intellect, and such a bent towards analysing and classifying dry facts, we do not look for much warmth of feeling. He is not likely to spend much of his time either in imagining objects of tender affection or in doting upon actual objects. The world has not yet seen the intellect of a Bacon combined with the sentimentality of a Sterne, or the philanthropy of a Howard. The works of Bacon afford very little food for ordinary human feelings. All the pleasure we gain from them is founded upon their intellectual excellences. Even the similitudes are intellectual rather than emotional, ingenious rather than touching or poetical. To adapt an image of Ben Jonson's—the wine of Bacon's writings is a dry wine. As we read, we experience the pleasure of surmounting obstacles; we are electrified by unexpected analogies, and the sudden revelations of new aspects in familiar things; and we sympathise more or less with the boundless exhilaration of a mind that pierces with ease and swiftness through barriers that reduce other minds to torpor and stagnancy.

Our author says of himself that he was not born "under Jupiter that loveth business;" "the contemplative planet carried him away solely." He had not the physical constitution needed to bear the worry and fatigue of the actual direction of affairs—not to say that he was so engrossed with his intellectual projects that practical drudgery was intolerably irksome. As Lord Chancellor, he cleared off a large accumulation of unheard cases with great despatch; but he proved unequal to the minuter duties of the office, and allowed subordinates to do as they pleased.[1]

Opinions.—The following is a bare outline of Bacon's great philosophical project: "The 'Instauratio' is to be divided into

probably drank in everything as he went along; or, if not everything, at least enough to keep him thinking about external things.

[1] So much has been made of certain specific charges of moral delinquency on the part of Bacon, that we cannot pass them over without some notice. Attentive readers will have anticipated our explanation. Take the case of Essex. Essex warmly patronised Bacon, pleaded with the Queen for his preferment, and made him a present of an estate. Yet when Essex was charged with treasonable practices, Bacon, as one of the Queen's Counsel, took part in the impeachment. We cannot enter here into minute casuistry; but it is easy to see that the impulsive Essex forced his patronage and his favours upon Bacon, and that Bacon, while he feared to discourage such a man's friendship, was acutely aware of its inconveniences. A man of high honour would have firmly declined Essex's services; a generous man, who had accepted such services, would have felt bound to stand by Essex to the last; and yet it would have been imprudent to have acted otherwise than as Bacon acted. His conduct in the Chancellorship is a plainer case. The faults that have been proved against him were faults of omission, not of commission. He was engrossed with his 'Novum Organum' and other projects, and closed his eyes to the doings of subordinates. He may even have received bribe-money from them without being at pains to inquire into the particulars. We can quite believe his declaration that he never gave judgment "with a bribe in his eye." He broke faith, not with justice, but with the giver of the bribe.

six portions, of which the first is to contain a general survey of the present state of knowledge. In the second, men are to be taught how to use their understanding aright in the investigation of nature. In the third, all the phenomena of the universe are to be stored up as in a treasure-house, as the materials on which the new method is to be employed. In the fourth, examples are to be given of its operation and of the results to which it leads. The fifth is to contain what Bacon had accomplished in natural philosophy without the aid of his own method, but merely" by what may be called common reason. In the sixth part "will be set forth the new philosophy—the result of the application of the new method to all the phenomena of the universe."

No sketch can here be attempted of his methods of induction. They possess little or no scientific value. He had no conception of valid proof. His own speculations are as rash as anything to be found in the schoolmen. Thus, among his 'Prerogative Instances' he lays down that precious stones, diamonds and rubies, are fine exudations of stone, just as the gum of trees is a fine straining through the wood and bark. He repeats this theory in the 'Sylva Sylvarum.' Of the thousand paragraphs in the 'Sylva' touching natural phenomena and their causes, there is hardly one that does not contain some speculation equally fanciful.

The opinions contained in his Essays[1]—observations and precepts on man and society—are perhaps the most permanent evidence of his sagacity. In this field he was thoroughly at home; the study of mankind occupied the largest part of his time. The Essays treat of a great variety of subjects—Truth, Death, Dissimulation, Superstition, Plantations, Masks and Triumphs, Beauty, Deformity, Vicissitudes of Things. To give any general idea of the contents of so many closely-packed pages of solid observation, is impossible within our limits. It may be said that to men wishing to rise in the world by politic management of their fellowmen, Bacon's Essays are the best handbook hitherto published. His own worldly wisdom was clenched by the significant aphorism, "By indignities men come to dignities."

His opinions in religion have been disputed. We know that his mother considered him remiss in the matter of family prayers, and in this respect not a pattern to his elder brother. But there is nothing in his writings at variance with the orthodox faith. It has been doubted whether a work called 'The Christian Paradoxes' was written by him; but if it was, it is only what it professes to be—a paradoxical expression of orthodoxy. He did not, as is sometimes stated, deny the argument from final causes. He

[1] The second part of the title—"Counsels Civil and Moral" is much more descriptive of the book, but it has been dropped, and would be difficult to revive. The original ten essays contained almost nothing but maxims of prudence.

only maintained that looking for final causes is a distraction from the investigation of physical causes. He would seem to have held that theology can be founded only on the Bible, and that whatever is affirmed there must be believed implicitly.

ELEMENTS OF STYLE.

Vocabulary.—Bacon's range of subjects was wide, and his command of words within that range as great as any man could have acquired. He took pains to keep his vocabulary rich. From some private notes that have been preserved, we see that he had a habit of jotting down and refreshing his memory with varieties of expression on all subjects that were likely to occur for discussion.

He uses a great many more obsolete words than either Hooker or Sidney. To be sure, the language of the feelings and the language of theology have changed less than the language of science. But in his narrative and in his Essays, as well as in his scientific writings, Bacon shows a decided preference now and then for "inkhorn terms." In his 'History of King Henry VII.' we meet with such words as "habilitate" for *qualified*, "the brocage of an usurper" for the *baits* or *panderings* of an usurper, "impatronise himself of" for *make himself patron of*, "difficile to" for *slow* to or *unwilling* to,—and suchlike. How archaic the scientific style is may be seen in the following passage from the 'Sylva Sylvarum'—perhaps an extreme case. It is headed, "Experiment Solitary touching Change of Aliments and Medicines:"—

> "It helpeth both in medicine and aliment, to change and not to continue the same medicine and aliment still. The cause is, for that nature, by continual use of anything, groweth to a satiety and dullness, either of appetite or working. And we see that assuetude of things hurtful doth make them lose their force to hurt; as poison which with use some have brought themselves to brook. And therefore it is no marvel though things helpful, by custom, lose their force to help. I count intermission almost the same thing with change; for that that hath been intermitted is after a sort new."

The phrase "for that" in place of *inasmuch as* is used so often by Bacon as almost to be a mannerism. The frequent use corresponds to his habit of accounting for things.

Sentences.—His general structure of sentence, as shown in his 'Advancement of Learning,' his History, and his occasional discourses, is less elaborate but more modern than in Hooker's average style. His sentences are shorter and more pointed; and being comparatively free from pedantic inversions, have a more modern flow. In the placing of qualifying clauses he is less awkward. The following period, from his "Discourse in praise of

Elizabeth," if somewhat intricate, is well built, and graduated to a climax :—

"The benefits of Almighty God upon this land, since the time that in His singular providence He led as it were by the hand, and placed in the kingdom, His servant, our Queen Elizabeth, are such, as not in boasting or in confidence of ourselves, but in praise of His holy name, are worthy to be both considered and confessed, yea, and registered in perpetual memory."

The next, from the 'Advancement of Learning,' is an average specimen of his long sentence :—

"And for matter of policy and government, that learning should rather hurt than enable thereunto, is a thing very improbable: we see it is accounted an error to commit a natural body to empiric physicians, which commonly have a few pleasing receipts whereupon they are confident and adventurous, but know neither the causes of diseases, nor the complexions of patients, nor peril of accidents, nor the true method of cures: we see it is a like error to rely upon advocates or lawyers, which are only men of practice and not grounded in their books, who are many times easily surprised when matter falleth out besides their experience, to the prejudice of the causes they handle: so by like reason it cannot be but a matter of doubtful consequence if states be managed by empiric statesmen, not well mingled with men grounded in learning."

The Essays, particularly the earlier ones, are full of balance and point, suiting their character as emphatic aphoristic precepts. The Essay on Studies, the first of the original ten, is more than usually balanced :—

"Read not to contradict and confute; nor to believe and take for granted; nor to find talk and discourse; but to weigh and consider. Some books are to be tasted, others to be swallowed, and some few to be chewed and digested; that is, some books are to be read only in parts; others to be read, but not curiously; and same few to be read wholly, and with diligence and attention. . . . Reading maketh a full man; conference a ready man; and writing an exact man. And therefore, if a man write little, he had need have a great memory; if he confer little, he had need have a present wit; and if he read little, he had need have much cunning, to seem to know that he doth not. Histories make men wise; poets witty; the mathematics subtile; natural philosophy deep; moral grave; logic and rhetoric able to contend."

The following is from his sagacious Essay "Of Negotiating:"—

"It is generally better to deal by speech than by letter. Letters are good, when a man would draw an answer by letter back again; or when it may serve for a man's justification afterwards to produce his own letter; or where it may be danger to be interrupted or heard by pieces. To deal in person is good, when a man's face breedeth regard, as commonly with inferiors; or in tender cases, where a man's eye upon the countenance of him with whom he speaketh may give him a direction how far to go; and generally, when a man will reserve to himself liberty either to disavow or to expound."

Again—

"All practice is to discover or to work. Men discover themselves in trust, in passion, at unawares, and of necessity, when they would have somewhat done and cannot find an apt pretext. If you would work any man, you must either know his nature and fashions, and so lead him; or his ends, and so persuade him; or his weakness and disadvantages, and so awe him; or those that have interest in him, and so govern him."

Paragraphs.—In connection with the paragraph may be noticed a peculiarity in the composition of the Essays. As a rule, Bacon's paragraphs are, comparatively, very good; he has a sense of method and good arrangement. In the 'Advancement of Learning' he adheres to a simple scheme; and the sentences of separate paragraphs are not inconsecutive nor complicated, as Hooker's sometimes are. But the Essays are of a peculiar structure. They are not, nor are they intended to be, consecutive expositions; each is a string of detached reflections and maxims bearing upon the same subject. The author's intention is more apparent in his first edition; he there distinguishes the transitions by the obsolete mark ¶. Thus, in the passage quoted from the Essay on Studies, there are four such marks, one at the head of each of the four different tacks—showing that he changed his tack advisedly, and not from confusion.

Figures of Speech—Similitudes.—Bacon's pages are very thickly strewn with similitudes. The first edition of the Essays is less figurative than the latest edition; the enlargements of the original ten often consist of additional figures.

That his earlier writings should be less figurative, accords with the character of his figures. They are not elaborated like the figures of Jeremy Taylor or Carlyle: his first care was the plain expression of his meaning; he made little effort to obtain similitudes, but took them rather when they came of themselves. He is sometimes spoken of as an imaginative writer; but this is not accurate if imagination is held to imply poetical feeling: his imagery is not evoked to gratify any poetical feeling refined or unrefined, but partly for purposes of illustration, and partly in the exercise of his incontinent quickness to discover analogy. This appears the moment we look at any number of his similitudes together. They are taken almost exclusively from familiar objects and operations in nature and human life. In his narrative their number is more within bounds, and they are usually very graphic; in the Essays they are often superfluous.

We shall exemplify his similitudes at some length, as the best way of showing that they are taken from familiar things, and that they are more illustrative than poetical:—

"For Pope Alexander, finding himself pent and locked up by a league and association of the principal States of Italy, that he could not make his way for the advancement of his own house (which he immoderately thirsted after), *was desirous to trouble the waters in Italy, that he might fish the better.*"

When Henry was threatened with a Scotch war, a Cornish insurrection, and the pretender Perkin Warbeck all at once, he judged it—

"His best and surest way to keep his strength together in the seat and centre of his kingdom; according to the ancient Indian emblem—in such a swelling season, *to hold his hand upon the middle of the bladder that no side might rise.*"

After recounting Henry's fine calculations regarding the action of Continental powers, he says:—

"But those things were too fine to be fortunate and succeed in all parts; for that *great affairs are commonly too rough and stubborn to be wrought upon by the finer edges or points of wit.*"

The following is the opening sentence of the fragment on Henry VIII.:—

"After the decease of that wise and fortunate king, King Henry the Seventh, who died in the height of his prosperity, there followed (as useth to do when the sun setteth so exceeding clear) one of the fairest mornings of a kingdom that hath been known in this land or anywhere else."

He very often uses these metaphors taken from the phenomena of the weather. At the outset of his reign, Henry, in his account of peace and calms, "did much overcast his fortunes, which proved for many years together full of broken seas, tides, and tempests." When the King has passed through any of his troubles, it is "fair weather" again. The news of Perkin Warbeck's claims "comes thundering and blazing" from abroad. So in the Essay on Seditions he says that "as there are certain hollow blasts of wind, and secret swellings of seas before tempests, so are there in States." Perhaps his most favourite figures are those taken from medicine and surgery: he is fond of likening individuals and societies to a body, and supposing them subject to disease, or operated on by a physician or surgeon. Thus—

"The King of Scotland laboured under the same disease that King Henry did (though more mortal, as it afterwards appeared), that is, discontented subjects, apt to rise and raise tumult."

So with King Henry, insurrection was "almost a fever that took him every year." In his punishment of treason, Henry "commonly drew blood (as physicians do), rather to save life than to spill it." A good many figures of this kind might be picked from the Essays. Thus—

"It were too long to go over all the particular remedies which learning doth minister to all the diseases of the mind—sometimes purging the ill humours, sometimes opening the obstructions, sometimes helping the digestion, sometimes increasing appetite, sometimes healing the wounds and ulcerations thereof, and the like."

Again, regarding seditions, he says :—

"To give moderate liberty for griefs and discontentments to evaporate (so it be without too great insolence or bravery) is a safe way. For he that turneth the humours back, and maketh the wound bleed inwards, endangereth malign ulcers and pernicious imposthumations."

His well-known figure concerning Truth has a more poetical tone than his figures usually have :—

"This same Truth is a naked and open daylight, that doth not show the masks and mummeries and triumphs of the world half so stately and daintily as candle-lights."

This was written after his fall. It is worth noticing that, in these latest Essays, both the subjects and the illustrations show a growing sense of the pleasures of retirement.

Other figures than similitudes occur in Bacon's writing. A "corrective spice" of antithesis runs through all his works; sometimes conducing to clearness and force, sometimes amusing with its ingenuity. It is illustrated in extracts under various heads. Of the abrupt figures he makes very little use; his style is too grave and sober. At the same time he knows their effect in declamation, and introduces them upon occasion. See an instance at p. 248.

QUALITIES OF STYLE.

Simplicity.—The best evidence of the general intelligibility of Bacon's style is that so little has been said about it. He is neither markedly Latinised nor markedly familiar; he is perhaps less affected than any of his contemporaries. In his 'Advancement of Learning,' addressed to King James, he seems to humour the pedantry of the monarch, and introduces not a few Latin quotations without translating them. In his other works there is less of this; there is little obstruction to our getting at his meaning, except an occasional technical term. And through all his writings the numerous homely and pointed illustrations make his meaning abundantly luminous.

Clearness.—In perspicuity of arrangement, he is much superior to any of the Elizabethan writers. To quote the arrangement of his 'Novum Organum' (see p. 240) is hardly pertinent, seeing that it was written in Latin; still, it may be referred to as an example of his orderly and simple method. The order of topics in the 'Advancement of Learning' is also both simple and free from confusion. His classification of the sciences, though deficient as a scientific classification for modern purposes, being superseded by the vast enlargement of the subjects of human knowledge in recent times, is a very lucid division so far as it goes, and as "a small globe of the intellectual world" was very serviceable in its day. The divisions are so clear, and proceed upon distinctions so familiar, that though the subdivision is carried to the eighth degree, there is not the least perplexity to any mind of ordinary education.

We cannot concede to him the praise of scientific precision; indeed he often affirms fundamental resemblance where the resemblance is only slender and superficial. Distinctness in the use of words was no part of his scheme of philosophical reformation; the confusion of ambiguous terms in science could not begin to be felt until science was more advanced.

Still, in one of the subjects that his practical life brought him to consider, we find him aware of the danger of loosely applying the same term to things not precisely alike. With reference to the religious disputes of the time, he objected to the term *priest* for a clergyman; *minister*, he said, or *presbyter*, would be better, and the term priest should be reserved for the sacrificing priests under the old law.

Apart from rigid exactness, Bacon has in an eminent degree what is called incisiveness of style; his words and figures go straight to the point. His remarks on Studies are a good example of making a statement clear by giving counter-statements. This art of style appears in all his writings. True, he often uses the "but" of contrast where there is no real opposition, and merely to indicate a fresh start: nevertheless he does make frequent and effective use of contrast for purposes of exact expression. Thus—

"There followed this year, being the second of the King's reign, a strange accident of state, whereof the relations which we have are so naked, as they leave it scarce credible; *not for the nature of it* (for it hath fallen out oft), *but for the manner and circumstance of it*, especially in the beginnings."

Here we have, in a less finished form, the scrupulosity of qualification that is so marked a feature in the style of De Quincey. The following sentence, which is more finished, contains a vividly incisive use of contrast:—

"Neither was the King's nature and customs greatly fit to disperse such mists, but contrariwise he had a fashion rather to create doubts than assurance."

The passages italicised in the two following contain ingenious distinctions clearly expressed:—

"For the opinion of plenty is amongst the causes of want, and the great quantity of books maketh a show rather of superfluity than lack; which surcharge nevertheless is *not to be remedied by making no more books, but by making more good books*, which, as the serpent of Moses, might devour the serpents of the enchanters."

Towards removing all hindrances to the pursuit of knowledge, he says :—

"The endeavours of a private man may be but as an image in a cross-way, that *may point at the way, but cannot go it.*"

Strength.—The quality of strength in his style is intellectual rather than emotional. In his narrative there is very little expression of feeling; the strength comes chiefly from conciseness, secured by comprehensive statement, pregnant metaphor, and occasional strokes of epigrammatic condensation. The following is a fair specimen of his way of relating events ; in disentangling a variety of motives or exhibiting negotiations, he allows himself greater amplitude :—

"At York there came fresh and more certain advertisement that the Lord Lovell was at hand with a great power of men, and that the Staffords were in arms in Worcestershire, and had made their approaches to the city of Worcester to assail it. The King, as a prince of great and profound judgment, was not much moved with it, for that he thought it was but a rag or remnant of Bosworth Field, and had nothing in it of the main party of the house of York. But he was more doubtful of the raising of forces to resist the rebels than of the resistance itself, for that he was in a core of people whose affections he suspected. But the action enduring no delay, he did speedily levy and send against the Lord Lovell to the number of three thousand men, ill armed, but well assured (being taken some few out of his own train, and the rest out of the tenants and followers of such as were safe to be trusted), under the conduct of the Duke of Bedford. And as his manner was to send his pardons rather before the sword than after, he gave commission to the Duke to proclaim pardon to all that would come in, which the Duke, upon his approach to the Lord Lovell's camp, did perform. And it fell out as the King expected ; the heralds were the great ordnance."

The effect of the vigorous expression is enhanced by the penetrating ingenuity and freshness of the thought. We spoke of this in our survey of his character. The pleasure of reading him is almost purely dependent upon the exercise of the intellect. How little gratification he affords to ordinary human feeling will be made apparent by a single example. Contrast the following with Hooker's manner of approaching a similar theme; Bacon's subtlety is at work to discover arguments where Hooker is lost in adoration :—

"First, therefore, let us seek the dignity of knowledge in the archetype or first platform, which is in the attributes and acts of God, as far as they are revealed to man, and may be observed with sobriety ; wherein we may not seek it by the name of learning ; for all learning is knowledge acquired, and all knowledge in God is original ; and therefore we must look for it by another name, that of wisdom or sapience, as the Scriptures call it.

"It is so, then, that in the work of the creation we see a double emanation of virtue from God ; the one referring more properly to power, the other to wisdom ; the one expressed in making the subsistence of the matter, and the other in disposing the beauty of the form. This being supposed, it is to be observed that for anything which appeareth in the history of the creation, the confused mass and matter of heaven and earth was made in a moment; and the order and disposition of that chaos or mass was the work of six days; such a note of difference it pleased God to put upon the works of power and the works of wisdom; wherewith concurreth that in the former it is not set down that God said, *Let there be heaven and earth*, as it is set down of the works following, but actually that God made heaven and earth: the one carrying the style of a manufacture, and the other of a law, decree, or counsel.

"To proceed to that which is next in order from God to spirits; we find as far as credit is to be given to the celestial hierarchy of that supposed Dionysius, the senator of Athens, the first place or degree is given to the angels of love, which are termed seraphim; the second to the angels of light, which are termed cherubim; and the third, and so following places, to thrones, principalities, and the rest, which are all angels of power and ministry, so as the angels of knowledge and illumination are placed before the angels of office and domination."

Though not naturally inclined to address the feelings so much as the reason, Bacon knew, and upon occasion practised, the arts of elevation. The chief English specimen of his more ambitious rhetoric is a discourse in praise of the Queen, written when he was about thirty. It is a very good example of artificial strength. In the following sample, the strength is gained chiefly by figures of speech proper,—by declamatory departure from the ordinary forms of speech:—

"To speak of her fortune, that which I did reserve for a garland of her honour; and that is that she liveth a virgin, and hath no children; so it is that which maketh all her other virtues and acts more sacred, more august, more divine. Let them leave children that leave no other memory in their times. *Brutorum æternitas, soboles.* Revolve in histories the memories of happy men, and you shall not find any of rare felicity, but either he died childless, or his line spent soon after his death, or else was unfortunate in his children. Should a man have them to be slain by his vassals, as the posthumus of Alexander the Great was? or to call them his imposthumes, as Augustus Cæsar called his? Peruse the catalogue—Cornelius Sylla, Julius Cæsar, Flavius Vespasianus, Severus, Constantinus the Great, and many more."

It is interesting to compare this forced declamation with the ingenious antithetic conceits on the same theme in his Essay on Parents and Children:—

"The perpetuity by generation is common to beasts; but memory, merit, and noble works are proper to men. And surely a man shall see the noblest works and foundations have proceeded from childless men, which have sought to express the images of their minds where those of their bodies have failed. So the care of posterity is most in them that have no posterity."

KINDS OF COMPOSITION.

Narrative.—Bacon's 'History of Henry VII.' was written upon a principle enounced in his 'Advancement of Learning.' After saying that history is of three kinds according as "it representeth a time, or a person, or an action," and that "the first we call chronicles, the second lives, and the third narrations or relations," he goes on—

"Of these, although the first be the most complete and absolute kind of history, and hath most estimation and glory, yet the second excelleth it in profit and use, and the third in verity and sincerity. For the history of times representeth the magnitude of actions, and the public faces and deportments of persons, and *passeth over in silence the smaller passages and motions of men and matters.* But such being the workmanship of God, as He doth hang the greatest weight upon the smallest wires, *maxima e minimis suspendens*, it comes therefore to pass that *such histories do rather set forth the pomp of business than the true and inward resorts* thereof. But lives, if they be well written, propounding to themselves a person to represent, in whom actions both greater and smaller, public and private, have a commixture, must of necessity contain a more true, native, and lively representation."

This ideal of history bears some resemblance to Carlyle's anti-Dryasdust views. Bacon, a more acute and dispassionate observer than the historian of Friedrich, and practically acquainted with the ends and expedients of kings, has left us what is probably the very best history of its kind. He wrote it in a few months, taking his facts from the Chroniclers, and having access to few, if any, original documents; and consequently its peculiar merit is not accuracy: still, even if it is taken on that ground, his sagacity and knowledge of state affairs proved so true a guide, that his views of the main actions have not been set aside by more patient investigators. Considered on its own claims as an explanation of events by reference to the feelings and purposes of the chief actor, it is perhaps a better model than any history that has been published since. "He gives," says Bishop Nicholson, "as sprightly a view of the secrets of Henry's Council as if he had been President of it."

In one respect Bacon's History is in strong contrast to Macaulay's. In relating the schemes and actions of such a king as Henry, Macaulay would have overlaid the narrative with strong expressions of approval or disapproval. Bacon writes calmly, narrating facts and motives without any comment of a moral nature. Sometimes, indeed, he criticises, but it is from the point of view of a politician, not of a moralist; a piece of cruelty or perfidy is either censured only as being injudicious, or not commented upon at all. On this ground he is visited with a sonorous declamation by Sir James Mackintosh—as if his not improving the occasion were a sign that he approved of what had been done. Bacon wrote upon a principle that is beginning to be pretty widely accepted as regards personal histories claiming to be impartial—namely, that "it is the true office of history to represent the events themselves together with the counsels, and to leave the observations and conclusions thereupon to the liberty and faculty of every man's judgment." He does not seek to seal up historical facts from the useful office of "pointing a moral;" he only held that the moralising should not interfere with the narrative.

Exposition.—We have said that the modern expositor has not much to learn from earlier writers. An exception in one respect may be claimed for Bacon. Though all his scientific matter has been superseded, and his style is now antiquated, the 'Advancement of Learning' might still be read as a general tonic for incisive expression and perspicuous method. At the same time, it would be a mistake for the student to go to Bacon before he had in some degree mastered the style of modern exposition. To read the productions of Bacon's vigorous and subtle intellect has a bracing influence, but we must first be confirmed against the affectation of trying to imitate.

The 'Sylva Sylvarum' has little value as regards expository style, being merely a record of experiments and observations, with speculations thereupon. The following on "the goodness and choice of waters" is an example of the style; it also illustrates the scientific worthlessness of many of his statements:—

"It is a thing of very good use to discover the goodness of waters. The taste, to those that drink water only, is somewhat: but other experiments are more sure. First, try waters by weight; wherein you may find some difference, though not much; and the lighter you may account the better. . . .

"Sixthly, you may make a judgment of waters according to the place whence they spring or come. The rain-water is by the physicians esteemed the finest and the best; but yet it is said to putrefy soonest, which is likely because of the fineness of the spirit; and in conservatories of rain-water (such as they have in Venice, &c.) they are found not so choice waters; the worse perhaps because they are covered aloft, and kept from the sun. Snow-water is held unwholesome; insomuch as the people that dwell at the foot of the snow-mountains or otherwise upon the ascent (especially the women), by drinking of snow-water, have great bags under their throats. Well-water, except it be upon chalk, or a very plentiful spring, maketh meat red, which is an ill sign. Springs on the top of high hills are the best; for both they seem to have a lightness and appetite of mounting; and besides, they are most pure and unmingled; and again are more percolated through a great space of earth. For waters in valleys join in effect underground with all waters of the same level; whereas springs on the tops of hills pass through a great deal of pure earth with less mixture of other waters."

Persuasion.—His power as an orator is attested by two eminent authorities. Sir Walter Raleigh says that he surpassed other men in speaking as much as he did in writing; and Ben Jonson, in his 'Discoveries,' affirms that—"His hearers could not cough or look aside from him without loss. He commanded when he spoke, and had his judges angry or pleased at his devotion. No man had their affections more in his power." Making every allowance for grateful exaggeration in Ben Jonson's eulogy, we can still believe that Bacon was indeed a very convincing speaker. He was not a declaimer; he would not seem to have spoken with heat and fervour: if we raise upon Ben Jonson's description a picture of a hushed audience listening to a glowing orator, we shall be very far from the probable reality. A studied orator, he affected gravity and weight; speaking "leisurely, and rather drawingly than hastily," on the principle that "a slow speech confirmeth the memory, addeth a conceit of wisdom to the hearers, besides a seemliness of speech and countenance." From all that we know, it seems unmistakable that he addressed chiefly the self-interest and confirmed passions of his audience. The main study of his life was how to "work" men.

His verbal ingenuity was great, and carefully cultivated. Under the title of 'Promus of Formularies and Elegancies,' Mr Spedding has published some specimens of his store of happy expressions, repartees, epigrams, quotations from all sources, laid up for use upon fitting occasions. His collection of apothegms was another part of the same elaborate preparation. In his Preface he says: "Certainly they are of excellent use. They are *mucrones verborum, pointed speeches.* Cicero prettily calls them *salinas, salt-pits;* that you may extract salt out of, and sprinkle it where you will. They serve to be interlaced in continued speech. They serve to be recited upon occasion of themselves. They serve if you take out the kernel of them, and make them your own."

Another of his studies for Persuasion appears in a fragment first published in 1597, entitled 'Of the Colours of Good and Evil,' or, more fully, 'A Table of Colours or Appearances of Good and Evil, and their Degrees, as places of Persuasion and Dissuasion, and their several Fallaxes and the Elenches of them." In the beginning he says that "the persuader's labour is to make things appear good or evil, and that in higher or lower degree; which as it may be performed by true and solid reasons, so it may be represented also by colours, popularities, and circumstances, which are of such force, as they sway the ordinary judgment either of a weak man, or of a wise man not fully and considerately attending and pondering the matter." One of these "Colours" may be quoted as an example of his ingenuity: he himself would probably have been prepared to use and enforce either side according as he found it necessary:—

"*That course which keeps the matter in a man's power is good; that which leaves him without retreat is bad; for to have no means of retreating is to be in a sort powerless; and power is a good thing.*

. . . .

"Appertaining to this persuasion, the forms are, *you shall engage yourself;* on the other side, *tantum quantum voles sumes ex fortuna,* &c.—you shall keep the matter in your own hands. The reprehension of it is, *that proceeding and resolving in all actions is necessary;* for as he saith well, *not to resolve is to resolve;* and many times it breeds as many necessities, and engageth as far in some other sort, as to resolve.

"So it is but the covetous man's disease translated into power; for the covetous man will enjoy nothing, because he will have his full store and possibility to enjoy more; so by this reason a man should execute nothing, because he should be still indifferent and at liberty to execute anything. Besides necessity and this same *jacta est alea*" ["the die is cast"] "hath many times an advantage, because it awaketh the powers of the mind, and strengtheneth endeavour."

OTHER WRITERS.

DIVINES UNDER JAMES.—During the reign of James the Puritans gave little trouble. Forbearing open controversy, they gained ground among the people by their exemplary lives, and left the literary champions of conformity to other employment. **Richard Field, 1561-1616,** celebrated at Oxford as a disputant, and a favourite royal chaplain under James, wrote a treatise to prove that the English Church was the Church of early Christianity, and that the Roman Catholic peculiarities were of modern origin. His style is periodic and sonorous, without containing unidiomatic inversions. He argues with considerable vigour, and occasionally warms into impressive declamation. **Lancelot Andrewes, 1555-1626,** Bishop of Winchester, and a Privy Councillor, was a man of greater vivacity. He was a favourite with Bacon, who records some of his witty apothegms. As a bishop he was hospitable and munificent. He was celebrated for his knowledge of languages. The fact that he was the most popular preacher at Court, both with Elizabeth and with James, shows us whence the fashions of cumbrously superfluous quotation and fanciful word-play came into the sermon-writing of this and the following period. In redundant display of learning he goes beyond even Jeremy Taylor; and his word-play is after the manner we have illustrated from Ascham and Lyly. **Bishop Morton, 1564-1659,** a descendant from Cardinal Morton, was a voluminous author, chiefly of controversial works; but the length, abstemiousness, and kindly generosity of his life, and the troubles of his later years, will do more to preserve his memory than genius either in thought or expression. **John Donne, 1573-1631,** the founder of the "Metaphysical" school of poetry, having ruined his prospects of advancement in secular office by an imprudent marriage, after some ten years' uneasy waiting for employment, was urged by King James to enter the Church, and was ordained in 1616. As compared with Andrewes, Donne has the same characteristics of excessive quotation and fanciful wit; still the two are very different. For one thing, though that is not so striking, they draw their quotations from different sources: Donne is specially read in the Latin classics. They differ chiefly in force of intellect. Donne is more powerful and original; divides and distinguishes with greater subtlety, and fetches his images from a greater distance. In Donne's sermons, an intellectual epicure not too fastidious to read sermons will find a delicious feast. Whether these sermons can be taken as patterns by the modern preacher is another affair. It will not be contended that any congregation is equal to the effort of following his subtleties. In short, as exercises in abstract subtlety, fanciful ingenuity, and scholarship, the sermons are admirable. Judged by the first rule of popular exposition, the style is bad—a bewildering maze to the ordinary reader, much more to the ordinary hearer. In the specimens that we quote there is no want of distinct order, but the expression is in the highest degree abstract and subtle. They are taken from a sermon on St Paul at Malta, the text being, "*They changed their minds, and said that he was a god:*"—

"The first words of our text carry us necessarily so far back as to see from what they changed; and their periods are easily seen: their *terminus a quo* and their *terminus ad quem*, were these; first that he was a murderer, then that he was a god. An error in morality; they censure deeply upon light evidence: an error in divinity; they transfer the name and estimation of a god upon an unknown man. Place both the errors in divinity (so you may justly do); and then there is an error in charity, a hasty and inconsiderate condemning; and an error in faith, a superstitious creating of an imaginary god. Now upon these two general considerations will this exercise consist; first that it is natural logic, an argumentation naturally imprinted in man, to argue, and conclude thus great calamities are inflicted, therefore God is greatly provoked. These men of Malta were but natural men, but barbarians (as S. Luke calls them), and yet they argue and conclude so: Here is a judgment executed, therefore here is evidence that God is displeased. And so far they kept within the limits of humanity and piety too. But when they descended hastily and inconsiderately to particular and personal applications,—This judgment upon this man is an evidence of his guiltiness in this offence, then they transgressed the bounds of charity; that because a viper had seized Paul's hand, therefore Paul must needs be a murderer.

. . . .

"So that for this doctrine" (the natural "argumentation" above spoken of) "a man needs not be preached unto, a man needs not be catechised; a man needs not read the fathers, nor the councils, nor the schoolmen, nor the ecclesiastical story, nor summists, nor casuists, nor canonists; no nor the Bible itself for this doctrine; for this doctrine, that when God strikes He is angry, and when He is angry He strikes, the natural man hath as full a library in his bosom as the Christian.

. . . .

"The same author of ours, Moses, tells us, 'The Lord our God is Lord of lords, and God of gods, and regardeth no man's person.' The natural man hath his author too, that tells him, *Semper virgines furiæ*,—the furies (they whom they conceive to execute revenge upon malefactors) are always virgins, that is, not to be corrupted by any solicitations. That no dignity shelters a man from the justice of God, is a natural conclusion, as well as a divine. We have a sweet singer of Israel that tells us, *Non dimidiabit dies*, 'The bloody and deceitful man shall not live out half his days;' and the natural man hath his sweet singer too, a learned poet, that tells him, that seldom any enormous malefactor enjoys *siccam mortem* (as he calls it), a dry, an unbloody death. That blood requires blood is a natural conclusion as well as a divine. Our sweet singer tells us again, that if he fly to the farthest ends of the earth, or to the sea, or to heaven, or to hell, he shall find God there; and the natural man hath his author that tells him, *Qui fugit, non effugit*, he that runs away from God does not scape God. That there is no sanctuary, no privileged place, against which God's *Quo Warranto* does not lie, is a natural conclusion as well as a divine. *Sanguis Abel*, is our proverb, that Abel's blood cries for revenge; and *Sanguis Æsopi* is the natural man's proverb, that Esop's blood cries for revenge; for Esop's blood," &c.

Besides his Sermons, Donne's most famous prose work is 'Biathanatos,' a treatise on Suicide.

DIVINES UNDER CHARLES I.—**Joseph Hall, 1574-1656,** is illustrious in the Church history of England chiefly through his efforts to reconcile Dissenters with the Established Church. Though professedly anxious for religious union, he was a stanch adherent to Episcopacy, and wrote in its defence against both Presbyterianism and Romanism. His literary career extends through nearly sixty years. His first work consisted of three books of 'Satires,' published in 1597, and other three published the following year—performances which are praised even by such an authority as Pope. In 1608-11 he published his 'Epistles.'[1] His best-known prose works are his 'Contemplations' on Scripture, often quoted in popular commentaries, and his 'Occasional Meditations,' one of his latest productions. Both as a writer and as a preacher his reputation stands high. With less scholarship and wit than Andrewes, and less original power than Donne or Taylor, he writes with great fluency and energy, and with much better taste than any of these writers. Some have called him the best preacher of that century—no small honour among such giants; and undoubtedly, for pulpit oratory, his strong feelings and fluent expression, guided by superior taste, would be more effective than the undisciplined profusion and originality of his great rivals. Certainly, though he had not the genius of Donne or Taylor, he is a man of great mark in the history of our literature. The variety as well as the power of his writings challenges attention. Over and above his voluminous works connected with religion, he claims to be the first English *Satirist*, the first English writer of *Epistles*,

1 These Epistles are sometimes said to be the first collection of "letters" in the English language. Such a statement involves a slight confusion of names. Hall's Epistles are not "letters" at all in the sense of correspondence on passing events, but are really moral and religious discussions in the epistolary form. To prevent confusion, they had better be allowed to keep their title of 'Epistles.'

and his 'Mundus Alter et Idem' (Another World yet the Same) is said (though *that* is disputed) to have furnished Swift with the idea of 'Gulliver's Travels.'[1]

The character and opinions of the "immortal **Chillingworth,"** **1602-1644,** attract interest; his style is as finished, clear, and vigorous as any that was written in his day; and he argues with great force. He was a distinguished student at Oxford, a versatile scholar, eminent both in mathematics and in poetry, and noted for the confident independence of his views, and fearlessness in asserting and acting up to them. His patron was Laud, and it needed no little policy to keep so erratic and independent a genius in the orthodox track. He was first gained over by the Roman Catholics; and when regained, he refused to sign the Church formulas, consenting only when it was urged that they were merely bonds of peace and union, and that subscription did not imply belief of the whole. At the siege of Gloucester, he showed his versatility by proposing certain siege engines on a Roman model. Before the King at Oxford, he boldly attacked the vices of the Cavaliers. His chief work is 'The Religion of Protestants a Safe Way to Salvation,' &c., 1637. It is a remarkably bold and liberal book. He is not tied down to his own Church; by the "religion of Protestants" he understands neither "the doctrine of Luther, or Calvin, or Melanchthon; nor the Confession of Augusta, or Geneva; nor the Catechism of Heidelberg, nor the Articles of the Church of England—no, nor the harmony of Protestant Confessions," but "the Bible, and THE BIBLE ONLY." His work is undoubtedly the germ of Taylor's 'Liberty of Prophesying,' published ten years later; and it breathes a still bolder and wider spirit of tolerance:—

"I see plainly, and with mine own eyes, that there are Popes against Popes, councils against councils, some fathers against others, the same fathers against themselves, a consent of fathers of one age against a consent of fathers of another age, the Church of one age against the Church of another age. . . . In a word, there is no sufficient certainty but of Scripture only for any considering man to build upon. . . . Propose me anything out of this Book, and require whether I believe or no, and seem it never so incomprehensible to human reason, I will subscribe it with hand and heart, as knowing no demonstration can be stronger than this. God hath said so, therefore it is true. In other things I will take no man's liberty of judgment from him; neither shall any man take mine from me. I will think no man the worse man nor the worse Christian: I will love no man the less for differing in opinion from me. . . . I am fully assured that God does not, and therefore that men ought not to require any more of any man than this, to believe the Scripture to be

[1] Like other writers of the time, he has his pedantic nickname. Sir Henry Wotton called him the English Seneca, probably because he wrote Satires, Epistles, and Moral Essays. Fuller says—"He was commonly called our English Seneca, for the pureness, plainness, and fulness of his style; not ill at controversies, more happy at comments, very good in characters, best of all in meditations."

God's Word, to endeavour to find the true sense of it, and to live according to it."

The "ever-memorable **John Hales," 1584-1656,** was before even Chillingworth in advocating tolerance. In his tract on "Schism and Schismatics," published in 1628, he boldly asserted that "Church authority is none." The chief public incident in his life was his attendance at the Synod of Dort, 1618-19; his letters written at the time contain perhaps the best account of its proceedings. He wrote little: some of his sermons and tracts were collected into a volume in 1659, after his death. He was a little man with "a most ingenuous countenance, sanguine, cheerful, and *full of air.*" He had a high reputation for learning, wit, and courteous manner. His style is simple and felicitous.

HISTORY.

This period very nearly saw the end of the last of the *Chroniclers*, **Sir Richard Baker, 1568-1645,** whose work, 'A Chronicle of the Kings of England, from the Time of the Romans' Government unto the Death of King James,' was published in 1641. Baker's name, though not his fame, has been kept alive by his connection with Sir Roger de Coverley in the 'Spectator:' Addison, ridiculing the simple ignorance of the Tory squires in the person of Sir Roger, makes him quote Sir Richard Baker as a great authority. Poor Sir Richard is visited quite as bitterly as his rustic admirer:—

"The glorious names of Henry the Fifth and Queen Elizabeth gave the Knight great opportunities of shining, and of doing justice to *Sir Richard Baker, who, as our Knight observed with some surprise, had a great many kings in him whose monuments he had not seen in the Abbey.*"

Baker's popularity with country gentlemen was probably due to his style, which is praised by such an authority as Sir Henry Wotton—"full of sweet raptures and researching conceits, nothing borrowed, nothing vulgar, and yet all glowing with a certain equal facility."

Two *antiquaries* survived from the illustrious knot of King James's reign through the whole of this generation and far into the next. **James Usher** or **Ussher,** Archbishop of Armagh, 1581-1656, and **John Selden,** lawyer and politician, Keeper of the Records in the Tower, 1584-1654, were intimate with Camden, Spelman, and Cotton. Both were men of some fortune: Usher inherited a good estate, but retained only a competency, resigning the rest to his brother; and Selden, having a lucrative practice as a consulting lawyer and a conveyancer, possessed, as Fuller said, "a number of coins of the Roman Emperors, and a good many more of the later English Kings." Their principal antiquarian works are in Latin. Usher is an authority in chronological matters: his 'Annales' (1650-54) settles the Chronology of Ancient History from the Creation to the Dispersion of the Jews. He wrote also voluminously on Church Antiquities. Further, he was a royalist, and wrote a denunciation of armed resistance to the King; this was not published till after his death. Sermons and Letters were also published posthumously. — Selden was an antiquary of more varied accomplishments, writing on the administration of Britain, international law, the legal antiquities of the Jews, the gods of Syria, the Arundel Marbles, old English Ballads, &c. In politics, both of State and of Church, he was opposed to Usher; his legal learning and skill are said to have been of service in the protestation against James, and in the Petition of Right against Charles. A cautious man, he held back from public business when his party went to an extreme. Selden's learning, prudence, and polite affable manner, made him perhaps the most generally respected man of his time—respected alike by Royalist and by Puritan. As a writer of English, he is known by his 'History of Tithes' (1618), which offended the clergy by denying their divine right to such revenue; but chiefly by his 'Table-Talk,' published after his death. The style of his writings is harsh, obscure, and antiquated; in conversation he seems to have been more felicitous, dealing in pointed sententious aphorisms and witty turns. The 'Table-Talk' is full of worldly wisdom and sarcasms against clerical bigotry.

Lord Herbert of Cherbury, 1581-1648, a high-minded diplomatist, known in philosophy as the author of a Latin deistical treatise, 'De Veritate,' wrote a history of the Life and Reign of King Henry VIII. Those that differ from Lord Herbert most widely, join in admiring the dignity and earnestness of his character. His history may be put side by side with Lord Bacon's 'History of Henry VII.,' as one of the best historical works published before 1660. His style is not so clear, flowing, and pointed as Bacon's, but the idiom is purer. His sagacity in the explanation of affairs is no less remarkable, and he is at greater pains to make sure of the facts.

MISCELLANEOUS.

"Rare" **Ben Jonson (1574-1637)** wrote a prose work entitled 'Timber; or, Discoveries made on Man and Matter'—a series of random jottings on various subjects, containing some very sensible literary criticism. He does not affect the abrupt discontinuous style of Bacon's Essays; he writes rather in a free and easy conversational style. The following are specimens of his literary notes:—

"And as it is fit to read the best authors to youth first, so let them be of the openest and clearest. As Livy before Sallust, Sidney before Donne: and beware of letting them taste Gower or Chaucer at first, lest falling too much in love with antiquity, and not apprehending the weight, they grow rough and barren in language only."

"Periods are beautiful when they are not too long: for so they have their strength too, as in a pike or javelin."

The following is partly an anticipation of Carlyle's metaphor about a plethoric style:—

"We say it is a fleshy style when there is much periphrasis and circuit of words: and when with more than enough, it grows fat and corpulent. It hath blood and juice when the words are proper and apt, their sound sweet, and the phrase neat and packed."

His criticism of Shakspeare is often quoted, almost always without the qualification, and too often as an evidence of Ben's jealousy:—

"I remember the players have often mentioned it as an honour to Shakspeare, that, in his writing (whatsoever he penned) he never blotted out a line. My answer has always been, Would he had blotted out a thousand. Which they thought a malevolent speech. I had not told posterity this but for their ignorance who chose that circumstance to commend their friend by, wherein he most faulted; and to justify mine own candour: for I loved the man, and do honour his memory on this side idolatry, as much as any."

In the 'Reliquiæ Wottonianæ,' the remains of **Sir Henry Wotton (1568-1639)**,—a wit of more polish than Overbury, King James's favourite diplomatist, and author of the definition of an ambassador as "an honest man sent to *lie* abroad for the good of his country"—we find a weighty balance of sentence almost as finished as Johnson's. The following is a sample:—

"Sometimes the possibility of preferment prevailing with the credulous, expectation of less expense with the covetous, opinion of ease with the fond, and assurance of remoteness with the unkind parents, have moved them, without discretion, to engage their children in adventures of learning, by whose return they have received but small contentment: but they who are deceived in their first designs deserve less to be condemned, as such who, after sufficient trial, persist in their wilfulness are noway to be pitied."

The use of the abstract noun makes the resemblance to the Johnsonian structure all the more complete. Here is another specimen:—

"The fashion of commending our friends' abilities before they come to trial, sometimes takes good effect with the common sort, who, building their belief on authority, strive to follow the conceit of their betters; but usually, amongst men of independent judgments, this bespeaking of opinion breeds a purpose of stricter examination, and if the report be answered, procures only a bare acknowledgment, whereas," &c.

Among the miscellaneous writers of the period may be mentioned two travellers: **George Sandys (1577-1643)**, son of Archbishop Sandys, translator of Ovid, and author of a book of 'Travels in the East' (1615); and **William Lithgow (d. 1640)**, a Scotsman, who, during the reign of James, spent nineteen years in walking through "the most famous kingdoms in Europe, Asia, and Africa." Sandys was an accomplished traveller, with a constant eye to literary effect; his 'Travels' went through many editions. Lithgow seems to have walked more for adventure, and for the pleasure of boasting how many places he had visited, and how many miles he had walked on foot.

We must also mention the author of the 'Anatomy of Melancholy,' the recluse student of Christ Church, Oxford, **Robert Burton (1576-1640)**. A grave dyspeptic man, and a great reader—"confusedly tumbling over divers authors in our libraries, with small profit for want of art, order, memory, judgment"—he was eccentric and original, and picked out of various authors an enormous mass of quotations suiting his peculiar moods. With an immense parade of divisions and subdivisions, there is no method in his book; the heading of a section is little clue to its contents. His enumeration of the acts characteristic of different forms of melancholy is wide enough to include every son of Adam in the category of gloom. The leading features of his style, if style it may be called, are profuse quotation—several authorities being quoted for the most trivial remark—and long strings of particular words by way of exhausting a general subject, poured out in successive sentences without break. Part of his account of himself may be quoted as a sample:—

"I am not poor, I am not rich; *nihil est, nihil deest*, I have nothing, I want nothing: all my treasure is in Minerva's tower. Greater preferment as I could never get, so am I not in debt for it, I have a competence (*laus Deo*) from my noble and munificent patrons, though I live still a collegiate student, as Democritus in his garden, and lead a monastic life, *ipse mihi theatrum*, sequestered from those tumults and troubles of the world, *Et tanquam in specula positus* (as he said) in some high place above you all, like *Stoicus Sapiens*, omnia sæcula, præterita præsentiaque videns, *uno velut intuitu*. . . . A mere spectator of other men's fortunes and adventures, and how they act their parts, which methinks are diversely presented unto me as from a common theatre or scene. I hear new news every day, and those ordinary rumours of war, plagues, fires, inundations, thefts, murders, massacres, meteors, comets, spectrums, prodigies, apparitions, of towns taken, cities besieged in France, Germany, Turkey, Persia, Poland, &c., daily musters and preparations and suchlike, which these tempestuous times afford, battles fought, so many men slain, monomachies, shipwrecks," &c.

The enumeration would stretch on through one of our pages. To the modern writer Burton is of use only as a quarry, and to this purpose he has been turned by many. Sterne is not the only writer that has used the 'Anatomy of Melancholy' as raw material.

The passage we have quoted is probably the germ of Steele and Addison's 'Spectator.'

Nathaniel Butter, bookseller and pamphleteer, is a personage of some importance, as being the father of newspapers. It used to be supposed that the 'English Mercury' of 1588 was the first of English printed newspapers, but it is proved to have been a forgery of later date. During the reign of Elizabeth annual summaries of the chief events upon the Continent were printed under the title of 'Gallo-Belgici.' The proceedings of Continental powers were always interesting, and letters from friends in London containing the latest news were eagerly passed from hand to hand. When the Thirty Years' War broke out, this interest may be supposed to have greatly increased; and express news-letters, written by booksellers and others to their customers in the provinces, were much in request. These occasional productions may sometimes have been printed. Butter is the first known author of a regular series of such printed papers of news; in 1622 he began the 'Weekly News,' which he "purposed to continue weekly by God's assistance, from the best and most certain intelligence." "Whosoever," he said, "will be cunning in the places and persons of Germany, and understand her wars, let him not despise my Corantoes." His "corantoes," or courants, however, were despised, and that intensely, by the wits of the period. There may have been no guile in Nathaniel himself, but his imitators and rivals, who soon became numerous, seem to have published letters from "an eminent Jew merchant in Germany," and other correspondents of doubtful authenticity. And Ben Jonson did not scruple to declare that their pamphlets of news were "made all at home, and no syllable of truth in them." The unfortunate name of Butter made him an inviting butt. Jonson called him the "butter-box," described his news as "rank Irish butter;" and Fletcher made one of his characters say that "the spirit of Butter shall look as if butter would not melt in his mouth." The hostility of the stage may have been partly roused by the dramatic criticisms of these embryonic journalists. Despite his name, Butter seems to have been an industrious and veracious man, and not by any means the fantastic liar that has been represented by the dramatists.[1]

[1] See Cornhill Magazine, July 1868.

CHAPTER IV.

FROM 1640 TO 1670.

THOMAS FULLER,

1608—1661.

In the exciting days of the first Charles and of the Commonwealth, the life even of a clergyman was subject to danger and adventure, if he happened to be a partisan. Fuller, the son of the Rector of All Winkle, in Northamptonshire, bred up in the usual course of school and college education, and appointed prebend of Salisbury and vicar of Broad Windsor at the age of twenty-three, spent the first thirty-three years of his life in the greatest imaginable freedom from care. Up to 1640 he was unmolested in his quiet existence—varying his parish duties with the literary plans that served to fill his hours of leisure. But by 1640 the political atmosphere became troubled; and Fuller was called from his retreat to uphold in the pulpits of the metropolis the duty of obedience to the King. He spent a year with the royal forces in the character of chaplain to Lord Hopton. Growing weary of this irregular life, in 1644 he withdrew to Exeter, and busied himself with his compositions. On the capitulation of Exeter, he removed to London. In 1655 he received from the Protector special permission to preach. He lived to see the Restoration, but did not long enjoy the reward given to his loyalty, dying on the 15th of August 1661.

His 'Holy War,' the first of his works, was written in the quiet of the parsonage at Broad Windsor. His other works[1] he com-

[1] The list of his principal works is as follow: 'History of the Holy War,' 1640; 'The Holy State,' 1642; 'Good Thoughts in Bad Times,' 1644-45; 'The Profane State,' 1648; 'Good Thoughts in Worse Times,' 1649; 'A Pisgah Sight

posed when his life was more unsettled; though during the excitement of the Civil War his energies were so far from being absorbed in the struggle, that he was quietly occupied in collecting materials for his 'Worthies,' and in laying up a heterogeneous store of anecdotes.

In person[1] Fuller seems to have been rather over the middle height, full-bodied, with light curling hair, florid complexion, and clear blue eyes. He had an erect easy carriage, as was natural in a man of confident good spirits. He was careless in his dress.

He had an astonishing memory. The anecdotes of his powers are probably, like all anecdotes of the kind, not a little over-coloured; still they show what an impression he made on those that knew him. "It is said that he could repeat five hundred strange words after twice hearing, and could make use of a sermon *verbatim* if he once heard it. He undertook once, in passing to and fro from Temple Bar to the farthest point of Cheapside, to tell at his return every sign as it stood in order on both sides of the way, repeating them either backwards or forwards; and he did it exactly." His quickness in discovering resemblance was no less remarkable. This power, however, was not exercised on subjects that test intellectual strength; he did not strain his intellect like a great rhetorician to find telling arguments, nor like a great poet to find harmonious images. He wandered at will over the great stores accumulated by his memory, and amused himself in picking out incongruities, playing upon names, making odd comparisons, and suchlike ingenious freaks.

The chief destination of his scholarship is to tickle the sense of the ludicrous; no writer in our literature, except perhaps Burton, applies so much scholarship to so singular a purpose. "Wit," Coleridge said, "was the stuff and substance of Fuller's intellect."

His outward appearance was, to use a phrase of his own, "hung out as a sign" of his disposition; the cheerful, careless, confident nature of the man was legible in his countenance. Though he lived in times of fierce excitement, and was violently thrust out from his quiet home by the Puritans, and not permitted to take even his books with him, yet he shows no stronger feeling towards the triumphant party than sly humorous ridicule of individual sectaries. His attachment to his friends was equally moderate; he probably had a bias for the Church of England, but he does

of Palestine,' 1650; 'Abel Redivivus' (a Martyrology), 1651; 'Church History of Britain,' 1656; 'Mixed Contemplations in Better Times,' 1660; 'Worthies of England' (posthumous), 1662. Fuller may be said to have been the first "writer of books" by profession. He acknowledges that one of his objects in writing was—"to get some honest profit to himself."

[1] It is difficult to make out the personal appearance of some eminent English divines. Even their good-looks are overrated by one party and underrated by another.

not uphold the fame of her champions with anything approaching jealous impatience of contradiction. His eye seems to have been ever open to the comic aspects both of friend and of foe. He made a habit of looking at the world through a humorous medium. He conveys abundance of solid information, but his information has the oddest possible frame of witty nonsense.

Confident and careless—careless in the sense of rising humorously superior to care—Fuller was not an idle man, disposed, like one of Charles Lamb's genial borrowing fellows, to live upon the generosity of his friends. He took no earnest part in the fierce contest of his times, but the list of his works is ample proof of his capacity for honest industry. He puts comical wrappages about his information, but it is unimpeachably substantial, and could not have been procured without steady application.

He was born a Churchman, and continued a Churchman; yet so moderate were his sentiments, that he was suspected of a leaning to Puritanism. Before the outbreak of the Civil War he preached in London, and offended the party of the Parliament by advising submission to royal authority. When the rupture came, he fled to the king at Oxford, and there offended the royalists by advising conciliation.

ELEMENTS OF STYLE.

Vocabulary.—A good many archaisms occur in Fuller, though upon the whole he writes with a more modern phrase than any clergyman and scholar of the time. In his easy manner he would probably use the first word that came to hand. We meet with such obsolete words as "authenticalness," "cowardness" (*cowardliness*), "diurnal" (*journal*), "extempory" (*extemporary*), "duncical" (*stupid*), "jocularly" (*jocular*), "farced" (*stuffed*), "misoclere" (*hater of the clergy*), "un-understood," "volant" (*volatile*). Such of his words as "minutary" (analogous to *momentary*), and "orderable," in the sense of submissive to orders, might with advantage have passed into general use.

In Fuller's time English had not yet settled down to the present form of inflections. He is not at all uniform in his mode of inflecting—sometimes he uses the modern forms, sometimes there stray across his page such forms as "took" for *taken*, "bleeded" (*bled*), "understanden," "understanded" (*understood*), "strick," "stroke," "strook" (*struck*), "sprongen" (*sprung*), "sungen" (*sung*). Sometimes he uses "his" instead of the possessive affix, "King James *his* reign." On one occasion he gives *whole* a comparative "wholler."

He mingled so much with the world, holding intercourse with all classes, and being a good listener to every form of garrulity, that he uses a larger admixture of Saxon than his more recluse contemporaries. Besides, as we shall see, the use of very homely words is one of his instruments of ridicule.

Sentences.—His sentences are not involved and intricate. In this respect he is much superior to Hooker, Taylor, or any theological writer of his time. The following, in his Church History, on the plan taken by James I. to reduce the power of the English nobility, is rather an exception; he has comparatively few so loose and involved as this:—

"But following the counsel of his English secretary there present, he soon found a way to abate the formidable greatness of the English nobility, by conferring honour upon many persons; whereby nobility was spread so broad, that it became very thin, which much lessened the ancient esteem thereof."

It must be allowed, however, that in a full statement, or in an argument pursued at any length, he is not so much more skilled in avoiding intricacies, than his contemporaries. He is orderly chiefly because he is brief—usually trying to despatch a statement of fact or an argument as succinctly as possible. He is seldom drawn into complicated statements by a desire of saying too much.

That he studied expressly to avoid the cumbrous effect of formally indicating connection and dependence, may be inferred from his Prefaces, where he is put upon his mettle, and writes with more care. Thus—

"Seamen observe, that the water is the more troubled the nearer they draw on to the land, because broken by repercussion from the shore. I am sensible of the same danger, the nearer I approach our times, and the end of this History."

Most writers before the Restoration would have thrown these two sentences into one.

He is a great master of short pointed sentences. His pages are strewn with pithy sayings, that stick in the mind like proverbs. Almost every paragraph is preceded by a short sentence giving the pith of the whole. Thus in his Essay on Tombs, he has the following aphorisms: "Tombs are the clothes of the dead. A grave is but a plain suit, and a rich monument is one embroidered." "Tombs ought in some sort to be proportioned, not to the wealth, but deserts of the party interred." "The shortest, plainest, and truest epitaphs are the best." "To want a grave is the cruelty of the living, not the misery of the dead." "A good memory is the best monument."

Paragraphs.—He often digresses to tell an anecdote, but is sensible of his transgression. Sometimes he apologises, and tries to make out a connection; at other times he throws himself on the reader's forbearance. Thus—"Reader, whether smiling or frowning, forgive the digression."

But there is this to be said for Fuller's digressions, they never confuse. He lightens his subject by numerous paragraph breaks, made with considerable though not perfect accuracy, and—which is his main preventive of confusion—with every considerable change of subject, he gives a summary italic heading, and makes a fresh start.

Figures of Speech.—His style is thickly interspersed with ingenious similitudes. "The chief diseases of the fancy," he says himself, "are either that it is too wild and high-soaring, or else too low and grovelling, or else too desultory and over-voluble." The last is his own "disease." Ingenious as is the play of his fancy, it is much more luxuriant than would be tolerated now, and did not escape censure even in his own day.

His figures, like Bacon's, are taken largely from his own observations of common life, only, unlike Bacon's, they are nearly all, in accordance with the author's ruling tendency, calculated to make the reader laugh or smile. So far from exalting the object they are applied to, their purpose is to set it in a whimsical light; the most serious subjects are set off with odd similitudes, and the reader is tempted to laugh where propriety requires him to be grave. The following are one or two examples. Of the good bishop he says:—

"He is careful and happy in suppressing of heresies and schisms. He distinguisheth of schismatics as physicians do of leprous people: some are infectious, others not; some are active to seduce others, others quietly enjoy their opinions in their own consciences. . . . To use force before people are fairly taught the truth, is to knock a nail into a board without wimbling a hole for it, which then either not enters, or turns crooked, or splits the wood it pierceth."

Again—

"Let us be careful to provide rest for our souls, and our bodies will provide rest for themselves. And let us not be herein like unto gentlewomen, who care not to keep the inside of the orange, but candy and preserve only the outside."

And, condemning the use of high-flown language with inferior matter, he says—

"Some men's speeches are like the high mountains in Ireland, having a dirty bog in the top of them."

He advises the young writer to take advice of a faithful friend:—

"When thou pennest an oration, let him have the power of the 'Index Expurgatorius' to expunge what he pleaseth; and do not thou, like a fond mother, cry if the child of thy brain be corrected for playing the wanton."

Fuller himself "plays the wanton" in similitudes so often that we see a touch of the ludicrous in nearly every comparison that he makes, just as in conversation we are tickled by every word that falls from an acknowledged wit.

A great many of his comparisons are historical parallels, or ingenious figurative applications of historical facts. The following is an instance. Writing of one of his Worthies, he says:—

"He obtained a plentiful estate, and thereof gave wellnigh three thousand pounds to Sidney College. Now as it is reported of Ulysses, returning from his long travel in foreign lands, that all his family had forgot him; so when the news of this legacy first arrived at the College, none then extant therein ever heard of his name (so much may the sponge of forty years blot out in this kind); only the written register of the College faithfully retained his name therein.

"This his gift was a gift indeed, purely bestowed on the College, as loaded with no detrimental conditions in the acceptance thereof. We read in the Prophet, 'Thou hast increased the nation, and not multiplied their joy.' In proportion whereunto, we know it is possible that the comfortable condition of a College may not be increased, though the number of the fellows and scholars therein be augmented, superadded branches sucking out the sap of the root; whereas the legacy of this worthy knight *ponebatur in lucro*, being pure gain and improvement to the College."

Here we see the same whimsical vein, the same tendency to make ludicrous comparisons of small things with great, and great things with small. The following, from his 'Mixt Contemplations,' is a sample of his elaborate similitudes; it also illustrates the ludicrous meanness of comparison that grave divines have pronounced unpardonable levity:—

"I have observed that children when they first put on new shoes, are very curious to keep them clean. Scarce will they set their feet on the ground for fear to dirt the soles of their shoes. Yea, rather they will wipe the leather clean with their coats; and yet, perchance, the next day they will trample with the same shoes in the mire up to the ankles. Alas, children's play is our earnest! On that day wherein we receive the sacrament, we are often over-precise, scrupling to say or do those things which lawfully we may. But we, who are more than curious that day, are not so much as careful the next; and too often (what shall I say?) go on in sin up to the ankles: yea, our sins go over our heads."

While the great majority of Fuller's similitudes have a whimsical turn, he often employs them to convey sound practical advice. Thus—

"Parents who cross the current of their children's genius (if running in no vicious channels), tempt them to take worse courses themselves."

QUALITIES OF STYLE.

Simplicity.—The drawback to Fuller's simplicity is the vice of his age—the parade of learned terms and unnecessary allusions. Expressions are quoted with chapter and verse when the quotation serves no purpose of illustration, and can excite in the reader only a pedantic pleasure that he has seen it before, or a whimsical surprise at seeing brought together two cases that have no material resemblance. It is, however, but just to say that he is much less pedantic than Taylor or Browne, and immeasurably less so than Burton. Only now and then do we come across such a passage as occurs in the following Dedication to Douse Fuller:—

"I cannot say certainly of you, as Naomi did of Boaz, 'He is near of kin unto us,' Ruth ii. 20; having no assurance, though great probability, of alliance unto you. However, sir, if you shall be pleased in courtesy to account me your kinsman, I will endeavour that (as it will be an honour to me) it may be to you no disgrace."

Or such as the following, where the homeliest Saxon rubs shoulders with canonical Latin:—

"First, soundly infix in thy mind what thou desirest to remember. What wonder is it if agitation of business jog that out of thy head which was there tacked rather than fastened? whereas those notions which get in by *violenta possessio*, will abide there till *ejectio firma*, sickness, or extreme age, dispossess them. It is best knocking in the nail over-night, and clinching it in the next morning."

Perspicuity.—One thing that helps largely to make Fuller's style so remarkably easy reading is his perspicuous arrangement. "Method," he says himself, "is the mother of memory." In all his works he follows a simple plan: there is consequently no confusion, no perplexity; we are not irritated by searching for a fact, and finding it out of its proper connection; we can find what we want in a moment. Take, for instance, his 'Worthies.' He there gives an account of the notabilities of England county by county, proceeding in each county after a fixed order, which he explains at the beginning of the book. How highly he valued the principle of order appears in his anxiety to show how well he had observed it. In an introductory chapter designed to anticipate objections to the "style and matter of the author," divided into heads and numbered, as is his manner with every subject, he supposes "Exception 16" to be as follows:—

"You lay down certain rules for the better regulating your work, and directing the reader, promising to confine yourself to the observation thereof, and break them often yourself. For instance, you restrain the topic of lawyers to capital judges and writers of the law; yet under that head insert Judge Paston and others, who were only puny judges in their respective courts. . . . Why did you break such rules, when knowing you made them? Why did you make such rules, when minding to break them?"

To this he returns the following—

"*Answer.*—I never intended to tie myself up so close, without reserving lawful liberty to myself upon just occasion. . . . I resolved to keep the key in my own hands, to enlarge myself when I apprehended a just cause thereof. However, I have not made use of this key to recede from my first limitations, save where I crave leave of and render a reason to the reader;

such anomalous persons being men of high merit, under those heads where they are inserted."

In giving an account of arguments, he states the two sides separately, often printing them in parallel columns. The reasonings of opposite parties in the Church are exhibited on this handy method. So when he argues himself, he analyses the positions of his adversary, and replies to them one by one, numbering each position, and labelling the argument and the answer with an italic heading to prevent every possibility of confusion, and to let the reader know where he is at a glance.

The 'Holy State' and the 'Profane State' are models of simple arrangement. In the 'Holy State' he describes a number of good characters, first an ideal unfolded in a number of maxims, then an example to correspond. Thus, for "the good servant" he lays down seven maxims—"(1) He doth not dispute his master's will, but doth it;" "(2) He loves to go about his business with cheerfulness;" "(3) He despatches his business with quickness and expedition,"—and so on. This is followed up by the life of Eliezer, the steward of Abraham's household. The 'Profane State' is the counterpart of the 'Holy State,' dealing with bad characters, the Harlot, the Heretic, the Traitor, &c. One of the books of the 'Holy State' deals with virtues and vices in the abstract, plentifully illustrated and embellished with anecdotes and fancies.

Strength.—Under this head little need be said of Fuller. His style has the vigour of brief statement and well-chosen words; but he never attempts to soar, and when he does, is soon tempted back to his homely level by some oddity of comparison.

Brevity is a very conspicuous feature in his style. In none of Fuller's works could we read three sentences on end without being reminded of the saying that "Brevity is the soul of wit."

Pathos.—His genius was more inclined to pathos than to strength: but his expression of tenderness is seldom direct; it is to be found in the disguise of humour, lurking in some droll conceit. There is a quaint kindliness in his conclusion of the 'Life of Philemon Holland,' the translator of Camden's 'Britannia.' "This venerable translator was translated to heaven in the year 16—."

But how little he could resist the attraction of comical allusions, even in the most pitiful circumstances, is seen in his account of an accident that happened to a Catholic congregation:—

"The sermon began to incline to the middle, the day to the end thereof; when on a sudden the floor fell down whereon they were assembled. It gave no charitable warning groan beforehand, but cracked, broke, and fell, all in an instant. Many were killed, more bruised, all frighted. Sad sight, to behold the flesh and blood of different persons mingled together, and the brains of one on the head of another! One lacked a leg; another an arm; a third whole and entire, wanting nothing but breath, stifled in the ruins."

As we noted in the case of Macaulay, his interest in unimportant facts overbears his interest in the tragic aspects of a scene. His account of the death of Charles is very matter-of-fact, and shows the antiquary predominating over the man. True, one or two of the facts are suggestive. Even the conclusion, the most dryasdust of the whole, will set some on the track of a reflection or a moral:—

"On the Wednesday se'nnight after, (February 7th), his corpse, embalmed and coffined in lead, was delivered to the care of two of his servants, to be buried in Windsor; the one Anthony Mildmay, who formerly had been his sewer, as I take it; the other John Joyner, bred first in his Majesty's kitchen, afterwards a parliament-captain, since by them deputed (when the Scots surrendered his person) cook to his Majesty. This night they brought the corpse to Windsor, and digged a grave for it in St George's Chapel, on the south side of the communion-table."

But certainly there is no superfluous sentiment on the part of the author. It might, indeed, have been dangerous to moralise under the circumstances; we could, however, have dispensed with the gossip about his Majesty's cook.

Wit and Humour.—The chief part of our author's reputation is based on his wit. A pleasant vein runs through everything he wrote, no matter what the subject, dignified or undignified, grave or gay. His very sermons are full of the same quaint humour. By some of his contemporaries, as we have said, he was frowned upon for treating solemn things in a tone of levity; but there is no better evidence of the power of wit to disarm resentment than the fact remarked by his recent editor, that Fuller "was permitted to give utterance to some strong sentiments, which less favoured individuals durst scarcely own to have found a lodgment within their breasts."

His wit is genial and good-natured; sometimes he burlesques the conduct of a sectary with considerable rudeness; but in general his laugh is kindly.

Nearly all Barrow's varieties of wit might be illustrated copiously from Fuller; indeed, he may have written his remarks on wit with Fuller's pages open before him. We have seen examples of the "odd similitude" and the "pat allusion to a known story." The "seasonable application of sayings," and the "forging of apposite tales," are of the same kind, and need not be farther illustrated. A large part of the wit consists in "playing in words and phrases, taking advantage from the ambiguity of their sense or the affinity of their sound." Laud is "a man of low stature, but of high parts;" Dr Field is "that learned divine whose memory smelleth like a Field the Lord hath blessed;" Nicholas

Sanders, being an enemy of the Church, is "more truly Slanders." Fuller never misses an opportunity of punning. Sometimes the puns are very elaborate, as in the following. Take first the seventh item in the character of the good widow:—

"*If she speaks little good of him*" (her dead husband) "*she speaks but little of him.* So handsomely folding up her discourse, that his virtues are shown outwards, and his vices wrapt up in silence; as counting it barbarism to throw dirt on his memory who hath moulds cast on his body."

Take next an item in the character of the good master:—

"*The wages he contracts for he duly and truly pays to his servants.* The same word in the Greek, *iòs*, signifies 'rust' and 'poison;' and some strong poison is made of the rust of metals; but none more venomous than the rust of money in the rich man's purse unjustly detained from the labourer, which will poison and infect his whole estate."

He is fond of constructing opportunities for droll rejoinders. In the introductory chapters to his 'Worthies,' already mentioned, he imagines and deals as follows with—

"*Exception* 9.—'Haste makes waste.' You have huddled your book too soon to the press, for a subject of such a nature. . . .

"——*Nonumque prematur in annum.*
"Eight years digest what you have rudely hinted,
And in the ninth year let the same be printed.

"*Answer.*—That ninth year might happen eight years after my death," &c.

The following is an unexpectedly conclusive evidence. By the beginning one is prepared only for some slight doubt of the suspicion:—

"The suspicion of making it" (something in the way of Church controversy) "fell on Gregory Martin: one probable enough for such a prank (as being Divinity Professor at Rheims) did not his epitaph there ensure me he was dead and buried two years before."

In the following he whimsically imagines, and objects to a strictness of literal interpretation that few would think of contending for:—

"St Paul saith, 'Let not the sun go down on your wrath,' to carry news to the antipodes in another world of thy revengeful nature. Yet let us take the apostle's meaning rather than his words, with all possible speed to dispose our passions; not understanding him so literally that we may take leave to be angry till sunset; then might our wrath lengthen with the days, and men in Greenland, where day lasts above a quarter of a year, have plentiful scope of revenge."

Wit is not the only comical seasoning of Fuller's amusing productions. Throughout his 'Church History' and his 'Worthies,' we are kept in a perpetual smile by the purposely undignified familiarity of his language. Sometimes this becomes open burlesque, as in his account of Brown, the founder of the "Brownists:"—

"Some years after Brown went over into Zealand, to purchase himself more reputation from foreign parts. For a smack of travel gives a high taste to strange opinions, making them better relish to the licorish lovers of novelty. Home he returns with a full cry against the Church of England, as, having so much of Rome, she had nothing of Christ in her discipline. Norfolk was the first place whereon Brown (new-flown home out of the Low Countries) perched himself, and therein," &c.

As another instance of this, note how he speaks of the Round Table legends:—

"As for his Round Table, with his knights about it, the tale whereof hath trundled so smoothly along for many ages, it never met with much belief among the judicious."

The strict method of his works, so far from being a shackle to his wit, furnishes him with additional opportunities for quaint turns. Thus he concludes his account of Brown by saying:—

"Thus to make our story of the troublesome man the more entire, we have trespassed on the two following years, yet without discomposing our chronology in the margin."

Again, writing of Bishop Barnes and Bernard Gilpin, he says:—

"Seeing they were loving in their lives, in my book their memories shall not be divided, though I confess the latter died some three years before."

No other quality of Fuller's style calls for special illustration. Brevity, point, simplicity, and wit, are his conspicuous characteristics. In the examples quoted, the reader will have noticed that he is fond of alliteration, an almost unconscious habit with nearly every writer of point. Taste is not a merit of Fuller's; he is an eccentric writer, setting good taste at defiance in the pursuit of his favourite effect. An historian and an antiquary in name, he is too easy and superficial to rank high in that species of composition: he has in his favour simplicity of language, and almost unique attention to arrangement; but the subject-matter of his works is only a field for the exercise of his extraordinary memory and his irrepressible wit.

JEREMY TAYLOR, 1613-1667.

A man of genius, the most distinguished prose writer of this period. He has been called "the Shakspeare of English prose," and "the Chrysostom of the English Pulpit:" and the designations are less fanciful than such designations often are.

Of his private life few particulars are known; he is said to have written an autobiography, but it has perished. Even the main dates in his public career have been traced with some difficulty. We know in general that he suffered in the temporary eclipse of the Episcopalian party, and that he lived to be rewarded at the Restoration.

He was born in Cambridge, of humble parentage; and educated there at the Grammar School and at Caius College. When only twenty years of age, he preached before Archbishop Laud, and his eloquence and youthful beauty made such an impression that the prelate at once took him under patronage, placed him at All Souls in Oxford, procured him a fellowship, and appointed him one of his own chaplains. In 1637-38, he was presented by the Bishop of London to the rectory of Uppingham, in Rutlandshire. At the breaking out of the Civil War, he repaid the favour of his patrons by a work in defence of Episcopacy; for this the king made him D.D., while the Presbyterians, then rapidly gaining strength, sequestrated his rectory.

About 1643 he retired to the residence of his mother-in-law in Wales; but before he had been long there, the tide of war rolling in that direction, he was taken prisoner by the forces of the Parliament, and kept for some time in confinement. On his release he supported himself by keeping a school, and during that time composed his 'Liberty of Prophesying.' Thereafter he found a patron in the Earl of Carbery, and lived for some years at that nobleman's seat, Golden Grove. There he wrote his 'Life of Christ,' and a work named after the place, 'Golden Grove.' An attack upon the Puritans in the 'Golden Grove' offended Cromwell; in 1654 he was apprehended, and during three or four years more than once suffered imprisonment. In 1658 he obtained from his friends an alternate lectureship at Lisburne, in the north of Ireland, where he remained till the Restoration. By Charles II. he was made Bishop of Down and Connor, and subsequently of Dromore. He died at Portmore, on the 3d of August 1667.

Most of his works were written during his virtual exile in Wales. The exceptions were strictly professional works: 'Episcopacy Asserted,' published in 1642; 'Discourse of Confirmation,' in 1663, after his elevation to the bishopric; and 'Dissuasive from Popery,' in 1664. His 'Liberty of Prophesying,' 'Life of Christ,' 'Holy Living and Holy Dying,' and 'Ductor Dubitantium,' were all composed during his seclusion, the last work being completed at Lisburne. His treatise on 'Repentance' was written between 1654 and 1658, during his imprisonments.

Taylor was a very handsome man, rather above the middle height, with a dark sparkling eye, and features almost feminine in their delicacy.

The characteristic of his intellect is luxuriant activity and productiveness rather than accuracy or taste.[1] For one that wrote so much and was not merely an unproductive dungeon of learning, his scholarship was enormous: but he does not seem to have verified his references with much care, and he has been detected in some ludicrously bad translations. Comparatively few items of his learning were allowed to sleep; all his works, whether technical, controversial, or practical, are crowded with superfluous quotations and allusions. As an evidence of his intellectual activity, consider what he wrote during his residence in Wales, the variety of subjects that he entertained; compare him in this respect with the "judicious" Hooker, a more careful scholar, but a much less active producer. The same characteristic appears in his impassioned flights; he is, says De Quincey, "restless, fervid, aspiring, scattering abroad a prodigality of life." He abandons himself without reserve to the inspiration of the moment, eagerly accumulating circumstances and similitudes, his free flight trammelled by no punctilious care to frame the particulars into a harmonious whole. In the filling out of his opulent pictures, he is equally unimpeded by a scrupulous regard for facts; in his telling illustrations of the decay of human splendour, he takes upon trust the most outrageous fables.

With all his scholarship and ingenuity, he had, if we may judge from his writings, a youthful freshness of sentiment. When thrust from his living by the great Rebellion, he did not acquiesce in silence, but, trusting probably to his distance from the centre of power and to the protection of Lord Carbery, he denounced the new Government as "disgracing the articles of religion, and polluting public assemblies," and stigmatised the new preachers as "impertinent and ignorant," fruitless "crabstocks." Thus warm in his expressions of dislike, he was no less warm in his expressions of affection: with all his learning, a vain, warm-hearted, childlike man. It seems strange that there should ever have been among biographers a dispute whether or not he was a woman-hater. Tenderness would seem to have been his ruling emotion. "There is nothing," he says, "can please a man without love." His works contain many passages of demonstrative affection. He expatiates with peculiar fondness upon children, and upon the delights of the

[1] We made a somewhat similar remark about Bacon, and as the two minds are so different in their general figure, in their appearance as wholes, it may be well to mention the more important analysed elements of difference. One vast difference lies in this, that Bacon was more original and constructive: Bacon, as his chaplain says, "never was a plodder upon books," and had comparatively little scholarship; Taylor's scholarship is a standing subject of wonder and admiration. Bacon had very little poetical feeling, Taylor had all the gifts of a poet except metre. The two men resemble each other in their enormous powers of intellectual work; they differ immeasurably in the quality and direction of that work.

"sanctuary and refectory" of the domestic circle, "his gardens of sweetness and chaste refreshment."

In a writer of casuistical morality, profoundly versed in the interminable dusty volumes of the schoolmen, we should not expect much sensibility to the beauties and grandeurs of nature. Yet Taylor shows this sensibility in rich abundance. He was not a dry, unmoved observer like Bacon. He had a profound susceptibility to the luxuries of the eye. In our illustrations of his style, we shall quote many evidences of his delighted contemplation of external life. It probably was the charm derived from this source that commended his writings so powerfully to the nature-poets of this century. Not only was he alive to beauties of form and colour, and to tender associations: he looked with delight upon the grandeurs of nature, upon the exciting phenomena of storms and tempests. Rarely indeed do we find such scholarship and subtlety combined with so fresh an interest in the outer world.

Of gentle disposition and ingratiating manners, he had not the hardihood required for the stir and bustle of practical life. He showed none of the political capacity of Whitgift or of Laud. His eloquence and personal grace made him a favourite: his learning and his services as a literary champion sanctioned his promotion to a bishopric. Warm in his expressions of resentment, he had not the courage of a martyr. When imprisoned for his outburst against the Puritans, he was not obdurate in his recriminations; he did not spend his imprisonment in the refractory occupation of composing further invectives, but quietly turned to his books, and wrote his treatise on Repentance.

The most generally celebrated of Taylor's opinions are those contained in his 'Discourse of the Liberty of Prophesying.' It is an elaborate argument for religious toleration. It does not recommend absolute freedom of opinion; it makes a stand upon the Apostles' Creed, and urges that no person subscribing to this should be denied communion by any Christian sect. It even allows difference of opinion as to the clause regarding Christ's descent into hell. The argument of the work is not abstract, *a priori:* he does not uphold freedom to differ as a "natural right;" this idea was of later growth. He reasons from experience; pointing out the difficulty of ascertaining the real truth; dilating upon, and, after his wont, copiously exemplifying, the fallibility of all human interpreters of Scripture—Popes, Councils, Fathers, or Writers Ecclesiastical. The work is not, as is sometimes stated, the first direct argument for toleration. It arose naturally at a time when difference of opinion, prolific of bitter dissensions for almost a century, had culminated in the distraction of civil war. While Taylor deserves and will ever receive all honour for his spirit of moderation, it would be unjust to Grindall, Hales, Chillingworth, and other tolerant Churchmen of former generations, to represent him as the first advocate of religious liberality.

His opinions on original sin made greater noise in his own day than his toleration. He was accused of being Pelagian, and seems to have held that original sin is "an effect or condition of nature, but no sin properly," that it cannot be repented of, in the proper sense of the word repent, and that no person shall be visited with eternal damnation for original sin only.

His 'Ductor Dubitantium' (Guide to the Scrupulous)—a work filling two closely-printed large octavo volumes, in Mr Eden's revision of Heber's edition—occupies a middle position between the casuistry of the schoolmen and the moral philosophy of such writers as Tucker and Paley. He deals more with the exposition of general principles than the scholastic casuists, and exhibits a larger number of cases and a greater subtlety in distinguishing degrees of guilt than Paley.

ELEMENTS OF STYLE.

Vocabulary.—The pedantic bookish element is very conspicuous in Taylor's language. He coins extensively both from Latin and from Greek. He uses "deturpated" for *deformed*, "clancularly" for *secretly*, "immorigerous" for *disobedient*, "intenerate" for *render soft*, "paranymph" for *lady's-maid*. In like manner he applies words according to their Latin etymology, and contrary to the growing usage—"insolent" in the sense of *unusual*, "extant figures" (figures *in relief*), an "excellent" pain (*surpassing, extreme*).

He has, besides, some few mannerisms. He goes beyond the extreme idiomatic licence in the way of forming plurals to abstract nouns—"aversenesses," "dissolutions," "prudencies," "strengths," "tolerations." Also, he uses abstract nouns in the same construction with concrete nouns, and where the construction is unidiomatic for abstract nouns. This occurs very often, and appears in several of our quotations. As an example for the present take the following: "The despised drops were grown into an artificial river *and an intolerable mischief*;" "the rivulet swelling into rivers *and a vastness*;" "the sea shall descend into *hollowness and a prodigious drought*." Another usage has been noted,—the comparative employed to express a degree short of the extreme; but this is not so peculiar. Examples are—"The Libyan lion drawn from his *wilder* foragings;" "a sad arrest of the looseness and *wilder* feasts of the French Court."

These "pedanterias" aside, Taylor has a powerful command of the language. There was no greater master of English in his day.

Sentences.—He is very careless in the structure of his sentences

In few passages even of his driest works is the syntax grammatical in six sentences upon end; and when he warms to his subject, he adds clause to clause as it were in a breath, without stopping to look back and see whether the accumulation has resulted in a coherent sentence. Inasmuch as he always writes with *verve*, this characteristic meets us in every page, indeed very often in the first sentence. As an example, take the first sentence in his 'Contemplations on Time,' where the connection of the clauses and the sequence of the tenses are alike irregular:—

"All philosophers which have thought of the nature of time, and which with much subtlety have disputed what it was, at length come to conclude, That they knew not what it is; the most they can reach unto is, That no time is long; and that can only be called time which is present, the which is but a moment; and how can that be said to be, since the only cause why it is, is because it shall not be, but is to pass into the *preterit*, so as we cannot affirm it to have a being?"

Very often his sentence is a string of statements bearing on the same subject, each joined to the preceding by the conjunction "and." The following is of unusual length, but otherwise is a fair specimen:—

"But when Christian religion was planted, and had taken root, and had filled all lands, then all the nature of things, the whole creation, became servant to the kingdom of grace; *and* the head of the religion is also the head of the creatures, and ministers all the things of the world in order to the spirit of grace: *and* now 'angels are ministering spirits sent forth to minister for the good of them that fear the Lord;' *and* all the violences of men, and things of nature, and choice, are forced into subjection and lowest ministries, and to co-operate as with an united design, to verify all the promises of the Gospel, and to secure and advantage all the children of the kingdom: *and* now he that is made poor by chance or persecution, is made rich by religion; *and* he that hath nothing,"—and so on.

One thing his sentences are free from; they are very rarely made intricate by elaborate involutions and suspensions such as we find in Hooker. He has many classical idioms and superfluous connectives, but the structure is simple.

Artificial condensations are pretty frequent. The peculiar use of the abstract noun (p. 275) is a mode of condensation. In many cases the condensation is more marked than in those quoted, as, for example, in the following:—

"And what can we complain of the weakness of our strengths, or the pressure of diseases, when we see a poor soldier stand in a breach almost starved with cold and hunger, and *his cold apt to be relieved only by the heats of anger, a fever, or a fired musket, and his hunger slacked by a greater pain and a huge fear?* This man shall stand in his arms, and wounds, *patiens luminis atque solis*, pale and faint, weary and watchful; and at night shall have *a bullet pulled out of his flesh, and shivers from his bones*, and endure his mouth to be *sewed up from a violent rent to its own dimension.*"

Figures of Speech.—Taylor's style is richly embellished with metaphors and similes taken from numerous sources, from familiar operations of life, from nature, and from books.[1] These need not be specially illustrated. On the figures taken from books, the remark may be made that they are often absurdly learned. This belongs to the parade of scholarship already mentioned as being fostered in English sermons by the taste of the Court. Taylor carries this pedantry to an extreme. Any of his contemporaries or predecessors might have said that "Nero might be called Most Clement with as much reason as some princes are styled Most Magnificent;" but perhaps none of them would have ventured to speak in their sermons of "the tender lard of the Apulian swine," or "garments stained with the Tyrian fish," or "garments made of the Calabrian fleece, and stained with the blood of the murex."

His most notable and characteristic figures are the elaborate similitudes from nature. In these he does not confine himself to the features of strict resemblance, but makes each similitude a complete picture in a single sentence, the circumstances being accumulated in the opulent irregular manner already described. The following are instances; others occur in the illustration of his pathos:—

"So we sometimes espy a bright cloud formed into an irregular figure; when it is observed by unskilful and fantastic travellers, it looks like a centaur to some, and as a castle to others; some tell that they saw an army with banners, and it signifies war; but another wiser than this fellow, says it looks for all the world like a flock of sheep, and foretells plenty; and all the while it is nothing but a shining cloud, by its own mobility and the activity of a wind cast into a contingent and inartificial shape; so it is in this great mystery of our religion, in which some espy strange things which God intended not, and others see not what God has plainly told."

"For so have I known the boisterous north wind pass through the yielding air which opened its bosom, and appeased its violence by entertaining it with easy compliance in all the regions of its reception: but when the same breath of heaven hath been checked with the stiffness of a tower, or the united strength of a wood, it grew mighty and dwelt there, and made the highest branches stoop, and make a smooth path for it on the top of all its glories. So is sickness, and so is the grace of God." (In reference to the subduing power of sickness and the evils of impatience.)

"For so doth the humble ivy creep at the foot of the oak, and leans upon its lowest base, and begs shade and protection, and leave to grow under its

---

[1] The fanciful conceits of the time appear in considerable numbers. Even Euphuism, in the restricted sense of similitudes from fabulous natural history, shows itself now and again. Thus, "No creature among beasts, but being smitten, will fall upon the way to relieve itself, except a blind incogitant sinner. Such as have written upon their sagacity in that kind, tell us that the fishes in the fresh water, being struck with a tool of iron, will rub themselves upon the glutinous skin of the tench to be cured. The hart wounded with an arrow runs to the herb dittany to bite it, that the shaft may fall out that stuck in his body. The swallow will seek out the green tetterwort to recover the eyes of her young ones when they are blinded. Only a stupid sinner forgets," &c.

branches, and pay a friendly influence for its mighty patronage; and they grow and dwell together, and are the most remarkable of friends and married pairs of all the leafy nation." (An illustration of the connection between Church and State.)

In these similitudes, as the reader will notice, he throws aside the purpose of close and pointed illustration, and luxuriates in filling up the picture for its own sake. Another instance shows a still more rapturous plenitude of picturesque details:—

"For thus the sun is the eye of the world; and he is indifferent to the negro or the cold Russian, to them that dwell under the line, and them that stand near the tropics, the scalded Indian, or the poor boy that shakes at the foot of the Riphean hills; but the flexures of the heaven and the earth, the conveniency of abode, and the approaches to the north or south, respectively change the emanations of his beams; not that they do not pass always from him, but that they are not equally received below, but by periods and changes, by little inlets and reflections; they receive what they can, and some have only a dark day and a long night from him; snows and white cattle, a miserable life, and a perpetual harvest of catarrhs and consumptions, apoplexies and dead palsies; but some have splendid fires and aromatic spices, rich wines and well-digested fruits, great wit and great courage, because they dwell in his eye, and look in his face, and are the courtiers of the sun, and wait upon him in his chambers of the east."

A great many such outbursts into gorgeous imagery occur in Taylor's writings; but the reader must not expect to find them in every page.

QUALITIES OF STYLE.

Simplicity.—Taylor's style, though not to be called simple, is not stiff, nor stately, nor Latinised; he uses more familiar language than either Hooker, or Milton, or Sir Thomas Browne. He introduces, as we have seen, many pedantic terms and bookish illustrations: further, in his sermons, and still more in his formal treatises, he carries to an extreme the then prevailing fashion of backing the most obvious statements with superfluous hosts of authorities, quoting scraps of Latin and Greek, sometimes with translations, sometimes without. The 'Ductor Dubitantium' is especially loaded with this cumbersome scholarship. Take as an example part of his exposition of the "rule" that "the virtual and interpretative consent of the will is imputed to Good or Evil:"—

"1. This rule is intended to explicate the nature of social crimes, in which a man's will is deeper than his hand, though the action of the will is often indirect and collateral, consequent or distant; but if by any means it hath a portion into the effect, it is entire in the guilt. And this happens many ways.

"2. (1) By ratihabition and confirmation.

"'In maleficio ratihabitio mandato comparatur,' saith the law: To command another to do violence is imputed to him that commands it more than to him that does it. So Ulpian, interpreting the interdict 'Unde tu illum vi dejecisti,' affirms 'eum quoque dejicere qui alteri mandavit vel jussit:' and therefore Ptolemy was guilty of the blood of Pompey, when he sent Photinus to kill him—

'Hic factum domino præstitit.'—MARTIAL.

Now because ratihabition is, by presumption of law, esteemed as a commandment, therefore Ulpian affirms of both alike, 'Dejicit et qui mandat, et dejicit qui ratum habet:' 'He that commands and he that consents after it is done, are equally responsible.' Now, though the law particularly affirms this only 'in maleficio,' in criminal and injurious actions, yet, in the edition of Holoander, that clause is not inserted, and it is also certain," &c.

The above is the beginning of a section in the 'Ductor Dubitantium,' and is a fair specimen of the beginnings of all the sections in that work.

The subjects discussed in the 'Ductor' are of the most abstruse kind, at least in their scholastic guise as problems regarding the Conscience and the Will; and were the book written throughout in the above style it would be still less read than it is. The above, however, though a fair sample of the beginning, is not a fair sample of the body of a section; having stated the problem in the above abstruse fashion, he proceeds to give copious exemplifications. Thus, to a reader once made acquainted with the peculiar psychology and the technical distinctions, the work is not so hopelessly perplexing. Still, with every allowance, it is a very abstruse production, never tempting the general reader, and perused only now and then by an antiquarian student of ethics; its principal use to the student of composition being to furnish an idea of the bad expository method of the schoolmen.

In works upon more familiar subjects—in his sermons and in his 'Holy Living and Holy Dying'—he reiterates so much, and presents his statements so much "dressed up in circumstances," that the heavy effect of his abstract language and Latin quotations is less felt: it is felt, but more as an encumbrance than as a source of perplexity. The general run of his language is simple. His sermons are much more easily followed than Donne's.

In respect of simple arrangement he is far from being equal to Fuller. Compare, for example, the 'Holy Living' with Fuller's 'Holy State.' Fuller is less pretentious: he takes up severally different ranks and conditions of men,—Servants, Masters, Husbands, Bishops, &c.—and lays down maxims for the guidance of each: and besides this, discusses certain virtues one after another in an easy way, with no attempt at classification. Taylor is more ambitious of a complete system of ethics. He takes a general view of the subject, maps it out into three divisions—*Christian Sobriety*, *Christian Justice*, and *Christian Religion* (corresponding to the common division—Duty to ourselves, Duty to others, Duty to God). Having mapped out the subject, he proceeds to consider various virtues—Modesty, Humility, Obedience to superiors, Faith, &c.—in minute detail. But while more complete and exhaustive than Fuller, he is much less easy to apprehend and remember; he multiplies subdivisions with extravagant minuteness. For example, he gives "Twenty-three Rules for employing our Time;" and the following is his analysis of "Section IV. of Humility:"—

"*Nine arguments against Pride, by way of Consideration.*
Nineteen Acts or Offices of Humility.
Fourteen Means and Exercises of obtaining and increasing the Grace of Humility.
Seventeen Signs of Humility."

With reference to the above, under the head of *Clearness*, it is to be observed that the want of simplicity in this tedious subdividing is not compensated by a gain of precision. On the contrary, both in the larger and in the smaller divisions, there is much overlapping and confusion. He is too hurried and careless to be either easy to understand or accurate in his divisions and classifications. Speed is everything with him: he seems to have written on impetuously, recording his first thoughts, and instead of obliterating what he saw to be incorrect, trying rather to square it with the truth by qualifications—a fertile source of intricacy and confusion.

Strength.—We have seen that our author's style has not the vigour of conciseness, precision, finished aptness of expression. His strength lies in quite an opposite direction: the style is animated and exhilarating from its rapidity and opulence of words and circumstances; not from succinct and telling brevity, but from prodigal profusion.

In every passage that we have quoted this has been conspicuously evident. Even in his technical works the unresting forward movement carries the reader away as on a rapid stream. Where the subject is hard and the thought difficult to follow, this irregular profusion grows bewildering; but upon an easy theme, the speed and fulness of the tide is exhilarating.

His design being usually didactic, it is chiefly in the illustrations and examples that he finds the greatest scope for the exhibition of his peculiar strength.[1] We shall see that in the choice of these extrinsic subjects he is ruled chiefly by the sentiment of tenderness: as regards the sentiment of power, he inclines rather to the agitation and excitement of horror than to calm grandeur, or even to any form of might unattended with turbulence and danger. I

1 With reference to this, De Quincey ranks Taylor among the princes of rhetoric as opposed to eloquence—rhetoric being the art of presenting a subject in its most imposing aspects, eloquence the utterance of deep feeling on a subject of intrinsically-absorbing interest.

speak only of ruling tendencies. I am aware that many examples of the telling description of beneficent powers might be quoted from his voluminous works. But, as a rule, in describing the operations of man or of nature, he chooses either objects of tenderness, or objects of horror, or movements of the "wilder" character.

Some examples may be quoted. For one of the "wilder" sort, we may refer to his animated description of the "boisterous north wind" (p. 277). As an instance of his piling up of circumstances of horror, take the following:—

"Apollodorus was a traitor and a tyrant, and the world wondered to see so bad a man have so good a fortune, but knew not that he nourished scorpions in his breast, and that his liver and his heart were eaten up with spectres and images of death; his thoughts were full of interruptions, his dreams of illusions: his fancy was abused with real troubles and fantastic images, imagining that he saw the Scythians flaying him alive, his daughters like pillars of fire, dancing round about a cauldron in which himself was boiling, and that his heart accused itself to be the cause of all those evils."

"Nature hath given us one harvest every year, but death hath two: and the spring and the autumn sends throngs of men and women to charnel-houses: and all the summer long men are recovering from their evils of the spring, till the dog-days come, and then the Syrian star makes the summer deadly; and the fruits of autumn are laid up for all the year's provision, and the man that gathers them eats and surfeits, and dies and needs them not, and himself is laid up for eternity; and he that escapes till winter only stays for another opportunity, which the distempers of that quarter minister to him with great variety. Thus death reigns in all the portions of our time. The autumn with its fruits provides disorders for us, and the winter's cold turns them into sharp diseases, and the spring brings flowers to strew our hearse, and the summer gives green turf and brambles to bind upon our graves. Calentures and surfeit, cold and agues, are the four quarters of the year, and all minister to death; and you can go no whither but you tread upon a dead man's bones."

In the description of the Day of Judgment, his imagination revels in elements of terror:—

"Then all the beasts and creeping things, the monsters and the usual inhabitants of the sea, shall be gathered together, and make fearful noises to distract mankind: the birds shall mourn and change their song into threnes and sad accents; rivers of fire shall rise from east to west, and the stars shall be rent into threads of light, and scatter like the beards of comets; then shall be fearful earthquakes, and the rocks shall rend in pieces, the trees shall distil blood, and the mountains and fairest structures shall return into their primitive dust; the wild beasts shall leave their dens, and shall come into the companies of men, so that you shall hardly tell how to call them, herds of men or congregations of beasts; then shall the graves open and give up their dead, and those which are alive in nature and dead in fear shall be forced from the rocks whither they went to hide them, and from caverns of the earth where they would fain have been concealed; because their retirements are dismantled and their rocks are broken into wilder ruptures, and admit a strange light into their secret bowels; and the men being forced abroad into the theatre of mighty horrors, shall run up and down distracted, and at their wits' end; and then some shall die, and some shall be changed; and by this time the elect shall be gathered together from the four quarters of the world, and Christ shall come along with them to judgment."

Pathos.—Tenderness is the ruling quality of Taylor's style—tenderness of a peculiar kind. Restless and hurried, he has little of the tranquil melancholy of Sir Thomas Browne. He is quick and versatile, hurrying from circumstance to circumstance, and from mood to mood. In accordance with this impetuosity, his expression of pity, affection, and charmed sense of beauty is, as it were, demonstrative and voluble. At times he shows the most exquisite delicacy of feeling, at other times he dwells too long upon disgusting details, though seldom without some redeeming touches; but whatever be the mode of the feeling, the expression is always eager and impetuous, never lingering upon one circumstance, but always hurrying off to another.

The following is a fair specimen of his versatile habit, and exemplifies the episodes of rare beauty that diversify passages of general gloom:—

"It is a mighty change that is made by the death of every person, and it is visible to us who are alive. Reckon but from the sprightfulnes of youth and the fair cheeks and the full eyes of childhood, from the vigorousness and strong flexure of the joints of five-and-twenty, to the hollowness and dead paleness, to the loathsomeness and horror of a three days' burial, and we shall perceive the distance to be very great and very strange. But so I have seen a rose newly springing from the clefts of his hood, and at first it was fair as the morning, and full with the dew of heaven, as a lamb's fleece: but when a rude breath had forced open its virgin modesty, and dismantled its too youthful and unripe retirements, it began to put on darkness, and to decline to softness and the symptoms of a sickly age; it bowed the head, and broke its stalk, and at night, having lost some of its leaves and all its beauty, it fell into the portion of weeds and outworn faces. The same is the portion of every man and every woman; the heritage of worms and serpents, rottenness and cold dishonour, and our beauty so changed, that our acquaintance quickly know us not; and that change mingled with so much horror, or else meets so with our fears and weak discoursings, that they who six hours ago tended upon us, either with charitable or ambitious services, cannot without some regret stay in the room alone where the body lies stript of its life and honour. I have read of a fair young German gentleman, who, living, often refused to be pictured, but put off the importunity of his friends' desire by giving way that after a few days' burial they might send a painter to his vault, and if they saw cause for it, draw the image of his death unto the life. They did so, and found his face half eaten, and his midriff and backbone full of serpents; and so he stands pictured amongst his armed ancestors. So does the fairest beauty change, and it will be as bad with you and me; and then, what servants shall we have to wait upon us in the grave? what friends to visit us? what officious people to cleanse away the moist and unwholesome cloud reflected upon our faces from the sides of the weeping vaults, which are the longest weepers for our funeral?"

The 'Holy Dying,' which sets forth all the miseries of the human lot as an inducement[1] "to look somewhere else for an

[1] See p. 285.

abiding city," is full of touching pity. The two following examples are among the best passages, being less disfigured with horrors than others that might be quoted; in both we mark the volubility already spoken of:—

"The wild fellow in Petronius that escaped upon a broken table from the furies of a shipwreck, as he was sunning himself upon the rocky shore, espied a man rolled upon his floating bed of waves, ballasted with sand in the folds of his garment, and carried by his civil enemy the sea towards the shore to find a grave: and it cast him into some sad thoughts: That peradventure this man's wife in some part of the continent, safe and warm, looks next month for the good man's safe return: or it may be his son knows nothing of the tempest; or his father thinks of that affectionate kiss which still is warm upon the good old man's cheek ever since he took a kind farewell, and he weeps with joy to think how blessed he shall be when his beloved boy returns into the circle of his father's arms. These are the thoughts of mortals, this the end and sum of all their designs: a dark night and an ill guide, a boisterous sea and a broken cable, a hard rock and a rough wind dashed in pieces the fortune of a whole family, and they that shall weep loudest for the accident are not yet entered into the storm, and yet have suffered shipwreck."

"A man may read a sermon, the best and most passionate that ever man preached, if he shall but enter into the sepulchres of kings. In the same Escurial where the Spanish princes live in greatness and power, and decree war or peace, they have wisely placed a cemetery where their ashes and their glory shall sleep till time shall be no more: and where our kings have been crowned, their ancestors lie interred, and they must walk over their grandsire's head to take his crown. There is an acre sown with royal seed, the copy of the greatest change, from rich to naked, from ceiled roofs to arched coffins, from living like gods, to die like men. There is enough to cool the flame of lust, to abate the heights of pride, to appease the itch of covetous desires, to sully and dash out the dissembling colours of a lustful, artificial, and imaginary beauty. There the warlike and the peaceful, and the fortunate and the miserable, the beloved and the despised princes mingle their dust and pay down their symbol of mortality, and tell all the world that, when we die, our ashes shall be equal to kings', and our accounts easier, and our pains for our crowns shall be less."

Much of his pathos is not mournful, but consists of the expression of tenderness for objects of beauty and affection. Most of his natural similitudes are of this character. He has a keen sense of the bright fresh pleasure of the eye. "The young man dances like a bubble empty and gay, and shines like a dove's neck, or the image of a rainbow;" drizzling rain-drops are "the descending pearls of a misty morning." In like manner he speaks with delight of "the beauty of the peacock's train, or the ostrich-plume," and of children "making garlands of useless daisies." In a passage already quoted he compares a procession of clouds to "an army with banners." His love for bright young children, and fresh but fragile natural things, is a kindred vein of sentiment:—

"Every little thing can blast an infant blossom; and the breath of the south can shake the little rings of the vine when first they begin to curl like the locks of a new-weaned boy: but when by age and consolidation they stiffen into the hardness of a stem, and have, by the warm embraces of the sun and the kisses of heaven, brought forth their clusters, they can endure the storms of the north and the loud noises of a tempest and yet never be broken."

"For so have I seen a lark rising from his bed of grass, and soaring upwards, singing as he rises and hopes to get to heaven, and climb above the clouds; but the poor bird was beaten back with the loud sighings of an eastern wind, and his motion made irregular and inconstant, descending more at every breath of the tempest, than it could recover by the libration and frequent weighing of his wings; till the little creature was forced to sit down and pant, and stay till the storm was over; and then it made a prosperous flight, and did rise and sing, *as if it had learned music and motion from an angel, as he passed sometimes through the air, about his ministries here below.*"

KINDS OF COMPOSITION.

Description.—Taylor never attempts the formal description of landscape; and we can suppose, from what we know of his irregular genius, that, if he had done so, his method would have been the reverse of perspicuous. It is well, however, in considering his style as applied to special modes of composition, to bear in mind his peculiar turn for accumulating picturesque circumstances. He possessed the love of nature that prompts to description, and had descriptive style been developed in his day, would probably have been among its masters.

Exposition.—Nothing need be added to what we have said in explaining his want of simplicity and clearness. He repeats a proposition again and again in an irregular fashion, in his own words and in the words of favourite authorities, intermingling his repeated statements with copious exemplification and illustration. His fault is the want of method; he is wastefully copious in all the means of exposition, if only he could have employed them on a better plan.

Persuasion.—As a moral orator he is not by any means effective. De Quincey, as we have said, considers that Taylor has carried off the highest honours of rhetoric; and he defines his peculiar meaning of rhetoric by saying that where conviction begins, the province of rhetoric ends, implying that the object of what he understands by rhetoric is to excite admiration rather than conviction. Whatever may be thought of the restriction of the term rhetoric to so narrow a signification, this is a good way of expressing the effect of Taylor's professed treatises on practical ethics. In the 'Holy Dying' we never tire of admiring the wide-ranging scholarship and the dazzling accumulation of instances, imagery, and circumstances; but the application is almost lost in the general blaze.

The truth is, that in these professedly practical treatises our author handles the subject more as a poet than as a moral preacher.

In the representation of misery, the end of the moral preacher is not only different from the end of the poet, but positively antagonistic. The preacher's vocation is to rouse our activities, to excite strenuous endeavour; the vocation of the poet is to gratify our feelings,—rather to make us weep over misery than to make us anxious for the relief of actual sufferers.

Now the effect of Taylor's representation of misery is poetical rather than practical. Dilating on the vanity and shortness of man's life, he represents "the thousand thousands of accidents in this world, and every contingency to every man and every creature." The reader asks whether this is not practical? whether it is not the most powerful means of urging us to improve our time? True, it might be so applied; but the application is not made by Taylor. He pictures the contingencies of the human lot in such a way as to put us into a brooding melancholy. He presents an array of unavoidable fatal possibilities—disease, shipwreck, unforeseen accident;[1] and by presenting them as unavoidable, at once quenches every motive to action. The effect upon readers that should give themselves up to the spirit of the preacher would be despair and horror, were it not that he mingles the dismal catalogue with expressions of pity, moves our tender feelings by painting the sorrow of friends over the unfortunate dead, and dwells upon the consolation of another and a better world. To be sure, he professes to "reduce these considerations" (of universal fatality) "to practice;" but the section that undertakes to do so is, in fact, another tale of possible misfortunes, the same "scene of change and sorrow a little more dressed up in circumstances."[2] He has formal heads of practical rules and considerations; but how far these exhortations are from being stimulating and practical, and what exquisite touches of poetry they contain, may be seen in the following example:—

"2. Let no man extend his *thoughts*, or let *his hopes* wander towards future and far-distant events and accidental contingencies. This day is mine and yours, *but ye know not what shall be on the morrow;* and every morning creeps out of a dark cloud, leaving behind it an ignorance and silence deep as midnight, and undiscerned as are the phantasms that make a crysome child to smile; so that we cannot discern what comes hereafter, unless we had a light from heaven brighter than the vision of an angel, even the spirit of prophecy. Without revelation we cannot tell whether we shall eat to-morrow, or whether a squinancy shall choke us: and it is written in the unrevealed folds of divine predestination, that many who are this day alive shall to-morrow be laid upon the cold earth, and the women shall weep over their shroud, and dress them for their funeral."

Such passages are certainly not the considerations that brace the

[1] See p. 281. [2] See p. 282.

moral energies. They tend rather to lower the moral tone, to throw the mind into a despondency;—a mournfully pleasing state, perhaps, but undoubtedly enervating. From the point of view of the poet, the above would be admirable if it were weeded of the coarse expression about the squinancy; from the point of view of the moral preacher,[1] it is not only useless, but positively harmful.

ABRAHAM COWLEY, 1618-1667.

Cowley holds perhaps a higher rank among prose writers than among poets. His Essays, written for the most part after the Restoration, mark an advance in the art of prose composition. The construction of the sentences is often stumbling and awkward, but the diction shows an increasing command over the language. No previous writer, not even Fuller, is so felicitous as Cowley in the combination of words. His prose has none of the extravagance of his poetry. "No author," says Johnson, "ever kept his verse and his prose at a greater distance from each other. His thoughts are natural, and his style has a smooth and placid equability, which has never yet obtained its due commendation. Nothing is far sought or hard-laboured; but all is easy without feebleness, and familiar without grossness."

Perhaps part of the explanation of this is, that for ten years he conducted the correspondence of the exiled royal family—a kind of experience likely to purify his language both from bookish terms and from poetical ornaments. Whatever be the reason, his combinations and turns of expression are remarkably modern; here and there short passages might be quoted that we should not be surprised to find in 'Blackwood' or in the 'Saturday Review.'

He was born in London, the son of a grocer ("his parents citizens of a virtuous life and sufficient estate"), and educated at Westminister school and at Trinity College, Cambridge. At the age of fifteen he had published a volume of poems; and while yet an undergraduate, he wrote two or three comedies, and the greater part of his 'Davideis.' When he had been seven years at Cambridge, and had proceeded to the degree of M.A., he was, in 1643, at the age of twenty-five, ejected from that university by the Puritan visitors, and took refuge in Oxford. "About the time when Oxford was surrendered to the Parliament, he followed the Queen to Paris, where he became secretary to the Lord Jermyn, afterwards Earl of St Albans, and was employed in such correspondence as the royal cause required, and particularly in cipher-

[1] Throughout the above we have used the word preacher as a preacher of moral conduct. It is not implied that moral preaching is the sole function of the pulpit. Another function is to console the wretched under their load of miseries. As a preacher of consolation our author is perhaps unrivalled.

ing and deciphering the letters that passed between the King and Queen—an employment of the highest confidence and honour. So wide was the province of his intelligence, that for several years it filled all his days and two or three nights in the week." In 1656 he returned to England, was arrested, liberated on bail, studied medicine, and took out a degree in 1657. He remained in London till Cromwell's death, suspected of being in secret communication with the exiled family. At the Restoration he was rewarded with a free lease of certain lands, yielding a rental of £300, and went to reside at Chertsea.

He found country life very different from his Arcadian ideal; but that he was positively unhappy in his solitude, we have no reason to believe. The letter to Dr Sprat that Johnson produces with a malicious chuckle, "for the consideration of all that may hereafter pant for solitude," is really a humorous caricature of his sufferings, evidently written in high spirits.

His prose remains are few; he considered "a little tomb of marble a better monument than a vast heap of stones and rubbish." Two prefaces, a short "Proposition for the Advancement of Experimental Philosophy," a "Discourse by way of Vision, concerning the Government of Oliver Cromwell," and eleven Essays, are the sum-total, and they are contained in a small volume.

We get no fair idea of Cowley's intellectual powers from reading merely his prose. There we are struck only by his singular ease in choosing apt words, and by the freshness and spirit of the combinations. In his poetry he is more "extravagant and Pindarical;" the predominating veins of sentiment are the same as we find in the Essays and the Discourse on Cromwell, but he gives a fuller licence to his ingenuity. Describing the style of the "metaphysical poets," Johnson says—"The most heterogeneous ideas are yoked by violence together; nature and art are ransacked for illustrations, comparisons, and allusions; their learning instructs, and their subtilty surprises:" and among the metaphysical poets he considers Cowley to be "undoubtedly the best." This implies no mean powers of intellect; yet we should not think of placing such a light horseman among the intellectual giants. He is entitled to the palm of fantastic breadth, swiftness, and subtlety of wit; and this was probably all the distinction that he coveted.

Indeed the soft easy nature of the man indisposed him to severe labour, whether of body or of mind. "Whatever was his subject, he seems to have been carried by a kind of destiny to the light and the familiar, or to conceits which require still more ignoble epithets." Even in his emotions he was easy and averse to excitement. He was not of an overflowing sociability, like Thomas Fuller; his ideal was to enjoy the company of a few friends in some "gentle cool retreat from all the immoderate heat in which the frantic world does burn and sweat." He never married; and his poems express no depth of affection: the only genuine pathos in his writings flows from his luxurious love of solitude and repose. Neither his prose nor his poetry gives evidence of strong antipathies: we shall quote some sharp invective, but it is not personal,—it is directed against abstractions. He loved to contemplate, in a soft indolent attitude, the spectacle of great power; royalist as he was, he could not refrain from admiring Cromwell. At the same time he would not, like Carlyle, have put himself to the trouble of searching the world for heroes; only when a hero comes across his path, he is not impervious to astonishment. Even in his admiration of Cromwell there is no depth of feeling; the rich and elevated language of the Discourse on that hero is dashed with touches of humour. He has none of Taylor's fresh delight in natural things: as Johnson says, he does not present pictures to the mind; he "gives inferences instead of images, and shows not what may be supposed to have been seen, but what thoughts the sight might have suggested."

In his younger days he wrote what he calls "a shrewd prophecy against himself:"—

"Thou neither great at court, nor in the war,
Nor at the exchange shalt be, nor at the wrangling bar."

The prophecy was shrewd enough; such a born epicurean was not likely to succeed in any mode of active life. As a royal secretary he probably discharged his duty sufficiently well, having the material furnished him, and experiencing none of the worry of contriving; but that he was not a particularly zealous and active servant is probably shown by the comparatively slender reward settled upon him at the Restoration. Of his natural indolence we have a very pretty evidence in his Essays. When he retired to the country, he says there was nothing he coveted so much as a small house and a large garden, where he might work and study nature; yet he confesses, "I stick still in the inn of a hired house and garden, among weeds and rubbish, and without that pleasantest work of human industry, the improvement of something which we call (not very properly, but yet we call) our own."

Cowley being neither a man of action, nor a moralist, nor a critic, nor an original student of science,[1] his opinions are not of consequence; in his humorous railing at ambition and advocacy of retirement, he is moved entirely by constitutional sentiment. The popularity of his Essays is a great tribute to the intrinsic power of style,—of manner as opposed to matter. It also indicates that

[1] His "Proposition for the Advancement of Experimental Philosophy" is merely a plan of a college and school, and contains nothing remarkable.

style can operate to most advantage when neither reader nor writer is impeded by difficulties in the matter.

ELEMENTS OF STYLE.

Vocabulary.—In his prose writings, the extent of his vocabulary is shown rather by skilful choice of words than by Shakspearian profusion. When we turn to his poetry, we see that his command of words, though great, is rather inferior for a writer of such reputation. The exertion of procuring variety would seem to have been too much for his easy temperament; and his range of emotion being so limited, he did not accumulate great stores of language except in the region of the light and familiar.

We have already said that his diction is noticeably less archaic than the diction of any preceding writer.

Sentences.—In his lighter compositions the sentence-structure is easy and careless, and has no marked rhythm. But in his serious writings the rhythm is more even. The preface to his poems published in 1656, and the Discourse on Cromwell, are written with a more even measure than any compositions prior to this date.

In Cowley we first notice very markedly the habit of adding to the simple statement an *obverse* or *inverse* statement, for the purpose of filling out the cadence. Thus, as an example of the *obverse* filling out:—

> "The Church of Rome, with all her arrogance, and her wide pretences of certainty in all truths, *and exemption from all errors,* does not clap on this enchanted armour of infallibility upon all her particular subjects, *nor is offended at the reproof of her greatest doctors.*"

As an example of the *inverse* filling out:—

> "A cowardly ranting soldier, an ignorant charlatanical doctor, a foolish cheating lawyer, a silly pedantical scholar, have always been, and still are, the principal subjects of all comedies, without any scandal given to those honourable professions, *or even taken by their severest professors.*"

These are not perhaps the best examples that might be selected, but they illustrate what is meant; other cases will appear in subsequent quotations.

While in Cowley we see the first extensive use of balanced yet idiomatic periods, and the first habitual practice of the chief arts of rhythmical balance, we must observe that measured structure and point are employed by him much more sparingly than by their great cultivator, Samuel Johnson. His rhythm is more varied, in this respect approaching nearer to the modern standard. Apart from an occasional weakness in the syntax, and a certain archaism in the phrase and in the thought, the following reads not unlike a good article in the 'Saturday Review:'[1]—

[1] From the Preface to 'The Cutter of Coleman Street.'

"As for all other objections, which have been or may be made against the invention or elocution, or anything else which comes under the critical jurisdiction; let it stand or fall as it can answer for itself, for I do not lay the great stress of my reputation upon a structure of this nature, much less upon the slight reparations only of an old and unfashionable building. There is no writer but may fail sometimes in point of wit; and it is no less frequent for the auditors to fail in point of judgment. I perceive plainly, by daily experience, that Fortune is mistress of the theatre, as Tully says it is of all popular assemblies. No man can tell sometimes from whence the invisible winds rise that move them. There are a multitude of people, who are truly and only spectators at a play, without any use of their understanding; and these carry it sometimes by the strength of their numbers. There are others who use their understandings too much; who think it a sign of weakness and stupidity to let anything pass by them unattacked, and that the honour of their judgments (as some brutals imagine of their courage) consists in quarrelling with everything. We are therefore wonderful wise men, and have a fine business of it, we who spend our time in poetry: I do sometimes laugh, and am often angry with myself when I think on it; and if I had a son inclined by nature to the same folly, I believe I should bind him from it by the strictest conjurations of a paternal blessing. For what can be more ridiculous, than to labour to give men delight, whilst they labour, on their part, more earnestly to take offence? To expose one's self voluntarily and frankly to all the dangers of that narrow passage to unprofitable fame, which is defended by rude multitudes of the ignorant, and by armed troops of the malicious? If we do ill, many discover it, and all despise us; if we do well, but few men find it out, and fewer entertain it kindly. If we commit errors, there is no pardon; if we could do wonders, there would be but little thanks, and that, too, extorted from unwilling givers."

The *Paragraph* structure, in the lighter essays, where there are no natural divisions in the subject-matter, is loose and rambling. In the Prefaces, when he has distinct topics to handle, such as different books of poetry, he naturally places them in separate paragraphs; but when there is no such marked guide, he is not more orderly than the looser sort of his predecessors, and often mixes up several subjects in the same paragraph. In the 'Cromwell,' the natural pauses in the flow of his declamation suggest paragraph breaks, and the sense of oratorical effect prevents rambling.

Figures of Speech.—Fantastic similitudes are almost the essence of Cowley's poetry; in his prose he is less exuberant. His prose, indeed, is less ornate than any fine writing of the century, prior, at least, to his own date; the similitudes are not quite so numerous, and they are not far-fetched, but seem to come easily to hand. Examples will be seen in the quotations that follow. In the Essays, which are familiar productions, he admits more embellishment than in the Prefaces or the Discourse; in the serious compositions, he gives his care to elaborate the plain statement of striking circumstances.

In declamatory passages he makes abundant use of the figures

Exclamation and Interrogation. These will be exemplified under the head of *Strength.*

QUALITIES OF STYLE.

Simplicity.—The subjects of the Essays are easy. Upon ambition, obscurity, procrastination, and suchlike, a writer can hardly produce new ideas; all his powers may be given to producing new turns of expression, illustrative anecdotes, historical allusions. If he is abstruse, the abstruseness must be wholly in the expression.

Cowley's treatment of his subjects is gay rather than grave, and the expression is easy and sprightly. He quotes a good deal of Latin, but he makes his quotations with a grace, and, apologising for "the pedantry of a heap of Latin sentences," provides us in most cases with fluent translations. The following on the Danger of Procrastination is a fair specimen:—

"A gentleman in our late civil wars, when his quarters were beaten up by the enemy, was taken prisoner, and lost his life afterwards, only by staying to put on a band, and adjust his periwig; he would escape like a person of quality or not at all, and died the noble martyr of ceremony and gentility. I think your counsel of 'Festina lente'[1] is as ill to a man who is flying from the world, as it would have been to that unfortunate well-bred gentleman, who was so cautious as not to fly undecently from his enemies; and therefore I prefer Horace's advice before yours—

Sapere aude,
Incipe—[2]

Begin; the getting out of doors is the greatest part of the journey. Varro teaches us that Latin proverb: . . . but to return to Horace—

. . . .
Begin; be bold, and venture to be wise;
He who defers this work from day to day,
Does on a river's bank expecting stay,
Till the whole stream, which stopt him, should be gone,
That runs, and as it runs, for ever will run on.

Cæsar (the man of expedition above all others) was so far from this folly, that whensoever, in a journey, he was to cross any river, he never went one foot out of his way for a bridge, or a ford, or a ferry; but flung himself into it immediately, and swam over: and this is the course we ought to imitate, if we meet with any stops in our way to happiness. Stay, till the waters are low; stay, till some boats come by to transport you; stay, till a bridge be built for you: you had even as good stay, till the river be quite past. Persius (who, you use to say, you do not know whether he be a good poet or no, because you cannot understand him, and whom, therefore, I say, I know to be not a good poet) has an odd expression of these procrastinators, which, methinks, is full of fancy—

. . . . .
Our yesterday's to-morrow now is gone,
And still a new to-morrow does come on;
We by to-morrows draw up all our store,
Till the exhausted well can yield no more.

---

[1] ["Take it easy;" lit. "Hasten slowly."]
[2] ["Have the courage to be wise,—begin."]

"And now, I think, I am even with you, for your 'Otium cum dignitate,' and 'Festina lente,' and three or four other more of your new Latin sentences; if I should draw upon you all my forces out of Seneca and Plutarch upon this subject, I should overwhelm you; but I leave those, as *Triarii*, for your next charge. I shall only give you now a light skirmish out of an epigrammatist, your special good friend; and so, *vale.*"

The above exemplifies the simple style of his familiar essays; we shall see that even in his most ambitious declamations there is a peculiar lightness and ease, a singular absence of stiffness and constraint.

Strength.—The passage just quoted from the Essays is an example of our author's sprightliness and animation. The passage quoted before to show how modern his expression is, exemplifies animation in a more serious vein, the animation of finished brevity and point.

In some parts of his Prefaces, and throughout the Discourse on Cromwell, he assumes a loftier tone of declamation. Some of these declamatory passages are highly finished. One of the finest of them, the summary of the striking paradoxes in the career of Cromwell, is quoted and analysed in Bain's 'Rhetoric.' In some remarks upon the 'Davideis,' he presents the fortunes of David in the same striking form, though the contrasts are not portrayed at the same length :—

"What worthier subject could have been chosen, among all the treasuries of past times, than the life of this young prince, who from so small beginnings, through such infinite troubles and oppositions, by such miraculous virtues and excellencies, and with such incomparable variety of wonderful actions and accidents, became the greatest monarch that ever sat on the most famous throne of the whole earth?"

His plea for dramatising the characters and incidents of the Old Testament, being an apology for his own practice, is written with all his powers of style. After enumerating the dramatic elements in the life of David, he continues :—

"What can we imagine more proper for the ornaments of wit or learning in the story of Deucalion, than in that of Noah? Why will not the actions of Sampson afford as plentiful matter as the labours of Hercules? Why is not Jephtha's daughter as good a woman as Iphigenia? and the friendship of David and Jonathan more worthy celebration than that of Theseus and Pirithous? Does not the passage of Moses and the Israelites into the Holy Land yield incomparably more poetical variety than the voyages of Ulysses or Æneas? Are the obsolete threadbare tales of Thebes and Troy half so stored with great, heroical, and supernatural actions (since verse will needs find or make such) as the wars of Joshua, of the Judges, of David, and divers others? Can all the transformations of the gods give such copious hints to flourish and expatiate on, as the true miracles of Christ, or of His prophets and apostles? Why do I instance in these few particulars? All the books of the Bible are either already most admirable and exalted pieces of poesy, or are the best materials in the world for it."

Perhaps the most effective piece of rhetoric in all his composition is the passage beginning with the simile of "Jack in the clock-house." The melodious solemnity of the rhythm, the vigour and propriety of the language, the fine similes, and the imposing examples, exhibit probably the utmost stretch of the author's power:—

"I have often observed (with all submission and resignation of spirit to the inscrutable mysteries of Eternal Providence) that, when the fulness and maturity of time is come, that produces the great confusions and changes in the world, it usually pleases God to make it appear, by the manner of them, that they are not the effects of human force or policy, but of the divine justice and predestination; and, though we see a man, like that which we call Jack of the clock-house, striking, as it were, the hour of that fulness of time, yet our reason must needs be convinced that his hand is moved by some secret, and, to us who stand without, invisible direction. And the stream of the current is then so violent, that the strongest men in the world cannot draw up against it; and none are so weak but they may sail down with it. These are the spring-tides of public affairs, which we see often happen, but seek in vain to discover any certain causes. And one man then, by maliciously opening all the sluices that he can come at, can never be the sole author of all this (though he may be as guilty as if really he were, by intending and imagining to be so); but it is God that breaks up the flood-gates of so general a deluge, and all the art then, and industry of mankind, is not sufficient to raise up dikes and ramparts against it. In such a time, it was, as this, that not all the wisdom and power of the Roman senate, nor the wit and eloquence of Cicero, nor the courage and virtue of Brutus, was able to defend their country, or themselves, against the unexperienced rashness of a beardless boy, and the loose rage of a voluptuous madman. The valour, and prudent counsels, on the one side, are made fruitless, and the errors, and cowardice, on the other, harmless, by unexpected accidents. The one general saves his life, and gains the whole world, by a very dream; and the other loses both at once, by a little mistake of the shortness of his sight. And though this be not always so, for we see that, in the translation of the great monarchies from one to another, it pleased God to make choice of the most eminent men in nature, as Cyrus, Alexander, Scipio, and his contemporaries, for his chief instruments, and actors, in so admirable a work (the end of this being, not only to destroy or punish one nation, which may be done by the worst of mankind, but to exalt and bless another, which is only to be effected by great and virtuous persons); yet, when God only intends the temporary chastisement of a people, he does not raise up his servant Cyrus (as he himself is pleased to call him), or an Alexander (who had as many virtues to do good, as vices to do harm); but he makes the Massaniellos, and the Johns of Leyden, the instruments of his vengeance, that the power of the Almighty might be more evident by the weakness of the means which he chooses to demonstrate it. He did not assemble the serpents, and the monsters of Afric, to correct the pride of the Egyptians; but called for his armies of locusts out of Æthiopia, and formed new ones of vermin out of the very dust; and, because you see a whole country destroyed by these, will you argue from thence they must needs have had both the craft of foxes, and the courage of lions?"

Wit and Humour.—Wit and humour are undoubtedly the ruling features of Cowley's prose. His ridicule is for the most part gay and genial. Here and there we meet with passages of keen satire;

but there is nothing approaching to personal spleen in his sarcasms. In his bitterest shots at Cromwell, he keeps in view rather what he supposed to be Cromwell's vices—tyrannous ambition and hypocrisy. The man himself he admits to be an extraordinary person, and professes to look upon him with no greater animosity than upon Marius or Sylla. Besides, the invective is supposed to be delivered in a dream, and to the face of a terrible angel professing to be an admirer of the late Lord Protector. The circumstances are managed with a kind of comic effect; and, keeping in mind the situation, we see the most bitter invective through a humorous medium.

As an example of his powers of sarcastic irony, take the following ludicrously-unexpected banter by the terrible apparition, the "North-West Principality." Cowley had been proceeding in a full tide of denunciation, accusing Cromwell of tyranny, craft, and other crimes:—

"Here I stopt; and my pretended protector, who, I expected, should have been very angry, fell a-laughing; it seems at the simplicity of my discourse, for thus he replied: 'You seem to pretend extremely to the old obsolete rules of virtue and conscience, which makes me doubt very much, whether, from this vast prospect of three kingdoms, you can show me any acres of your own. But these are so far from making you a prince, that I am afraid your friends will never have the contentment to see you so much as a justice of peace in your own country. For this, I perceive, which you call virtue, is nothing else but either the forwardness of a Cynic, or the laziness of an Epicurean. I am glad you allow me at least artful dissimulation, and unwearied diligence in my hero; and I assure you that he, whose life is constantly drawn by these two, shall never be misled out of the way of greatness. But I see you are a pedant, and Platonical statesman, a theoretical commonwealth's-man, an Utopian dreamer. Was ever riches gotten by your golden mediocrities? or the supreme place attained to by virtues that must not stir out of the middle? Do you study Aristotle's politics, and write, if you please, comments upon them; and let another but practise Machiavel: and let us see, then, which of you two will come to the greatest preferments. If the desire of rule and superiority,'" &c.

The satire of the Essays is never long kept up; some good-humoured familiarity of expression comes in after a short passage of keener language, and puts us into a humorous mood by revealing the easy unexcited temper of the satirist. Thus, in the Essay on Obscurity:—

"If we engage into a large acquaintance and various familiarities, we set open our gates to the invaders of most of our time: we expose our life to a quotidian ague of frigid impertinencies, which would make a wise man tremble to think of. Now, as for being known much by sight and pointed at, I cannot comprehend the honour that lies in that: whatsoever it be, every mountebank has it more than the best doctor, and the hangman more than the lord chief justice of a city. Every creature has it, both of nature and art, if it be any ways extraordinary. It was as often said, 'This is that Bucephalus,' or 'This is that Incitatus,' when they were led prancing through the streets, as 'This is that Alexander,' or 'This is that Domitian;' and truly, for the latter, I take Incitatus to have been a much more honourable beast than his master, and more deserving the consulship, than he the empire."

He can be humorous at his own expense, as in the description of his country experiences:—

"One would think that all mankind had bound themselves by an oath to do all the wickedness they can; that they had all (as the Scripture speaks) *sold themselves to sin:* the difference only is, that some are a little more crafty (and but a little, God knows) in making of the bargain. I thought, when I went first to dwell in the country, that, without doubt, I should have met there with the simplicity of the old poetical golden age; I thought to have found no inhabitants there, but such as the shepherds of Sir Philip Sidney in Arcadia, or of Monsieur d'Urfé, upon the banks of Lignon; and began to consider with myself, which way I might recommend no less to posterity the happiness and innocence of the men of Chertsea: but to confess the truth, I perceived quickly, by infallible demonstrations, that I was still in Old England, and not in Arcadia, or La Forrest; that, if I could not content myself with anything less than exact fidelity in human conversation, I had almost as good go back and seek for it in the Court, or the Exchange, or Westminster-hall. I ask again then, whither shall we fly, or what shall we do?"

The Essay on Agriculture is written in his happiest vein. He searches out the authorities for the dignity of agricultural life with great pleasantry:—

"From Homer, we must not expect much concerning our affairs. He was blind, and could neither work in the country, nor enjoy the pleasures of it; his helpless poverty was likeliest to be sustained in the richest places; he was to delight the Grecians with fine tales of the wars and adventures of their ancestors; his subject removed him from all commerce with us, and yet, methinks, he made a shift to show his goodwill a little. For though he could do us no honour in the person of his hero Ulysses (much less of Achilles), because his whole time was consumed in wars and voyages; yet he makes his father Laertes a gardener all that while, and seeking his consolation for the absence of his son in the pleasure of planting, and even dunging his own grounds. Ye see, he did not contemn us peasants; nay, so far was he from that insolence, that he always styles Eumæus, who kept the hogs, with wonderful respect, δῖον ὑφορβον, the divine swine-herd: he could have done no more for Menelaus or Agamemnon."

OTHER WRITERS.

The justification of departing from the usual chronological arrangement, which dates a period from the Restoration, is that by the present arrangement we get a more compact grouping of our authors relatively to the great Rebellion. By annexing to the period of the Commonwealth the first ten years of the reign of Charles II., we bind together those that wrote during the agitation of the political storm, and those whose literary activity was greatest, indeed, when that storm was laid, but whose thoughts and style were powerfully influenced by the experience of their early manhood, and who belong in every way to the generation of the Commonwealth.

The writers of the Commonwealth—and they are remarkably numerous — may, indeed, be divided into three classes: recluse or easy-tempered students, like Thomas Browne and Fuller, who were hardly influenced at all by the surrounding excitement; men of bold speech, like Milton, who made their voices heard in the strife; and men, like Cowley, who composed their works when the agitation had subsided. The division is more a loose help to the understanding and the memory than one that can be marked out with sharp and clear lines: it makes an interesting distribution of a few great men, and it is so far a clue to their character; but it cannot be made a principle of classification for the mass of writers without leading to unprofitable refinements. We here follow the same plan as for the other periods.

THEOLOGY.

Hall, Hales, and Chillingworth, all survived into this period. The Church of England boasted also two of her most famous divines, **Robert Sanderson (1587-1663)**, and **John Pearson (1613-1686)**. At the outbreak of the Civil War, Sanderson was Regius Professor of Divinity at Oxford, Canon of Christ Church, and a royal chaplain. Upon the Restoration he was appointed Bishop of Lincoln, and he was one of the commissioners at the Savoy Conference in 1661. His principal work in English is 'Nine Cases of Conscience.' He is the chief of Protestant casuists. Pearson, who after the Restoration succeeded Dr Wilkins in the Mastership of Trinity and in the see of Chester, published in 1659 an 'Exposition of the Creed,' which still holds its ground as a standard production. The work is laborious, calm, and acute, written in simple and clear language; it follows the easy arrangement of taking each word in order. He was profoundly versed in patristic literature; and in that department criticised with such acuteness that Bentley said "his very dross was gold."

The most eminent of the Nonconforming divines of this generation was **Richard Baxter (1615-1691)**. He was ordained in the Church of England, and at the beginning of the Civil War was pastor of Kidderminster. He sided with the Parliament, was attached as chaplain to a regiment, and saw some active service; but his health failing, he returned to his pastoral charge, and buried himself in study. In this retirement he wrote the 'Saint's Everlasting Rest,' a volume of pious thoughts that have a peculiar interest when we view them as the aspirations of an infirm man turning wearily from the distractions of a time so utterly out of joint. The violent breaking to pieces of the old monarchy and the usurpation of Cromwell were painful things to a man thirsting for quiet and security; and in a celebrated interview with the Protector he had the courage to remonstrate. After the Restoration he was offered a bishopric, but declined the offer. Subsequently, when penal enactments were passed against Dissenters, his quiet ministrations in London were interfered with, and he was exposed to considerable hardships. At last, in 1685, he was thrown into prison, taken before the infamous Judge Jeffreys, and shamefully bullied: he was released by the special intervention of the king. All his life through he was an indefatigable writer: of his multitudinous works, numbering in all 168, only the 'Saint's Rest' and the 'Call to the Unconverted' have had a durable popularity. His autobiography—'Memorable Passages of my Life and Times'—affords an interesting picture of an ardent impulsive nature tamed down by rude experience and infirm health to greater sobriety of judgment and closeness of observation. In the following passage he frankly owns that had his works been less numerous, their fame might have been more durable:—

"Concerning almost all my writings, I must confess that my judgment is, that fewer, well studied and polished, had been better; but the reader who can safely censure the books, is not fit to censure the author, unless he had been upon the place, and acquainted with all the occasions and circumstances. Indeed, for the 'Saint's Rest,' I had four months' vacancy to write it, but in the midst of continual languishing and medicine; but, for the rest, I wrote them in the crowd of all my other employments, which would allow me no great leisure for polishing and exactness, or any ornament; so that I scarce ever wrote one sheet twice over, nor stayed to make any blots or interlinings, but was fain to let it go as it was first conceived; and when my own desire was rather to stay upon one thing long than run over many, some sudden occasions or other extorted almost all my writings from me."

Another eminent Dissenter was **John Owen (1616-1683)**, first a Presbyterian, thereafter an Independent. He was a man of singular moderation and sweetness of temper. He was a special favourite with Cromwell, who took him to Ireland to organise the College of Dublin, and subsequently to Scotland. After the Restoration, Clarendon offered him preferment in the Church if he would conform, and Charles himself desired his acquaintance. His voluminous writings are exclusively on religious subjects. The style is bad. "I can't think how you like Dr Owen," said Robert Hall. "I can't read him with patience; I never read a page of Dr Owen, sir, without finding some confusion in his thoughts, either a truism or a contradiction in terms." "Sir, he is a double Dutchman, floundering in a continent of mud."

Less accommodating and pliable, less sweet if not less enlightened, was **George Fox (1624-1690)**, the Founder of the Society of

Friends, an illegitimate son of the Church in a time of religious excitement, one of the most extraordinary men of genius in this eccentric generation. He was a grave, sober, reflective man, with no outgoings of volatile imagination, buoyant egotism, or healthy energy in any shape; as passive, unexcited, vacuous, as Bunyan was active, excitable, teeming with creative energy,—not pouring out force, but letting the world flow in upon him, judging and measuring the traditions and opinions floating about him, and striving in a calm way to reduce the bewildering mass to consistent clearness. Probably the more he pondered, the more he entangled himself in perplexing mazes, and he finally ceased to ponder, and took refuge in a set of arbitrary dogmas. He originated the prominent ideas of Quakerism, the use of "thou," the objection to uncover the head before dignitaries, the objection to oaths, the aversion to war, the doctrine that inner light and not the Bible is the rule of life. Like Bunyan he was an illiterate artisan of an inferior craft, a cobbler or shoe-mender—holding to the shoemaker the same relation that the tinker holds to the brazier. His style is more compact, and has greater graphic felicity of plain language, than Bunyan's, but it has none of the Pilgrim's figurative richness.

Another character of the time, of wider reputation than George Fox, was the man just mentioned, **John Bunyan (1628-1688),** "the wicked tinker of Elstow." We need not dwell upon the incidents of his early life and conversion, minutely and vividly related in his autobiographic 'Grace Abounding to the Chief of Sinners.' His later biographers accuse himself and his early biographers of exaggerating his youthful enormities by way of magnifying the divine grace. He says himself that "he did still let loose the reins of his lust, and delighted in all transgressions against the law of God; so that until he came to the state of marriage, he was the very ringleader in all manner of vice and ungodliness." The only sins that he specifically confesses to are Sabbath-breaking and swearing. From another sin pretty plainly stated in the above passage, Southey, followed by Macaulay, exculpates him on the ground of a subsequent specific denial—exculpates him somewhat hastily; for though the natural interpretation of one plain-spoken sentence is that the denial covers his whole life, yet, when we reflect and look closely, we see that the charge was pointed at his conduct after conversion and marriage, and that, in the course of his indignant denial, he brings in the qualifying clause "from my first conversion until now," and so does not contradict his previous confession that he was not better than he should have been *before* he "came to the state of marriage." "After he had been about five or six years awakened," "he was desired, and that with much earnestness, that he would be willing at sometimes to take in hand, in one of the meetings, to speak a word of exhortation unto them;"

and with much private irresolution, he consented to their request, and "discovered his gift amongst them" with such effect that after a time he "was more particularly called forth, and appointed to a more ordinary and public preaching of the Word." Five years after his ordination, in 1660, he was apprehended under the Conventicle Act of the restored Government, taken before the quarter-sessions, and "indicted for an upholder and maintainer of unlawful assemblies and conventicles, and for not conforming to the national worship of the Church of England; and after some conference there with the justices, they, taking his plain-dealing with them for a confession, as they termed it, of the indictment, did sentence him to a perpetual banishment, because he refused to conform. So being again delivered up to the gaoler's hands, he was had home to prison, and there lay complete twelve years, waiting to see what God would suffer those men to do with him." During this long imprisonment, the latter half of which was very lenient and virtually no imprisonment at all, he began the 'Pilgrim's Progress.' After he was set at liberty, he was chosen pastor of the Dissenters at Bedford, and lived there for the most part, preaching by stealth and visiting the dwellings of his flock. When in 1687 the penal laws against Dissenters were relaxed, a church was built for him at Bedford, and attended by multitudes from all parts of the neighbourhood. He was particularly noted for his tact in reconciling differences, and often was called long journeys for that purpose. One of those benevolent errands was the indirect cause of his death; he caught cold from exposure, and died of fever on the 12th of August 1688. His principal work, besides the 'Pilgrim's Progress' and 'Grace Abounding,' is the 'Holy War,' an account of the fall and redemption of mankind under figure of a war waged by Satan for the possession of the town of Mansoul. His immense popularity was not posthumous; he rose into fame before his death. "The 'Pilgrim's Progress,'" says Macaulay, "stole silently into the world. Not a single copy of the first edition is known to be in existence. The year of publication has not been ascertained. It is probable that during some months the little volume circulated only among poor and obscure sectaries. . . . In 1678 came forth a second edition with additions; and then the demand became immense. In the four following years the book was reprinted six times. The eighth edition, which contains the last improvements made by the author, was published in 1682, the ninth in 1684, the tenth in 1685." In learned circles doubts were expressed whether a poor ignorant tinker could be the author of such a work; which doubts he refuted by publishing the second part in 1684. In his metrical preface to the 'Holy War,' which followed soon after, he strongly asserted his originality—declaring that "None in all the world, without a lie, can say that this is mine, excepting I." The character of such a man is an interesting study. Many of his peculiarities lie upon the surface. He was naturally of vehement, ardent temper; we need not the evidence of his early habits to assure us that his temper was one that an oath gave a natural relief to. He was often conscious of an uncontrollable impulse to blaspheme and imprecate. The imagination that reared the wonderful fabric of his allegories rendered his youth miserable by its ungovernable activity in creating images of fear; at times he was as full of terrible apprehensions as a horse in a forest at midnight. It was part of the impulsive nature of the man that he could not refrain from acting upon his fancies with the force of belief; he would turn aside from a house under the strength of a sudden apprehension that it would fall upon him. Not until he had obtained assurance of God's favour was this imaginative energy turned into more profitable channels. Once released from his fearful anticipations of the wrath of God, his active mind found employment in new directions. We are apt to view him too exclusively as the author of the 'Pilgrim's Progress,' and to search there, and there only, for the signs of his intellectual power. In addition to the abundant evidence therein exhibited of his power of entering into the thoughts and feelings of men in different circumstances, we may glean significant particulars here and there in the records of his life. There is a telling hint of his restless versatility in the catalogue of "abominations" that to the last he "found in his heart;" in the "inclining to unbelief," in the "wanderings and coldness in prayer," and in the being "apt to murmur because he had no more, and yet ready to abuse what he had." And what better testimony could there be to penetration and address than his fame in later life as a mediator in family quarrels? Imaginative power and knowledge of men (which may be said to be different aspects of the constructive faculty) are the main secrets of his success as a writer. Perhaps too much has been made of his style, viewed merely as written composition. His language is simple and often forcible, and, particularly in 'Grace Abounding,' has a soft melodious flow. The most pleasing element is the graphic force of the similitudes. And this is almost all that can be said. Macaulay's estimate is expressed with characteristic slap-dash extravagance: "No writer has said more exactly what he meant to say. For magnificence, for pathos, for vehement exhortation, for subtle disquisition, for every purpose of the poet, the orator, and the divine, this homely dialect—the dialect of plain working men—was perfectly sufficient. There is no book in our literature on which we would so readily stake the fame of the old unpolluted English language, no book which shows so well how rich that language is in its own proper wealth, and how little it has been improved by all that it has borrowed." Even the assertion that "the vocabulary is the vocabulary of the common people" is inconsiderate and erroneous. The language is homely, indeed, but it is not the everyday speech of hinds and tinkers; it is the language of the Church, of the Bible, of Fox's 'Book of Martyrs,' and whatever other literature Bunyan was in the habit of perusing. As for the "old unpolluted English language," it needs no microscopical eye to detect in the 'Pilgrim's Progress' a considerable sprinkling of vulgar provincialisms, and even of such Latin idioms as are to be found in his favourite old martyrologist Fox.

Two other devotional writers of this period retain their hold on pious readers, especially among the lower orders: — **Samuel Rutherford (1600-1661)**, a Scotch minister (author of the 'Trial and Triumph of Faith'); and **Sir Matthew Hale (1609-1676)**, an English judge (author of 'Contemplations, Moral and Divine').

HISTORY.

The great historian of the peried was **Edward Hyde, Lord Clarendon (1609-1674)**, who had some share in making material for the history that he wrote. The son of a country gentleman, he was bred to the law, and in 1640 began his public career in Parliament. He supported the moderate opposition to the arbitrary measures of the King; but when Parliament raised its tone and demanded the abolition of Episcopacy, he went over to the King's party. He accompanied the Prince and the Queen-mother to France. After the Restoration, which was brought about chiefly by his skilful management, he was appointed Chancellor; but in the course of a few years he became unpopular both with the King and with the people, and in 1667 he was impeached of high treason by the Commons, ordered by the King to quit the kingdom, and pursued by the Lords with a bill of banishment. He was never permitted to return; he spent four years of his exile at Montpellier, and the remaining three years at Rouen. It was during his two periods of exile that he composed his various works. His 'History of the Grand Rebellion' was begun at Jersey—his first place of refuge on the failure of the King's cause—and completed during his final banishment. His 'Life and Continuation of the History' was published from his manuscripts in 1759. He wrote, besides, several brief works now fallen into neglect. He seems to have been a man of great practical sagacity and singular tenacity of purpose—a hard, austere, and, on the whole, upright man; too unyielding and too little disposed to regard the feelings of others. His manner was reserved and dictatorial. He comments upon the transactions of the time from his own point of view, animadverting severely upon the enemies of the King; but it is universally allowed that he wrote with a high-principled regard for truth: he was probably too magnanimous, too loftily convinced of the right of his own cause, to seek to pervert the facts. His style is dry and rather prolix. In the history our interest is drawn chiefly to the judgments of men and measures; the veteran politician was a penetrating observer, and his estimates of character and motive will always attract readers to his work.

Two minor historians deserve a passing mention. **Thomas May (1595-1650)**—commended by Dr Johnson as one of the earliest English writers of Latin verse able "to contest the palm with any other of the lettered nations"—was secretary to the Parliament, and published in 1647 'The History of the Parliament of England which began November 3, 1640.' **Arthur Wilson (1596-1652)**, secretary to the Parliamentary General Essex, left a work on 'The Life and Reign of James I.'

The two chief antiquaries were **Sir William Dugdale (1605-1686)**, and his son-in-law **Elias Ashmole (1617-1692)**.

MISCELLANEOUS.

James Howell (1596-1666), a versatile writer of dictionaries, grammars, histories, biographies, poems, and political pamphlets, is now known chiefly as the author of the first volume of 'Familiar Letters' in our language. Howell had something of the versatile activity of Defoe: like Defoe he travelled on the Continent for commercial purposes, and like Defoe he was often employed on political missions. Only, Howell had less power than the later adventurer, and was less intensely political, observing men good-humouredly, and recording his observations with sparkling liveliness. As an example of the purposely-familiar strain of his letters, take his account of the rise of the Presbyterians, in a letter written from the Fleet prison to a grave inquirer:—

"The first broacher of the presbyterian religion, and who made it differ from that of Rome and Luther, was Calvin; who being once banished Geneva was revoked, at which time, he no less petulantly than profanely applied to himself that text of the holy prophet which was meaned of Christ, *The stone which the builders refused, is made the headstone of the corner*, &c. Thus Geneva lake swallowed up the episcopal sea, and church lands were made secular; which was the white they levelled at. This Geneva bird flew thence to France, and hatched the Hugonots, which make about the tenth part of that people. It took wing also to Bohemia and Germany high and low, as the Palatinate, the land of Hesse, and the confederate provinces of the States of Holland, whence it took flight to Scotland and England. It took first footing in Scotland, when King James was a child in his cradle; but when he came to understand himself, and was manumitted from Buchanan, he grew cold in it; and being come to England, he utterly disclaimed it, terming it in a public speech of his to the parliament a sect, rather than a religion. To this sect may be imputed all the scissures that have happened in Christianity, with most of the wars that have lacerated poor Europe ever since; and it may be called the source of the civil distractions that now afflict this poor island."

Howell, as is evident from the above, was a royalist: and when he wrote it, he lay in prison by order of the Parliament.

When Fuller's 'Church History' was published, it was attacked by a somewhat flippant and self-confident controversialist, **Peter Heylin (1600-1662)**, author of a 'History of the Reformation in England.' Heylin began to write at an early age, publishing 'Microcosmus; or, a Description of the World,' a popular geographical work, in 1621; and to the end of his life he continued a prolific and varied writer. In 1625 he published an account of a six weeks' tour in France—a very flippant and superficial affair, with occasional dashes of clever expression. In his history he is a bitter partisan on the royalist side. He was in holy orders, and is said to have died partly of chagrin at not being recognised after the Restoration.

John Earle (1601-1665), chaplain and tutor to Prince Charles II., appointed at the Restoration Bishop of Worcester, and subsequently promoted to Salisbury, followed in the wake of Overbury, Dekker, and others, as a writer of essays and characters. His 'Microcosmography; or, a Piece of the World discovered in Essays and Characters,' was published about 1628, and became popular. An eleventh edition was printed in 1811. The characters are such as an Antiquary, a Carrier, a Country Fellow, a University Dun. He writes in the same punning antithetical strain as Overbury, but caricatures more, and has a much less delicate fancy.

Long after the death of **Samuel Butler**, author of 'Hudibras' **(1612-1680)**, in 1759, appeared his 'Genuine Remains in Prose.' The principal of them are "Characters" in the style of Overbury and Earle. Butler belongs to this generation through his satires on the Puritans. His prose has something of the coarse satiric vigour of his poetry; the wit has a much stronger flavour than either Overbury's or Earle's.

Owen Felltham (1608-1677 ?) put forth in 1628 a second edition of a work called—'Resolves' (that is, "Solutions"); 'Divine, Moral, and Political,'—consisting of essays on the model of Bacon's. The work made little noise at the time, but being reprinted in 1707, it went through twelve editions in less than two years. The thoughts are commonplace, the method bad, being the disjointed method of Bacon's essays without the natural clearness; and there is a constant straining after imagery. Their popularity in Queen Anne's reign is accounted for by their high moral tone, and their occasionally felicitous application of Baconian imagery to common themes, such as moderation in grief, evil-speaking, industry, and meditation.

Sir Thomas Browne (1605-1682).—Were this book intended as a guide to the intellectual epicure, it should give a large space to the works of Sir Thomas Browne, the curiously-learned, meditative, and humorous physician of Norwich.[1] Born in London the son of a rich merchant, he lost his father early, and was defrauded by one of his guardians, but was taken up by his step-father and sent to Winchester school, and thence to Oxford. He studied medicine, practised for some time near Oxford, travelled on the Continent, received M.D. at Leyden in 1633, returned to England, practised for a short time near Halifax, settled in Norwich, and there spent the remainder of his life. His first work, 'Religio Medici,'—The Religion of a Physician—published in 1643,[2] made an immediate sensation, was translated into Latin, and "very eagerly read in England, France, Italy, Belgium, and Germany." It is remarkable for its equanimity and tranquil warmth of sentiment; he avows himself an orthodox believer in the English Church, yet he loves the symbols of Catholic worship; he is elevated in spirit at hearing "the Ave-Mary bell," and is moved to tears at sight of a solemn procession; when others, "blind with opposition and prejudice, fall into an excess of scorn and laughter," he "cannot laugh at but rather pities" the asceticism of pilgrims and friars, because there is in it "something of devotion." He did not like to hear that the Anglican religion began with Henry VIII.—he desired for it a longer antiquity; and he disapproved of the "popular scurrilities and opprobrious scoffs at the Bishop of Rome"—"though he call me heretic, I will not return to him the name of antichrist, man of sin, or whore of Babylon." For all his moderation the book was placed on the 'Index Expurgatorius.'[3] His other works made less immediate noise, though they contain equally fine passages; their themes are less exciting, run counter to no vested interests. The 'Pseudodoxia Epidemica,' or 'Enquiries into Vulgar and Common Errors,' 1646, deals with physical, not moral, errors:—false beliefs concerning the properties of gems, of plants, of animals, of men; mistakes in popular pictures (the conventional dolphin, pelican, &c., the conventional temptation of Eve, sacrifice of Isaac, &c.); cosmographical and geographical errors (concerning the seasons, the river Nilus, the blackness of Negroes, &c.); historical errors, chiefly touching Scripture (that a man hath one rib less than a woman, that John the Evangelist should not die, &c.) 'The Garden of Cyrus, or

[1] See p. 94.

[2] A surreptitious copy, published in 1642, he disowned as imperfect.

[3] The fate of his refined moderation is a warning. Hating nobody, he was hated and attacked by the extreme adherents of all parties; denounced as an atheist, as a Papist, and as a Presbyterian. On the other hand, a certain Quaker was hopeful of bringing him over to the Society of Friends, because he disliked strife, and with all his love of symbolic acts, would not lift his hat to a crucifix.

the Quincuncial Lozenge, or Network Plantations of the Ancients, artificially, naturally, mystically considered,' 1658, is a fanciful search through nature for his favourite figure the Quincunx: he finds, says Coleridge, "quincunxes in heaven above, quincunxes in earth below, quincunxes in the mind of man, quincunxes in tones, in optic nerves, in roots of trees, in leaves, in everything." 'Hydriotaphia,' Urn-burial, published along with the 'Garden of Cyrus,' is a discourse upon the ancient practice of incremation, occasioned by the discovery of certain urns in Norfolk; in the concluding chapter, the solemn impassioned rhetoric on the shortness of life, and of posthumous memory, is considered his finest effort.

Browne's character is drawn by De Quincey in its points of contrast with the character of Jeremy Taylor. He is "deep, tranquil, and majestic as Milton, silently premeditating and 'disclosing his golden couplets,' as under some genial instinct of incubation." The reference to Milton is not so happy: Browne had not the passionate fervour of Milton; grave, solemn, meditative, without fire or freshness of sentiment, he would have shrunk from Milton's vituperative scorn, and could never have conceived the tender and graceful fancies of Milton's smaller poems. The prevailing characteristic of his style is tranquil elaboration. He abounds in carefully-constructed periods, intermixed with short pointed sentences that have a singularly Johnsonian sound, from the fulness of the rhythm. His sentence-structure is more "formed" than in any previous writer, perhaps more so than in any writer anterior to Johnson. His figures are original, ingenious, and peculiarly apt; he does not err in excess of similitudes. Felicitous and complete expression, comparatively free from tautology, inspires a general feeling of vigour; and here and there we are carried away by flights of high and solemn elevation. The great drawback for the modern reader is his excessive use of words coined from the Latin. Even Johnson condemns him on this score. His Latinised diction is all the more remarkable because he expressly condemns Latin quotations, saying that "if elegancy still proceedeth, and English pens maintain that stream we have observed to flow from many, we shall within few years be fain to learn Latin to understand English, and a work will prove of equal facility in either." His offences have probably been exaggerated, extreme passages being tendered as fair examples; still in every page there are at least two words that have not been naturalised—*improperations*, *amit*, *depilous*, *manuduction*, and suchlike.

Another recluse, more sensitive and egotistic, and less full of power than the tranquil sage of Norwich, was Dr **Henry More (1614-1687)**, Fellow of Christ's College, Cambridge. He was obstinately attached to the cloister: he might have had a bishopric; and he refused even the Mastership of his College. His favourite meditations were mystical speculations about the soul, first evolved in his poem 'Psychozoia,' or "the first part of the song of the Soul, containing a Christiano-Platonical display of life." He was an admirer of Descartes. He and a few congenial spirits formed in the reign of Charles II. a school known as the Platonising or Latitudinarian Divines.

Bishop Wilkins (1614-1672) is known as the author of an "Essay towards a real Character, and Philosophical Language." He was one of our earliest physical speculators: he contended that the moon was inhabited ('Discovery of a New World,' 1638); and in a work published in 1640, one of the earliest systematic defences of the Copernican system, he maintained that the earth is probably one of the planets. During the Civil War and the Protectorate, he sided with the Parliament, and in 1656 married a widowed sister of Oliver Cromwell. He was appointed Warden of Wadham, Oxford, and afterwards Master of Trinity, Cambridge. From this preferment he was degraded at the Restoration, but he afterwards regained the royal favour, and was elevated to the bench. He is illustrious as one of the founders of the Royal Society: the scientific enthusiasts afterwards incorporated with this institution held their first meetings in the lodgings of Dr Wilkins. In the Church he was an eminent member of the Latitudinarian school. But his name is most widely known in connection with his "discourse concerning the possibility of a passage to the moon."

Sir Kenelm Digby (1603-1665) deserves a word among the half-mystic, half-scientific men of his time. He was a strange compound of dashing soldier, accomplished courtier, successful lover, and occult philosopher. There are passages in his treatise—'Of Bodies and Man's Soul'—hardly surpassed in Sir Thomas Browne. He was one of the original Council of the Royal Society.

Izaak Walton (1593-1683), already mentioned as the biographer of Hooker, was another quiet and peaceable man in an age of excitement. He wrote also the lives of Donne, Sir Henry Wotton, George Herbert, and Bishop Sanderson: the respective dates of publication being, "Donne," 1640; "Wotton," 1651; "Hooker," 1662; "Herbert," 1670; "Sanderson," 1678. But the work usually coupled with his name is 'The Complete Angler' (1653), still read by the followers of "the gentle craft" for its information, and interesting to the general reader as disclosing the character of the writer—quiet, humorous, and enamoured of fresh pastoral scenery. Walton was a retired London linen-draper; he had married into a clerical family, and spent the greater part of his retirement at the houses of country clergymen.

John Milton (1608-1674) wrote a good many works in prose, although, as he said, "in this manner of writing, knowing myself inferior to myself, led by the genial power of nature to another task, I have the use, as I may account it, but of my left hand." His first appearance was on the Puritan side, in a treatise entitled 'Of Reformation,' 1641. In the same year he put forth a treatise 'Of Prelatical Episcopacy,' as his contribution in the warfare raised by Joseph Hall's 'Humble Remonstrance' in favour of Episcopacy. This work he had to back up with two tracts: "Animadversions on a 'Defence' of the Remonstrance;" and "An Apology for Smectymnuus," in reply to a criticism of the Animadversions. In 1642 he came forward with a larger work—'The Reason of Church Government urged against Prelacy.' This was for the time his last word on the Church government controversy. In 1644 he wrote his 'Areopagitica, a Speech for the Liberty of Unlicensed Printing,' the first formal plea for the freedom of the press. In 1645 he wrote his famous works advocating greater freedom of Divorce—'Doctrine and Discipline of Divorce,' 'Judgment of Martin Bucer concerning Divorce,' 'Tetrachordon,' and 'Colasterion.' After the exertion of writing these works—

"I imagined," he says, "that I was about to enjoy an interval of uninterrupted ease, and turned my thoughts to a continued history of my country, from the earliest times to the present period. I had already finished four books; when after the subversion of the monarchy, and the establishment of a republic, I was surprised by an invitation from the Council of State, who desired my services in the office for foreign affairs. A book appeared soon after, which was ascribed to the King, and contained the most invidious charges against the Parliament. I was ordered to answer it, and opposed the 'Eikonoclastes' to the 'Eikon.'"

This was in the end of 1649. Before this, in the beginning of the year, immediately after the King's execution, he published his 'Tenure of Kings and Magistrates.' Thereafter he engaged in a Latin controversy with Salmasius, a rhetorical Leyden Professor, said to have been hired to defend the memory of the King, and asperse his executioners; the titles of Milton's works were, 'A Defence of the People of England' (1651), and 'A Second Defence' (1654). An earnest champion up to the last moments of the dissolving Commonwealth, he wrote in 1659—'A Treatise of Civil Power in Ecclesiastical Causes,' 'Considerations towards the likeliest Means to remove Hirelings out of the Church,' and 'A Letter to a Friend concerning the Ruptures of the Commonwealth.' Next year he addressed a letter to Monk—'The present means and brief declaration of a free Commonwealth, easy to be put in practice, and without delay.' When the fatal moment came nearer, he issued a last appeal—'The ready and easy way to establish a free Commonwealth, and the excellence thereof compared with the inconvenience and dangers of readmitting kingship in this nation. The author J. M.' Immediately after the Restoration he was busy with his 'Paradise Lost.' His remaining works in prose are—a 'History of Britain, down to the Norman Conquest' (1670); a treatise—'Of True Religion, Heresy, Schism, Toleration, and what best Means may be used against the growth of Popery;' and a 'Brief History of Muscovia, and of other less known Countries lying eastward of Russia, as far as Cathay.' He wrote also in Latin a 'Treatise on Logic;' published a collection of Latin Familiar Letters; spent several years on an extensive Latin Dictionary; and left at his death a system of Christian Doctrine, the discovery of which, in 1823, and its publication by royal order, gave an opportunity for Macaulay's celebrated Essay.

Concerning Milton's style the most diverse opinions have been pronounced. Everything depends upon the point of view. Rich and powerful it is undeniably, coming from such a master of words, and yields in the highest degree the pleasure of luxurious expression. But the student need hardly be warned that Milton's prose is to be enjoyed without being imitated: for modern purposes the language and idiom are too stiffly Latinised, and the imagery too fantastic. Further, for a work of controversy the style is too ornate, too unmethodical, and too coarsely vituperative to have much convincing or converting power. In Milton still more than in Taylor the application is lost in the gorgeous splendour of words and imagery, and all but decided adherents are repelled by the unmeasured discharge of abuse and ridicule.

The author of 'Eikon Basilike; or the Portraiture of his Most Sacred Majesty in his Solitude and Sufferings,' was **Bishop Gauden (1605-1662).**[1] Purporting to be written by Charles himself, and published a few days after his execution, this work had a prodigious effect, fifty editions being sold within the year. There is nothing in the style deserving notice; it professes to be a simple record of the King's meditations.

Thomas Hobbes (1588-1679), "the philosopher of Malmesbury," is notorious for his views of human nature, and of the relations between the governing power and the subject. His long life covers three generations. The works that have immortalised his name were written between 1640 and 1660: the dates of publication being—'De Cive,' privately circulated in 1642, published with notes in 1647, and translated into English in 1650; 'Treatise on Human Nature,' 1650; 'De Corpore Politico,' a concise summary in English of his main political views, 1650; 'Leviathan, or the Matter, Power, and Form of a Commonwealth, Ecclesiastical and Civil,' 1651; 'De Corpore,' the fundamental work of his philosophical system, 1655, done into English 1656.

Malmesbury was the place of his birth. It is said that his

1 The authorship of the 'Eikon Basilike' was the great literary puzzle of the seventeenth century, as 'Junius' was of the eighteenth.

mother, overpowered by the national excitement at the coming of the Armada, brought him forth prematurely. He mentions this himself to account for a certain constitutional timidity that never left him. He was a precocious child. He graduated at Oxford in 1608; and being almost immediately appointed half tutor, half companion to the son of the first Earl of Devonshire, he spent the next twenty years of his life in ease, travelling on the Continent, and at home forming the acquaintance of the most eminent men of the time, Bacon, Lord Herbert, Ben Jonson, and others. His pupil and patron died in 1628, and in that year he made his first publication, a translation of Thucydides, undertaken to show the evils of popular rule. From 1631 to 1637 he was tutor to the third Earl of Devonshire, a boy; and travelling in that capacity, made the acquaintance of Galileo, Mersenne, and other eminent men, in whose company he had his thoughts turned towards physical science. For eleven years, from 1640 to 1651, he sought shelter in Paris from the apprehended hostility of the Long Parliament, having by this time become known as a political thinker, and was active, as we have said, in the composition of his leading works. In 1651, fearing persecution at Paris in consequence of his obnoxious opinions, he ventured back to England, and lived unmolested with the Devonshire family through the remainder of the Commonwealth, and the first nineteen years of the restored monarchy. Though free from material discomfort, his old age was not a little troubled. He was assailed by swarms of hostile critics for his obnoxious views of human nature and politics, and his works were formally censured by Parliament in 1666. To add to this vexation, he had provoked a quarrel with mathematicians, Dr Wallis and others, maintaining that he had discovered the quadrature of the circle, and defying the whole race of geometers and natural philosophers with acrimonious contempt. In extreme old age he "wrote in Latin metre a history of the Romish Church and an autobiography; and in his eighty-sixth year, amid other occupations, translated the 'Odyssey' and 'Iliad' into vigorous, if not elegant, English verse." After his death was published his last work, entitled 'Behemoth; or a History of the Civil Wars from 1640 to 1660.'

The merits ascribed to his style are brevity, simplicity, and precision. These merits are sometimes extravagantly overrated. Sir James Mackintosh says:—

"A permanent foundation of his fame remains in his admirable style, which seems to be the very perfection of didactic language. Short, clear, precise, pithy, his *language never has more than one meaning, which it never requires a second thought to take.* By the help of his exact method, it takes so firm a hold on the mind that it will not allow attention to slacken."

This is mere reckless hyperbole. The words put in italics describe an ideal that every expositor should try to attain, but which no expositor can hope to reach. Undoubtedly Hobbes took great pains to be simple and precise. He makes an effort to express himself in familiar words, explains his general positions by examples, and his order of exposition is such as can be easily followed. Having a deep sense of the evils of ambiguous language, he is careful to define his terms. Further, he has great powers of terse and vigorous statement, his figures are studied and apt, and his didactic strain is enlivened by ingenious and occasionally sarcastic point. Yet he is far from being a perfect expositor, as he is by no means always a consistent thinker. When he enters upon details, he is often perplexed, does not keep his main subject prominent, and introduces statements out of their proper order. There are passages in his works that Sir James could not have taken up at first sight without a superhuman quickness of apprehension. The truth is, that Hobbes owes his reputation for simplicity and clearness in a very large measure to the simplicity of his leading ideas. The plain language and exact method would not have made the style so famous had not the matter been simple to the degree of slurring over difficulties. Both upon mind and upon politics he superinduces simple and plausible theories, assembles the facts that support them, and says nothing about the facts that they do not explain. That there is an external world and a mental experience; that thought consists merely in a continuance of movements communicated to the organs of sense by the external world; that man's motives are originally selfish; that the aboriginal men lived in war and anarchy; that government arose when they came to an understanding, and entered into a contract to observe certain rules; that these rules constitute right, and must at all risks be obeyed,—such doctrines are simple, immediately and clearly intelligible, but their simplicity is gained by glossing over the complicacy of the actual problems. Not that Hobbes had any conscious desire to skip over difficulties. The inaccurate simplicity of his doctrines is to be attributed to his strong feeling of the vagueness of previous speculations, his endeavour to attain greater certainty by applying the method of mathematics, and his failure to verify his results by an appeal to actual life.

Along with Hobbes may be mentioned, as a political speculator, **James Harrington** (1611-1677), author of 'Oceana' (published 1656), an ideal republic. In his review of the literature of the period, Hume has the following:—

"Harrington's 'Oceana' was well adapted to that age, when the plans of imaginary republics were the daily subjects of debate and conversation; and even in our time it is justly admired as a work of genius and invention. The style of this author wants ease and fluency, but the good matter which his work contains makes compensation."

Another republican, a more fiery man of action than Harrington, was **Algernon Sidney** (1622-1683), author of a 'Discourse on Government.' Sidney inherited headstrong blood from both parents. His father was Robert, Earl of Leicester, and his mother a daughter of Percy, Earl of Northumberland. He was a most determined foe to monarchy; engaged vehemently on the side of the Parliament, refused to take office under the usurpation of Cromwell, and fled to the Continent at the Restoration, refusing the mediation of his friends with the restored monarch. Obtaining permission to return in 1677, he threw himself into the opposition to the Government, and in his furious zeal for the accomplishment of his aims, engaged, if the papers of the French Ambassador are to be trusted, in unscrupulous intrigues with France. In 1683 he was condemned, on very partial evidence, upon the charge of conspiring to assassinate the King, and was executed on Tower-hill. He is regarded as a martyr to republican principles. His 'Discourse' was first published in 1698.

Marchmont Needham (1620-1678) is the chief representative of journalism in this generation. Public events favoured the growth of newspapers: the Thirty Years' War on the Continent was not concluded when topics of more powerful interest arose at home with the outbreak of the Civil War. Many sheets, with every variety of piquant title, started into existence to meet the public thirst for intelligence. On the 1st of January 1642 the 'Mercurius Aulicus' was issued from Oxford, avowedly as the organ of the King's party. It was edited by one Birkenhead, then a Fellow of All-Souls, and for a short time Professor of Moral Philosophy. He was appointed licenser of the press after the Restoration. In 1643, Needham, another Oxonian, appeared with an opposition "Mercury," entitled 'Mercurius Britannicus.' His paper was exceedingly popular; but the Puritans were stern censors of the press, and the gay and restless Needham, after serving them for four years, went over to the King, and turned his wit against his former masters. He stood by the King to the last, and was imprisoned and condemned to death; but being offered his life by the Independents upon condition of giving them his services against the Presbyterians, he accepted the offer, and remained "Parliamentary intelligencer" until the Restoration. Both Birkenhead and Needham are abused for raillery, buffoonery, and want of principle; but facts do not show them to have differed much from their contemporaries, except in a clever faculty of gaining the popular ear.[1] Needham's changes of party are explicable without the supposition that he was worse than other men. He seems to have been a gay, versatile creature, and is mentioned by Anthony à Wood as possessing considerable humour and convivial qualities.

[1] Cornhill Magazine, July 1868.

CHAPTER V.

FROM 1670 TO 1700.

SIR WILLIAM TEMPLE,

1628—1699.

DIPLOMATIST, statesman, and miscellaneous writer, one of the most remarkable men under the reign of Charles II. Swift, not given to over-praising, said: "It is generally believed that this author has advanced our English tongue to as great a perfection as it can well bear." And Johnson is reported to have laid down in conversation that "Sir William Temple was the first writer who gave cadence to English prose. Before this time they were careless of arrangement, and did not mind whether a sentence ended with an important word or an insignificant word, or with what part of speech it was concluded." Spoken in the hurry of conversation, this dictum asserts several merits. Usually the first part is quoted and the second passed over, although the second is the higher compliment. Better general method, and greater attention to details of expression, are more valuable improvements than superior regularity of cadence.

To the family of Temple belong some of the most eminent names in our political history. The late Lord Palmerston was descended from a brother of Sir William's. In last century three Privy Councillors—Sir Richard Temple, Baron Cobham; Earl Temple; and Lord Grenville—came from another branch of the same family. "There were times," says Macaulay, "when the cousinhood, as it was once nicknamed, would of itself have furnished almost all the materials necessary for the construction of an efficient Cabinet." The lineal descendants of Sir William himself ended with the third generation. The family has been continued chiefly through the female line.

Our author's ancestors did not rise to the highest offices of state, yet they were men of considerable mark. It is interesting to know that his grandfather was the chosen companion of Sir Philip Sidney during the Flemish war, and was present at that hero's untimely death. His father was made Master of the Rolls of Ireland by Charles I., and retained the office, with a short interval, throughout the Commonwealth, dying in 1677, of the same age as the century.

Sir William was born in London. His tutor at Cambridge, where he resided two years, was the learned Cudworth. From 1648 to 1654 he travelled on the Continent, making himself master of French and Spanish. His first public employment was as a member of the Irish Convention in 1660: there he gained distinction by taking the lead against an exorbitant tax proposed by the new and popular Government. In 1665 began his career as a diplomatist. In that year he displayed such address as envoy to the Bishop of Munster that he was appointed Resident at the vice-regal Spanish Court of Brussels. In 1668 he accomplished with unparalleled speed the famous negotiation usually coupled with his name, the Triple Alliance between England, Holland, and Sweden. Immediately after this he was made Ambassador at the Hague, and completed the Treaty of Aix-la-Chapelle. In 1670, in consequence of the King's dishonest intrigues with France, he was recalled, and spent three years in retirement at Sheen. In 1673 he concluded the peace that followed upon Charles's second war with Holland; and, declining an offer of the embassy to Spain, and also the Secretaryship of State, was again, in June 1674, appointed Ambassador at the Hague. He had the credit of bringing about during that embassy the marriage between William of Orange and the Princess Mary. In 1678 he represented England in an endeavour to settle the complicated relations of Continental powers; but his efforts to uphold the dignity of our Government as an arbitrating power were baffled by the distractingly crooked policy of the King and his Ministers. He maintained his integrity by refusing to sign the Treaty of Nimeguen. In 1679 he was summoned from Holland to take office as Secretary of State, but ingeniously contrived to evade the hazardous dignity. His only other public service was the plan of a Privy Council of thirty to renew the confidence of the nation in King Charles. When this scheme worked ill from the multiplicity of intrigue at the Court, he retired altogether from public business. He was frequently consulted during his retirement by Charles II., James II., and William; but nothing could induce him to resume office. No man, he said, should be in public business after fifty; and ten years before this he had declared that he knew enough of Courts to see "that they were not made for one another." Having purchased Moor Park, near Farnham in Surrey, he went there in 1686, and amused himself with literature, architecture, Dutch gardening, and other employments of retired leisure. At the Revolution he was much pressed to take office, but steadfastly refused, and lived in retirement at Moor Park till his death in 1699.

The various works he has left us were composed in his periods of retirement. During his temporary seclusion, between 1670 and 1673, he wrote his 'Observations on the United Provinces,' and some miscellaneous pieces. In his final retirement he selected and prepared for the press his public correspondence during the years of his active life. He also wrote 'Memoirs of the Treaty of Nimeguen,' with an account of the difficulties that this Treaty was designed to solve. To complete his record of what passed during his public employment, he wrote other Memoirs, "from the peace concluded 1679, to the time of the author's retirement from public business." He wrote also various Miscellanies—"Upon the Gardens of Epicurus;" "Of Heroic Virtue;" "Of Poetry;" "On the Cure of the Gout by Moxa," &c.

"Sir William Temple's person," says the nameless writer of "a short character" prefixed to his works, "is best known by his pictures and prints. He was rather tall than low; his shape, when young, very exact; his hair a dark brown, and curled naturally, and, whilst that was esteemed a beauty, nobody had it in greater perfection; his eyes grey, but lively; and his body lean, but extreme active, so that none acquitted themselves better at all sorts of exercise."

What principally strikes us in Temple's intellect is its singular measure, solidity, sagacity. In negotiating he timed his movements with admirable skill; he succeeded in whatever he undertook; he was the author of the most famous alliance in that generation, and nobody has detected a flaw in his plans, or proved that in his diplomacy he should have acted otherwise than he did. The same sagacity appears in his political speculations; he keeps close to the facts, and does not begin to speculate till he has mastered them. Such he was as a man of practice and a thinker, attempting comparatively little, and doing what he attempted with thoroughness. When we view him on the æsthetic side, we see the same characteristic appearing in the shape of refined taste. He did not attempt works of the imagination, but he studied the beauties of order and finished rhythm, and even in his most didactic compositions the language and the similitudes have a refined elevation.

He seems to have been a man of deep tenderness and strong

personal feelings, a great favourite with children, a passionate lover, a fond husband, a constant friend. As his likes were strong, so were his dislikes; he had such an aversion for some men as to be impatient of their conversation.

But however strong his feelings might be, he kept the expression of them under control. He was not extravagant in his professions of attachment, but sprightly and humorous; and he had, as even Macaulay admits, a good command of his naturally irritable temper. So with his love of power; he did not rush actively into the struggle of ambition, and he would not seem to have occupied his imagination with ambitious dreams. He was equally moderate in his admiration of power: he could admire; he was not an envious disappointed man; but he admired with a just appreciation of the actors and the circumstances. Unprincipled, egotistic ambition he could not admire; his sympathies and general human kindliness were too predominant for that. In his political treatises, his personality comes little to the surface; he is grave and dignified as becomes his subject, and criticises in the impersonal spirit of a statesman warmly interested in humanity, but elevated above party or national feeling by the comprehensiveness of his views. In the Preface to the 'Observations on the United Provinces,' he states how far he looks upon History as a field of scenic interest.[1] His published letters abound in graceful compliments and strokes of wit. But in nearly all his formal essays he has an eye to instruction rather than pleasure: "I can truly say, that, of all the paper I have blotted, which has been a great deal in my time, I have never written anything for the public without the intention of some public good."

In the discharge of public business he showed the measure that seems to us his most striking characteristic. That he could act with vigour and decision upon an emergency was proved in more than one trying situation. He ascribed the failure of his constitution in middle life partly to "unnecessary diligences in his employments abroad;" and doubtless one-half of his success as a diplomatist was due to his promptitude in seizing the favourable moment. But he kept his energies strictly in hand; he lived temperately, he was distinguished for his frankness and truthfulness, and showed no propensity to grasp momentary advantages by unscrupulous craft. He refrained immovably from affairs that he knew to be beyond his power. When the Court was in confusion from the intrigues of unscrupulous rivals and the unpatriotic policy of the King, nothing could induce him to accept office. He joined neither the unprincipled struggle for power, nor the hopeless endeavours under the name of patriotism. He boldly lectured the King on the duties of his position, and steadily wound himself

[1] See p. 318.

out of the imbroglio. He could act with vigour, but action was not a necessity of his nature. After his fixed resolution "never more to meddle with any public employment," he busied himself with his garden and his books, "taking no more notice of what passed upon the public scene than an old man uses to do of what is acted on a theatre, where he gets as easy a seat as he can, entertains himself with what passes on the stage, not caring who the actors are, nor what the plot, nor whether he goes out before the play be done."

In practical politics the most important of Temple's views are those regarding England's best Continental policy in the then existing situation. The Triple Alliance, between England, Holland, and Sweden, is a clear and easily-remembered index. As Sidney and Raleigh had to urge the growing power of Spain upon the Government of Elizabeth, so Temple had to urge the growing power of France upon the Government of Charles. He advocated alliance with Holland in opposition both to commercial jealousy and to the French proclivities of the Court. As a speculator upon the 'Original and Nature of Government,' he writes with characteristic sagacity. Concerning the origin of Government, his leading views coincide with what is now generally accepted. He dismisses the theory of an original contract, and treats political communities as an expansion of the family system. The existence of aristocracies he ascribes in most cases to an incoming of conquerors. As regards the best form of government, he holds that there are but two leading forms, the rule of one and the rule of several; that experience gives little light as to the best system in detail. He lays down the seeming truism that "those are generally the best governments where the best men govern." But farther, he considers that all government rests ultimately on the will of the people, however propitiated, and that the most stable government is the *pyramidal*, the government that rests on the widest basis of popular confidence. He is not misled into overrating the importance of Greek and Roman history to the political student; he regards the classical governments as short-lived political failures, and considers the more stable institutions of China, of the Ottomans, of the Goths, and of Peru, as at least equally deserving of attention.

His Essay on Ancient and Modern Learning maintains that the ancient literature is superior to the modern. We must remember that it was written before 1688. He was not the originator of the comparison; it was a favourite theme among members of the French Academy and of the English Royal Society. Our author dwells chiefly on general considerations. He rebuts the argument that the moderns *must* be better than the ancients because intellects are very much the same in all ages and countries, and because the moderns have always the advantage of the experience of their predecessors. He argues that the Greeks had before them the wisdom of the Egyptians and the Hindus; that "many circumstances concur to one production that do not to any other, in one or many ages;" and that in recent times learning had been discouraged by ecclesiastical disputes, civil dissensions, want of royal patronage, and general contempt of scholarship, owing to the excessive pedantry of some scholars. He considers Sidney, Bacon, and Selden the three greatest "wits" among the English moderns; he does not mention Shakspeare.

ELEMENTS OF STYLE.

Vocabulary.—In Temple we meet with very few words that are not to be found in good modern prose. But some of the phrases and combinations are rather old-fashioned,—such as, "I am not in pain" for *I am under no alarm;* "wits possessed of the vogue;" "it is all a case" for *it is all one;* "the bottom and reach of the design," where a modern writer would probably say—"the foundation and object of the plot (or of the conspiracy);" "these spirits were fed and heightened" for "this state of feeling was inflamed (or encouraged)."—Any reader comparing Temple's diction with ordinary modern diction cannot fail to notice in how many cases Saxon expressions have been superseded by Latin.

His style is sometimes decried as being tainted with Gallicisms. The accusation should be limited. In his 'Memoirs' he uses a good many French terms and turns—such as, "with all the *secret* imaginable" (for *secrecy*), "*resentment* of kindness shown me" (for *gratitude*), "this testimony is justly due to all that *practised* him" (for *all that had much intercourse* with him). As Swift tells us, he used these expressions unconsciously, being led into them naturally from carrying on diplomacy in French. But when the fault was pointed out to him, he took pains to correct it, and, except in his 'Memoirs,' there are few traces either of French terms or of French idiom.

Sentences.—Comparing Temple's composition with any publication of anterior date, we remark that the placing of words is better attended to; the cadence being more regularly filled out, and the balance of the clauses more neatly finished. In especial, we remark a peculiar finish of pointed balance—greater pains to bring two opposed words or phrases into corresponding places in the syntax of two successive clauses, and so more *pointedly* direct attention to the antithesis.

We must not suppose from Johnson's panegyric that Temple was the inventor of rhythmical balance and point. It has been seen that these arts of style were practised under Elizabeth; every age, indeed, can produce at least one representative of the pointed style. Temple's merit lies in improving and perfecting. In his composition the recurrence of clauses formed after the same model is more measured and regular. After reading a part of any of his highly-finished passages, our ear comes to expect something more or less pointed in every sentence, and we are seldom disappointed. Were the subject-matter trifling, this would soon become tiresome; but as the matter is usually weighty, and the language dignified and varied, the play of antithesis is rather an agreeable addition.

To illustrate the superior dignity and finish of his pointed sentences, one or two passages may be quoted. Our quotations under this head are longer than usual, because this is really the chief distinction of the author's style.

The following is from the Preface to his 'Observations on the United Provinces.' He is upholding the dignity of History:—

"Nor are we to think Princes themselves losers, or less entertained, when we see them employ their time and their thoughts in so useful speculations, and to so glorious ends: but that rather thereby they attain their true prerogative of being happier, as well as greater, than subjects can be. For all the pleasures of sense that any man can enjoy, are within the reach of a private fortune and ordinary contrivance; grow fainter with age, and duller with use; must be revived with intermissions, and wait upon the returns of appetite, which are no more at call of the rich than the poor. The flashes of wit and good-humour that rise from the vapours of wine, are little different from those that proceed from the heats of blood in the first approaches of fevers or frenzies, and are to be valued, but as (indeed) they are, the effects of distemper. But the pleasures of imagination, as they heighten and refine the very pleasures of sense, so they are of larger extent and longer duration; and if the most sensual man will confess there is a pleasure in pleasing, he must likewise allow there is good to a man's self in doing good to others: and the further this extends the higher it rises, and the longer it lasts. Besides, there is beauty in order, and there are charms in well-deserved praise: and both are the greater by how much greater the subject; as the first appearing in a well-framed and well-governed state, and the other arising from noble and generous actions. Nor can any veins of good-humour be greater than those that swell by the success of wise counsels, and by the fortunate events of public affairs; since a man that takes pleasure in doing good to ten thousand, must needs have more than he that takes none but in doing good to himself."

Our next passage is from the "Original and Nature of Government," expounding why the country population is less democratic than the town:—

"The contrary of all this happens in countries thin inhabited, and especially in vast Campanias, such as are extended through Asia and Afric, where there are few cities besides what grow by the residence of the kings or their governors. The people are poorer, and having little to lose, have little to care for, and are less exposed to the designs of power or violence. The assembling of persons, deputed from people at great distances one from another, is trouble to them that are sent, and charge to them that send. And, where ambition and avarice have made no entrance, the desire of leisure is much more natural than of business and care; besides, men conversing all their lives with the woods, and the fields, and the herds, more than with one another, come to know as little as they desire; use their senses a great deal more than their reasons; examine not the nature or the tenure of power and authority; find only they are fit to obey, because they are not fit to govern; and so come to submit to the will of him they found in power, as they do to the will of heaven, and consider all changes of conditions that happen to them under good or bad Princes, like good or ill seasons, that happen in the weather and the air."

His letter of consolation to the Countess of Essex is one of his most finished productions. The following paragraph illustrates at once the rhythmical finish of his style and the soundness of his judgment:—

"But, Madam, though religion were no party in your case, and that for so violent and injurious a grief, you had nothing to answer to God, but only to the world and yourself; yet, I very much doubt, how you would be acquitted. We bring into the world with us a poor, needy, uncertain life, short at the longest, and unquiet at the best; all the imaginations of the witty and the wise have been perpetually busied to find out the ways how to revive it with pleasures, or relieve it with diversions; how to compose it with ease, and settle it with safety. To some of these ends have been employed the institutions of lawgivers, the reasonings of philosophers, the inventions of poets, the pains of labouring, and the extravagances of voluptuous men. All the world is perpetually at work about nothing else, but only that our poor mortal lives should pass the easier and happier for that little time we possess them, or else end the better when we lose them. Upon this occasion, riches came to be coveted, honours to be esteemed, friendship and love to be pursued, and virtues themselves to be admired in the world. Now, Madam, is it not to bid defiance to all mankind, to condemn their universal opinions and designs; if, instead of passing your life as well and easily, you resolve to pass it as ill and miserably as you can? You grow insensible to the conveniences of riches, the delights of honour and praise, the charms of kindness or friendship, nay to the observance or applause of virtues themselves; for who can you expect, in these excesses of passion, will allow you to show either temperance or fortitude, to be either prudent or just? and for your friends, I suppose you reckon upon losing their kindness, when you have sufficiently convinced them, they can never hope for any of yours, since you have none left for yourself or anything else. You declare upon all occasions, you are incapable of receiving any comfort or pleasure in anything that is left in this world; and, I assure you, Madam, none can ever love you that can have no hopes ever to please you."

The following is a balanced comparison between Homer and Virgil; the order is well kept up:—

"Homer was, without dispute, the most universal genius that has been known in the world, and Virgil the most accomplished. To the first must be allowed the most fertile invention, the richest vein, the most general knowledge, and the most lively expression; to the last, the noblest ideas, the justest institution, the wisest conduct, and the choicest elocution. To speak in the painter's terms, we find, in the works of Homer, the most spirit, force, and life; in those of Virgil, the best design, the truest proportions, and the greatest grace; the colouring in both seems equal, and indeed is in both admirable. Homer had more fire and rapture, Virgil more light and swiftness; or at least the poetical fire was more raging in one, but clearer in the other, which makes the first more amazing, and the latter more agreeable. The ore was richer in one, but in the other more refined, and better allayed to make up excellent work. Upon the whole, I think it must be confessed, that Homer was of the two, and perhaps of all others, the vastest, the sublimest, and the most wonderful *genius;* and that he has been generally so esteemed, there cannot be a greater testimony given, than what has been by some observed, that not only the greatest masters have found in his works the best and truest principles of all their sciences or arts, but that the noblest nations have derived from them the original of their several races, though it be hardly yet agreed whether his story be true or a fiction. In short, these two immortal poets must be allowed to have so much excelled in their kinds, as to have exceeded all comparison, to have even extinguished emulation, and in a manner confined true poetry, not only to their two languages, but to their very persons."

We have noticed only the merits of Temple's sentences. These are not uniformly sustained. The sentence-structure of his 'Memoirs' is not so good. Our quotations are fair specimens of his general style, and even they have not the grammatical accuracy and finish that Johnson introduced into the language. In his 'Memoirs' he aims at Thucydidean compactness and brevity, and so falls into the error of condensations that are too forced, and sentences that are deficient in unity. I shall quote the most faulty condensation that I have observed:—

"This, I suppose, gave the occasion for reflections upon what had passed in the course of my former embassies in Holland and at Aix; and his Majesty, and his ministers, the resolution to send for me out of my private retreat, where I had passed two years (as I intended to do the rest of my life), and to engage me in going over into Holland, to make the separate peace with that State."

Paragraphs.—Our author has a certain apprehension, however faint, of paragraph method. If we except Fuller, he makes his paragraphs more orderly and consecutive than any writer before Johnson. His Essay on the "Original and Nature of Government" is a favourable example of his method. He has five large breaks, at each of which he introduces a new proposition. But the passages between the breaks are far from being perfectly consecutive, or strictly confined to the subject enounced in the first proposition; although, to do them justice, they are quite as orderly as many compositions of much later date. As an example of the minuter paragraph arrangement, may be quoted one of these larger divisions. It will be seen that the first paragraph is not a complete introduction, and that towards the end the arrangement becomes more confused:—

"Authority arises from the opinion of wisdom, goodness, and valour in the persons who possess it.

"Wisdom is that which makes men judge what are the best ends, and what the best means to attain them; and gives a man advantage among the weak and the ignorant; as sight among the blind, which is that of counsel and direction; this gives authority to age among the younger, till these begin at certain years to change their opinion of the old and of themselves. This gives it more absolute to a pilot at sea, whom all the passengers suffer to steer them as he pleases.

"Goodness is that which makes men prefer their duty and their promise, before their passions or their interest; and is properly the object of trust: in our language it goes rather by the name of honesty; though what we call an honest man, the Romans call a good man; and honesty in their language, as well as in French, rather signifies a composition of those qualities which generally acquire honour and esteem to those who possess them.

"Valour, as it gives awe, and promises protection to those who want either heart or strength to defend themselves: this makes the authority of men among women; and that of a master-buck in a numerous herd, though perhaps not strong enough for any two of them; but the impression of single fear holds when they are all together by the ignorance of uniting.

"Eloquence, as it passes for a mark of wisdom; beauty of goodness, and nobility of valour (which was its original) have likewise ever some effect upon the opinion of the people; but a very great one, when they are really joined with the qualities they promise or resemble.

"There is yet another source from which usually springs greater authority than from all the rest; which is the opinion of divine favour, or designation of the persons or of the races that govern. This made the kings among the heathens ever derive themselves, or their ancestors, from some god; passing thereby for heroes—that is, persons issued from the mixture of divine and human race, and of a middle nature between gods and men; others joined the mitre to the crown, and thereby the reverence of divine, to the respect of civil power.

"This made the Caliphs of Persia and Egypt, &c.

"Piety, as it is thought a way to the favour of God, and fortune, as it looks like the effect either of that, or at least of prudence and courage, beget authority. As likewise splendour of living in great palaces, with numerous attendance, much observance, and rich habits differing from common men: both as it seems to be the reward of those virtues already named, or the effect of fortune; or as it is a mark of being obeyed by many.

"From all these authority arises, but is by nothing so much strengthened and confirmed as by custom," &c.

Figures of Speech—Similitudes.—Temple and Cowley did much to confirm the reaction against the indiscriminate figurative profusion of the preceding generations. Neither can be called ornate. But while they agree in using similitudes with moderation, they differ widely in another respect. Temple's similitudes are much more apt and striking than Cowley's, and have not the same appearance of being fetched from a distance. They are not light ornaments, but substantial additions, having usually both an illustrative and an emotional force.

One or two examples may be quoted. Remarking on the interest attaching to the United Provinces, he says:—

"And such a revolution as has since happened there, though it may have made these discourses a little important to his Majesty or his council; yet it will not have rendered them less agreeable to common eyes, who, like men that live near the sea, *will run out upon the cliffs to gaze at it in a storm, though they would not look out of their window to see it in a calm.*"

"I knew and esteemed a person abroad, who used to say, a man must be a mean wretch that desired to live after threescore years old. But so much, I doubt, is certain, that, *in life, as in wine, he that will drink it good, must not draw it to the dregs.*"

"I have said that the excellency of genius must be native, because it can never grow to any great height if it be only acquired or affected: but it must be ennobled by birth to give it more lustre, esteem, and authority; it must be cultivated by education and instruction, to improve its growth, and direct its end and application; and it must be assisted by fortune, to preserve it to maturity. . . . *Now, since so many stars go to the making up of this constellation, 'tis no wonder it has so seldom appeared in the world; nor that when it does, it is received and followed with so much gazing, and so much veneration.*"

Contrast.—We have seen that Temple makes abundant use of antithesis, and that he studies how to give antithesis effective point. In this place we may quote some examples where the antithesis is more paradoxical and epigrammatic. His antitheses very often have an epigrammatic turn:—

"The subsidies from France bore no proportion to the charge of our fleets; and our strength at sea seemed rather lessened than increased by the conjunction of theirs: our seamen fought without heart, and were more afraid of their friends than their enemies; and our discontents were so great at land, that the assembling of our militia to defend our coasts was thought as dangerous as an invasion."

Concerning the Cabal, he drily remarks—"And thus, instead of making so great a king as they pretended by this Dutch War and French Alliance, they had the honour of making only four great subjects."

The Dutch having inundated their country to check the French invasion, he says that "they found no way of saving their country but by losing it."

"Some ages produce many great men and few great occasions; other times, on the contrary, raise great occasions but few or no great men."

"Following this uncertain course, they succeeded, as such counsels must ever do: instead of pleasing all, they pleased none; and, aiming to leave no enemies to their settlement of Ireland, they left it no friends."

Climax.—Our author's grave composed style is as far as possible opposed to abrupt and startling figures of speech, exclamation, apostrophe, and suchlike. It is all the more compatible with the careful building up of climaxes. The reader will notice a steady graduation and culmination in every passage where the subject calls for more than usual stateliness. See under *Strength*, p. 325.

QUALITIES OF STYLE.

Simplicity.—This quality is incompatible with the dignity and elevation of Temple's style. His diction is very different from the light familiar diction of Cowley.

In one respect he is more simple than Cowley. He is thoroughly free from the pedantry of superfluous Latin quotations. This does credit to his taste; he was a scholar, and might have quoted. Dryden quotes a little, and probably would have quoted more had he possessed the requisite scholarship. No scholarly writer before Johnson makes so few Latin quotations as Temple.

In the choice and treatment of subjects, he departs from the easy and familiar tracks. An Essay on the "Original and Nature of Government" cannot be made so light and entertaining as an essay on Ambition. On subjects not naturally abstruse—in the 'Memoirs' of his diplomacy and in his Observations on the United Provinces, he writes with two aims more or less antagonistic to popular treatment—a desire to be thorough and a desire to be brief. He is not content with mentioning the chief and obvious circumstances that concur to an event; while his compact pages want the easy diffuseness of picturesque details. In this last respect particularly he differs from the popular historians and essayists of our century: he condenses both narrative and exposition at least three times as much.

Clearness is a distinguishing quality of our author's style. He is both perspicuous and precise. We have spoken of the comparatively good order of his paragraphs. His precision, for one whose works are not upon technical subjects, is no less remarkable. Writing with leisure and composure, he calmly chooses the aptest words and similitudes; sober and sagacious, he seldom leaves his meaning open to doubt.

We have already remarked the propriety of his similitudes. That he squared the circumstances of a comparison deliberately and not by accident, would appear from the following manipulation of a commonplace:—

"The comparison between a State and a ship has been so illustrated by poets and orators that 'tis hard to find any point wherein they differ; and yet they seem to do it in this, that, in great storms and rough seas, if all the men and lading roll to one side, the ship will be in danger of oversetting by their weight: but, on the contrary, in the storms of State, if the body of the people, with the bulk of estates, roll on one way, the nation will be safe. For the rest, the similitude holds."

He shows great steadiness in keeping close to facts, rising above verbal quibbling, and calmly setting aside misleading associations. His rejection of the factitious simplicity of the scholastic division of governments into Monarchies, Aristocracies, and Democracies, showed no small power of looking beneath the surface to the underlying distinctions: his more accurate division was unheeded until revived and made precise by recent authorities. Many examples might be quoted of his steady superiority to plausible appearances and irrelevant disputes. The beginning of his essay on Poetry is not perhaps the best, but here it is:—

"The two common shrines, to which most offer up the application of their thoughts and their lives, are profit and pleasure; and by their devotions to either of these, they are vulgarly distinguished into two sects, and called either busy or idle men. Whether these terms differ in meaning or only in sound, I know very well may be disputed, and with appearance enough, since the covetous man takes perhaps as much pleasure in his gains as the voluptuous does in his luxury, and would not pursue his business, unless he were pleased with it, upon the last account of what he most wishes and desires, nor would care for the increase of his fortunes, unless he thereby proposed that of his pleasures too, in one kind or other; so that pleasure may be said to be his end, whether he will allow to find it in his pursuit or no. Much ado there has been, many words spent, or (to speak with more respect to the ancient philosophers) many disputes have been raised upon this argument, I think to little purpose, and that all has been rather an exercise of wit, than enquiry after truth; and all controversies, that can never end, had better perhaps never begin. The best perhaps is to take words as they are most commonly spoken and meant, like coin, as it most currently passes, without raising scruples upon the weight of the alloy, unless the cheat or the defect be gross and evident. Few things in the world, or none, will bear too much refining; a thread too fine spun will easily break, and the point of a needle too finely filed. The usual acceptation takes profit and pleasure for two different things, and not only calls the followers or votaries of them by several names of busy and of idle men, but distinguishes the faculties of the mind that are conversant about them, calling the operations of the first wisdom, and of the other wit. . . . . To the first of these are attributed the inventions or productions of things generally esteemed the most necessary, useful, or profitable to human life, either in private possessions or public institutions: to the other, those writings or discourses which are the most pleasing or entertaining to all that read or hear them."

The following passage may be contrasted with Carlyle's theory of laughter:—

"If it" (laughter) "were always an expression of good-humour or being pleased, we should have reason to value ourselves more upon it; but 'tis moved by such different and contrary objects and affections, that it has gained little esteem, since we laugh at folly as well as wit, at accidents that vex us sometimes, as well as others that please us, and at the malice of apes, as well as the innocence of children; and the things that please us most, are apt to make other sorts of motions both in our faces and hearts, and very different from those of laughter."

Strength.—Our author's style has a certain animation, arising chiefly from brevity and point. This is less felt in the severely didactic works, partly because the reader's attention is more heavily taxed, and partly because the writer, having an eye to the main object of presenting the facts, is less able to attend to charms of expression. It is more decidedly pleasing in his Letters, and in the lively essay on the "Cure of the Gout," which also is in the form of a letter.

Not animation, however, but dignity, is the ruling characteristic. Of the general composure and elevation of his tone, the reader will judge best from passages quoted without an eye to this particular quality. When the subject requires a more intense or a loftier tone, he answers easily to the call, providing harmonious language and imagery without any appearance of straining. Thus—

"I have sometimes thought, how it should have come to pass, that the infinite swarm of that vast northern hive, which so often shook the world like a great tempest, and overflowed it like a torrent; changing names, and customs, and government, and language, and the very face of nature, wherever they seated themselves; which, upon record of story, under the name of Gauls, pierced into Greece and Italy, sacking Rome, and besieging the Capitol in Camillus's time; under that of the Cimbers, marched through France to the very confines of Italy, defended by Marius; under that of Huns or Lombards, Visigoths, Goths, and Vandals, conquered the whole forces of the Roman empire, sacked Rome thrice in a small compass of years, seated three kingdoms in Spain and Afric, as well as Lombardy; and under that of Danes or Normans, possessed themselves of England, a great part of France, and even of Naples and Sicily: how (I say) these nations, which seemed to spawn in every age, and at some intervals of time discharged their own native countries of so vast numbers, and with such terror to the world, should, about seven or eight hundred years ago, leave off the use of these furious expeditions, as if on a sudden they should have grown barren, or tame, or better contented with their own ill climates."

Again, describing the spread of Mohammedanism :—

"To be short, this contagion was so violent, that it spread from Arabia into Egypt and Syria, and his power increased with such a sudden growth as well as his doctrine, that he lived to see them overspread both those countries, and a great part of Persia; the decline of the old Roman empire making easy way for the powerful ascent of this new comet, that appeared with such wonder and terror in the world, and with a flaming sword, made way wherever it came, or laid all desolate that opposed it."

The following long sentence may be quoted as an example of sustained strength. No ordinary resources of language are needed to prevent a break-down in the conclusion of what opens with such grandeur. He is moralising on the victorious invasion of the Netherlands by Louis XIV. :—

"When we consider such a power and wealth, as was related in the last chapter, to have fallen in a manner prostrate within the space of one month; so many frontier towns, renowned in the sieges and actions of the Spanish wars, entered like open villages by the French troops, without defence or almost denial; most of them without any blows at all, and all of them with so few; their great rivers that were esteemed an invincible security to the provinces of Holland and Utrecht, passed with as much ease, and as small resistance, as little fords; and in short, the very heart of a nation, so valiant of old against Rome, so obstinate against Spain, now subdued, and in a manner abandoning all before their danger appeared: we may justly have our recourse to the secret and fixed periods of all human greatness, for the account of such a revolution; or rather to the unsearchable decrees and irresistible force of divine providence; though it seems not more impious to question it, than to measure it by our scale; or reduce the issues and motions of that eternal will and power to a conformity with what is esteemed just, or wise, or good, by the usual consent or the narrow comprehension of poor mortal men."

Pathos.—In his grave treatises he is too composed and stately for the lively expression of affection, sorrow, or a fresh sense of beauty. Yet he never passes by a touching occasion without some sign of feeling. The mood of the writer appears in the temperate and refined mournfulness of the language. Thus—

"The noblest spirit of genius in the world, if it falls, though never so bravely, in its first enterprises, cannot deserve enough of mankind to pretend to so great a reward as the esteem of heroic virtue. And yet perhaps many a person has died in the first battle or adventure he achieved, and lies buried in silence and oblivion; who, had he outlived as many dangers as Alexander did, might have shined as bright in honour and fame."

"When all is done, human life is, at the greatest and the best, but like a froward child, that must be played with and humoured a little to keep it quiet till it falls asleep, and then the care is over."

Wit.—As under *Strength* passages may be singled out where the grave vigour and dignity of his style gains the ascendancy, and soars into a loftier strain, so under *Wit* we may single out passages where his pointed animation gains the ascendancy, and becomes keener and more sparkling.

He is too grave and temperate to turn anybody or anything into violent ridicule. The fine flavour of polished wit is always uppermost. The following is an example:—

"A man that tells me my opinions are absurd or ridiculous, impertinent or unreasonable, because they differ from his, seems to intend a quarrel instead of a dispute, and calls me fool or madman with a little more circumstance, though, perhaps, I pass for one as well in my senses as he, as pertinent in talk, and as prudent in life; yet these are the common civilities, in religious argument, of sufficient and conceited men, who talk much of right reason, and mean always their own; and make their private imagination the measure of general truth. But such language determines all between us, and the dispute comes to end in three words at last, which it might as well have ended in at first, That he is in the right, and I am in the wrong."

Examples of his more genial point are to be found chiefly in his letters. The essay on the "Cure of the Gout" is written in a sprightly vein. For example:—

"All these things put together, with what a great physician writes of cures by whipping with rods, and another with holly, and by other cruelties of cutting and burning, made me certainly conclude, that the gout was a companion that ought to be treated like an enemy, and by no means like a friend, and that grew troublesome chiefly by good usage; and this was confirmed to me by considering that it haunted usually the easy and the rich, the nice and the lazy, who grow to endure much, because they can endure little; that make much of it as soon as it comes, and yet leave not making much of themselves too; that take care to carry it presently to bed, and keep it safe and warm, and indeed lay up the gout for two or three months, while they give out that the gout lays up them. On the other side it hardly approaches the rough and the poor, such as labour for meat, and eat only for hunger; that drink water, either pure or but discoloured with malt; that know no use of wine, but for a cordial, as it is, and perhaps was only intended: or if such men happen by their native constitutions to fall into the gout, either they mind it not at all, having no leisure to be sick; or they use it like a dog, they walk on, or they toil and work as they did before, they keep it wet and cold; or if they are laid up, they are perhaps forced by that to fast more than before, and if it lasts, they grow impatient, and fall to beat it, or whip it, or cut it, or burn it; and all this while, perhaps, never know the very name of gout."

Taste.—As might be inferred from his character, our author's style is very highly refined. Affectation of terms or phrases, abruptness, extravagance, maudlin sentimentality, coarse invective, are as foreign as may be to his characteristic manner. If the standard of a good English style is the style that shall please the majority of educated Englishmen, he errs on the side of too great refinement. In many respects he is a contrast to Macaulay, still more to Carlyle.

KINDS OF COMPOSITION.

Narrative.—In a preface to the third part of Temple's 'Memoirs,' Swift claims him as the first Englishman "(at least of any consequence) who ever attempted that manner of writing." Though it is a personal record, the style, as already noticed, is not gossiping and diffuse, but on the contrary compact and brief to the verge of abstruseness. As the principal actor in some of the transactions, he had exceptional advantages for knowing the hidden springs of events.

At one time he intended to write a History of England, having often felt the want of a good general history, and being far from satisfied with the Chroniclers. Obliged by pressure of other employments to abandon this design, he completed an 'Introduction to the History of England,' "from the first originals, as far as he could find any ground of probable story, or of fair conjecture," "through the great and memorable changes of names, people, customs, and laws that passed here, until the end of the first Norman reign." The work is instructive, abounding in sagacious criticism of social and political institutions. It is interesting to contrast his views of history with Macaulay's:—

"I have likewise omitted the accounts and remarks wherein some writers have busied their pens, of strange comets, inclemencies of seasons, raging diseases, or deplorable fires that are said to have happened in this age and kingdom; and are represented by some as judgments of God upon the king's reign, because I rather esteem them accidents of time or chance, such as happen in one part or other of the world, perhaps every age, at some periods of time, or from some influence of stars, or by the conspiring of some natural or casual circumstances, and neither argue the virtues or vices of princes, nor serve for example or instruction to posterity, which are the great ends of history, and ought to be the chief care of all historians."

His 'Observations upon the United Provinces of the Netherlands' is an example of a conspectus, or general view of a state of society in all its parts at a particular time. It is a model of painstaking observation and search, and is full of sagacious remarks. After recounting the rise and progress of the Federation, he delineates their condition towards 1672 under six heads:—their *Government*, their *Situation*, their *People and Dispositions*, their *Religion*, their *Trade*, their *Forces and Revenues.* The performance is very different from the third chapter of Macaulay's History. It is as severely didactic and thorough as Macaulay's is pictorial and superficial.

JOHN DRYDEN, 1631-1700.

From the beginning to the end of his poetical career, Dryden, not content to leave his works to the chances of criticism, loved to defend in prose his principles of composition, and issued hardly anything without an apologetic or explanatory preface or dedication. In this casual form he has left some ingenious special pleading for his own practice, as well as many valuable remarks on his predecessors, and interesting comparisons of the most eminent names. Besides these stray pieces, he published, in 1668, a formal 'Essay of Dramatic Poesy'—"a little discourse in dialogue, for the most part borrowed from the observations of others"—which, says Johnson, "was the first regular and valuable treatise on the art of writing." It is now interesting chiefly for its defence of rhyming in tragedies—a style abandoned in the author's later works. It also contains some clever argument in favour of the superiority of modern to ancient playwriters.

After his conversion to the Catholic Church, he was employed by James II. to defend against Stillingfleet a paper found in the strong-box of the deceased king, purporting to be written by the Duchess of York in explanation of her departure from the Protestant faith. In this controversy there was little that could be called argument on either side—it was very much like other controversies of that time, a pitched battle of abuse; and Dryden, in the exuberant and careless "horseplay" of his raillery, laid himself fatally open to the cool retorts of his antagonist.

In the list of his prose works are included two translations from the French—Bouhours' 'Life of Francis Xavier' (1687), and Du Fresnoy's 'Art of Painting' (1695). He also wrote the life of Plutarch prefixed to what is known as 'Dryden's Translation' of Plutarch's Lives. But the only prose works of his that are now read are his Prefaces and the 'Essay of Dramatic Poesy.'

The fact that these are still worth reading has been fixed in our minds by Byron's happy doggerel lines—

> " Read all the Prefaces of Dryden,
> For these the critics much confide in,
> Though only writ at first for filling,
> To raise the volume's price a shilling."

Dryden's prose, as well as Temple's, is a marked improvement on the prose of the Commonwealth generation. His expressions have not the curious felicity of Cowley's; but the sentences are much more flowing. He displays to some extent what Dr Blair considered such a beauty in Temple's composition—the "harmonious pause," the measured sentence of several members. He aims very much at antithetic point, reserving emphatic statements for the close of the sentence, and practising occasionally the abrupt introduction of a general statement before its application is known. The peculiarities of his sentence-structure may be studied in the following extract from his Preface to 'Absalom and Achitophel,' published in 1681: in it we see the rudiments of certain abrupt arts of style more fully developed by Johnson and Macaulay:—

"It is not my intention to make an apology for my poem: some will think it needs no excuse, and others will receive none. The design, I am sure, is honest; but he who draws his pen for one party must expect to make enemies of the other: for wit and fool are consequents of Whig and Tory; and every man is a knave or an ass to the contrary side. There is a treasury of merits in the Fanatic church, as well as in the Popish, and a pennyworth to be had of saintship, honesty, and poetry, for the lewd, the factious, and the blockheads: but the longest chapter in Deuteronomy has not curses enough for an Anti-Bromingham. My comfort is, their manifest prejudice to my cause will render their judgment of less authority against me. Yet if a poem have genius, it will force its own reception in the world; for there is a sweetness in good verse which tickles even while it hurts; and no man can be heartily angry with him who pleases him against his will. The commendation of adversaries is the greatest triumph of a writer, because it never comes unless extorted. But I can be satisfied on more easy terms: if I happen to please the more moderate sort, I shall be sure of an honest party, and in all probability of the best judges; for the least concerned are probably the least corrupt. And I confess I have laid in for those, by rebating the satire (where justice would allow it) from carrying too sharp an edge. They who can criticise so weakly as to imagine I have done my worst, may be convinced, at their own cost, that I can write severely with more ease than I can gently. I have but laughed at some men's follies, where I could have declaimed against their vices; and other men's virtues I have commended as freely as I have taxed their crimes. . . . The violent on both sides will condemn the character of Absalom, as either too favourably or too hardly drawn: but they are not the violent whom I desire to please. The fault, on the other hand, is to extenuate, palliate, and indulge; and, to confess freely, I have endeavoured to commit it. Besides the respect which I owe his birth, I have a greater for his heroic virtues; and David himself could not be more tender of the young man's life than I would be of his reputation. But since the most excellent natures are always the most easy, and, as being such, are the soonest perverted by ill counsels, especially when baited with fame and glory, it is no more a wonder that he withstood not the temptations of Achitophel, than it was for Adam not to have resisted the two devils, the serpent and the woman. The conclusion of the story I purposely forbore to prosecute, because I could not obtain from myself to show Absalom unfortunate. The frame of it was cut out but for a picture to the waist, and if the draught be so far true, it is as much as I designed.

"Were I the inventor, who am only the historian, I should certainly conclude the piece with the reconcilement of Absalom to David; and who knows but this may come to pass; things were not brought to an extremity where I left the story; there seems yet to be room left for a composure, hereafter there may be only for pity. I have not so much as an uncharitable wish against Achitophel, but am content to be accused of a good-natured error, and to hope, with Origen, that the devil himself may at last be saved; for which reason, in this poem, he is neither brought to set his house in order, nor to dispose of his person afterwards as he in wisdom shall think fit."

Dryden had no idea of observing paragraph law; his genius was the reverse of methodical. He rambles on, making a point here and a point there, and dashing heartily away from his immediate subject whenever he sees an opening for his vigorous wit. His prose has something of the irregular zigzag lightning vigour and splendour of his verse. Any one reading his prose fragments for the strokes of comprehensive terseness, brilliant epigram, and happy aptness of expression, should be on their guard against the infection of his negligent manner; none should take it for granted that their genius is, like his, sufficient to hide any number of irregularities.

The following remarks on Laughter, from his 'Parallel between Poetry and Painting,' prefixed to the translation of Du Fresnoy, exemplify his rather incoherent agglomeration of vigorous sentences:—

"Laughter is indeed the propriety of a man, but just enough to distinguish him from his elder brother with four legs. It is a kind of bastard-pleasure too, taken in at the eyes of the vulgar gazers, and at the ears of the beastly audience. Church painters use it to divert the honest countryman at public prayers, and keep his eyes open at a heavy sermon; and farce scribblers make use of the same noble invention, to entertain citizens, country-gentlemen, and Covent Garden fops. If they are merry all goes well on the poet's side. The better sort go thither too, but in despair of sense and the just images of nature, which are the adequate pleasures of the mind; but the author can give the stage no better than what was given him by nature; and the actors must represent such things as they are capable to perform, and by which both they and the scribbler may get their living. After all, it is a good thing to laugh at any rate; and if a straw can tickle a man, it is an instrument of happiness. Beasts can weep when they suffer, but they cannot laugh."

His remarks on Invention are more to the purpose:—

"The principal parts of painting and poetry next follow. Invention is the first part, and absolutely necessary to them both; yet no rule ever was or ever can be given, how to compass it. A happy genius is the gift of nature: it depends on the influence of the stars, say the astrologers; on the organs of the body, say the naturalists; it is the particular gift of heaven, say the divines, both Christians and heathens. How to improve it, many books can teach us; how to obtain it, none; that nothing can be done without it, all agree—

Tu nihil invita dices faciesve Minerva.

Without invention, a painter is but a copier, and a poet but a plagiary of others. Both are allowed sometimes to copy, and translate; but as our author tells you, that is not the best part of their reputation. 'Imitators are but a servile kind of cattle,' says the poet; or at best, the keepers of cattle for other men: they have nothing which is properly their own: that is a sufficient mortification for me, while I am translating Virgil. But to copy the best author, is a kind of praise, if I perform it as I ought; as a copy after Raffaelle is more to be commended than an original of any indifferent painter."

And yet, on principle, he was opposed to unnecessary digressions on the larger scale:—

"As in the composition of a picture the painter is to take care that nothing enter into it which is not proper or convenient to the subject, so likewise is the poet to reject all incidents which are foreign to his poem and are naturally no parts of it; they are wens and other excrescences, which belong not to the body, but deform it. No person, no incident in the piece or in the play, but must be of use to carry on the main design. All things else are like six fingers to the hand, when nature, which is superfluous in nothing, can do her work with five. A painter must reject all trifling ornaments, so must a poet refuse all tedious and unnecessary descriptions. A role which is too heavy is less an ornament than a burthen."

We might expect to find the prose diction of a poet highly coloured, and profusely embellished with imagery. Dryden's is the reverse of this—familiar, clear, vigorous, and full of epigrammatic point. "I have endeavoured," he says, "to write English as near as I could distinguish it from the tongue of pedants and that of affected travellers." He expressly apologises for the "poetical expressions" in his translation of Du Fresnoy; he "dares not promise that some of them are not fustian, or at least highly metaphorical," but the fault lay with the original.

There is little geniality in his style; he knew as well as anybody where his power lay, and he said of himself that "he could write severely with more ease than he could write gently." When he girds on his sword for a sarcastic onslaught, he goes to work with all his heart. In the controversy with Stillingfleet, his intense feeling sometimes betrays him into bare unadorned abuse; he calls his adversary, by comparison with "the meekness, devotion, and sincerity" of the pious lady's declaration, "disingenuous, foul-mouthed, and shuffling." But this is a passage of exceptional heat; most of the sarcasm is clothed in fresh and splendid language, and takes the form of rough but brilliant wit, throwing his tamer rival into the shade: indeed, had his cause not been so hopelessly unpopular, the attack would have been overwhelming.

OTHER WRITERS.

THEOLOGY.

The most eminent divine in the early part of this period was **Isaac Barrow (1630-1677)**, a man of extremely fertile and versatile talents. He was the son of a linen-draper in London. In 1649 he was elected a Fellow of Trinity College, Cambridge, and for some time thereafter studied medicine. In 1652 he was a candidate for the Greek Professorship, but was disappointed. He then spent some years in travelling along the shores of the Mediterranean. In 1660 he again tried for the same post, and was successful. He had been but two years Professor of Greek when he discovered his preference for mathematics by accepting the Professorship of Geometry in Gresham College. In 1663 he was appointed Lucasian Professor of Mathematics in Cambridge. In 1669, having not yet found his life-work, he vacated his professorship in favour of his pupil Isaac Newton, and thereafter devoted himself exclusively to divinity. In 1670 he was made D.D. by royal mandate, receiving at the time a high compliment from the lips of the King. In 1672 he was nominated to the Mastership of Trinity. He published several mathematical works in Latin. His English writings are all theological, consisting of seventy-seven Sermons; Expositions of the Apostles' Creed, The Lord's Prayer, The Decalogue, &c.; a 'Treatise on the Pope's Supremacy:' and a 'Discourse concerning the Unity of the Church.' "He was in person of the lesser size, and lean; of extraordinary strength, of a fair and calm complexion, a thin skin, very sensible of the cold; his eyes grey, clear, and somewhat short-sighted; his hair of a light auburn, very fine and curling." He was abstracted in his manner, and of slovenly habits. Anecdotes are told of his personal courage and presence of mind. He was a great smoker, and an immoderate eater of fruit. He died of fever, to which he was subject. The most striking things in his sermons are the extraordinary copiousness and vigour of the language, and the exhaustiveness and subtlety of the thought. He is a perfect mine of varied and vigorous expression. His sentences are thrown up with a rough careless vigour; an extreme antithesis to the polished flow of language and ideas in Addison. In his love of scrupulous definitions and qualifications we discover the mathematician; he divides and subdivides with Baconian minuteness, and in drawing parallels adjusts the compared particulars with acute exactness.

The simple and felicitous diction of **John Tillotson**, Archbishop of Canterbury (**1630-1694**), was praised by Dryden and by Addison, and long held up as a model.[1] Born in Yorkshire, of Puritan parents, he was educated at Cambridge, submitted to the Act of Uniformity in 1662, and entered the Church. Going to London in 1663, his preaching soon drew attention, and he was rapidly promoted. At the Revolution he was made Dean of St Paul's, and in 1691 was raised to the supreme height of ecclesiastical dignity. He was a man of great moderation and good sense, without excitability or enthusiasm, "loving neither the ceremony nor the trouble of a great place." Though he received preferment in the reign of Charles, he was not an extravagant royalist: his wife was the niece of Oliver Cromwell, and daughter-in-law of Bishop Wilkins. Ready to serve his friends, he was literary executor to Wilkins and to Barrow, gave an opinion on Burnet's 'History of the Reformation' before it was published, and edited the 'Discourses' of Dr Hezekiah Burton. A good, easy, clear-headed man, with not a little of the character of Paley. The merits of his style are simplicity, and a happy fluency in the choice and combination of words. He probably had no small influence in forming the style of Addison. The defects are considerable. In his easy way he lingers upon an idea, and gives two or three expressions where one would serve the purpose; passing on, he rambles back again, and presents the idea in several other different aspects. The result is an enfeebling tautology and want of method. Taken individually, the expressions are admirably easy and felicitous; but there are too many of them, and they are ill arranged.

Edward Stillingfleet (1635-1699), made Bishop of Worcester in 1689, was much before the public as a controversialist during this period. He fought against Atheists, Unitarians, Papists, and Dissenters, and rendered distinguished service to his cause. His best-known engagements were with Dryden and Locke. Against Dryden, though far inferior in style, he had the best of the argument;

[1] Dryden is said to have "owned with pleasure that if he had any talent for English prose it was owing to his having often read the writings of Archbishop Tillotson." This is but a random compliment; Dryden showed his talent for English prose before Tillotson had published a line, and long before he became famous.

but in the encounter with Locke he sustained a defeat so signal and humiliating that it was said to have hastened his death. He wrote with great vigour, but his expressions are neither original nor felicitous. To a modern reader his manner seems too arrogant and personal to be persuasive. Although Clarendon professes himself "exceedingly delighted with the softness, gentleness, and civility of his language," this word-praise is not borne out by facts; there is no evidence that he had Tillotson's power of bringing over opponents.

William Sherlock (1641-1707), who succeeded Tillotson as Dean of St Paul's, was another champion of the Church against dissent and infidelity, and wrote a 'Vindication of the Trinity' in 1691; but he is now known only by his devotional works. His 'Discourse concerning Death' is a standing article in second-hand book-stalls. This continued popularity is due more to the matter than to the manner. His son Thomas was more distinguished than himself.

Sherlock's 'Vindication' was attacked with great wit and fury by a man far his superior in literary genius, **Robert South (1633-1716).** South, a brilliant Oxonian scholar, the son of a London merchant, was an ultra-royalist, appointed at the Restoration Public Orator of his University, and chaplain to the Earl of Clarendon. He accompanied Lawrence Hyde to Poland in 1676. On his return he was presented to the rectory of Islip, and, having some private fortune, steadily declined farther preferment. He has been called the last of the great English divines of the century. A quick and powerful intellect, solid erudition, a superlative command of homely racy English, and wit of unsurpassed brilliancy, make a combination that, in a literary point of view, places the possessor at least on a level with Taylor and Barrow. Doubtless his fame would have been equal to his powers had he not mistaken his vocation. He shows little religious earnestness, and without *that*, devotional, and even controversial, religious works can hardly pretend to the first rank. He was an earnest Churchman, but not an earnest Christian. Against sectaries his abuse was hearty and hot—"villanous arts," "venomous gibberish," "treacherous cant," "a pack of designing hypocrites," are samples of his phrases. Satirical wit is his distinguishing quality. Even his sermons are brilliantly lighted up with flashes of ingenious mockery; he was always glad to have a victim.

Thomas Sprat, D.D. **(1636-1713),** Fellow of Wadham, Bishop of Rochester, friend and biographer of Cowley. Besides his 'Life of Cowley,' he wrote a 'History of the Royal Society,' of which he was a member, as well as sermons and political tracts. He is praised by Macaulay as "a great master of our language, and possessed at once of the eloquence of the orator, of the controversialist, and of the historian." He also receives a high tribute from Johnson. There is indeed a certain flow and rotund finish about his diction. Some of his sentences would pass for Johnson's. Had the matter been more substantial, he might have taken a higher place in our literature; but he was a good genial fellow, rather fond of the bottle, and his lubricated eloquence perished with him.

Thomas Burnet (1635-1715), Master of the Charter-house, is known in literature by his 'Sacred Theory of the Earth' (pub. in Latin 1680, in English 1691). It is the outcome of a poetic mind excited by the gathering interest in physical science. The theory is merely a framework for extravagant sublimities of description. He represents the antediluvian globe as disposed in regular concentric belts, the heavy solid parts in the centre, then the liquid, then on the top of the liquid a floating crust of solidified oily matter, "even and uniform all over," without rocks or mountains, "wrinkle, scar, or fracture." On this smooth surface, fresh, fruitful, overhung by a calm and serene atmosphere, men lived till the Flood; that calamity was caused by the generation of steam in the subterraneous water and the rupture of the crust, when "the whole fabric broke," and tumbled in fragments into the abyss. The accounts of the Flood and of the final conflagration of the existing earth are given in language worthy of such bold and spacious conceptions.

Of little importance in literature, but of considerable importance in the history of opinion, are the two chief literary defenders of the Quaker faith, **William Penn (1644-1718)** and **Robert Barclay (1648-1690)**, both men of good position by birth. Penn, the son of an admiral, imbibed the proscribed views at Oxford, and was expelled the University. A course of travel on the Continent made him a fine gentleman again; the Plague reconverted him; a trip to Ireland restored him to fashionable circles; a sermon from an old master converted him a third time. This last conversion was in 1668: from that date he remained Quaker for life. In 1669 he was imprisoned for eight months. For some years thereafter his life was prosperous. He was reconciled to his father, who left him a good estate, and some claims on the Government, in liquidation of which he received a grant of Pennsylvania in America. In the later years of Charles and under James he was a great favourite at Court: his conduct there is assailed by Macaulay and warmly defended by Paget and others. The remaining thirty years of his life were spent in private, not a little imbittered by personal griefs and losses.—Barclay was a Scotsman, of the family of Barclay of Ury. He several times suffered imprisonment. His works are, 'Truth Cleared of Calumnies,' 1670; and 'An Apology for the People called in scorn Quakers.' Neither Penn nor Barclay has any special grace or vigour of style. Penn is lively and pointed, Barclay grave and argumentative.

Thomas Ellwood (1639-1713), another of the Quakers, a meek, industrious man, of a feeble constitution, is interesting, not from his style, but from his intercourse with Milton. He was one of the blind poet's readers. He wrote an autobiography, and controversial and devotional treatises.

PHILOSOPHY.

John Locke (1632-1704). The famous author of the 'Essay on the Human Understanding' (pub. 1690) was the son of a small proprietor in the west of England. He took the degree of B.A. at Oxford in 1655, and was elected a student of Christ Church. His chief studies were medicine and physical science, on which subjects he became an authority. His approbation of Sydenham's theory of acute diseases was considered worth boasting of by this "father of English medicine;" and he signified a desire to succeed, in the event of a vacancy, to the Physic Professorship at Gresham College. His chief patron was the Earl of Shaftesbury. He divided his time between Oxford and London, living in the most cultivated society. He spent four years in France. When Shaftesbury's fortunes declined, Locke also fell into difficulties with the Government, and had to take refuge in Holland. While there he wrote in Latin his famous 'Letter on Toleration.' After the Revolution, having recommended himself by his liberal principles, he was rewarded with the Commissionership of Stamps; and also held for five years a more lucrative office as one of the Commissioners of Trade. His 'Two Treatises on Government,' opposing the divine right of kings, and advancing the ideas of a social compact and of the natural rights of man, appeared in 1690. In the same year were published the Essay, and the 'Treatise on Education.' The 'Conduct of the Understanding' was not published till after his death. Locke's health was never robust; an elder brother died young of consumption, and he himself, in spite of the utmost care, died of a decline. He was an agreeable, well-bred man, a sprightly talker, and fond of company chiefly for the pleasures of talking. At college he associated with the lively and agreeable in preference to the scholarly. He was frugal, and regular in his habits. His sagacity and powers of expression were very great. All the works above mentioned drew immediate attention, and are still read by everybody professing an acquaintance with their topics. He is one of the most simple of philosophical writers. Authorities complain that this popular simplicity is bought at the expense of exactness; that his use of terms is vacillating; and that his notions are ill defined.

The learned **Ralph Cudworth (1617-1688)**, a student of Cambridge, and Professor of Hebrew there from 1645 to 1675, published in 1678 his 'Intellectual System of the Universe.' He seems to have been a shy, retiring man, with something of Hooker's disposition; like Hooker, also, an industrious and profound scholar. He was not of a controversial turn, but was pressed by his friends to take the field against Hobbes, Atheism, and every form of heterodoxy. He stated the opinions of his opponents at such length and with such candour that his sincerity was suspected; and he was so alarmed at the outcry raised by his honourable and ingenuous fashion of polemic, that he refrained from farther publication. His 'Treatise of Eternal and Immutable Morality' was not published till 1731.

Another opponent of Hobbes was **Richard Cumberland (1632-1718)**, Bishop of Peterborough, author of a work on the 'Laws of Nature.' His doctrines have an independent place in the history of philosophy; but as he wrote in Latin, he has but a quasi-legitimate standing in the history of English literature.

HISTORY.

Gilbert Burnet (1643-1715), Bishop of Salisbury, an active politician, and author of several religious and other works known only to antiquarians, received the thanks of Parliament for his 'History of the Reformation' in 1676, and earned a durable fame by his posthumous 'History of my own Times, from the Restoration of Charles II. to the conclusion of the Treaty of Peace at Utrecht, in the Reign of Queen Anne.' He belonged to an ancient Aberdeenshire family, and was educated at Marischal College, Aberdeen. At the age of twenty-six (1669) he was made Professor of Divinity in Glasgow, and before he was thirty he was twice offered a Scottish bishopric. About 1673 he resigned his professorial chair and went to London, where his powers as a preacher, no less than as a sagacious observer of politics, soon made him conspicuous. During the reign of James, he thought it prudent to retire to the Continent, and received a flattering invitation to the Hague. He came back with the Prince of Orange, and in 1689 was appointed Bishop of Sarum. He was a shrewd, sagacious Scotchman, and throughout life acted with a prudence that was disturbed neither by impetuosity nor by strong feeling. Yet he displayed at times a steady courageous sincerity where many of the sneerers at his prudence would have kept discreetly in the background. He had a peculiar power of reading character, and of insinuating himself into the confidence of the great. A tall, well-built, fine-looking man, with extraordinary powers of extempore address, he was one of the most popular preachers of the metropolis: he "was often," says Macaulay, "interrupted by the deep hum of his audience; and when, after preaching out the hour-glass, he held it up in his hand, the congregation clamorously encouraged him to go on till the sand had run off once more." Natural temper and varied education concurred to make his views anti-despotic; he was a steady supporter of the Revolution; by his considerate behaviour he made himself extremely popular among the clergy of his diocese. We have evidence that he was careful about his written style, purposely aiming at "aptness of words and justness of figures," and striving to avoid "the fulsome pedantry under which the English language laboured long ago, the trifling way of dark and unintelligible wit that came after that, the coarse extravagance of canting that succeeded this, and the sublime pitch of a strong but false rhetoric, which had much corrupted not only the stage but even the pulpit, but was almost worn out" when he wrote.[1] He may be said to have realised this ideal; his words are generally well chosen, his illustrations appropriate, and his diction copious without being in any way extravagant; but his dry correctness is not made up for by fluent melody or by happy originality of combination. The great charms of his 'History of my own Times' lie in the gossip from behind the scenes, and the skilful delineation of character. He had something of Boswell's faculty for noting characteristic incidents, besides the power of showing them briefly in a connected portraiture. None of our historians surpass, if any equal him, in this respect. When we compare his vivid delineations of the men of the Revolution with Macaulay's jumble of characteristic traits and high-flown moral commonplaces, we at once recognise the hand of a natural master of the art.

Along with Burnet may be mentioned **Sir George Mackenzie, 1636-1691,** Lord Advocate under Charles II. and James II., author of 'Memoirs of the Affairs of Scotland, from the Restoration of Charles II.,' not printed till 1821. Mackenzie was familiar with Dryden and the literary society of the time, and wrote several lively miscellaneous essays: "The Virtuoso or Stoic," "Moral Gallantry," "The Moral History of Frugality," &c. A composition in praise of Solitude led to a friendly passage of arms with *John Evelyn*, who entered the lists in defence of active life.

Two famous DIARISTS are usually reckoned in this generation—**Samuel Pepys (1632-1703)** and **John Evelyn (1620-1706)**. Pepys was Secretary to the Admiralty in the reigns of Charles II. and James II. His Diary, which extends from 1660 to 1669, was written in shorthand, and was deciphered by Lord Braybrooke in 1825. This delightful book of gossip is one of the most interesting memorials of the domestic life of the time. Evelyn's Diary is

1 Preface to his translation of More's 'Utopia,' 1684.

the work of a more accomplished man (though a less interesting and instructive gossip), and extends through a longer period. It is, indeed, an autobiography extending from 1620 to 1706. From 1641 he was in the habit of setting down with considerable detail everything that interested him. Only extracts of so voluminous a work have been published. Evelyn is now known chiefly by his Diary. In his own day he was called "Sylva" Evelyn, from a 'Discourse on Forest-Trees, and the Propagation of Timber in his Majesty's Dominions,' published in 1664. He was a man of independent fortune, and held public employment under Charles and James.

Among the chief ANTIQUARIES of the period were **Anthony à Wood (1632-1695)**, the great authority on the antiquities of Oxford (*Athenæ Oxonienses*, 1691), and **John Aubrey (1626-1700)**, a fellow-labourer with Dugdale and Wood, and an authority on popular superstitions. **Thomas Rymer (1638-1714)**, compiler of Carlyle's favourite butt, Rymer's 'Fœdera,' also flourished in this period. He began life as a tragic poet and dramatic critic. Appointed historiographer-royal in 1692, he was employed to prepare a collection of the documents of our public transactions with foreign powers. He lived to publish seventeen folio volumes of the series, the first appearing in 1703.

MISCELLANEOUS.

Sir Roger L'Estrange (1616-1704) was the leading newspaper writer throughout the reigns of Charles and James. An enterprising royalist soldier, who had suffered not a little in the cause, he was appointed licenser or censor of the press in 1663, and at the same time received a monopoly of public intelligence in favour of his own newspaper, 'The Public Intelligencer.' He worked hard to make his paper a thorough repertory of news, and to extend its circulation; and it was a great discouragement to the growth of newspapers when in 1665 his monopoly and his censorship were taken from him and given to a duller rival in Court favour. The disgrace did not extinguish his loyalty. He continued to support the Court with various effusions; and in his 'Observator,' which appeared in 1681, rendered valuable service in defending the royal family from the charge of Popery. He excelled in the coarse derision and invective—the rough give-and-take of the time; so much so, that he has been, absurdly enough, accused of corrupting the English language. He earned the hatred of lovers of freedom by his opposition to the emancipation of the press (which was accomplished in 1694), and by his rude exercise of authority while he was himself censor; but these offences may fairly enough be considered the accidents of his time and his position.

Charles Blount (1654-1693), son of Sir Henry Blount, a Hertfordshire gentleman, author of Travels and various poetical pieces, came more than once into collision with L'Estrange. He rendered himself notorious by various deistical publications—among others, a history of opinions concerning the soul, and an exposition of his own views, under the title of 'Religio Laici.' A trick that he played on the licenser of books in 1693, led to the abolition of all restrictions on the freedom of the press. He committed suicide because the sister of his deceased wife, to whom he was passionately attached, would not marry him without the consent of the Church, and that was not to be obtained.

Walter Charleton (1619-1707), physician to Charles II., and a friend of Hobbes, besides several works on Theology, Natural History, Natural Philosophy, Medicine, and Antiquities, wrote 'A Brief Discourse concerning the Different Wits of Men' (1675). Traces of Hobbes's materialism appear in the work. He ascribes differences in character to differences in the form, size, and quality of the brain. His style is rather pedantic, chiefly from a peculiar habit of beginning his sentence with the predicate adjective ("Somewhat slow they are"—"Barren they are not," &c.); but he writes with vigour, clearness, and wit.

The witty, sagacious, and versatile **George Saville**, Marquis of Halifax **(1630-1695)**, in the course of his active public life wrote some short treatises that show him to have been an easy master of the best English of the time. His 'Character of a Trimmer' (a humorous defence of moderate courses) is the most famous of these productions.

Robert Boyle (1627-1691), "the father of chemistry, and brother to the Earl of Cork," is the author of six quarto volumes of scientific observations and religious advices and meditations. He was one of the most active of the original members of the Royal Society. His favourite subjects were chemistry and pneumatics. His religious musings are very commonplace: it was to get clear of the annoyance of reading them aloud to a lady admirer that Swift wrote his famous parody, 'Meditation on a Broomstick.' His style is prolix and unmethodical.

Sir Isaac Newton (1642-1727), the most distinguished of English mathematicians, inventor of the method of fluxions, and discoverer of gravitation and the dispersion of light, need only be mentioned here. He was born in Lincolnshire; like Hobbes, a premature and sickly child. His mechanical and mathematical powers were soon conspicuous. In 1669 he succeeded Barrow as Lucasian Professor of Mathematics at Cambridge. In recognition of his services to science, he was appointed Warden of the Mint in 1695, and Master in 1699. In 1703 he was elected President of the Royal Society, to which he had early been admitted as a member. In 1705 he received the honour of knighthood. His best-known mathematical work, the 'Principia,' or Mathematical Principles of Natural Philosophy, published in 1687, was written in Latin. In addition to his mathematical labours, he turned his ingenuity to thorny questions in Scripture, writing 'Observations on the Prophecies;' the 'Chronology of Ancient Kingdoms;' and 'An Historical Account of Two Notable Corruptions of Scripture;'—which works were published after his death. His style is plain and clear.[1]

John Ray (1628-1705), the son of a blacksmith in Essex, was the great English naturalist of the century, and is regarded as one of the founders of botany. A work published in 1691, 'The Wisdom of God, manifested in the Works of the Creation,' was exceedingly popular until superseded by Paley's 'Natural Theology.' It is written with considerable neatness and spirit.

[1] A vexed question in the life of Newton is whether or not his mind was deranged about the year 1693. Sir David Brewster, in his 'Life of Newton,' inclines to think that it was but a temporary excitement. In one of his letters Newton complains of not having slept "an hour a-night for a fortnight together, and for five days together not a wink." About this time he wrote some incoherent letters, on which principally is founded the story of his madness.

CHAPTER VI.

FROM 1700 TO 1730.

THROUGHOUT last century this period was venerated as the Augustan Age in English Literature, the idea being that it had reached a crowning pitch of refinement in the arts of composition, and that in this respect the Augustan Age was its prototype. The present century has not sanctioned the venerable title: our critics will not allow that Pope, Swift, and Addison are equal in literary power either to their great predecessors of the age of Elizabeth, or to their great successors of more recent times; and on that ground refuse them the dignified appellation of Augustan. We may agree with the criticism of this century and yet leave the Queen Anne celebrities in possession of their coveted title. In the quality of careful finish the Queen Anne men were undoubtedly as much superior to their predecessors as the Augustan men were to *their* predecessors. In other and more universally impressive qualities the Shakspeare period and the Byron period surpass both Queen Anne and Augustus—rising, if not "above all Greek," certainly "above all Roman fame."

We have here to do only with prose; and, in that department, even the doctrine that the Queen Anne men are superior to their predecessors in elaborate finish may be assailed with plausible, if not destructive casuistry. Defoe was probably as careless and hurried in composition as any author that ever lifted pen in the Elizabethan or in any other age. Addison probably committed more errors in syntax than Thomas Fuller. Swift finished his great compositions with extreme care, but he learned the habit of painstaking from his master Sir William Temple. One cannot be too careful in making sweeping generalisations about the characteristics of a period. Probably all that can be affirmed with safety about Queen Anne prose is that, taken as a whole, the prose written by this generation contained fewer grammatical errors, and was, within certain limits, more varied in expression than the prose written by the preceding generation; and this can probably be affirmed of any generation of writers in the history of our literature. We are too apt to attribute the characteristics of a leading writer to his age; because Addison wrote with refined wit and elegant simplicity, and had a certain number of imitators, we are not to ascribe these qualities to the whole prose literature of the reign of Queen Anne.

DANIEL DEFOE, 1661-1731.

One of the most indefatigable and productive of our prose writers,[1] pamphleteer, journalist, writer of Commercial Treatises, of Religious Treatises, of History, and of Fiction. He is so well known as the author of 'Robinson Crusoe' that many think of him in no other capacity; and forget, if they ever hear of, the extraordinary number and variety of his works. He is reputed author of 250 distinct publications. He was nearly sixty years old when he published his first novel; and before that time he had written some hundred and fifty treatises on politics, religion, commerce, and what not.

He is sometimes represented as an illiterate London tradesman with no education but what he gave himself after leaving school. His own account is that he was educated by his father, a well-to-do butcher in St Giles's, Cripplegate, with a view to the Dissenter ministry, and that he studied for five years with that express aim. At whatever time or times he had picked up his knowledge, he was well informed, and even accomplished: being (by his own account) master of five languages—including Latin; widely read in books of history and travel; and acquainted with such science as was known in his day.

His life was stirring and eventful, although comparatively few of the incidents are known. His enemies taunted him with beginning business as a hosier. This he denied, describing himself as a trader. From other authority we know that in course of business he visited Portugal, and perhaps other parts of the Continent. Whatever his trade may have been, he was too volatile to stick to it. An ardent politician, he wrote in 1683 a political pamphlet on the war between the Turks and the Austrians; and in 1685 rode out (at least so he says) and joined the western rising for the Duke of Monmouth. In 1692 he had to compound with his creditors. It is a fair conjecture that about this time he began to

[1] He is sometimes called the first author by profession; but this is hardly correct. Fuller had little to depend upon but the sale of his works, and Birkenhead, Needham, and L'Estrange, lived by their literary services to a party.

cherish, with or without encouragement, hopes of patronage from the Minister of State. Some friends offering to settle him as a factor at Cadiz, he preferred his prospects at home. Another business speculation was unsuccessful: he started a pantile work, but, according to his own account, it lost him £3000. In 1695 he was appointed accountant to the commissioners for managing the duties on glass; and held that office till the duty was abolished in 1699. In 1701 his metrical satire 'The True-Born Englishman' —an energetic defence of King William, the Dutch, and the Revolution—brought him into high favour with the King. In 1702 an ironical proposal—'The Shortest Way with the Dissenters'—gave such offence that he was put in the pillory, fined, and imprisoned. During his imprisonment he collected and revised twenty-one of the numerous tracts that he had written up to that date, and projected a weekly periodical called the 'Review,' the prototype of the 'Tatler' and the 'Spectator.' The first number of the 'Review' was published on 19th February 1704, and it was continued single-handed for eight years. In 1704, through the intervention of Harley, he was not only released, but was taken into the confidence of Government, and employed on secret services. In 1706-7 he spent four months in Edinburgh as an agent for promoting the Union, and his skilful advocacy of the commercial advantages of the measure is supposed to have exercised no small influence on the happy result. Through the changes of administration during the latter years of Queen Anne, he continued in the secret service of Government, all the time writing periodicals and pamphlets with his characteristic prolific industry. Nor did he lose this profitable connection with the ruling powers on the accession of George I. and the Whigs. Till a discovery made by Mr William Lee in 1869, it was supposed that at this date he retired from politics, and wrote his more elaborate works: his 'Family Instructor' (1715), 'Religious Courtship' (1722), 'Complete English Tradesman' (1726), 'Political History of the Devil' (1726); and his novels—the foundation of his literary fame—'Robinson Crusoe' (1719), 'Captain Singleton' (1720), 'Duncan Campbell' (1720), 'Moll Flanders' (1721), 'Colonel Jack' (1721), 'Journal of the Plague' (1722), 'Roxana' (1724), 'Memoirs of a Cavalier' (undated). But it seems that for several years after 1715 he played a very double game; being paid by the Whig statesmen to insinuate himself into the staff of an extreme Jacobite paper, 'Mist's Journal,' and repress its most obnoxious attacks. In one of the newly-discovered letters he says, "I ventured to assure his Lordship the Sting of that mischievous Paper should be entirely taken out, though it was granted that the style should continue Tory, as it was, that the Party might be amused, and not set up another, which would have destroyed the design. And this

Part I therefore take entirely on myself still." He continued his prodigious literary activity to the very last, dying in April 1731.[1]

In a proclamation offering a reward for his capture in 1703 (after his "Shortest Way with the Dissenters"), Defoe is described as "a middle-sized spare man about forty years old, of a brown complexion, and dark-brown hair, though he wears a wig, having a hook nose, a sharp chin, grey eyes, and a large mole near his mouth."

His constitution must have been very robust to endure the enormous amount of work that he went through in the course of his threescore and ten years of life. Not only was he constantly engaged in literary work, but, as a secret agent of the Government, he managed harassing negotiations and braved considerable danger—sometimes, as he said in his hyperbolical way, "running as much risk as a grenadier on a counterscarp." Of his domestic life we know nothing, except that he was married and had six children.

The number, variety, freshness, and popularity of Defoe's works, furnish the best possible evidence of the fertility and ingenuity of his intellect. For thirty years always ready with something upon every political and social question that was passing, he still had energy, when this excitement was over, to conquer a new field of literature; and was quite as prolific on subjects of perennial and universal interest as he had been on the more exciting topics of the hour. The nature no less than the number of his works conveys the impression of amazing versatile energy. Little trouble has been taken with the mere literary workmanship; the author of 'Robinson Crusoe' can never be classed among the masters of carefully-elaborated prose. The labour has been expended on making his narrative minutely circumstantial—his reflection of life a picture of unparalleled fidelity and detail. His novels are in the autobiographical form; and the circumstances of the various situations, the adventures encountered by the supposed narrator, and the feelings of different moments, are detailed with such minuteness that all his fictions would pass for records of actual experience. None of our writers, not even Shakspeare, shows half such a knowledge of the circumstances of life among different ranks and conditions of men; none of them has realised with such fidelity how so many different persons lived and moved. He displays especial subtlety in tracing the gradual growth of an opinion or a purpose, from its first suggestion to its full development: this power meets us in all his works, and perhaps nowhere is more con-

[1] I have mentioned only the most prominent of Defoe's writings. To mention them all is impossible within our limits; the titles alone would occupy at least thirty or forty of our pages.

spicuous than in his representation of the growth of religious conviction in the 'Family Instructor.'

Supple and versatile of intellect, he was not distinguished for either intensity or delicacy of feeling. He seems to have been a vain, impulsive, audaciously boastful sort of man. His controversial works are brimful of happy egotism; he exults in his ingenuity and clearness of vision, and boils over in ironical mockery of his duller opponents. It is a tribute to his powers of imagination, but few people will consider it a compliment to his honesty, to say that we can believe hardly a word that he tells us about himself. The stories that he gives about his youthful enthusiasm in joining the Duke of Monmouth, and about the unheard-of persecutions that he suffered in later life, are probably no less fictitious than the adventures of Robinson Crusoe.

The characteristics of his intellect come out strongly in his active life. If the precepts in the 'Complete English Tradesman' were drawn from his own practice, he must have been a most adroit man of business. His insinuating address was fully appreciated by those that employed him on secret affairs of state. In dealing with men, his fertile ingenuity and profound observation left him never at a loss. He would seem to have been a most consummate dissembler; his easy success in playing the hypocrite gave him the fullest confidence, and his daring effrontery well entitled him to Pope's epithet—"*unabashed* Defoe." He was one of the most audaciously shifty and supple of men.

It is but just to his fair fame to add that his hypocrisy was not turned to malevolent objects: if he was not persecuted so much as he represents, he is not accused of persecuting others. He was probably too magnanimous for personal grudges. What is more, no discoveries that have yet been made implicate him in transactions detrimental to the public good.

Our author, as we have seen, wrote something like 150 treatises on passing questions between 1688 and 1715; an exhaustive account of his opinions would take us over the entire political, social, and commercial history of that period. A few of the more notable of his views may be singled out. He was a strong supporter of the Revolution; his 'True-Born Englishman' was a reply to a personal attack on the "foreigner" ruler and his Dutch favourites. He strongly opposed the war with France; we shall quote from the 'Consolidator,' of date 1705, a satirical passage that might have been the basis of Swift's famous 'Conduct of the Allies' in 1711.[1] By birth a Dissenter, he frequently made the *High-fliers*, as the High Churchmen were called, the objects of his ridicule; one of these attacks, we have seen, landed him in the

[1] See p. 371.

pillory and in Newgate. His most considerable political achievement was his share in effecting the union between England and Scotland; his principal means of persuasion would seem to have been the advantages to Scottish traders.

His active mind was fertile in practical projects. In 1697 he published an 'Essay on Projects.' "He wrote," says Mr George Chalmers, "many sheets about the coin; he proposed a register for seamen, long before the Act of Parliament was thought of; he projected county banks, and factories for goods; he mentioned a proposal for a commission of inquiries into bankrupts' estates; he contrived a pension office for the relief of the poor." One of the projects in his 'Essay' was a society on the model of the French Academy—"for encouraging polite learning, for refining the English language, and for preventing barbarisms of manners."

ELEMENTS OF STYLE.

Vocabulary.—A good many of Defoe's phrases are old-fashioned, and have long since dropped out of current English. We should not be safe to use an expression upon his authority. He is an excellent representative of the colloquial style of the time; but colloquial phrases have their day. Owing to his frequent use of homely idioms, his writings are a very rewarding study to verbal reformers, who desire to weed the language of slip-shod idioms that have indolently been allowed to establish themselves, and who are anxious to back their proposed reforms with the practice of elder writers.

As we should expect in an author writing upon such a variety of topics, his command of English is prodigious. If one may judge from a general impression of variety, no writer comes nearer to the Shakspearian profusion of language. His sympathies were so catholic that it is difficult to find out in what region he was deficient. He is seldom declamatory or pathetic, but when he is, the words seem to flow in the choicest abundance. The rich vein in his vocabulary is easier to discover. From his wide practice as a controversialist, he is a great master of the language of sarcasm and abuse; even Swift's range is probably not more extensive, as his powers of ridicule were less versatile.

He was too popular a writer to be eccentric in his general language; yet sometimes in the extravagance of high spirits he whimsically coins words that are not unlike some of the eccentricities of Carlyle. The following is an example:—

"The yet further extravagances which naturally attend the mischief of wit, are beauism, dogmaticality, whimsification, impudensity, and various kinds of fopperosities (according to Mr Boyle), which, issuing out of the brain, descend into all the faculties, and branch themselves by infinite variety into all the actions of life."

Sentences and Paragraphs.—In this mechanical part of composition our author is singularly negligent, especially in his hurried political tracts. Had he been, like Temple, a careful builder of sentences—studious of the arts of arrangement—he could not have produced one-tenth of what he wrote. His ungrammatical laxity would not be allowed in any modern writer.

He is so careless that it would answer no purpose to exemplify his errors, and so irregular that it would not be easy to discover peculiarities of structure.

His only merit lies in his being consecutive. Whatever be the distribution of the matter into sentences and paragraphs, he is desirous that the connection be clearly apparent, and is very explicit in his phrases of reference.

Figures of Speech—Similitudes.—Illustrative force is the most remarkable thing in Defoe's similitudes. In conjunction with the general spirit and vigour of his language, their effect is electrifying. Agreeably to the wonderful discursiveness of his intellect, they are taken from all sources, not forcibly hunted out for embellishment, but used for illustration when they present themselves. As suited a vigorous popular style, his preference was for the homely, and even the coarse. His allusions are sometimes learned, but always easily understood from the homeliness of the expression.

We may quote a few examples :—

"Dryden might have been told his fate that, *having his extraordinary genius slung and pitched upon a swivel*, it would certainly turn round as fast as the times, and instruct him how to write elegies to Oliver Cromwell and King Charles the Second with all the coherence imaginable; how to write 'Religio Laici' and the 'Hind and Panther,' and yet be the same man, every day to change his principle, change his religion, change his coat, change his master, and yet never change his nature."

He describes, in the following metaphorical terms, the wonderful psychological revelations of the Chinese philosopher, Mira-cho-cholasmo :—

"There you have that part of the head turned inside outward, in which nature has placed the materials of reflecting; and, *like a glass beehive*, represents to you all the several cells in which are lodged things past, even back to infancy and conception. There you have the repository, with all its cells, classically, annually, numerically, and alphabetically disposed. There you may see how, when the perplexed animal, on the loss of a thought or a word, scratches his poll, every attack of his invading fingers knocks at nature's door, alarms all the register-keepers, and away they run, unlock all the classes, search diligently for what he calls for, and immediately deliver it up to the brain; if it cannot be found, they entreat a little patience, till they step into the revolvary, where they run over little catalogues of the minutest passages of life, and so, in time, never fail to hand on the thing; if not just when he calls for it, yet at some other time."

As an example of his more ambitious illustrations, take his comparison between the doctrine of passive obedience and the Copernican system :—

"I take the doctrines of passive obedience, &c., among the statesmen, to be like the Copernican system of the earth's motion among philosophers, which, though it be contrary to all ancient knowledge, and not capable of demonstration, yet is adhered to in general, because by this they can better solve and give a more rational account of several dark phenomena in nature than they could before.

"Thus our modern statesmen approve of this scheme of government; not that it admits of any rational defence, much less of demonstration, but because by this method they can the better explain, as well as defend, all coercion in cases invasive of natural right than they could before."

Contrast.—Although our author is not a studious cultivator of point or epigram, yet these arts form one among his many instruments of ridicule. We shall produce two examples. The first is an account of some of the things that he saw when he visited the moon, through a wonderful glass that penetrated beneath all disguises :—

"Here we saw the state of the war among nations; here was the French giving sham thanks for victories they never got, and somebody else addressing and congratulating the sublime glory of running away; here was Te Deum for sham victories by land, and there was thanksgiving for ditto by sea; here we might see two armies fight, both run away, and both come and thank God for nothing. Here we saw a plan of a late war like that in Ireland; there was all the officers cursing a Dutch general, because the damned rogue would fight and spoil a good war, that, with decent management and good husbandry, might have been eked out this twenty years; there were whole armies hunting two cows to one Irishman, and driving off black cattle declared the noble end of the war. Here we saw a country full of stone walls and strong towns, where, every campaign, the trade of war was carried on by the soldiers with the same intriguing as it was carried on in the council-chambers; there were millions of contributions raised, and vast sums collected, but no taxes lessened; whole plate-fleets surprised, but no treasure found; vast sums lost by enemies, and yet never found by friends; ships loaded with volatile silver, that came away full and got home empty; whole voyages made to beat nobody, and plunder everybody; two millions robbed from the honest merchants, and not a groat saved for the honest subjects. There we saw captains listing men with the Government's money, and letting them go again for their own; ships fitted out at the rate of two millions a-year, to fight but once in three years, and then run away for want of powder and shot."

The next seems to be an extravagant parody of the epigram :—

"He told me, as the inhabitants were the most numerous, so they were the strangest people that lived; both their natures, tempers, qualities, actions, and way of living, was made up of innumerable contradictions; that they were the wisest fools and the foolishest wise men in the world; the weakest, strongest, richest, poorest, most generous, covetous, bold, cowardly, false, faithful, sober, dissolute, surly, civil, slothful, diligent, peaceable, quarrelling, loyal, seditious nation that ever was known."

QUALITIES OF STYLE.

Simplicity.—The use of homely language is one of the most remarkable features in Defoe's style. It is one of the secrets of the continued popularity of 'Robinson Crusoe.'

Two things may be specially exemplified under this head. One is, the coarse plainness of language that he sometimes adopted for purposes of ridicule; and the other, his orderly colloquial exposition of subjects that might have been treated in a more pretentious and abstruse style.

As an example of a very undignified tone of banter, take the beginning of his 'Reasons against the Succession of the House of Hanover,' another ironical piece that was taken for earnest, and led to his temporary imprisonment:—

> "What strife is here among you all? And what a noise about who shall or shall not be king, the Lord knows when? Is it not a strange thing we cannot be quiet with the queen we have, but we must all fall into confusion and combustions about who shall come after? Why, pray folks, how old is the queen, and when is she to die? that here is this pother made about it. I have heard wise people say the queen is not fifty years old, that she has no distemper but the gout, that that is a life-long disease, which generally holds people out twenty, or thirty, or forty years; and let it go how it will, the queen may well enough linger out twenty or thirty years, and not be a huge old wife neither. Now, what say the people? must we think of living twenty or thirty years in this wrangling condition we are now in? This would be a torment worse than some of the Egyptian plagues, and would be intolerable to bear, though for fewer years than that. The animosities of this nation, should they go on, as it seems they go on now, would by time become to such a height, that all charity, society, and mutual agreement among us, will be destroyed. Christians shall we be called? No; nothing of the people called Christians will be to be found among us. Nothing of Christianity, viz., charity, will be found among us! The name Christian may be assumed, but it will be all hypocrisy and delusion; the being of Christianity must be lost in the fog, and smoke, and stink, and noise, and rage, and cruelty, of our quarrel about a king. Is this rational? Is it agreeable to the true interests of the nation? What must become of trade, of religion, of society, of relation, of families, of people? Why, hark ye, you folk that call yourselves rational, and talk of having souls, is this a token of your having such things about you, or of your thinking rationally? if you have, pray what is it likely will become of you all? Why, the strife is gotten into your kitchens, your parlours, your shops, your counting-houses, nay, into your very beds. You gentlefolks, if you please to listen to your cook-maids and footmen in your kitchens, you shall hear them scolding, and swearing, and scratching, and fighting among themselves; and when you think the noise is about the beef and the pudding, the dish-water, or the kitchen-stuff, alas, you are mistaken! the feud is about the more mighty affairs of the government, and who is for the Protestant succession, and who for the Pretender. Here the poor despicable scullions learn to cry, High Church, No Dutch Kings, No Hanover, that they may do it dexterously when they come into the next mob. Here their antagonists of the dripping-pan practise the other side clamour, No French Peace, No Pretender, No Popery. The thing is the very same up," &c.

Examples of his simple expositions may be found in any page of the 'Complete Tradesman.' The following is a very fair specimen :—

"Another trading license is that of appointing and promising payments of money, which men in business are oftentimes forced to make, and forced to break, without any scruple ; nay, and without any reproach upon their integrity. Let us state this case as clearly as we can, and see how it stands as to the morality of it, for that is the point in debate.

"The credit usually given by one tradesman to another, as particularly by the merchant to the wholesale-man, and by the wholesale-man to the retailer, is such, that, without tying the buyer up to a particular day of payment, they go on buying and selling, and the buyer pays money upon account, as his convenience admits, and as the seller is content to take it. This occasions the merchant or the wholesale-man to go about, as they call it, *a-dunning* among their dealers, and which is generally the work of every Saturday. When the merchant comes to his customer the wholesale-man, or warehouse-keeper, for money, he tells him, 'I have no money, sir ; I cannot pay you now ; if you call next week, I will pay you.' Next week comes, and the merchant calls again ; but it is the same thing, only the warehouseman adds, 'Well, I will pay you next week, *without fail.*' When the week comes, he tells him he has met with great disappointments, and he knows not what to do, but desires his patience another week : and when the other week comes, perhaps he pays him, and so they go on.

"Now, what is to be said for this ? In the first place, let us look back to the occasion. This warehouse-keeper, or wholesale-man, sells the goods which he buys of the merchant—I say, he sells them to the retailers, and it is for that reason I place it first there. Now, as they buy in smaller quantities than he did of the merchant, so he deals with more of them in number, and he goes about among them the same Saturday, to get in money that he may pay his merchant, and he receives his bag full of promises, too, everywhere instead of money, and is put off from week to week, perhaps by fifty shopkeepers in a day ; and their serving him thus obliges him to do the same to the merchant.

"Again, come to the merchant. Except some, whose circumstances are above it, they are by this very usage obliged to put off the Blackwellhall factor, or the packer, or the clothier, or whoever they deal with, in proportion ; and thus promises go round for payment, and those promises are kept or broken as money comes in, or as disappointments happen : and all this while there is no breach of honesty, or parole ; no lying, or supposition of it, among the tradesmen, either on one side or other.

"But let us come, I say, to the morality of it. To break a solemn promise is a kind of prevarication ; that is certain, there is no coming off of it ; and I might enlarge here upon the first fault, namely of making the promise, which, say the strict objectors, they should not do. But the tradesman's answer is this : all those promises ought to be taken as they are made —namely, with a contingent dependence upon the circumstances of trade, such as promises made them by others who owe them money, or the supposition of a week's trade bringing in money by retail, as usual, both of which are liable to fail or at least to fall short ; and this the person who calls for the money knows, and takes the promise with those attending casualties ; which if they fail, he knows the shopkeeper, or whoever he is, must fail him too."

Clearness.—The last-quoted passage is a specimen of our author's most distinct style of expression. When, as in the above case, he is put upon his mettle to be perspicuous, he observes a certain precision of method, giving express notice when he passes from one consideration to another: "In the first place, let us look back to the occasion;" "Again, come to the merchant;" "But let us come, I say, to the morality of it." But he writes too hurriedly to be precise in expression. When we study for a little what he writes, we can see that he has a clear and vigorous mind, and is seldom oppressed by confusion of thought. But his expression is often imperfect. He hurries on, and is content to leave it incomplete. The above phrases of transition, for example, are incomplete—the first particularly. We see what they mean after we have read the paragraph they introduce, but not before.

Strength.—Defoe's general style may be described as nervous. It has the strength arising from variety, copiousness, and vigorous fitness of plain words and metaphors, with an occasional "tang" of antithesis.

He wants the power of sonorous declamation; as may be seen in the coarse vigour of his familiar expostulation with the people of England concerning their political dissensions. In his 'Seasonable Warning and Caution,' touching the same theme, he attempts a loftier flight, but mars the effect by occasional expressions in his more usual tone of familiarity. Thus—

"Why, how now, England! what ailest thee now? What evil spirit now possesseth thee? O thou nation famous for espousing religion, and defending liberty; eminent in all ages for pulling down tyrants, and adhering steadily to the fundamentals of thy own constitution: that has not only secured thy own rights, and handed them down unimpaired to every succeeding age, but has been the sanctuary of other oppressed nations; the strong protector of injured subjects against the lawless invasion of oppressing tyrants.

"To thee the oppressed Protestants of France owed, for some ages ago, the comfort of being powerfully supported, while their own king, wheedled by the lustre of a crown, became apostate, and laid the foundation of their ruin among themselves; in thee their posterity find a refuge, and flourish in thy wealth and trade, when religion and liberty find no more place in their own country.

"To thee the distressed Belgii owe the powerful assistance by which they took up arms in defence of liberty and religion against Spanish cruelty, the perfidious tyranny of their kings, and the rage of the bloody Duke d'Alva.

" . . . But what has all this been for? And to what intent and purpose was all this zeal, if you will sink under the ruin of the very fabric ye have pulled down? If ye will give up the cause after ye have gained the advantage, and yield yourselves up after you have been delivered; to what purpose then has all this been done? Why all this money expended? Why all this blood spilt? To what end is France said to be reduced, and peace now concluded, if the same Popery, the same tyranny, the same arbitrary methods of government shall be received among you again? Sure your posterity will stand amazed to consider how lavish this age has been of their money and their blood, and to how little purpose; since no age since the creation of the world can show us a time whenever any nation spent so much blood and treasure to end just where they begun: as, if the arts of our enemies prevail, we are like to do."

His homely nervous style is well suited to the relation of lively horrors, or of exciting commotions, such as riots and mutinies. In recording the alarms caused by the fear of infection during the Great Plague of 1666, he is incomparably graphic and impressive. He produces his effects not by ponderous epithets, or impressive reflections, but by the accumulation of striking details in homely language. As an example:—

"Another infected person came and knocked at the door of a citizen's house, where they knew him very well; the servant let him in, and being told the master of the house was above, he ran up, and came into the room to them as the whole family were at supper. They began to rise up a little surprised, not knowing what the matter was; but he bade them sit still, he only came to take his leave of them. They asked him, 'Why, Mr ——, where are you going?' 'Going,' says he, 'I have got the sickness, and shall die to-morrow night.' It is easy to believe, though not to describe, the consternation they were all in; the women and the man's daughters, which were but little girls, were frightened almost to death, and got up, all running out, one at one door and one at another, some down-stairs and some up-stairs, and getting together as well as they could, locked themselves into their chambers, and screamed out at the window for help, as if they had been frighted out of their wits. The master, more composed than they, though both frighted and provoked, was going to lay hands on him and throw him down-stairs, being in a passion; but then considering a little the condition of the man, and the danger of touching him, horror seized his mind, and he stood like one astonished. The poor distempered man, all this while, being, as well, diseased in his brain as in his body, stood still like one amazed; at length he turns round, 'Ay!' says he, with all the seeming calmness imaginable, 'is it so with you all? Are you all disturbed at me? Why then I'll e'en go home and die there.' And so he goes immediately down-stairs. The servant that had let him in goes down after him with a candle, but was afraid to go past him and open the door, so he stood on the stairs to see what he would do; the man went and opened the door, and went out and flung the door after him."

The Ludicrous.—The extravagance of Defoe's sense of the ludicrous is in proportion to the marvellous energy of the man. He deals in the same kind of undisguised banter as Macaulay; only he is more exuberant, stands less upon his dignity, hits fearlessly at greater antagonists, and altogether has a more magnanimous air. At the risk of being formal, we may compare him with the other three great prose wits in this age of wits, Addison, Steele, and Swift. He is more openly derisive and less bitter than Addison, having no mastery of the polite sneer: he is not a loving humorist like Steele, but sarcastically and derisively humorous; and he is more magnanimous and less personal than Swift, dealing with public not with private conduct, and carrying into the warfare a spirit less savagely ferocious.

Passages already quoted illustrate the extravagance of his humour, as it appears in epigrammatic paradox, and in the application of very homely language to affairs usually treated with stiff dignity. His 'Consolidator, or Memoirs of Sundry Transactions from the Moon,' is, as we should expect from the title, full of extravagant fun—so extravagant that the satire is converted into humour. In the passage quoted concerning the Irish and French wars (p. 349), the satire is predominant; but very often he loses sight of his polemical purpose, and gives a loose rein to his powers of ludicrous invention. The metaphorical description of the discoveries of the great psychologist (p. 348) is a fair example. Here is another:—

"If these labours of mine shall prove successful, I may, in my next journey that way, take an abstract of their most admirable tracts in navigation, and the mysteries of Chinese mathematics; which outdo all modern invention at that rate, that it is inconceivable; in this elaborate work I must run through the 365 volumes of Augro-machi-lanquaro-zi, the most ancient mathematician in all China; from thence I shall give a description of a fleet of ships of a hundred thousand sail, built at the expense of the emperor Tangro the XVth.; who, having notice of the general deluge, prepared these vessels, to every city and town in his dominions one, and in bulk proportioned to the number of its inhabitants; into which vessel all the people, with such movables as they thought fit to save, and with a hundred and twenty days' provisions, were received at the time of the flood; and the rest of their goods being put into great vessels made of China ware, and fast luted down on the top, were preserved unhurt by the water: these ships they furnished with six hundred fathom of chain instead of cables, which being fastened by wonderful arts to the earth, every vessel rid out the deluge just at the town's end; so that when the waters abated, the people had nothing to do but to open the doors made in the ship-sides and come out, repair their houses, open the great China pots their goods were in, and so put themselves *in statu quo.*"

One of the most striking features in our author's wit is his power of irony. Of this power he received very disagreeable proof: his ironical proposal, 'The Shortest Way with the Dissenters,' was praised by the extreme High-fliers as an admirable idea, and the mocking author imprisoned when they discovered to their fury how they had been cheated; and eleven years later, his ironical 'Reasons against the Succession of the House of Hanover' was misinterpreted by the Government, and much to his surprise, he was incarcerated as a genuine Jacobite. We have quoted the opening of the latter piece. The following is a portion of the mock declamation of his 'Shortest Way:'—

"It is now near fourteen years that the glory and peace of the purest and most flourishing church in the world has been eclipsed, buffeted, and disturbed, by a sort of men who God in His providence has suffered to insult over her, and bring her down; these have been the days of her humiliation and tribulation. She was born with an invincible patience, the reproach of the wicked, and God has at last heard her prayers, and delivered her from the oppression of the stranger.

"And now they find their day is over, their power gone, and the throne of this nation possessed by a royal, English, true, and ever-constant member of, and friend to the Church of England. Now that they find they are in danger of the Church of England's just resentments; now they cry out peace, union, forbearance, and charity, as if the Church had not too long harboured her enemies under her wing, and nourished the viperous brood, till they hiss and fly in the face of the mother that cherished them.

"No, gentlemen, the time of mercy is past, your day of grace is over; you should have practised peace, and moderation, and charity, if you expected any yourselves.

"We have heard more of this lesson for fourteen years past. We have been huffed and bullied with your Act of Toleration; you have told us that you are the church established by law, as well as others; have set up your canting synagogues at our church-doors, and the church and members have been loaded with reproaches, with oaths, associations, abjurations, and what not; where has been the mercy, the forbearance, the charity, you have shown to tender consciences of the Church of England, that could not take oaths as fast as you made them? that having sworn allegiance to their lawful and rightful King, could not dispense with that oath, their King being still alive, and swear to your new hodge-podge of a Dutch government? These have been turned out of their livings, and they and their families left to starve; their estates double taxed, to carry on a war they had no hand in, and you got nothing by. What account can you give of the multitudes you have forced to comply, against their consciences, with your new sophistical politics, who, like new converts in France, sin because they can't starve? And now the tables are turned upon you, you must not be persecuted, 'tis not a Christian spirit!

"Your management of your Dutch monarch, whom you reduced to a mere king of cl——s, is enough to give any future princes such an idea of your principles, as to warn them sufficiently from coming into your clutches; and, God be thanked, the Queen is out of your hands, knows you, and will have a care of you."

KINDS OF COMPOSITION.

Defoe, as is testified by every page of his writings, excelled in the graphic presentation both of concrete things and of states of mind. He did not attempt comprehensive formal delineations of complicated scenes, and so does not exhibit *Descriptive method* in its most difficult application; yet he must be allowed to be one of our greatest masters of single descriptive touches.

One variety of descriptive method, indeed, he may be said to have employed, and that with the highest success—the presentation of scenes from the traveller's point of view. He puts before us the various features of a country as they turn up in his narrative. There is no full description of Robinson Crusoe's island in any one place, but particular is added to particular as they occurred to Robinson himself, and before the close of the narrative we know the island from shore to shore. He acts upon the same plan in all his narratives. One of his narratives in particular, his 'Voyage Round the World,' is framed expressly for descriptive purposes; in that work his main object is to present a systematic body of his multifarious knowledge concerning foreign countries, foreign trade, and foreign adventures, by sea and by land.

It is worthy of remark that he observes the cardinal rule of description, the inaugural presentation of a comprehensive view. He fills in the picture by degrees, but he begins by drawing the general outline. One of the first things that Robinson Crusoe does is to go to the top of a hill and view the country:—

"After I had with great labour and difficulty got to the top, I saw my fate, to my great affliction, viz., that I was in an island environed every way with the sea, no land to be seen except some rocks, which lay a great way off, and two small islands, less than this, which lay about three leagues to the west. I found also that the island I was in was barren, and, as I saw good reason to believe, uninhabited, except by wild beasts, of whom, however, I saw none."

Another thing worth observing in his descriptions is that he has a Herodotean knack of giving numerical measures of extent, and of indicating the lie of a country by a reference to the points of the compass. This is one of his arts for giving an air of reality to his narratives.

The *Narrative* art of so successful a story-teller as Defoe deserves careful study. He chooses the simplest form of narration, the record by an individual of incidents that have happened within his personal knowledge. His narratives are all autobiographical. In his 'Memoirs of a Cavalier,' and others of his works, he mingles general accounts of public transactions that the Cavalier took part in with the narrative of personal adventures; but it is in the narrative of personal adventures that the interest of the work consists.

The question arises, Does he show any art beyond the accumulation of interesting incidents: does he show skill in the order of presenting them? Apart from the question of interest,—which, it is superfluous to say, Defoe sustains with unique power,—his narrative is eminently perspicuous. He has, to be sure, no complicated difficulties to overcome, but he observes all the conditions of perspicuity for the simple forms of narrative that he professes: when he shifts the scene, he gives the reader distinct intimation of the change; when new agents are introduced, their appearance is expressly announced; and he does not depart from the order of events without an apology and ample explanation. And as he is tolerably exact in his measurement of space, so he is tolerably exact in his measurement of time: the assigning of definite dates also helps to keep up the air of reality. We have mentioned these various items of lucidity without qualification: it should be added, that though Defoe observes these conditions in the main, his narratives were for the most part written hurriedly, and the close reader finds an occasional confusion.

For popular *Exposition*, apart from his general felicity of language, Defoe had two strong cards: a multifarious, and, comparatively speaking, inexhaustible command of examples and comparisons. His 'Complete English Tradesman' is a manual of advice that still finds readers.

JONATHAN SWIFT, 1667-1745.

The author of 'Gulliver's Travels,' the eccentric Dean of St Patrick's in Ireland, has been all but universally acknowledged as the most vigorous and grammatical writer of English anterior to Johnson.

He was born in Dublin, the posthumous son of Jonathan Swift, a native of Yorkshire, said to be second cousin to the poet Dryden; and was educated by the charity of an uncle at the school of Kilkenny, and at Trinity College, Dublin. He entered the world, at the age of twenty-one, as private secretary to Sir William Temple, who had married a relative of his mother. This post he held, with a brief interval, for eleven years, remaining in the Moor Park family till the death of Sir William in 1699. Again thrown on his own resources, he was for a short time chaplain in the family of Lord Berkeley, and from him obtained in 1700 the livings of Laracor and Rathbeggin in the diocese of Meath. He rose to no higher preferment till made Dean of St Patrick's by his Tory friends in 1713.

Like other literary men of the time, he took an interest in politics, and wrote with a political aim. His first publication, 'Dissensions in Athens and Rome,' appeared in 1701, when the author was thirty-four years of age: it relates the evil consequences of dissensions between Nobles and Commons in the ancient states, and points a moral against the quarrelsome behaviour of the English Commons. The anonymous 'Tale of a Tub,'—a satire on religious dissensions and the self-sufficiency of the different Churches, filled out with numerous satirical digressions on various subjects,—was written about 1696, and first published in 1704. Along with the 'Tale of a Tub' appeared 'The Battle of the Books'—a burlesque on Temple's opponents in the Ancient *versus* Modern controversy. In 1708 he took a leading place among the wits by his ridicule of John Partridge, the Philomath or Astrologer. This performance made the name of Isaac Bickerstaff one of the most popular in town, for which reason it was assumed by Steele when he began the 'Tatler.' From 1710 to 1714, the four last years of Queen Anne's reign, he was the chief literary support of the Tory Administration, writing the 'Conduct of the Allies,' the 'Letter to the October Club,' the 'Examiner,' and other telling compositions. His 'Journal to Stella' was written during his residence in London at this period. When George came to the throne, and the power of government passed to the Whigs, he retired to his Irish deanery. Ten years thereafter he made a great sensation in the political world, and gained unexampled popularity in Ireland, by his 'Drapier's Letters,' written against Wood's patent for a copper coinage. The letters raised such a commotion that the patent had to be revoked. 'Gulliver's Travels' was published in 1726-27, and "was received with such avidity that the price of the first edition was raised before the second could be made."

Swift's relations with Stella and Vanessa—Miss Johnson and Miss Vanhomrigh—are too complicated to be here entered upon at length. Stella passed as a daughter of Sir William Temple's steward, but was believed to be the natural daughter of Sir William himself. When Swift went to Ireland he persuaded her to come and live near him under the charge of Mrs Dingley, kept up with her all the intimacy of a Platonic friendship, and latterly was united to her by a private marriage, though the connection was for some reason or other never publicly acknowledged. His relations with Miss Vanhomrigh were less mysterious, but more tragical. As her literary tutor, he suffered or encouraged her to fall passionately in love with him. Warm-hearted and impetuous, she made him an offer of marriage; and when he equivocated and urged delay, she threw reserve aside, and pursued the unusual suit with warm entreaty and argument. She died of a broken heart, on discovering the Dean's intimacy with Stella.

Swift is described by Sir Walter Scott as "in person tall, strong, and well made, of a dark complexion, but with blue eyes, black and bushy eyebrows, nose somewhat aquiline, and features which remarkably expressed the stern, haughty, and dauntless turn of his mind."

It needed considerable constitutional strength to support the astonishing force of his character; yet there would seem to have been some radical disorder in his system. From our earliest records of his behaviour, he was excessively irritable, at times even savagely so. He could not endure to accommodate himself to people; he either gloomily held his tongue, or overbore opposition with fierce impatience. We can hardly explain this without supposing some radical distemper; it may have been the uneasy beginnings of the brain disease that afterwards unhinged his reason.

Taken as a whole, his writings leave upon our minds a wonderful impression of persistent originality, analogical power, effective eloquence, and wit. We feel his originality most vividly when we compare his works with the works of writers less powerful or less persistently concentrated; when, for example, we compare his 'Tale of a Tub' with Defoe's 'Shortest Way with Dissenters,' or his 'Gulliver's Travels' with Defoe's 'Voyage to the Moon.' Defoe's performances have the originality of first thoughts dashed off hastily—originality, as it were, of the first remove. Swift's performances appear as the outcome of strong powers working up to a high ideal; remodelling first thoughts and still remaining unsatisfied; climbing, stage after stage, to a transcendently imposing altitude above the common level. A man with his quickness of thought would probably find *some* ludicrous parallel upon the first endeavour; but he was not content until he had discovered a parallel that should be supremely ludicrous. The surprising persistence and power of his efforts appears not less in the quantity than in the quality of his analogies. In the 'Tale of a Tub' and in 'Gulliver's Travels,' the multitude as well as the aptness of the parallels between the imaginary narrative and the facts allegorised are absolutely unrivalled among works of that nature, and could have been conceived only by the greatest powers at the maximum of intense concentration. He was famous for quick flashes of extempore wit; in an age of brilliant talkers, he held one of the highest places. But the requirements for his sustained compositions embraced something over and above this: 'Gulliver's Travels' needed steady application as well as quickness of analogical energy. There were men in the Queen Anne period that held their own with Swift in the social interchange of wit, as there were men more delicate in criticism and more sagacious in statecraft; but he stood alone in the rare combination of subtle wit with demoniac perseverance.

In some of his writings he displays intense feeling; we read hardly a page without encountering some stroke of passion. Strong egotism is more or less involved in all his emotional manifestations. He was, as we have said, savagely impatient of the slightest contradiction. If either a person or an institution jarred with his notions of what it ought to be or ought to do, his rage was instantaneous and irrepressible.[1] In his Journal to Stella, indeed, he expressed himself with the most passionate fondness But this was not inconsistent with the irritable egotism that elsewhere displayed itself as the ruling passion of his nature. It was, indeed, an outcome of the same passion in an *allotropic* form: intense affection for an intimate companion is describable as an

[1] The gross violations of decency in his writings are referable to the same intense egotism; he delighted to shock conventional notions, and to brave contradiction or rebuke.

expanded egotism. While Swift was in London, Stella was to him an *alter ego*, another self; there were none of the irritations of actual companionship to break the flow of his tenderness.

His conduct both in public and in private was determined by imperious irritable pride. He was immoderately fond of the exercise of power, and ungovernably restless under authority. He must have his own way for the moment, come what would. He has not been proved guilty of mean selfishness or of malice. On the contrary, he showed himself on several occasions public-spirited and charitable. But both his public spirit and his charity were to this extent egotistic that he insisted dictatorially upon his own schemes for the good of the party interested. As a clergyman, "discharging his duties with punctuality," his ruling passion came out in dictatorial schemes for improving the condition of his parishioners, and savage contempt for the idleness and over-populating fecundity that marred his plans. During his four years' importance at Court, he is described as lording it over the highest officers of state, treating them with the air of a patron, "affecting rather to dictate than advise." In private company, though esteemed the greatest wit of the age, he behaved at times with the same rude imperiousness. A story is told of his peremptorily bidding Lady Burlington "sing him a song," and, when she refused, threatening to make her sing when he bade her. In the rampant moments of this towering egotism, he was blind to every other interest. When he suspected his patron Lord Berkeley, and Berkeley's secretary, Bushe, of playing false to him in the matter of a clerical presentation, he left their presence in a fury, crying—"God confound you both for a couple of scoundrels!" When his butler, who copied the Drapier letters, seemed to presume upon his knowledge of the terrible secret, he dismissed the man with "Do the worst you dare, sir!"—an infuriated braving of consequences which it would be hard to parallel.

Opinions.—Macaulay brands our author as "an apostate politician." He coquetted with the Whigs, it is said, and went over to the Tories when the Whig leaders showed an imperfect respect for his powers. It is not pretended that he ever wrote for the Whigs, or ever received favours from them. In his choice of a party he probably was determined not a little by personal feelings and his natural love of opposition.

His religious sincerity has been questioned. The presumptions are drawn solely from the satirical and gross tone of his writings. Macaulay terms him "a ribald priest." Against the presumptions thus derived is the fact that he is often sarcastic with disbelievers in Christianity. His 'Tale of a Tub' supports the Church of England against Papist and Presbyterian.

We may quote one or two of his "Thoughts on various subjects:"—

"We have just enough religion to make us hate, but not enough to make us love, one another."

"When we desire or solicit anything, our minds run wholly on the good side or circumstances of it; when it is obtained, our minds run wholly on the bad side."

"The stoical scheme of supplying our wants by lopping off our desires, is like cutting off our feet when we want shoes."

"The latter part of a wise man's life is taken up in curing the follies, prejudices, and false opinions he had contracted in the former."

"All fits of pleasure are balanced by an equal degree of pain or languor; it is like spending this year part of next year's revenue."

"Would a writer know how to behave himself with relation to posterity, let him consider in old books what he finds that he is glad to know."

"A very few men, properly speaking, live at present, but are providing to live another time."

"Matrimony has many children; Repentance, Discord, Poverty, Jealousy, Sickness, Spleen, Loathing," &c.

In his letter to a Young Clergyman, he gives the following advice:

"I should likewise have been glad if you had applied yourself a little more to the study of the English language than I fear you have done; the neglect whereof is one of the most general defects among the scholars of this kingdom, who seem not to have the least conception of a style, but run on in a flat kind of phraseology, often mingled with barbarous terms and expressions peculiar to the nation. . . . Proper words in proper places make the true definition of a style."

ELEMENTS OF STYLE.

Vocabulary.—Swift's mastery of the language for purposes of ridicule is universally allowed to be unsurpassed. His range is indeed somewhat too wide for ordinary tastes; in the process of "debasing and defiling," he sometimes condescends to use the language of the brothel. The propensity to shock decorum cost him the favour of Queen Anne and a bishopric.

His diction is praised for its grammatical purity. We have just seen that he was particular about not using barbarous terms. "He studied purity; and though perhaps all his strictures" [his syntax] "are not exact, yet it is not often that solecisms can be found; and whoever depends on his authority, may generally conclude himself safe."

Sentences and Paragraphs.—In point of syntax, our author is so much more correct than any writer before Johnson that he sometimes gets the credit of establishing modern grammar. Doubtless he profited greatly by his residence with the finically-studious Temple. If his syntax is more uniformly correct than Temple's, he certainly owes to Temple the habit of being particular in this matter. We can distinctly trace his master's influence in the finished compacting of his sentences.

It is matter of praise that no other peculiarity calls for special remark. He is neither strikingly periodic, nor strikingly loose, nor strikingly pointed. His education under Temple taught him the period and point; his natural love of simplicity kept him from pushing these forms to an extreme. The consequence is, that the reader's attention is not specially drawn to any one form, which is so far the perfection of sentence style. Farther, with his natural clearness, he is fairly attentive to the placing of words, and to the unity of his sentences.

From Temple also he learned to study method, both in the general arrangement of a discourse and in the disposition of paragraphs. Almost vehemently anxious to be followed and understood, he is explicit in referring us to what has been said, what is to come, and what is the connection of one thing with another.

One of his paragraph arts deserves to be exemplified. He often, but not obtrusively often, reserves a telling point for the end. This art is seen in the three following paragraphs from his letter of advice to a Young Lady on her marriage:—

"I must likewise warn you strictly against the least degree of fondness to your husband before any witness whatsoever, even before your nearest relations, or the very maids of your chamber. This proceeding is so exceeding odious and disgustful to all who have either good breeding or good sense, that they assign two very unamiable reasons for it; the one is gross hypocrisy, and the other has too bad a name to mention. If there is any difference to be made, your husband is the lowest person in company either at home or abroad, and every gentleman present has a better claim to all marks of civility and distinction from you. Conceal your esteem and love in your own breast, and reserve your kind looks and language for private hours; which are so many in the four-and-twenty, that they will afford time to employ a passion as exalted as any that was ever described in a French romance.

"Upon this head I should likewise advise you to differ in practice from those ladies who affect abundance of uneasiness while their husbands are abroad; start with every knock at the door, and ring the bell incessantly for the servants to let in their master; will not eat a bit of dinner or supper if the husband happens to stay out; and receive him at his return with such a medley of chiding and kindness, and catechising him where he has been, that a shrew from Billingsgate would be a more easy and eligible companion.

"Of the same leaven are those wives who, when their husbands are gone a journey, must have a letter every post, upon pain of fits and hysterics; and a day must be fixed for their return home, without the least allowance for business, or sickness, or accidents, or weather; upon which I can only say that in my observation those ladies who are apt to make the greatest chatter on such occasions, would liberally have paid a messenger for bringing them news that their husbands had broken their necks on the road."

Figures of Speech—Similitudes.—No general statement can be made regarding our author's use of figures of similarity. Some of his writings are very plain, and some of them are very figurative. Setting aside 'Gulliver's Travels,' which affects the blunt diction of a seafaring captain, and not forgetting that the work as a whole is one sustained similitude, we may say that when he writes seriously his language is simple, unadorned, and designed above everything to convey his meaning directly; and that when he writes in a spirit of ridicule he gives free play to his fancy.[1] Even this needs modification. His gravest didactic is enlivened by strong and apt similes and metaphors. Nothing could be more absurd than the idea that he never uses metaphors. It is said to be a boast of his own; if so, he must have meant by metaphors—euphemisms for "nasty ideas." In that quarter he always calls a spade a spade.

One thing is very remarkable and characteristic in his similitudes; they never elevate a subject, except in irony. On the other hand, they frequently debase, and that to no ordinary depth. His allusions are often extremely gross.

A quotation or two will illustrate the character of his similitudes. The first is on the worship of Clothes, which Carlyle acknowledges as a "dim anticipation" of his Philosophy:—

"The worshippers of this deity had also a system of their belief, which seemed to turn upon the following fundamentals. They held the universe to be a large suit of clothes, which invests everything: that the earth is invested by the air; the air is invested by the stars, and the stars are invested by the *primum mobile*. Look upon this globe of earth, you will find it to be a very complete and fashionable dress. What is that which some call land, but a fine coat faced with green? or the sea, but a waistcoat of water tabby? Proceed to the particular works of the creation, you will find how curious a journeyman Nature has been to trim up the vegetable beaux; observe how sparkish a periwig adorns the head of a beech, and what a fine doublet of satin is worn by the birch. To conclude from all, what is man himself but a microcoat, or rather a complete suit of clothes with all its trimmings? As to his body there can be no dispute; but examine even the requirements of his mind, you will find them all contribute in their order towards furnishing out an exact dress: to instance no more; is not religion a cloak, honesty a pair of shoes worn out in the dirt, self-love a surtout, vanity a shirt, and conscience a pair of breeches, which, though a cover," &c.

"The most accomplished way of using books at present is twofold: either, first, to serve them as some men do lords, learn their titles exactly, and then brag of their acquaintance; or, secondly, which is indeed the choicer, the profounder, and politer method, to get a thorough insight into the index, by which the whole book is governed and turned, like fishes by the tail. For to enter the palace of learning at the great gate requires an expense of time and forms; therefore men of much haste and little ceremony

[1] Dr Johnson places the 'Tale of a Tub' by itself for "copiousness of images and vivacity of diction;" but others of his ironical pieces are of the same character. See the "Letter to a Young Poet."

are content to get in by the back-door. For the arts are all in a flying march, and therefore more easily subdued by attacking them in the rear. Thus physicians discover the state of the whole body, by consulting only what comes from behind. Thus men catch knowledge by throwing their wit on the posteriors of a book, as boys do sparrows, with flinging salt upon their tails. Thus human life is best understood by the wise man's rule of always regarding the end."

"To my certain knowledge, some of our greatest wits in your poetical way have not as much real learning as would cover sixpence in the bottom of a basin; nor do I think the worse of them; for, to speak my private opinion, I am for every man's working upon his own materials, and producing only what he can find within himself, which is commonly a better stock than the owner knows it to be. I think flowers of wit ought to spring, as those in a garden do, from their own root and stem, without foreign assistance. I would have a man's wit rather like a fountain, that feeds itself invisibly, than a river, that is supplied by several streams from abroad.

"Or if it be necessary, as the case is with some barren wits, to take in the thoughts of others in order to draw forth their own, as dry pumps will not play till water is thrown into them; in that necessity, I would recommend some of the approved standard authors of antiquity for your perusal as a poet and a wit, because maggots being what you look for, as monkeys do for vermin in their keepers' heads, you will find they abound in good old authors, as in rich old cheese, not in the new; and for that reason you must have the classics, especially the worm-eaten of them, often in your hands."

Allegory.—The 'Tale of a Tub' and 'Gulliver's Travels' are the two most finished allegories in our language. Perhaps greater constructive skill is shown in the Tale than in the Travels. The Dean is said to have exclaimed in his old age, "What a genius I had when I wrote that book!" In the Travels he has no fixed order to observe, and can introduce his satirical allusions when and where he pleases; but in the Tale he undertakes to allegorise a history. A father dies leaving three sons, Peter, Martin, and Jack (Popery, Episcopalianism, and Presbyterianism, represented by the apostle *Peter*, *Martin* Luther, and *Jack* Calvin). He has no great property to bequeath, so he bequeaths them each a coat (a system of worship), with a body of directions how to preserve it. This will of his represents the Bible. The three sons soon fall into the ways of the world, and overlay their coats with all the fashionable trimmings—at first evading the will by ingenious interpretations, but finally locking it up and never referring to it. By-and-by Martin and Jack have thoughts of reforming; steal a copy of the will; and are kicked out of doors by Peter. They then reform in earnest, Martin cautiously, Jack impetuously: Martin picking off the adventitious gold-lace, silver fringes, flame-coloured lining, &c., carefully, so as not to injure the garment; Jack tearing off these ornaments with such violence as to leave his coat in tatters. Jack quarrels with Martin for his want of zeal, separates from him in a rage, runs mad, and sets up all kinds of strange doctrine. [The bias of the allegory, it may be remarked, is strongly in favour of the English Church.]

One of the most ingenious, and at the same time one of the coarsest, chapters is the account of Jack's doctrine of Æolism (from Æolus, the god of wind). It is a satire on the Puritan belief in the special inspiration of preachers by the Holy Ghost. The beginning is an example of his ingenuity in bringing scattered particulars under a common idea:—

"The learned Æolists maintain the original cause of all things to be wind, from which principle this whole universe was at first produced, and into which it must at last be resolved; that the same breath which had kindled and blew up the flame of nature, should one day blow it out. This is what the *adepti* understand by their *anima mundi;* that is to say, the spirit, or breath, or wind of the world; for, examine the whole system by the particulars of nature, and you will find it not to be disputed. For whether you please to call the *forma informans* of man by the name of *spiritus, animus, afflatus,* or *anima;* what are all these but several appellations for wind, which is the ruling element in every compound, and into which they all resolve upon their corruption? Farther, what is life itself but, as it is commonly called, the breath of our nostrils? whence it is very justly observed by naturalists, that wind still continues of great emolument in certain mysteries not to be named," &c.

The following seems intended for an allegorical description of General Assemblies among the Presbyterians:—

"At certain seasons of the year you might behold the priests among them in vast numbers, with their mouths gaping wide against a storm. At other times were to be seen several hundreds linked together in a circular chain, with every man a pair of bellows applied to his neighbour's breech, by which they blew up each other to the size of a tun; and for that reason, with great propriety of speech, did usually call their bodies their vessels. When, by these and the like performances, they were grown sufficiently replete, they would immediately depart, and disembogue, for the public good, a plentiful share of their acquirements into their disciples' chaps."

Irony.—Of this art Swift is a consummate master. The best known specimens of his skill are—'An Argument to prove that the abolishing of Christianity in England may, as things now stand, be attended with some inconveniences, and perhaps not produce those many good effects proposed thereby;' and 'A Modest Proposal for preventing the children of poor people in Ireland from being a burden to their parents or country, and for making them beneficial to the public.' As compared with Defoe's irony, the wit of these pieces is more subtle and surprising. The opening of the "Argument" is inimitably happy; he affects to be in a minority, and apologises for venturing to oppose the general opinion:—

"I am very sensible what a weakness and presumption it is to reason against the general humour and disposition of the world. I remember it was, with great justice and due regard to the freedom both of the public and the press, forbidden upon several penalties to write or discourse, or lay wagers against the Union even before it was confirmed by Parliament; because that was looked upon as a design to oppose the current of the people, which, besides the folly of it, is a manifest breach of the fundamental law that makes this majority of opinion the voice of God. In like manner, and for the very same reasons, it may perhaps be neither safe nor prudent to argue against the abolishing of Christianity at a juncture when all parties appear so unanimously determined upon the point, as we cannot but allow from their actions, their discourses, and their writings. However, I know not how, whether from the affectation of singularity, or the perverseness of human nature, but so it unhappily falls out, that I cannot be entirely of this opinion. Nay, though I were sure an order were issued for my immediate prosecution by the Attorney-General, I should still confess that, in the present posture of our affairs at home or abroad, I do not yet see the absolute necessity of extirpating the Christian religion from among us.

"This perhaps may appear too great a paradox even for our wise and paradoxical age to endure; therefore I shall handle it with all tenderness, and with the utmost deference to that great and profound majority which is of another sentiment.

. . . .

"Every candid reader will easily understand my discourse to be intended only in defence of nominal Christianity; the other having been for some time wholly laid aside by general consent as utterly inconsistent with our present schemes of wealth and power."

In his "Modest Proposal" about the Irish children, he begins by a description of the miseries of over-population, reminds us of "the prodigious number of children in the arms, or on the backs, or at the heels of their mothers," and declares that—

"Whoever could find out a fair, cheap, and easy method of making these children sound useful members of the Commonwealth, would deserve so well of the public as to have his statue set up for a preserver of the nation."

He then puts in his claim to the distinction of such a discovery. He proposes—

"To provide for them in such a manner as, instead of being a charge upon their parents or the parish, or wanting food and raiment for the rest of their lives, they shall on the contrary contribute to the feeding, and partly to the clothing, of many thousands."

What, then, is the scheme?

"I have been assured by a very knowing American of my acquaintance in London, that a young healthy child, well nursed, is, at a year old, a most delicious, nourishing, and wholesome food, whether stewed, roasted, baked, or boiled; and I make no doubt that it will equally serve in a fricassee or a ragout.

"I do therefore humbly offer it to public consideration, that of the 120,000 children already computed, 20,000 may be reserved for breed, whereof only one-fourth part to be males, which is more than we allow to sheep, black cattle, or swine; and my reason is, that these children are seldom the fruits of marriage, a circumstance not much regarded by our savages, therefore one male will be sufficient to serve four females. That the remaining 100,000 may, at a year old, be offered in sale to the persons of quality and fortune through the kingdom, always advising the mother to let them suck plentifully in the last month, so as to render them plump and fat for a good table. A child will make two dishes at an entertainment for friends; and when the family dines alone, the fore or hind quarter will make a reasonable dish, and, seasoned with a little pepper or salt, will be very good boiled on the fourth day, especially in winter.

"I grant this food will be somewhat dear, and therefore very proper for landlords, who, as they have already devoured most of the parents, seem to have the best title to the children.

"Those who are more thrifty (as I must confess the times require), may flay the carcase; the skin of which, artificially dressed, will make admirable gloves for ladies, and summer boots for fine gentlemen.

"As to our City of Dublin, shambles may be appointed for this purpose in the most convenient parts of it, and butchers, we may be assured, will not be wanting; although I rather recommend buying the children alive, then dressing them hot from the knife, as we do roasting-pigs."

The above are perhaps the more horrible details of this horrible proposal. The conclusion is a very fine stroke of wit, as carrying out the consistency of the irony to the greatest possible height:—

"I profess, in the sincerity of my heart, that I have not the least personal interest in endeavouring to promote this necessary work, having no other motive than the public good of my country, by advancing our trade, providing for infants, relieving the poor, and giving some pleasure to the rich. I have no children by which I can propose to get a single penny, the youngest being nine years old, and my wife past child-bearing."

QUALITIES OF STYLE.

Simplicity.—"His delight was in simplicity. His style was well suited to his thoughts, which are never subtilised by nice disquisitions, decorated by sparkling conceits, elevated by ambitious sentences, or variegated by far-sought learning. . . . He always understands himself, and his readers always understand him: the peruser of Swift wants little previous knowledge; it will be sufficient that he is acquainted with common words and common things; he is neither required to mount elevations nor to explore profundities; his passage is always on a level, along solid ground, without asperities, without obstruction."[1]

The Drapier Letters were written in peculiarly familiar style. Whoever wishes to model upon Swift in this respect, must not forget that his simplicity verges on coarseness.

Clearness.—It is not always Swift's desire to make his meaning distinct. One of his arts is to hide it away under similitudes. When he does wish to be beyond possibility of mistake, he knows how to accomplish the object. He does not deal with subjects where single words are much open to different interpretations by different readers, and so has not much room for showing his skill in preventing ambiguity. But he is careful to make his words fit

[1] Johnson, Life of Swift.

close to his ideas, and often brings out his meaning sharply, by contrasting it with what he does not mean.

Strength.—His diction is emphatic and copious, and the intense force of his satire is unsurpassed. Johnson's saying, that "he pays no court to the passions, he excites neither surprise nor admiration,"[1] is a hasty judgment that needs qualification. If we accept it, we must understand by passion—sublimity; and by surprise and admiration, the elevation of sublimity. Nothing could be more surprising or impressive than the flashes of Swift's wit; and of passion, in one sense, there is enough, and more than enough, in the Drapier's Letters:—

> "Good God! who are this wretch's advisers? Who are his supporters, abettors, encouragers, or sharers? Mr Wood will oblige me to take fivepence-halfpenny of his brass in every payment; and I will shoot Mr Wood and his deputies through the head, like highwaymen or housebreakers, if they dare to force one farthing of their coin on me in the payment of £100. It is no loss of honour to submit to the lion; but who, with the figure of a man, can think with patience of being devoured alive by a rat? He has laid a tax upon the people of Ireland of 17s. at least in the pound; a tax, I say, not only upon lands, but interest-money, goods, manufactures, the hire of handicraftsmen, labourers, and servants.
>
> "Shopkeepers, look to yourselves!" &c.

Pathos.—Swift had such a hatred of insincere sentiment, and such a tendency to believe every open profession of sentiment to be insincere, that he seldom, if ever, wrote a word either of affection or of compassion in any work intended for publication. The only exceptions that I have remarked are in the Drapier Letters, where he expresses an indignant pity for the sufferings of Ireland, and makes a lofty profession of the disinterestedness of his public spirit. The Journal to Stella was not intended for the public eye. There he indulges without constraint in infantine expressions of fondness: Stella is "sirrah Stella," "Stellakins," "rogue Stella," "pretty Stella," "MD," "little MD," "dearest MD," "dear, roguish, impudent, pretty MD."

> "How now, sirrah, must I write in a morning to your impudence?
>
> Stay till night
> And then I'll write
> In black and white
> By candle-light
> Of wax so bright
> It helps the sight
> A bite, a bite!
>
> Marry come up, Mrs Boldface."

---

[1] Sir W. Scott is more exact—"He never attempted any species of composition in which either the sublime or the pathetic were required of him. But in every department of poetry where wit is necessary, he displayed, as the subject chanced to require, either the blasting lightning of satire, or the lambent and meteor-like coruscations of frolicsome humour."

The Ludicrous.—He is pre-eminently a satirist; nobody can pretend to dispute his title of the prince of English Satirists.

In the ludicrous degradation of his victims, he makes no affectation of kindliness, and parades rather than disguises his contempt. Readers that are not subdued by the charms of his wit pronounce him coarse, insolent, unfeeling, and turn from his pages with aversion. This is one difference between him and Addison; they agree in being derisive rather than humorous.

From Addison he differs still more in the extent and force of his satire. Addison has a few pet objects of ridicule. Swift exempts from his ridicule no profession, no foible, hardly any institution, hardly any character. Clergymen, lawyers, doctors, authors, politicians, wits, demonstrative affection, coxcombry, the behaviour of ladies, bad manners, Popery, Presbyterianism, education, and, one may say in general, every individual that crosses his opinions—all come in for a cut of his stinging lash.

There are some fair specimens of insulting sarcasm among his 'Thoughts on various subjects:'—

"Query, whether churches are not dormitories of the living as well as of the dead?"

"Apollo was held the god of physic and sender of diseases. Both were originally the same trade, and still continue."

"The two maxims of any great man at court are, always to keep his countenance, and never to keep his word."

"A very little wit is valued in a woman, as we are pleased with a few words spoken plain by a parrot."

"A nice man is a man of nasty ideas."

"If the men of wit and genius would resolve never to complain in their works of critics and detractors, the next age would not know that they ever had any."

His advice "to a very young lady on her marriage" is an excellent specimen of rough sarcastic counsel, wholesome, but not in the slightest accommodated to the palate. See p. 362.

A very favourite stroke at the free-thinkers and the wits is to set forth ironically the advantages of the Church and of Christianity:—

"It is objected, as a very absurd, ridiculous custom, that a set of men should be suffered, much less employed and hired, to bawl one day in seven against the lawfulness of those methods most in use towards the pursuit of greatness, riches, and pleasure, which are the constant practice of all men alive on the other six. But the objection is, I think, a little unworthy of so refined an age as ours. Let us argue this matter calmly: I appeal to the breast of any polite free-thinker, whether, in the pursuit of gratifying a predominant passion, he has not always felt a wonderful incitement by reflecting that it was a thing forbidden; and therefore we see, in order to cultivate this taste, the wisdom of the nation has taken special care that the ladies should be furnished with prohibited silks, and the men with prohibited wine. And indeed it were to be wished that some other prohibitions were promoted, in order to improve the pleasures of the town; which, for want of such expedients, begin already, as I am told, to flag and grow languid, giving way daily to cruel inroads from the spleen."

He is dissatisfied with modern education:—

"From frequently reflecting upon the course and method of educating youth in this and a neighbouring kingdom, with the general success and consequence thereof, I am come to this determination; that education is always the worse in proportion to the wealth and grandeur of the parents; nor do I doubt in the least, that if the whole world were now under the dominion of one monarch (provided I might be allowed to choose where he should form the seat of his empire), the only son and heir of that monarch would be the worst educated mortal that ever was born since the creation; and I doubt the same proportion will hold through all degrees and titles, from an emperor downwards to the common gentry."

"Another hindrance to good education, and I think the greatest of any, is that pernicious custom in rich and noble families, of entertaining French tutors in their houses. These wretched pedagogues are enjoined by the father to take special care that the boy shall be perfect in his French; by the mother, that master must not walk till he is hot, nor be suffered to play with other boys, nor be wet in his feet, nor daub his clothes, and to see the dancing-master attends constantly and does his duty; the father insists that he be not kept too long poring on his book, because he is subject to sore eyes, and of a weakly constitution."

In his treatise on good manners, he is very contemptuous about the practice of duelling:—

"I should be exceedingly sorry to find the legislature make any new laws against the practice of duelling; because the methods are easy and many for a wise man to avoid a quarrel with honour, or engage in it with innocence. And I can discover no political evil in suffering bullies, sharpers, and rakes, to rid the world of each other by a method of their own, where the law has not been able to find an expedient."

By nature extremely impatient of whatever was troublesome, he hated over-civility. One of his Tatlers is a coarse exaggeration of overdone hospitality. When sneering at the multiplication of ceremonies, he relates a ridiculous accident, without caring to conceal names:—

"Monsieur Buys, the Dutch envoy, whose politics and manners were much of a size, brought a son with him, about thirteen years old, to a great table at Court. The boy and his father, whatever they put on their plates, they first offered round in order to every person in company; so that we could not get a minute's quiet during the whole dinner. At last their two plates happened to encounter, and with so much violence that, being china, they broke in twenty pieces, and stained half the company with wet sweatmeats and cream."

His personal sarcasms are very contemptuous. He alludes to Defoe as "the fellow that was pilloried, I forget his name." He is merciless on poor John Dennis:—

"One Dennis, commonly called 'the critic,' who had writ a threepenny pamphlet against the power of France, being in the country, and hearing of a French privateer hovering about the coast, although he were twenty miles from the sea, fled to town, and told his friends they need not wonder at his haste; for the King of France, having got intelligence where he was, had sent a privateer on purpose to catch him."

One of the special objects of his pitiless dislike was Burnet the historian. He ridiculed the 'History of my own Times' under the allegory of the 'Memoirs of P. P., Clerk of this Parish.' Swift's copy of the history has been preserved; the marginal comments are good specimens of the peculiar turn of his wit. I quote one or two as they are given in Collet's 'Relics of Literature:'—

Preface, p. 3. *Burnet.*—"Indeed, the peevishness, the ill-nature, and the ambition of many clergymen, have sharpened my spirits perhaps too much against them; so I *warn* my readers to take all that I say on those heads with some grains of allowance." *Swift.*—"I will take his *warning.*"

P. 28. *Burnet.*—"The Earl of Argyle was a more solemn sort of man, grave and sober, and free of all scandalous vices." *Swift.*—"As a man is free of a corporation, he means."

P. 5. *Burnet.*—"Upon the King's death, the Scots proclaimed his son king, and sent over Sir George Wincan, *that married my great aunt*, to treat with him while he was in the Isle of Jersey." *Swift.*—"Was *that* the reason why he was sent?"

P. 163. *Burnet* (speaking of 'Paradise Lost').—"It was esteemed the beautifullest and perfectest poem that ever was writ, at least in *our* language." *Swift.*—"A mistake! for it is in *English.*"

KINDS OF COMPOSITION.

Persuasion.—Swift's pamphlet on 'The Conduct of the Allies' is said to have told with unexampled effect; to have revolutionised public feeling, and overturned a powerful Ministry. For ten years, in union with Germany and Holland, we had fought against the succession of a French prince to the Spanish throne; we had won four splendid victories, and yet seemed in no hurry to make reasonable overtures of peace. Dazzled by Marlborough's success, the people had no suspicion that the war was protracted to fill his pockets. Swift's pamphlet changed the aspect of things as by enchantment; it was read everywhere, and raised popular indignation to such a height, that, within a year after its appearance, a new Government was formed, which concluded the famous Treaty of Utrecht.

Johnson thinks that "the efficacy of this wonder-working pamphlet was supplied by the passions of its readers; that it operated by the mere weight of facts with a very little assistance from the hand that produced them." But the art of the pamphleteer lay in bringing the popular passions into exercise—in picking out, and showing in strong light, facts that were escaping general notice—in relieving the public from the fascination of military success, and fixing their eyes on the other side of the picture.

If the 'Conduct of the Allies' gained its end by a skilful presentation of facts in a calm statement, the Drapier Letters were performances of a very different kind. A Mr Wood, a large owner of mines, had obtained from Government a patent for issuing, under certain regulations, a copper coinage of halfpence for Ireland. In Ireland, then as now, there was strong jealousy of England; and Swift, striking in against the project, took full advantage of the national feeling. The need of a copper coinage was glaring and urgent—he could say nothing on that score; but he represented that the Irish Houses of Parliament had previously requested leave to coin and issue the needful money, and had been refused. What was refused to the nobility and gentry of Ireland had been granted to this man—"a mean ordinary man, a hardware dealer." Swift makes no attempt to argue the justice of the proceeding. He heaps abuse upon Wood,[1] asserts against him audaciously groundless charges, pictures the most unreasonable consequences of the measure, and pours out hot appeals to the passions of his readers.

The following quotations illustrate the kind of reasoning he used. When to these ludicrous exaggerations of the inconvenience of exchange the simple answer was made that nobody would be obliged to take more than fivepence-halfpenny in copper, Swift blustered about confining the liberty of the subject. But for the strong feeling existing against England, which blinded the Irish to every consideration of reason, the Drapier would have been laughed at. As it was, had the Government refused to give way, his violent and hot exaggerations would have raised an armed rebellion, and his apparent patriotism made him a national hero:—

"Suppose you go to an alehouse with that base money, and the landlord gives you a quart for four of those halfpence, what must the victualler do? his brewer will not be paid in that coin; or, if the brewer should be such a fool, the farmers will not take it from them for their bere, because they are bound by their leases to pay their rent in good and lawful money of England; which this is not, nor of Ireland neither; and the 'squire their landlord will never be so bewitched to take such trash for his land; so that it must certainly stop somewhere or other; and wherever it stops, it is the same thing, and we are all undone."

"If a squire has a mind to come to town to buy clothes, and wine, and spices, for himself and family, or perhaps to pass the winter here, he must bring with him five or six horses well laden with sacks, as the farmers bring their corn; and when his lady comes in her coach to our shops, it must be followed by a car loaded with Mr Wood's money. And I hope we shall have the grace to take it for no more than it is worth."

---

[1] See p. 368.

"And let me in the next place apply myself particularly to you who are the poorer sort of tradesmen. Perhaps you may think you will not be so great losers as the rich if these halfpence should pass; because you seldom see any silver, and your customers come to your shops or stalls with nothing but brass, which you likewise find hard to be got. But you may take my word, whenever this money gains footing among you, you will be utterly undone. If you carry these halfpence to a shop for tobacco or brandy, or any other thing that you want, the shopkeeper will advance his goods accordingly, or else he must break and leave the key under the door. 'Do you think I will sell you a yard of tenpenny stuff for twenty of Mr Wood's halfpence? no, not under 200 at least; neither will I be at the trouble of counting, but weigh them in a lump.' I will tell you one thing further, that if Mr Wood's project should take, it would ruin even our beggars; for when I give a beggar a halfpenny, it will quench his thirst, or go a good way to fill his belly; but the twelfth part of a halfpenny will do him no more service than if I should give him three pins out of my sleeve."

JOSEPH ADDISON, 1672-1719.

Speaking of the age of William and Anne, Macaulay says—"There was, perhaps, never a time at which the rewards of literary merit were so splendid, at which men who could write well found such easy admittance into the most distinguished society, and to the highest honours of the State." Nobody profited more than Addison by this accident of the times. His abilities were very soon recognised by the Whig leaders. The son of Lancelot Addison, Rector of Lichfield, educated at Charterhouse and Magdalen College, Oxford, he was dissuaded from his design of entering the Church by Charles Montagu, afterwards Earl of Halifax, who procured him a pension from King William, and sent him to travel in France and Italy (1699-1702). Returning to England on the death of William, which had stopped his pension, he gained some reputation by a poem commemorating the victory of Blenheim (1704); and, having thus proved his value to a party, was in 1705 made Under-Secretary of State. Thereafter he held various political offices: was appointed Keeper of the Records of Ireland in 1709; Secretary to the Regency on the demise of Queen Anne in 1714; one of the Lords of Trade under George I.; one of the Chief Secretaries of State in 1717. From these high posts he drew a large income, while he had considerable leisure for writing. He died in 1719, leaving one daughter by the Countess Dowager of Warwick, whom he had married three years before, and who added little to his comfort while he was alive.

Addison's first prose composition, his 'Dialogues on Medals,' was written during his Continental travels. In 1702 he published an account of his travels in Italy, remarkable for happy allusions to ancient Roman history and literature. His fame as a prose writer rests on his contributions to periodical papers—

the 'Tatler,' the 'Spectator,' and the 'Guardian.' The 'Tatler' was commenced on April 12, 1709, by Sir Richard Steele, under the assumed name of Isaac Bickerstaff. Addison, who was then in Ireland, detected the author by a passage in the sixth number, and sent his first ascertained contribution to No. 20, May 26. The paper appeared three times a-week. Addison did not become a regular contributor till his return from Ireland in September. The last number of the 'Tatler' appeared on January 2, 1711. On the demise of the 'Tatler,' Steele projected the 'Spectator,' to be issued daily: it continued from March 1, 1711, to December 6, 1712, and during all that time Addison was a frequent contributor, writing more than half of the numbers. The 'Guardian,' also a daily paper, extended from March 12 to October 1, 1713; Addison's contributions were chiefly to the later numbers. In 1714 came out what is known as the Eighth Volume of the 'Spectator;' of this nearly all the first half was written by Addison.

The 'Tatler,' the 'Spectator,' and the 'Guardian' formerly excluded politics; their professed purpose was to discuss the fashions and manners of society, the pulpit, the theatre, the opera, and general literature; in short, they were open to all the subjects now discussed in the 'Saturday Review,' the 'Spectator,' or the 'Examiner,' except politics. In this respect they differed from the 'Review' of Defoe, the real prototype of modern periodicals. But while they excluded politics in form, Addison, as we shall see, in many of his papers was in no small degree influenced by political prejudices.

Besides these universally-known performances, Addison wrote some strictly political papers: in 1707, a pamphlet on the 'Present State of the War;' the 'Whig Examiner,' a weekly tract, not carried beyond the fifth number; the 'Trial of Count Tariff,' a satire on the commercial treaty of Utrecht, 1713; and 'The Freeholder,' a bi-weekly, carried through 55 numbers, 1715-16.

Addison's personal appearance has not been very vividly recorded. Thackeray speaks of "his chiselled features, pure and cold." We know also that he was a fair man, of a full habit of body, soft and flabby from wine-bibbing and want of exercise. He was so weakly a child that he was christened on the day of his birth, not being expected to live.

The most general characteristic of his intellect is happily expressed by Johnson—"He thinks justly, but he thinks faintly." He is a great contrast to the prolific and vigorous Defoe. Not only had he little spontaneous activity of intellect, little impulsiveness: this might be said of the cautious and sober Temple. More than this, he had not sufficient constitutional energy to be equal to the mere effort requisite for forming a clear and profound judgment on any question of difficulty. With his languid vitality, he was content to be superficial. He had naturally a fine memory for words, and was, in his quiet way, an accurate observer of what passed before him. His chief intellectual exercise was the study of "putting things"—whether things that he had seen and heard, reflections that he had made upon them, or thoughts that he had met with in the course of his reading. He had neither scholarship nor original thought—"a fine gentleman living upon town, not professing any deep scholastic knowledge of literature," and employing his leisure in writing elegant periodical articles.[1]

Like Cowley, he had no depth of sentiment for imagination to work upon. Not only so, but he was deficient in constitutional power of enjoyment; he was by nature shy, irritable, and captious, sitting in company reserved and taciturn, until his cups had raised him to the point of geniality. Even his panegyrist Thackeray admits—"I do not think Addison's heart melted very much, or that he indulged very inordinately in the 'vanity of grieving.'" "This great man was also one of the lonely ones of the world." The chief emotion that he cultivated may be described in the words of Johnson as "gay malevolence and satirical humour:" the malevolence being due to his constitutional incapacity for enjoyment—to ill-nature, in the strict sense of the words; while the gaiety or humour arises chiefly from the delicate elegance of his language, and the writer's pleasure in the exercise of his gift. His essays on Milton and on the Pleasures of the Imagination would seem to show that, though he had not energy to write with sublimity himself,[2] he enjoyed sublime writing when it was presented to him; he could at least utter the formula of indolent admiration—"There is a pleasure in what is great, in what is beautiful, and in what is new."

Although engaged in politics, he had no natural gifts for active

[1] "With reference to Addison in particular, it is time to correct the popular notion of his literary character, or at least to mark it by severer lines of distinction. It is already pretty well known that Addison had no very intimate acquaintance with the literature of his own country. It is known, also, that he did not think such an acquaintance any ways essential to the character of an elegant scholar and *littérateur*. Quite enough he found it, and more than enough for the time he had to spare, if he could maintain a tolerable familiarity with the foremost Latin poets, and a very slender one indeed with the Grecian. *How* slender, we can see in his Travels."—De Quincey, xv. 8.

[2] "Though Addison generally hated the impassioned, and shrank from it as from a fearful thing, yet this was when it combined with forms of life and fleshly realities (as in dramatic works), but not when it combined with elder forms of eternal abstractions. Hence he did not read, and did not like, Shakspeare—the music was here too rapid and lifelike; but he sympathised profoundly with the solemn cathedral-chanting of Milton. An appeal to his sympathies which exacted quick changes in those sympathies he could not meet, but a more stationary key of solemnity he *could*."—De Quincey, vii. 56. This is explained by his want of constitutional energy, and consequent incapability of supporting excitement.

life. He could not have made his own position; the accident of the times rendered literary service valuable, and he was virtually nothing more than the literary retainer and *protégé* of the leaders of a party. His easy indolent habits, with some other features of his character, appear in the following sketch by Johnson:—

"Of the course of Addison's familiar day, before his marriage, Pope has given a detail. He had in the house with him Budgell, and perhaps Philips. His chief companions were Steele, Budgell, Philips [Ambrose], Carey, Davenant, and Colonel Brett. With one or other of these he always breakfasted. He studied all morning; then dined at a tavern; and went afterwards to Button's. Button had been a servant in the Countess of Warwick's family, who, under the patronage of Addison, kept a coffee-house on the south side of Russell Street, about two doors from Covent Garden. Here it was that the wits of the time used to assemble. It is said, when Addison had suffered any vexation from the Countess, he withdrew the company from Button's house. From the coffee-house he went again to a tavern, where he often sat late, and drank too much wine. In the bottle discontent seeks for comfort, cowardice for courage, and bashfulness for confidence. It is not unlikely that Addison was first seduced to excess by the manumission which he obtained from the servile timidity of his sober hours."

His conduct generally was marked by great prudence. He made few enemies. He was at great pains to conciliate Swift. "Of his virtue it is a sufficient testimony that the resentment of party has transmitted no charge of any crime." Yet his irritable temper was not under thorough control. On one occasion he put an execution in force against Steele for a hundred pounds that his improvident friend had borrowed, and he has never been cleared of the charge of jealous intriguing against Pope. De Quincey, in his 'Life of Pope,' says that "Addison's petty manœuvring against Pope proceeded entirely from malignant jealousy. That Addison was more in the wrong even than has generally been supposed, and Pope more thoroughly innocent as well as more generous, we have the means at a proper opportunity of showing decisively."

Opinions.—In practical politics he adhered steadfastly to the Whigs. In 1707 he elaborately justified the war with France, maintaining that France and Britain were natural enemies. He strongly supported the Hanoverian succession, and turned his most malicious and unqualified ridicule against the "Pretender" and his foreign adherents. With equal animosity he satirised the Tory country gentlemen, or Tory fox-hunters, as he delighted to nickname them.

Party politics, as we have said, had no place in the 'Tatler,' the 'Spectator,' and the 'Guardian.' The professed object of our author in these periodicals was "to banish vice and ignorance out of the territories of Great Britain," and "to bring philosophy out of closets and libraries, schools and colleges, to dwell in clubs and assemblies, at tea-tables and coffee-houses."

The minor immoralities that he attacked were such as affectation, presumption, foppery, fashionable extravagance, upstart vulgarity. As "vices" of the same class, he contrived to satirise the rustic manners of the objects of his constant aversion, the Tory squires, "who had never seen anything greater than themselves for twenty years."

In criticising polite literature, he gave his opinions on the Opera, on Tragedy, on True and False Wit, on Sappho, on Ovid, on Milton, and on the Pleasures of the Imagination. He "decided by taste rather than by principles;" and the taste of such a man, while elegant in the highest degree, had a tendency to be captious and narrow. He sneered at the scenery and stage-machinery both of the opera and of the theatre, considering that the effect upon the audience should be produced mainly by the language of the play. He ridiculed the use of Italian in the opera; for which De Quincey makes some game of him. Under False Wit he reckoned Puns, Anagrams, Acrostics, Chronograms, Crambo, and other agreeable ingenuities. In the case of Milton, his application of Aristotle's rules for epic poetry, and his selection of fine passages, have the credit of first drawing general notice to 'Paradise Lost.'[1] His papers on the Pleasures of the Imagination have no analytic value; he gets no farther than that there is a pleasure in beholding the great, the beautiful, and the new.

ELEMENTS OF STYLE.

Vocabulary.—Were we to judge from the papers on Milton, we should pronounce Addison's command of language rather under than above the average of eminent literary men.[2] He is constantly repeating the same epithets "inexpressibly beautiful," "wonderfully poetical," "wonderfully fine and pleasing." Upon lighter themes his vocabulary is more varied. Choiceness and not profusion is at all times his characteristic; yet we find him varying his expression with the greatest ease on simple themes. Thus, in his paper in the 'Lover' upon the female passion for china-ware, he describes it with considerable variety—"brittle ware," "frail furniture," "perishable commodity," "all china-ware is of a weak and transitory nature," "the fragility of china is such as a reasonable being ought by no means to set its heart upon."

[1] It is sometimes said that Addison was the first to discern Milton's excellence. This is saying too much. Defoe had praised Milton several years before; and Steele, in one of his early 'Tatlers,' had expressed his admiration.

[2] Lord Lytton is of opinion that Addison's command of expression was not first-rate.

Sentences.—Among our classic prose writers, Addison is the standing example of a loose style. He is ostentatiously easy and flowing, making no effort to be periodic, but rather studiously avoiding the periodic structure. In his expository papers, when he is not expressly aiming at point, he takes the utmost freedom in adding clauses of explanation and amplification after he has made a full statement. Thus—

"Everything that is new or uncommon raises a pleasure in the imagination, because it fills the soul with an agreeable surprise, gratifies its curiosity, and gives it an idea of which it was not before possest. We are indeed so often conversant with one set of objects, and tired out with so many repeated shows of the same things, that whatever is new or uncommon contributes a little to vary human life, and to divert our minds for a while, with the strangeness of its appearance: it serves us for a kind of refreshment, and takes off from that satiety we are apt to complain of in our usual and ordinary entertainments."

Here the structure is very loose, and the easy way of adding clause to clause betrays the writer into not a little confusion, which we shall notice in the proper place. The following is another example of a loose tautologous sentence:—

"They here began to breathe a delicious kind of ether, and saw all the fields about them covered with a kind of purple light, that made them reflect with satisfaction on their past toils, and diffused a secret joy through the whole assembly, which showed itself in every look and feature."

The vice of this careless structure, which within proper limits is not without its advantages, is the misplacing of clauses. The two following examples are from Irving's 'Elements of Composition:'—

"This kind of wit was very much in vogue among our countrymen, about an age or two ago, who did not practise it for any oblique reason, but purely for the sake of being witty."

Here the clause "about an age or two ago" comes very awkwardly between the relative and its antecedent, and would be much better disposed of at the beginning—"About an age or two ago, this kind of wit," &c.

"The Knight, seeing his habitation reduced to so small a compass, and himself in a manner shut out of his own house, upon the death of his mother, ordered all the apartments to be flung open, and exorcised by his chaplain."

Irving remarks that here the clause "upon the death of his mother" is so placed as to be ambiguous, and proposes to remedy this by another arrangement—namely, "seeing his habitation, &c., the Knight, upon the death of his mother, ordered all the apartments," &c. This gets rid of the ambiguity, but is rather a clumsy arrangement; it would be better to begin with the clause of time—"Upon the death of his mother, the Knight," &c.

It is chiefly in the papers on the Pleasures of the Imagination that the inconvenience of this loose style is felt, and there chiefly because it goes along with a vague and rambling train of thought. On a light theme he is often smart and pointed, as will be sufficiently illustrated in the examples of his Wit.

Even in the expository papers there are occasional touches of pointed expression. In the following we see two forms of expression that are very largely used by Johnson:—

"A man of a polite imagination is let into a great many pleasures that the vulgar are not capable of receiving. *He can converse with a picture and find an agreeable companion in a statue.* He meets with a secret refreshment in a description, *and often feels a greater satisfaction in the prospect of fields and meadows than another does in the possession.*"

Sometimes, but not often, he makes the effort of a careful balanced comparison. The following comparison between Homer and Virgil is from a paper where he exhibits Homer, Virgil, and Ovid as specimens respectively of "what is great, what is beautiful, and what is new." It is a much simpler comparison than either Temple's or Pope's, being more superficial—dealing with fewer circumstances; besides, it is less just, the facts being adapted to suit the author's theory:—

"Homer is in his province when he is describing a battle or a multitude, a hero or a god. Virgil is never better pleased than when he is in his Elysium or carrying out an entertaining picture. Homer's epithets generally mark out what is great, Virgil's what is agreeable. Nothing can be more magnificent than the figure Jupiter makes in the first Iliad, nor more charming than that of Venus in the first Æneid." [Here the passages are quoted]. "Homer's persons are most of them godlike and terrible; Virgil has scarce admitted any into his poem who are not beautiful, and has taken particular care to make his hero so—

And gave his rolling eyes a sparkling grace,
And breathed a youthful vigour on his face.

In a word, Homer fills his readers with sublime ideas, and, I believe, has raised the imagination of all the good poets that have come after him. I shall only instance Horace, who immediately takes fire at the first hint of any passage in the 'Iliad' or 'Odyssey,' and always rises above himself when he has Homer in his view. Virgil has drawn together, into his 'Æneid,' all the pleasing scenes his subject is capable of admitting; and in his 'Georgics,' has given us a collection of the most delightful landscapes that can be made out of fields and woods, herds of cattle, and swarms of bees."

QUALITIES OF STYLE.

Simplicity has always been alleged as a great merit of Addison's style—"familiar," says the imperious dictator, "but not coarse." "His prose is the model of the middle style; on grave subjects not formal, on light occasions not grovelling, pure without scrupulosity, and exact without apparent elaboration; always equable, always easy, without glowing words or pointed sentences. Addison never deviates from his track to snatch a grace; he seeks no ambitious ornaments, and tries no hazardous innovations."

To this merit in the expository papers, there are considerable drawbacks. I would not insist with De Quincey on his superficial treatment of Milton and of the Imagination. It is probably but a slight exaggeration to say that he was "the man of all that ever lived most hostile even to what was good in pedantry, to its tendencies towards the profound in erudition, towards minute precision, and the non-popular; . . . the champion of all that is easy, natural, superficial." And it is but fair to say, that if, as he boasted, he brought "Philosophy out of closets and libraries, schools and colleges, to dwell in clubs and assemblies, at tea-tables and coffee-houses," it certainly was Philosophy in a very diluted form. But in a periodical such as the 'Spectator' the superficiality and dilution were not out of place; "an instructor like Addison was now wanting, whose remarks, being superficial, might be easily understood, and being just, might prepare the mind for more attainments."

Still, it should be possible, without going into more abstruse considerations, to make such papers as those on the Pleasures of the Imagination not only more accurate, but even more intelligible and more easily remembered.

One great improvement in the way of rendering the papers more perspicuous would be to state explicitly their real character; to lower their pretensions; to declare them to be not a philosophic explanation of æsthetic pleasures, but an enumeration of objects that give pleasure to the imagination as being great, beautiful, or new. Were this done, the reader would go on smoothly:—receiving first an account of pleasing objects in nature; then in artificial works, gardens, and buildings; then in the Fine Arts, statuary, painting, music, poetry, history, natural philosophy. Once aware that the papers were nothing more than a catalogue of things "apt to affect the imagination," the reader could pass lightly over the moral reflections and crude attempts at deeper explanation, as being but irregular excrescences upon the plan.

Such, we say, is the real character and value of the papers—the divisions become simple only when looked upon in this light; and had the author consulted the ease and instruction of the reader, he would have indicated this at the beginning, and repeated the indication as he went on. But the truth is that he did not know their real character—he imagined he was going deeper than he really went; and in perplexing the reader with a futile straining after explanation, he was but repeating his own perplexity.

A good deal might be done to make the papers more *exact*, without going deeper into the matter.

His statements are frequently ambiguous. For example—

"The prettiest landscape I ever saw was one drawn on the walls of a dark room, which stood opposite on one side to a navigable river, and on the other to a park."

This gives as good an opening for ingenious conjecture as the most involved passages in the ancient classics; a collection of such passages would be no mean substitute for classical discipline of the ingenuity. At first sight one wonders how he could see a picture in a dark room, and what the river and the park had to do with it. If the ingenious student refer to the context,[1] he may be able to see the meaning without the help of a commentator; but if so, he must be very ingenious indeed. As an example not so hopelessly puzzling, but very misleading, take the following opening of one of the Essays, marking an important transition in the subject:—

"I at first divided the pleasures of the imagination into such as arise from objects that are actually before our eyes, or that once entered in at our eyes, and are afterwards called up into the mind either barely by its own operations, or on occasion of something without us, as statues or descriptions. We have already considered the first division, and shall therefore enter on the other, which, for distinction sake, I have called the secondary pleasures of the imagination."

The first sentence states the two divisions: let the reader try to discover them without reading through the whole paper, and the chances are that the expression misleads him. Without attempting to recast the sentence, which might lead to an irrelevant scrutiny of the division itself, the following modification will make the meaning plainer:—

"I at first divided the pleasures of the imagination into such as arise from objects that are actually before our eyes, *and such as arise from objects* that, once *having* entered in at our eyes, are afterwards," &c.

Another breach of accuracy, too, often committed in these papers on the Imagination, is to repeat the same statement in a different form as if it were a different statement. Look back for an example of this tautology to a passage quoted among the Sentences (p. 378)—"Everything that is new or uncommon," &c. In the first sentence three expressions are identical, and the fourth is only slightly different—"new or uncommon raises a pleasure in the imagination," "fills the soul with an agreeable surprise,' "gratifies its curiosity," "gives it an idea of which it was not

[1] Spectator, No. 414. The Essays on the Imagination are reprinted separately.

before possest:" — yet the three last of those expressions are given as the explanation of the first. So much confused feebleness we discover when we take the sentence to pieces with charitable latitude — "a novelty is agreeable when it is agreeable." Were we to take the sentence in its grammatical strictness, we should find him affirming a more questionable principle—namely, that "every novelty is agreeable." The second sentence in this passage is equally unfitted for close examination.

He makes comparatively little use of contrast for the purpose of giving clearness to his views. This makes his pages smoother reading for such as are averse to the trouble of close thinking and dislike squareness of form; but it is no small drawback to perspicuity. At least when he does make a contrast, the form ought to be clear, and very often it is not. Thus—

"By greatness I do not only mean the bulk of any single object, but the largeness of a whole view"—

should be—

"By greatness I mean not only the bulk of a single object, but the largeness of a whole view;"

or, more perspicuously—

"I apply the term greatness to a whole view as well as to a single object."

Again—

"I must confess, after having surveyed the antiquities about Naples and Rome, I cannot but think that our admiration of them *does not so much arise out of their greatness as uncommonness.*"

This should be—"Arises not so much from their greatness as from their uncommonness."

Take yet another example of this careless use of the forms of contrast—

"There is as much difference between comprehending a thought clothed in Cicero's language, and that of an ordinary writer, as between seeing an object by the light of a taper and the light of the sun."

Here the form of the expression implies exactly the opposite of what he means.

Sometimes, from an affectation of polite ease, he does not choose the aptest word. Thus—

"Those who look into Homer are surprised to find his battles still rising one above another, and *improving in horror* to the conclusion of the 'Iliad.' Milton's *fight* of the angels is wrought up with the same *beauty.*"

Such improprieties are a source of feebleness rather than of confusion. As a rule, Addison's papers, particularly those on lighter themes, are distinguished by the aptness of the phraseology. The chief thing that tempts him to err is the study of elegance.

Strength is not a feature of Addison's prose. He has neither sublimity nor vigour: "a model" as Johnson says, "of the middle style," "always equable, always easy, without glowing words or pointed sentences."

In the matter of *Pathos* he is very unlike his warm-hearted coadjutor Steele.

The Ludicrous.—It is upon the witty vein in his writings that Addison's fame is durably founded. His elegant satires on the manners of his time will be read with delight when his grave essays are glanced at as productions that made no small noise on their first appearance, but were too superficial to be permanent.

He is the great English example of polite ridicule. The poignancy of his sarcasm is so disguised and softened by elegance of language, ingenuity of wit, and affectation of kindliness, that he is often pointed out as a crowning instance of amiable humour. The error would probably have less often been committed had he not been conjoined with Steele, a writer of genuinely amiable humour. However that may be, it is an error, and one that needs little discernment for its discovery. Not a single paper of Addison's can be pointed out that does not contain some stroke of malice—"gay malevolence," perhaps, but nevertheless malevolence. The wit and polish are exquisite. The satire is usually pointed at classes, and not at individuals; if it is pointed at individuals, they are not real personages, but imaginary types of classes. He sometimes affects kindliness for the object of his shafts. All these arts keep the sufferer out of view, and enable us to enjoy the witty sallies without scruple. Still, in characterising his humour, the critic must not sink the fact that it is at basis malicious—it is "humorous satire." If we call it amiable humour, we must remember that it is a kind of humour that may be amiable to the reader or hearer, but is far from appearing amiable to the object.

In exemplifying his satire, we shall follow the order of Criticism, Politics, and Society.

In No. 5 of the 'Spectator,' he opens his batteries on the scenery and stage-machinery of the opera:—

"As I was walking in the streets about a fortnight ago, I saw an ordinary fellow carrying a cage full of little birds upon his shoulder; and, as I was wondering with myself what use he would put them to, he was met very luckily by an acquaintance, who had the same curiosity. Upon his asking him what he had upon his shoulder, he told him that he had been buying sparrows for the opera. 'Sparrows for the opera,' says his friend, licking his lips, 'what, are they to be roasted?' 'No, no,' says the other, 'they are to enter towards the end of the first Act, and to fly about the stage.' This strange dialogue awakened my curiosity so far, that I immediately bought the opera, by which means I perceived that the sparrows were to act the part of singing-birds in a delightful grove; though upon a nearer enquiry I found the sparrows put the same trick upon the audience that Sir Martin Mar-all practised upon his mistress; for though they flew in sight, the music proceeded from a consort of flageolots and bird-calls which were planted behind the scenes. . . . But to return to the sparrows; there have been so many flights of them let loose in this opera, that it is feared the house will never get rid of them; and that in other plays they make their entrance in very improper scenes, so as to be seen flying in a lady's bed-chamber, or perching upon a king's throne; besides the inconveniences which the heads of the audience may sometimes suffer from them."

Writing of English translations of Italian operas, and maliciously remarking on the blunders of the translators, he says:—

"I remember an Italian verse that ran thus word for word—

And turned my rage into pity;

which the English for rhyme sake translated—

And into pity turned my rage.

By this means the soft notes that were adapted to *pity* in the Italian, fell upon the word *rage* in the English, and the angry sounds that were turned to *rage* in the original were made to express *pity* in the translation. It oftentimes happened likewise, that the finest notes in the air fell upon the most insignificant words in the sentence. I have known the word *and* pursued through the whole gamut, have been entertained with many a melodious *the*, and have heard the most beautiful graces, quavers, and divisions bestowed upon *them*, *for*, and *from*, to the eternal honour of our English particles."

This exquisitely-worded criticism is somewhat malicious towards the poor singers and their audience; the satire was no doubt wholesome, and the arch satirist could plead the sanction of good sense, but there is not much amiability in the spirit of such ridicule. His ridicule of the Tory squires is by no means so delicate. He had carefully studied the character, with the sharp insight of inveterate dislike, and exposes all the weak points of their rusticity with unmerciful exaggeration. One of his first contributions to the 'Tatler' is an account of a visit paid him in his own apartment by Sir Harry Quickset, Sir Giles Wheelbarrow, Knight, Thomas Rentfree, Esquire, Justice of the Quorum, Andrew Windmill, Esquire, and Mr Nicholas Doubt, of the Inner Temple, Sir Harry's grandson. He had been forewarned of his distinguished company by a letter from Sir Harry's steward:—

"The hour of nine was come this morning, and I had no sooner set chairs, by the steward's letter, and fixed my tea-equipage, but I heard a knock at my door, which was opened, but no one entered; after which followed a long silence, which was broke at last by, 'Sir, I beg your pardon, I think I know better;' and another voice, 'Nay, good Sir Giles.' I looked out from my window, and saw the good company all with their hats off, and arms spread, offering the door to each other. . . . But they are now got to my chamber-door, and I saw my old friend Sir Harry enter. I met him with all the respect due to so reverend a vegetable; for, you are to know, that is my sense of a person who remains idle in the same place for half a century. I got him with great success into his chair by the fire, without throwing down any of my cups. . . . I had the misfortune, as they stood

> cheek by jowl, to desire the squire to sit down before the justice of the quorum, to the no small satisfaction of the former, and resentment of the latter." [On the squire's refusing to take tea, the steward proposed an adjournment to some public-house.] "We all stood up in an instant, and Sir Harry filed off from the left, very discreetly, countermarching behind the chairs towards the door. After him, Sir Giles in the same manner. The simple squire made a sudden start to follow; but the justice of the quorum whipped between upon the stand of the stairs. A maid going up with coals, made us halt, and put us into such confusion that we stood all in a heap, without any visible possibility of recovering our order. . . . We were fixed in this perplexity for some time, until we heard a very loud noise in the street; and Sir Harry asking what it was, I, to make them move, said 'it was fire.' Upon this, all ran down as fast as they could, without order or ceremony, into the street, where we drew up in very good order, and filed off down Steer Lane; the impertinent templar driving us before him as in a string, and pointing to his acquaintance who passed by."

Another of his rustic characters in the 'Tatler' is Tom Bellfrey, the fox-hunter, who gives an imitation of a fox-chase in a London drawing-room, and "calls all the neighbouring parishes into the square." The most frequently quoted of these caricatures is the "Tory Fox-hunter," drawn with unsparing skill in the 'Freeholder.' Upon this character Dr Nathan Drake remarks:—

> "The character of the Tory Fox-hunter is, it must be confessed, in every respect less amiable and respectable than that of Sir Roger de Coverley; we neither love nor esteem him; for, instead of the sweet and benevolent temper of the knight, we are here presented with a vulgar, rough, and totally uneducated squire, whose credulity and absurd prejudices are not softened down or relieved by those mild and tender feelings which so greatly endear to us almost every incident in the life of Sir Roger."

Yet Addison's share in the character of Sir Roger is really a caricature of rusticity, not one whit better-natured than the Fox-hunter. We shall notice more fully, in treating of Steele, that "the sweet and benevolent temper," "the mild and tender feelings," are Steele's contributions to the character of the knight. This is not the only instance where Addison has profited by his alliance with Steele.

His character of Will Wimble is a sharp and considerably overcharged satire on the younger sons of the aristocracy. While he professes deep compassion that "so good a heart and such busy hands were wholly employed in trifles," he exposes those trifling occupations with anything but a loving hand. Will "generally lives with his elder brother *as superintendent of his game;*" "is extremely well versed in all the little handicrafts *of an idle man;*" "is a good-natured, *officious* fellow;" "carries a tulip-root in his pocket from one to another, or exchanges a puppy between a couple of friends that live perhaps in the opposite sides of the country." This is said to be "the case of many a younger brother of a great family, who had rather see their children starve like gentlemen, than thrive in a trade or profession that is beneath their quality." To profess compassion after drawing such a picture is to add keenness to the sting.

Of his satires on society, very short examples must suffice. Any of his papers will illustrate the poignancy of the strokes, and the exceeding delicacy and ingenuity of the expression. Perhaps the most characteristic examples of this vein of his satire are seen in his delicate application of caustic to the foibles of women. He was animated by nothing like Steele's chivalrous gallantry towards the sex. Take the following on the female passion for china, his contribution to Steele's short-lived 'Lover:'—

"There are no inclinations in women which more surprise me than their passions for chalk and china. The first of these maladies wears out in a little time; but when a woman is visited with the second, it generally takes possession of her for life. China vessels are playthings for women of all ages. An old lady of fourscore shall be as busy in cleaning an Indian mandarin, as her great-granddaughter is in dressing her baby.

"The common way of purchasing such trifles, if I may believe my female informers, is by exchanging old suits of clothes for this brittle ware. The potters of China have, it seems, their factors at this distance, who retail out their several manufactures for cast clothes and superannuated garments. I have known an old petticoat metamorphosed into a punch-bowl, and a pair of breeches into a teapot," &c.

In this example the wit is not quite worthy of Addison, and the derision borders on coarseness. As an extreme contrast, take a passage from the exquisitely graceful paper on the 'Use of the Fan:'—

"Women are armed with fans, as men with swords, and sometimes do more execution with them. To the end therefore that ladies may be entire mistresses of the weapon which they bear, I have erected an academy for the training up of young women in the exercise of the fan, according to the most fashionable airs and motions that are now practised at Court. The ladies who *carry* fans under me are drawn up twice a-day in my great hall, where they are instructed in the use of their arms, and *exercised* by the following words of command:—

Handle your fans,
Unfurl your fans,
Discharge your fans,
Ground your fans,
Recover your fans,
Flutter your fans,

By the right observation of these few plain words of command, a woman of a tolerable genius who will apply herself diligently to her exercise for the space of but one half-year, shall be able to give her fan all the graces that can possibly enter into that little modish machine.

. . . . "The *Fluttering of the Fan* is the last, and indeed the masterpiece of the whole exercise; but if a lady does not misspend her time, she may make herself mistress of it in three months. I generally lay aside the dog-days and the hot time of the summer for the teaching this part of the exercise, for as soon as ever I pronounce *Flutter your Fans*, the place is filled with so many zephyrs and gentle breezes as are very refreshing in that season of the year, though they might be dangerous to ladies of a tender constitution in any other.

"There is an infinite variety of motions to be made use of in the Flutter of a Fan: there is the angry flutter, the modest flutter, the timorous flutter, the confused flutter, the merry flutter, and the amorous flutter. Not to be tedious, there is scarce any emotion in the mind which does not produce a suitable agitation in the fan; insomuch, that if I only see the fan of a disciplined lady, I know very well whether she laughs, frowns, or blushes."

Not content with satirising the ladies of his own generation, he carries his cynical raillery of the sex into imaginary generations before the Flood. In his papers on the loves of Shalum and Hilpah, the humour receives a satirical turn from the imputation of unworthy motives to Hilpah.

Besides the redeeming graces of expression, two things may be urged in extenuation of the malicious or satirical basis of Addison's wit. First, his ridicule is not personal; it is aimed at what the author takes to be vice, folly, or bad taste, not at an actual offender. Secondly, "it is justly observed by Tickell that he employed wit on the side of virtue and religion."

Melody.—A good deal of Johnson's panegyric of Addison's style is really the picture of an ideal to which, in his opinion, Addison approaches; but many of the particulars are happy, and none more so than this—that "it was his principal endeavour to avoid all harshness and severity of diction; he is therefore sometimes verbose in his transitions and connections, and sometimes descends too much to the language of conversation." The melodious flow of the diction is a very striking quality of our author's style; and doubtless his endeavour after this beauty accounts for many of his sins against precision. In the Appendix to Bain's 'Rhetoric,' a passage is analysed with a view to this quality, and it is traced to the fewness of abrupt consonants or harsh combinations, the variety of the vowels, and "the rhythmical construction, or the alternation of long and short, emphatic and unemphatic sounds."

Taste.—Elegance is the ruling quality of Addison's style. He sacrifices everything to the unctuous junction of syllables, and the harmonious combination of ideas. The pedantic scholarship of Taylor, the rough vigour and profusion of Barrow, are illustrative by extreme contrast. But we might go the round of our great writers without finding such another example of superficial smoothness. We have remarked the studied refinement of Temple; but in Temple refinement is united with majesty and depth of feeling. Cowley's diction is studied, and his thoughts light and trivial; but as compared with Addison, his rhythm is often awkward and stumbling, his fancy exuberant, and his ridicule bare and undisguised.

The following is at once an illustration of his elegant treatment of a theme that might easily be made pedantic, and an example of the principles that guided his own composition:—

"Allegories, when well chosen, are like so many tracks of light in a discourse, that make everything about them clear and beautiful. A noble metaphor, when it is placed to an advantage, casts a kind of glory round it, and darts a lustre through a whole sentence. These different kinds of allusion are but so many different manners of similitude, and that they may please the imagination, the likeness ought to be very exact, or very agreeable, as we love to see a picture where the resemblance is just, or the posture and air graceful. But we often find eminent writers very faulty in this respect; great scholars are apt to fetch their comparisons and allusions from the sciences in which they are most conversant, so that a man may see the compass of their learning in a treatise on the most indifferent subject. I have read a discourse upon love which none but a profound chymist could understand, and have heard many a sermon that should only have been preached before a congregation of Cartesians. On the contrary, your men of business usually have recourse to such instances as are too mean and familiar. They are for drawing the reader into a game of chess or tennis, or for leading him from shop to shop, in the cant of particular trades and employments. It is certain there may be found an infinite variety of very agreeable allusions in both these kinds; but for the generality, the most entertaining ones lie in the works of nature, which are obvious to all capacities, and more delightful than what is to be found in arts and sciences."

SIR RICHARD STEELE, 1675-1729.

"When Mr Addison was abroad," writes Thackeray, "and after he came home in rather a dismal way to wait upon Providence in his shabby lodging in the Haymarket, young Captain Steele was cutting a much smarter figure than that of his classical friend of Charterhouse Cloister and Maudlin Walk." Steele, born in Dublin, of English parents, was also a Charterhouse boy and an Oxonian, his college being Merton. A gay, impetuous youth, overflowing with wit and good-nature, and fond of company, he yet gained some celebrity as a scholar, and before he graduated had written a poem and a comedy. When he had to choose a profession he fixed upon the army; and his friends refusing to buy him a commission, he enlisted as a private in the Horse Guards. His wit making him a general favourite, he had, by the year 1701, been promoted to the rank of captain in the Fusiliers. He is said to have passed a dissipated and reckless life: he "probably wrote and sighed for Bracegirdle, went home tipsy, in many a chair, after many a bottle, in many a tavern—fled from many a bailiff." But if this debauchery was as bad as has been represented, in the midst of it all he kept up his literary tastes. In 1701 he published 'The Christian Hero,' a curious production for a dissipated officer, and an indication of the sinning and repenting character of the man. In the following year he produced a comedy, 'The Funeral, or, Grief à la Mode,' a satire on hired mourners and will-making lawyers. By the death of King William he lost his chances of promotion in the army, and turned all his powers to literature and politics. In 1703 appeared his comedy of 'The Tender Husband;' in 1704 the 'Lying Lovers,' a piece too tame and moralising to succeed on the stage of those days. About 1705, through the influence of his friend Addison, he was appointed Gazetteer—"the lowest Minister of State," as he facetiously styled himself. We shall not follow the windings of his fortunes chronologically. His literary projects were—'The Tatler,' 'The Spectator,' 'The Guardian,' and 'The Lover,' already mentioned; 'The Englishman' and 'The Crisis,' 1714 (two intense political pamphlets, which led to his expulsion from the House of Commons); 'The Reader,' 1714, also political, like Addison's 'Whig Examiner,' an opposition print to the Tory 'Examiner;' occasional political and anti-Popery tracts; a collection of his political writings, 1715; 'The Town-Talk,' 'The Tea-Table,' 'The Chit-Chat,' short-lived periodicals, 1716; in 1719 'The Plebeian,' which was opposed by Addison in the 'Old Whig,' and produced a quarrel between the two friends; 'The Theatre,' a periodical, 1719-20, under the feigned name of Sir John Edgar; 'The Conscious Lovers,' his best comedy, 1722. His Government appointments were, after the Gazetteership, Commissionership of Stamps, 1710; Surveyorship of the Royal Stables at Hampton Court, and Governorship of the Royal Company of Comedians, 1715; Commissionership of Forfeited Estates in Scotland, 1717.

His personal appearance would seem to have been rather unfavourable. The satirical portrait by John Dennis is said by Thackeray to bear "a dreadful resemblance" to the original—"Sir John Edgar, of the county of ——, in Ireland, is of a middle stature, broad shoulders, thick legs, a shape like the picture of somebody over a farmer's chimney—a short chin, a short nose, a short forehead, a broad flat face, and a dusky countenance."

As we may judge from this picture, he possessed great bodily energy, and his constitutional vigour supported him in the heartiest enjoyment of life. Living in a whirl of social dissipation, he yet, as Gazetteer, as editor of periodicals, and in other offices, went through a great deal of worrying business; and in the hurry of his active life was constantly snatching moments to despatch little notes to his "dearest Prue." Of these affectionate billets, Mrs Steele preserved no less than 400.

His intellect was of a rougher cast than his friend's. It is the emotional character of the man that renders him interesting, and entitles him to a good secondary place among our great writers of prose. Probably a large fraction of his energy was spent in the rollicking enjoyment of existence; otherwise his rank would have been higher than it is. His contributions to the 'Spectator' and allied periodicals take their distinction from his prevailing tenderness of heart and wide acquaintance with human life. To him these papers owe their pathos, their humour, and their extraordinary variety of characters. He loved company, and the quickness of his sympathies made him constantly alive to differences in the personalities of his companions.

His habits were irregular; he had not the familiar routine and select circle of Addison. He was under no necessity of economising his energies; he seems to have been capable of bearing practically any amount of work and dissipation. He had small power of resisting the impulses of emotion. His plans for the day were easily disconcerted by the entrance of a good companion. In politics, when any of his darling principles seemed to be in danger, he rushed to the rescue without regard to consequences.

In this place we shall remark upon and exemplify chiefly his pathos and his humour. His characters are really artistic creations, and belong to poetry and fiction.

On the other qualities of his style we remark cursorily. In command of words he is not equal to Addison; his choice is much less felicitous. His sentence composition is irregular and careless, often ungrammatical: writing in the character of a Tatler, he thought it incumbent to assume "incorrectness of style, and an air of common speech"—a style very agreeable to his own inclinations. He has not the polished and felicitous melody of Addison. His language and sentiments are much more glowing and extravagant; his papers may be distinguished by this feature alone.

The chief differences between his own style and Addison's are well summed up by himself—"The elegance, purity, and correctness in his writings were not so much my purpose as, in any intelligible manner as I could, to rally all those singularities of human life, through the different professions and characters in it, which obstruct anything that was truly good and great."

Pathos.—Steele is one of the most touching of our writers. Himself of a nature the reverse of melancholy, he yet at certain seasons "resolved to be sorrowful;" and when the sorrowful mood was upon him, the incidents that he recalled or imagined were of the most heartrending character. The kind of pathos that we find in him would not be pathetic at all, in a poetic sense, to the more delicate order of sensibilities: it would be a pain, and not an æsthetic pleasure. There are not many of these affecting papers in either 'Tatler,' 'Spectator,' or 'Guardian.' Most of those that do appeal to our tender sensibilities lay before us situations of extreme anguish. We shall quote two examples, in which the extreme painfulness of the incidents is relieved only by the exhibition of extreme devotedness. The first is the story of Unnion and Valentine ('Tatler,' No. 5):—

"At the siege of Namur by the Allies, there were in the ranks, of the company commanded by Captain Pincent, in Colonel Frederick Hamilton's regiment, one Unnion, a corporal, and one Valentine, a private centinel; there happened between these two men a dispute about a matter of love, which, upon some aggravations, grew to an irreconcileable hatred. Unnion, being the officer of Valentine, took all opportunities even to strike his rival, and profess the spite and revenge which moved him to it. The centinel bore it without resistance, but frequently said he would die to be revenged of that tyrant. They had spent whole months thus, one injuring, the other complaining; when, in the midst of this rage towards each other, they were commanded upon the attack of the castle, where the corporal received a shot in the thigh, and fell; the French pressing on, and he expecting to be trampled to death, called out to his enemy, 'Ah, Valentine! can you leave me here?' Valentine immediately ran back, and in the midst of a thick fire of the French, took the corporal upon his back, and brought him through all that danger, as far as the abbey of Salsine, where a cannon-ball took off his head: his body fell under his enemy whom he was carrying off. Unnion immediately forgot his wound, rose up, tearing his hair, and then threw himself upon the bleeding carcase, crying, 'Ah, Valentine! was it for me, who have so barbarously used thee, that thou hast died? I will not live after thee!' He was not by any means to be forced from the body, but was removed with it bleeding in his arms, and attended with tears by all their comrades who knew their enmity. When he was brought to a tent, his wounds were dressed by force; but the next day, still calling upon Valentine, and lamenting his cruelties to him, he died in the pangs of remorse and despair."

This story is given "in order to inspire the love and admiration of worthy actions," and "as an instance of the greatness of spirit in the lowest of her Majesty's subjects." The next is a deathbed scene, from an account of a family where Mr Bickerstaff was very intimate ('Tatler,' Nos. 95, 114):—

"I went up directly to the room where she lay, and was met at the entrance by my friend, who, notwithstanding his thoughts had been composed a little before, at the sight of me turned away his face and wept. The little family of children renewed their expressions of their sorrow according to their several ages and degrees of understanding. The eldest daughter was in tears, busied in attendance upon her mother; others were kneeling about the bedside; and what troubled me most was, to see a little boy, who was too young to know the reason, weeping only because his sisters did. The only one in the room who seemed resigned and comforted was the dying person. At my approach to the bedside, she told me, with a low broken voice, 'This is kindly done. Take care of your friend—do not go from him.' She had before taken leave of her husband and children, in a manner proper for so solemn a parting, and with a gracefulness peculiar to a woman of her character. My heart was torn in pieces, to see the husband on one side suppressing and keeping down the swellings of his grief, for fear of disturbing her in her last moments; and the wife, even at that time, concealing the pains she endured, for fear of increasing his affliction. She kept her eyes upon him for some moments after she grew speechless, and soon after closed them for ever. In the moment of her departure, my friend, who had thus far commanded himself, gave a deep groan, and fell into a swoon by her bedside."

We have evidence that Steele himself was overpowered by the painfulness of his own creations. It is said that after writing the above deathbed scene he was so affected as to be unable to proceed: the commonplace consolations that follow in the original are said to have been appended by Addison. Sometimes he seeks relief from his painful recollections or imaginations by violent expedients. In one paper a most touching soliloquy is interrupted by a knock at the door, and the arrival of a hamper of wine; whereupon he sends for three of his friends, and restores himself to cheerfulness by the generous warmth of two bottles. In another he works upon his reader's feelings till they reach the point of agony, and then suddenly transfers the horrible scene to dreamland:—

"I was once myself in agonies of grief that are unutterable, and in so great a distraction of mind, that I thought myself even out of the possibility of receiving comfort. The occasion was as follows. When I was a youth in a part of the army which was then quartered at Dover, I fell in love with an agreeable young woman of a good family in those parts, and had the satisfaction of seeing my addresses kindly received, which occasioned the perplexity I am going to relate.

"We were in a calm evening diverting ourselves upon the top of the cliff with the prospect of the sea, and trifling away the time in such little fondnesses as are most ridiculous to persons in business, and most agreeable to those in love.

"In the midst of these our innocent endearments, she snatched a paper of verses out of my hand, and ran away with them. I was following her; when on a sudden the ground, though at a considerable distance from the verge of the precipice, sank under her, and threw her down from so prodigious a height, upon such a range of rocks, as would have dashed her into ten thousand pieces, had her body been made of adamant. It is much easier for my reader to imagine my state of mind upon such an occasion than for me to express it. I said to myself, It is not in the power of Heaven to relieve me! *when I awaked, equally transported and astonished, to see myself drawn out of an affliction which, the very moment before, appeared to me altogether inextricable.*"

The Ludicrous.—Steele's humour is distinguished from Addison's chiefly by two circumstances—unaffected geniality and heartiness, and less delicate elaboration.

Steele was a kindly observer of human frailties. Against what he considered to be heartlessness and vice he was openly indignant: his natural tendency was to use the lash freely in hot blood—not to introduce galling points of satire with a smiling countenance. Minor faults, affectation, presumption, a dictatorial manner, and suchlike, he ridiculed with good-humour, with a certain fellow-feeling for the objects of his ridicule.

At the same time, he had not enough patient skill to work out a ludicrous conception into the exquisite details that give such a charm to the papers of Addison. By comparison with his coadjutor, he is sketchy and declamatory.

It is not difficult to find illustrations of both of these points. In several cases Addison has taken up Steele's conception, and worked it out with more elaborate skill, at the same time turning it into a more slyly-malicious, or at least a colder, vein.

For example, we have quoted (p. 386) Addison's exquisite paper on the use of the Fan. Let us look now at the original conception in the 'Tatler.' The "beauteous Delamira" being about to be married, the "matchless Virgulta" beseeches her to tell the secret of her manner of charming:—

"Delamira heard her with great attention, and with that dexterity which is natural to her, told her that 'all she had above the rest of her sex and contemporary beauties was wholly owing to a fan (that was left her by her mother, and had been long in the family), which, whoever had in possession, and used with skill, should command the hearts of all beholders; and since,' said she, smiling, 'I have no more to do with extending my conquests or triumphs, I will make you a present of this inestimable rarity.' Virgulta made her expressions of the highest gratitude for so uncommon a confidence in her, and begged she would 'show her what was peculiar in the management of that utensil, which rendered it of such general force while she was mistress of it.' Delamira replied, 'You see, madam, Cupid is the principal figure painted on it; and the skill in playing this fan is, in your several motions of it, to let him appear as little as possible; for honourable lovers fly all endeavours to ensnare them; and your Cupid must hide his bow and arrow, or he will never be sure of his game. You may observe,' continued she, 'that in all public assemblies, the sexes seem to separate themselves, and draw up to attack each other with eye-shot: that is the time when the fan, which is all the armour of a woman, is of most use in our defence; for our minds are construed by the waving of that little instrument, and our thoughts appear in composure or agitation, according to the motion of it. . . . Cymon, who is the dullest of mortals, and though a wonderful great scholar, does not only pause, but seems to take a nap with his eyes open between every other sentence in his discourse: him have I made a leader in assemblies; and one blow on the shoulder as I passed by him has raised him to a downright impertinent in all conversations. The airy Will Sampler is become as lethargic by this my wand, as Cymon is sprightly. Take it, good girl, and use it without mercy.'"

Compare this with Addison's railing proposal to teach the use of the fan, and his elaborate exposure of all the arts. A gallant tenderness for the sex shines through "good-hearted Dick's" mock-heroic humour. Addison politely holds the sex up to ridicule; Steele sympathises with their little artifices, and even insinuates a piece of genuine good advice as to the best means of success.

As another field for comparison, take their sketches of Clubs. None of Addison's Clubs have the rollicking humour of the *Ugly Club*, and none of Steele's have the mean and sordid insinuations contained in the rules of the *Twopenny Club*. On the other hand, even the Ugly Club, which was a favourite conception,[1] is far from having the minute finish of the *Everlasting Club.*

The difference between the humour of the two writers is nowhere more conspicuous than in the papers upon Sir Roger de Coverley. Steele's Sir Roger is quite a different person from Addison's Sir Roger. All that is amiable in the conception belongs to Steele. His first paper ('Spectator,' No. 2) represents Sir Roger as a jolly country gentleman, "keeping a good house both in town and country;" a lover of mankind, with such a mirthful cast in his behaviour, that he is beloved rather than esteemed; unconfined to modes and forms, disregarding the manners of the world when he thinks them in the wrong; when he enters a house, calling the servants by their names, and talking all the way up-stairs to a visit. He had been a man of fashion in his youth, but being crossed in love by a beautiful widow, had grown careless of his person, and never dressed afterwards. Steele's subsequent papers, Nos. 6, 107, 109, 113, 118, 174, bear out this description—give examples of his common-sense, of his considerate treatment of his servants, of his gratitude to one of them for saving his life, and of his occasional singularities of behaviour. The knight is made to explain his own eccentricities as a result of his love disappointment—"Between you and me," he says, "I am often apt to imagine it has had some whimsical effect upon my brain, for I frequently find that, in my most serious discourse, I let fall some comical familiarity of speech or odd phrase, that makes the company laugh." Such is Sir Roger according to Steele—an easy, good-natured gentleman, of good sense, purposely setting at nought the conventions of fashion, singular and eccentric, but aware of his eccentricities. In Addison's hands he becomes a very different character. He is transformed into a good-natured Tory fox-hunter. He retains the good-nature and the eccentricity; he drops, except in name, the good sense, and the familiar knowledge of town life. Addison makes him a thorough rustic; autocratic, self-important, ignorant, credulous. True, he is at great pains to repeat that Sir Roger was much esteemed for his universal benevolence—"at peace within himself,

[1] The Ugly Club, and the difficulties met with in finding members, form one of the best specimens of Steele's rollicking humour. In giving an account of it, he makes the following humorous confession in the person of the Spectator: "For my own part, I am a little unhappy in the mould of my face, which is not quite so long as it is broad. Whether this might not partly arise from my opening my mouth much seldomer than other people, and by consequence not so much lengthening the fibres of my visage, I am not at leisure to determine. However it be, I have been often put out of countenance by the shortness of my face, and was formerly at great pains in concealing it by wearing a periwig with a high foretop, and letting my beard grow. But now I have thoroughly got over the delicacy, and could be contented were it much shorter, provided it might qualify me for a member of the Merry Club, which the following letter gives me an account of."

and esteemed[1] by all about him." But this affectation of respect for the knight is a sly artifice to bring him into ridiculous situations. No. 106, the first of Addison's papers, is the most amiable part of the picture, and seems designed to let Steele's conception down softly. Yet even this paper shows Sir Roger in a ridiculous light, inconsistent with the following paper, No. 107, by Steele. Both knight and servants are pleasantly caricatured in No. 106—"You would take his *valet de chambre* for his brother, his butler is grey-headed, his groom is one of the gravest men that I have ever seen, and his coachman has the looks of a privy councillor." His chaplain was chosen for his "good aspect, clear voice, and sociable temper:" "at his first settling with me," says Sir Roger, "I made him a present of all the good sermons which have been printed in English, and only begged of him that every Sunday he would pronounce one of them in the pulpit." Among these venerable domestics the good knight is treated like an infant. "When he is pleasant upon any of them, all his family are in good humour, and none so much as the person whom he diverts himself with: on the contrary, if he coughs or betrays any infirmity of old age, it is easy for a stander-by to observe a secret concern in the looks of all his servants." After this opening sketch of Sir Roger's good-nature, we are presented with some exquisitely-wrought pictures of his ridiculous doings. He exorcises the shut-up rooms of his house, by making the chaplain sleep in them. In church "he suffers nobody to sleep besides himself; for if by chance he has been surprised into a short nap at sermon, upon recovering out of it he stands up and looks about him, and if he sees anybody else nodding, either wakes them himself, or sends his servant to them;" he lengthens out a verse half a minute after the rest of the congregation, says *Amen* three or four times, and calls out to John Matthews to mind what he is about, and not disturb the congregation. He had been a great fox-hunter in his youth. He would have given over Moll White, the witch, to the County Assizes, had he not been dissuaded by the chaplain. Perhaps the most exquisitely ludicrous of his adventures are his journey to the Assizes, and his speech there (No. 122); his visit to Westminster Abbey (329); his observations on "The Distressed Mother," in the playhouse: in all these situations he is merely a good-natured, credulous, unsophisticated butt for the delicate ridicule of his companion the Spectator.

While there is such a difference between the conceptions of the two writers, there is a still greater difference in the execution. In

[1] *Esteemed.*—Steele had said that Sir Roger was rather beloved than esteemed. But this was estimating the knight by the standard of his town friends. Addison places him entirely in the country; and represents him as an object of great admiration and respect to the simple country-people, thereby getting a double gratification for his contempt of the country or Tory party.

point of literary skill, any one of Addison's papers is worth all Steele's put together. Steele is sketchy and rude, and mars the portraiture with patches of moralising. Addison fills in the minute touches with his most exquisite skill.[1]

OTHER WRITERS.

THEOLOGY.

Towards the end of the seventeenth century the Church of England began to rest from her labours against Papacy, and to turn her forces against a new enemy. A new topic engaged all clergymen of a literary and controversial disposition, and the general tone of their sermons underwent a corresponding change. For such changes one cannot assign a definite year; it takes time to give a new direction to the energies of a large body of different men. We must be content to say that a religious revolution took place during the end of the seventeenth century and the beginning of the eighteenth. If we dip into the writings of Churchmen twenty years before the end of the century, we find their polemic tracts burning with zeal against Papacy, and their sermons administering the consolations and warnings of Christianity, in full assurance of its divine origin. Twenty years after the end of the century we breathe a different atmosphere. The Church was then on the alert against a new antagonist—the all-absorbing topic was the controversy with the Deists. Tracts poured from the press; young aspirants to the bench were eager to break a lance with Toland or with Collins. Sermons were largely influenced by the prevailing controversy. Devotional ardour was replaced by polemical ardour, by a desire to "prove the reasonableness" of Christianity. Whatever was the preacher's text, his anxiety was to "prove" that it was eminently suited to the condition of men, eminently calculated to make them happy. Sublimity and pathos were banished from the pulpit, and argument reigned in their stead. The great majority of the sermons preached in the eighteenth century were "tedious moral essays:" their favourite exhortations were "to abstain from

[1] It is an example of the injustice done to Steele by the admirers of Addison, and also of the want of discrimination in their homage, that they give Addison credit for the amiability of the character as well as for the skill of the portraiture. There can be no doubt that, in this as in other cases, Addison profited greatly by his alliance with Steele; the original suggestiveness of discursive "Dick" gave many a hint for the elaborating skill of his friend. The laborious Dr Drake thinks it a subject for regret that Steele's first draughts do not combine better with Addison's full and accurate picture; condescends to say that Nos. 107 and 109 "carry on the costume and design of Addison with undeviating felicity;" and thinks it "an *ingenious conjecture* of Dr Aikin, that Addison intended, through the medium of Sir Roger's weakness, to convey an indirect satire on the confined notions and political prejudices of the country gentleman!"

vice, to cultivate virtue, to fill our station in life with propriety, to bear the ills of life with resignation, and to use its pleasures moderately."

Not a few of the theologians of this period might be grouped together as taking part in the trial of the Bible by common reason. Towards the end of the seventeenth century rationalism was predominant among learned students of religion, whether in the Church or out of it. By nearly all theologians it seemed taken for granted that the Bible was not to be received without question as the authoritative word of God, but was to be tried by its agreement with reason. Some accepted these evidences, some did not; orthodoxy was sharply assailed by heterodoxy, and issued numerous sharp replies. The controversy did nothing appreciable for the advancement of English style. None of the combatants could be called great masters of language.[1]

The three most distinguished Churchmen of this generation, Atterbury, Hoadley, and Clarke, did not win their reputation in the war against the Deists. Atterbury is known chiefly as a politician; Hoadley by his views regarding Church and State; Clarke as a scholar, and a writer on Natural Theology and Ethics. In literary power they are much inferior to the three great divines of the preceding age, Barrow, Tillotson, and South.

Francis Atterbury (1662-1732), Bishop of Rochester, was an uncompromising champion of the High Church and Tory party. The son of a rector in Buckinghamshire, he was sent to Westminster School and to Christ Church. As a scholar, he was, according to Macaulay, more brilliant than profound. He took part in the celebrated "Battle of the Books." He was tutor to Charles Boyle, the editor of 'Phalaris,' and is generally understood to have written the reply to Bentley's first short criticism of the Letters (1694). He distinguished himself greatly in 1700 by supporting the High Church view of the powers of the Lower House of Convocation. He is supposed to have borne a chief part in framing the speech pronounced by Sacheverell at the bar of the House of Lords. When the Tories rose into power, he was made Dean of Christ Church, and afterwards Bishop of Rochester. After the accession of George, he was suspected of intriguing with the Pretender, and formally banished in 1723. He died in France. He was a bold, turbulent man, having an ambition that would not rest short of the highest power; eloquent, a dazzling master of controversial fence; so audacious in his statements and clever in his personalities, that on two occasions he vanquished his superiors in learning, and made the worse appear the better reason. "Such arguments

[1] The best succinct account of the religious thought of this generation and the following is contained in Mr Mark Pattison's "Tendencies of Religious Thought in England, 1688-1750," one of the 'Essays and Reviews.'

as he had he placed in the clearest light. Where he had no arguments, he resorted to personalities, sometimes serious, generally ludicrous, always clever and cutting. But whether he was grave or merry, whether he reasoned or sneered, his style was always pure, polished, and easy." His diction is not quite so pure as Swift's or Addison's; and it is easy in the sense of fluent and racy, not in the sense of languid.

Benjamin Hoadley or **Hoadly (1676-1761)**, successively Bishop of Bangor, Hereford, Salisbury, and Winchester, wrote *against* the pretensions of High Churchmen and Tories. On more than one occasion he crossed swords with Atterbury. His most famous work was a sermon preached before George I. soon after his elevation to the bench, on the 'Nature of the Kingdom of Christ.' The text—"My kingdom is not of this world"—was a good clue to the contents. He strongly advocated the subordination of the Church to the State. The sermon made a great sensation. It drew upon the author a formal censure from the Lower House of Convocation, whose independent privileges had been maintained by Atterbury; and it originated what is known as the Bangorian controversy, an engagement of some forty or fifty pamphlets. His collected works occupy three volumes, published by his son in 1773. His style is in general vigorous and caustic; he seems careless of elegance, and his dry sarcasms have lost their interest.

The other eminent divine of the period is **Dr Samuel Clarke (1675-1729)**, the pupil and friend of Newton. As a scholar, he translated Rohault's 'Physics' into English, Newton's 'Optics' into Latin, edited Cæsar's 'Commentaries,' and published the first twelve books of the 'Iliad' with a Latin version. As a theologian, he is known chiefly by an illusory attempt to give a mathematical demonstration of the existence of God, which he undertook upon the suggestion of Sir Isaac Newton. In the Boyle Lectures (1704-5) he promulgated an ethical system whose chief proposition is that goodness and virtue consist in the observance of certain "eternal fitnesses." In 1715 he joined Newton in a famous controversy with Leíbnitz, who had represented the Newtonian philosophy as both false and subversive of religion. His views on the Trinity and on some other points hindered his advancement in the Church. As regards style, Clarke's sermons may almost be said to have been the models of the Scotch "moderate" school of preachers — heavy, prolix, argumentative, full of practical good sense, and possessing none of the ardour familiar to us under the name "Evangelical."

The leading "Deists" (so-called) were Toland, Collins, Woolston, and Tindal. With these might be reckoned Shaftesbury: only he, from his rank (as Mr Pattison thinks), was refuted with less warmth, and had not the same notoriety as a controversialist.

John Toland (1669-1722) was born near Londonderry, of Catholic parents, took a degree at Glasgow, and studied afterwards at Leyden and Oxford. His 'Christianity not Mysterious,' 1696, caused none the less excitement that its quarrel with orthodoxy was chiefly concerning the word "mysterious." He accepted the Bible theory of the origin of sin, only labouring to make out that there was nothing mysterious about it. He did not repudiate miracles; he only held that there was nothing mysterious in an all-powerful Being breaking through the order of nature. Professor Ferrier styles him "but a poor writer," and charges him with "dulness, pedantry, vanity, and indiscretion."

Anthony Collins (1676-1729), a gentleman of independent fortune, with an Eton and Cambridge education, and the training of a barrister, an esteemed young friend of Locke, wrote several works that engaged him in controversy with the most eminent divines of the time. In 1707 he discussed the value of testimony, making polemical capital out of the 30,000 doubtful readings that Dr John Mill had set down in his edition of the New Testament. In 1710, in a 'Vindication of the Divine Attributes,' he contended that predestination is incompatible with "freedom" of the human will, and that the will is not "free." In 1713 his 'Discourse on Free Thinking' claimed unlimited permission to discuss the problems of religion. In 1724 appeared his most notorious work—'Discourse on the Grounds and Reasons of the Christian Religion;' this publication was replied to by all the talent of the Church. "The moral character of this writer stands extremely high for temperance, humanity, and benevolence; and both as a magistrate and a man he acquired general esteem." Though not orthodox, he was religious; he declared on his deathbed that he had endeavoured to serve both God and his country. His style is simple, clear, and concise; he has none of the iconoclastic violence of other objectors to established faith.

In 1726, amid the storm of hostile criticism, there appeared on the side of Collins a *Moderator between an Infidel and an Apostate.* This was **Thomas Woolston** (1669-1733), Fellow and Tutor of Sidney Sussex, Cambridge. Woolston had long made theology his favourite study, but till more than fifty had shown no symptoms of acute heterodoxy. He had indeed taken up Origen's view of the Old Testament as a spiritual allegory, and in 1723 had made acrimonious attacks on the clergy. But now he pushed the idea of allegory into the New Testament, maintaining that the miracles also were fictitious allegories. In the four following years, in 'Six Discourses on the Miracles of Christ,' he assailed the gospel narrative with ridicule. He also issued some ironical defences of Christian tenets. His manner was offensive; he was prosecuted for blasphemy, fined, and imprisoned.

In the last year of this period, 1730, **Matthew Tindal (1657-1733)**, a Fellow of All Souls, published a dialogue, 'Christianity as old as the Creation, or the Gospel a republication of the Religion of Nature.' This is perhaps the most elaborate of the deistical works of the period. The author holds the startling doctrine that Christianity is useless where it is not mischievous; that man has always been able to distinguish right and wrong with regard to his special circumstances; and that to lay down a system of general rules is certain to conduct to error.

The Deists were opposed by the whole force of the clergy, as well as by a considerable number of laymen. Among those that more particularly distinguished themselves — apart from such champions as Hoadley, Clarke, and Bentley, who achieved distinction in other fields—may be mentioned **Charles Leslie (1650-1722)**, author of a famous work provoked chiefly by Toland, entitled 'Short and Easy Method with the Deists;' **John Norris (1657-1711)**, rector of Bemerton, one of the earliest critics of Locke, who replied to Toland's 'Christianity not Mysterious;' **Peter Brown**, Bishop of Cork, also a critic of Locke and Toland; **Edward Chandler (d. 1750)**, Bishop of Lichfield, who in 1725 wrote a 'Defence of Christianity' against Collins; **Thomas Sherlock (1678-1761)**, Bishop of London, who wrote a 'Trial of the Witnesses of the Resurrection of Jesus' in reply to Woolston. But the most able apologists belong to our next period; they came forward to repel the assault made by Tindal. The fight began to rage hotly about 1720, after the subsidence of the Bangorian controversy; Tindal's work was the culminating charge, after which the battle became fainter.

PHILOSOPHY.

Bernard de Mandeville (1670-1733) is famed as the author of 'The Fable of the Bees, or private Vices public Benefits.'[1] "This work is a satire upon artificial society, having for its chief aim to expose the hollowness of the so-called dignity of human nature." He endeavours with cynical humour to explain away all alleged cases of disinterested conduct. He regards pride and vanity as

[1] The received bibliography of this Fable is inaccurate. It appeared originally in 1706 (not in 1714, the received date), as a small sixpenny pamphlet of doggerel verses, entitled 'The Grumbling Hive; or Knaves turned Honest.' Soon after, it was pirated, and hawked about the streets in a halfpenny sheet. In 1714 the author republished it with some two hundred small pages of remarks, and an 'Enquiry into the Origin of Moral Virtue:'—the whole under the title—'The Fable of the Bees, or private Vices public Benefits.' In 1723 the work was entirely recast, but the title, 'The Fable of the Bees,' was not then given to it for the first time.

the chief incentives that delude men into what is called public spirit. His humour is the coarsest of the coarse; but he cannot be denied great wit, happy expression, and ingenious illustrations. A happy saying of his stuck to Addison—"a parson in a tye-wig;" which has much the same force as our familiar "a policeman in plain clothes," the tye-wig being unclerical in the reign of Queen Anne.

William Wollaston (1659-1724), a clergyman, was bequeathed an ample fortune when he was about thirty, settled in London, and passed a life of study—so very regular that he is said not to have slept out of his own house for thirty years. Roused, like Clarke, by the ethics of Hobbes, he wrote a treatise entitled 'The Religion of Nature Delineated.' His ethical system is at bottom the same with Clarke's, though differently expressed. According to him, immorality consists in the violation of truth, truth consisting in the observance of certain eternally-fixed relations between man and man and between man and God.

Anthony Ashley Cooper, third **Earl of Shaftesbury,** grandson of the first Earl ("Achitophel") **(1671-1713)**, made a considerable reputation as an ethical writer. He was for a few years in Parliament, but the greater part of his life was spent in study. His works are,—'Inquiry concerning Virtue' (1699); 'Letter on Enthusiasm' (1708); 'Moralists, a Philosophical Rhapsody'—a Platonic vindication of Deity and Providence, highly praised by Leibnitz (1709); 'Essay upon the Freedom of Wit and Humour'—advocating the trial of religious as well as other doctrines by the test of ridicule (also 1709); 'Advice to an Author' (1710). The title of his collected works, excluding the 'Inquiry,' which contains his ethical theories, is 'Characteristics of Men, Manners, Opinions, and Times.' He was a man of feeble constitution, but cheerful and witty. His ethical speculations show no great power of analysis. He may be called the first of the intuitional school, writing without being at all aware of the difficulties of his position. Cudworth had been alarmed at the attempt of Hobbes to restrict the term moral to actions commanded by a supreme power; Shaftesbury disliked Locke's theory that our ideas of morality are got by reflection upon our experience. He calls himself a *Moral Realist;* and holds not only that the distinctions between virtue and vice are "real," but that we have a special *moral sense*, whereby we distinguish what is virtuous and what is vicious. Into the origin of this sense he does not profess to inquire.—His style is highly elaborated. His first care is to be delicately melodious. He strives also to avoid the very appearance of harshness in the union of ideas. As a consequence, he is rather wanting in vigour, is driven upon affected inversions, and is obliged often to prolong his sentences to a tedious length before his smooth circumlocutions amount to a complete expression.

George Berkeley (1684-1753), Bishop of Cloyne, established himself in a high philosophical reputation. Born in Ireland, he was educated at Kilkenny School and at Trinity College, Dublin. A precocious youth, he published his first work at the age of twenty-three—'An Attempt to demonstrate Arithmetic without the aid of Algebra or Geometry.' In 1709 (at age twenty-five) he wrote his first psychological work, 'The Theory of Vision,' remarkable as the earliest attempt to distinguish in an act of vision between what we actually see with the eye and what we supply from former experience. In the following year (1710) he published his 'Principles of Human Knowledge,' containing views so original that they have become identified with his name. He assailed the independent existence of Matter, and maintained that sensation, or perception, is a mental fact or product, a phase or aspect of mind, and cannot have any existence apart from mind. After the age of twenty-seven, he published no farther novelty in psychology, although in some of his other works he expounded his Idealism at greater length. He wrote in favour of passive obedience and non-resistance; travelled on the Continent; and is said to have literally been the death of Malebranche in Paris, arguing with that philosopher while he was suffering from inflammation of the lungs. About 1722 he became acquainted with Miss Vanhomrigh, Swift's Vanessa, who left him half of her fortune. In 1728 he set out on a philanthropic scheme to convert the American Indians to Christianity by establishing a college in the Bermudas. This scheme failing through breach of faith on the part of Sir R. Walpole, Berkeley returned, and was soon preferred to the see of Cloyne. He took part in the deistic controversy; his 'Minute Philosopher' is a most acute attack on the deistic positions.—He is described as "a handsome man, with a countenance full of meaning and benignity, remarkable for great strength of limbs; and, till his sedentary life impaired it, of a very robust constitution." The characteristic of his intellect was extraordinary subtlety rather than solid judgment. He had, perhaps, too warm an imagination to arrive at sound and sober conclusions. Something of this caprice of imagination appears in his conduct; contrast his philandering scheme to convert the Indians with morose Swift's endeavours to improve the condition of the Irish peasants. Berkeley, too, was an Irish clergyman; and in the elevation of his parishioners might have found an ample field for the strongest "enthusiasm of humanity." His style has always been esteemed admirable; simple, felicitous, and sweetly melodious. The dialogues are sustained with great skill.

HISTORY.

There is no historian of any note in this period. **Lawrence Echard (1671-1730),** an English clergyman, wrote several historical works, but none of them have kept a place among general readers. His 'History of Rome,' 'General Ecclesiastical History,' and 'History of England to the Revolution,' all obtained considerable praise and circulation in their day, but have been superseded by the works of more eminent writers.

The most famous ANTIQUARY of the period is **John Strype (1643-1737),** a most industrious collector of ecclesiastical antiquities relating to the Reformation in England: author of 'Annals of the Reformation,' and of separate 'Lives' of the various founders of the Anglican Church.

With Strype may be mentioned **Dr Humphrey Prideaux** (**1648-1724**), author of a 'Connection of the History of the Old and New Testament' (1715-17), a work still used by students of divinity. He wrote also a highly popular 'Life of Mahomet' (1707), and other works.

Dr Potter (**1674-1747**), Archbishop of Canterbury, wrote a manual of the 'Antiquities of Greece,' which was the standard work among students until superseded in some points by more thorough researches. **Basil Kennett** (**1674-1714**) wrote a similar work on 'Roman Antiquities,' which held its ground for nearly a century.

MISCELLANEOUS.

Richard Bentley (**1662-1742**) is one of the most famous of English critics. He was a graduate of Cambridge. In 1693 he published sermons against atheism, which he had preached as Boyle Lecturer. About this time he was appointed Keeper of the Royal Library of St James. When Charles Boyle published his edition of 'Phalaris,' he animadverted on the incivility of Bentley in suddenly recalling a book that he had borrowed from the library. Bentley took pungent notice of this, and of the general value of the 'Epistles of Phalaris,' in a dissertation appended to Wotton's 'Reflections on Temple's Ancient and Modern Learning' (1697). This was the beginning of the famous controversy burlesqued by Swift in his 'Battle of the Books.' Boyle, with the assistance of Atterbury and Aldrich, replied to the dissertation, and was thought to have demolished his antagonist. But Bentley, after two years' silence, came forward with an irrefragably thorough exposure of the spuriousness of the Letters, seasoned with the most cutting and unsparing ridicule of his opponents. There had never been in

English criticism such a display of scholarship and arrogant wit; and Bentley's fame was at once established. His other great performance was an attack on Collins, under the name of 'Phileleutherus Lipsiensis,' pointing out that the text of the New Testament is less corrupt than the text of any classical author, and exulting in the Free-thinker's unscholarly mistakes. Bentley was a man of imperious and capricious temper; and, as Master of Trinity, Cambridge, was involved in constant squabbles with the Fellows. His critical scholarship is universally allowed to have been prodigious. His sagacity in textual emendations is also highly extolled, though with the qualification that he is too bold. We laugh at many of his courageous liberties with the text of Milton; a Roman might have been equally amused with some of his emendations of Horace. His style has surprising force and wit, formed upon the scholastic models of unsparingly personal acrimony. The times allowed great freedom of abuse in controversy, and Bentley's natural temper had full scope.

The two principal coadjutors of Addison and Steele in the 'Spectator' were **John Hughes (1667-1720)** and **Eustace Budgell (1685-1737).** Both held Government appointments. Hughes was a refined poetical soul, wrote poems and dramas, and translated from Latin, French, and Italian polite literature. His papers in the 'Spectator' approach very near to Addison's in finish and happy expression. The difference between them lies chiefly in simplicity. Hughes has longer and more involved sentences, and clogs the smooth flow of his rhythm with a greater number of epithets.—Budgell was a rough, vigorous, dissipated barrister, who preferred making a figure in the coffee-houses and in literature to the practice of his profession. His humour is comparatively obstreperous, of the Defoe and Macaulay type, which the French seem to consider peculiarly English. It is genial rather from the author's hearty enjoyment of the fun he is making than from any sympathy with the objects of his derision. The 'She Romp Club' and the rural sports of Sir Roger are from his pen. He came to an unfortunate end. Tindal, the deist, having bequeathed him £2000, he was suspected of having tampered with the will; and, unable to bear the disgrace of such a suspicion, committed suicide by throwing himself into the Thames.

Over against these literary Whigs may be mentioned the literary Tories, the associates of Swift in the 'Examiner' and elsewhere. Passing over **Mrs Manley,** the novelist, who conducted the 'Examiner' after Swift, and who had been prosecuted for a satire on the Whig statesmen, we may single out **Dr John Arbuthnot (1667-1735)** as being, next to Swift, and excluding Pope, by far the ablest writer on the Tory side. His best performance, 'The History of John Bull,' a satire on Marlborough and the war, was ascribed to Swift, and is usually printed among Swift's works. Swift said of him—"He has more wit than we all have, and his humanity is equal to his wit." Arbuthnot was one of the northern Scots that were now beginning to push their fortunes in London. He was born in Kincardineshire, at a town of his own name, and studied medicine in Aberdeen. Immediately after completing his studies he went to London, and made a livelihood at first by teaching mathematics. He soon brought himself into notice by some tracts on mathematical and medical subjects. In 1705 he was appointed physician extraordinary to Queen Anne; in 1709 physician ordinary. He became a leading wit in the coffee-houses. When Swift came over from Ireland in 1708, and the Tories concerted a grand assault upon the Whigs, Arbuthnot's ready pen supplied some of the most effective missiles of offence. The 'History of John Bull' by Arbuthnot, the 'Conduct of the Allies' by Swift, and 'The Defence of Sacheverell' by Atterbury, were the three great literary contributions to the fall of the Whig Government: the eulogist of Arbuthnot usually gives the honour to Arbuthnot's performance, the eulogist of Swift to Swift's, the eulogist of Atterbury to Atterbury's. Arbuthnot's other great production is his share in the writings of 'Martinus Scriblerus,' sometimes printed with Swift's works, sometimes with Pope's. The Scriblerus Club was instituted in 1714 by Pope, Swift, Arbuthnot, Gay, Parnell, Atterbury, Congreve, and others. The object was to satirise the absurdities of literature. The members were actuated a good deal by the spirit of Pope's 'Dunciad.' Arbuthnot bore a large share in the works published under the signature of Scriblerus. In the essay on the 'Art of Sinking,' his hand can be traced in several of the chapters.—Arbuthnot's fortunes declined at the accession of George, and his later days were made unhappy by poverty and ill-health.—There is no collected edition of his works. The 'John Bull' is usually printed in Swift's works, the 'Scriblerus' papers partly in Swift's, partly in Pope's. He was exceedingly careless of what he wrote; all was done to serve a passing purpose, and he took no pains to preserve either manuscript or print. He must have been a man of great social tact and amiability. Swift seems to have loved him like a brother—"If the world had a dozen Arbuthnots in it," he wrote in one of his letters, "I would burn my Travels." The power of his satire was proved by its effects. He is the most versatile, as regards mood, of all the great wits of the period. When his feelings are not specially roused he is genial, lambent, good-humoured; but he was capable of genuine indignation, and sometimes lays on the lash with unsparing severity. His paper on the 'Altercation or Scolding of the Ancients' is in very happy humour; his 'Art of Political Lying' is more sarcastic; and some sallies usually attributed to him against Bishop Burnet, the favourite butt of Swift, are worthy of the savage Dean himself.

One imposing figure in the public transactions of the time also demands a high place in the history of our literature—**Henry St John, Viscount Bolingbroke (1678-1751).** His chief philosophical and political works were written during the forced inaction of the latter half of his life, and in this manual he should, in strict method, be placed in the following generation; but he is so thoroughly identified with the Queen Anne men that it would be an unprofitable violation of the usual arrangement not to mention him here.

Entering Parliament in 1701 at the age of twenty-three, he had not to watch and wait for distinction; his splendid powers placed him at once in the front rank. He gained a seat in the Cabinet in 1704 as Secretary at War, and remained in office four years. During the four last years of Queen Anne, he and Harley were the leaders of the Administration. He quarrelled with Harley, and supplanted him as formal head of the Government about a week before the Queen's death. With the death of the Queen his power came to an end: he was suspected of having intrigued for the succession of the Pretender Prince, and had to flee the country. For some time he was secretary to the Pretender; and, turning to literary composition, produced 'Reflections on Exile,' and a defence of his conduct in the form of a letter to Sir William Wyndham. After seven years' exile, he was permitted to return, but was not suffered to resume his place in the House of Lords. Upon his return he wrote in the 'Craftsman' a series of letters, afterwards reprinted as 'A Dissertation on Parties,' and busied himself with other studies and writings. In 1735 he went to France, this time voluntarily, and lived there for seven years, during which he published 'Letters on the Study of History' and a 'Letter on the True Use of Retirement.' On his final return to England in 1742, he settled at Battersea; wrote 'Letters on the Spirit of Patriotism;' the 'Idea of a Patriot King' (pub. in 1749); and the various philosophical and other works published after his death by his literary executor, David Mallet.—Much has been said of the splendid personality of Bolingbroke. Pope gave poetic expression to a very general feeling when he said that, on the appearance of a comet, he could not help thinking that it had been sent as a chariot to take his friend St John away. "Nature," writes Goldsmith, "seemed not less kind to him in her external embellishments, than in adorning his mind. With the graces of a handsome person, and a face in which dignity was happily blended with sweetness, he had a manner of address that was very engaging. His vivacity was always awake, his apprehension was quick, his wit refined, and his memory amazing; his subtlety in thinking and reasoning was profound; and all these talents were adorned with an elocution that was irresistible." His constitutional energy was prodigious, appearing in the wild excesses of his dissolute youth, no less than in his hard work and complicated intrigues as a Minister of State. The most striking feature of his style is splendour of declamation. All his works, philosophical as well as political, are written in a declamatory strain, and read like elaborate speeches. Not only have the words an oratorical glow and vehemence, but the general structure is the structure of spoken rather than of written style. The dedication of his 'Dissertation on Parties,' addressed to Sir Robert Walpole, is an extreme example:—

> "Let me now appeal to you, sir. Are these designs which any man, who is born a Briton, in any circumstances, in any situation, ought to be ashamed or afraid to avow? You cannot think it. You will not say it. That never can be the case, until we cease to think like freemen, as well as to be free. Are these designs in favour of the Pretender? I appeal to the whole world; and I scorn with a just indignation to give any other answer to so shameless and so senseless an objection. No; they are designs in favour of the constitution; designs to secure, to fortify, to perpetuate that excellent system of government. I court no other cause; I claim no other merit."

Here not only the vehement eloquence, but the short sentences, the pointed balance, the repetition of the leading word (as in "designs"), the figures of interrogation and exclamation—all belong to oratory. We meet some or all of these characteristics in every page. Although, however, in almost every page we meet with the short oratorical sentence familiar to readers of Macaulay, his sentences are not in general so short as in the above extract. On the contrary, he is rather famous for long sentences—remarkable on this ground, that the conclusion of the predicate is put off by one clause after another, and yet these clauses are so admirably placed that there is seldom the least confusion. The structure of these long sentences is all the more simple that very often the latter part is a paraphrase or extension in apposition to some word in the former part. Thus—

> "How different the case is, on the other side, will appear not only from the actions, but from the principles of the Court party, as we find them avowed in their writings; principles more dangerous to liberty, though not so directly, nor so openly levelled against it, than even any of those, bad as they were, which some of these men value themselves for having formerly opposed."

This structure is also oratorical.[1] To call Bolingbroke a splendid

[1] In singling out certain features of Bolingbroke's style as oratorical, I do not mean to imply that these are confined to oratory. I call them oratorical because they are such as occur in nearly every Parliamentary speech of the eighteenth century, and because they are peculiarly fitted to spoken address.

declaimer is to give him little more than half his due. He is also a wit; and at every turn he electrifies the reader with some felicitous stroke of brevity, or happy adjustment of words to his meaning.

To enumerate all the miscellaneous writers of this time would be as much out of place in the present work as to enumerate all that have written to newspapers or magazines within the nineteenth century. A great many periodicals, weekly, bi-weekly, or daily, some continued for a few weeks, some for one or two years, were published contemporaneously with, and after the decease of, Defoe's 'Review;' Steele's 'Tatler,' 'Spectator,' and 'Guardian;' and Swift's 'Examiner.' A long list is given in the beginning of vol. iv. of Drake's Essays on Steele, Addison, and Johnson. The names that we meet with are such as—'The Re-Tatler;' 'The Female Tatler;' 'The Tory Tatler;' 'The Grumbler;' 'The Medley' (conducted by an accomplished man, Mr Maynwaring); 'The Lay Monastery' (conducted by the poet Sir Richard Blackmore); 'The Censor' (conducted by Lewis Theobald, the annotator of Shakspeare); 'The Free-thinker (supported by Ambrose Phillips, the friend of Addison, and George Stubbs, a scholarly elegant recluse clergyman); 'The Plain Dealer' (started by Aaron Hill); 'The Intelligencer' (by Dr Sheridan, the friend and biographer of Swift). Most of the periodicals of the day were political; others diversified politics with literature, on the plan of the 'Review;' and some consisted of a few numbers directed against an object of aversion in literature, manners, or even commerce. Periodicals were the fashion; most of them very short-lived. A periodical sheet was started to vent an opinion that, in the present day, would be expressed in a letter, or a series of letters, to a daily newspaper; and expired either when the author had exhausted the idea, or when the public had received enough and refused to purchase more.

CHAPTER VII.

FROM 1730 TO 1760.

SAMUEL JOHNSON,

1709—1784.

THE great "Moralist" and "Lexicographer" was the son of a respectable bookseller in Lichfield, where he was born on the 18th of September. The mistress of a dame's school there praised him as the best scholar she ever had. After five years at a higher school in Lichfield, one year at the school of Stourbridge, and two years loitering at home, he was sent, at the age of nineteen, to Pembroke College, Oxford. He was too desultory to confine himself to the studies of the place, and continued in the library of the college the wide miscellaneous reading he had practised in his father's shop. Yet his fluent command of Latin procured him marked attention. A Latin hexameter version of Pope's 'Messiah,' which he executed as a Christmas exercise, was considered so good that Pope is said to have declared that posterity would be in doubt which was the original and which the translation. Owing to poverty, he left Oxford in 1731 without taking a degree. Too constitutionally irregular to settle down to a profession, he lived at home for several months; acted for several months as an usher; lived with a friend in Birmingham; translated for a Birmingham bookseller 'Lobo's Journey to Abyssinia' (pub. in 1735); returned to Lichfield; married Mrs Porter of Birmingham, a widow with £800; and set up a boarding-school near Lichfield. Finally, the school not succeeding, he removed to London in 1737, and for the next quarter of a century maintained himself by his pen.

Had he been born a generation sooner, and gone to London in

the reign of Queen Anne, he might have been retained as a party-writer, and well rewarded. Bolingbroke or Harley might have employed him to abuse Marlborough or browbeat the 'Freeholder.' But in 1737 party-writers were not in demand. The man of letters might possibly meet with a wealthy patron, but his trust was chiefly in the booksellers, who were beginning to compete for the favour of the public with periodicals, editions, translations, and every sort of compilation that was likely to sell. There was plenty of employment, though at a low rate of remuneration, for men of ability; and had Johnson possessed ordinary business habits and industry, he might have lived comfortably. During the first ten years of his London life he wrote chiefly for CAVE, the publisher of the 'Gentleman's Magazine' (established in 1731), composing prefaces, lives of eminent men, abridgments, and miscellaneous papers. He succeeded William Guthrie as writer of the Parliamentary Debates (which were forbidden to be reported, but which Cave introduced into his Magazine as the proceedings of the Senate of Lilliput, sending men to the House to bring away what they could remember, and getting a clever man to compose speeches according to their reports). In 1738 he published his poem "London." In 1747 his fame was well established, and he was engaged by a combination of London booksellers for £1575 to prepare his famous Dictionary. In 1750, before this was completed, he began the work that raised his fame to its full height, a periodical under the title of 'The Rambler.' This he carried on single-handed twice a-week for two years. In 1753 he made several contributions to 'The Adventurer.' The Dictionary was completed in 1755; and, to grace his name on the title-page, the University of Oxford presented him with the degree of M.A. Thereafter he continued his multifarious writings for a livelihood. In 1756 he wrote several reviews and other papers for the newly-started 'Literary Magazine.' From 1758 to 1760 he wrote the papers known as 'The Idler' for Payne's 'Universal Chronicle.' In 1759 he wrote 'Rasselas.'

The year 1762 relieved him from his quarter of a century of literary drudgery, bringing him from Government an annual pension of £300. From that date he wrote comparatively little; his chief productions were the Notes to his edition of Shakspeare, 1765; his 'Journey to the Western Islands of Scotland,' and 'Taxation no Tyranny,' 1775; and the last and best of his works, 'The Lives of the Poets,' prefixed as detached Prefaces to an edition of the English Poets, 1779-81. After being made independent by the pension, he spent a great part of his time in social enjoyment, becoming the conversational oracle of a circle of distinguished literary friends. In 1763 he met Boswell, to whose painstaking record he is mainly indebted for the perpetuation of his fame. In 1764 he founded the Literary Club (still existing), which met every Monday at the Turk's Head. In 1765 he made the acquaintance of the Thrales; dined with them frequently; and finally came to be considered as a member of their family. At his own house in Bolt Court, where Boswell found him on his return from the Hebrides, he charitably kept a number of humble dependants—Mrs Williams, Mrs Desmoulins, Dr Robert Levett, Black Frank, and a cat called Hodge. Among the intimate associates of his latter years were Burke, Goldsmith, Gibbon, Topham Beauclerk, Langton, Sir John Hawkins, Sir Joshua Reynolds, Arthur Murphy. He died in his house in Bolt Court.

Johnson's appearance was far from prepossessing. "He is, indeed," says Miss Burney, "very ill-favoured. He has naturally a noble figure, tall, stout, grand, and authoritative; but he stoops horribly; his back is quite round, his mouth is continually opening and shutting as if he were chewing something; he has a singular method of twirling his fingers and twisting his hands; his vast body is in constant agitation, see-sawing backwards and forwards; his feet are never for a moment quiet; and his whole great frame looks often as if it were going to roll itself quite voluntarily from its chair to the floor." One of his cheeks was disfigured by the marks of scrofula; and his face showed the peculiar nervous twitching known as St Vitus's Dance. His gait was rolling and clumsy; he seemed to be struggling with fetters.

Along with the scrofulous taint, he had inherited from his father a disposition to melancholy, which came upon him in cruel fits. During these gloomy seasons he was more imperious and irritable than Swift. He had inherited, also, a deep-rooted indolence and a hatred of regular work. His ambition, his desire to excel, was not alone sufficient to overcome this constitutional indolence. He needed to be "well whipt" at school, and when grown to manhood he did little more than enough to keep himself and his wife from starving. England gave him but "fourpence-halfpenny a-day," if she gave him no more, chiefly because he was too lazy to work for more.

His intellectual powers must not be judged by what he produced. He was indolent not in the sense of dozing away his time without thinking or reading, but in the sense of being averse both to productive exertion and to regular application. In his father's shop at Lichfield, in the college library at Pembroke, and in arranging the vast Harleian library of books and pamphlets, he was thoroughly in his element; ranging with luxurious pleasure from book to book, and insatiably storing up miscellaneous knowledge. Partly in consequence of thus reserving his strength, he was capable of intense concentration when he did apply his mind to production.

In dashing off a definition, a criticism, or a general precept, he seized with great force upon the leading features. In these moments of intense concentration, he had the power of doing in a wonderfully short time what Lord Brougham describes as seizing the kernel and leaving the husk. This habit of making short work with a subject gives his writings their most distinctive character. The bold comprehensive grasp, right usually in the main, has always deeply impressed the admirers of force. On the other hand, his hardihood in making untenably sweeping assertions, his inevitable omission of many considerations in the course of his intense but hurried survey, has severely tried the patience of the lovers of delicate accuracy.

His naturally powerful reason was a good deal clouded by various prejudices. He would believe no good either of republican or of infidel. He did injustice to Milton; he abused Bolingbroke without reading him; and Boswell mentions his having uttered about Hume a remark too gross to be committed to paper. He hated and ridiculed the French and the Scotch, and refused to be persuaded that anybody could live happily out of London. In these things, as in many others, he showed gross egotism and want of sympathy. Swift was not more overbearing nor more intolerant of contradiction. He had a peculiar horror of death, and if anybody was said to feel differently, he at once pronounced them either mad or mendacious. He was a humane, warm-hearted man, at least towards cases of extreme distress brought on by no fault of the sufferer; he opened his house as a retreat for several "infirm and decayed" persons; amused himself with their quarrels, and patiently endured their caprices. He had a few strong attachments. But even in his displays of benevolence and kindly affection, you see his natural love of domineering; he allowed nobody but himself to praise his favourites, and he treated them roughly when they deviated from his ideal of propriety. He was frequently humorous at his own expense, but he would allow nobody else to take liberties with him; he made boisterous mirth at the expense of certain of his friends, but he would not endure that the slightest air of ridicule should be thrown upon any of his own sayings or doings. Often in his writings he enforced the "vanity of human wishes." His 'Rasselas' is virtually a sermon on the impossibility of finding perfect happiness in this world; one of its professed objects is the benevolent achievement of damping the ardour of youth. Yet when anybody else ventured to complain in his presence, he was ready to avow that the world is a very enjoyable world, and to denounce all complaints as mere sentimental whining.

Though renowned as a biographer, he was far from being carried away by hero-worship. He is rather chary than enthusiastic in his allowance of merit, and scatters without mercy any air of romance or exaggeration that may have been gathered about an eminent name by the zeal of admirers. When Sir Thomas Browne, whom Johnson is said to have admired and imitated, declares that "his life has been a miracle of thirty years; which to relate were not history, but a piece of poetry, and would sound like a fable," —Johnson remarks somewhat sarcastically that "self-love, co-operating with an imagination vigorous and fertile as that of Browne's, will find or make objects of astonishment in every man's life."

Opinions.—In politics Johnson was a bigoted Tory. He could not repress his political leanings even in writing the definitions for his Dictionary. When writing the Parliamentary Debates for Cave, he "took care that the Whig dogs should not have the best of it." He wrote little in direct support of the Tories. After he received his pension he conceived himself bound to do something, and composed a few pamphlets—'The False Alarm,' 'The Falkland Islands,' 'The Patriot,' and 'Taxation no Tyranny.' In these he stated his views of true liberty and true patriotism, and maintained that the English Parliament had a right to tax the Americans without their consent.

Naturally a pious man, he was a bigoted Churchman. He hated Dissenters as "honestly" as he hated Whigs, infidels, French, and Scotchmen.

Though called the Great Moralist, he expounded nothing that could be called an ethical system. He simply applied strong good sense to the common situations of life. His first principles were understood, not stated.

The merits of his literary criticisms were the result of his good sense, their defects the result of his narrow sympathies and fragmentary knowledge. He seldom or never erred on the side of extravagant praise. He admired the wonderful powers of Shakspeare, defended the violation of the "unities," and the mixture of comedy with tragedy; but, along with the great dramatist's virtues he enumerated considerable failings—occasional "tumour, meanness, tediousness, and obscurity," wearisome narration, and the introduction of frigid conceits and quibbles, to the ruin of true sublimity and pathos. His tendency was to banish from poetry everything that would not be approved of by sober reason. In some points his principles of criticism were better than his practice. He laid down that "in order to make a true estimate of the abilities and merits of a writer, it is always necessary to examine the genius of his age and the opinions of his contemporaries." But this was a perfection-height of critical qualification that indolence would not suffer himself to attain. He wrote his notes on Shakspeare without having read a single one of the contemporary dramatists. He had plenty of time, but he preferred to indulge his appetite for social talk and desultory reading. Sometimes, too, he laid down principles that he broke habitually in his own composition. He satirised plays "where declamation roars and passion sleeps;" yet his own 'Irene' belongs to the category. He condemned the practice of filling out the sound of a period with unnecessary words. It is but fair to say that in later life he recognised his own faults. On one occasion, when some person read his 'Irene' aloud, he left the room, saying he did not think it had been so bad; and in his 'Lives of the Poets' he tried hard to work himself out of the sonorous grandiloquence of the 'Rambler.'

ELEMENTS OF STYLE.

Vocabulary.—Johnson's memory for words, and consequent command of language, was amazing. In this respect he stands in the very first rank. One might suppose, from what is usually said concerning the great preponderance of Latin words in his diction, that he failed in command of homelier language; but this is a mistake. His 'Rambler' is highly Latinised; but in his Preface to Shakspeare, 1768, we trace the beginnings of a homelier style. In his 'Lives of the Poets' the style is not so Latinised as the average style of the present day. The proportion of Latin words is not above half as great as in a leader of the 'Times.' He is often studiously homely, and shows a perfect command of homely diction. Perhaps the less pompous diction of his latest productions is partly a result of his great practice in conversation. As we have just said, he was conscious of the blemish in his 'Rambler,' and endeavoured to amend.

As an example of studied variety of expression, take the following comparison between punch and conversation:—

"The spirit, volatile and fiery, is *the proper emblem* of vivacity and wit; the acidity of the lemon will *very aptly figure* pungency of raillery and acrimony of censure: sugar is *the natural representative* of luscious adulation and gentle complaisance; and water is *the proper hieroglyphic* of easy prattle, innocent and tasteless."

Sentences and Paragraphs.—The often-remarked mannerism of Johnson's sentences does not consist in one particular, but in the combination of several.

(1.) The frequent use of the balanced structure. He employs liberally all the arts of balance both in sound and in sense. In the 'Lives of the Poets' he is much less elaborate and sonorous in his balances than in the 'Rambler.' In the following sentence from the 'Rambler' there are five different balances:—

"It is easy to laugh at the folly of him who refuses *immediate* ease for *distant* pleasure, and *instead of enjoying* the blessings of life, lets life glide away *in preparations to enjoy them ;* it affords such opportunities of triumphant exultation, to exemplify the uncertainty of the human state, to rouse mortals from their dream, and inform them of the silent celerity of time, that we may believe authors willing *rather to transmit than examine* so advantageous a principle, and *more* inclined to pursue a track so smooth and so flowery, *than* attentively to consider whether it leads to truth."

In the 'Lives of the Poets' there are few sentences of such sonorous amplitude. In this later work balances are numerous; but, on the whole, it may be said that there the cadence is more varied, and that we have a greater proportion of curt, short sentences and balances, in the following emphatic form :—

"Observation daily shows that much stress is not to be laid on hyperbolical accusations and pointed sentences, which even he that utters them desires to be *applauded rather than credited.*"

Such balances as the following are very common—"If his jests are coarse, his arguments are strong;" "too judicious to commit faults, but not sufficiently vigorous to attain excellence;" "his figures neither divert by distortion, nor amaze by exaggeration;" "however exalted by genius, or enlarged by study."

(2.) Short comprehensive sentences. These appear plentifully in all his works, but, partly from the nature of the subject, are especially plentiful in the 'Lives of the Poets.' The following short passage is a fair illustration :—

"In the poetical works of Swift, there is not much upon which the critic can exercise his powers. They are often humorous, almost always light, and have the qualities which recommend such compositions, easiness and gaiety. They are, for the most part, what their author intended. The diction is correct, the numbers are smooth, and the rhymes exact. There seldom occurs a hard-laboured expression, or a redundant epithet; all his verses exemplify his own definition of a good style; they consist of 'proper words in proper places.'"

(3.) One of the most striking mannerisms in Johnson's composition belongs strictly to the paragraph—to the arrangement of sentences rather than the arrangement of clauses. He has a habit of abruptly introducing a general principle before the particular circumstances that it applies to. We have remarked this as a peculiarity in Macaulay's style. If Johnson did not orginate this form of composition, he was at least the first to bring it into prominence. After him it was extensively adopted. Macaulay is hitherto his most celebrated imitator.

The following passage concerning Cowley is an example of his abrupt introduction of general principles. It exemplifies also a cognate practice of abruptly bringing in a person or thing contrasted or compared with the subject of the discourse :—

"In the year 1647, his 'Mistress' was published; for he imagined, as he declared in a preface to a subsequent edition, that 'poets are scarcely thought freemen of their company, without paying some duties, or obliging themselves to be true to love.'

"This obligation to amorous ditties owes, I believe, its original to the fame of Petrarch, who, in an age rude and uncultivated, by his tuneful homage to his Laura, refined the manners of the lettered world, and filled Europe with love and poetry. *But the basis of all excellence is truth: he that professes love ought to feel its power. Petrarch was a real lover, and Laura doubtless deserved his tenderness. Of Cowley* we are told by Barnes, who had means enough of information, that, whatever he may talk of his own inflammability, and the variety of characters by which his heart was divided, he in reality was in love but once, and then never had resolution to tell his passion.

"This consideration cannot but abate in some measure the reader's esteem for the works and the author. *To love excellence is natural; it is natural likewise for the lover to solicit reciprocal regard by an elaborate display of his own qualifications. The desire of pleasing has in different men produced actions of heroism, and effusions of wit; but* it seems as reasonable to appear the champion as the poet of 'an airy nothing,' and to quarrel as to write for what Cowley might have learned from his master Pindar to call 'the dream of a shadow.'"

To make up what is called the "Johnsonian manner," or "Johnsonese," we must take not only these striking peculiarities of sentence-structure, but certain other peculiarities, especially a peculiar use of the abstract noun, and vigorous comprehensive brevity. Macaulay's sentence-structure is modelled in a considerable degree upon Johnson's, yet the resemblance is not at first so striking, because Macaulay is a concrete and diffuse writer, whereas Johnson is extremely abstract and condensed.

Figures of Speech—Similitudes.—Our author's prose is not ornate. He studies condensed expression rather than embellishment or illustration. None of our great prose writers is so sparing of similitudes. In the 'Rambler' there are pages that contain hardly a single metaphor.

The few similitudes that he does use are in harmony with the general loftiness of his style. Thus, Imlac is represented as saying to Rasselas—

"The world, which you figure to yourself smooth and quiet as the lake in the valley, you will find a sea foaming with tempests, and boiling with whirlpools; you will be sometimes overwhelmed by the waves of violence, and sometimes dashed against the rocks of treachery."

Again, writing of the subversion of the Roman Empire by the Northern barbarians, he says that had America then been discovered, and navigation sufficiently advanced, "*the intumescence of nations would have found its vent, like all other expansive violences, where there was least resistance.*"

Allegory.—There are several allegories in the 'Rambler' on the model of the allegories in the 'Spectator.' One in the 'Rambler' on "Wit and Learning" is the model of Dr Campbell's allegory on "Probability and Plausibility," examined minutely in the Appendix to Bain's 'Rhetoric.' The allegoric style of composition, though still occasionally used, now makes its appearance in composition much less frequently than in the age of Johnson. The following is an example of the artificial manufacture, from 'Rambler' 96—"Truth, Falsehood, and Fiction, an Allegory:"—

"While the world was yet in its infancy, TRUTH came among mortals from above, and FALSEHOOD from below. TRUTH was the daughter of JUPITER and WISDOM; FALSEHOOD was the progeny of FOLLY impregnated by the wind. . . .

"It sometimes happened that the antagonists met in full opposition. In these encounters, FALSEHOOD always invested her head with clouds, and commanded FRAUD to place ambushes about her. In her left hand she bore the shield of IMPUDENCE, and the quiver of SOPHISTRY rattled on her shoulder. All the passions attended at her call; VANITY clapped her wings before, and OBSTINACY supported her behind," &c.

Contrast.—From his earliest composition to his last, Johnson shows a liking for strong antithesis. It is frequently combined with balance, and has been already to some extent illustrated. He is particularly fond of antithesis in his succinct expositions of character and style. Goldsmith is "a man who had the art of being minute without tediousness, and general without confusion; whose language was copious without exuberance, exact without constraint, and easy without weakness." Rowe "seldom moves either pity or terror, but he often elevates the sentiments; he seldom pierces the breast, but he always delights the ear, and often improves the understanding." "The 'Thessalia' of Rowe deserves more notice than it obtains, and as it is more read will be more esteemed." We have already quoted his account of Addison.

QUALITIES OF STYLE.

Simplicity.—Perhaps the most common objection to Johnson's style is that it contains too many heavy words of Latin origin. The objection is just, but there are one or two things that the objectors commonly overlook. One is that his earlier style is much more Latinised than his later: as already remarked, his 'Lives of the Poets' contains more of the Saxon element than the average style of the present day. Another thing is that his Latin derivatives are not of his own coining: he told Boswell that he had not taken upon him to add more than four or five words to the language; and being, as a lexicographer, brought painfully face to face with gaps in our language, he must in this respect have practised no little self-denial. Finally, he is much less Latinised than several writers of note both before and after him—than Sir Thomas Browne, for instance, or Robertson, or Gibbon.

The 'Rambler' certainly is a very ponderous composition. Reviewing it himself later in life, he shook his head, and exclaimed that it was "too wordy." Take as an example the following, which is not an extreme case:—

"In cities, and yet more in courts, the minute discriminations which distinguish one from another are for the most part effaced, the peculiarities of temper and opinion are gradually worn away by promiscuous converse, as angular bodies and uneven surfaces lose their points and asperities by frequent attrition against one another, and approach by degrees to uniform rotundity."

Compare this with a passage from Sterne, where you have the same idea:—

"The genius of a people, where nothing but the monarchy is *salique*, having ceded this department, with sundry others, totally to the women, by a continual higgling with customers of all ranks and sizes from morning to night, like so many rough pebbles shook along together in a bag, by amicable collisions they have worn down their asperities and sharp angles, and not only become round and smooth, but will receive, some of them, a polish like a brilliant."

Again, take the following, which is rather an extreme example, and reads almost like caricature "Johnsonese:"—

"The proverbial oracles of our parsimonious ancestors have informed us, that the fatal waste of fortune is by small expenses, by the profusion of sums too little singly to alarm our caution, and which we never suffer ourselves to consider together. Of the same kind is the prodigality of life; he that hopes to look back hereafter with satisfaction upon past years, must learn to know the present value of single minutes, and endeavour to let no particle of time fall useless to the ground."

A simple writer would have expressed this in some such way as the following:—

"Take care of the pennies," says the thrifty old proverb, "and the pounds will take care of themselves." In like manner we might say, Take care of the minutes, and the years will take care of themselves.

The heaviness of Johnson's style does not arise from any abstruseness in the subject-matter. The 'Rambler' took up mainly subjects suitable for light reading. The explanation seems to be that his ear was enamoured of a measured ponderous movement, of a lofty departure from the simple pace of common speech, and that he was not versatile enough to adopt any other, even when this was flagrantly unsuitable to the occasion. Myrtilla, a young lady of sixteen, is made to state her case as follows:—

"Sir, you seem in all your papers to be an enemy of tyranny, and to look with impartiality upon the world; I shall therefore lay my case before you, and hope by your decision to be set free from unreasonable restraints, and enabled to justify myself against the accusations which spite and peevishness produce against me.

"At the age of five years I lost my mother, and my father, being not qualified to superintend the education of a girl, committed me to the care of his sister, who instructed me with the authority, and, not to deny her what she may justly claim, with the affection of a parent. She had not very elevated sentiments or extensive views, but her principles were good, and her intentions pure; and though some may practise more virtues, scarce any commit fewer faults."

In the above extract, we see one good example of the peculiar use of the abstract noun that has already been spoken of as peculiarly Johnsonian. He uses the abstract noun with an active verb as if it were the name of a person—"the accusations which *spite and peevishness produce against me.*" Another example is seen in the extract immediately preceding—"sums too little singly *to alarm our caution.*" This is one of Johnson's most characteristic peculiarities, and appears no less in his later than in his earlier works.

Clearness.—Writing with an intense concentration of his energies upon the work in hand, he is generally successful in seizing upon the most apposite words to express his meaning. He is also anxious to be understood, and guards the reader from misapprehension by stating what he does *not* mean. (We have already exemplified his frequent use of contrast to explain qualities of style.) But he was too hurried to be a minutely accurate writer. His assertions are too unqualified. He had little of the scrupulous precision of De Quincey: the utmost we can say is, that his expressions are accurate in the main, and that he had an honest dislike to vague language. He ridicules the vague use of the word Nature, a supposititious entity not unfrequently appealed to even in our time. Rasselas asks a philosopher what is meant by "living according to nature," and receives the following caricature in answer:—

"To act according to nature, is to act always with due regard to the fitness arising from the relations and qualities of causes and effects; to concur with the great and unchangeable scheme of universal felicity; to co-operate with the general disposition and tendency of the present system of things."

Strength.—Johnson's style is seldom or never impassioned. He delivers himself with severe magisterial dignity and vigorous authoritative brevity.

Robert Hall, in his early days, made Johnson a model, but soon gave him up, complaining of a want of fervour in his morality. Though profoundly convinced of the doctrines of Religion, he seldom dilates on her "august solemnities," or on the grandeur of her hopes and fears. What he keeps principally in view is the beneficial effect of religious belief on human conduct, laying down the law in sonorous dogmas.

In the presence of objects that raise emotions of sublimity in other men, he was on the watch to lay hold of general rules. Instead of giving way to the æsthetic influences of the situation, he pondered on the causes or the moral value of them, and meditated dictatorial, high-sounding, general propositions. He acknowledged himself impressed by the ruins of Icolmkill; but instead of giving expression to the sublime thoughts awakened by the place, he fabricated the following sentence:—

"Whatever withdraws us from the power of the senses; whatever makes the past, the distant, or the future predominate over the present, advances us in the dignity of thinking beings."[1]

One may choose examples of his severity and comprehensive vigour from any page of the 'Rambler' or of the 'Lives of the Poets.'

Pathos.—A certain softness is thrown over the stern moralising of the 'Rambler' by the humane designs of the moralist. Good advice, however roughly given, if it is honest and not ill-natured, has a kindly effect. Farther, there is a pathetic air of gloomy melancholy about his sonorous reflections on the vanity of human wishes. But there is little in any part of Johnson's writings to touch the warmer affections.

On themes of sorrow, as on themes of sublimity, his power to move is paralysed by his constant tendency to reason and moralise. Instead of sympathising with distress, he seems to ask himself, Is distress in these circumstances reasonable? Rasselas in the happy valley reasons acutely on the causes of his discontent:—

"I can discover within me no power of perception which is not glutted with its proper pleasures, yet I do not feel myself delighted. Man surely has some latent sense for which this place affords no gratification, or he has some desires distinct from sense, which must be satisfied before he can be happy."

But though he is said to "bewail his miseries with eloquence," his lamentations are not very touching:—

"As he passed through the fields, and saw the animals around him, 'Ye,' said he, 'are happy, and need not envy me that walk thus among you, burdened with myself; nor do I, ye gentle beings, envy your felicity; *for it is not the felicity of man.* I have many distresses from which ye are free; I fear pain when I do not feel it; I sometimes shrink at evils recollected, and sometimes start at evils anticipated: *surely the equity of Providence has balanced peculiar sufferings with peculiar enjoyments.*'"

So when the Princess Nekayah loses her favourite maid Pekuah, and "sinks down inconsolable in hopeless dejection," she is represented as holding her own in an argument with the philosopher Imlac as to whether she "does well" to be sorrowful:—

[1] This proposition is an example of the sounding tautology that Johnson was sometimes betrayed into by his powerful command of expression. It might be analysed and translated into—"Whatever makes us think more, gives increased occupation to our thoughts." Similarly, his famous couplet—

"Let observation with extensive view
Survey mankind from China to Peru,"

is rendered—"Let observation, with extensive observation, observe mankind extensively."

"'Since Pekuah was taken from me,' said the princess, 'I have no pleasure to reject or to retain. She that has no one to love or trust, has little to hope. *She wants the radical principle of happiness.* We may, perhaps, allow, that what satisfaction this world can afford, must arise from the conjunction of wealth, knowledge, and goodness. Wealth is nothing but as it is bestowed, and knowledge nothing but as it is communicated: they must therefore be imparted to others, and to whom could I now delight to impart them? Goodness affords the only comfort which can be enjoyed without a partner, and goodness may be practised in retirement.'"

In the expression of impassioned affection he is as "uncouth and tumultuous" as Garrick described him to have been in his conjugal endearments. See, for example, the passionate lament of the devoted Anningait on leaving his mistress Ajut:—

"'O life!' says he, 'frail and uncertain! where shall wretched man find thy resemblance but in ice floating on the ocean? It towers on high, it sparkles from afar, while the storms drive and the waters beat it, the sun melts it above, and the rocks shatter it below. What art thou, deceitful pleasure! but a sudden blaze streaming from the north, which plays a moment on the eye, mocks the traveller with the hopes of light, and then vanishes for ever? What, love, art thou, but a whirlpool, which we approach without knowledge of our danger, drawn on by imperceptible degrees, till we have lost all power of resistance and escape? Till I fixed my eyes on the graces of Ajut, while I had not yet called her to the banquet, I was careless as the sleeping morse, I was merry as the singers in the stars. Why, Ajut, did I gaze upon thy graces? why, my fair, did I call thee to the banquet? Yet, be faithful, my love, remember Anningait, and meet my return with the smiles of virginity. I will chase the deer, I will subdue the whale, resistless as the frost of darkness, and unwearied as the summer sun. In a few weeks I shall return prosperous and wealthy; then shall the roe-fish and the porpoise feast thy kindred; the fox and hare shall cover thy couch; the tough hide of the seal shall shelter thee from cold; and the fat of the whale illuminate thy dwelling.'"

The Ludicrous.—The 'Rambler' is much more serious in its tone than the 'Spectator.' There is a greater proportion of gravely didactic papers. Not that the 'Rambler' has not considerable variety of topics. He does not confine himself to rebuking and satirising vices: like the 'Spectator,' he aims at being a censor of minor immoralities. Humorous satire of the follies of young men and young women of fashion alternates with grave rebuke to scepticism, and grave advice to young and old of both sexes and of different occupations. But the prevailing tone is serious.

His sarcasm is very different from the "gay malevolence" of Addison, and his humour very different from the good-natured sympathy of Steele. When his indignation is roused, his vituperation is round and unqualified. When he is in a pleasant mood, his humour is broad and arrogant. The most pleasing form of his humour is when he is humorous at his own expense.

The review of 'A Free Enquiry into the Nature and Origin of Evil, by Soame Jenyns,' is a well-known example of his bullying ridicule:—

"He calls it a *Free Enquiry*, and indeed his *freedom* is, I think, greater than his modesty. Though he is far from the contemptible arrogance, or the impious licentiousness, of Bolingbroke, yet he decides too easily upon questions out of the reach of human determination, with too little consideration of mortal weakness, and with too much vivacity for the necessary caution."

"I am told that this pamphlet is not the effort of hunger: what can it be then but the product of vanity? and yet how can vanity be gratified by plagiarism or transcription? When the speculatist finds himself prompted to another performance, let him consider whether he is about to disburthen his mind or employ his fingers; and if I might venture to offer him a subject, I should wish that he would solve this question, Why he that has nothing to write, should desire to be a writer?"

The above shows the Great Moralist in his most unfavourable aspect. He appeared thus only when his deep prejudices were crossed. Many of the 'Ramblers' are full of genuine humour, broad and hearty, and of happy strokes of wit. The following account of "The Busy Life of a Young Lady," purporting to be written by herself, is a favourable specimen. It forms one of the latest 'Ramblers,' and is written in an appropriately simple style, as if he had been warned of the incongruity of his sounding periods on similar occasions before:—

"Dear Mr Rambler,—I have been four days confined to my chamber by a cold, which has already kept me from three plays, nine sales, five shows, and six card-tables, and put me seventeen visits behind; and the doctor tells my mamma, that if I fret and cry, it will settle in my head, and I shall not be fit to be seen these six weeks. But, dear Mr Rambler, how can I help it? At this very time Melissa is dancing with the prettiest gentleman:—she will breakfast with him to-morrow, and then run to two auctions, and hear compliments, and have presents; then she will be dressed, and visit, and get a ticket to the play; then go to cards and win, and come home with two flambeaux before her chair. Dear Mr Rambler, who can bear it?

"My aunt has just brought me a bundle of your papers for my amusement. She says you are a philosopher, and will teach me to moderate my desires and look upon the world with indifference. But, dear Sir, I do not wish nor intend to moderate my desires, nor can I think it proper to look upon the world with indifference, till the world looks with indifference on me. I have been forced, however, to sit this morning a whole quarter of an hour with your paper before my face; but just as my aunt came in, Phyllida had brought me a letter from Mr Trip, which I put within the leaves; and read about *absence* and *inconsolableness*, and *ardour*, and *irresistible passion*, and *eternal constancy*, while my aunt imagined that I was puzzling myself with your philosophy, and often cried out, when she saw me look confused, 'If there is any word which you do not understand, child, I will explain it.'

. . . .

"But their principal intention was to make me afraid of men; in which they succeeded so well for a time, that I durst not look in their faces, or be left alone with them in a parlour; for they made me fancy that no man ever spoke but to deceive, or looked but to allure; that the girl who suffered him that had once squeezed her hand, to approach her a second time, was on the brink of ruin; and that she who answered a billet without consulting her relations, gave love such power over her, that she would certainly become either poor or infamous.

. . . .

"But I am most at a loss to guess for what purpose they related such tragic stories of the cruelty, perfidy, and artifices of men, who, if they ever were so malicious and destructive, have certainly now reformed their manners. I have not, since my entrance into the world, found one who does not profess himself devoted to my service, and ready to live or die as I shall command him. They are so far from intending to hurt me, that their only contention is who shall be allowed most closely to attend, and most frequently to treat me; when different places of entertainment or schemes of pleasure are mentioned, I can see the eye sparkle and the cheek glow of him whose proposals obtain my approbation; he then leads me off in triumph, adores my condescension, and congratulates himself that he has lived to the hour of felicity. Are these, Mr Rambler, creatures to be feared? Is it likely that any injury will be done me by those who can enjoy life only while I favour them with my presence?"

KINDS OF COMPOSITION.

Description.—Johnson rarely attempts to describe natural scenery, and where he does try, as in the description of the "Happy Valley," in 'Rasselas,' the clumsiness and poverty of the language betray his want of familiarity with the work. His interest, as he boasted, centred in man.

Narration.—He never attempted national history. Indeed he had a positive dislike to the subject; and rudely put down anybody that introduced it into conversation. As a biographer, he had great reputation in his own day. His Life of Savage, and his Lives of the great naval heroes, Blake and Drake (contributed to the 'Gentleman's Magazine'), were so much admired and talked of, that the king specially desired him to write the lives of his literary predecessors.

The excellence of his Lives consists not in narrative skill, nor in power of showing in varied lights the prominent features of character, but in the numerous maxims, moral and literary, attached to the biographical incidents. The narrative is really secondary. Such is his propensity to moralise, that the events in his biographies seem reduced to the importance of so many texts.

Exposition.—Johnson had not the qualifications of a popular expositor. His diction was too Latinised, and he did not sufficiently relieve the dryness of general statements by examples and illustrations.

The only art of exposition that he excels in is the putting of a statement obversely. We have already remarked his love of antithesis. In the review of Jenyns (which is also a good measure of his logical power) this is particularly apparent.

The short political tract entitled "The Patriot" is a very favourable specimen of his expository style. He considers with much vigour the various distinguishing marks of a true patriot, what he will do, and what he will not do; and then, obversely, "what will prove a man to be *not a patriot.*"

In expounding various delusive signs of patriotism, he proceeds almost entirely by repetition in pointed forms, direct and obverse. The following is a specimen:—

"Some claim a place in the list of patriots by an acrimonious and unremitting opposition to the Court.

"This mark is by no means infallible. Patriotism is not necessarily included in rebellion. A man may hate his king, yet not love his country. He that has been refused a reasonable or unreasonable request, who thinks his merit underrated, and sees his influence declining, begins soon to talk of natural equality, the absurdity of *many made for one*, the original compact, the foundation of authority, and the majesty of the people. As his political melancholy increases, he tells, and perhaps dreams, of the advances of the prerogative, and the dangers of arbitrary power; yet his design in all his declamation is not to benefit his country, but to gratify his malice."

Even this, which is in his later style, and is much more simple and concrete than the 'Rambler,' would have been more popularly effective if enlivened by examples. Macaulay would certainly have produced cases in point, if any were to be had. The following extract is more lively towards the end:—

"It is the quality of patriotism to be jealous and watchful, to observe all secret machinations, and to see public dangers at a distance. The true lover of his country is ready to communicate his fears, and to sound the alarm whenever he perceives the approach of mischief. But he sounds no alarm when there is no enemy; he never terrifies his countrymen till he is terrified himself. The patriotism, therefore, may be justly doubted of him, who" [better, we may justly doubt the patriotism of him that] "professes to be disturbed by incredulities; who tells that the last peace was obtained by bribing the Princess of Wales; that the King is grasping at arbitrary power; and that, because the French in their new conquests enjoy their own laws, there is a design at Court of abolishing in England the trial by juries."

Persuasion.—Johnson's faulty exposition diminished his influence with the generality of readers. The magisterial air of his 'Rambler' probably awed many into reading him with respect, and trying to profit by his doctrine; but the dry abstract character of the exposition must have made the perusal anything but a labour of love.

His political tracts must have exercised the very minimum of influence for the productions of so great a writer. He was the last man in the world to conciliate opposition, and his strong powers of argument were warped by prejudice. His 'Taxation no Tyranny,' written to defend the taxation of the American colonists against their will, is at once overbearing and sophistical. It might inflame and imbitter partisans, but it was too abusive and too unreasonable to make converts.

OTHER WRITERS.

THEOLOGY.

At the beginning of this period the controversy with the Deists was at its height. Tindal's 'Christianity as old as the Creation' had wrought the excitement to a frenzy. There was no lack of replies in various degrees of power; Leland enumerates as "valuable treatises" that appeared within the year 1730, works by Dr Thomas Burnet, Dr Waterland, Mr Law, Mr Jackson, Dr Stebbing, Mr Balguy, James—afterwards Dr—Foster, and a "pastoral letter" by Bishop Sherlock. There were many others. One of the most elaborate defences was made by **Dr John Conybeare (1691-1757),** afterwards Bishop of Bristol. This is praised by Warburton as "one of the best-reasoned books in the world."

The Deists were reinforced by **Thomas Morgan** and **Thomas Chubb.** Morgan published in 1737 'The Moral Philosopher, a dialogue between Philalethes, a Christian Deist, and Theophanes, a Christian Jew.' He does not hold with Tindal that the Christian republication of the law of nature is superfluous. He holds that Christ's promulgation of "the true and genuine principles of nature and reason" "were such as the people had never heard or thought of before, and never would have known, without such an instructor, such means and opportunities of knowledge." He calls himself a Christian Deist. But he repudiates both miracles and prophecy: Christ, he holds, attained moral truth by "the strength and superiority of his own natural faculties," and in that sense may be said to have had the light of revelation! He attacks Judaism. "He representeth the law of Moses as 'having neither truth nor goodness in it, and as a wretched scheme of superstition, blindness, and slavery, contrary to all reason and common-sense, set up under the specious popular pretence of a divine instruction and revelation from God.' And he endeavours to prove that this was the sentiment of St Paul." Further, he attacks the preaching of the apostles—"pretends that they preached different gospels, and that the New Testament is a jumble of inconsistent religions." Morgan was specially refuted by Joseph Hallet, Dr John Chapman, and Dr Leland. **Thomas Chubb (1679-1747)** was a self-educated man, journeyman to a tallow-chandler, yet much taken notice of for his "strong natural parts and acuteness" by wealthy patrons of letters. In his 'True Gospel of Jesus Christ asserted,' and in his 'Discourse on Miracles,' he takes much the same ground as Morgan. He left for publication after his death a variety of tracts on the most important subjects of religion. In these tracts, among other sceptical views, he expresses uncertainty regarding a future life.

Among the Deists it is usual to reckon Lord Bolingbroke. His philosophical works, containing his arguments against orthodox theology, were not published till 1754. By that time the excitement had died down. His declamations against religion, which went far beyond all previous attacks, were replied to by Leland and Warburton.

By far the ablest of the Christian Apologists was **Joseph Butler (1692-1752),** Bishop of Bristol and Dean of St Paul's. His 'Analogy' (1736) is so compact and exhaustive, that it has superseded and destroyed the reputation of all the replies to the Deists then current. It was directed chiefly against Tindal's 'Christianity as old as the Creation.' In the first part he proves elaborately that there is a Moral Governor of the universe who has placed man in a state of probation, and rebuts any argument from the incomprehensibility of parts of the scheme of the world to the untruth of the leading doctrines of natural theology. In the second part he maintains Christianity to be a divine republication of natural religion, and marshals the various evidences. The work is most thorough. It is a sagacious digest of all that had been said in the course of the controversy. "It is no paradox to say that the merit of the 'Analogy' lies in its want of originality. It came (1736) towards the end of the deistical period. It is the result of twenty years' study—the very twenty years during which the deistical notions formed the atmosphere which educated people breathed. The objections it meets are not new and unseasoned objections, but such as had worn well, and had borne the rub of controversy, because they were genuine. And it will be equally hard to find in the 'Analogy' any topic in reply which had not been suggested in the pamphlets and sermons of the preceding half-century." "Butler's eminence over his contemporary apologists is seen in nothing more than in that superior sagacity which rejects the use of any plea that is not entitled to consideration singly. In the other evidential books of the time, we find a miscellaneous crowd of suggestions of very various value; never fanciful but often trivial; undeniable, but weak as proof of the point they are brought to prove."[1] The matter of the work must indeed be of sterling value to retain it in the place it has permanently assumed as a text-book of Natural Theology. The style, as a style designed for general reading, could hardly be worse. It would hardly be possible to make a book more abstruse and difficult. This probably arises partly, as Mr Pattison points out, from his aiming at logical precision, at arranging the arguments so that each shall have its exact weight, and no more. He is probably entitled to the merit of precision. But his sins against simplicity, against ready intelligibility, are heinous. His sentences are long

[1] Mr Pattison—Essays and Reviews, p. 287, 289.

and intricate, he studies to express himself in the most abstract form possible, and there are very few examples or illustrations to relieve the dry press of general statements. His defects as a popular expositor are most vividly felt when he is compared with Paley, who may be said to have interpreted him to the multitude.

In **William Warburton (1698-1779)**, Bishop of Gloucester, we see a controversialist very different from the abstract and dignified Butler, a bold man, of great intellectual force and wide erudition. In his youth he was articled to an attorney. He took orders in 1727, and soon after obtained the rectory of Brand Broughton, in Lincoln. His first work was, in 1736, on the alliance between Church and State. His masterpiece is 'The Divine Legation of Moses' (1738). The leading idea, which immediately involved him in controversy, is the paradox that there is no mention of a future state in the Old Testament, and that this, so far from being an argument against its divine origin, is an argument in favour. With much learning and ingenuity he seeks to establish that no ruler except Moses has ever kept a people in subjection without the sanction of punishments in a future life, and argues that Moses could not have done so without supernatural assistance. Besides this great work, he published sermons and controversial tracts chiefly in defence of the Legation, and in refutation and abuse of Bolingbroke. One of his most famous exploits was his defence of Pope against the charge of Deism. Pope, it is said, had been led on the ice by his friend Bolingbroke, and had adopted doubtful tenets without being fully aware of their bearing. Warburton went opportunely to the rescue, and proved a redoubtable champion. In Warburton force predominated very much over judgment. He delighted in upholding paradoxes and hopeless causes—arguing with great ingenuity, eking out his argument with plentiful abuse, and, when violently excited, even going the length of threatening his opponent with the cudgel. His command of language, if used with greater discretion, would have given him one of the highest places in literature. His style is simple, emphatic, and racy; diversified with clever quotations and pungent sarcasm (often taking the form of irony).

Dr John Leland (1691-1766), a Presbyterian minister in Dublin, acquired considerable fame in the deistical controversy, which he made the chief occupation of his life. He wrote separate works against Tindal, Morgan, Dodwell, and Bolingbroke. His 'View of the Deistical Writers' (1754), a brief work written in a spirit of praiseworthy moderation, is still a text-book for students of divinity. His great work, 'On the Advantage and Necessity of a Christian Revelation' (1764), is long since forgotten.

Dr Nathaniel Lardner (1684-1768), also a Dissenting minister, published between 1730 and 1757 his voluminous 'Credibility of the Gospel History.' This vast quarry of learning supplied Paley with the material for his more neat and substantial 'Evidences.'

Dr James Foster[1] **(1697-1753)**, another Dissenting minister —who, when he preached in London, drew wits and beaux to hear him, making something like the sensation afterwards produced by Edward Irving—took part against the Deists in various tracts.

While the deistical controversy was raging, sacred literature was not wholly neglected. **Bishop Robert Lowth (1710-1787)** acquired great fame as a Biblical critic, translator, and commentator. **Dr Kennicot (1718-1783)** began in 1753 his great work of collating the MSS. of the Hebrew Bible. **Bishop Thomas Newton (1704-1782)**, the editor of Milton, published in 1754 his famous 'Dissertations on the Prophecies.' **Archbishop Secker (d. 1768)**, a man of somewhat eventful life, wrote lectures on the Catechism of the Church of England, which were widely circulated in their day. **Bishop Edmund Law (1703-1787)**, who edited the works of Locke, and whose life is written by Paley, published 'Considerations on the Theory of Religion, and Reflections on the Life and Character of Christ.'

Three or four devotional writings (or works in "hortatory theology," as Dr Johnson calls them) that were written during this period still hold their ground. Law's 'Serious Call to a Holy Life' (**William Law, 1686-1761**) is remarkable, as the book that is said to have converted Johnson from youthful levity. Watts's 'On Improvement of the Mind' (**Dr Isaac Watts, 1674-1748**, a youthful prodigy, a well-known author of religious hymns) was published about the beginning of this period. Doddridge's 'Rise and Progress of Religion in the Soul' (**Dr Philip Doddridge, 1702-1751**, one of the most distinguished of Nonconformist divines, and author of numerous religious works) was published in 1745. Hervey's 'Meditations on the Tombs' (**James Hervey, 1714-1758**, took part against Bolingbroke, and had with Sandeman a controversy of his own concerning the nature of faith), upon its publication in 1746, achieved immediate popularity, and is still to be found in nearly every Scotch household—its somewhat bombastic ornaments being no blemish in the eyes of uncritical readers.

The most celebrated pulpit orators of this generation, with the exception perhaps of James Foster, belonged to the Methodists. The germ of the Methodist Society was the "Holy Club" at Oxford, which, in 1732, included the two Wesleys, John and Charles, Whitefield, and "Meditation" Hervey, and drew inspiration from the author of the 'Serious Call,' the spiritual father

[1] All these three D.D.'s received the honour from Aberdeen.

of John Wesley. The name Methodist was first given to Charles Wesley,[1] and from him extended to his companions.

John Wesley (1703-1791), the son of an English clergyman, studied at Oxford and took orders. After officiating for some years as curate to his father, he returned to Oxford, was introduced by his brother Charles to the young "Methodists," and entered into their enthusiasm. He spent two years in evangelising the newly-established colony of Georgia (1735-37). Returning to England, he found himself one of the leaders of an impetuous religious awakening. In 1741 he and Whitefield agreed to separate. Wesley was comparatively a cold man, with a genius for ruling, and strove rather to restrain the impetuosity of his followers, acting as a drag upon their estrangement from the Church of England. He did not permit the independent organisation of Methodism till 1784. His preaching had not the melting power of Whitefield's. It would seem to have been more strenuous; at least it had the peculiar effect of throwing excitable hearers into convulsions.

George Whitefield (1714-1770), the founder of Calvinistic Methodism, was celebrated for the marvellous power of his oratory. He preached in many parts of England, America, and Scotland. Everybody is familiar with the anecdotes of his preaching; with his drawing tears from the eyes of the Bristol colliers, and money from the pocket of Benjamin Franklin. His published sermons are far from equal to his reputation; the charm seems to have been in his voice, elocution, and gesture.

The founders of the Secession Church in Scotland, the two brothers, **Ebenezer** and **Ralph Erskine**, were also noted preachers, especially Ebenezer. They were deposed by the General Assembly in 1740. The chief cause of the quarrel with the Established Church was the law of patronage. They are usually spoken of as heading in Scotland a religious revival such as Wesley and Whitefield began in England.

PHILOSOPHY.

The present is quite a flowering period in ethical and metaphysical literature. Hutcheson was in full vigour at the commencement of it; Edwards, Hartley, and Hume were publishing before it was far gone; Price and Adam Smith began to publish just before its close.

Francis Hutcheson (1694-1747), a native of Ireland, a student at Glasgow, received in 1729 the appointment of Professor of

[1] Charles Wesley was six years older than Hervey and Whitefield, and was the originator of the Club. When he introduced his brother John to the Club, John, being a senior of about thirty years of age, was looked up to with respect, and soon became their leader.

Moral Philosophy in Glasgow. He usually receives the credit of having by his eloquence and enthusiasm given the first great stimulus to mental philosophy in Scotland. His chief works were —'Inquiry into the Original of our Ideas of Beauty and Virtue,' first published in 1725; 'Essay on the Nature and Conduct of the Passions and Affections,' 1728; 'A System of Moral Philosophy,' published in 1755, after his death, containing the completest exposition of his views. He adopted and worked out Shaftesbury's suggestion of a *Moral Sense*. He maintained the existence of disinterested feelings. He placed the Highest Good in the pleasures of sympathy, moral goodness, and piety—exalting these against "creature comforts," Epicurean "enjoyment of life." His style was copious and glowing. He tries to engage the attention of the reader by great abundance of examples and comparisons.

David Hartley (1705-1757), a physician, was the first to bring into prominence the doctrine of the association of ideas, explaining by this theory the growth of moral sentiments. He is still more famous as the first English writer to bring into prominence the doctrine that the brain and the nerves are the instruments of the mind. Not much has been added to his proofs. He held that the impressions of sense are conveyed along the nerves by a vibratory movement. His 'Observations on Man' was published in 1749. The style of this work is sober, and possesses few attractions. It is, however, sufficiently clear, and the doctrines not being abstruse, it is, for a psychological work, comparatively easy reading.

Jonathan Edwards (1703-1758) is notable in Philosophy for his arguments against the so-called Freedom of the Will, and in Theology for his defence of the doctrine of Original Sin. He was born in Windsor, Connecticut, became a preacher, was closely connected with the great religious revival, though himself too feeble and awkward to address multitudes, conducted a mission to the Indians, and died President of New Jersey College. His 'Inquiry into the Freedom of the Will' was published in 1754; his work on Original Sin in 1758. He was of a severe ascetic turn. He was driven from his first charge as a minister in consequence of his rigorous purging of the sacramental tables. His controversial acuteness and subtlety in drawing distinctions entitle his works to their high rank. He had little turn for style. Dry and precise, without either felicity or ornament, his writings are calculated to repel all but hard students of their particular subjects.

David Hume (1711-1776) is in this generation what Berkeley, Locke, and Hobbes were in theirs. He belonged to a good Scottish family. His strong literary turn appeared at an early age. He tried to learn first law and then commerce, but found both uncongenial. He spent three years in France at Rheims and at the Jesuit College of La Fleche. Immediately thereafter, in 1739, he published his 'Treatise of Human Nature.' In 1741-42 appeared his 'Essays Moral and Political;' in 1748 his 'Inquiry concerning Human Understanding;' in 1751 his 'Inquiry concerning the Principles of Morals;' from 1754 to 1762 the various volumes of his 'History of England.' While these were in course of preparation he did not make his living by literature alone. During one year he had charge of an insane young nobleman; for two years he was secretary to General St Clair, accompanying him on an expedition to the coast of France and on a mission to Turin. Thereafter he had important appointments in the service of the Government. From 1763 to 1766 he was Secretary to the British Embassy at Paris, and on his return home became Under-Secretary of State for the Northern Department. The last six years of his life he spent in the pleasant society of Edinburgh. His 'Dialogues on Natural Religion' were published by his nephew in 1779, three years after his death. Hume is described as a corpulent man, "of happily-balanced temper," "of simple, unaffected nature, and kindly disposition." He says of himself—"I was, I say, a man of mild disposition, of command of temper, of an open, social, and cheerful humour, capable of attachment, but little susceptible of enmity, and of great moderation in all my passions." He was not a very productive writer. He did not so much teem with ideas; he rather gave himself to the steady elaboration of a few. His philosophical writings, whatever may be their scientific value, have the merit of being clear and consistent. He was very painstaking with his composition. His manuscripts bear evidence of the most careful revision and fastidious choice of words and phrases. Especially was he anxious to weed his diction of Scotticisms, inviting criticism and correction with a genuine desire to profit thereby. He offends chiefly by using terms peculiar to Scotch law. The great beauty of his style is its perspicuity. His choice of words is often very apt, and the combinations felicitous. The heavy character of his subjects is enlivened by a constant dry sparkle of antithesis, and occasional touches of quiet sarcasm and humour. He is highly eulogised by Dr Nathan Drake—"The Essays of Hume, in fact, sometimes present the reader with the grace and sweetness of Addison, accompanied with a higher finishing and more accurate tact in the arrangement and structure of periods; so that no language is more clear and lively, more neat and chaste, more durably and delicately pleasing to the ear, than what may be produced from the best portions of those elaborate but very sceptical disquisitions."

Adam Smith and Price published ethical works towards the close of this period, but they belong properly to the next generation.

HISTORY.

The most famous historical work of this period is **Hume's** 'History of England,' from the earliest times down to the Revolution. The author's original idea was to write this History from the Union of the Crowns to the accession of George I. He never brought it farther down than the Revolution; and when he had brought it to that point he enlarged his scheme in the other direction—went back to the invasion of Julius Cæsar, and carried down the narrative to the Union. The work was highly popular. It is sometimes compared with the 'History of England' by Macaulay, who began where Hume left off, and who is said to have been ambitious of proving a worthy continuator of the elder historian. The style, though more abstract and much less spirited than Macaulay's, and though the writer aimed at being "concise after the manner of the ancients," was brilliant and sparkling as compared with the ordinary historical performances of that or of prior date. There was also in the work a great feature of novelty. Hume was the first to mix with the history of public transactions accounts of the condition of the people, and of the state of arts and sciences. Although these supplementary chapters of his are very imperfect, and though he had neither materials for the task nor a just conception of the difficulty of it, still the little that he gave was a pleasing innovation. Like Macaulay, he is accused of partiality in his explanation of events, but in the opposite direction. He is accused of giving a favourable representation of the despotic conduct of the Stuarts, and of trying to throw discredit on the popular leaders.

A 'Complete History of England,' also from the invasion of Julius Cæsar, but brought down to a later period than Hume's—to 1748 (afterwards to 1765), was published by **Tobias Smollett,** the novelist, in 1758. A narrative from Smollett's pen could not fail to be attractive. But such a work written in fourteen months could hardly compete in manner, and still less in matter, with the eight years' careful labour of Hume. The style is fluent and loose, possessing a careless vigour where the subject is naturally exciting, but composed too hastily to rise above dulness in the record of dry transactions. As regards matter, the historian can make no pretension to original research. He executed the book as a piece of hack-work for a London bookseller, availing himself freely of previous publications, and taking no pains to bring new facts to light. He was in too great a hurry even to compare and check authorities: the history is said to be full of errors and inconsistencies. The concluding part of the work is sometimes printed as a continuation of Hume.

Among the minor historians of the period were **Thomas Carte (b. 1686)**, an intense Jacobite, secretary to Bishop Atterbury, author of a 'General History of England' (1747), and of a 'History of the Life of James, Duke of Ormond;' **Nathaniel Hooke (d. 1763)**, who assisted the famous Duchess of Marlborough in the vindication of her life, compiler of a 'History of Rome' (1733-1771), remarkable as taking the side of the plebeians; **William Harris (1720-1770)**, author of memoirs of James I., Charles I., Oliver Cromwell, and Charles II.; and the compilers of a 'Universal History,' published about 1760—namely, three Scotsmen (**Archibald Bower, John Campbell,** and **William Guthrie**),[1] **George Sale** (translator of the Koran), and **George Psalmanazar,** the pretended native of Formosa. With these we may reckon **Lord Hervey**, the Sporus of Pope, whose 'Memoirs of the Reign of George II., from his Accession to the Death of Queen Caroline,' were published by Mr Croker in 1848.

The writer of the 'Life of Cicero,' a historical biography, **Dr Conyers Middleton (1683-1750)**, receives high praise for his style from Dr Nathan Drake, when that work is said to be "the earliest *classical* production which we possess in the department of history." This, however, is considerably modified in what follows:—

"Its reputation, however, as a specimen of fine writing, is on the decline. . . . The chief defects of the composition of the 'Life of Cicero' have arisen from the labour bestowed upon it. The sentences are too often, in their construction, pedantic and stiff, owing in a great measure to the perpetual adoption of circumlocutions, in order to avoid customary phrases and modes of expression. The author has indeed, upon this plan, given a kind of verbose dignity to his style; but, at the same time, frequently sacrificed ease, perspicuity, and spirit. In grammatical construction, he is for the most part pure and correct; but in his choice of words he has exhibited frequent marks of defective taste. He is occasionally elegant and precise, but more commonly appears majestic, yet encumbered, struggling under the very mass of diction which he has laboured to accumulate. He has contributed, however, to improve English composition by affording examples of unusual correctness in the construction of his sentences, and of that roundness, plenitude, and harmony of period for which his favourite Cicero has been so universally renowned."

Middleton was a Fellow of Trinity College, Cambridge, an implacable enemy of the Master, Richard Bentley, with whom he had several lawsuits, and whose New Testament he attacked with extreme bitterness. He wrote several works of some note in their day. He is severely handled by De Quincey, who calls him "the most malignant of a malignant crew," rejoices that his gross unac-

[1] Mentioned by Boswell as a political writer of such power that Government "thought it worth their while to keep him quiet by a pension." He was one of the first authors by profession, unconnected with politics, though he did not scruple to enlarge his income by taking a side. He is praised as the first historian that made extensive searches among original documents.

knowledged plagiarisms were detected, denounces him for being a free-thinker all the time that he drew his bread from the Church, and says that his style "at one time obtained credit through the caprice of a fashionable critic."

The antiquaries of the period were,—**William Stukeley (1687-1765)**, author of an Itinerary; **Dr Thomas Birch (1705-1765)**, an industrious and faithful Dryasdust, associated with Sale in editing Bayle's Dictionary, writer of biographical memoirs, editor of Milton, of Dr Robert Boyle, of Thurloe's State Papers, &c. &c.; **Thomas Blackwell (1701-1757)**, Principal of Marischal College, Aberdeen, a great enthusiast, who gave a new impulse to classical studies in the North, and whose 'Memoirs of the Court of Augustus' was ridiculed by Johnson for its affectations of style.

MISCELLANEOUS.

Benjamin Franklin (1706-1790), the famous discoverer of the identity of lightning with the electrical spark, wrote several miscellaneous papers, scientific and political, which have doubtless had no small influence in forming American style. His chequered life is pretty generally known. He made his fortune as a printer, solely by his own sagacity, industry, and prudence, and bore a distinguished part in the assertion of American independence, acting as ambassador to France. His writings are remarkable for simplicity, terseness, and force. Both the language and the illustrations fit the meaning with emphatic closeness. He affects no graces of style: a hard-headed, practical man, he seeks to convey his meaning as briefly and as emphatically as possible. Thus—

"Be studious in your profession, and you will be learned. Be industrious and frugal, and you will be rich. Be sober and temperate, and you will be healthy. Be in general virtuous, and you will be happy; at least you will, by such conduct, stand the best chance for such consequences."

"He that spits against the wind, spits in his own face."

"He that for giving a draught of water to a thirsty person should expect to be paid with a good plantation, would be modest in his demands compared with those who think they *deserve* heaven for the little good they do on earth."

A writer of a very different stamp is **William Melmoth (1710-1799)**, the elegant translator of Pliny and Cicero, and author of 'Letters of Sir Thomas Fitzosborne on several Subjects' (1742). "The style of Melmoth," says Dr Nathan Drake, "both in his original and translated works, is easy, perspicuous, and elegant. He is more correct in grammatical construction, more select in his choice of words, than any preceding writer; but he is sometimes languid and verbose. His taste, which was very refined and pure, has seldom permitted him to adopt ornament not congenial to the subject of discussion, and his diction is therefore singularly chaste and free from inflation."

James Harris (1709-1780), a man of fortune, who rose to be a Lord of the Treasury, was celebrated as a writer on Art, Grammar, and Logic. His most famous work is entitled 'Hermes, or a Philosophical Inquiry concerning Language and Universal Grammar.'

Dr John Brown (1715-1766), a friend of Warburton and Pope, a critic of the Earl of Shaftesbury, is praised by Wordsworth as the first to appreciate and describe the scenery of the English Lakes.

CHAPTER VIII.

FROM 1760 TO 1790.

EDMUND BURKE,

1728—1797.

UNTIL the publication of Mr Macknight's 'Life of Burke,' the biographies of this eminent orator, writer, and statesman were full of minute errors. Contradictory statements prevailed concerning the date and place of his birth, the religion of his parents, his early education, his employments before he entered Parliament, and many other points wherein assurance is to be desired regarding a man of such eminence.

He was born in a house on Arran Quay, Dublin, most probably on January 12, 1728 or 1729.[1] His supposed ancestors were wealthy citizens of Limerick, who adhered to the Catholic faith, and lost their possessions in the time of Cromwell. His father was a solicitor in good practice, and belonged to the Protestant communion. His mother's name was Nagle; she was a Roman Catholic. It is of some consequence to note that Burke's earliest years were spent under the care of his Catholic uncles, who farmed some land of their own in the south of Ireland, and that his schoolmaster (Abraham Shackleton, of Ballitore, in Kildare) was a Quaker. He had thus the best possible training in the toleration of different creeds. From 1743 to 1748 he was a student in Trinity College, Dublin. He was too desultory to excel in the studies of the place; he had occasional fits of application to mathematics and logic; and he was awarded a scholarship in classics: but he did not carry off the highest honours in any one department.

[1] 1728 according to the register of Trinity College; 1729 according to the tablet in Beaconsfield Church.

Not that, like his contemporary the gay Goldsmith, he wasted his time in frolic and dissipation; but he gave himself up to miscellaneous reading, especially of poetry, to verse-making, and to day-dreaming. In 1747 he entered his name at the Middle Temple, and in 1750 went to London to keep law terms; but in this new study he showed equally little diligence, and for some years is to be conceived "as a young Templar, in delicate health, fond of jaunting about England, fond of literature, and anything but fond of law."[1]

His first literary productions appeared in 1756. 'A Vindication of Natural Society,' intended as a parody of Bolingbroke's reasonings on religion, is sometimes praised as a successful piece of mimicry; but it contains more of the real Burke than of the sham Bolingbroke. It may be viewed as an exercise in the style that the author ultimately adopted as his habitual manner of composition. The 'Essay on the Sublime and Beautiful' has much less glow and sweep of style; the writer's flow of words seems to be painfully embarrassed by the necessity of observing order and proportion of statement. In 1757 he married. The same year he wrote 'An Account of European Settlements in America,' and an unfinished 'Essay towards an Abridgment of English History.' Next year he suggested to Dodsley the 'Annual Register,' a yearly summary of notable facts. He is supposed to have written the whole of this annual for 1758 and for 1759, and to have contributed the political summary for a good many years after.

In 1759 he was introduced more intimately to political life. In that year he became connected with "Single-Speech" Hamilton as private secretary, or, as he was nicknamed, "jackal," his previous studies making him well qualified to act as political tutor. He accompanied Hamilton to Ireland in 1761, and is supposed to have been the original prompter of the efforts then instituted by Government to relax the inhuman penal laws against the Roman Catholics. In 1765, his connection with Hamilton having ended in an open rupture, he was fortunate enough to obtain the higher appointment of private secretary to the Prime Minister, Lord Rockingham, who continued his friend and patron to the last.

He entered Parliament in 1766 as member for Wendover. Our space will not allow us to trace his career minutely. During his first session he supported Rockingham's conciliatory policy towards the irritated colonies of North America in speeches that fairly rivalled the eloquence of the veteran Chatham. Thereafter he vigorously defended this policy both in Parliament and out of it, with speech and with pamphlet, through several stormy years until the final rupture and Declaration of Independence. 'Observations

[1] The story that in 1751 he applied for the Professorship of Logic in Glasgow is discredited as absurd, and its origin sufficiently accounted for.

on a late Publication, intituled The Present State of the Nation,' a reply to a jeremiad supposed to be written by Grenville, appeared in 1769; 'Thoughts on Present Discontents' in the following year. His patronage of the colonies was widely acknowledged. In 1771 he was appointed agent for the state of New York, with a salary of £500 a-year; and in 1774 he was returned to Parliament free of expense by the peace-loving merchants of Bristol. His famous speech "on conciliation with America" was made in support of certain resolutions that he introduced in 1775.

In 1778 he supported Lord Nugent's proposals for freeing the trade of Ireland from certain restrictions. The credit of this action—which, indeed, "the impartial historian" would have expected from any Irishman of moderately patriotic feelings—is not a little diminished by his factious opposition to Pitt's endeavours in 1785 to procure the abolition of the remaining restrictions.

In 1780 he brought forward his great scheme of economical reform. The ministers of the Crown had at their disposal a large number of lucrative sinecures, nominal posts in the royal household, and suchlike. On this patronage—a gigantic system of corruption, used by the Government to bribe adherents—Burke proposed to make considerable curtailments. Only a small part of his scheme was carried.

About the same time his attention was powerfully drawn to Indian misgovernment by his kinsman William Burke. In 1781 he sat on a committee of inquiry. In 1783 he assisted in concocting Fox's India Bill, which proposed to abolish the East India Company and vest the government in seven commissioners appointed for life. Shortly afterwards he opposed the more constitutional and judicious Bill introduced by Pitt. One of the most memorable events of his life was the conduct of the impeachment of Warren Hastings for tyrannical abuse of his power as Governor of India. The trial lasted from 1788 to 1794, judgment not being pronounced till 1796.

Much has been said regarding his views of the French Revolution, and his consequent separation from his political associates. In a debate on the Army Estimates in 1790, Fox took occasion to praise the French Guards, because, during the late commotions, they had sided, not with the Court, but with the people; they "had shown that men, by becoming soldiers, did not cease to be citizens." In the course of the same debate Burke deprecated this praise, called them "not citizens, but base hireling mutineers, and mercenary sordid deserters," and warmly asserted that rather than give the least countenance in England to the distemper of France, he would "abandon his best friends, and join with his worst enemies." Afterwards, when the leading members of his party avowed a decided sympathy with the Revolution, he openly and violently broke with them, and employed his eloquence in decrying that event with such effect that he has been called the leader of the reactionary movement throughout Europe. His most famous writings on the subject are 'Reflections on the French Revolution,' 1790; 'An Appeal from the New to the Old Whigs,' 1791; and 'Letters on a Regicide Peace,' 1796.

In 1794 he retired from Parliament. Shortly after, he sustained a great blow in the death of his only son, who had just been elected for Malton in his stead. Towards the end of the same year he received a pension from Government; and the apparent inconsistency of an economical reformer accepting such a boon having been attacked by the Duke of Bedford in the House of Lords, he replied in his famous "Letter to a Noble Lord," February 1795. He died at Beaconsfield on July 8, 1797.

Burke's appearance is described by Mr Macknight in the following terms: "Tall, and apparently endowed with much vigour of body, his presence was noble and his appearance prepossessing. In later years, the first peculiarity which caught the eye as Burke walked forwards, as his custom was, to speak in the middle of the House, were his spectacles, which, from shortness of sight, seemed never absent from his face. . . . His dress, though not slovenly, was by no means such as would have suited a leader of fashion. He had the air of a man who was full of thought and care, and to whom his outward appearance was not of the slightest consideration. But as a set-off to this disadvantage, there was in his whole deportment a sense of personal dignity and habitual self-respect. . . . His brow was massive. . . . They who knew how amiable Burke was in his private life, and how warm and tender was the heart within, might expect to see these softer qualities depicted on his countenance. But they would have been disappointed. It was not usual at any time to see his face mantling with smiles; he decidedly looked like a great man, but not like a meek or gentle one. . . . All his troubles were impressed on his working features, and gave them a somewhat severe expression, which deepened as he advanced in years, until they became to some observers unpleasantly hard. The marks about the jaw, the firmness of the lines about the mouth, the stern glance of the eye, and the furrows on the expansive forehead, were all the sad ravages left by the difficulties and sorrows of genius, and by the iron which had entered the soul."

"During his boyhood, and even for some years after he had reached manhood, his health was very delicate." He had an athletic frame, but a tendency to consumption threatened him in his childhood, and again when first he went to reside in London.

De Quincey justly describes Burke as "the supreme writer of his century." No writer of that century is to be compared with him as regards command of English expression. With equal justice, as it seems to us, he is described by Carlyle as "a man vehement rather than earnest; a resplendent, far-sighted Rhetorician, rather than a deep, sure Thinker." Others, who eagerly and somewhat perversely question this judgment of Carlyle's, maintain him to have been "a man of the highest genius, taking rank with Shakspeare and Bacon." There is no necessary discrepancy between these views, if only we recognise diversity of gifts, and cease to advance impossible claims for our favourite authors. Burke *may* have had as much intellectual force as either Shakspeare or Bacon, although it displayed itself in a different line. To be such a rhetorician as he was implies no common powers—immense resources of expression and illustration, a wide and ready command of facts, and fertile and far-sighted ingenuity in arranging facts and principles for the purposes of persuasion. To be among the foremost rhetoricians demands, probably, as great intellectual power of its kind as to be among the foremost poets or the foremost men of science. Be this as it may, one cannot read much of Burke's writings without seeing that they are essentially rhetorical. His 'Vindication of Natural Society' is obviously an exercise in the art of special pleading. Even his 'Essay on the Sublime and Beautiful' is the work of a rhetorician rather than a clear-sighted analyst. It is not a profound analysis of æsthetic emotions, but a wide assemblage of facts, and an ingenious pleading in favour of some very fanciful theories. His various pamphlets and speeches are, as Mr Arnold says, "saturated with ideas;" but the ideas are all brought out with polemical objects. Many of them appear to have occurred in the heat of pressing his point, and sometimes their application even carries an air of sophistry. The claim of high political sagacity, so often advanced in his favour, is not incompatible with this splendid ingenuity in accumulating substantial and insubstantial arguments in support of his views. Yet one may well doubt whether Burke's political sagacity was of the first rank. Certain of his predictions are sometimes quoted as evidence of this sagacity; but not to mention that many of his predictions were oracular failures, the very fact of making confident political predictions is in itself an evidence of want of sagacity. It is, of course, unprofitable to argue regarding a term so vague; yet we are safe to say that the highest honours of sagacity cannot be awarded to a man confessedly one-sided. He was too vehement and passionate to be always master of his sagacity. "When his passions were asleep," says an able editor of his works, "and his judgment calm, no man could display more perspicacity; the range and comprehensiveness of his intellect peculiarly fitted him for grappling with the most difficult and complicated subjects. *But his imagination was capable of leading him into the wildest extravagances.*" We can understand his vehemence against the French Revolution: for a quarter of a century he had been the persistent champion of constitutional conservatism, and a persistent enemy to the realisation of political ideals; and in the close of his life he found his lessons violently infringed, and his favourite pupils applauding the infringement as the highest achievement of political wisdom. Nothing could have been more exasperating to a man of proud sensibilities. But his views of the French Revolution are not the only evidence of his strong partiality for his own schemes. His opposition to Pitt's India Bill, and to Pitt's Bill for relieving the commerce of Ireland, offers perhaps stronger evidence of blind attachment to preconceived opinions. Doubtless he saw many aspects of a question, but he insisted upon throwing over them all a colour favourable to his own conclusions. The inability to look with the eyes of other men is universally admitted to have marred his influence in Parliament. Mr Macknight, who writes the life of Burke with somewhat of a biographer's partiality, allows that "his vehemence indeed was frequently injurious to the object he had in view. With his friends in a hopeless minority, his cherished measures entirely defeated, and his policy abhorred both by the Court and the nation, instead of growing apathetic, or at least quiescent, during this summer, he became only the more pertinacious, and even violent in his denunciations of the Indian interest and the Government which it supported. His speeches at this time abound in imagery, philanthropy, wisdom, all the noblest characteristics of his genius; yet was the manner of their delivery so impetuous and fervent, that plain men, who knew nothing, and cared less about the crimes which he declared to have been perpetrated in India, thought his zeal, remaining, as it did, unseconded by the two leaders of the House, to be almost incompatible with soundness of mind."

In many respects Burke presents a strong contrast to the social open-hearted Goldsmith. Both were compassionate and generous, and both were extremely sensitive to kindness and to affronts. But Burke had much more pride and reserve about him than Goldsmith; he was a much more dignified character. Goldsmith, with his keen sense of the ridiculous, and his power and habit of looking at himself from a spectator's point of view, often made a butt of his own failings. Burke bore himself with decorous self-respect. When Goldsmith wanted money, he borrowed openly and without shame; Burke died heavily in debt, yet somehow we never hear the circumstance mentioned. There was a corresponding difference between the men in their social demeanour. Goldsmith bestowed his affections, one might almost say, promiscuously; he was ready to fraternise with almost anybody: Burke, on the contrary, was a man of intense personal attachments, a devoted husband, a fond father, a firm adherent to the interests of his patron. Volatile in his likings, Goldsmith was equally volatile in his dislikings. He was eminently a placable man, incapable of a sustained grudge. Burke hated with a vehemence corresponding to the warmth of his attachments, and thought no expression too coarse, no comparison too degrading, for the objects of his resentment. To complete the parallel, Goldsmith's wit is light, and his style very seldom endeavours to soar; Burke deals rather in dignified irony or direct personal ridicule, and often soars to the highest heights of rhetorical sublimity.

Burke possessed great industry, great powers of acquisition. "He used to boast that he had 'none of that master-vice, *sloth*,' in his disposition." "The most minute provisions of a comprehensive act of legislation — the most wearisome drudgeries of Parliamentary committees—the driest and most tedious investigations necessary for drawing up elaborate reports,—to all this his patience and industry were fully equal. Some of the public documents he drew up are generally allowed to be perfect models of that species of composition."

His ideal polity was government by a patriotic aristocracy. He was never weary of maintaining that the end of government is the good of the people, not the aggrandisement of the governing body. At the same time, he did not recognise what the majority of voices has since declared to be the best means of securing this. He resisted Parliamentary reform. Looking to the corruption and venality of the electors, he was disposed rather to lessen their number with a view to increasing their weight and independence. Against the selfishness of rulers, in case they were inclined to pursue their own interests and forget their duties to the country, he provided no check but unembodied public opinion.

From the beginning to the end of his political life he frequently declaimed against the immediate practical application of what he called "metaphysical theories" of government. He was particularly hostile to the obtrusion of "natural rights" as a basis for legislation. The statesman has to consider not what is right in the abstract, but what is expedient in given circumstances. For his own part, the British constitution came near his ideal polity, and he vehemently contended that no change should be made except to remedy specific grievances. The disabilities of the Catholics, hardships in the Penal Code, financial extravagance, the iniquities of the Slave Trade, were unmistakable definite evils, and should be redressed; deficient representation in Parliament was but an imaginary evil—a hardship in speculation, not in practice.

With all his contempt for "visionary politicians," "metaphysical theorists," "legislators of the schools," "sophisters," and suchlike, he must not be classed with such "practical men" as Macaulay, who profess to dispense with theory altogether. "I do not," he says, "put abstract ideas out of the question, because I well know that under that name I should dismiss principles, and that without the guide and light of sound, well-understood principles, all reasonings in politics, as in everything else, would be only a confused jumble of particular facts and details, without the means of drawing out any theoretical or practical conclusion." Again—

"I do not vilify theory and speculation—no, because that would be to vilify reason itself. No; whenever I speak against theory, I always mean a weak, erroneous, fallacious, unfounded, or imperfect theory; and one of the ways of discovering that it is a false theory is to compare it with practice. This is the true touchstone of all theories which regard man and the affairs of men."

True, his language is not always so guarded; and unless we happen to light upon the right passages, we shall suppose him to have embraced in his contempt for metaphysical politics all works on the theory of government, from Locke downwards. If we read attentively, we find that in his calm moments he was far from despising political theories; his real aversion was for attempts to give immediate effect to political ideals in all their completeness:—

"I do not mean to condemn such speculative enquiries concerning this great object of the national attention" (the Constitution). "They may tend to clear doubtful points, and possibly *may lead, as they have often done, to real improvements.* What I object to, is their introduction into a discourse relating to the immediate state of our affairs, and recommending plans of practical government."

One great feature in his statesmanship was his consistent endeavour to introduce into the conduct of affairs between nation and nation higher principles of morality. Nations should be humane, just, and generous in their dealings with nations, as men should be humane, just, and generous in their dealings with men; what is immoral for a man is equally immoral for a nation. He ignored the fact that there is no earthly tribunal to preside over international disputes; no executive to punish international delinquencies; no higher power to guarantee nations in the possession of life and property should their neighbours be less generous and just than themselves.

ELEMENTS OF STYLE.

Vocabulary.—Burke's command of expression is strikingly rich. He rejoices in multiform repetitions, in varied presentations of the subject-matter:—

"It may be safely said that there never was a man under whose hands language was more plastic and ductile. No matter what his subject—no matter what the modification of thought which demands expression—he has always at command language at once the most appropriate and the most beautiful. As to the materials of his style, his vocabulary was as extensive as his knowledge,—and that was boundless. It consisted of the accumulated spoils of many languages and of all ages. Not only so, the technicalities and appropriated phraseology of almost all sciences and arts, professions and modes of life, were familiar to him, and were ready to express in the most emphatic manner the exhaustless metaphors which his imagination supplied from these sources. What is not a little remarkable, he could employ with equal power all the elements of our copious language, combining the eloquence and richness of a classical diction with all the nerve and energy of our Saxon vernacular. For lofty or dignified sentiment, he has at command all the magnificence of the former; while to give point and energy to sarcasm, and ridicule, and invective, he can employ the full powers of the latter."

We have already said that we regard such unqualified panegyrics as hopeless but profitable ideals, rather than descriptions of anything that has been or can be actually achieved. Perfect command of English, like any other perfection, is hard to attain; we must be content to rank Burke among the few that have come nearest to that perfection.

The following are two examples of his habit of urging the same fact in many different forms. The first is from his reply to the political pamphlet supposed to have been written by Grenville:—

"The piece is called 'The Present State of the Nation.' It may be considered as a sort of digest of the avowed maxims of a certain political school, the effects of whose doctrines and practices this country will feel long and severely. It is made up of a farrago of almost every topic which has been agitated on national affairs in Parliamentary debate, or private conversation, for these last seven years. The oldest controversies are hauled out of the dust with which time and neglect had covered them. Arguments ten times repeated, a thousand times answered before, are here repeated again. Public accounts formerly printed and reprinted revolve once more, and find their old station in this sober meridian. All the commonplace lamentations upon the decay of trade, the increase of taxes, and the high price of labour and provisions, are here retailed again and again in the same tone with which they have drawled through columns of Gazetteers and Advertisers for a century together. Paradoxes which affront common-sense, and uninteresting barren truths which generate no conclusion, are thrown in to augment unwieldy bulk without adding anything to weight. Because two accusations are better than one, contradictions are set staring one another in the face without even an attempt to reconcile them. And, to give the whole a sort of portentous air of labour and information, the table of the House of Commons is swept into this grand reservoir of politics."

Our other example is taken from the famous 'Letter to a Noble Lord:'—

"Making this protestation, I refuse all revolutionary tribunals, where men have been put to death for no other reason than that they had obtained favours from the Crown. I claim, not the letter, but the spirit, of the old English law—that is, to be tried by my peers. I decline his Grace's jurisdiction as a judge. I challenge the Duke of Bedford as a juror to pass upon the value of my services. Whatever his natural parts may be, I cannot recognise in his few and idle years, the competence to judge of my long and laborious life. If I can help it, he shall not be upon the inquest of my *quantum meruit*. Poor rich man! He can hardly know anything of public industry in its exertions, or can estimate its compensations when its work is done. I have no doubt of his Grace's readiness in all the calculations of vulgar arithmetic; but I shrewdly suspect that he is little studied in the theory of moral proportions; and has never learned the rule of three in the arithmetic of policy and state."

Sentences.—Giving his strength to the choice of words and of illustrations, he seems to have paid little attention to the mechanism of his sentences. Clumsily-constructed sentences occur frequently in his essay on the 'Sublime and Beautiful,' and occasionally in his later productions. He cannot be said to write in a formed style. In many of his vehement passages the sentences move with an abruptness and rapidity resembling the habitual mannerism of Macaulay. Nearly all the 'Letter to a Noble Lord' is written in this style. The following extract is a good specimen:—

"In one thing I can excuse the Duke of Bedford for his attack upon me and my mortuary pension. He cannot readily comprehend the transaction he condemns. What I have obtained was the fruit of no bargain; the production of no intrigue; the result of no compromise; the effect of no solicitation. The first suggestion of it never came from me, mediately or immediately, to His Majesty or any of his ministers. It was long known that the instant my engagements would permit it, and before the heaviest of all calamities had for ever condemned me to obscurity and sorrow, I had resolved on a total retreat. I had executed that design. I was entirely out of the way of serving or of hurting any statesman or any party when the ministers so generously and so nobly carried into effect the spontaneous bounty of the Crown. Both descriptions have acted as became them. When I could no longer serve them, the ministers have considered my situation. When I could no longer hurt them, the Revolutionists have trampled on my infirmity. My gratitude, I trust, is equal to the manner in which the benefit was conferred. It came to me, indeed, at a time of life, and in a state of mind and body, in which no circumstance of fortune could afford me any real pleasure. But this was no fault in the royal donor, or in his ministers, who were pleased, in acknowledging the merits of an invalid servant of the public, to assuage the sorrows of a desolate old man."

Figures of Speech.—Burke's profusion of figurative language has been the theme of endless admiration. His mind was a repertory of things generally known concerning history, sciences, professions, manufactures, handicrafts; and he drew illustrations from all classes of subjects in his multifarious knowledge. It is too much to say that "abstract and physical science, the most familiar and domestic arts, the professions, nay, the handicrafts practised by all classes of men, must yield up *their peculiar mysteries*, *their most recondite and technical phraseology*, to furnish the materials of his illustrations." Such things need "illustration" rather than afford it. To make obscurities plain, we do not have recourse to the most recondite and technical phraseology of special occupations. Burke does, indeed, occasionally use very technical terms—such as "lixiviated" and "aphelion;" but it is misleading to speak of this in the language of admiration.

It is usually said that his later writings are much more figurative than his earlier. In the hands of Macaulay this paradoxical circumstance has been greatly exaggerated. The figurative language of his earlier productions is more subdued, and attracts comparatively little attention; but the figurative turn is unmistakably there. And the language of his youthful letters is quite as extravagant as the most extravagant of his fulminations against the French Revolution.

Like Carlyle, he makes abundant use both of tropes and of the explicit figures. He is especially rich in metaphors: he has been called "the greatest master of metaphor that the world has ever seen;" and, if we except Carlyle, we may allow that he is the most metaphorical of our prose writers.

We shall not attempt to give a classified illustration of his figures. They are taken, as we have said, from many sources. A few extracts from his 'Letter to a Noble Lord' will give the reader a fair idea of their character. We must, however, remember that this composition was written at fever-heat, with the flaming vehemence of insulted sensibility, and that the illustrations have a corresponding temperature. Otherwise the specimen is sufficiently representative:—

"Let me tell my youthful censor that the necessities of that time required something very different from what others then suggested, or what his Grace now conceives. Let me inform him that it was one of the most critical periods in our annals.

"Astronomers have supposed, that if a certain comet, whose path intercepted the ecliptic, had met the earth in some (I forget what) sign, it would have whirled us along with it, in its eccentric course, into God knows what regions of heat and cold. Had the portentous comet of the Rights of Man (which 'from its horrid hair shakes pestilence and war,' and 'with fear of change perplexes monarchs'), had that comet crossed upon us in that internal state of England, nothing human could have prevented our being irresistibly hurried out of the highway of heaven into all the vices, crimes, horrors, and miseries of the French Revolution.

"Happily, France was not then jacobinised. Her hostility was at a good distance. We had a limb cut off; but we preserved the body. We lost our colonies; but we kept our constitution. There was indeed much intestine heat; there was a dreadful fermentation. Wild and savage insurrection quitted the woods, and prowled about our streets in the name of reform.

. . . .

"Had [certain 'Parliamentary reforms'] taken place, not France, but England, would have had the honour of leading up the death-dance of democratic revolution.

. . . .

"My measures were, what I then truly stated them to the House to be, in their intent, healing and mediatorial. I heaved the lead every inch of way I made.

. . . .

"The French revolutionists complained of everything; they refused to reform anything; and they left nothing, no, nothing at all *unchanged.* The consequences are *before* us—not in remote history, not in future prognostication: they are about us; they are upon us. The revolution harpies of France, sprung from night and hell, or from that chaotic anarchy which generates equivocally 'all monstrous, all prodigious things,' cuckoo-like, adulterously lay their eggs, and brood over and hatch them in the nest of every neighbouring State. These obscene harpies, who deck themselves in I know not what divine attributes, but who in reality are foul and ravenous birds of prey (both mothers and daughters), flutter over our heads, and souse down upon our tables, and leave nothing unrent, unrifled, unravaged, or unpolluted with the slime of their filthy offal.

. . . .

"I was not, like his Grace of Bedford, swaddled, and rocked, and dandled into a legislator; *Nitor in adversum* is the motto for a man like me. At every step of my progress in life (for every step was I traversed and opposed), and at every turnpike I met, I was obliged to show my passport, and again and again to prove my title to the honour of being useful to my country.

. . . .

"The grants to the house of Russel were so enormous as not only to outrage economy, but even to stagger credibility. The Duke of Bedford is the leviathan among all the creatures of the Crown. He tumbles about his unwieldly bulk; he plays and he frolics in the ocean of the royal bounty. Huge as he is, and whilst 'he lies floating many a rood,' he is still a creature. His ribs, his fins, his whalebone, his blubber, the very spiracles through which he spouts a torrent of brine against his origin, and covers me all over with the spray—everything of him and about him is from the throne. Is it for *him* to question the dispensation of the royal favour?

. . . .

"The persons who have suffered from the cannibal philosophy of France are so like the Duke of Bedford, that nothing but his Grace's probably not speaking quite so good French, could enable us to find out any difference. . . . I assure him that the Frenchified faction, more encouraged than others, are warned by what has happened in France. Look at him and his landed possessions as an object at once of curiosity and rapacity. He is made for them in every part of their double character. As robbers, to them he is a noble booty; as speculatists, he is a glorious subject for their experimental philosophy. He affords matter for an extensive analysis in all the branches of their science, geometrical, physical, civil, and political. . . . . Deep philosophers are no triflers: brave sans-culottes are no formalists. They will no more regard a Marquis of Tavistock than an Abbot of Tavistock; the Lord of Woburn will not be more respectable in their eyes than the Prior of Woburn; they will make no difference between the superior of a Covent Garden of nuns, and of a Covent Garden of another description. They will not care a rush whether his coat is long or short; whether the colour be purple or blue and buff. They will not trouble *their* heads with what part of *his* head his hair is cut from; and they will look with equal respect on a tonsure and a crop. Their only question will be, that of their *Legendre*, or some other of their legislative butchers, how he cuts up? how he tallows in the caul or on the kidneys?

"Is it not a singular phenomenon, that whilst the sans-culotte carcase-butchers, and the philosophers of the shambles, are pricking their dotted lines upon his hide, and like the print of the poor ox that we see at the shop-windows at Charing-Cross, alive as he is, and thinking no harm in the world, he is divided into rumps, and sirloins, and briskets, and into all sorts of pieces for roasting, boiling, and stewing, that all the while they are measuring *him*, his Grace is measuring *me*; is invidiously comparing the bounty of the Crown with the deserts of the defender of his order, and in the same moment fawning on those who have the knife half out of the sheath—poor innocent!

'Pleas'd to the last, he crops the flow'ry food,
And licks the hand just raised to shed his blood.'"

QUALITIES OF STYLE.

Simplicity.—From the nature of his subjects, and the imperious necessity of being directly intelligible to an audience, the public speaker generally uses a more familiar diction than the writer of recondite books; and when he takes his pen in hand to produce a political pamphlet, his style is likely to have something of the easy intelligibility of his speeches. Burke cannot be classed among the more abstruse writers of our language. But he may be said to be abstruse for an orator. His turn of expression is often abstract; and in the pursuit of loftiness and dignity, he introduces a large mixture of unfamiliar words from Latin sources.

Not, however, that he is invariably magniloquent. He frequently unbends, and then becomes homely enough. Especially when he wishes to cover anything with ridicule, his words are taken from everyday speech, and his figures from the commonest objects; indeed, both words and figures are often plain to the degree of being coarse.

He is the model of Macaulay in his abundant use of facts and statistics. But his facts and statistics have not the simple effect of Macaulay's; he is more thoroughgoing, enters more into detail; his 'Observations on the State of the Nation,' and his speech on 'Economical Reform,' are not superficial productions, but discuss their respective topics with the fulness of a speech on the Budget.

Clearness, Perspicuity.—His earlier writings are arranged with great clearness. His later works, like Carlyle's political rhapsodies, are less perspicuous. He was aware of the importance of method; in his 'Reflections on the French Revolution,' he adopted the form of a letter advisedly, that he might have greater scope. "A different plan, he was sensible, might have been more favourable to a commodious division and distribution of the matter." In such a work, rigid obedience to a plan would have been a cold obstruction to the warm flow of his eloquence.

Precision.—It may be doubted whether, with all his industry, he had patience enough to be a precise writer. His treatise on the 'Sublime and Beautiful' is very much wanting in the exactness required for scientific discussion. He shows himself conscious of the principle that in scientific writing each word should be used in a definite sense; and himself proposes to give the loose word "delight" a distinctive signification; but before many pages are over he violates his own definition.

Strength.—Strength is the prominent quality in Burke's style, as it is in our literature generally. The peculiar mode is difficult to express; but it may be said that Burke's strength has something of the quality of Macaulay's, although possessing greater body and less rapidity and point. We have already mentioned the similarity in the structure of their sentences. They have also a similar declamatory energy, a similar concreteness, and something of the same mixture of original turns of expression with a copious use of stock-phrases. Before we can feel the resemblance, we must leave out of sight the differences in opinion and in depth and range of thought; when we succeed in disregarding these differences in subject-matter, the resemblance otherwise is very striking.

The following is a fair specimen of the general style of the 'Reflections.' In it we can easily trace all the above points of resemblance to Macaulay:—

"I find a preacher of the Gospel profaning the beautiful and prophetic ejaculation commonly called *nunc dimittis*, made on the first presentation of our Saviour in the Temple, and applying it with an inhuman and unnatural rapture, to the most horrid, atrocious, and afflicting spectacle that perhaps ever was exhibited to the pity and indignation of mankind. This '*leading in triumph*,' a thing in its best form unmanly and irreligious, which fills our preacher with such unhallowed transports, must shock, I believe, the moral taste of every well-born mind. Several English were the stupefied and indignant spectators of that triumph. It was (unless we have been strangely deceived) a spectacle more resembling a procession of American savages, entering into Onondago, after some of their murders called victories, and leading into hovels hung round with scalps, their captives, overpowered with the scoffs and buffets of women as ferocious as themselves, much more than it resembled the triumphal pomp of a civilised, martial nation;—if a civilised nation, or any men who had a sense of generosity, were capable of a personal triumph over the fallen and the afflicted. . . . I must believe that the National Assembly find themselves in a state of the greatest humiliation in not being able to punish the authors of this triumph or the actors in it; and that they are in a situation in which any inquiry they may make upon the subject must be destitute even of the appearance of liberty or impartiality. The apology of that Assembly is found in their situation; but when we approve what they *must* bear, it is in us the degenerate choice of a vitiated mind.

"With a compelled appearance of deliberation they vote under the dominion of a stern necessity. They sit in the heart, as it were, of a foreign republic; they have their residence in a city whose constitution has emanated neither from the charter of their king, nor from their legislative power. There they are surrounded by an army not raised either by the authority of their crown, or by their command; and which, if they should order to dissolve itself, would instantly dissolve them. There they sit, after a gang of assassins had driven away some hundreds of the members; whilst those who held the same moderate principles, with more patience or better hope, continued every day exposed to outrageous insults and murderous threats. There a majority, sometimes real, sometimes pretended, captive itself, compels a captive king to issue as royal edicts, at third hand, the polluted nonsense of their most licentious and giddy coffee-houses. It is notorious that all their measures are decided before they are debated. It is beyond doubt that under the terror of the bayonet, and the lamp-post, and the torch to their houses, they are obliged to adopt all the crude and desperate measures suggested by clubs composed of a monstrous medley of all conditions, tongues, and nations. Among these are found persons, in comparison of whom Catiline would be thought scrupulous, and Cethegus a man of sobriety and moderation. Nor is it in the clubs alone that the public measures are deformed into monsters. They undergo a previous distortion in academies, intended as so many seminaries for these clubs, which are set up in all the places of public resort. In these meetings of all sorts, every counsel, in proportion as it is daring, and violent, and perfidious, is taken for a mark of superior genius. Humanity and compassion are ridiculed as the fruits of superstition and ignorance. Tenderness to individuals is considered as treason to the public. Liberty is always to be estimated perfect as property is rendered insecure. Amidst assassination, massacre, and confiscation, perpetrated or meditated, they are forming plans for the good order of future society. Embracing in their arms the carcases of base criminals, and promoting their relations on the title of their offences, they drive hundreds of virtuous persons to the same end, by forcing them to subsist by beggary or by crime."

In passages specially laboured, where Burke's individual genius is at its height, and the figures and turns of expression are peculiarly his own, we cannot profess to trace any appreciable likeness. The following is quoted by De Quincey, with the remark that Burke is said to have acknowledged spending more labour upon it than upon any passage in all his writings, and to have been tolerably satisfied with the result:—

"As long as the well-compacted structure of our Church and State, the sanctuary, the holy of holies of that ancient law, defended by reverence, defended by power, a fortress at once and a temple, shall stand inviolate on the brow of the British Zion; as long as the British monarchy, not more limited than fenced by the orders of the State, shall, like the proud keep of

Windsor, rising in the majesty of proportion, and girt with the double belt of its kindred and coeval towers, as long as this awful structure shall oversee and guard the subjected land, so long the mounds and dykes of the low flat Bedford level will have nothing to fear from all the pickaxes of all the levellers of France. As long as our sovereign lord the king, and his faithful subjects the lords and commons of this realm, the triple cord which no man can break ; the solemn sworn constitutional frank-pledge of this nation ; the firm guarantees of each other's being and each other's rights ; the joint and several securities, each in its place and order for every kind and every quality of property and of dignity,—as long as these endure, so long the Duke of Bedford is safe, and we are all safe together ; the high from the blights of envy and the spoliation of rapacity ; the low from the iron hand of oppression and the insolent spurn of contempt. Amen ! and so be it : and so it will be,

> 'Dum domus Æneæ Capitoli immobile saxum
> Accolet ; imperiumque pater Romanus habebit.' "

The great element of power in Burke, over and above what he has in common with Macaulay, is his extravagant splendour of imagery. This, especially in the picked passages usually quoted from him, gives such a flavour to his composition, that readers, forming their judgment upon these passages, would refuse to believe how much Macaulay had made him a model. He rises to a pitch of wild excitement that Macaulay was incapable of. The images thrown off in these ungovernable moments were such as Macaulay could never have imitated. The following, from the 'Letters on a Regicide Peace,' describing the embassy to the French Minister, is a well-known quotation :—

"To those who do not love to contemplate the fall of human greatness, I do not know a more mortifying spectacle than to see the assembled majesty of the crowned heads of Europe waiting as patient suitors in the ante-chamber of regicide. They wait, it seems, until the sanguinary tyrant *Carnot* shall have snorted away the fumes of the indigested blood of his sovereign. Then, when, sunk on the down of usurped pomp, he shall have sufficiently indulged his meditations with what monarch he shall next glut his ravening maw, he may condescend to signify that it is his pleasure to be awake ; and that he is at leisure to receive the proposals of his high and mighty clients for the terms on which he may respite the execution of the sentence he has passed upon them. At the opening of those doors, what a sight it must be to behold the plenipotentiaries of royal impotence, in the precedency which they will intrigue to obtain, and which will be granted to them according to the seniority of their degradation, sneaking into the regicide presence, and, with the relics of the smile, which they had dressed up for the levee of their masters, still flickering on their curled lips, presenting the faded remains of their courtly graces, to meet the scornful, ferocious, sardonic grin of a bloody ruffian, who, whilst he is receiving their homage, is measuring them with his eye, and fitting to their size the slider of his guillotine ! These ambassadors may easily return as good courtiers as they went : but can they ever return from that degrading residence, loyal and faithful subjects ; or with any true affection to their master, or true attachment to the constitution, religion, or laws of their country ? There is great danger that they, who enter smiling into this Trophonian cave, will come out of it sad and serious conspirators ; and such will continue as long as they live. They will become true conductors of contagion to every country which has had the misfortune to send them to the source of that electricity."

Pathos.—Burke is often said to excel in pathos as in every other quality of style; but if we take tranquillity and composure to be part of the essence of pathos, there is very little of it to be found within the range of his published works. It was inconsistent with his purposes as an orator to draw soothing pictures of distress. In the conclusion of the celebrated Begum charge in the trial of Warren Hastings, he is said to have made "an affecting appeal to the feelings and the passions of their lordships;" but his object was to horrify and inflame them, not to fill them with luxurious feelings of compassion. The soft tranquillity of pathos was inconsistent with his purposes as an orator. It was no less inconsistent with his nature. An excitable man, of ungovernable sensibility, when his feelings were moved he was ever prone to run into wild extravagance. He probably possessed the power of communicating his own excitement to such as were not repelled by it; but the effect produced went very far beyond the tranquil borders of pathos.

His well-known allusion to Marie Antoinette is very touching, but it touches our sensibilities more keenly than pathos. The emotion cannot sustain itself in the melting mood, but passes into fiery indignation.

The Ludicrous.—During his quarter of a century of polemical life, he made abundant use of the weapon of ridicule. In his earlier writings he had recourse chiefly to dignified irony—irony that shows no great wit, but is always pleasing and effective from the copiousness and vigour of the language. The ridicule of his later writings, of which we have had a specimen in the quotations from his 'Letter to a Noble Lord,' is extravagantly excited and personal. "If by wit," says Mr Rogers, "be meant any of its lighter and more playful species, then it can hardly be doubted that in these Burke did not excel; at least whatever powers of this kind he might possess, they were in no sort of proportion to his other intellectual endowments. It is true that Burke was fond of punning; his success, however, was not equal to his ardour in the pursuit. Again, if by wit be meant that caustic and subtle irony, which is the more powerful from the calmness of the style, and stings the deeper from the collected manner of him who utters it—neither did Burke possess much of this. But if by wit be meant any of its forms compatible with fierce invective, his speeches abound with innumerable instances of the highest merit." His invective, as we see in his attack upon the Duke of Bedford, is of the most direct and unvarnished kind. He does not scruple to make the most grossly offensive comparisons in the plainest terms. Frequently, indeed, by his vehemence, he defeated his own ends. Only partisans could have applauded his recriminations on the Duke of Bedford, and his unmeasured abuse of Hastings provoked a reaction in favour of the victim.

The following are examples of the licence that he ventured to take in his invective against Hastings. We quote from the collection of his speeches :—

"What (said Mr Burke) could make this proud and haughty ruler of India submit to such language, and bear with such opprobrium? Guilt, conscious guilt! The cursed love of money had got possession of his soul; and in the contemplation of his detested wealth, he found sufficient consolation for the loss of character and of honour. Under the lash of Sir John Clavering, and the execration of all Asia, he seemed to say with the poet—

'——*Populus me sibilat, at mihi plaudo*
Ipse domi, simul ac nummos contemplor in arca.' [1]

It was this love of money that made him deaf to the calls of glory, and callous to the feelings of honour. It was this unbounded and insatiable passion for money that had seared his conscience and his feelings; and happy in the accumulation of wealth, even by the foulest means, he could bear, unmoved, the most cutting reproaches of Sir John Clavering. He lay down in his stye of infamy, wallowed in the filth of disgrace, and fattened upon the offals and excrements of dishonour."

Again—

"Mr Burke then cited passages from a variety of Oriental authors, proving the right of property in India, and showing that that property had been respected by the greatest princes and conquerors, by Tamerlane, Gengis Khan, Khouli Khan, and others. But (said Mr Burke) the Council have fancied that we compared Mr Hastings to Tamerlane and others, and they have told your lordships of the thousands of men slaughtered by the ambition of those princes. Good God! have they lost their senses? Can they suppose that we meant to compare a fraudulent maker of bullock-contracts with an illustrious conqueror? We never compared Hastings to a lion or a tiger; we have compared him to a rat or a weasel. When we assimilate him to such contemptible animals, we do not mean to convey an idea of their incapability of doing injury. When God punished Pharaoh and Egypt, it was not by armies, but by locusts and by lice, which, though small and contemptible, are capable of the greatest mischiefs."

Such puerile meanness of invective must inevitably recoil upon the author. In a cooler frame of mind, Burke himself would have been the first to condemn it; and we cannot suppose that he ever indulged in it without to some extent bullying his artistic as well as his prudential conscience.

His fury against Hastings carried him to lengths still more outrageous :—

"He made some very sarcastic similes as to the connection between Mr Hastings and the Begums, quoting Dean Swift's 'Progress of Love' as

[1] "The people hiss me, but when I go home and feast my eyes upon the coins in my safe, I cry 'Bravo!' to myself."

applicable on the occasion. The humour touching the Munny Begum flowed something in this way: 'Age has its comforts—the consolations of debility and ugliness may be found in brandy. The old lady had therein a monopoly. She was a great dealer in the article. But mark the transition—a youth of sentiment and love; an old age reposing upon the brandy-cask.' He then ironically adverted to the passion of great men for strumpets. 'Antony had his Cleopatra, and Mr Hastings his Munny Begum. It might be so; for aged, shrivelled, bony deformity had its relish for some palates; but, good God! no man ever fell in love with his own banyan[1]!'"

We have seen that he compared Hastings to a wallowing sow. He also compared him to "the keeper of a pig-stye, wallowing in filth and corruption." Towards the conclusion he became so violent as to apply the epithets "rogue, common cheat, swindler;" and to declare—"You must repeal this Act of Parliament, you must declare the Legislature a liar, before you can acquit Warren Hastings."

Taste.—In his more excited compositions Burke frequently offends against good taste. His abuse of the Duke of Bedford, of Warren Hastings, and of the principal actors in the French Revolution, is often outrageously coarse. His comparison of the Duke to a whale, his comparison of Hastings to a sow, and his imagining Carnot to have drunk the blood of a king, and to be "snorting away the fumes of indigestion" in consequence, cannot be paralleled except from "the scolding of the ancients;" and these are not perhaps his worst violations of taste. Lord Brougham produces the following tit-bit concerning Mr Dundas:—

"With six great chopping bastards" ('Reports of Secret Committee'), "each as lusty as an infant Hercules, this delicate creature blushes at the sight of his new bridegroom, assumes a virgin delicacy; or to use a more fit, as well as a more poetical, comparison, the person so squeamish, so timid, so trembling lest the winds of heaven should visit too roughly, is expanded to broad sunshine, exposed like the sow of imperial augury, lying in the mud with all the prodigies of her fertility about her, as evidence of her delicate amour."

These occasional infractions of taste, gross though they be, must not be allowed to detract from his just fame as "the supreme writer of his century." Taste is certainly not the special virtue of English literature: there is none of our greatest masters of prose that does not offend in some particular. Burke was far from being prone "to revolve ideas from which other minds shrink with disgust," at least in cold blood; only when excited he could not find images too disgusting to express his aversion.

KINDS OF COMPOSITION.

Description.—Burke's descriptive *forte* is very like Macaulay's. There is no method in his descriptions; his works contain none of

[1] "Money-broker."

the elaborate word-painting to be found in Carlyle; but he details impressive circumstances with his characteristic fulness of expression, and profusion and boldness of imagery.

He gives the following picturesque account of the ancient manner of catering for the royal household:—

"These old establishments were formed also on a third principle, still more adverse to the living economy of the age. They were formed, sir, on the principle of *purveyance*, and *receipt in kind*. In former days, when the household was vast, and the supply scanty and precarious, the royal purveyors, sallying forth from under the Gothic portcullis to purchase provision with power and prerogative instead of money, brought home the plunder of a hundred markets, and all that could be seized from a flying and hiding country; and deposited their spoils in a hundred caverns, with each its keeper."

The present condition of the royal palaces he describes as follows:—

"But when the reason of old establishments is gone, it is absurd to preserve nothing but the burthen of them. . . . Our palaces are vast, inhospitable halls. There the bleak winds, there 'Boreas, and Eurus, and Caurus, and Argestes loud,' howling through the vacant lobbies, and clattering the doors of deserted guard-rooms, appal the imagination, and conjure up the grim spectres of departed tyrants—the Saxon, the Norman, and the Dane; the stern Edwards and fierce Henries—who stalk from desolation to desolation, through the dreary vacuity, and melancholy succession of chill and comfortless chambers. . . . They put me in mind of *Old Sarum*, where the representatives, more in number than the constituents, only serve to inform us that this was once a place of trade, and sounding with 'the busy hum of men,' though now you can only trace the streets by the colour of the corn; and its sole manufacture is in members of Parliament."

Persuasion.—Our author's qualifications as an orator are elaborately analysed by Mr Rogers, from whom we make the following extracts:—

"As an orator, Burke will never be ranked among the very first masters of the art, so long as the professed object of oratory shall be *conviction and persuasion.* Not that we for a moment assert that the degree of eloquence possessed by an orator is always to be estimated by his success. By no means; for as on the one hand there are many cases in which the divinest eloquence will in vain contend against the prejudices of an audience predetermined not to be convinced, so there are many where the passions have already spoken more eloquently than the orator. The question, in such instances, is not how much, but how little, oratorical skill is necessary to success."—Treating eloquence and oratorical skill as synonymous—a somewhat questionable usage—Mr Rogers goes on to remark that Burke's eloquence was not "adapted to produce success."

For purposes of persuasion he erred in not appealing to principles of action. He allowed his reason and his imagination to play freely upon the subject, and did not confine himself to the orator's chief end—namely, to guide his audience to a particular resolution. "He can seldom confine himself to a simple *business-like* view of the subject under discussion, or to close, rapid, compressed argumentation on it. On the contrary, he makes boundless excursions into all the regions of moral and political philosophy; is perpetually tracing up particular instances and subordinate principles to profound and comprehensive maxims; amplifying and expanding the most meagre materials into brief but comprehensive dissertations of political science, and incrusting (so to speak) the *nucleus* of the most insignificant fact with the most exquisite crystallisations of truth; while the whole composition glitters and sparkles again with a rich profusion of moral reflections, equally beautiful and just." "His exuberance of fancy" was "equally unfavourable to the attainment of the highest oratorical excellence. When a speaker indulges in very lengthened or elaborate imagery, a suspicion is sure to be engendered (and, except in one or two instances of very extraordinary mental structure, that suspicion is uniformly just) that he is scarcely in earnest; that if he has an object, it is to commend his own eloquence rather than to convince his audience; that his inspiration is not the inspiration of *nature;* and for this very sufficient reason, that it is *not* natural for intense emotion to express itself in the fantastic forms of laboured imagery. . . . When illustration is very abundant and elaborate, even the admiration it may excite will often be anything but friendly to the speaker's *professed* object, nay, the very reverse; the admiration will resemble that which is excited by a fine piece of poetry. . . . That it is possible to indulge in such exuberance of illustration, as to suspend the current of strong passions, and defeat the orator's avowed object, it is needless to say."

Farther, he was either ignorant of the feelings of his audience, or too vehement and self-willed to try to conciliate them. "As a political tactician, Burke was far inferior to many of his contemporaries. There was, in fact, a singular disproportion between his knowledge of human nature in general, and his knowledge of individual character; or, if he possessed the latter at all, he was strangely incapable of using it to any practical purpose. None understood better than he did, that abstract principles of policy must be modified by actually existing circumstances; yet this very same maxim, of such profound truth and such immense value, he showed a singular inability to apply to individual conduct, on the small scale and within the limited sphere of *parties.* In the conduct of any measure, he never deigned to consult prejudices or to soften enmity. He had no patience to bear with folly; he was only irritated by it. So far from any attempt to conciliate his political opponents, he often exasperated hostility by setting them all at open defiance, and would frequently pour out the most bitter scorn and invective, when the most guarded and temperate style of expression was essential to success. Never checking the impetuosity of his passions, he often contended for mere trifles with a pertinacity which could only have been justified in the defence of principles of vital importance; trifles, the timely and graceful concession of which would have insured success, which would have far more than counterbalanced such a sacrifice. He never seemed nicely to calculate, with a view to his own conduct, the temper and conduct of the House, or the exact relation of parties in it; thus he never cared to conceal or disguise his opinions on any subject whatever, but uniformly expressed them boldly and fully. Now, though we may admire the blunt honesty of such conduct, none can commend its prudence; nothing but the most imperious necessity could justify it."

OLIVER GOLDSMITH, 1728-1774.

Goldsmith's life offers an exception to the usual even tenor of the literary career. His fortunes were as chequered as restless imprudence and romantic generosity could make them. His father was a good-hearted Irish clergyman, the supposed original of Dr Primrose in the 'Vicar of Wakefield,' and of the kindly old preacher in the 'Deserted Village.' Oliver was born at Pallas, in Longford, the fourth of a family of seven. When he was two years old his father removed to the more comfortable living of Lissoy, in West Meath. His first teacher was a garrulous old soldier, who had served under Marlborough, and delighted to entertain the boys with tales of marvellous adventure. He entered Trinity College, Dublin, as a sizar, in the year of the great Jacobite rising, 1745. What he afterwards said of Parnell's college course may be applied to his own—"His progress through the college course of study was probably marked with but little splendour; his imagination might have been too warm to relish the cold logic of Burgersdicius, or the dreary subtleties of Smiglesius; but it is certain that as a classical scholar few could equal him." He had no liking for mathematics, but, as he afterwards boasted, he could "turn an ode of Horace with any of them." He is said to have more than once been in difficulties with the heads of the college from his love of boisterous frolic. He left college with no fixed aim. His father designed him for the Church, but after he had spent two years at home in preparation, he failed to give satisfaction to the bishop, and could not obtain orders. He next thought of the law, and set off for London; but falling into good company at Dublin, he spent all his money there, and returned home in disgrace. He was then fitted out for the study of medicine in Edinburgh, but was much too restless to pass decorously through the ordinary curriculum and settle down into a quiet practice. After studying (or at least staying) two years in Edinburgh, he went off to the Continent, and spent some time in the medical schools of Leyden and Louvain. Thereafter, in a restless spirit of adventure, he wandered through Switzerland, Italy, and France, supporting himself mainly, it is said, by playing on the flute for food and lodging. In 1756 he returned to London, and there tried various ways of making a livelihood; being successively assistant to an apothecary, physician (among the poorer orders), proof-corrector in Richardson's press, usher in Dr Milner's school at Peckham, critic for the 'Monthly Review,' and usher again. In 1758 he tried to pass at Surgeon's Hall as a hospital mate, but was rejected, and thus driven back finally on literature. His first independent work was 'The Inquiry into the State of Polite Learning in Europe,' which appeared anonymously in 1759. From that date till his death, in 1774, he received steady work from the booksellers, and but for his imprudent generosity and love of finery, might have lived in comfort, if not in luxury. His chief productions were—'The Bee,' a weekly periodical, which reached only eight numbers, lasting through October and November, 1759; 'Chinese Letters,' contributed to Newbery's 'Public Ledger' in 1760, and afterwards published separately under the title of 'The Citizen of the World;' 'The History of England, in a series of Letters from a Nobleman to his Son,' 1762; 'The Vicar of Wakefield,' written and sold in 1764, but not published till 1766; 'The Traveller,' 1764; the comedy of 'The Good-Natured Man,' performed in 1768; 'History of Rome,' 1769; 'The Deserted Village,' 1770; 'History of England,' in four volumes, 1771; 'She Stoops to Conquer,' performed in 1773; 'History of Animated Nature,' 1774.

"The Doctor," as he was called, had not a handsome exterior. Miss Reynolds once toasted him as "the ugliest man she knew." Boswell says—"His person was short, his countenance coarse and vulgar, his deportment that of the scholar awkwardly affecting the easy gentleman." Judge Day's description is more favourable: "In person he was short—about five feet five or six inches; strong but not heavy in make; rather fair in complexion, with brown hair—such, at least, as could be distinguished from his wig. His features were plain but not repulsive—certainly not so when lighted up by conversation. His manners were simple, natural, and perhaps on the whole, we may say, not polished; at least, without the refinement and good-breeding which the exquisite polish of his compositions would lead us to expect."

His naturally strong constitution was soon impaired by his hardships. At the age of thirty-one he wrote thus to his brother: "Though I never had a day's sickness since I saw you, yet I am not that strong active man you once knew me. You scarcely can conceive how much eight years of disappointment, anguish, and study, have worn me down." The climate of London was trying to him, and he frequently had to recruit by taking lodgings in the country.

The strong points of Goldsmith's intellect centred in his power of easy and graceful literary composition. He was not a profound scholar, and his mind was neither very comprehensive nor very productive. His fame rests upon the charms of his style: he tried nearly every kind of composition—poetry, comedy, fiction, history, essay-writing, natural science—and, as Johnson said in his well-known epitaph, "whatever he touched he adorned." He criticised, as he wrote, with exquisite taste. The fragments that Mr Forster has reprinted from the 'Monthly Review,' Goldsmith's earliest performances, are models of just criticism. His delicately-sympathetic nature was a peculiar qualification for appreciating the works of others. This also gave him his singular power of reading character. His drawing of the members of the Literary Club, in the poem "Retaliation," is a supreme work of art. On the strength of Garrick's well-known epigram—

> "Here lies poet Goldsmith, for shortness called Noll,
> Who wrote like an angel, but talked like poor Poll"—

it has sometimes been said that he was very dull in conversation, and that in the Literary Club he was often made a butt. As Boswell admits, his conversational dulness has been much exaggerated. Undoubtedly he was quicker with his pen than with his tongue. A man of fine taste needs time to mature his thoughts; and Goldsmith, careless of his reputation, often opened his mouth without the least premeditation. As to his being made a butt, it was part of his peculiar humour to sacrifice himself for the amusement of the company by affecting ridiculous vanity and stupidity. Many of the anecdotes of his vanity bear evidence of the stolidity of the narrators—their incapability of understanding a joke or entering into the fun of humorous affectation.

In the matter of emotion, he was one of those beings that are often found in extremes. When fortune went well with him, he was as happy as the day was long. So mobile were his sympathies that he could not be sad in merry company, and was easily beguiled out of his sorrows. Yet he was also easily dispirited, and often took dark views of the future. Self-respect kept him from making many confidants of his heartless anticipations. He often assumed an appearance of gaiety when there was no small anxiety within; but we find him, in an affectionate letter to his brother in Ireland, complaining of a "settled melancholy" and "gloomy habits of thinking;" and he sometimes laid his cares before his sturdy friend Johnson. After a happy deliverance from gloomy apprehensions, he would entertain his friends with ludicrous pictures of his previous distress. He was a warm friend and a generous enemy; quick to take offence, and easily pacified. His heart overflowed with tenderness: he loved the happy faces of children, and could not bear to see misery. With his rare skill in divining the thoughts of others, and detecting what they prided themselves upon, he might have been a stinging satirist; but his tenderness, though it could not restrain, always induced him to soften the dart.

The imprudence of his conduct has often been dilated upon. As a young man he was flighty, and more bent upon seeing the world than willing to subside into a staid professional career. His life was one long battle with imprudence. He was thirty-one when he finally settled down to authorship; and then he never thought of laying up money for an evil day, but spent faster than he earned, and died two thousand pounds in debt. "His purse replenished," says Judge Day, "the season of relaxation and pleasure took its turn, in attending the theatres, Ranelagh, Vauxhall, and other scenes of gaiety and amusement. When his funds were dissipated—and they fled more rapidly from his being the dupe of many artful persons, male and female, who practised upon his benevolence—he returned to his literary labours, and shut himself up from society to provide fresh matter for his bookseller, and fresh supplies for himself." There are several well-known anecdotes of his imprudent generosity. On one occasion about the beginning of his career as an author, he pawned a suit of clothes that he had on loan to save his landlady from an execution for debt. Throughout all his struggles he continued to send money to his poor mother in Ireland; and when he died, "on the stairs of his apartment there was the lamentation of the old and infirm, and the sobbing of women, poor objects of his charity, to whom he had never turned a deaf ear."

Opinions.—Goldsmith is not known to have held strong opinions, as Johnson did, either in politics or in sectarian religion. He was more of an observer than of a doctrinaire. He had seen much of mankind, and interested himself more in noting characteristic expression and conduct than in gaining adherents to any favourite views. The point of view of the Chinese Letters is characteristic. Himself emancipated by temperament and education from nearly every mode of traditionary prejudice, he regarded as absurd and mischievous many of the English opinions, customs, and institutions. But he did not attack these directly, as Mr Matthew Arnold has lately done, in his own proper person. He assumed the person of a philosophic Chinaman, and showed, in the form of letters to friends in the East, how English ways appeared in the eyes of a "Citizen of the World." In these letters he not only expresses surprise at superficial absurdities in dress, in public ceremonies, and suchlike, and at such incongruities as charging admission-fees to tombs and other memorials of great men, but also strikes at graver subjects, at the law of divorce, at iniquities in the administration of justice, at the abuses of Church patronage, at the frivolous causes of great wars, and similar matters of more serious import.

ELEMENTS OF STYLE.

Vocabulary.—The best evidence of Goldsmith's wide command of language is his excellence in so many different kinds of composition. The remarkable thing is his combination of purity with copiousness. He is more copious than Addison; and, while no less simple than that master of simple language, he never is affectedly easy, never condescends to polite slang. One is safe to assert that no writer of English is at once so copious and so pure.

Sentences and Paragraphs.—The light and graceful structure of Goldsmith's sentences cannot be too much admired. It would be interesting to find out what preceding writer he is most indebted to. We may concede to Boswell and to Dr Nathan Drake that in some respects he belongs to the "Johnsonian school." Had Goldsmith written before Johnson, he would probably have constructed his sentences as loosely as Addison. He may have learnt from Johnson to observe grammar more strictly than was usual with the Queen Anne writers, to balance clauses, and to round off his sentences without leaving inelegant tags. Probably he caught these parts of his skill from Johnson, though none but the greater grammatical accuracy can be said to have been originated by "the great lexicographer." But in other respects his style is so unlike Johnson's that it needs some practice in criticism to discover any resemblance whatsoever. Not to speak of Goldsmith's simple diction and exquisite melody, which make a sufficient disguise for the general reader, his sentences are much shorter, less condensed, and less abrupt. When we remember Goldsmith's acquaintance with French literature, we can hardly help ascribing some of the merits of his style to the influence of the French.

In the following specimens of his style, taken from his earliest work, the 'Inquiry into the Present State of Polite Learning,' we catch an occasional echo of Johnson; but the general structure is much lighter and more graceful:—

"If we examine the state of learning in Germany, we shall find that the

Germans early discovered a passion for polite literature; but unhappily, like conquerors who, invading the dominions of others, leave their own to desolation, instead of studying the German tongue, they continued to write in Latin. Thus, while they cultivated an obsolete language, and vainly laboured to apply it to modern manners, they neglected their own.

"At the same time, also, they began at the wrong end,—I mean by being commentators; and though they have given many instances of their industry, they have scarcely afforded any of genius. If criticism could have improved the taste of a people, the Germans would have been the most polite nation alive. We shall nowhere behold the learned wear a more important appearance than here; nowhere more dignified with professorships, or dressed out in the fopperies of scholastic finery. However, they seem to earn all the honour of this kind which they enjoy. Their assiduity is unparalleled; and did they employ half those hours on study which they bestow on reading, we might be induced to pity as well as praise their painful pre-eminence. But, guilty of a fault too common to great readers, they write through volumes while they do not think through a page. Never fatigued themselves, they think the reader can never be weary; so they drone on, saying all that can be said on the subject, not selecting what may be advanced to the purpose. Were angels to write books, they never would write folios."

Again—

"The French nobility have certainly a most pleasing way of satisfying the vanity of an author, without indulging his avarice. A man of literary merit is sure of being caressed by the great, though seldom enriched. His pension from the Crown just supplies half a competence, and the sale of his labours makes some small addition to his circumstances. Thus the author leads a life of splendid poverty, and seldom becomes wealthy or indolent enough to discontinue an exertion of those abilities by which he rose. With the English it is different. Our writers of rising merit are generally neglected, while the few of an established reputation are overpaid by luxurious affluence. The young encounter every hardship which generally attends upon aspiring indigence; the old enjoy the vulgar and perhaps the more prudent satisfaction of putting riches in competition with fame. Those are often seen to spend their youth in want and obscurity; these are sometimes found to lead an old age of indolence and avarice. But such treatment must naturally be expected from Englishmen, whose national character is to be slow and cautious in making friends, but violent in friendships once contracted."

Once more, in a criticism of Gray's Odes, he says—

"We cannot without regret behold talents so capable of giving pleasure to all, exerted in efforts that at best can amuse only the few: we cannot behold this rising poet seeking fame among the learned, without hinting to him the advice that Isocrates used to give his scholars, *Study the people.* This study it is that has conducted the great masters of antiquity up to immortality. Pindar himself, of whom our modern lyrist is an imitator, appears entirely guided by it. He adapted his works exactly to the dispositions of his countrymen. Irregular, enthusiastic, and quick in transition, he wrote for a people inconstant, of warm imagination, and exquisite sensibility. He chose the most popular subjects, and all his allusions are to customs well known in his days to the meanest person."

Figures of Speech.—Goldsmith resembles Johnson in the neglect of ornamental similitudes. To say so is, however, to use "similitudes" in the sense of similes, or formal similitudes. The remark does not apply as regards metaphors. Goldsmith's style is too much elevated by metaphors to be called plain. He is not so plain a writer as Addison ; his style has (to use Ben Jonson's expression) more "blood and juice." Thus—

"The other countries of Europe may be considered as immersed in ignorance or making but feeble efforts to rise. Spain has long fallen from amazing Europe with her wit, to amusing them with the greatness of her catholic credulity."

Again—

"Men like these, united by one bond, pursuing one design, spend their labour and their lives in making their fellow-creatures happy, and in repairing the breaches caused by ambition. In this light, the meanest philosopher, though all his possessions are his lamp or his cell, is more truly valuable than he whose name echoes to the shout of the million, and who stands in all the glare of admiration. In this light, though poverty and contemptuous neglect are all the wages of his good-will from mankind, yet the rectitude of his intention is an ample recompense; and self-applause for the present, and the alluring prospect of fame for futurity, reward his labours. The perspective of life brightens upon us, when terminated by an object so charming. Every intermediate image of want, banishment, or sorrow, receives a lustre from its distant influence. With this in view, the patriot, philosopher, and poet, have often looked with calmness on disgrace and famine, and rested on their straw with cheerful serenity. Even the last terrors of departing nature abate of their severity, and look kindly on him who considers his sufferings as a passport to immortality, and lays his sorrows on the bed of fame."

Contrast.—As sufficiently appears in the preceding quotations, he was taken with the charm of rhetorical antithesis, and laboured to deliver his sayings in an antithetical form. In his 'Polite Learning' we can read but few sentences without encountering a formal "point;" and here and there we find the general sparkle condensed into the brilliancy of an epigram.

The following are examples of his epigrams :—

"Cautious stupidity is always in the right."

"We see more of the world by travel, more of human nature by remaining at home."

"We grow learned, not wise, by too long a continuance at college."

"To imitate nature was found to be the surest way of imitating antiquity."

"The true use of speech is not so much to express our wants as to conceal them."[1]

The peculiar artifice of ending off a sentence with an unexpected turn is of the nature of epigram. Of this artifice we might cull numerous examples from Goldsmith. It peculiarly suited his gay volatility. We take the three following from the narrative of the Man in Black.[2]

[1] Epigrams similar to this occur in South, Butler, Young, and Voltaire.

[2] The Man in Black is usually said to be modelled on the real character of Goldsmith's father. The father of the Man in Black is obviously drawn from Goldsmith's father; the Man in Black is no less obviously intended by Goldsmith for a portrait of himself.

"After I had resided at college for seven years, my father died, and left me—his blessing."

"O Friendship! thou fond soother of the human breast, to thee we fly in every calamity; to thee the wretched seek for succour; on thee the care-tired son of misery fondly relies; from thy kind assistance the unfortunate always hopes for relief, and may ever be sure of—disappointment!"

"A soldier does not exult more when he counts over the wounds he has received, than a female veteran when she relates the wounds she has formerly given: exhaustless when she begins a narrative of the former death-dealing power of her eyes. She tells of the knight in gold lace, who died with a single frown, and never rose again till—he was married to his maid; of the squire who, being cruelly denied, in a rage flew to the window, and lifting up the sash, threw himself in an agony—into his arm-chair; of the parson who, crossed in love, resolutely swallowed opium, which banished the stings of despised love—by making him sleep."

Minor Figures.—Goldsmith sometimes assumes a declamatory style, with oratorical interrogation and answer, and paragraphs in the form of a climax. In these declamations there is usually a tincture of mock-heroism. Thus—

"What, then, are the proper encouragements of genius? I answer, Subsistence and respect; for these are rewards congenial to its nature. Every animal has an aliment suited to its constitution. The heavy ox seeks nourishment from earth; the light cameleon has been supposed to exist on air; a sparer diet than even this will satisfy the man of true genius, for he makes a luxurious banquet upon empty applause. It is this alone which has inspired all that ever was truly great and noble among us. It is, as Cicero finely calls it, the echo of virtue. Avarice is the passion of inferior natures; money the pay of the common herd. The author who draws his quill merely to take a purse, no more deserves success than he who presents a pistol."

QUALITIES OF STYLE.

Simplicity.—The specimens already quoted afford a fair measure of his simple language and simple structure. Goldsmith is among the simplest of our writers. In one aspect he differs from Addison: his diction is more metaphorical, farther elevated above the language of common life. This is borne out by our quotations. But in another and more striking aspect he resembles Addison: his simplicity is an elegant simplicity. He is not homely like Paley, nor coarse like Swift. This, also, is sufficiently apparent without farther illustration.

To write with simplicity on some of Goldsmith's themes was comparatively easy. Others could not have been treated in a simple style without a considerable effort. In particular, some of his 'Animated Nature' must have tried his powers of simple exposition. Where he had objects to describe—birds, beasts, or fishes—he probably experienced no difficulty except in mastering the details. But sometimes he is called upon to expound general principles, and then we have an opportunity of seeing the extent of his art. The following is his account of the attraction of gravity. In some parts the language might possibly be made more familiar without becoming less exact; but his manner of approaching the subject, and the easy sequence of the thoughts, are eminently popular. He seems at the end of every sentence to place himself in the position of the reader—to weigh its effect from the reader's point of view, to study what might be expected next, and how to carry the reader easily forward to the next idea:—

"Modern philosophy has taught us to believe, that when the great Author of nature began the work of creation, he chose to operate by second causes; and that, suspending the constant exertion of his power, he endued matter with a quality by which the universal economy of nature might be continued, without his immediate assistance. This quality is called attraction, a sort of approximating influence, which all bodies, whether terrestrial or celestial, are found to possess; and which, in all, increases as the quantity of matter in each increases. The sun, by far the greatest body in our system, is, of consequence, possessed of much the greatest share of this attracting power; and all the planets, of which our earth is one, are of course entirely subject to its superior influence. Were this power, therefore, left uncontrolled by any other, the sun must quickly have attracted all the bodies of our celestial system to itself; but it is equally counteracted by another power of equal efficacy; namely, a progressive force which each planet received when it was impelled forward by the divine Architect upon its first formation. The heavenly bodies of our system being thus acted upon by two opposing powers—namely, by that of attraction, which draws them towards the sun, and that of impulsion, which drives them straight forward into the great void of space—they pursue a track between these contrary directions; and each, like a stone whirled about in a sling, obeying two opposite forces, circulates round its great centre of heat and motion."

Clearness.—As we have frequently noticed in treating of simple writers, it is vain to expect in union with simplicity the somewhat antagonistic merit of precision. Goldsmith is no exception: he is not careful to observe mathematical accuracy. Thus, in the above passage, a mathematician would object to the phrase, "equally counteracted by another power of equal efficacy," as an expression for the action of centrifugal relatively to centripetal force. In exact language, it would rather apply to two equal forces acting in direct opposition, and so bringing things to a stand-still.

Strength.—Had the bent of Goldsmith's genius been for the sublime, the works that he undertook gave him ample opportunities of displaying his powers. His periodical essays, as their purpose demanded, were chiefly upon the lighter topics. But in his 'History of the Earth and of Animated Nature' (to quote the title at full length), he was free to describe the grandeurs of nature as well as the beauties and the curiosities; and he preferred the beautiful, the odd, and the instructive to the sublime.

So in his histories there was plenty of room for lofty declamation; but he shows no inclination to avail himself of such opportunities. Let us take, for instance, his reflections on the death of Cæsar, and on the extinction of the Western Empire of Rome—both good openings for the eloquent worshipper of greatness. The following is his peroration on Cæsar, more remarkable for sound judgment than for eloquence:—

"Cæsar was killed in the fifty-sixth year of his age, and about fourteen years after he began the conquest of the world. If we examine his history, we shall be equally at a loss whether most to admire his great abilities or his wonderful fortune. To pretend to say that from the beginning he planned the subjection of his native country, is doing no great credit to his well-known penetration, as a thousand obstacles lay in his way, which fortune, rather than conduct, was to surmount. No man, therefore, of his sagacity, would have begun a scheme in which the chances of succeeding were so many against him: it is most probable that, like all very successful men, he only made the best of every occurrence; and his ambition rising with his good fortune, from at first being contented with humbler aims, he at last began to think of governing the world, when he found scarce any obstacle to oppose his designs. Such is the disposition of man, whose cravings after power are always most insatiable when he enjoys the greatest share."

He dismisses the Roman Empire at the conclusion of his 'History of Rome' with two sentences:—

"Such was the end of this great empire, that had conquered mankind with its arms, and instructed the world with its wisdom; that had risen by temperance, and that fell by luxury; that had been established by a spirit of patriotism, and that sunk into ruin when the empire was become so extensive, that a Roman citizen was but an empty name. Its final dissolution happened about five hundred and twenty-two years after the battle of Pharsalia; an hundred and forty-six after the removal of the imperial seat to Constantinople; and four hundred and seventy-six after the nativity of our Saviour."

Bolingbroke, Burke, or De Quincey would have concluded in a much loftier strain.

Pathos.—Considering Goldsmith's natural tenderness and wide acquaintance with distress, one would expect his writings to be deeply tinged with pathos. In reality, however, he is not so pathetic a writer as Sterne. His benevolence was probably more active than sentimental, just as Sterne's was more sentimental than active. His poems and his novel contain some of our very finest touches of pathos, but in his ordinary prose we meet with comparatively few. The only deeply-touching letter in his 'Citizen of the World' is one entitled "A City Night Piece," and it in some parts is too distressing to be lingered over with melancholy pleasure, rather serving the moralist's end of making the reader uncomfortable:—

"The clock just struck two, the expiring taper rises and sinks in the socket, the watchman forgets the hour in slumber, the laborious and the happy are at rest, and nothing wakes but meditation, guilt, revelry, and despair. The drunkard once more fills the destroying bowl, the robber walks his midnight round, and the suicide lifts his guilty arm against his own sacred person.

"Let me no longer waste the night over the pages of antiquity or the sallies of contemporary genius, but pursue the solitary walk, where Vanity ever changing, but a few hours past walked before me, where she kept up the pageant, and now like a froward child, seems hushed with her own importunities. . . .

"How few appear in those streets which but some few hours ago were crowded! and those who appear now no longer wear their daily mask, nor attempt to hide their lewdness or their misery.

"But who are those who make the streets their couch, and find a short repose from wretchedness at the doors of the opulent? These are strangers, wanderers, and orphans, whose circumstances are too humble to expect redress, and whose distresses are too great even for pity. Their wretchedness excites rather horror than pity. Some are without the covering even of rags, and others emaciated with disease: the world has disclaimed them; society turns its back upon their distress, and has given them up to nakedness and hunger. . . .

"Why was I born a man, and yet see the sufferings of wretches I cannot relieve! Poor houseless creatures! the world will give you reproaches, but will not give you relief. The slightest misfortunes of the great, the most imaginary uneasiness of the rich, are aggravated with all the power of eloquence, and held up to engage our attention and sympathetic sorrow. The poor weep unheeded, persecuted by every subordinate species of tyranny; and every law which gives others security, becomes an enemy to them.

"Why was this heart of mine framed with so much sensibility? or why was not my fortune adapted to its impulse? Tenderness, without a capacity of relieving, only makes the man who feels it more wretched than the object which sues for assistance."

The Ludicrous.—Goldsmith surpasses all our humorists in the combination of delicate wit with extravagant fun. His fancy was of the lightest and airiest order, and his volatile spirit was easily warmed to the boiling-point of comical extravagance. "His comic writing," says Leigh Hunt, "is of the class which is perhaps as much preferred to that of a staider sort by people in general, as it is by the writer of these pages—comedy running into farce. . . . It is that of the prince of comic writers, Molière. The English have no dramatists to compare in this respect with the Irish. Farquhar, Goldsmith, and Sheridan surpass them all; and O'Keefe, as a farce-writer, stands alone."

The following passage from a letter written about the time when he commenced author, may be quoted as characteristic. He was far from being a happy self-complacent man, but the mere excitement of writing to a friend was enough to elevate him "o'er a' the ills o' life victorious." The sturdier, less inflammable spirit of Burns, required stronger stimulants to raise it to the same pitch:—

"God's curse, sir! who am I? Eh! what am I? Do you know whom you have offended? A man whose character may one of these days be mentioned with profound respect in a German comment or Dutch Dictionary; whose name you will probably hear ushered in by a Doctissimus Doctissimorum, or heel-pieced with a long Latin termination. Think how Goldsmithius, or Gubblegurchius, or some such sound, as rough as a nutmeg-grater, will become me. . . . I must own my ill-natured contemporaries have not hitherto paid me those honours I have had such just reason to expect. I have not yet seen my face reflected in all the lively display of red and white paints on any sign-posts in the suburbs. Your handkerchief weavers seem as yet unacquainted with my merits or my physiognomy, and the very snuff-box makers appear to have forgot their respect. Tell them all from me, they are a set of Gothic, barbarous, ignorant scoundrels. There will come a day, no doubt it will," &c.

His works contain many traces of this airy conquest of the ills of life. Beau Tibbs is made to describe his garret as "the first floor down the chimney;" the Man in Black, when imprisoned, reflects that "he is now on one side the door, and those who are unconfined are on the other; that is all the difference between them:" and both are strokes of wit that may have consoled the author himself in similar circumstances. His incomparable "description of an author's bed-chamber," ending with the couplet—

"A night-cap decked his brows instead of bay,
A cap by night—a stocking all the day"—

may also be taken as a humorous transfiguration of his own experience. Take also the following anecdote related in the "Club of Authors:"—

"I'll tell you a story, gentlemen, which is as true as that this pipe is made of clay. When I was delivered of my first book, I owed my tailor for a suit of clothes; but that is nothing new, you know, and may be any man's case as well as mine. Well, owing him for a suit of clothes, and hearing that my book took very well, he sent for his money, and insisted on being paid immediately. Though I was at the time rich in fame, for my book ran like wild-fire, yet I was very short in money, and being unable to satisfy his demand, prudently resolved to keep my chamber, preferring a prison of my own choosing at home, to one of my tailor's choosing abroad. In vain the bailiffs used all their arts to decoy me from my citadel; in vain they sent to let me know that a gentleman wanted to speak with me at the next tavern; in vain they came with an urgent message from my aunt in the country; in vain I was told that a particular friend was at the point of death, and desired to take his last farewell. I was deaf, insensible, rock, adamant; the bailiffs could make no impression on my hard heart, for I effectually kept my liberty by never stirring out of my room."

"This was all very well for a fortnight;" but at the end of that time the unfortunate author was entrapped by "a splendid message from the Earl of Doomsday." He took coach and rode in high expectation to the residence, as he thought, of his noble patron; but on alighting, found himself, to his horror, at the door of a spunging-house. All the proceedings of this club of authors are in Goldsmith's happiest vein, and form a good illustration of his power of throwing a ludicrous colour over incidents uncomfortably near the reality of his own life.

Goldsmith is also the most amiable of our satirists. He was full of "the milk of human kindness," and the range of his sympathies was wide. His ridicule is always on the side of good sense and good feeling. And he handles even his embodiments of folly and weakness "tenderly, as if he loved them;" as if, at least, he had a lurking toleration for them, and secretly recognised their claim to exist in their own way as varieties of multiform humanity.

The most exquisite of his humorous creations is Beau Tibbs, who figures in the letters of the 'Citizen of the World.'

OTHER WRITERS.

THEOLOGY.

Few of the theologians that we reckon in this period were men of high literary celebrity. The reason probably is that there was no exciting topic to vex the theological world, and put its foremost intellects upon their mettle. The Deists had been a hundred times answered before 1760, and no other heresy equally dangerous and exciting appeared until the ferment of the French Revolution. The great religious revival begun by Wesley and Whitefield gained no distinguished champions during the first half of the reign of George III.

One of the most eminent divines of the generation was **Samuel Horsley (1733-1806)**, who has been called "the last of the race of polemical giants in the English Church—a learned, mighty, fearless, and haughty champion of the theology and constitution of the Anglican establishment." His first efforts in authorship were some mathematical tracts. In 1776 he published proposals for a new edition of the works of Sir Isaac Newton. About the same time he wrote on Man's Free Agency. His charge to the clergy of his archdeaconry in 1783 involved him in a controversy with Priestley concerning the divinity of Christ: in which controversy he is said to have displayed great learning, masterly reasoning, and impetuous dogmatism. He was made Bishop of St David's in 1788. When the French Revolution broke out, he stood forth in the front rank of alarmists, and declaimed with great vehemence against the "twin furies"—Jacobinism and Infidelity. His declamations against conventicles, and his disposition to favour penal laws against Dissent, brought him into collision with Robert Hall, who assails him as "the apologist of tyranny, and the patron of passive obedience," and describes a sermon of his as a "disgusting picture of sanctimonious hypocrisy and priestly insolence." Horsley had an arrogance and dogmatism even fiercer than Warburton's, without anything like Warburton's genius for style. His sermons procured him respect from many that disapproved of his violence as a polemic; they are distinguished by breadth of view and clear racy expression.

Beilby Porteous (1731-1808), Bishop of London, was a divine of a much milder type, author of a poem "On Death," which gained the Seatonian prize in 1759, and the intimate associate of Hannah More, whom he is said to have assisted in the composition of her religious novel, 'Cœlebs in search of a Wife.' He wrote a life of his patron, Archbishop Secker, and published a variety of sermons, charges, and other devotional tracts. His 'Evidences' is still used as a class-book in schools.

The most distinguished Scottish theologian of the time was **George Campbell,** author of an able 'Dissertation on Miracles,' written in reply to Hume's Essay on Miracles, and a 'New Translation of the Gospels, with Preliminary Dissertations,' a work displaying the highest critical sagacity. We shall notice him again among the writers on Rhetoric.

PHILOSOPHY.

By far the most eminent psychologist of this generation is **Thomas Reid (1710-1796)**, the founder of what is known as the Philosophy of Common Sense. He was a native of Kincardineshire, and was educated at Marischal College, Aberdeen. He studied for the Church, and in 1737 was presented to the living of New Machar, a parish near Aberdeen. In 1752 he was appointed Professor of Philosophy in King's College, Aberdeen. While in this office he took part in the meetings of a literary coterie, of great local celebrity, which comprised several men that attained eminence in the world of letters—himself, Campbell, Beattie, and Gerard. In 1763 he was invited to succeed Adam Smith as Professor of Moral Philosophy in Glasgow. His 'Inquiry into the Human Mind,' which had been discussed by his friends in Aberdeen, and had been in part submitted to Hume, was published in 1764. The impulse to this work was given, as he said in the dedication, by Hume's 'Treatise of Human Nature.' He had not previously "thought of calling in question the principles commonly received with regard to the human understanding;" but finding that, "by reasoning which appeared to him to be just," there was built upon those principles "a system of scepticism which leaves no ground to believe any one thing rather than its contrary," he proceeded to subject the principles themselves to a close examination. "For my own satisfaction, I entered into a serious examination of the principles upon which the sceptical system is built; and was not a little surprised to find, that it leans with its whole weight upon a hypothesis which is ancient indeed, and hath been very generally received by philosophers, but of which I could find no solid proof. The hypothesis I mean is, That nothing is perceived but what is in the mind which perceives it: that we do not really perceive things that are external, but only certain images and pictures of them imprinted upon the mind, which are called *impressions and ideas.*" The 'Inquiry' has a polemical tone throughout, and contains a good deal of humorous banter directed against Hume upon the assumption that the arch-sceptic is bound in consistency to believe "neither his own existence nor that of his reader," and that "the intention of his work is to show that there is neither human nature nor science in the world."—Without attempting to define Reid's position relatively to modern analysts of the mind, we may give his views concerning the origin of knowledge in his own words. Against the opinion that all knowledge concerning external things is derived from the phenomena of Sense and the operations of the Intellect upon the phenomena, he contends that "many original principles of belief" are "*suggested* by our sensations." "Sensation suggests the notion of present *existence*, and the belief that what we perceive or feel does now *exist*. . . . A beginning of existence, or any change in nature, suggests to us *the notion of a cause*, and compels our belief of its existence. And, in like manner, certain sensations of touch, by the constitution of our nature, suggest to us *extension*, *solidity*, *and motion*, which are nowise like to sensations, although they have been hitherto confounded with them."—After teaching in his Professorship till 1781, Reid prepared a more systematic exposition of the Mind, which appeared in two parts—'Essays on the Intellectual Powers,' in 1785; and 'Essays on the Active Powers,' in 1788. He continued his studious activity till the very close of his long life, writing philosophical essays, working mathematical problems, and following the progress of physical science.—"In point of bodily constitution, few men have been more indebted to nature than Dr Reid. His form was vigorous and athletic; and his muscular force (though he was somewhat under the middle size) uncommonly great; advantages to which his habits of temperance and exercise, and the unclouded serenity of his temper, did ample justice." The mere fact of his originating a school of philosophy, even though we allow that his conclusions were supported by popular feeling, argues a large measure of intellectual force, in one direction or another; but very different opinions have been expressed as to his capacities for mental analysis. Various particulars in his style and in his favourite studies indicate a tendency to dwell by preference upon the concrete. He had no great turn for style; his composition deserves the praise of "ease, perspicuity, and purity;" it is, besides, neat and finished, and often moves with considerable spirit: but it has neither the incisive vigour of Campbell, the copiousness of Smith, nor the original freshness of Tucker.

Abraham Tucker (1705-1774), author of 'The Light of Nature Pursued, by Edward Search, Esq.'—a work in seven volumes, four of which were published in 1765, and the remainder after his death—is in point of style one of the most pleasing of our philosophical writers. The son of a wealthy London merchant, having received an Oxford education and acquired many elegant accomplishments, he bought an estate near Dorking, and there lived a "retired and undiversified" life, "the exercise of his reason being his daily employment." He declined the political business that Burke held to be a duty intrusted to men of his station, and spent his time in a soft Epicurean endeavour to realise the maximum of tranquil happiness. He "apportioned his time between study and relaxation;" and, when in London, "commonly devoted much of his evenings to the society of his friends, relations, and fellow-collegians, among whom he was particularly distinguished for his dexterity in the Socratic method of disputation." We may indicate his philosophical position in a loose compendious way by saying that he based his psychology upon Hartley's, and that his original ethical views are adopted, digested, and systematised in Paley's 'Moral Philosophy.' Paley candidly acknowledges his obligations. "There is one work to which I owe so much, that it would be ungrateful not to confess the obligation; I mean the writings of the late Abraham Tucker, Esq. I have found in this writer more original thinking and observation upon the several subjects that he has taken in hand, than in any other, not to say in all others put together. His talent also for illustration is unrivalled. But his thoughts are diffused through a long, various, and irregular work. I shall account it no mean praise, if I have been sometimes able to dispose into method, to collect into heads and articles, or to exhibit in more compact and tangible masses, what in that otherwise excellent performance is spread over too much surface."—Tucker's style has several charms rarely met in philosophical works—charms, indeed, that are more or less incompatible with rigorous scientific precision. The diction is simple, thickly interspersed with colloquial idioms, and has an exquisitely musical flow. In every other sentence we are delighted with some original felicity of expression or of illustration. The loose and often ungrammatical structure of the sentences, and the diffusive rambling character both of the work as a whole and of the several divisions, forbid his being taken as a model for strict scientific exposition; but the popular expositor of practical wisdom might learn a great deal from his copious and felicitous language and imagery. Obviously, however, it will not do even for popular purposes to imitate him closely. The expense of his voluminous treatise may have something to do with the general neglect of so ingenious a writer; but at any rate it is significant against close imitation of his style that the views of Happiness and Virtue in Paley's 'Moral Philosophy,' which are simply Tucker's summarised and formulated, are never referred to their original author.

Richard Price (1723-1791)—a Dissenting minister in London, who supported the cause of American Independence, and who was vehemently abused by Burke because from his pulpit in Old Jewry Lane he hailed the French Revolution as the advent of Liberty —made himself a considerable name in Ethical Philosophy. His 'Review of the Principal Questions and Difficulties in Morals' was published in 1758. "He appears as the antagonist of the empiricism popularly associated with the name of Locke, and as the leading representative of his time in England of the double origin of knowledge. The doctrine of Price with respect to the Good and the True reminds us more of the Pure Reason of his great German contemporary Kant, than of the internal and common-sense school of Hutcheson and Reid." He also "reveals affinities to Platonism."[1] His style displays in no eminent degree either of the cardinal virtues of a philosophical work; he is not remarkably perspicuous, and he is far from being remarkably precise. His numerous political and economical pamphlets are written with considerable energy, "not unfitly typified by the unusual muscular and nervous activity of his slender person."

Joseph Priestley (1733-1804), a Unitarian minister, illustrious in Natural Science as the discoverer of oxygen and other elementary substances, was an irrepressibly voluminous writer not only in science but in theology, philosophy, history, politics, and whatever happened to engage his interest. At the age of 22 he became pastor to a Dissenting congregation, and from that time till 1773 he occupied various situations as minister and as tutor, and began to make himself a name by his theological and scientific writings. From 1773 the patronage of the Earl of Shelburne enabled him to devote the most of his time to scientific and literary pursuits. He made his discovery of oxygen in 1774. In the same year he wrote a severe examination of the Common-Sense Philosophy, defending the principles of Locke and Hartley. In his 'Disquisitions relating to Matter and Spirit,' 1777, he avowed himself a materialist, and showed that materialism did not affect the arguments for the existence of God, or for the belief in a future state. His 'History of the Corruptions of Christianity,' 1782, was attacked, as we have said, by Horsley, and a hot war in pamphlets was carried on through more than one stage of rejoinder and surrejoinder. During the excitement of the French Revolution, his advanced opinions made him an object of aversion; his house in Birmingham

[1] Professor Fraser, in the 'Imperial Dictionary of Biography.'

was sacked by a mob; and he was ultimately obliged to betake himself to America. He died at Northumberland in Pennsylvania. —He is said to have been a man of mild, urbane manners, and to have won the personal favour of very bigoted antagonists when he met them face to face. Brougham rather misrepresents him in describing him as "a fierce and angry polemic." He often writes severe things, but he writes with perfect command of temper. He cannot be charged with unprovoked abuse: his asperities are called forth by what he considers arrogance, conceit, or misrepresentation on the part of others. "Those," he says, "who are disposed to be civil to me shall meet with civility from me in return; and as to those who are otherwise disposed, I shall behave to them as I may happen to be affected at the time." For his own part, whether right or wrong, he is exceedingly fair and candid. His style is idiomatic, compact, incisive, and vigorous. He is eminently easy to follow: he usually describes the progress of his thoughts, explains by what circumstances he was led to take such and such a view, and thus introduces us from the known to the unknown by an easy gradation.

James Beattie (1735-1803), one of Dr Reid's Aberdonian coterie, whose reputation rests chiefly on his poetry, first came before the public in 1770 as an antagonist to Hume. He was a man of intensely personal, not to say spiteful feelings, intemperately sensitive; and his 'Essay on Truth' is written with anything but philosophic calm. On the title-page he describes his work as "written in opposition to sophistry and scepticism," and throughout ascribes to his opponent the basest motives, and to his opponent's writings the most degrading influences; claims for himself and his side the exclusive possession of love for truth, learning, mankind, and honourable fairness; and declares repeatedly that none of Mr Hume's admirers understand him: in short, he offensively assumes a superiority to Hume in morals, and a superiority to Hume's followers in intellect. His style has considerable power of the rotund declamatory order; copious, high-sounding, and elegant; occasionally in its appeals to established feeling throwing out rhetorical interrogations, followed by brief, abrupt answers. His Essay was very popular with the English clergy, and exasperated the easy-minded Hume more perhaps than any of the numerous replies to his obnoxious opinions. Beattie wrote also in prose several miscellaneous essays—'On Poetry and Music' (1762); 'On Laughter' (1764); 'On Classical Learning' (1769); and 'Dissertations Moral and Critical' (1783).

Another of the Aberdonian coterie, perhaps the most powerful mind of the number, and of a very different temper from Beattie, was **George Campbell (1719-1796)**, already mentioned as an antagonist to Hume's 'Essay on Miracles.' Originally destined for the law, he changed his mind and entered the Church, was appointed minister of Banchory-Ternan, was subsequently translated to one of the city charges in Aberdeen, and in 1759 became Principal of Marischal College. His first work was the 'Dissertation on Miracles,' 1762. After several less-known performances, he published in 1776 his 'Philosophy of Rhetoric,' which is often spoken of as the most original work on that subject that had appeared since Aristotle. His 'New Translation of the Gospels' was published in 1778.—Campbell was a man of sturdy, sagacious intellect, and tolerant temper. In controversy he was candid and generous, imputing no unworthy motives, and making no offensive claims to superior powers of discernment. His style is perspicuous and terse; he writes as one possessing a clear comprehensive grasp of his subject, and an abundant choice of language.

Along with Campbell may be mentioned Henry Home, **Lord Kames** (1696-1782), and **Hugh Blair** (1718-1799); both, like him, best known in general literature by their works on English Composition. Home was an Edinburgh lawyer of great social wit and literary tastes, who employed his leisure after his elevation to the bench in composing various works, metaphysical, social, and critical—'Principles of Morality and Natural Religion' (1751), 'Art of Thinking' (1761), 'Elements of Criticism' (1762), 'Sketches of the History of Man' (1773), 'The Gentleman Farmer' (1777), 'Loose Hints on Education' (1781). His diction is tolerably copious, and his turns of expression often have something of the crisp ingenuity of Hume's, but his sentences are not very skilfully put together; his style wants flow. Curiously enough, his analysis of the mechanical artifices of sentence-making is one of the most substantial parts of his 'Elements;' it supplied both Campbell and Blair with all that they have to say on sentence-mechanism, and contains some ingenuities that they did not see fit to adopt.—Blair was a highly popular minister in Edinburgh, who, in 1759, following the example of Adam Smith, and also under the patronage of the benevolent Mæcenas, Lord Kames, began to read a course of lectures on Belles Lettres. A Chair of Rhetoric being endowed in 1762, Blair was appointed the first Professor. He published his course of lectures in 1783. He was the most popular sermon-writer of his day. His sermons, the first volume of which was published in 1777, were received with delighted applause in England; were commended by Johnson; and were translated into almost every language of Europe. His reputation is now considerably faded: works for which their admirers fondly predicted classical immortality, are now universally neglected. He was a flowing, elegant writer, with no great pretensions to depth or originality: his 'Rhetoric' is a very vapid performance compared with Campbell's—"Campbell's," says Whately, "is incomparably superior, not only in depth of thought and ingenious original research, but also in practical utility to the student."

Adam Smith (1723-1790) is an important figure in the history of Ethics, and, as the author of the first systematic treatise on Political Economy, is entitled to the honour of being called the founder of that science. He was born at Kirkcaldy in Fifeshire, a posthumous child. At the age of fourteen he entered Glasgow College, and after a curriculum of three years, proceeded thence with a Snell Exhibition to Oxford. He was expected to take orders in the English Church, but he preferred returning to Scotland and taking his chance of getting a professorship in one of the Universities. Settling in Edinburgh in 1748, he began to read lectures on Rhetoric under the patronage of Lord Kames; and soon after, in 1751, was elected Professor of Logic in the University of Glasgow. In 1752 he obtained the more coveted Chair of Moral Philosophy, a post made illustrious by Carmichael and Hutcheson. His 'Theory of Moral Sentiments' was published in 1759. In 1763 he was induced to resign his professorship and undertake the education of the young Duke of Buccleuch. He travelled with his pupil for two or three years, and on his return withdrew to his native town of Kirkcaldy, and applied himself for ten years, with little interruption, to solitary study, the fruits of which at length appeared, in 1776, in his great work 'The Wealth of Nations.' During the last twelve years of his life he held the office of Commissioner of Customs. Before his death he burnt all his unpublished manuscripts with the exception of a few comparatively unimportant essays.—In person he was a grave preoccupied-looking man, of a stout middle size, with large features and large grey eyes, absent-minded in company, often incontinently talking to himself, and keeping up his rather poor constitution by strict regularity and temperance. He was warm and affectionate in disposition, exceedingly unreserved, with simple frankness expressing the thoughts of the moment, and with ready candour retracting his opinion if he found that he had spoken without just grounds. His intellectual proceedings were calm, patient, and regular: he mastered a subject slowly and circumspectly, and carried his principles with steady tenacity through multitudes of details that would have checked many men of greater mental vigour unendowed with the same invincible persistence. He was noted for his strength of memory, and had a wide acquaintance with English, French, and Italian literature, his tastes inclining him to the so-called classical school of Corneille, Racine, Pope, and Gray. The principal feature of his ethical work is his tracing the operation of sympathy as the prime constituent of moral sentiments. "The purely scientific inquiry is overlaid by practical and hortatory dissertations, and by eloquent delineations of character and of beau-ideals of virtuous conduct. His style being thus pitched to the popular key, he never pushes home a metaphysical analysis; so that even his favourite theme, Sympathy, is not philosophically sifted to the bottom." The most striking doctrine in his 'Wealth of Nations' was his advocating the abolition of commercial restrictions—the doctrine of "Free Trade." Concerning the sometimes disputed originality of this work, his editor, Mr M'Culloch, remarks: "Some of the most important doctrines embodied in the 'Wealth of Nations' had been distinctly announced; and traces, more or less faint, of the remainder, may be found in various works published previously to its appearance. But this has little or nothing to do with the peculiar merits of Smith, and in no respect invalidates his claim to be considered as the real founder of the science of political economy. Some of the *disjecta membra* had, indeed, been discovered, with indications of the others. But their importance, whether in a practical or scientific point of view, and their dependence, were all but wholly unknown. They formed an undigested mass, without order or any sort of rational connection, what was sound and true being frequently (as in the theory of the economists) closely linked to what was false and contradictory. Smith was the enchanter who educed order out of this chaos. And in such complicated and difficult subjects, a higher degree of merit belongs to the party who first establishes the truth of a new doctrine, and traces its consequences and limitations, than to him who may previously have stumbled upon it by accident, or who had dismissed it as if it were valueless."—Smith's style is perspicuous and melodious, and both the language and the imagery are chosen with admirable taste. Perhaps its chief value to the student arises from its copiousness, which sometimes amounts to diffuseness. He is particularly rich in subjective language. It is a good exercise for the ethical or the economical expositor to run over his pages and note his various modes of expressing the same facts or principles. The construction of his sentences is loose, and wanting in vigour.

HISTORY.

During this period two historians sustained and advanced the higher ideal of historical composition furnished by David Hume. Robertson published his 'History of Scotland' in the last year of the reign of George II. (1759), and Gibbon his 'Decline and Fall of the Roman Empire' in the first year of the last quarter of the century (1776). Robertson's History was the greatest success that had been achieved by any historical work up to that time; and Gibbon's was still more successful than Robertson's.

William Robertson (1721-1793), the son of an Edinburgh

minister, received the usual Scotch school and college education, entered the Established Church, and at the early age of twenty-two was ordained to the charge of the small parish of Gladsmuir in East Lothian. The lightness of his clerical duties left him ample time for study as well as for extra-parochial activity: he read and wrote with methodical industry, attended the meetings of a distinguished literary society in Edinburgh, and made such a figure in the debates of the General Assembly of the Church, that he soon was recognised as the leader of the "Moderates." In 1759 appeared his 'History of Scotland,' the first edition of which was sold within a month; and in the same year he was translated to the charge of Old Greyfriars' in Edinburgh. In 1762 he was appointed Principal of the University. In 1769 he completed what is generally regarded as his masterpiece, the 'History of Charles V.;' in 1777 his 'History of America,' which grew naturally out of the 'History of Charles.' His only other published work, the 'Disquisition on Ancient India,' appeared in 1791, about two years before his death.—Robust in personal build, a broad, square-shouldered man, rather over the middle height, with a large head and large features, Robertson was no less robust in intellect. He seems to have been well fitted for active life: he displayed great sagacity and firmness as a leader in the General Assembly; and the common saying about him is that he would have been better employed in acting history than in writing it. He took great pains both with the composition of his History and with the collection of the facts. He particularly prided himself, and with justice, upon his accuracy. After all the labour that he spent upon his style, and all the praises that have been lavished upon its purity and correctness, it is not of much value to the student of composition. It is undoubtedly pure and correct: it contains no Scotch idioms and no grammatical inaccuracies; but neither does it contain many peculiarly English idioms; and it possesses little original charm of expression. Some of the admirers of Robertson allege as a peculiar merit of his style that it can be readily turned into Latin; and this is another way of saying that it is not distinctively idiomatic. Indeed nothing else was to be expected: he had no opportunities of hearing English as it was spoken, and learned it almost as a foreign language from books. The wonder is that he succeeded in freeing himself so completely from peculiar Scotch idioms. The chief merit of his narrative, apart from its superior accuracy, is perspicuous arrangement: this was so much dwelt upon by contemporary critics that we must suppose it to have been a very sensible improvement on preceding Histories. Among other things that have been mentioned as coefficient causes of his extraordinary success, besides the correctness and perspicuity of his style, and the accuracy of his research, are the comprehensiveness of his views, his singular insight into political transactions, and the management of his narrative so as to excite the interest of a dramatic plot.

The first year of the last quarter of the eighteenth century is rather a memorable year in prose literature; it witnessed the death of Hume and the publication of three remarkable works, Smith's 'Wealth of Nations,' Campbell's 'Philosophy of Rhetoric,' and Gibbon's 'Roman Empire.'

Edward Gibbon (1737-1794), the son of a wealthy proprietor in Surrey and Hampshire, was born at Putney. He was an infirm child, the only survivor of a family of seven, and being sent to school at irregular intervals, was allowed very much to educate himself. Having free access to good libraries, he read voraciously, particularly in historical works; and when he went to Oxford at the age of fifteen, he possessed "a stock of knowledge that might have puzzled a doctor, and a degree of ignorance of which a schoolboy would have been ashamed." At Oxford he had resided but fourteen months, when meeting in the course of his multifarious reading with two productions from the pen of Bossuet, he was by them converted to the Roman Catholic faith, and consequently obliged to quit the University. He would not seem to have lost much by this forced separation: "To the University of Oxford," he says, "I acknowledge no obligation; and she will as cheerfully renounce me for a son, as I am willing to disclaim her for a mother." Removed from Oxford, he was placed at Lausanne, in Switzerland, under the care of a pious clergyman, who persuaded him to return to the Protestant communion. At Lausanne he remained nearly five years. On his return to England in 1758, he lived chiefly at his father's house in Hampshire; and, entering no profession, continued the miscellaneous studies that had occupied him in Switzerland. In 1761 he made his first appearance as an author in an essay on 'The Study of Literature,' written in French; a work that made no impression at home, but was very favourably received abroad. About the same time he was appointed a captain in the Hampshire Militia: he afterwards said that this experience was of use to him when he came to write his history—"The discipline and evolutions of a modern battalion gave him a clearer notion of the phalanx and the legion." Some three years after this, in the course of a tour in Italy, he conceived the idea of his famous work: "It was at Rome, on the 15th of October 1764, as I sat musing amidst the ruins of the Capitol, while the bare-footed friars were singing vespers in the Temple of Jupiter, that the idea of writing the decline and fall of the city first started to my mind." He did little towards the fulfilment of this conception till 1770, when the death of his father left him master of an ample fortune.

The first volume appeared in 1776, and was received with unprecedented favour; the first edition was disposed of in a few days. He completed the work at Lausanne in 1787, and it was published in 1788, on his fifty-first birthday. His death took place in the beginning of 1794, about ten months before the birth of Grote, the historian of Greece.

Gibbon is described as having been in his early years of feeble constitution and slender frame, with a disproportionately large head. In after-life he presented an obese figure, fashionably dressed, with a small mouth, a mellifluous voice, and elegant and dignified manners. "His honourable and amiable disposition," says Brougham, who is far from being a generous critic, "his kind and even temper, was praised by all, displayed as it was in the steadiness of his friendships, and the generosity of his conduct towards Deyverdun, and indeed all who needed whatever help his circumstances enabled him to give. Perhaps the warmth of his affection was yet more strikingly exemplified in his steady attachment to his kind aunt, Miss Porten, and towards his venerable stepmother." The same authority objects to Mackintosh's off-hand opinion that Gibbon "might have been cut out of a corner of Burke's mind, without being missed;" and affirms that Burke's "whole writings, excellent as they are for some qualities, will never stand nearly so high in the estimation of mankind, either for profound learning or for various usefulness, as the 'Decline and Fall.' As regards the peculiar opinions of this work, its hostility to Christianity has been widely reprobated and deplored: the author's insidious way of accounting for the spread of Christianity by "secondary causes" —that is, by circumstances apart from the inherent power of the religion—has always given especial offence. His excuse that he might have softened the two obnoxious chapters (the 15th and 16th) if he had thought that "the pious, the timid, and the prudent, would feel, or affect to feel, with such exquisite sensibility," was more aggravating than apologetic.—Apart altogether from the character of his opinions, his style is very remarkable—"copious, splendid, elegantly rounded, distinguished by supreme artificial skill." That it cannot be recommended as a general model, is no more than must be said of almost all English authors. In spite of its singularities, it must be considered a valuable contribution to the wealth of the language. He possessed in the largest measure the author's first great requisites—a full command of words, and the power of striking out fresh combinations. His chief mechanical peculiarities are an excessive use of the abstract noun, and an unusually abundant employment of descriptive and suggestive epithets. This last peculiarity is the main secret of what is often described as the "pregnancy" of his style; it forms one of the principal arts of condensation, brevity, compression. He conveys incidentally, by a passing adjective, information that Macaulay would have set forth in a special sentence: from its form, the expression seems to take for granted that the reader is already acquainted with the facts referred to, but substantially in an allusive way it adds to the knowledge of the most uninitiated.

To this period belongs also the most successful biography in our language. It was not published till 1791, but probably everything except the printing was executed before the last year of the present division.

James Boswell (1740-1795), the only son of the laird of Auchinleck, in Ayrshire, who was an Edinburgh lawyer, and rose to be one of the Lords of Session, was born in Edinburgh, and educated for the law. He showed from early manhood less fondness for business than for travel and literary company. At the age of twenty-three, he set out to make the tour of Europe, was introduced to Johnson as he passed through London, and shaped the course of his travels so as to obtain introductions to many of the chief European celebrities, including Voltaire and Rousseau. On his return, he published in 1768 'An Account of Corsica, with Memoirs of General Paoli;' his enthusiasm for the Corsicans and their general procuring him the nickname of "Corsica Boswell." In 1773 he accompanied Johnson on his famous tour through the Hebrides; his journal of this tour he published in 1785, the year after Johnson's death. His great work, 'The Life of Johnson,' appeared, as we have said, six years later. With all the praise that is lavished upon this biography, the author himself is rather an underrated man. It is pretty generally supposed that little intellectual power was required for such a production—that it is merely an affair of memory and observation. Now such powers of memory and observation are certainly no common endowment; but these are far from being the only powers displayed in the work. Casual readers are apt to undervalue the skill shown in the arrangement and the narrative of the facts and the conversations; and Macaulay, who dilates upon the meanness of spirit shown in the drawing out of Johnson's opinions, gives no credit to the ingenuity. Boswell was undoubtedly a man of much social tact, possessing great general knowledge of human nature, and a most penetrating insight into the thoughts and intents of his habitual companions. He played upon the prejudices of Johnson, and gained his own ends, with consummate adroitness. It is but a fair retort to Macaulay, that whoever considers Boswell a "great fool," lays himself open, as regards that judgment at least, to a similar imputation. His habit of thrusting himself upon celebrated men was not such an immorality as has sometimes been represented; it was at least the most amiable and disinterested form of tuft-hunting. And it is rather a hasty judgment to set down the fact that he could live on friendly terms with celebrated men of every variety of character and opinions to innate servility of disposition; a better-advised, not to say a more generous judgment, would accept his own explanation—that he "ever delighted in that intellectual chemistry which can separate good qualities from evil in the same person," and that he endured the evil for the sake of the good.

MISCELLANEOUS.

Horace Walpole, Earl of Oxford **(1717-1797),** the son of Sir Robert Walpole, is one of the most felicitous of our minor writers of prose. The peculiarities of his easy sauntering disposition were a great puzzle to Lord Macaulay: that energetic writer pronounced him "the most eccentric, the most artificial, the most fastidious, the most capricious of men," and said that "his mind was a bundle of inconsistent whims and affectations." His inconsistencies are not so startling when we bear in mind the character and station of the man; he was too fond of ease, too much averse to effort, to take the trouble of being consistent. His endeavour was to gratify his various tastes at the minimum of exertion. He had a taste for pictures and for articles of antiquarian value, and haunted print-shops and auction-rooms; he frequented clubs and went into society, and amused himself with retailing the gossip and the *bon-mots* to lady and other correspondents; he procured introductions to eminent and notorious individuals; in political circles he enjoyed the mischievous fun of setting people together by the ears. He purposely refrained from forming opinions, or purposely dissembled them, that he might be saved the trouble of maintaining them. He was ambitious of literary distinction, and wrote books: but he pretended that they were valueless, and disclaimed the title of author; partly, no doubt, for the pleasure of so doing, but partly also that he might be saved the effort of supporting a character for learning. He is described as a very tall, slender man, with dark, lively, penetrating eyes, and complexion of a most unhealthy paleness. His observant faculty and freedom from excitement gave him a great advantage in witty repartee and impromptu turning of compliments. One of his greatest beauties of style is his skill in hitting off characteristic traits. His works are rather voluminous: writing would seem to have been his favourite employment: 'Catalogue of Royal and Noble Authors,' 1758; 'Anecdotes of Painting,' 1761-71; 'Catalogue of Engravers,' 1763; 'Castle of Otranto,' 1764; 'Mysterious Mother,' 1768; 'Historic Doubts on the Life and Reign of Richard III.,' 1768. Several volumes of his Letters have also been published.

'Junius.'—The first of the celebrated Letters of Junius appeared on the 21st of January 1769, in the 'Public Advertiser,' one of the leading newspapers of the time. The same writer had been, under various signatures, an active correspondent for at least two years before, and is supposed to have written some of the shorter letters that appeared in explanation and reinforcement of the views of Junius. The letters under the signatures of "Junius" and "Philo-Junius" had a certain unity of theme, were more studied in composition, and, from a combination of circumstances, made by far the greatest sensation in the political world. At the time when they appeared, there was an almost unparalleled disorganisation among the rulers of the country:—an obstinate king bent upon asserting and extending his prerogative; Parliament distracted by opposite policies, and still more by personal enmities; difficulties with more than one European power; a growing quarrel with our American colonies; and at home an imbittered struggle for the freedom of the press. Junius attacked the conduct and character of the leading politicians with unprecedented freedom. The mere splendour of his language and the energy of his sarcasm would have made him a reputation; but what chiefly attracted interest and raised consternation was the knowledge that he showed of State secrets and of the private life of his victims. The excitement grew when the name of this apparent traitor to his order baffled the most determined inquiries.

The authorship of Junius was never acknowledged, either publicly or privately. There are several traditions of great persons who professed to know all about it; but none of them are said to have committed themselves to an express declaration. In 1804, the Marquess of Lansdowne asserted that "he knew Junius, and knew all about the writing and production of those letters;" that Junius had never been publicly named; and that he purposed one day to write a pamphlet and disclose the secret: but he died and gave no sign. The evidence for the authorship is thus wholly circumstantial.

In the day and generation of Junius himself, nearly every man of distinction was named by one person or another as the "Great Unknown." The preliminary essay to the 1812 edition of Junius —issued by the son of Woodfall, the publisher of the 'Public Advertiser,' and containing Junius's private letters to Woodfall, along with fac-similes of his handwriting—discusses the pretensions of some twelve or more individuals. Since 1812 many volumes have been written, solving the mystery with equal confidence in favour of different claimants. Colonel Barré, Lauchlin Macleane, Thomas Lord Lyttleton, Lord Temple (with Lady Temple as amanuensis), are among the authors more recently put forward at considerable length.

The pretensions of **Sir Philip Francis** have been countersigned by an overwhelming number of authorities. His name was never mentioned in connection with the celebrated Letters until 1814; in 1816, Mr John Taylor, in his "Junius Identified with a celebrated Living Character," produced a body of evidence that has since been very generally accepted as conclusive. Brougham, Lord Campbell, De Quincey, Macaulay, Earl Stanhope, and many others have declared themselves satisfied. De Quincey is perhaps the most decided. Lord Brougham, he says, does not "state the result with the boldness which the premises warrant. Chief Justice Dallas, of the Common Pleas, was wont to say that a man arraigned as Junius upon the evidence here accumulated against Sir Philip Francis, must have been convicted in any court of Europe. But I would go much farther; I would say that there are single proofs, which (taken separately and apart from all the rest) are sufficient to sustain the whole onus of the charge."

The arguments in favour of the title of Francis are such as the following:—"Junius" shows an acquaintance with the forms of the Secretary of State's Office, and with the business of the War Office; Francis began life as a clerk in the Secretary of State's Office, and was a clerk in the War Office at the time of the appearance of the Letters. "Junius" shows a minute acquaintance with the private life of statesmen and with secret political manœuvres; Francis had means of access to such knowledge through his father, as well as through other channels. Francis thus possesses the preliminary requisites for a claimant to the honour or dishonour of the authorship. It was possible for him, from his situation in life, to obtain the very special and startling knowledge displayed by "Junius." Farther, it is contended that the character of Francis was consistent with the characteristic temper of "Junius." Francis was an ambitious man, of proud, imperious disposition, with a certain generosity of public spirit, but of intense personal animosity, and very exacting in his ideal of human virtue, especially as regarded his superiors in public station;—a young man in a humble office jealously measuring himself with higher officials, and savage because he had to drudge for men that he considered inferior to himself. Again, it is contended that Francis possessed the requisite ability. "Junius" was evidently a cultivated and practised writer; and Francis was in a peculiar manner bred to the pen by his father, and seems to have begun at an early age to send letters to the newspapers on passing events. In addition to these considerations, which do no more than show that Francis was capable of writing "Junius," and had a motive in his own jealous ambitious temper, there are various alleged coincidences that bring the charge more nearly home. "The tendency of all the external arguments," says De Quincey, "drawn from circumstantial or personal considerations, from local facts, or the records of party, flows in the very same channel; with all the internal presumptions derived from the style, from the anomalous use of words, from the anomalous construction of the syntax, from the peculiar choice of images, from the arbitrary use of the technical shorthand for correcting typographical errors, from capricious punctuation, and even from penmanship (which, of itself, taken separately, has sometimes determined the weightiest legal interests). Proofs, in fact, rush upon us more plentiful than blackberries; and the case ultimately becomes fatiguing, from the very plethora and riotous excess of evidence. It would stimulate attention more, and pique the interest of curiosity more pungently, if there were some conflicting evidence, some shadow of presumptions against Francis. But there are none, absolutely none."

One of the chief arguments against the title of Francis is that he was an exceedingly vain man, and yet expressly denied the authorship. In reply to this argument De Quincey is particularly ingenious. He points out, in the first place, that the denial is ambiguous—"most jesuitically adapted to convey an impression at variance with the strict construction which lurks in the literal wording." Secondly, he urges that Francis was debarred from making the avowal by fear and shame. He had obtained his information by treachery, and he had directed his ill-nature against some of his principal benefactors. To disclose the secret would have been to declare himself a detestable villain. And this consideration is one of the strongest corroborative proofs of the identity of Junius with Francis; for who else had the same motive to perpetual secrecy? "Upon such an account only is it possible to explain the case. All other accounts leave it a perpetual mystery, unfathomable upon any principles of human nature, why Junius did not, at least, make his claim by means of some last will and testament."

The principal opponent of the "Franciscan" theory of Junius, as it is called, is Mr Hayward. Those who wish to see all that can be pleaded against the verdict of the majority should consult his "More about Junius," reprinted from 'Fraser's Magazine,' Vol. LXXVI. The Franciscans have recently received strong support from the 'Professional Investigation of the Handwriting of Junius,' by Mr Charles Chabot, Expert. Mr Chabot is of opinion that the handwriting of Junius is the handwriting of Francis disguised.

Dr Francis, the father of Sir Philip, was an Irish clergyman, who settled in London as author and teacher about the middle of the century. He is known as the translator of Horace, Demosthenes, and Æschines. He was an active party-writer, was intimate with Lord Holland and other statesmen, and was always well stored with political gossip. Philip, born in Dublin in 1740, was brought by his father to London, and received his principal schooling at St Paul's, where he was the master's most admired pupil. In 1756 he obtained, through his father's patron, Lord Holland, a junior clerkship in the Secretary of State's Office, and remained there, with certain brief interruptions, until 1762, when he was appointed first clerk in the War Office. He held his clerkship in the War Office for ten years, during which he is supposed to have written the "Candor" letters, "Junius," and many letters under other signatures. He resigned the clerkship in 1772, for reasons that are somewhat obscure. The Franciscans hold that the motive was resentment at the appointment of Chamier as Deputy-Secretary, and connect this with the attacks of Junius upon that individual. In 1773 he obtained an extraordinary preferment, which the Franciscans suppose to be somehow connected with his authorship of Junius. He was made a member of the Supreme Council in Bengal, with a salary of £10,000 a-year. In India he persistently opposed Warren Hastings, and was wounded by him in a duel. Returning to England in 1780, he entered Parliament, and became an active supporter of the Whigs. He died in 1818.

The leading feature in the mechanical part of the style of "Junius" is the predominance of the balanced structure—"the poised and graceful structure of the sentences;" and the leading "quality" of the style is sarcasm, sometimes elaborately polished, sometimes inclining to coarse, unvarnished abuse. The imagery is also much admired, and the expression is often felicitous, though far from being of the first order of originality.

John Horne Tooke (1736-1812) is best known in literature by a philological work, 'The Diversions of Purley' (pub. 1786); but his general fame rests more upon his political activity. Made a clergyman against his will by his father, a wealthy London poulterer, he nevertheless engaged actively in politics on the Radical side; and finding himself trammelled by the clerical character, he resigned his living in 1773, and studied law. He twice suffered for his "advanced" opinions. He was fined and imprisoned in 1777 for accusing the king's troops of having "murdered" the American insurgents at Lexington; and in 1794 he was tried for high treason, mainly on account of his connection with the Constitutional Society during the excitement of the French Revolution. Yet, upon the whole, he prospered. Having rendered some service to Mr Tooke of Purley, he was made that gentleman's heir, and assumed his name; and he spent his latter years in literary leisure and genial society at Wimbledon. During his active life he made several unsuccessful attempts to gain a seat in Parliament, and at last entered as representative of the rotten borough of Old Sarum in 1801. In 1802 he was excluded from the House; his exclusion being a most startling exemplification of two principles—one that no priest can lay aside his orders and become a layman,[1] and the other (enacted in 1802 for the express purpose of ousting Tooke) that no one in priest's orders can sit in the House of Commons. His etymological 'Diversions' arose out of his political career. He began to theorise in prison upon the construction by the judges of certain propositions in a case quoted against him on his trial in 1777. This perhaps accounts for his proceeding upon what is justly described as the "monstrous" principle that "the etymological history of words is our true guide, both as to the present import of the words themselves, and as to the nature of those things which they are intended to signify." Apart from this, he is very ingenious in his attempts to trace how the language of mind has been borrowed from the language of external things, and how conjunctions and other syntactic particles of speech have been derived from significant nouns and verbs. But the main interest of the 'Diversions' to the general reader lies in the witty intermixture of political thrusts and declamations.

No other prose writers within this period have any special interest. The writings of the eccentric **James Burnet**, Lord Monboddo (1714-1799), contain interesting passages, such as his theory about the origin of man, and his humorously extravagant defence of the superiority of ancient over modern writers; but the interest is more in the matter than in any felicity or original force of expression.

[1] Repealed in 1870.

CHAPTER IX.

FROM 1790 TO 1820.

WILLIAM PALEY,

1743—1805.

THE middle thirty years of Paley's life coincided very nearly with the preceding period; but as most of his works[1] were published in the beginning of this period, we take him as belonging to it.

His life was easy and prosperous, without any striking turns either of hardship or of good fortune. He was born at Peterborough, his father being a minor canon in the Cathedral. His father was afterwards appointed head-master of the grammar-school of Giggleswick in Yorkshire, and the family removed there. Though not very precocious as a boy, he gave such proofs of shrewdness and intellectual force as to raise high expectations of his future eminence. At the age of 15 he was entered as a sizar at Christ's College, Cambridge. It is said on his own authority that he was at first an idle student, and loved company better than his books, and that he made a remorseful resolution to read hard when one of his idle companions reproved him for wasting his talents. He probably exaggerated the effect of this reprimand; but however that may be, he did become a hard student, and eventually came out senior wrangler. He taught Latin for three years in an academy at Greenwich. In 1766 he was elected to a fellowship in his college, and appointed a lecturer. One of his college friends was a son of Bishop Law, and through the bishop's influence he

[1] The list is: 'Moral and Political Philosophy,' 1785; 'Horæ Paulinæ, or The Truth of the Scripture History of St Paul evinced,' 1790; 'A View of the Evidences of Christianity,' 1794; 'Natural Theology,' 1802. There are published also several of his Sermons.

was preferred from one benefice to another in the see of Carlisle. His 'Moral Philosophy' was based upon the lectures he delivered in his college. Upon the publication of his 'Evidences of Christianity' in 1794, he was rewarded by three several bishops with preferments amounting in all to considerably more than £2000. From some unknown cause or causes, he never obtained a bishopric. In the course of his leisure he found time to write the works we have mentioned. He died at Bishop Wearmouth on the 25th of May 1805.

In person Paley was above the middle height, of a stout make, inclining in his later years to corpulence. A good, easy man, he was rather careless about his attire, and his homely manners and provincial accent are said to have stood in the way of his elevation to the bench.

His intellect was clear and steady. He is a shining example of the form of practical good sense characteristic of Englishmen. He did not hunt after paradoxes and subtleties, nor did he throw himself with eagerness into original investigations. He liked to walk on sure ground, and made abundant use of the labours of others. Good sense is the distinguishing quality of his 'Moral and Political Philosophy.' In the case of such a question as the existence of a *moral sense*, he enters into no subtle disquisition, but puts the thing at once to a rough and simple test; and such theories as that of "natural right" he at once sets aside as groundless. In his 'Evidences of Christianity,' which has long been the textbook on the subject, he does little more than popularise the condensed Butler and the voluminous Lardner. The 'Horæ Paulinæ' and the 'Natural Theology' are the product of no more subtle qualities of mind than patient industry and shrewdness.

He was sober and temperate in his feelings, a most unromantic and unpoetic man. At school and at the university he was much sought after as a boon companion; his good humour and drollery, set off by his rather cumbrous and slovenly exterior, making him a great favourite. Throughout life he retained his social, neighbourly ways, keeping up acquaintance with his parishioners in homely, unostentatious intercourse. His writings contain little or nothing to satisfy the emotions; occasionally we cross a pleasant vein of irony or sarcasm, and we are constantly entertained with homely facts, but high-flown sentiment is totally wanting.[1]

[1] Discoursing on Human Happiness in his Philosophy he openly disclaims refined sentiment: "I will omit much usual declamation on the dignity and capacity of our nature; the superiority of the soul to the body, of the rational to the animal part of our constitution; upon the worthiness, refinement, and delicacy of some satisfactions, or the meanness, grossness, and sensuality of others; because I hold that pleasures differ in nothing but in continuance and intensity."

His easy compliant temper, and shrewd steady intellect, were the ruling principles of his conduct. True, he was ambitious of literary distinction, but he pursued his ambition by safe and easy paths. He was eminently "loyal to facts;" he recognised their supremacy without a struggle. At college he proposed to defend the thesis that eternity of punishment is contrary to the divine attributes; but when his tutor expressed disapproval, he simply placed a "*not*" before "contrary," and reversed his arguments. Later in life, when charged with some inconsistency, he made the humorous remark that "he could not afford to keep a conscience." As clergyman and author, he got through his work by steady regularity. Everything had its allotted time, and in his untroubled existence there were few interruptions to his settled plans.

Opinions.—It is probably owing to the prestige of Paley's doctrines that Utilitarianism is so often and so obstinately identified with selfishness. To class Paley with the Utilitarians of the present day is misleading. He agrees with them fully in one point, and in one point only—namely, in repudiating Innate moral distinctions. On a very fundamental point he is utterly at variance with them; he allows no merit to disinterested action, as such. In Paley's view, they only are praiseworthy that act from a regard to their own everlasting happiness. In matters of religion, whatever may have been Paley's private opinions, he published nothing inconsistent with the Thirty-Nine Articles. In one solitary point he showed a tendency to be latitudinarian; he wrote, in defence of his patron Bishop Law, a pamphlet against the propriety of requiring Subscription to Articles of Faith.

He was eminently free from bigotry, and wrote in favour of the most enlightened tolerance, with an exception against works of "ridicule, invective, and mockery." "Every species of intolerance which enjoins suppression and silence, and every species of persecution which enforces such injunctions, is adverse to the progress of truth." In the matter of Church government he held that "if the dissenters from the establishment become a majority of the people, the establishment itself ought to be altered or qualified."

He had the humanity to write strongly against the slave trade, and to refute every shred of argument that could be urged in its favour.

ELEMENTS OF STYLE.

Vocabulary.—Although Paley's language is not studiously varied, he never seems to be in want of words, and the combinations are often agreeably fresh. His preference is for homely words; but he does not scruple to use the most technical terms, and now and then even quotes Latin, trusting to make himself intelligible to the ordinary capacity by the power of his homely illustrations.

Sentences and Paragraphs.—The chief thing worth noticing about Paley's sentences is that they are not constructed upon a few favourite forms, or with any leaning to a favourite rhythm. His is not a "formed" style; he is studious to express himself in simple language, without regard to measure or fluent melody.

It might be expected that, having no misleading desire for euphonious combinations, he would adopt the best arrangement for emphasis. But it is not so; he had not much natural turn for point, and does not seem to have been aware of the advantage of calling special attention to a word by its position.

The construction of his paragraphs is worth examining minutely. (1.) The first thing that strikes us in turning over his pages with an eye to the paragraph division is the unusual number of paragraphs. Every statement that he wishes to make prominent, he places in a paragraph by itself. Thus—

"It will be our business to show, if we can,

"I. What Human Happiness does not consist in:

"II. What it does consist in.

"FIRST, then, Happiness does not consist," &c.

Again—

"The above account of human happiness will justify the two following conclusions, which, although found in most books of morality, have seldom, I think, been supported by any sufficient reasons:—

"FIRST, That happiness is pretty equally distributed amongst the different orders of civil society:

"SECONDLY, That vice has no advantage over virtue, even with respect to this world's happiness."

Once more—

"The four CARDINAL virtues are, *prudence*, *fortitude*, *temperance*, and *justice*.

"But the division of virtue, to which we are in modern times most accustomed, is into duties:—

"Towards *God;* as piety, reverence, resignation, gratitude, &c.

"Towards *other men* (or relative duties); as justice, charity, fidelity, loyalty, &c.

"Towards *ourselves;* as chastity, sobriety, temperance, preservation of life, care of health, &c."

The above short extracts show his arts of giving prominence to leading statements and leading words. He uses separate paragraphs; he makes divisions conspicuous sometimes by figures—I., II., &c., sometimes by numbers printed in small capitals—FIRST, SECONDLY, &c.; he emphasises leading words by printing them in small capitals or in italics. The first chapter of the book on 'Moral Obligations' upon the question, *Why am I obliged to keep my word?* is a very happy example of his perspicuous method. His chief defect in this respect is in the arts of indicating degrees of subordination. He has nothing but the difference between capitals and italics, and the difference between Roman numbers (I., II., &c.) and Arabic (1, 2, &c.) Owing to this defect, the multiplicity of small paragraphs is not a little confusing when we attempt to take in a chapter at a comprehensive glance. It would be a great advantage if the most important statements were printed in larger type.

(2.) The next thing that strikes us is the fulness of his phrases of reference, and the consequent ease of following his exposition. We are constantly kept to the point by such phrases as—"We will explain ourselves by an example or two;" "This will serve for one instance; another is the following;" "For this is the alternative. Either . . . or . . . ;" and so forth.

(3.) When we take special paragraphs in detail, we find that the exposition is not so perspicuous as we should expect from the perspicuity of the larger divisions. On examination we find the reason to be that he does not always keep the main subject prominent, but in his easy way changes the point of view. In the following passage, though the separate statements are simple, they cannot be put together coherently without an effort:—

> "The art in which the secret of human happiness consists, is to *set* the habits in such a manner that every change may be a change for the better. The habits themselves are much the same; for whatever is made habitual, becomes smooth and easy, and nearly indifferent. The return to an old habit is likewise easy, whatever the habit be. Therefore the advantage is with those habits which allow of an indulgence in the deviation from them."

Here the remark about the return to an old habit is not so put as to show its relevance. It were better omitted at that particular stage. Perhaps the following would be a simpler statement:—

> "The great art of human happiness is to *set* the habits in such a manner that every change may be a change for the better. In a habit itself there is little either of pleasure or of pain; whatever is made habitual becomes smooth, easy, and nearly indifferent. The pleasure or pain lies in the departure from a habit. This being so, our wisdom is to form such habits as may be changed for the better, and are not likely to be changed for the worse."

To be sure, the difference between the two modes of statement is slight; still in exposition every little helps, and changes that seem trifling in a short passage, may, if carried through a chapter, make a very substantial difference to the ease of the reader. It is only by slight changes that Paley's method can be improved upon; and the student of popular exposition would do well to attend to such improvements.

QUALITIES OF STYLE.

Simplicity and *Perspicuity* are the eminent qualities of Paley's style. We have already said that the diction, though occasionally Latinised and technical, is upon the whole familiar, and that the structure, with certain possibilities of improvement, is upon the whole perspicuous and easy to follow. But the simple diction and perspicuous structure are by no means the only elements of his popular style.

(1.) It is somewhat of a paradox to say concerning a writer on Moral and Political Philosophy, Christian Evidences, and Natural Theology, that his subject-matter is not abstruse. Of course, Paley's subject-matter is abstruse compared with the subject-matter of mere narrative, or of essays on the minor morals. But it is not so abstruse as it might be, considering the professed themes. He is careful not to take up any doctrine that is too deep or too subtle for popular exposition. He knows either by instinct or by definite purpose where to stop. He makes no pretence of going to the very root of a matter. In discussing moral obligation he does not enter upon the Freedom of the Will. In his 'Natural Theology' he does not enter upon external perception. In considering cases of conscience, he restricts himself to "the situations which arise in the life of an inhabitant of this country in these times." "I have," he says, "examined no doubts, I have discussed no obscurities, I have encountered no errors, I have adverted to no controversies, but what I have seen actually to exist." In saying all this, we must not forget that such subjects as Paley does think fit to discuss might be treated in a very abstruse manner. Only it is necessary to remember that the popular character of his exposition depends to some extent upon the choice of subject-matter.

(2.) He has a habit of stating principles in their application to a concrete case, and he chooses very homely illustrations. These are undoubtedly the main secrets of the simplicity of his style.

A good example of his simple way of stating disputed principles by bringing them to bear on a supposed case, is seen in his chapter on the "moral sense." He begins the chapter by relating the story of Caius Toranius, who in the proscription by the triumvirate was betrayed to the executioners by his own son. He then proceeds :—

"Now the question is, whether, if this story were related to the wild boy caught some years ago in the woods of Hanover, or to a savage without experience, and without instruction, cut off in his infancy from all intercourse with his species, and, consequently, under no possible influence of example, authority, education, sympathy, or habit ; whether, I say, such a one would feel, upon the relation, any degree of *that sentiment of disapprobation of Toranius's conduct* which we feel, or not ?

"They who maintain the existence of a moral sense; of innate maxims; of a natural conscience; that the love of virtue and hatred of vice are instinctive; or the perception of right and wrong intuitive; (all which are only different ways of expressing the same opinion,) affirm that he would.

"They who deny the existence of a moral sense, &c., affirm that he would not.

"And upon this, issue is joined.

"As the experiment has never been made, and, from the difficulty of procuring a subject (not to mention the impossibility of proposing the question to him, if we had one), is never likely to be made, what would be the event, can only be judged of from probable reasons."

He then proceeds to state the pros and cons.

No better instance could be had of the simplicity of his examples and comparisons than the well-known pigeon illustration. It constitutes the first chapter of the book on 'Relative Duties,' and is headed *On Property*:—

"If you should see a flock of pigeons in a field of corn; and if (instead of each picking where and what it liked, taking just as much as it wanted, and no more) you should see ninety-nine of them gathering all they got into a heap; reserving nothing for themselves but the chaff and the refuse; keeping this heap for one, and that the weakest, perhaps worst, pigeon of the flock; sitting round and looking on, all the winter, whilst this one was devouring, throwing about, and wasting it: and if a pigeon more hardy or hungry than the rest, touched a grain of the hoard, all the others instantly flying upon it, and tearing it to pieces; if you should see this, you would see nothing more than what is every day practised and established among men. Among men, you see the ninety-and-nine, toiling and scraping together a heap of superfluities for one (and this one, too, oftentimes the feeblest and worst of the whole set, a child, a woman, a madman, or a fool), getting nothing for themselves all the while but a little of the coarsest of the provision which their own industry produces; looking quietly on, while they see the fruits of all their labour spent or spoiled; and if one of the number take or touch a particle of the hoard, the others joining against him, and hanging him for the theft." [1]

Clearness.—Perspicuity is possessed by Paley in a very high degree, but the *precision* of his statements and definitions is a good deal affected by his paramount desire to be popular. Too clear-headed to run into confusion, he is at the same time anxious to accommodate himself to the plainest intelligence, and, like many simple writers, purchases simplicity at the expense of exactness. His purpose is to be easily understood by the mass, and he deliberately and avowedly prefers a division or definition because it is common and popular. His classification of the virtues is an example (see p. 491). His consideration of "*what*

[1] An account of Paley can hardly be considered complete without this illustration. It has a historic interest. It is said that when Paley's name was suggested to George III. as one that might deserve a bishopric, the King cried—"Paley?—hae! hae! *pigeon* Paley?" whereby our author's hopes of such promotion were ruined for ever.

we mean to say when a man is OBLIGED *to do a thing*" is a favourable specimen of his popular way of defining, and of his care to be as exact as is consistent with popular usage:—

"A man is said to be *obliged* '*when he is urged by a violent motive resulting from the command of another.*'

"FIRST, 'The motive must be violent.' If a person who has done me some little service, or has a small place in his disposal, ask me upon some occasion for my vote, I may possibly give it him, from a motive of gratitude or expectation: but I should hardly say that I was *obliged* to give it him; because the inducement does not rise high enough. Whereas, if a father or a master, any great benefactor, or one on whom my fortune depends, require my vote, I give it him of course, and my answer to all who ask me why I voted so and so is, that my father or my master *obliged* me; that I had received so many favours from, or had so great a dependence upon, such a one, that I was *obliged* to vote as he directed me.

"SECONDLY, 'It must result from the command of another.' Offer a man a gratuity for doing anything—for seizing, for example, an offender—he is not *obliged* by your offer to do it; nor would he say he is; though he may be *induced*, *persuaded*, *prevailed upon*, *tempted*. If a magistrate or the man's immediate superior command it, he considers himself as *obliged* to comply, though probably he would lose less by a refusal in this case than in the former.

"I will not undertake to say that the words *obligation* and *obliged* are used uniformly in this sense, or always with this distinction: nor is it possible to tie down popular phrases to any constant signification; but wherever the motive is violent enough, and coupled with the idea of command, authority, law, or the will of a superior, there, I take it, we always reckon ourselves to be *obliged*.

"And from this account of obligation, it follows, that we can be obliged to nothing, but what we ourselves are to gain or lose something by: for nothing else can be a 'violent motive' to us. As we should not be obliged to obey the laws or the magistrate, unless rewards or punishments, pleasure or pain, somehow or other depended upon our obedience; so neither should we, without the same reason, be obliged to do what is right, to practise virtue, or to obey the commands of God."

Strength, &c.—The preceding extracts give a fair idea of the amount of force in Paley's composition; he never soars or declaims. No other quality of his style need be specially noticed. We have already remarked his indifference to melody in the structure of his sentences. Unless in the vulgarity of his illustrations, he cannot be said to offend against good taste; he is a homely expositor who never even in an illustration makes any pretence to touch the finer sensibilities, and never being in the region of art, cannot be caught trespassing.

KINDS OF COMPOSITION.

Description.—Paley's anatomical descriptions in his 'Natural Theology' have been much admired. There is nowhere, perhaps, a better field for the display of perspicuous descriptive power than in describing the complicated mechanism of the human body. It is, however, hardly fair to compare Paley with systematic writers on anatomy, and to praise the lucidity of his descriptions at their expense. He has an advantage over them in taking up the contrivances of the human mechanism only in so far as they subserve certain ends, confining himself to their obvious points of suitability to those ends, and not entering into puzzling intricacies of detail. On the other hand, it is but justice to his extraordinary powers of perspicuous arrangement to say that systematic writers might often take a lesson from him.

He seems to have been aware of the great art of preventing confusion in complicated descriptions—the art of keeping the leading features prominently before the reader. This he was enabled to effect more easily in many cases by the intention of his work. He wished to show how exquisitely various parts are adapted to particular ends, and thus had ready to his hand an easy principle of lucid arrangement. He treats the body simply as a piece of machinery, or rather as an assemblage of machines, and describes each part only in so far as it performs some particular function. Take, for example, his description of the spine or backbone. He does not attempt to deal with all its complications at once; he separates its contrivances into three groups according to the purposes that they serve, according as they contribute to stability or firmness, to flexibility, or to the safe conveyance of the spinal marrow.

His mastery of familiar figures was of signal service to him in his endeavours to put the reader at starting in possession of a comprehensive idea of the subject of his description. To illustrate this we shall quote the beginning of his account of the circulation of the blood. The quotation also illustrates what may be laid down as a principle in the description of mechanical contrivances—namely, that we should begin by stating the purpose, as giving the most comprehensive idea of the mechanism:—

"The utility of the circulation of the blood, I assume as an acknowledged point. One grand purpose is plainly answered by it; the distributing to every part, every extremity, every nook and corner of the body, the nourishment which is received into it by one aperture. What enters at the mouth finds its way to the fingers' ends. A more difficult mechanical problem could hardly, I think, be proposed, than to discover a method of constantly repairing the waste, and of supplying an accession of substance to every part of a complicated machine at the same time.

"This system presents itself under two views: first, the disposition of the blood-vessels, *i.e.*, the laying of the pipes; and, secondly, the construction of the engine at the centre—viz., the heart, for driving the blood through them."

Exposition.—All Paley's works became popular standards, and his 'Evidences' and 'Natural Theology' have not yet been superseded. No writer has surpassed him in popularising the subjects that he treated of. He may not rank high as an original thinker; but as a popular expositor he may still be said to be "the first of the first rank." The fact that he is far from perfect even in that capacity, should be an inducement for authors of kindred genius to surpass him, or at least to bring similar subjects up to the level of more recent thought.

We have seen that his great art of exposition is the production of homely examples and comparisons. This appears in every extract that we have considered, and needs not be farther enlarged upon. It needs only be remarked, that trusting to this way of making himself intelligible, he is not always so careful as he might be in his general statements.

He does not often repeat a statement, either directly or obversely. His ideal seems to be to give a single statement, and then follow up with one or more illustrations, as the case may require.

Of course, his power of homely illustration would not have insured his popularity as the expounder of a technical subject had he not been so orderly and methodical, and had he not avoided the most abstruse inquiries.

Over and above all this, he must also have possessed some means of imparting popular interest. Putting aside the intrinsic interest of the subjects, which must always be supposed in a popular work, we can see little in Paley's manner of exposition to attract interest except its simplicity, and its contrast in that respect to other works on the same subjects. When we wish to know something of a subject, and can find nothing but dry, abstruse expositions, it is a great pleasure to meet with an instructor that sympathises with our difficulties, and is studiously careful to make the path of knowledge easy. Such an instructor is Paley. Take, for example, his most technical work, the 'Moral and Political Philosophy.' Instead of scaring us in the Preface with a parade of the difficulties of the subject, and apologies for his temerity in undertaking such a task, he understates the difficulties, and takes the task upon him with easy confidence. We are told that the design of the work is to "direct private consciences in the general conduct of human life," "to instruct individuals in their duty." There is not a hint of any perplexity about what "conscience" is, or what "duty" is. The discussion of the difficult points, such as the Moral Sense, is managed with such consummate simplicity, that we read the work through as a shrewd body of good advice, and wonder how there could be so much hot controversy about questions so plain. Our conductor never indicates, by any faltering in his tone, that he is in any difficulty. When he starts a subject on which moralists have shown a perplexing difference of opinion, he confidently assures us that the differences are more in name than in reality. It is refreshing to turn to the Book on 'Moral Obligations,' and find the first chapter—which is headed, "The Question, *Why am I obliged to keep my word*, considered"—effect such an easy reconciliation of conflicting views:—

"Why am I obliged to keep my word?

"Because it is right, says one.—Because it is agreeable to the fitness of things, says another.—Because it is conformable to reason and nature, says a third.—Because it is conformable to truth, says a fourth.—Because it promotes the public good, says a fifth.—Because it is required by the will of God, concludes a sixth.

"Upon which different accounts, two things are observable:—

"FIRST, that they all ultimately coincide.

"The fitness of things, means their fitness to produce happiness: the nature of things, means that actual constitution of the world, by which some things, as such and such actions, for example, produce happiness, and others misery; reason is the principle by which we discover or judge of this constitution: truth is this judgment, expressed or drawn out into propositions."

Persuasion.—As might be inferred from what we have said, Paley is much more successful in convincing the reason than in captivating the fancy or touching the feelings. As a preacher he is "moderate" and "rationalistic," insisting much upon the *prudence* of living in accordance with the Christian faith. He excels more as a controversial writer. His fairness and clear good sense always produce a favourable impression; and in his steady way of going to work, he gives a succinct presentation of an opponent's arguments before proceeding to state his case in reply. The 'Evidences' are generally allowed to be nearly exhaustive from their particular point of view, and in the 'Natural Theology' he makes the most of his knowledge.

He shines especially in refutation. He was perhaps hardly energetic enough to show much original ingenuity in discovering arguments. His power in what may be called "constructive" argument lay rather in effective statement and arrangement, and in the elaborate filling-out of the skeleton-ideas of others. It is in refutation, in "destructive" argument, that he appears to most advantage. He has a mercilessly steady eye for inconsistency; and, from his habit of referring every general statement to its basis of facts, often makes short work of very specious generalities.

His power lies most conspicuously in the happy use of particular facts to demolish groundless generalities. In this way, for example, he conclusively exposes the commonplace outcry against theoretical politicians, which has been taken up even by such men as Macaulay:—

"I am not ignorant of an objection that has been advanced against all abstract speculations concerning the origin, principle, or limitation of civil authority—namely, that such speculations possess little or no influence upon the conduct either of the State or of the subjects, of the governors or the governed, nor are attended with any useful consequences to either; that in times of tranquillity they are not wanted; in times of confusion they are never heard. This representation, however, in my opinion, is not just. Times of tumult, it is true, are not the times to learn; but the choice which men make of their side and party, in the most critical occasions of the commonwealth, may nevertheless depend upon the lessons they have received, the books they have read, and the opinions they have imbibed, in seasons of leisure and quietness. Some judicious persons, who were present at Geneva during the troubles which lately convulsed that city, thought they perceived, in the contentions there carrying on, the operation of that political theory which the writings of Rousseau, and the unbounded esteem in which these writings are holden by his countrymen, had diffused among the people. Throughout the political disputes that have within these few years taken place in Great Britain, in her sister kingdom, and in her foreign dependencies, it was impossible not to observe, in the language of party, in the resolutions of public meetings, in debate, in conversation, in the general strain of those fugitive and diurnal addresses to the public which such occasions call forth, the prevalency of those ideas of civil authority, which are displayed in the works of Mr Locke."

He was not the man to rush into every controversy affecting the Church; but, once aroused, he was an able champion of his cause. His paper on 'Subscription to Articles of Faith,' written in defence of his patron, Bishop Law, against some animadversions, is a model of cool and thorough refutation. An extract or two will show how vigorously he argues, and how carefully he has mastered his opponent's positions:—

"The author of the 'Considerations'" (the title of Bishop Law's work) "contends very properly that it is one of the first duties a Christian owes to his Master, 'to keep his mind open and unbiassed' in religious inquiries. Can a man be said to do this who must bring himself to assent to opinions proposed by another? who enters into a profession where both his subsistence and success depend upon his continuance in a particular persuasion? In answer to this we are informed that these articles are no 'rule of faith' (what! not to those who subscribe them?); that 'the Church deprives no man of his right of private judgment' (she cannot; she hangs, however, a dead weight upon it); that it is 'a very unfair state of the case to call subscription a declaration of our full and final persuasion in matters of faith;' though if it be not a 'full' persuasion, what is it? and ten to one it will be 'final,' when such consequences attend a change. That 'no man is hereby tied up from impartially examining the Word of God,' *i.e.*, with the 'impartiality' of a man who must 'eat' or 'starve,' according as the examination turns out; an 'impartiality' so suspected that a court of justice would not receive his evidence under half of the same influence: nor from altering his opinion if he finds reason so to do; which few, I conceive, will find, when the alteration must cost them so dear. If one could give credit to our author in what he says here, and in some other passages of his Answer, one would suppose that, in his judgment at least, subscription restrained no man from adopting what opinion he pleased, provided 'he does not think himself bound openly to maintain it;' that 'men may retain their preferments, if they will but keep their opinions to themselves.' If this be what the Church of England means, let her say so.

"It seemed to add strength to this objection that the judgment of most thinking men, being in a progressive state, their opinions of course must many of them change; the evil and iniquity of which the answerer sets forth with great pleasantry, but has forgot at the same time to give us any remedy for the misfortune, except the old woman's receipt, to leave off thinking for fear of thinking wrong.

"Our author, good man, 'is well persuaded that the generality of the clergy, when they offer themselves for ordination, consider seriously what office they take upon them, and firmly believe what they subscribe to.' I am persuaded much otherwise. But as this is a 'fact,' the reader, if he be wise, will neither take the answerer's word for it nor mine, but form his own judgment from his own observation. Bishop Burnet complained above sixty years ago, that 'the greater part,' even then, 'subscribed the Articles without ever examining them, and others did it because they must do it.' Is it probable that, in point either of seriousness or orthodoxy, the clergy have much mended since?"

ROBERT HALL, 1764-1831.

One of the most eminent, if not the most eminent, preacher of his generation. He was the son of a Baptist minister at Arnsby, near Leicester, the youngest of fourteen children. He seems to have been a very precocious boy: he is related to have been a great talker at the age of *three*, to have told amusing stories at *six*, to have studied Butler's 'Analogy' and Jonathan Edwards 'On the Will' at *nine*, and to have learnt all that his schoolmaster could teach him at *eleven*. He received his higher education at a Baptist academy in Bristol, and at King's College, Aberdeen, where he passed through the regular course of study and took the degree of A.M. At Aberdeen he was the class-fellow and intimate companion of Sir James Mackintosh—the two young men often walking together and debating questions in metaphysics and general literature. For five years he officiated at Broadmead, near Bristol, as assistant-minister to a Baptist congregation, acting at the same time as classical tutor in the Baptist Academy. In 1790 he received a call from a congregation in Cambridge, and remained there for fifteen years, acquiring great fame as a preacher. While there he published some tracts and sermons,—'Christianity Consistent with the Love of Freedom' (1791); 'Apology for the Freedom of the Press' (1793); 'Modern Infidelity considered with respect to its Influence on Society' (1799); 'Reflections on War' (1802); 'The Sentiments Proper to the Present Crisis' (1803). What with hard study, and what with the excitement of preaching and talking, he overtaxed his strength: in 1804, and again in 1805, he had an attack of insanity. When his health was reestablished, he became associated with a congregation in Leicester, and preached there with such acceptance that the church had to be enlarged. He remained at Leicester for nearly twenty years. In 1826 he removed to Bristol, upon an invitation from the church where he had been assistant nearly forty years before. He died at

Bristol in 1831. His collected works, edited with a Life by Dr Olinthus Gregory, contain the pieces above mentioned; two small volumes of sermons (among which may be singled out the 'Funeral Sermon for the Princess Charlotte,' and 'The Glory of God in Concealing'); 'Terms of Communion' (an attempt to promote free communion among Christian Churches); and other pieces of minor importance.

Hall had a large-built, robust-looking figure. When in repose, his features wore a stern expression, his large mouth having a peculiarly formidable appearance; but when he was engaged in friendly talk, the lines were soft and winning.

With so much of the appearance of robust health, his constitution was far from being strong in all its parts. All his life through he suffered from acute pains in the side and loins; and when he died, the cause of his sufferings was found to be extensive disease of the heart and the right kidney. The other vital organs were found to be quite healthy; and this probably explains why he was able to endure his acute pains so long, and to enjoy life, to maintain even a buoyant flow of spirits, in the intervals of the keener paroxysms. He supported nature further by large doses of stimulants and narcotics, drinking enormous quantities of tea (as many as thirty cups in an afternoon), smoking hard, and in his later years, when his pains increased, taking as much as a thousand drops of laudanum in a night.

As in the case of Johnson, still more in the case of Hall, it would be unfair to estimate his intellectual powers by his published writings. These contain much clear and vigorous argument, copiousness of expression, and here and there passages of splendid declamation; but they do not bear out the reputation he held among his contemporaries, both in his peculiar brotherhood and out of it. He never concentrated his powers long upon any one theme. He was very unlike the steady, sagacious Paley, who threw the greater part of his energy into his books. He was ready to spend himself upon "labour that profiteth not," at least for posthumous reputation. He went through a laborious course of reading in Latin and Greek authors, "because he thought himself especially defective in a tasteful and critical acquaintance with them;" sparing not even "the best treatises on the Greek metres then extant." He went through a similarly laborious course of reading in mathematics, in order to comprehend Sir Isaac Newton's philosophical discoveries. When Macaulay wrote his celebrated article on Milton, Hall set to work at Italian, that he might be able to verify the comparison between Milton and Dante. A man so discursive could not be expected to write much at a high standard of excellence. Nearly all his published writings were composed rather hastily. He prepared only one or two of his sermons for publication: most of them were published after his death from notes taken by hearers. The intellectual power displayed in what he has written is very unequal; but there are passages that show us what he was capable of, and entitle him to a high rank in literature.

Like Jeremy Taylor, Hall was at once a hard student and a man of warm feelings. He had, as we have said, in spite of all his acute sufferings, a keen enjoyment of life. He said of himself that he "enjoyed everything." He liked company extremely—"Don't let us go yet," he was often heard to say; "the present place is the best place." He took pleasure in the dry treatises of Jonathan Edwards, and spoke with enthusiasm of Chillingworth's 'Religion of Protestants'—"It is just," he said, "like reading a novel." His likes, dislikes, and admirations were numerous, and expressed with vehemence. In argument he was excitable, and often lost his temper: when his companions differed from him on a point that he had considered well, he closed the debate with a peremptory deliverance of his opinion. When excited, he indulged freely in personal sarcasms. In genial company he was the gayest of companions; uttering his opinions without reserve, playing on his friends with affectionate raillery, and showing a grateful sense of the regard paid to his talents. With unaffected piety he often took himself to task for not making his conversation more spiritually edifying, and made good resolutions to amend; but though he entered a company with the best intentions, his genial impulses were too strong.

For active life he was eminently unqualified. He was tolerably methodical in his studies, and there is no record of his being diverted by other interests from the due preparation of his weekly discourses. But in the matter of active duties he needed constant supervision. He became absorbed in his books, and forgot his engagements. His deacons often had to look for him in his study. He was sometimes ignorant of the day of the week: and if he went to London, and engaged to deliver letters for his friends, the chances were that he brought them back in his pocket.

Opinions.—Hall caused some suspicion and anxiety among his graver brethren by the liberality of his views, and his free remarks on names venerable in the Church. There was no moroseness, no austerity, in his religious opinions: as we have seen, he was by nature lively and full of gay spirits. He was latitudinarian in his views of Church government, inclining to Pope's epigram, "Whate'er is best administered is best." In his 'Terms of Communion,' he advocated the admission of every denomination of Christians to the communion-tables of every other. There his indulgence stopped. He had Johnson's hatred of infidelity and infidels.

He wrote with great spirit against the ecclesiastical and the political intolerance to Dissenters.

He took little part in political controversies. His first work, 'Christianity consistent with a Love of Freedom,' was designed to vindicate the exertions of Christian ministers in the cause of political freedom; but though he defended the principle, he himself had no natural turn for the work. In his 'Apology for the Freedom of the Press and for General Liberty,' he appears as one of the earliest advocates for Parliamentary Reform.

ELEMENTS OF STYLE.

Vocabulary.—His command of language is sufficiently copious, though not by any means of the first order. This is perhaps due in no small measure to the course of his reading. He spent comparatively little time upon the masters of the English language. His favourite authors were the writers of systematic and controversial theology and metaphysics. From this circumstance his command of the great popular body of the language is limited in comparison with what might be expected with his powers of verbal memory. And from the same circumstance his diction is Latinised and heavily encumbered with the technical phrases of argumentation.

Sentences.—In the structure of his sentences he is a close imitator of Johnson. He acknowledged that in his youth he "aped Johnson, and preached Johnson," but said that he found the diction too cumbrous, and abandoned all attempts to make it a model. His sentences, however, although shorter, bear unmistakable traces of Johnson. He has not the same abrupt way of introducing generalities, but he imitates all the arts of balance, from the ponderous swing to the sharp emphatic point.

QUALITIES OF STYLE.

Simplicity.—Hall's diction is not suited for a popular style. Not only does it want pictorial embellishments, except in the more highly wrought passages: it is positively dry; he has a preference for heavy Latin derivatives, and for abstract forms of expression—the result, as we have said, in some measure, of his favourite studies. Such expressions as—"The author knows not with certainty to whom to ascribe it. *He believes it fell from the pen of an illustrious female*, Mrs More"—belong to a stilted order of composition very shocking to modern advocates of the Queen's English. Apart from the occasional use of stilted and unfamiliar words, the general cast of the expression is excessively abstract. Any passage will illustrate this: let us take (from the 'Sentiments proper to the Present Crisis') some remarks upon our reasons for expecting to be victorious over the French:—

"They appear to entertain mistaken sentiments, who rely with too much confidence for success on our supposed superiority in virtue to our enemies. Such a confidence betrays inattention to the actual conduct of Providence. Wherever there is conscious guilt, there is room to apprehend punishment; nor is it for the criminal to decide where the merited punishment shall first fall. The cup of divine displeasure is, indeed, presented successively to guilty nations, but it by no means invariably begins with those who have run the greatest career in guilt. On the contrary, 'judgment often begins at the house of God;' and He frequently chastises His servants with severity before He proceeds to the destruction of His enemies. He assured Abraham his seed should be afflicted in Egypt for four hundred years, and that after their expiration, 'the nation that afflicted them He would judge.'"

There is undeniably a certain dignity in this mode of expression, but it is very much unsuited to the easy apprehension of people generally. A simple writer would probably prefer some such beginning as this:—

"We do wrong to trust in our being more virtuous than our enemies. Even though we are more virtuous, *that* is no reason for believing that Providence, in the first instance at least, will fight on our side. We may be better than our enemies, yet we cannot pretend to be perfect: if we are guilty, we deserve to be punished, and we have no right to complain if we are punished before others more guilty than ourselves. Consider the dealings of Providence in past times. Have the most wicked nations always been the first to receive punishment? No; on the contrary, 'judgment often begins at the house of God,'" &c.

Clearness.—Hall's mind had a natural craving for broad comprehensive views, and he usually states his case with great perspicuity. His pursuit of abstract argumentative literature also, while it confirmed him in the use of unfamiliar language, accustomed him to a certain exactness of expression. In his controversial works he makes copious use of logical formalities, and gives evidence of a concentrated effort to be clear in his phrases of reference and in the general conduct of his discourse, as well as precise and discriminate in the employment of doubtful terms.

Strength.—The distinguishing excellence of Hall's style consists in general vigour and elevation of language. His astonishing popularity was probably due to the occasional bursts of splendid eloquence.

His 'Apology for the Freedom of the Press' is written with great spirit. The following bears out what we say as regards general vigour and elevation:—

"Between the period of national honour and complete degeneracy, there is usually an interval of national vanity, during which examples of virtue are recounted and admired without being imitated. The Romans were never more proud of their ancestors than when they ceased to resemble them. From being the freest and most high-spirited people in the world, they suddenly fell into the tamest and most abject submission. Let not the name of Britons, my countrymen, too much elate you ; nor even think yourselves safe while you abate one jot of that holy jealousy by which your liberties have hitherto been secured. The richer the inheritance bequeathed you, the more it merits your care for its preservation. The possession must be continued by that spirit with which it was at first acquired ; and as it was gained by vigilance, it will be lost by supineness. A degenerate race repose on the merits of their forefathers ; the virtuous create a fund of their own. The former look back to their ancestors to hide their shame ; the latter look forward to posterity, to levy a tribute of admiration. In vain will you confide in the forms of a free constitution. Unless you reanimate these forms with fresh vigour, they will be melancholy memorials of what you once were, and haunt you with the shade of departed liberty. A silent stream of corruption poured over the whole land, has tainted every branch of the administration with decay. On your temperate but manly exertions depend the happiness and freedom of the latest posterity. That Assembly which sits by right of representation, will be little inclined to oppose your will, expressed in a firm, decisive manner. You may be deafened by clamour, misled by sophistry, or weakened by division, but you cannot be despised with impunity. A vindictive ministry may hang the terrors of criminal prosecution over the heads of a few with success ; but at their peril will they attempt to intimidate a nation. The trick of associations, of pretended plots, and silent insurrections, will oppose a feeble barrier to the impression of the popular mind."

The concluding expression is an example of our author's peculiar failing, the introduction here and there of an incongruous meanness of expression, of a word or phrase out of tune as it were. "*The impression of the popular mind*" is a feeble ending; "*the will of a whole people*," or some such phrase, would have been more in keeping. These occasional lapses are probably the results of his chronic malady; when an acute paroxysm came upon him, he must often have ended off a sentence with the first form that occurred, having no patience to see that it harmonised.

A good example of his loftiest flights is the animated address at the close of 'Sentiments proper to the Present Crisis.' The passage is often quoted:—

"By a series of criminal enterprises, by the successes of guilty ambition, the liberties of Europe have been gradually extinguished : the subjugation of Holland, Switzerland, and the free towns of Germany, has completed that catastrophe ; and we are the only people in the eastern hemisphere who are in possession of equal laws and a free constitution. Freedom, driven from every spot on the Continent, has sought an asylum in a country which she always chose for her favourite abode ; but she is pursued even here, and threatened with destruction. The inundation of lawless power, after covering the whole earth, threatens to follow us here ; and we are most exactly, most critically placed, in the only aperture where it can be successfully repelled, in the Thermoplyæ of the universe. As far as the interests of freedom are concerned, the most important by far of sublunary interests, you, my countrymen, stand in the capacity of the federal representatives of the human race ; for with you it is to determine (under God) in what condition the latest posterity shall be born ; their fortunes are entrusted to your care, and on your conduct at this moment depends the colour and complexion of their destiny. If liberty, after being extinguished on the Continent, is suffered to expire here, whence is it ever to emerge in the midst of that thick night that will invest it? It remains with you then to decide whether that freedom, at whose voice the kingdoms of Europe awoke from the sleep of ages, to run a career of virtuous emulation in everything great and good; the freedom which dispelled the mists of superstition, and invited the nations to behold their God; whose magic touch kindled the rays of genius, the enthusiasm of poetry, and the flame of eloquence; the freedom which poured into our lap opulence and arts, and embellished life with innumerable institutions and improvements, till it became a theatre of wonders; it is for you to decide whether this freedom shall yet survive, or be covered with a funeral pall, and wrapt in eternal gloom. It is not necessary to await your determination. In the solicitude you feel to approve yourselves worthy of such a trust, every thought of what is afflicting in warfare, every apprehension of danger must vanish, and you are impatient to mingle in the battles of the civilised world. Go, then, ye defenders of your country, accompanied with every auspicious omen; advance with alacrity into the field, where God Himself musters the hosts to war. Religion is too much interested in your success not to lend you her aid; she will shed over this enterprise her selectest influence. While you are engaged in the field, many will repair to the closet, many to the sanctuary; the faithful of every name will employ that prayer which has power with God; the feeble hands which are unequal to any other weapon will grasp the sword of the Spirit; and from myriads of humble, contrite hearts, the voice of intercession, supplication, and weeping, will mingle in its ascent to heaven with the shouts of battle and the shock of arms."

The continuation of this passage, which is not so often quoted, exhibits no falling off of power. There is not perhaps in the whole range of oratory anything more inspiring than the concluding invocations:—

"While you have everything to fear from the success of the enemy, you have every means of preventing that success, so that it is next to impossible for victory not to crown your exertions. The extent of your resources, under God, is equal to the justice of your cause. But should Providence determine otherwise, should you fall in this struggle, should the nation fall, you will have the satisfaction (the purest allotted to man) of having performed your part; your names will be enrolled with the most illustrious dead; while posterity, to the end of time, as often as they revolve the events of this period (and they will incessantly revolve them), will turn to you a reverential eye, while they mourn over the freedom which is entombed in your sepulchre. I cannot but imagine the virtuous heroes, legislators, and patriots, of every age and country, are bending from their elevated seats to witness this contest, as if they were incapable, till it be brought to a favourable issue, of enjoying their eternal repose. Enjoy that repose, illustrious immortals! Your mantle fell when you ascended; and thousands inflamed with your spirit, and impatient to tread in your steps, are ready *to swear by Him that sitteth upon the throne, and liveth for ever and ever*, they will protect freedom in her last asylum, and never desert that cause which you sustained by your labours, and cemented with your blood. And thou, sole Ruler among the children of men, to whom the shields of the earth belong, *gird on thy sword, thou Most Mighty:* go forth with our hosts in the day of battle! Impart, in addition to their hereditary valour, that confidence of success which springs from thy presence! Pour into their hearts the spirit of departed heroes! Inspire them with thine own; and while led by thine hand, and fighting under thy banners, open thou their eyes to behold in every valley and in every plain, what thy prophet beheld by the same illumination—chariots of fire and horses of fire! *Then shall the strong man be as tow, and the maker of it as a spark; and they shall both burn together, and none shall quench them.*"

In the Funeral Sermon for the Princess Charlotte there are several soaring passages. The following is one of the most striking:—

"What, my brethren, if it be lawful to indulge such a thought, what would be the funeral obsequies of a lost soul? Where shall we find the tears fit to be wept at such a spectacle? or, could we realise the calamity in all its extent, what tokens of commiseration and concern would be deemed equal to the occasion? Would it suffice for the sun to veil his light, and the moon her brightness; to cover the ocean with mourning, and the heavens with sackcloth? or were the whole fabric of nature to become animated and vocal, would it be possible for her to utter a groan too deep, or a cry too piercing, to express the magnitude and extent of such a catastrophe?"

Another of his most celebrated flights occurs in the magnificent sermon on 'The Glory of God in Concealing.'

Pathos.—We remarked that Jeremy Taylor describes the miseries of human life more as a poet than as a preacher of morality. Hall was opposed to this on principle. He thought that the preacher should endeavour not so much to be tender and touching, as to stir his hearers to virtuous action. He distinguishes clearly the pathetic and the practical treatment of distress:—

"There are kinds of distress founded on the passions, which, if not applauded, are at least admired in their excess, as implying a peculiar refinement of sensibility in the mind of the sufferer. Embellished by taste, and wrought by the magic of genius into innumerable forms, they *turn grief into a luxury, and draw from the eyes of millions delicious tears.* . . . Nor can I reckon it among the improvements of the present age, that, by the multiplication of works of fiction, the attention is diverted from scenes of real to those of imaginary distress; from the distress which demands relief, to that which admits of embellishment: in consequence of which the understanding is enervated, the heart is corrupted, and *those feelings which were designed to stimulate to active benevolence are employed in nourishing a sickly sensibility.* . . . Though it cannot be denied that by diffusing a warmer colouring over the visions of fancy, sensibility is often a source of exquisite pleasures to others, if not to the possessor, yet it should never be confounded with benevolence. . . . A good man may have nothing of it; a bad man may have it in abundance."

Wherever, therefore, Hall describes scenes of misery, he does so in such a way as to "stimulate to active benevolence," and makes no attempt to diffuse over them the warmer colouring that "draws from the eyes of millions delicious tears." His well-known picture of the horrors of war is an example.

Besides, his genius inclined much more to sublimity than to

pathos. In the Funeral Sermon for the Princess Charlotte, from which we have already given a quotation, he passes lightly over the affecting aspects of death, dilates in magnificent strains on such collateral themes as the grandeurs of eternity, and exhibits "the uncertainty of human prospects, and the instability of earthly distinctions," as considerations to "check our presumption, and appal our hearts."

And again, for purposes of pathos, his diction is too Latinised: language can hardly be touching unless it is simple. His frequent use of controversial forms is peculiarly jarring, when the theme is of a tender nature. Take for example his 'Reflections on the Inevitable Lot of Human Life.' He begins in a determined tone, as if he meant to overbear a very obstinate opponent—"*There is nothing better established by universal observation*, than that the condition of man upon earth is less or more an afflicted condition: 'Man is born unto trouble as the sparks fly upward.'" Throughout the sermon the melancholy train of reflection is harshly broken by these disputatious turns of expression. Thus—"If we are tempted to repine at seeing others in peace and prosperity, while we are harassed and distressed, *we form a most inadequate and premature judgment*. Their period of trial will arrive," &c. In expressing the pathos of pious confidence he introduces the same fatal intellectual hardness. The effect of the following passage is destroyed by the two clauses marked in italics—a chilling limitation, and a no less lowering comparison:—

"That the Lord reigns, is one of those truths which lie at the very basis of piety; nor is there any more consoling. It fills the heart, *under a right impression of it*, with a cheerful hope and unruffled tranquillity, amidst the changes and trials of life, *which we shall look for in vain from any other quarter.*"

The last sentence should have been expressed in some such way as follows:—

"Amidst the changes and trials of life, it fills the heart with cheerful hope and unruffled tranquillity."

KINDS OF COMPOSITION.

Persuasion.—Hall's Latinised diction and argumentative forms were against his popularity as a preacher. How it came about that he was popular in spite of these drawbacks is explained by John Foster:—

"There was a remission of strict connection of thought towards the conclusion, where he threw himself loose into a strain of declamation, always earnest, and often fervid. This was of great effect in securing a degree of favour with many, to whom so intellectual a preacher would not otherwise have been acceptable; it was this that reconciled persons of simple piety and little cultivated understanding. Many who might follow him with very imperfect apprehension and satisfaction through the preceding parts, could *reckon* on being warmly interested at the end."

On the whole, however, his was not a style of preaching that was likely to have much practical effect on the conduct of his hearers. He was much too general both in his exaltation of virtue and in his denunciation of vice. John Foster relates that after a sermon on the sin and absurdity of covetousness, one of the hearers observed to another—"An admirable sermon—yet why was *such* a sermon preached? For probably not one person in the congregation, though it is not wanting in examples of the vice in question, would take the discourse as at all applicable to himself." "Too many of the attendants," says Foster, "witnessed some of the brightest displays rather with the feeling of looking at a fine picture than of being confronted by a faithful mirror; and went away equally pleased with a preacher that was so admirable, and with themselves for having the intelligence and taste to admire him."

"It appeared a serious defect in Mr Hall's preaching, that he practically took on him too little of this responsibility of distinguishing degrees of Christian virtue. In temporary oblivion of the rule that theoretic description should keep existing fact so much in view that a right adjustment may be made between them, he would expatiate in eloquent latitude on the Christian character, bright and 'full-orbed' in all its perfections, of contempt of the world, victory over temptation, elevated devotion, assimilation to the divine image, zeal for the divine glory, triumphant faith, expansive charity, sanctity of life; without an intimation, at the time or afterward, that all this, so sublime if it were realised, so obligatory as the attainment toward which a Christian should be, at whatever distance, aspiring, is yet unhappily to be subjected, on behalf of our poor nature, to a cautious discussion of modifications and degrees; especially when the anxious question comes to be, *What deficiencies prove a man to be no Christian?*"

OTHER WRITERS.

THEOLOGY.

About the beginning of this period the Evangelical movement inaugurated by Wesley and Whitefield among the lower classes, began to make itself powerfully felt in higher circles. One of its chief leaders was **Charles Simeon (1759-1836)**, appointed vicar of Trinity Church in Cambridge in 1782. Simeon was, in the face of very bitter opposition, an energetic preacher of evangelical doctrine, and a generous patron of pious young men, such as Henry Martin and Henry Kirke White. He bore the chief part in originating the missionary schemes of the English Church. His 'Horæ Homileticæ' (complete in 21 vols., 1832) is a representative exposition of evangelical views.—Another representative work of this school of religious thought, of a more popular character, is Wilberforce's 'Practical Christianity,' published by the great agitator for the abolition of the Slave Trade in 1797. This work has gone through fifty editions in England and America, and has been translated into several European languages.

To the same school belonged the brothers Milner,—**Joseph Milner (1744-1797)**, vicar of Hull, and **Isaac Milner (1751-1820)**, Senior Wrangler, Master of Queen's College, and Dean of Carlisle,—two sturdy-minded natives of Yorkshire, who raised themselves from humble life. The 'History of the Church' was begun by the elder brother in 1794, and finished by the younger in 1812. Isaac Milner is said to have been the means of converting Wilberforce to evangelical piety, and he was an honoured member of the society that we have already mentioned as influencing the youth of Macaulay.

With these may be linked, as an Evangelical of a different type, **John Foster (1770-1843)**, a Baptist clergyman, a friend of Robert Hall's, known in general literature as a writer of essays. Foster was far from having Hall's reputation as a preacher: he was a reserved kind of man, and his power lay more exclusively with the pen. The best known of his essays, which have passed through many editions, is one "On Decision of Character." He cultivated originality both in thought and in expression. His command of language and illustration is copious, but his style has a want of flow, an air of labour. He repeats an idea again and again, but the successive repetitions do not, like the varied expression of Chalmers, make the meaning more and more luminous; they often burden rather than illuminate the general reader, and they strike the critic as a laboured exercise in the accumulation of synonyms and similitudes.

We may place in another group the divines that engaged deeply in politics. Chief among these (excluding Bishop Horsley, who remained during the first half of this period the Jupiter of Conservative Churchmen) stands **Dr Samuel Parr (1747-1825)**, known in his day as the Whig Samuel Johnson, but by the present generation hardly distinguished from the founder of "Parr's Life Pills." Parr was a man of unquestionable ability, and the oblivion that has overtaken his name is due to his having left no great work on any great subject. His fame rested upon two accomplishments, both perishable foundations,—Latin scholarship and powers of conversation. His pre-eminence in Latin composition was universally acknowledged: although a Whig, he was selected to write the epitaphs of Johnson and of Burke. His powers of conversation are attested by evidence equally unequivocal: although he held no higher station than the curacy of Hatton, he was received at the tables of the Whig nobility, and corresponded with "nearly one-half of our British peerage, and select members of the royal family." His talents secured this admission to high life in spite of a rude dogmatic manner, a homely person, and eccentricity in the matter of dress. Besides this indirect evidence of his social acceptability, we have the direct evidence of Johnson, whom the lesser Samuel imitated in the rudeness of his manner—"Sir," he said to Langton, "I am obliged to you for having asked me this evening. Parr is a fair man. I do not know when I have had an occasion of such free controversy." With all this it is strange that Parr never received the coveted distinction of a bishopric: the explanation probably is that his chief patron, Fox, died just as the Whigs came into power, and that his other friends in high circles were not so indulgent to his arrogant eccentricities and classical licence of personal invective. His style was grandiloquent to an extravagant extreme. De Quincey speaks of "his periodic sentences, with their ample volume of sound and self-revolving rhythmus;" and of "his artful antithesis, and solemn anti-libration of cadences." And Sydney Smith, who reviewed his 'Spital Sermon' in the first number of the 'Edinburgh Review,' characterises the style as follows: "The Doctor is never simple and natural for a single instant. Everything smells of the rhetorician. He never appears to forget himself, or to be hurried by his subject into obvious language. Every expression seems to be the result of artifice and intention; and as to the worthy dedicatees, the Lord Mayor and Aldermen, unless the sermon be *done into English by a person of honour*, they may perhaps be flattered by the Doctor's politeness, but they can never be much edified by his meaning. Dr Parr seems to think that eloquence consists not in an exuberance of beautiful images—not in simple and sublime conceptions—not in the language of the passions; but in a studious arrangement of *sonorous*, *exotic*, and *sesquipedal* words."

Another clergyman and politician, more successful in the world than Parr, was **Richard Watson (1737-1816)**, successively Second Wrangler at Cambridge, Professor of Chemistry, Professor of Divinity, and Bishop of Llandaff. In politics he was a moderate Whig; he vindicated the principles of the French Revolution at the outset, but in 1798 he issued 'An Address to the People of Great Britain, warning them of the danger which the French Revolution taught them.' He also wrote 'An Apology for Christianity,' in reply to Gibbon; and 'An Apology for the Bible,' in reply to Paine. His own orthodoxy was suspected. He was an exceedingly ambitious man, and although more than once in his life he received undeserved promotion, yet in his autobiography he is indignant that the Whigs did not prefer him to a more lucrative see.—Watson's anti-revolutionary address was fiercely commented on by **Gilbert Wakefield (1756-1801),** the son of an English rector, who took orders in the Church, but left it from conscientious scruples. He was a very scholarly man, and published a translation of the New Testament, and 'An Inquiry concerning the Person of Christ.' An earnest creature, of sensitive excitable temperament, he felt warmly, and gave fearless expression to his convictions. He was prosecuted for his reply to the Bishop of Llandaff, and imprisoned for two years. He survived his imprisonment only a few months.

PHILOSOPHY.

In this generation the philosophy of Reid was upheld by **Dugald Stewart (1753-1828),** Professor of Mathematics, and subsequently, from 1785 to 1810, Professor of Moral Philosophy, in Edinburgh. He propounded little that was original in philosophy; his opinions were for the most part modifications of Reid; but as an expositor of philosophical doctrines, his reputation stands deservedly high. Most of his works were composed after his retirement from the Chair of Philosophy in 1810. A remark is sometimes made that his best works were his pupils; the plain paraphrase of which is that he was a person of stately manners and polished oratory, and —a rare thing then for a man in his position—a Whig in politics, and that several scions of the Whig nobility were placed in Edinburgh under his care. Along with a fine presence, Stewart possessed great natural eloquence. James Mill used to declare that though he had heard Pitt and Fox deliver some of their most admired speeches, he never heard anything nearly so eloquent as some of the lectures of Professor Stewart. While his account of Mind coincides in the main with Reid's, the statement and illustration of the doctrines, and the arguments on points of dispute, are his own. He is the most ornate and elegant of our philosophical writers. His summaries of philosophical systems are sometimes praised as being especially perspicuous and interesting. His manner as a controversialist is peculiarly agreeable when taken in contrast to the hard-hitting and open ridicule of such controversialists as Priestley: Stewart's copious lubricated eloquence is much better fitted to conciliate opponents and win assent.

Thomas Brown (1778-1820) was appointed colleague to Stewart in the Moral Philosophy Chair in 1810, and discharged the duties of the office till his death in 1820. Brown is an often-quoted case of precocious genius: he composed and published 'Observations on Darwin's Zoonomia' before he had completed his twentieth year. He was one of the band of young men that originated the 'Edinburgh Review,' and he wrote a paper on Kant in the second number; but he took offence and seceded before the Review was many months old. In 1805 he published an 'Inquiry into the Relation of Cause and Effect.' During the ten years of his professoriate, he published several poems, which possessed little original merit, and soon relapsed into the province of the antiquarian. In his philosophy, Brown agreed with Reid and Stewart in ascribing an intuitive origin to certain beliefs, and differed from them in some minor points of nice distinction relating to external perception. He was a very popular lecturer: he was more sentimental than Stewart, his style was more florid, and his criticism of his predecessors was acrimonious and racy, not to say flippant.

The most influential and original philosopher of this generation was **Jeremy Bentham (1748-1832)**, the founder of the science of Jurisprudence, and the first to make a thorough application of the principle of Utility to practical affairs. The son of a London solicitor, he was sent to Westminster School, and to Oxford, and bred to the law; but, cherishing a strong repugnance to legal abuses, he refrained from the practice of his profession, and lived the life of a studious recluse.

His character and writings are very impartially discussed in a well-known essay by Mr John Stuart Mill ('Dissertations,' vol. i.) "Bentham has been in this age and country the great questioner of things established. It is by the influence of the modes of thought with which his writings inoculated a considerable number of thinking men, that the yoke of authority has been broken, and innumerable opinions, formerly received on tradition as incontestable, are put upon their defence, and required to give an account of themselves." He "carried the war of criticism and of refutation, the conflict with falsehood and absurdity, into the field of practical abuses." Nor was he merely a negative, destructive, or subversive philosopher. His mind was eminently positive, constructive, synthetic. He never pulled down without building up. After showing that an institution was inconsistent with his fundamental principles, he always suggested a substitute that was consistent therewith. His method of procedure was more important than his results. His method "may be shortly described as the method of detail; of treating wholes by separating them into their parts, abstractions by resolving them into things,—classes and generalities by distinguishing them into the individuals of which they are made up; and breaking every question into pieces before attempting to solve it." The method was not by any means absolutely original; but "whatever originality there was in the method, in the subjects he applied it to, and in the rigidity with which he adhered to it, there was the greatest." Again, "the generalities of his philosophy itself have little or no novelty. To ascribe any to the doctrine that general utility is the foundation of morality, would imply great ignorance of the history of philosophy, of general literature, and of Bentham's own writings. He derived the idea, as he says himself, from Helvetius; and it was the doctrine, no less, of the religious philosophers of that age, prior to Reid and Beattie." As regards the results, those achieved in the field of Ethics are not nearly so valuable as those achieved in the field of Jurisprudence. [The value of Bentham's labours in Jurisprudence is univerally admitted. Even his somewhat unfriendly critic Macaulay says, with characteristic sweep, that he "found jurisprudence a gibberish and left it a science."] In Ethics his conclusions are marred by the peculiarities of his own character. "Bentham's contempt, then, of all other schools of thinkers, his determination to create a philosophy wholly out of the materials furnished by his own mind, and by minds like his own, was his first disqualification as a philosopher. His second was the incompleteness of his own mind as a representative of universal human nature. In many of the most natural and strongest feelings of human nature he had no sympathy; from many of its graver experiences he was altogether cut off;" and he was deficient in the power by which one human being enters into the mind and circumstances of another. "His knowledge of human nature is wholly empirical; and the empiricism of one who has had little experience. He had neither internal experience nor external; the quiet, even tenor of his life, and his healthiness of mind, conspired to exclude him from both. He never knew prosperity and adversity, passion nor satiety. He never had even the experiences which sickness gives; he lived from childhood to the age of eighty-five in boyish health. He knew no dejection, no heaviness of heart. He was a boy to the last. . . . Other ages and other nations were a blank to him for purposes of instruction. He measured them but by one standard; their knowledge of facts, and their capability to take correct views of utility, and merge all other objects in it."—His style is much better in his early writings than in his later. His 'Fragment on Government,' published anonymously, was so well written that it was attributed to some of the greatest masters of style at the time. Even in the most involved of his later writings we meet with many happy turns of expression, and with imagery "quaint and humorous, or bold, forcible, and intense." His great fault is intricacy. The origin of this is well explained by Mr Mill: "From the same principle in Bentham came the intricate and involved style, which makes his later writings books for the student only, not the general reader. It was from his perpetually aiming at impracticable precision. Nearly all his earlier, and many parts of his later writings, are models, as we have already observed, of light, playful, and popular style: a Benthamiana might be made of passages worthy of Addison or Goldsmith. But in his later years and more advanced studies, he fell into a Latin or German structure of sentence, foreign to the genius of the English language. He could not bear, for the sake of clearness and the reader's ease, to say, as ordinary men are content to do, a little more than the truth in one sentence, and correct it in the next. The whole of the qualifying remarks which he intended to make, he insisted upon embedding as parentheses in the very middle of the sentence itself. And thus, the sense being so long suspended, and attention being required to the accessory ideas before the principal idea had been properly seized, it became difficult, without some practice, to make out the train of thought."

With Bentham, Mr Mill ranks as the other great "seminal mind" of England in that generation the poet **Samuel Taylor Coleridge (1772-1834).** Bentham's leading purpose was to provide good substitutes for the bad side in existing institutions. Coleridge insisted rather upon the good side, and the propriety of making the most of *that.* Coleridge was also the first great English champion of German transcendental philosophy. It was principally through conversation that he exercised his influence. To some extent, also, he disseminated his opinions in print, although he was too confirmed an opium-eater to be a persistent worker. In 1796 he issued nine numbers of a Radical weekly paper, called 'The Watchman;' in 1809-10 twenty-seven numbers of the 'Friend,'—an unfinished project designed to convey a consistent body of opinions in Theology, Philosophy, and Politics; in 1816 'The Statesman's Manual, or the Bible the best Guide to Political Skill and Foresight, a Lay Sermon;' in 1817 'A Second Lay Sermon,' "on the existing distresses and discontents;" in 1817 'Biographia Literaria,' a history of the development of his own opinions;' in 1825 'Aids to Reflection.' His prose style is copious, and has something of the soft melody of his verse.

To this period belong also two well-known names in Political Economy, the **Rev. T. R. Malthus (1766-1836)** and **David Ricardo (1772-1823).** Malthus's celebrated work on 'Population' appeared in 1798. Ricardo's 'Political Economy' was published in 1817. Both are moderately perspicuous writers, but neither of them possessed any special gift of style.

Archibald Alison (1757-1839), son of an Edinburgh magistrate, educated at Glasgow and at Oxford, latterly an Episcopal clergyman in Edinburgh, is known in letters as the father of the historian, Sir Archibald, and as the author of an 'Essay on Taste,' published in 1790, and in 1811 commended and adopted in its leading positions by the critical potentate, Francis Jeffrey. Alison denied that there is any intrinsic pleasure either in sound, in colour, or in form. He resolved the emotions of sublimity and beauty into associations with primitive sensibilities.

The 'Essay' is written in a very readable style for a work of abstruse analysis.

Another literary man of this generation, best known through his son, is **Isaac Disraeli (1766-1848)**, author of 'Curiosities of Literature,' 'Literary Miscellanies,' 'Quarrels of Authors,' 'Calamities of Authors,' &c. His 'Literary Character,' an attempt to analyse the constituents of literary genius, was a favourite with Byron. In the writings of the elder Disraeli we meet with occasional touches of the felicity of expression so conspicuous in his more distinguished son.

HISTORY.

The most considerable history published in the early part of this period was Mitford's 'History of Greece.' **William Mitford (1744-1827)** was the son of an English proprietor near Southampton, served with Gibbon as an officer in the Hampshire militia, and sat for many years in Parliament. His History appeared in successive volumes at long intervals between 1784 and 1818. The writer was a stanch Conservative, and part of the success of the work, in those days of political apprehension, was due to the use he made of the proceedings and the disasters of the Grecian republics to point a moral against democracy. The work was very derisively reviewed by the young Whig Macaulay in one of his first efforts, and it was humorously pronounced by the Conservative De Quincey to be "choleric in excess, and as entirely partial, as nearly perfect in its injustice, as human infirmity would allow." Mitford's style is in general verbose, periodic, and heavy. There is, however, a certain animation in his narratives of striking events; and his expression sometimes receives a warm colour from the strength of his feelings as a political partisan. He is included by De Quincey among "orthographic mutineers," eccentrics in the matter of spelling.

The history of Greece was written also by **John Gillies (1747-1836)**, an alumnus of Glasgow, and travelling tutor to a son of the Earl of Hopetoun, who in 1793 succeeded Robertson as historiographer-royal for Scotland, and figured in the literary society of "Modern Athens" during the first quarter of this century. His 'History of Greece' was published in 1786. He published also translations from Aristotle, wrote upon Frederick the Great, and continued his history down to the reign of Augustus. All his works have been eclipsed, as regards both matter and manner.

MISCELLANEOUS.

William Cobbett (1762-1835) raised himself, by the force of his self-educated literary powers, from the station of a private soldier to a seat in Parliament. He could not remember a time when he did not earn his own living. An impulsive, self-willed lad, working with his father, a small farmer in Surrey, he first made an abortive attempt to go to sea; then ran away to London and obtained employment as an attorney's clerk; from that enlisted as a private soldier, and went abroad with his regiment. Obtaining his discharge after eight years' service, he emigrated to America in 1792, and soon distinguished himself as a violent political writer, standing up with a characteristic love of contradiction against the ruling democratic faction. The extreme virulence of his abuse soon made the States too hot for him: after two trials for libel and one conviction, with sweeping damages, he returned to England in 1800, and commenced political writer in London under his American nickname "Peter Porcupine." For a short time he wrote on the side of the Conservatives; but he soon quarrelled with them, and became, what he ever afterwards continued, an ultra-Radical. His famous paper, 'The Weekly Political Register,' was begun in 1802, and continued till his death. He exercised great influence upon the working classes, and raised intense hostility among those opposed to his opinions: he was several times prosecuted for libel, and in 1817 he had to recross the Atlantic to evade the pressure of a short-lived Act of Parliament, which he asserted to have been passed for his special annoyance. After several unsuccessful attempts to gain a seat in Parliament, he was returned for the borough of Oldham in 1832, but he lived only three years to enjoy his honours, and made no figure in the House. Besides his political writings, he composed a French Grammar and an English Grammar, and towards the close of his life wrote 'Rural Rides' and 'Advice to Young Men.'—Cobbett has been called "The Last of the Saxons," and the designation may be allowed if the essence of the Saxon character is taken to be dogged, impracticable, unaccommodating energy, and indomitable courage. Exceedingly impetuous, he needed only opposition to make his most random impulses persistent. He was a man destined to excite strong feelings wherever he went, troubling the political world as a strongly-charged electrical cloud troubles the atmosphere. He was a great master of clear and forcible idiomatic English. His 'Rural Rides' expounds the homely aspects of English scenery with much picturesqueness and graphic neatness of touch. In his political diatribes he indulged in a licence of invective and abuse almost incredible to newspaper readers of this generation, although it was not so much above the ordinary heat of his time.

A strong contrast to the pragmatic Cobbett was the amiable, indolent, speculative **Sir James Mackintosh (1765-1832).** A native of Inverness-shire, he was a student, along with Robert

Hall, at King's College, Aberdeen; went to Edinburgh in 1784 to qualify for the practice of Physic; and in 1788 set out for London with a doctor's degree, to push his fortunes. He failed to establish himself in medical practice, and was obliged to depend for a livelihood mainly on his literary abilities. He was first brought into notice by his 'Vindiciæ Gallicæ,' a glowing defence of the French Revolution against the denunciations of Burke. Soon after, he abandoned medicine for law, and was called to the bar in 1795. In 1803 he distinguished himself by his defence of Peltier against a prosecution for a libel on Bonaparte. In 1804 he was appointed Recorder of Bombay. After seven years of "sickly vegetation" in India, he returned with an impaired constitution; entered Parliament; was appointed Professor of Law in the East India College at Haileybury; wrote philosophical dissertations for the 'Encyclopædia Britannica,' and miscellaneous articles for the 'Edinburgh Review;' and remained for twenty years a very acceptable member of general society. The great literary ambition of his life was to write the History of England: for this he had accumulated many materials, but he left only a fragment on the Causes of the Revolution of 1688. He wrote also for 'Lardner's Cyclopædia' a Life of Sir Thomas More, and an abridgment of English History, carried down as far as the Reformation. Mackintosh was an amiable and able man, humorously introspective and tolerant, fond of reading and of society, and an observant critic both of books and of men. Easy, good-humoured indolence, aggravated by his residence in India, stood between him and durable reputation. His fame, like Dr Parr's, rests chiefly on perishable traditions of his conversational power: he had no Boswell to preserve specimens for us, and we have only such reports as the testimony of Sydney Smith—"His conversation was more brilliant and instructive than that of any human being I ever had the good fortune to be acquainted with." His rank is not high either as a philosopher or as a historian: he was naturally averse to vigorous exertion, whether in reasoning or in research; his authority was weakened, as he himself knew and admitted, by an amiable propensity to eulogistic declamation.

Miscellaneous writing received a new impulse in the early part of the nineteenth century by the establishment of the Reviews and the Magazines—namely, 'Edinburgh Review' in 1802; 'Quarterly Review' in 1808; 'Blackwood's Magazine' in 1817; 'London Magazine' in 1820; and 'Westminster Review' in 1823. We give some account of a few of the principal writers in our concluding chapter.

CHAPTER X.

SELECT WRITERS OF THE EARLY PART OF THIS CENTURY.

THEOLOGY.

Thomas Chalmers, D.D., LL.D., (1780-1847), is the most celebrated name among the preachers of the Church of Scotland. A native of Anstruther, in the county of Fife, he was sent at the age of twelve to the University of St Andrews, and was licensed to preach in 1799. In 1802 he was presented to the charge of Kilmany in Fife. During his college course, and the first six years of his ministry, he seems to have held no serious views in religion; in fact, he seems to have entered the Church in heartless scepticism, simply as a means of securing a livelihood. His favourite studies were scientific. In the interval between his obtaining licence and his coming of age, he studied chemistry, natural philosophy, and moral philosophy under the Edinburgh professors of the time. During the winter after his presentation to Kilmany, he taught the mathematical class in the University as assistant to a superannuated professor: during the following winter, having quarrelled with the University authorities, he set up opposition lectures in the town; and not satisfied with lecturing in the winter at St Andrews, he also lectured on chemistry to his parishioners at Kilmany during the summer. He was an unsuccessful candidate for the Professorship of Mathematics at St Andrews, and subsequently for a similar post in the University of Edinburgh. He was lieutenant and chaplain to a regiment of Volunteers. He published a book on 'The Extent and Stability of the National Resources.' Altogether his life was at this time most laborious and eccentric. His composition of the article "Christianity" for the 'Edinburgh

Encyclopædia' seems to have been a turning-point in his career. The death of a sister in 1808, and a lingering illness in the following year, are also mentioned as circumstances that helped to fix his thoughts more upon the peculiar work of the ministry. From about that time dates the beginning of his fame as a preacher. In 1815 he accepted a call to the Tron Church in Glasgow. During the eight years of his ministry there, he acquired as a preacher and a social reformer, a wider reputation than had ever before attended the labours of a minister of the Church of Scotland. His 'Astronomical Discourses' raised universal admiration; and when he visited London, the leading wits of the day, and notably Canning and Wilberforce, "formed part of his congregation wherever he preached, and vied with one another in their anxiety to do him honour in society." His 'Commercial Discourses' also had an enormous circulation. As a social reformer he was known by his advocacy of Malthusianism, his extraordinary energy in organising the voluntary contributions for the relief of the poor, and his personal efforts to "excavate the practical heathenism of our large cities." In 1823 he was appointed Professor of Moral Philosophy in St Andrews; in 1827 declined an offer of a chair of Moral Philosophy in University College, London; and in 1828 accepted a Divinity Professorship in Edinburgh. The first extra-official work of his professorial life was a continuation of papers on the 'Christian and Civic Economy of Large Towns,' begun before he left Glasgow: this was soon followed in the same direction by a course of lectures on Political Economy, which, when published in 1832, were highly praised by the authorities in that subject. He also published his lectures on Natural Theology and on Christian Evidences, and wrote the Bridgewater Treatise on "the adaptation of the world to the mental constitution of man. In addition to his professorial and literary labours, he played a prominent part in the Courts of the Church: he was particularly distinguished by his schemes for Church extension, and by the lead that he took in the controversies terminating in the Disruption. He was chosen by acclamation Moderator of the first Free Church Assembly, and spent his latter years as Principal of the Free Church College in Edinburgh. He had no small influence in raising and establishing what is known as the Sustentation Fund. His collected works fill thirty-four duodecimo volumes.

We have mentioned his extraordinary fame as a preacher. His appearance is described as being by no means prepossessing; he had a hard voice and a broad pronunciation; his gestures were uncouth; and, unlike Robert Hall, he brought a written sermon to the pulpit, and confined his eyes to the manuscript. The charm seems to have lain in his fervid nervous energy. The hearers were laid hold of by his extraordinary concentrated emphasis and graphic expression, and brought almost mesmerically under his influence. As an author, he is distinguished more for his exposition of the views of others than for the excogitation of anything profoundly original. It may with confidence be pronounced that he had a greater genius for style than any other Scotchman of this century except Carlyle.[1] We cannot read a page of Chalmers without feeling ourselves in the hand of a master of luminous and varied exposition. Himself possessing the clearest grasp of his subject, he fully comprehended and kept steadily in view the difficulties of the reader: he sought to unfold his matter in the most luminous sequence, and to make sure that one point was thoroughly expounded before he proceeded to the next. He insisted upon being vividly understood. His habit of persistent repetition, of turning over each proposition and presenting it in many different shapes, is the most remarkable feature in his style. Robert Hall is reported to have dwelt upon this in conversation: "He often reiterates the same thing ten or twelve times in the course of a few pages. Even Burke himself had not so much of that peculiarity. His mind resembles . . . a kaleidoscope. Every turn presents the object in a new and beautiful form; but the object presented is still the same. . . . He may be said to indulge in this repetition to a faulty excess. His mind seems to move on hinges, not on wheels. There is incessant motion, but no progress. When he was at Leicester, he preached a most admirable sermon, on the necessity of immediate repentance; but there were only two ideas in it, and on these his mind revolved as on a pivot." Whether Chalmers carries repetition to excess is matter of opinion: in a popular expositor excessive repetition is an error upon the right side. It is incorrect to say that there is no progress in his expositions; there is progress, but it is slow and thorough.

HISTORY.

In 1817-18 was published the 'History of British India,' by **James Mill (1773-1836)**, celebrated afterwards as a writer on psychology, ethics, and sociology. "An ampler title to distinction in history and philosophy," writes the late Mr Grote, "can seldom be produced than that which Mr James Mill left behind him. We know no work which surpasses his 'History of British India' in the main excellences attainable by historical writers: industrious accumulation, continued for many years, of original authorities—careful and conscientious criticism of their statements, and

[1] It is rather a remarkable fact that both these men in their younger days were distinguished as mathematicians. Such combinations of high scientific with the highest literary aptitude are rare.

a large command of psychological analysis, enabling the author to interpret phenomena of society, both extremely complicated and far removed from his own personal experience." Born in Kincardineshire, not far from the birthplace of Thomas Reid, Mill was educated after a fashion and with a purpose very common in Scotland: he was sent to the school of his native parish, Logie-Pert; to the grammar-school of the nearest town, Montrose; and to the University of Edinburgh; and he was destined to the ministry of the Kirk. But after receiving licence as a preacher, he relinquished his intended profession, and took, about the beginning of this century, a step that Jeffrey about the same time had thoughts of taking—went to London, and settled there as, to use Jeffrey's expression, a literary "grub." He became editor of the 'Literary Journal,' a short-lived adventure, and wrote for the 'Eclectic Review,' the 'Edinburgh Review,' and other periodicals. He made the acquaintance of Jeremy Bentham, and for a number of years he and his family lived during the summer in Bentham's country-house. His 'History of British India' was commenced in 1806. In 1819, the year after the publication of this work, he was offered the high post of Assistant-Examiner of Correspondence in the India House, in which he was ultimately Chief Examiner, an office nearly equivalent to the Under-Secretaryship of State for Indian Affairs. Shortly after his appointment to the India House he contributed to the 'Encyclopædia Britannica' the articles on Government, Jurisprudence, Liberty of the Press, Prison Discipline, Colonies, Law of Nations, and Education. He was one of the principal contributors to the 'Westminster Review,' which was founded in 1823. His chief works on more abstruse subjects are—'Elements of Political Economy,' 1821-22; 'Analysis of the Human Mind,' 1829; and 'Fragments on Mackintosh,' 1835.—Mill was endowed with eminent powers of expression and illustration. Bentham judged rightly in helping him on as a promising expositor of utilitarian principles. His strength, however, lay more in the logical, scientific faculty: men were drawn to his books more by the severe and penetrating rationality of the matter than by the attractions of the style. The severity of his style was probably deepened by a lurking cynicism that on several occasions made itself disagreeably conspicuous: a man of clear insight and intense reserved disposition, he had something like a passionate hatred of superficial knowledge and gushing sentimentality, and he opposed the philosophy of Sir James Mackintosh and the amiable Hindu extravagance of Sir William Jones with too much asperity, and in the case of Jones with some disadvantage to the truth. His style possesses very little figurative ornament; it aims at brief and clear expression as the main chance;

and its principal charms are the severe charms of sententious incisiveness and occasional strokes of epigrammatic point. His 'Encyclopædia' essays have always been exceedingly popular among hard-headed people: they have none of the softer graces of style, but they are almost unrivalled as efforts at the concise application of general principles to practical life; and, in addition to their "pithy" character, their constant endeavour to give the pith of the matter in the briefest possible statement, they contain sharp stimulating touches of epigram and of cynical paradox. Macaulay's criticism that "his arguments are stated with the utmost affectation of precision, his divisions are awfully formal, and his style is generally as dry as that of Euclid's elements," is, like too many of Macaulay's criticisms, an extreme caricature. The main defect in these essays is pointed out by the author's son, Mr John Stuart Mill, in the chapter on the "Geometrical method of reasoning in Politics" (Logic, ii. 471). The 'History of British India' is a perspicuous, well-arranged narrative, written without much pretence to fine composition. As in his essays, the style is enlivened chiefly by epigrammatic turns, succinct maxims, and sharp cynical criticisms. The value of the work consists mainly in its clear analysis of institutions, and its reviews of legal and political transactions by the light of general principles.[1] Concerning Mill's other principal works we quote the opinion of Mr Grote: "Mr James Mill's 'Elements of Political Economy' were, at the time when they appeared, the most logical and condensed exposition of the entire science then existing. Lastly, his latest avowed production, the 'Analysis of the Phenomena of the Human Mind,' is a model of perspicuous exposition of complex states of consciousness, carried farther than by any other author before him."

Henry Hallam (1777-1859) is the author of three celebrated historical works. The son of a dignitary of the English Church, he received his education at Eton and Oxford, and afterwards studied law in the Inner Temple; but possessing some private fortune, and holding besides a Government sinecure, he was independent of professional emolument, and devoted himself to literature. He attached himself to the Whig party, wrote for the 'Edinburgh Review,' took an active part in the Anti-slavery

[1] Its value was much increased some twenty years ago by the annotations of Mr Wilson, Boden Professor of Sanscrit in Oxford, who followed Mill step by step over the field with a superior knowledge of Hindu literature. It appears that Mill, while his work is fully entitled to the praise of extensive research, was somewhat prejudiced against the Hindus by his antipathy to what he considered the over-estimate of them formed by Sir William Jones. Mr Wilson not only corrects Mill's errors in matters of fact, but pursues him throughout with a sharp criticism of his conclusions regarding men and measures; and while he cannot be said to show the same superiority in judgment that he shows in scholarship, the caustic criticising of the critic forms an interesting by-play in the perusal of the book. Mr Wilson also continues the history up to his own time.

agitation, and was united with Brougham, Mackintosh, Russell, Althorp, and other notabilities of his party, in the establishment of the Society for the Diffusion of Useful Knowledge. His 'View of the State of Europe during the Middle Ages,' pronounced by foreign critics to be "beyond contradiction" the best of his works, was published in 1818; his 'Constitutional History of England' in 1827; his 'Introduction to the Literature of Europe during the 15th, 16th, and 17th Centuries,' in 1838-39. In 1830 George IV. instituted two gold medals for the best historical works of his reign; and Hallam and Washington Irving were the historians that his Majesty delighted to honour. Hallam's works are praised for industrious research and dignified impartiality; his Constitutional History is accepted as the standard work on that subject. He had great reputation as a scholar; Byron calls him "classic Hallam much renowned for Greek:" but it may be doubted whether his Introduction to the Literature of Europe was not too ambitious a work for any one man not possessed of the resources of Faust. Certainly his criticisms of English writers, though always expressed with elegance, will not always bear close examination, and too often give evidence of very superficial and second-hand knowledge.[1] Ornate, dignified elegance is the characteristic of his style: for popular purposes it is perhaps too Latinised.

Sir Archibald Alison, Bart., the historian of Modern Europe, born December 29, 1792, was the son of the Rev. Archibald Alison, author of the 'Essay on Taste,' who, at the time of his birth, was vicar of Kenley in Shropshire. His father removing to Edinburgh when he was five years old, he received his school and university education there, and became, in 1814, an advocate at the Scotch bar. He was at Paris in 1814, "when Talma played before a pitful of kings;" and there conceived the idea of recording from its first beginnings the stirring series of events that was supposed to have terminated in the meeting of the Allied sovereigns. The prosecution of this idea cost him "fifteen subsequent years of travel and study, and fifteen more of composition;" the first instalment of his 'History of Europe from 1789 to the Restoration of the Bourbons in 1815' making its appearance in 1833, and the concluding volumes in 1844. Meantime this was far from being his sole occupation: he published 'Principles of the Criminal Law of Scotland' in 1832, and 'Practice of the Criminal Law' in 1833; and from 1834 he discharged the duties of the sheriffdom of Lanarkshire. He was a frequent contributor to 'Blackwood's Magazine;' a selection of his contributions in three volumes was published in 1850. He wrote also 'Principles of Population,' 1840; 'Free Trade and Protection,' 1844; 'England in 1815 and in 1845;' 'Life of the Duke of Marlborough,' 1847.

[1] For example see p. 210 of this work.

In the latter years of his busy life he continued his History to the accession of Louis Napoleon in 1852; the successive volumes appearing between 1852 and 1859. He was created a baronet by Lord Derby's Ministry in 1852. His death took place on the 23d of May 1867.—Sir Archibald was in politics an extreme Conservative: he remained an uncompromising opponent to the principles of Free Trade, and he never ceased to represent the Reform Bill of 1832 as inaugurating an era of disorganisation and decay. Two of his opinions in particular have been subjected to much criticism: one that crime is increased rather than diminished by merely intellectual education—a doctrine inculcated also by Auguste Comte, and which presents a considerable field for casuistry; and the other relating to the amount of harm done to British commercial interests by the return to a metallic currency after the conclusion of the Napoleonic wars. His peculiar views are strongly enounced in the later continuation of his History. But, as is admitted by the sharpest critics of this work, his Toryism and his crotchets are not allowed to interfere with the fairness and candour of his narrative, or with his estimates of political opponents. The 'Edinburgh Review' credits him with "an entire freedom from all mean and petty jealousies or rancorous sentiments towards his antagonists;" and affirms that "he has a generous and hearty appreciation of all merit which he perceives, and can bestow praise in no stinted measure even on those most opposed to him." In addition to this, one of the first requisites for the supremely difficult task of writing contemporary history, Sir Archibald displayed the greatest industry in collecting materials for his work; all agree in bearing testimony to the thoroughness of his researches. Very little exception has been taken to the accuracy of his facts, as regards either omission or positive error—less than has been taken in the case of Macaulay's 'History of England;' adverse critics have confined themselves principally to his opinions. His style has been exposed to considerable animadversions: grammarians have cited from his pages numerous violations of grammar, and the 'Edinburgh Review' charges him with verbosity, and with excessive pomp in the enunciation of his general reflections. These, however, are faults that occur chiefly to the critic and the cynic; and the critics of Sir Archibald's style do not appear to have sufficiently accounted for the extraordinary world-wide popularity of the work. The 'History of Europe,' widely circulated at home, has been translated into all European languages, and also into Arabic and Hindustani: in a work designed for general reading, such popularity may be taken as a proof of excellence, unless good reasons can be assigned to the contrary. The intrinsic interest of the events narrated, absorbing as that undoubtedly was, and the author's industrious accuracy, great as that was, do not constitute a sufficient explanation; the interesting story is undeniably told with high narrative skill. When we disregard minute errors of structure, and look to general effects, we find many excellences of style that help to explain his popularity. The historian possesses a flowing command of simple and striking language, always equal to the dignity and spirit of the events related, and enlivened by happy turns of antithesis and epigram. He had a feeling for dramatic contrasts, and introduces them with striking effect. He visited the scenes of all the important engagements, and his descriptions have the freshness and animation of pictures drawn from nature. Finally, what is of prime importance in such a work, though he deals with highly complicated affairs involving the interaction of several different powers, he keeps the concurring streams of events lucidly distinct, and brings the reader without perplexity to their joint conclusion. His explanatory episodes are peculiarly elaborate and luminous. In short, it has been well said that "if the art of engaging the reader's attention, and sustaining it by the vigour, spirit, and vivacity of the narrative be a high merit, many popular and many great historians must cede superiority of this kind to Sir Archibald Alison."

PHILOSOPHY.

Sir William Hamilton, Bart. (1788-1856), the greatest British supporter of *a priori* philosophy in this century, was the son of Dr W. Hamilton, Professor of Anatomy in the University of Glasgow. He was the lineal representative and was adjudged heir to the title of Sir Robert Hamilton, the leader of the Covenanting forces at Drumclog. His father died when he was two years old. He received his schooling partly at home, partly at the public schools of Glasgow, and partly at private schools in England. He passed through the curriculum of Arts in Glasgow, and spent a winter at Edinburgh in the study of medicine, which he was inclined to make his profession. In 1807 he went to Oxford as an exhibitioner on the Snell Foundation. There he became engrossed in the study of mental philosophy, and in the final examination professed a knowledge of an unusual (though currently very much exaggerated) list of books, and was passed with the highest distinction. About this time he abandoned his design of entering the profession of medicine, and ultimately settled at Edinburgh as a lawyer, being called to the bar in 1814, three years after his graduation as B.A. at Oxford. In 1820 he was an unsuccessful candidate for the Chair of Moral Philosophy, vacated by the death of Brown, the appointment being given to John Wilson. In the following year he was appointed to the poorly-salaried Chair of Civil History. His appointment to the Chair of Logic did not take place till 1836.

By this time, through articles contributed to the 'Edinburgh Review,' and subsequently reprinted under the title of 'Dissertations and Discussions in Philosophy,' he had obtained European reputation as a philosopher. In 1844 his health was much shattered by an attack of paralysis of the right side, which, while it left his mind uninjured, permanently disabled the side affected, impairing his eyesight and his speech, and leaving him with an imperfect use of his right arm and right leg. "He had so far recovered from his illness in the winter of 1844-45 as to be able to resume his studies, and he continued the work of reading and thinking with but slight interruptions till a few days before his death in May 1856. The editing of Reid, which had suffered so much from interruptions, was resumed. The work was finally published—though without being completed—in November 1846. The supplementary dissertations D* * and D* * * had been written before his illness." His class lectures on Logic and Metaphysics were published after his death, under the editorial charge of the late Dean Mansel and Professor Veitch, his pupils.—In his youth Hamilton was a very handsome, athletic man. He is described by Carlyle as having "a fine firm figure of middle height; one of the finest cheerfully-serious human faces, of square, solid, and yet rather *aquiline* type; and a pair of the beautifullest kindly-beaming hazel eyes, well open, and every now and then with a lambency of smiling fire in them, which I always remember as if with trust and gratitude." "He was finely social and human in these walks or interviews. His talk was forcible, copious, discursive, careless rather than otherwise; and on abstruse topics, I observed, was apt to become embroiled and revelly, much less perspicuous and elucidative than with a little deliberation he could have made it. . . . By lucid questioning you could get lucidity from him on any topic." In company he had no pretensions to shine as a talker, and listened quietly without showing any disposition to strike in, unless he had a special interest in the subject, when he became animated and fluent. "He did not accommodate himself to the prevailing opinions of the company; but rather took delight in running atilt against them in a good-humoured way. He had great pleasure in stating and defending some paradox or startling opinion (of which he would perhaps afterwards make a joke), not because it exactly represented his own opinion, but sometimes merely for the sake of argument, and more frequently with the wish to uphold the unpopular side of a question under discussion."[1] "The prevailing opinion on a subject, when strongly put, had a tendency to arouse in him a feeling of opposition." "As in intellect he was critical, so in temperament he was strongly polemical, even finding a certain enjoyment in conflict for its own sake." "His views on

[1] Mr Veitch's Memoir of Sir William Hamilton, p. 142.

University matters brought him pretty frequently into sharp collision with some of his colleagues. For with all his lovableness, even tenderness of nature, Hamilton was yet a man of resolute will, and high and somewhat uncompromising temper." From the time of his extraordinary examination at Oxford, his erudition and encyclopedic reading became a subject of wonder and exaggerated rumour. He seems to have had something of the same book-devouring turn as Johnson. Johnson is described as "tearing out the heart" of a book, and Sir William, in a coarser modification of the phrase, as "tearing out the entrails"—expressions that point to the same habit of glancing at the table of contents, the index, or the marginal annotations, and reading only what one happens to be interested in. The two men agreed further in combining with this literary epicureanism (or rather gluttony) a reluctance to compose; but Hamilton, who had a decided mechanical turn, preserved the results of his reading in an elaborately ingenious commonplace-book,[1] whereas Johnson left what he read to the chances of resuscitation by his powerful memory. Of late years both the extent and the accuracy of Hamilton's scholarship have been questioned, but with all deductions he still remains what he was represented to De Quincey as being—"a monster of erudition."—We do not here attempt any outline of his philosophy; and his philosophical abilities are still matter of dispute.—As regards style, he had, with his prodigious memory, a fine command of language; his command of the language of controversy, especially for the purpose of summarily "putting down" an antagonist, is at least as good as his command of the language of philosophical exposition. In both operations he is masterly. He had a taste for antithesis and pithy compression. He was also notably studious of method, of good arrangement; more, apparently, from a love of mechanical symmetry, than from any lively sympathy with the difficulties of the reader.

MISCELLANEOUS.

Francis Jeffrey (1773-1850), the chief of the originators of the 'Edinburgh Review,' was the son of a depute-clerk of the Court of Session, and received his early education at the Edinburgh High School. He pursued university studies partly at Glasgow, partly at Oxford, and partly at Edinburgh, exercising himself all the while voluminously in English composition. At Oxford he remained only nine months, and left with a sense of relief, finding the routine subjects of study very uncongenial. He was called to the Edinburgh bar in 1794. Entertaining the then unpopular principles of the Whig party, his career was for several years the re-

[1] Mr Veitch's Memoir of Sir William Hamilton, p. 386.

verse of prosperous, and more than once he had serious thoughts of abandoning the profession. The establishment of the 'Edinburgh Review' in 1802 was the making of his fame and fortune. "Without patronage, without name, under the tutelage of no great man; propounding heresies of all sorts against the ruling fancies of the day, whether political, poetical, or social; by sheer vigour of mind, resolution of purpose, and an unexampled combination of mental qualities—five or six young men in our somewhat provincial metropolis laid the foundation of an empire to which, in the course of a few years, the intellect of Europe did homage." The sociable and clear-sighted Jeffrey was admirably fitted to keep together and direct the energies of this fortuitous concourse of unemployed talent. His fame grew with the fame of the work. He rose rapidly to a first-rate position at the bar. His election to the Rectorship of Glasgow University in 1820 was a proof of the general admiration of his powers. His election as Dean of the Faculty of Advocates in 1829 was a proof that he enjoyed the highest popularity among his brother lawyers. From 1830, for about three years and a half, he held office in the Whig Ministry as Lord Advocate. In 1833 he was appointed one of the Judges of the Court of Session, and lived in the quiet discharge of his judicial duties and the pleasant society of "Modern Athens" until his seventy-seventh year, when he died, after a brief illness, on the 26th of January 1850.[1]—Jeffrey was a dark, wiry, little creature, with small mobile features, black sparkling eyes, and a remarkably long, narrow head. His voice was high-pitched, his speech somewhat mincing, and his movements exceedingly animated. "Jeffrey's manner," wrote his friend Horner, "almost irresistibly impresses upon strangers the idea of levity and superficial talents." His appearance, however, did not do him justice. "He has indeed a very sportive and playful fancy, but it is accompanied with an extensive and varied information, with a readiness

[1] The following is his own account of his connection with the 'Edinburgh Review:' "I wrote the first article in the first number of the Review in October 1802, and sent my last contribution to it in October 1840! It is a long period to have persevered in well—or in ill doing! But I was by no means equally alert in the service during all the intermediate time. I was sole editor from 1803 till late in 1829; and during that period was no doubt a large and regular contributor. In that last year, however, I received the great honour of being elected, by my brethren of the bar, to the office of Dean of the Faculty of Advocates; when it immediately occurred to me that it was not quite fitting that the official head of a great Law Corporation should continue to be the conductor of what might be fairly enough represented as, in many respects, a party journal; and I consequently withdrew at once and altogether from the management. . . . I wrote nothing for it for a considerable time subsequent to 1829; and during the whole fourteen years that have since elapsed, have sent in all but four papers to that work, none of them on political subjects. I ceased in reality to be a contributor in 1829."—*Preface to the collected edition of his contributions to the 'Edinburgh Review,'* 1843.

of apprehension almost intuitive, with judicious and calm discernment, with a profound and penetrating understanding." To this it must be added, that the range of his apprehension, discernment, or penetration was not of the widest order: a man of great activity and decision, with much knowledge of the world, and skill in the management of men, he yet did not display, at least in literature, the highest power of entering into the feelings of others, of understanding the position of men very different in character from himself. In his criticisms of Wordsworth we see vividly at once his own character and his failure to appreciate a character very different from his own. He was an affectionate man, intensely attached to his friends, and uncontrollably fond of their society; and the passages that he admires in Wordsworth are chiefly passages of tenderness. He loved natural scenery, too, in a way, and does justice to Wordsworth's more striking word-pictures; but he was too much attached to "the busy haunts of men" to follow the raptures of a genuine nature-worshipper, and he found Wordsworth's minute descriptions intolerably tedious. But what he chiefly failed to understand, and what chiefly offended him, were the meditations natural to a recluse, and the glorification of children and of country personages to a degree altogether out of keeping with their conventional place in the social scale. He was constantly accusing Wordsworth of clothing the commonest commonplaces with unintelligible verbiage, and of debasing tenderness with vulgarity. A similar narrowness, the same tendency to lay down the law without a suspicion that other people were differently constituted from himself, appears in his essay on 'Beauty.' Himself defective in the feeling for colour, he denies that colour possesses any intrinsic beauty, and is utterly sceptical regarding the statements of artists and connoisseurs, suspecting them of pedantry and jargon. His style is forcible and copious, without any pretence to finished or elegant structure. His diction is perhaps too overflowing; his powers of amplification and illustration sometimes ran away with him; "his memory," says Lockhart, "appeared to range the dictionary from A to Z, and he had not the self-denial to spare his readers the redundance which delighted himself." His collected works give but a feeble idea of the cleverness of his ridicule; he refused to republish the most striking specimens of his satirical skill.

Conjoined with Jeffrey in the origination of the 'Edinburgh Review' was the Rev. **Sydney Smith** (1771-1845), the most brilliant wit of his generation. The son of an eccentric English gentleman, he was educated at Winchester and at Oxford, and then set adrift to push his own fortunes. He wished to study for the bar, but was under the necessity of entering the Church. For three years he acted as curate in a small village in the midst of

Salisbury Plain. In 1797, being appointed travelling tutor to the son of the parish squire, he set out with his pupil for the University of Weimar, but was forced by the political storm then raging on the Continent to put into Edinburgh. Here he found a congenial group of aspiring young men, most of them fortuneless like himself, and linked together by agreement in unpopular political views: among these, some four or five years after his arrival, he suggested the idea of a quarterly periodical as a vent for their opinions and their ambition, and himself took a leading part in writing and in choosing articles for the first number of the 'Edinburgh Review.' He contributed to this periodical for a quarter of a century, until he became a dignitary of the Church; and his strong sense and wit are justly credited with a large share of its popularity. In 1804-5-6 he lectured at the Royal Institution on Moral Philosophy. Very slender recognition was given to his powers and his connection with the rising Whig Review: although his political friends were then in office, he had to accept the small living of Foxton-le-Clay in Yorkshire; and even it was obtained with some difficulty. There he remained for twenty-two years. In 1828 he was presented by Lord Lyndhurst, a Conservative, to the canonry of Bristol Cathedral, and from that time ceased to write for the 'Edinburgh Review.' Through the influence of the same nobleman he was enabled to exchange Foxton for the living of Combe Florey, near Taunton. All that his Whig friends did for him was to make him a prebend of St Paul's: this piece of promotion he received in 1831. His case is sometimes mentioned along with Swift's as an example of political ingratitude; the excuse for not making him a bishop was that his writings were generally regarded as being inconsistent with clerical decorum. He died on the 22d of February 1845. Like De Quincey, Jeffrey, Wilson, and many other less distinguished contributors to periodical literature, he has left no great work as a pre-eminent monument of his genius; his Peter Plymley's "Letters on the subject of the Catholics," which appeared in 1808, are his most elaborate efforts on any one subject, and they do not extend beyond fifty closely-printed octavo pages. It is perhaps a vain regret to wish that his powers had been spent upon sustained compositions of greater length; he wrote briefly upon questions of passing interest with extraordinary immediate effect; he influenced as well as gratified his contemporaries; and now that his objects have been attained and the interest of his themes has been succeeded by other interests, the lovers of wit are as much entertained by his short effusions as they would have been by more ambitious performances.—Both physically and mentally Sydney Smith belonged to the race of giants. He was a man of a large build, and of a constitution that retained to his latest years a hearty enjoyment of life. His wit and great convivial powers did not prevent him from making more solid attainments: though not by any means a profound scholar, or a logician of scholastic subtlety, he did not disdain to master the dry facts of what he professed to discuss; and he argued with strong good sense: his papers on political questions are instructive and convincing, as well as witty. "He never came into society without naturally and easily taking the lead as, beyond all question, the most agreeable, sensible, and instructive guest and companion that the oldest person living could remember." His straitened means and the enforced solitude of country life were doubtless efficacious in giving earnestness and solidity to his character; had genial company been always within his reach, he would probably now have been known only as a convivial spirit of happy memory. Regarding the mechanical part of his style, Mr Hayward[1] makes the following criticism: "His sermons, which are mostly free from mannerism, prove that he could combine purity and correctness with force of language when he thought fit. But his humorous writings are often deficient in ease, smoothness, grace, rhythm, and purity, because he constantly aimed at effect by startling contrasts, by the juxtaposition of incongruous images or epithets, or by the use of odd-sounding words and strange compounds of Greek and Latin derivation. Thus he describes a preacher wiping his face with his cambric '*sudarium*,' and asks, 'why this *holoplexia* on sacred occasions alone?' A weak and foolish man is 'anserous' and 'asinine.' Dr Parr's wig is the μέγα θαῦμα of barbers," &c. On these defects in his composition it would be easy to insist too much; they are part and parcel of the pervading quality of his style. He takes rank among our greatest masters of the ludicrous. He has been surpassed as a wit, surpassed as a humorist, surpassed as a satirist; but taken all in all, both in his writings and in private society, he probably never has been surpassed in the power of exciting hearty laughter. In private company he seems to have been irresistible; the more so that "there was always plenty of bread to his sack; the coruscations of his humour were relieved not by flashes of silence, but by the moonlight beams of good feeling and good sense." With his unfailing buoyancy of spirits, he could keep up the flow of wit and clever nonsense long after men of ordinary constitution would have been exhausted; out of the mere wealth of his constitution he could do what was impossible for Theodore Hook without an extreme use of stimulants. His style has something of the reported character of his conversation; mixed up with the "infinite humour," we have clear statement of pertinent facts and sound arguments. We are not conscious of any awkwardness of transition from the comic to the serious; he usually writes with a serious purpose—with the object of discrediting, both by reason and by

[1] Biographical and Critical Essays, i. 50.

ridicule, something that he disapproves of. He is often humorous, purely for the sake of the humour, but his prevailing purposes are serious. What is more, he did not, like the 'Spectator,' the 'Rambler,' and the 'Citizen of the World,' attack ignorance, folly, bigotry, and vice with inoffensive generality, directing his ridicule against imaginary types; but he openly assailed and turned to scorn living men, and laws, parties, and institutions that were in actual existence. He was far from surveying mankind with the artistic impartiality of Goldsmith; he used his wit unmercifully on the side of a party; he was one of the most aggressive of the Edinburgh Reviewers. Anti-revolutionary alarmists, the upholders of Catholic disabilities, fanatical Methodists, Indian missionaries, the abuse of classical study, female education, public schools, the Game-laws, the Poor-laws, the state of prisons, the cruel treatment of untried prisoners—these and suchlike were the objects of his witty satire and humorous derision. Although a good-natured man, without a trace of the sourness and fierceness of Swift, and now recognised as having used his powers in the main on the side of good sense and good feeling, he was most provokingly and audaciously personal in his strictures. This point must be especially attended to in an estimate of Sydney Smith as a master of the ludicrous; the mere fact of overt personality distinguishes him from all our great humorists or satirists except Swift, and he is distinguished from Swift by his greater heartiness of nature. He is too complacent, too aboundingly self-satisfied, too buoyantly full of spirits, to hate anybody; but he burlesques them, derides them, and abuses them with the most exasperating effrontery—in a way that is great fun to the reader, but exquisite torture to the victim. For short characteristic specimens we may refer to his review of Dr Langford's sermon, and his Letters on the American Debts.

A humorist of a much less robust and boisterous type than Sydney Smith, a *humorist* in a more restricted sense of the word, was the author of the 'Essays of Elia,' **Charles Lamb (1775-1834)**. The son of a lawyer's clerk in the Inner Temple, he was, along with Coleridge, a scholar on the foundation of Christ's Hospital, went from that to the South Sea House, and in 1792 obtained an appointment in the India House, where he remained for thirty-three years. While his public life was thus uneventful, the course of his domestic life was altered and saddened by a well-known tragical calamity, the result of an outbreak of insanity in his only sister. This took place in 1796. "For a time Mary was confined in an asylum; but, the fit passing off, she was released, on her brother giving a solemn undertaking to watch over her through life. . . . For the sake of his sister, he gave up the brighter prospects of life, . . . abandoning, it is thought, a passion he had conceived for a young lady who is apparently alluded to in his

Essays under the designation of 'Alice W.' The history of the long association between brother and sister, broken from time to time by a fresh accession of the fatal malady, is one of the most touching things in fact or fiction." Lamb's first appearance as an author was in 1797; in that year he contributed some poems to a volume issued by Coleridge and Lloyd. In 1798 appeared his prose tale of 'Rosamond Gray;' in 1801 his tragedy of 'John Woodvil,' an imitation of the Elizabethan style, which was mercilessly ridiculed by the Edinburgh Reviewers. Shortly afterwards he wrote a farce, which also proved a failure. In 1807 he published his 'Tales from Shakspeare,' written in conjunction with his sister. He made several contributions to Leigh Hunt's 'Reflector.' The papers that established his reputation with the public were his 'Essays of Elia,' which originally appeared in the 'London Magazine,' and were reprinted in a collected form in 1823. In 1825 he retired from his clerkship with a handsome pension. He gives a very humorous account of his sensations on thus obtaining liberty from the routine of the desk, and of the unhappiness that soon overtook him from his having nothing to do. He lived through nine years of his uneasy leisure, occasionally writing verses and periodical articles, but adding little to his literary reputation. His sister Mary survived till 1847; but after his death her lunacy returned, and she had to be placed under restraint.—Lamb was a very different man from the robust, hearty, buoyant Sydney Smith: a spare, slender person, of extremely excitable nervous temperament, of shy melancholy air, his humour not an outcome of healthy animal spirits, but a provision of the fancy to make up for the poverty of the constitutional sources of pleasure. He had a tinge of the insanity that was developed in his sister; a melancholy capricious turn; an excitability that might easily have been pushed beyond the limits of self-control. Two or three glasses of wine excited him; and, once excited, he carried out the most comical whims with an utter recklessness of consequences and appearances. Shy in general society, he was a man of warm and deep affections, as was evinced not only by his lifelong devotion to his sister, but by his excessive fondness for the company of a few intimate friends. As we often see in an excitable nature not endowed with a constitution capable of sustaining much excitement, he hated bustle, agitation, change—all the associations of vigorous energy; his feelings were all in favour of quiet and repose. He loved things that had been passively abandoned to the operations of nature—tattered old books, crazy old houses, old-fashioned pumps and statues; he disliked brand-new books, and execrated modern improvements. Narrative, he said, teased him; he had little concern in the progress of events; he loved to hang "*for the thousandth time* over some passage in old Burton, or one of his strange contemporaries." His sociability and his old habits led him to prefer the town to the country, and his whimsical humour to exaggerate this preference in the presence of the Lakers; but in the town his favourite haunts were suburban lanes and the quiet gardens of the Temple; and he had a genuine longing for the "pretty pastoral walks in hearty, homely, loving Hertfordshire." Akin to his dislike of rigorous energy, was his fondness for oddities, for things that were not braced up by an effort to a conventional standard, but seemed as if they had whimsically followed their own sweet will—"out-of-the-way humours and opinions—heads with some diverting twist in them"—"things quaint, irregular, out of the road of common sympathy," and particularly the oddities of authorship, such as "the beautiful obliquities of the Religio Medici." He liked the "artificial comedy" of Congreve and Wycherly, as a region "where no cold moral reigns," "out of which our coxcomical moral sense is for a little transitory ease excluded." He wished people to enjoy in imagination the comical invasions of strict morality, and professed for himself that after "an airing beyond the diocese of the strict conscience," he "came back to his cage and his restraint the fresher and more healthy for it." With all Lamb's whims and oddities, the foundations of his being were serious and substantial. He was a most penetrating observer and critic; his eye was not easily diverted from the heart of a subject. Readers of poetry are pre-eminently indebted to him for his services in the work of exhuming the old dramatic writers of the Shakspearian age. "He threw," it has been said, "more and newer light upon the genuine meaning of the great masterpieces of the theatre than any other man; and yet we do not remember a single instance in which his positions have been gainsaid."

Walter Savage Landor (1775 - 1864), author of the poems 'Gebir' and 'Count Julian,' and who, as Byron said, "cultivated much private renown in the shape of Latin verses," is by some authorities placed in the first rank among writers of prose. His life has recently been written with great minuteness by Mr John Forster. He was born in the year of the outbreak of the American War (1775), on the 30th January, the anniversary of the execution of Charles I. From his youth up he gave evidence of an insubordinate spirit; he had to quit Rugby, and subsequently Oxford, in consequence of misdemeanours, aggravated by dogged defiance of authority. After his rustication from Oxford in the summer of 1794, he declined his father's desire that he should choose a profession, by way of having something to do; and being heir to considerable estates, preferred being put upon a yearly allowance, with liberty to travel where he pleased. His poem 'Gebir' was published in 1797; it was highly praised by Southey in the 'Critical Review,' but it made no impression on the general public. As he sympathised with the anti-monarchical enthusiasts of the period, his help was solicited for the current newspaper warfare, and he made several contributions to journals then supported by Coleridge and Southey. The death of his father in 1805 made him a wealthy man, and for a year or two thereafter he lived chiefly at Bath in great splendour. In 1808 he suddenly set out for Spain to assist in the war of liberation, but soon quarrelled with some of his associates and came back again. Shortly after his return, he sold his paternal estates, bought Llanthony in Monmouthshire, and married "a pretty little girl, of whom he seems literally to have had no other knowledge than that she had more curls on her head than any other girl in Bath." In 1812 appeared his tragedy of 'Count Julian,' the legendary traitor who introduced the Moors into Spain. While Wilson was living in supreme happiness at Elleray, poor Landor at Llanthony was in a Tartarean broil of bitter quarrels with his tenants and his neighbours, the final result of which was his departure from England and his settlement in Italy in 1815. Twenty years he remained in Italy, during which his only productions worthy of note were the 'Imaginary Conversations' (1824-29) and 'Pericles and Aspasia' (1835). Throughout this period his factious temper involved him in frequent quarrels with various Florentine officials and others; and in 1835 an irreconcilable quarrel with his wife drove him back to England. He lived chiefly at Bath for twenty-one years, and published in 1853 'Last Fruit off an Old Tree,' a volume containing a few more conversations, and miscellaneous odds and ends. In 1858 he withdrew from England to escape an action for libel raised at the instance of a lady he had quarrelled with; and spent the remaining six years of his life in Italy.—Landor, as De Quincey remarks, is one of those authors about whose personal appearance we have a special curiosity. He was, then, an erect, stout-set man, of middle height, with a broad head retreating in front but very full behind, fair-complexioned and grey-eyed, wearing in later years a peculiarly venerable look from his grey hairs, broad bald forehead, and erect carriage. The headstrong, overbearing, quarrelsome, ungregarious side of his character, is made apparent by the briefest outline of his social career. Towards his few friends he seems to have been generous and overflowingly affectionate. Yet even among friends admitted to his intimacy he was so exacting and "touchy," that they never knew the moment when they might strike against a torpedo that should make an irreparable breach. His most intimate friendships were states of unstable equilibrium. His prose writings are better known than his poetry; yet it is probably his poetry that is the most secure basis of his reputation. His crowning excellence is sublimity of conception: the character of Count Julian is his masterpiece, and it is ranked by so sober a judge as De Quincey with the Satan of Milton and the Prometheus of Æschylus. In his 'Imaginary Conversations,' as was to be expected from so wilful an egotist, dramatic exhibition of character is no part of their excellence. Some critics, indeed, profess to see a great deal of character in some of the dialogues. But the concession is made that it is not impossible that in many cases he first wrote the opinions and then looked about for a passably consistent mouthpiece; and in many cases personages are credited with opinions that they are very unlikely to have entertained. The 'Conversations' are interesting not from their dramatic propriety or significance, but as the vehicles of Landor's own opinions. He does not attempt to imitate the style of literary interlocutors: in the dialogue between Sir Philip Sidney and Fulke Greville, Greville talks the language of Sidney's 'Arcadia,' and Sidney the language of Walter Landor. In his prose style two points of excellence may be singled out—the aphoristic force of his general propositions, and the felicitous force of his imagery. In the opinion of many, his style has too much *force.* In addition to the vigour and occasional vehemence of the meaning, the minute observer will remark that the words are studiously chosen for emphatic articulation, containing an unusual proportion of energetic "labials," a choice doubtless apt and consistent, but, like all obtrusive arts, liable to be overdone.[1]

William Hazlitt (1778-1830), an eminent critic, born at Maidstone, in Kent, was the son of a Dissenting minister, and was carefully educated by his father with a view to the same profession. As he grew up, his own wishes did not ratify his father's choice, and at the age of seventeen he was permitted to change the direction of his studies, and to indulge an ambition of becoming a great painter. He persevered in the study and practice of painting for several years, and is said to have been prevented from attaining eminence only by a too fastidious spirit of criticism, and a despair of working up to his high ideals. His first literary effort was a metaphysical work on the 'Principles of Human Action,'

[1] Landor is the chief of De Quincey's "orthographic mutineers" (De Quincey's Works, xiii. 95): "As we are all of us crazy when the wind sits in some particular quarter, let not Mr Landor be angry with me for suggesting that he is outrageously crazy upon the one solitary subject of spelling." Landor's views about spelling and purity of language in general are to be found in the dialogue between Archdeacon Hare and Walter Landor in 'Last Fruit off an Old Tree,' and in two 'Imaginary Conversations' between Johnson and Horne Tooke.

published in 1805, remarkable as advocating the disinterested side in human nature. From that date he subsisted by literature. He wrote an abridgment of Tucker's 'Light of Nature' in 1807; compiled a selection of Parliamentary speeches, under the title of 'The Eloquence of the British Senate,' in 1808; and did other "journey-work" for the booksellers. In 1813 he delivered at the Russell Institution a series of lectures on English Philosophy; a fact worth mention, as showing that for many years the chief studies of the future critic were philosophical. About this time he became connected with the press as a contributor of political and theatrical criticisms, some of which were afterwards worked up into the volumes 'Political Essays' and 'A View of the English Stage.' He was first brought prominently into notice by his lectures at the Surrey Institution on the "English Poets" (1818), on the "English Comic Writers" (1819), and on the "Dramatic Literature of the Age of Elizabeth" (1821). About the same time appeared his 'Characters of Shakspeare's Plays.' His other principal works were—'Table-Talk,' 1821-22; the 'Spirit of the Age' (a series of criticisms on contemporaries, bitterly condemned by nearly all reviewers), 1825; the 'Plain Speaker,' a collection of Essays, 1826; and his last and greatest performance, 'The Life of Napoleon,' 1828-30. During the last ten years of his life he was a frequent contributor to various periodicals—the 'London Magazine,' the 'Edinburgh Review,' the 'New Monthly,' and the 'Monthly.' He died on the 18th of September 1830.—"In person Mr Hazlitt was of the middle size, with a handsome and eager countenance, worn by sickness and thought; and dark hair which had curled stiffly over the temples, and was only of late years sprinkled with grey. His gait was slouching and awkward, and his dress neglected; but when he began to talk he could not be mistaken for a common man. In the company of persons with whom he was not familiar, his bashfulness was painful; but when he became entirely at ease, and entered on a favourite topic, no one's conversation was ever more delightful." He was an excitable man, of intense and vehement feelings, nursing and indulging excitement to dangerous excess. He did not criticise in cold blood. The reviewers of his own time dwelt upon his intense love and admiration for great authors as one of his "noblest" qualifications for the office of critic. "He did not square and measure out his judgments by the pedantries of dry and lifeless propositions—his taste was not the creature of schools and canons, it was begotten of Enthusiasm by Thought." Critics who admired this qualification, as applied to the great men of former times, sharply resented its application in the 'Spirit of the Age' to the author's contemporaries. Enthusiasm was then spoken of as "bad taste" and "affectation;" and poor Hazlitt was told the bitter truth that it was his worst enemy. His criticisms of his contemporaries seem to us to be, taken all in all, neither more nor less just than his criticisms of departed poets, comic writers, and dramatists. In all his criticisms alike he strikes us as a man of extravagant sentiment and hyperbolical expression, widely read in philosophy and in general literature, a habitual and acute student of human character, more alive to varieties of excellence than any of his critical contemporaries, excepting De Quincey and John Wilson, and more, perhaps, than even these, alive to what may be called varieties of mood. His judgment was liable to be "deflected" by intemperate feeling, generous or splenetic. His criticisms must be taken with some grains of allowance on this score before we appreciate their substantial body of sound discernment. He often puts things graphically and incisively; but his composition strikes the general taste of critics as wearing too much an appearance of effort, and straining too much at flashing effects. "Hazlitt," says De Quincey, "was not eloquent, because he was discontinuous. No man can be eloquent whose thoughts are abrupt, insulated, capricious, and non-sequacious. . . . Now Hazlitt's brilliancy is seen chiefly in separate splinterings of phrase or image which throw upon the eye a vitreous scintillation for a moment, but spread no deep suffusions of colour, and distribute no masses of mighty shadow. A flash, a solitary flash, and all is gone." De Quincey objects also to Hazlitt's habit of trite quotation, of ornamenting his pages with "tags of verse and 'cues' of rhyme."

James Henry Leigh Hunt (1784-1859), journalist, essay-writer, book-compiler, and poet, may be placed with Hazlitt as another distinguished member of what was derisively termed "The Cockney School." He was the son of a West Indian lawyer, settled at Southgate in Middlesex, and received his schooling at Christ's Hospital. His father published a collection of his verses in 1802, under the title of 'Juvenilia,' when he was but eighteen—a collection which met with a much more favourable reception than Byron's 'Hours of Idleness,' published some five years later. Throughout his life his aspirations and pursuits were exclusively literary. The short trial that was made of his business abilities in a law office, and subsequently in the War Office, could hardly be said to be an interruption. When he was little more than twenty he made a sensation as a dramatic critic in his brother's paper, the 'News.' In 1808 he joined with his brother in setting up the 'Examiner,' designed as a weekly organ for political views more advanced than were then current in the press. The attacks of the 'Examiner' upon the Government involved it in more than one prosecution for libel; and in 1813 our author was indicted for certain sarcastic comments on the Prince Regent, and suffered imprisonment for two years, glorying in his bonds, and declining several offers from friends to pay his fine and procure his release. In 1816 his 'Story of Rimini' presented him to the public as a poet; and as he had, some years before, in his 'Feast of the Poets,' rather captiously insulted the whole of that irritable race, his performance was reviewed and himself reviled with the utmost spirit. In 1819-21, he published the 'Indicator,' a weekly series of essays on the model of the 'Spectator.' The most notorious event in his life, next to his imprisonment for a political offence, was his connection with Lord Byron. He set sail for Italy in 1821 to assist Byron and Shelley in establishing the 'Liberal,' a projected new light in matters social, political, and religious; but the scheme failed through want of congeniality among the collaborateurs; and Hunt, after his return to England, published 'Recollections of Lord Byron,' in which he tried to exculpate himself at the expense of his friend. He returned to England in 1825. For the remaining thirty-four years of his life he lived as a man of letters in London, the fruits of his pen being eked out by occasional contributions from his friends, and after 1847 by a Government pension of £200, bestowed by Lord John Russell. He projected periodicals—the 'Companion' (shortly after his return, a continuation of the 'Indicator'), the 'Tatler' (1830-33), the 'London Journal' (1834), and wrote to periodicals already established; composed a fictitious autobiography of Sir RALPH ESHER, a gentleman of the Court of Charles II. (1832), a poem, 'Captain Sword and Captain Pen,' 1839, and a play, 'The Legend of Florence,' 1840; and published various compilations, criticisms, and books of gossip—'Imagination and Fancy,' 1845; 'Wit and Humour,' 1846; 'Stories from the Italian Poets,' 1846; 'Men, Women, and Books' (a collection from his periodical essays), 1847; 'A Jar of Honey from Mount Hybla,' 1847; 'The Town,' 1848; 'Autobiography,' 1850; 'The Religion of the Heart,' 1853; 'The Old Court Suburb,' 1855. He died on the 28th of August 1859.—He is described as a rather tall man, of dark complexion, with erect carriage, and engaging liveliness and suavity of address. "His hair was black and shining, and slightly inclined to wave; his head was high, his forehead straight and white, his eyes black and sparkling." The inner as well as the outer man differed considerably from the typical John Bull. He was ruled by sentiment. His capacities for business were of the poorest order. He had no sense of the value of money, and would often have been in great distress had not the amiability of his character procured him relief from the generosity of his friends. As a youth he was spoiled by the praise of his precocity; overweeningly self-complacent, he sat in judgment with a patronising air upon his elders and superiors, and, meaning no harm in the world, made hosts of enemies on every side. When his eyes were opened to the unconscious offensiveness of his behaviour, he appeared in a more amiable aspect. His 'Autobiography' is brimming with expressions of goodwill to all mankind, and frank confession of youthful offences. His philanthropic sentiment was overflowing. Uncle Toby was his ideal —"divine Uncle Toby." "He who created Uncle Toby was the wisest man since the days of Shakspeare." "As long as the character of Toby Shandy finds an echo in the heart of man, the heart of man is noble." In point of style, his model was Addison. In simplicity and felicitous grace of expression he may be contrasted with the more robust and careless vigour predominant in the early days of the 'Edinburgh Review' and 'Blackwood.' He particularly excels in graceful touches of humorous caricature.

John Wilson, "Christopher North" **(1785-1854)** was the son of a prosperous manufacturer in Paisley. When he was six or seven years old, he was placed under the care of the minister of the neighbouring parish of Mearns, and displayed from the first his singular union of muscular vigour with love of intellectual distinction. Jack was anything but a dull boy; his enthusiasm for angling and other sports,[1] and his rattling youthful eloquence, were no less conspicuous than his quickness in book-learning. He studied at Glasgow, and subsequently at Oxford. At Glasgow he carried off the first prize in the Logic class; and at Oxford, besides being distinguished as a boxer and as the best far-leaper of his day in England, he was said to have passed for his degree "the most illustrious examination within the memory of man." He left Oxford in 1807, and soon after, having purchased the beautiful residence of Elleray on the banks of the Windermere, he married, and lived there for several years in Utopian health and happiness, surrounded by the finest of scenery, and varying his poem-writing and halcyon peace with walking excursions and jovial visits from friends that, like himself, entered with zest into the hearty enjoyment of life. During this period he wrote his 'Isle of Palms,' a beautiful reflection of the soft passage of his days. In 1815, in consequence of pecuniary embarrassment, brought on by the misfortunes of the trustee of his father's property, he was under the necessity of choosing a profession, and decided for the Scottish bar. He made no effort to secure a practice. In 1820 he was appointed Professor of Moral Philosophy in Edinburgh. The duties of this Chair he discharged till 1851, when he retired upon a pension of £300, all the more gratifying as a mark of public respect that it was bestowed by his political enemies. But the most brilliant side of his life was his activity in connection with 'Blackwood's Magazine,' which, after a short tentative flight,

[1] See Recreations of Christopher North.

was in 1817 fairly started in its present character with "Christopher North" as its leading contributor. When Wilson gave up his residence at Elleray, he was, writes Professor Ferrier,[1] "after sundry pleasant overtures from Jeffrey, and the composition of one eloquent article on 'Childe Harold' for the 'Edinburgh Review,' induced finally to cement a perpetual treaty with Mr Blackwood, and to act, for months and years, as the animating soul of his celebrated Magazine." It was not, however, by a jump, or even rapidly, that Wilson attained to the full command of his powers, or the Magazine to a lucrative circulation. It was established in 1817; but it was not until 1825 that that brilliant succession of articles from Wilson's pen began to appear, which brought fame to him and a shoal of subscribers to the Magazine. For the ten following years his industry never flagged. About 1836 it became somewhat intermittent, although, until near the close of his life, it was still powerfully exerted. "Dies Boreales" were the last contributions from his pen to 'Blackwood's Magazine.'[2] All his prose writings made their first appearance in 'Maga,' as he delighted to call the Magazine; after his death the principal of them were collected and published by the Messrs Blackwood under the editorship of his son-in-law Professor Ferrier.—The numerous floating traditions of "Christopher North's" commanding personal appearance and physical prowess have always made him one of the most popular of literary characters. The graceful dignity of his carriage, and the length of limb and peculiar formation of heel that gave him his extraordinary superiority as a far-leaper, are recorded with characteristic minuteness in De Quincey's sketch. De Quincey also dwells upon the popularity of his manners—his frank, open affability to all comers, his "infinite gamut" of acquaintance from college "Don" to groom, ostler, and stable-boy. His writings were no less popular than his person. As a critic he did not possess De Quincey's subtle power of entering into characters different from his own (in that respect De Quincey probably stood alone among his contemporaries); but his sympathies were so broad that it is not easy to define their limits. His strong pleasure in natural scenery, the native susceptibility of his eye to colour and form, gave him a wider compass than Jeffrey, and was the secret of his enthusiastic advocacy of Wordsworth, as a corresponding deficiency was the secret of Jeffrey's no less earnest depreciation. When we compare his review of Mr Tennyson's early poems with Lockhart's

[1] In Mackenzie's Imperial Dictionary of Biography.

[2] Among the early contributors to this Magazine, which introduced a new era in periodical writing, being the first parent of all the magazines that now swim the literary stream, were John Gibson Lockhart, Captain Hamilton (author of 'Cyril Thornton,' a brother of Sir William Hamilton), John Galt (author of 'Annals of the Parish'), Mrs Hemans, David M. Moir ("Delta"), Sir Archibald Alison, De Quincey, and other well-known names.

review of the same publication in the 'Quarterly,' we see that this nature-interest, this additional "bump" or bumps, overbalanced his repugnance to the admixture of the "Cockney" element, and the pseudo-metaphysical "drivel," that irreconcilably offended his early friend and associate. As regards Wilson's style, it has been said by Mr Hallam that "his eloquence is like the rush of mighty waters." He greatly admired Jeremy Taylor; and while, from temperament, he does not display the same habitual breathless eagerness in the accumulation of words, but pours out his full eloquence with less appearance of excitement, he often reminds us of Taylor's manner in his way of following out picturesque similitudes. Comparing them upon one point only, and disregarding other characteristics, we should say that of the two Taylor is the more rhetorical, and Wilson the more eloquent: Taylor rather accumulates his wealth of expression upon given themes; Wilson flows out spontaneously and often somewhat irrelevantly to the subject in hand, concerning what strongly interested him in real life: Taylor can flexibly bring his powers to bear upon any subject; Wilson, although from the width of his interests the distinction is not glaringly obtrusive, is copious only when he happens to strike a plentiful spring in his own nature. With all Wilson's Nimrod force and abounding animal spirits, perhaps his richest and most original vein of expression is connected with his love of peaceful beauties in natural scenery. A very high tribute both to his judgment and to his powers of illustration is paid by De Quincey when he says that from Wilson's contributions to 'Blackwood's Magazine,' and more especially from his meditative examinations of great poets ancient and modern, a *florilegium* might be compiled of thoughts more profound and more gorgeously illustrated than exist elsewhere in human composition.

John Gibson Lockhart (1794-1854), already mentioned in connection with 'Blackwood's Magazine,' was editor of the 'Quarterly Review' for more than a quarter of a century, from 1826 to 1853. The son of a Scotch parish minister in Lanarkshire, he was a distinguished student at Glasgow College, and at the close of his curriculum was presented to one of the Snell exhibitions for Balliol College, Oxford. In the final examination at Oxford in 1813, he took a first-class in classics. After a visit to Germany, in the course of which he made the acquaintance of Goethe, he fixed his residence in Edinburgh, and was called to the Scotch bar in 1816. Like several other young lawyers of the same date, his profession was more literature than law. He co-operated with Wilson in the inauguration of 'Blackwood's Magazine' in 1817. He had a principal hand in the famous 'Chaldee Manuscript.'[1] In 1819 he published

[1] This pungent production appeared in the seventh number of 'Blackwood's Magazine,' the first number contributed to by Wilson and Lockhart. It was

'Peter's Letters to his Kinsfolk,' satirical sketches of Edinburgh men of the time. In the following year he married the eldest daughter of Sir Walter Scott, who fitted up for the reception of the youthful pair the little cottage of Chiefswood, near Abbotsford. Here he produced in rapid succession his 'Metrical Translations of Spanish Ballads,' and his four novels, 'Valerius,' 'Adam Blair,' 'Reginald Dalton,' and 'Matthew Wald.' From 1826, when he accepted the editorship of the 'Quarterly Review,' he resided in London; and besides his editorial duties and his own contributions to the periodical, which were upwards of a hundred in number, he found time to write his 'Life of Burns' for 'Constable's Miscellany' (1827), his 'Life of Napoleon' for 'Murray's Family Library' (1829), and his greatest work, the 'Life of Scott,' the last volume of which appeared in 1838.—Lockhart was a thin, dark, erect figure, proud and reserved in general society, and regarded with some fear on account of his sarcastic ways; but among his chosen companions, at least in his earlier and happier years, loved for his exuberance of animal spirits and his irrepressible flow of wit and humour. The kindliness that was not distributed promiscuously, made itself felt all the more strongly within the chosen circle. He made numerous enemies, especially during his career in Edinburgh, by the tormenting force of his ridicule, by his ingenuity in driving rusty nails into the most vulnerable parts of his victims; yet more acts of generous kindness and high integrity are recorded of him than can be placed to the credit of many men of more philanthropic professions and greater general suavity of manner. As a critical potentate "he was kind and considerate towards unpretending merit, ready to recognise and welcome real talent in friend or foe, and severe only where presumption went hand in hand with ignorance." Much of his power as a writer depended upon his penetrating knowledge of character. The most notable feature in his novels and tales is the development of thought, feeling, and purpose, under the influence of circumstances: he loves particularly to play upon natural mistakes, and the consequences of natural mistakes, in the interpretation of appearances. His most-admired articles in the 'Quarterly' are biographical. Throughout his life the study of character seems to have been his prevailing study: we trace the natural bent towards it in his boyish caricatures, and we have the first memorable fruits of it in 'Peter's Letters.' The 'Life of Burns' is a good specimen of his power: when we compare this work with Dr Currie's, we are most forcibly struck with Lockhart's skill in weaving out of crude material a coherent narrative of characteristic incidents. No student of

written in the style of the Old Testament. Its clever personalities made such a sensation that it was withdrawn from the second edition of the number. (See Wilson's Works, vol. iv.)

biography can afford to overlook Lockhart. Apart from his skill in choosing significant circumstances, he is peculiarly distinguished by his faithful adherence to reality: his biographies are remarkably free from the distortions of romance and hero-worship. He objected on several grounds to the writing of the lives of persons recently deceased; but he held that if "contemporaneous biography," as he called it, is to be permitted, the biographers should be peculiarly careful not to make in favour of the hero suppressions that might do injustice to other persons concerned. It was probably in pursuance of this principle that he made revelations concerning Scott which extreme admirers of the poet would rather he had left unsaid. Lockhart's is not a studied, finished style, but he had a great mastery of language, and is exceedingly fresh and varied in his diction. His characteristic qualities are keen incisive force, and sarcastic exuberant wit.

INDEX OF PRINCIPAL NAMES.